HANDBOOK OF RESEARCH METHODS IN CORPORATE SOCIAL RESPONSIBILITY

Handbook of Research Methods in Corporate Social Responsibility

Edited by

David Crowther
Leicester Business School, De Montfort University, UK

Linne Marie Lauesen
Water and Waste Svendborg, Denmark

Edward Elgar PUBLISHING

Cheltenham, UK • Northampton, MA, USA

© David Crowther and Linne Marie Lauesen 2017

All rights reserved. No part of this publication may be reproduced, stored in a retrieval system or transmitted in any form or by any means, electronic, mechanical or photocopying, recording, or otherwise without the prior permission of the publisher.

Published by
Edward Elgar Publishing Limited
The Lypiatts
15 Lansdown Road
Cheltenham
Glos GL50 2JA
UK

Edward Elgar Publishing, Inc.
William Pratt House
9 Dewey Court
Northampton
Massachusetts 01060
USA

Paperback edition 2019

A catalogue record for this book
is available from the British Library

Library of Congress Control Number: 2017936562

This book is available electronically in the Elgaronline
Business subject collection
DOI 10.4337/9781784710927

ISBN 978 1 78471 091 0 (cased)
ISBN 978 1 78471 092 7 (eBook)
ISBN 978 1 78471 093 4 (paperback)

Typeset by Servis Filmsetting Ltd, Stockport, Cheshire
Printed by CPI Group (UK) Ltd, Croydon CR0 4YY

Contents

List of contributors	viii
Introduction *David Crowther and Linne Marie Lauesen*	1

PART I   METHODOLOGY PLANNING

1	Grounded theory in corporate social responsibility research *Vilma Žydžiūnaitė and Loreta Tauginienė*	29
2	Using a mixed methods approach for corporate social responsibility research *Jane Claydon*	44
3	Imperative of meta-study for research in the field of corporate social responsibility and emerging issues in corporate governance *Lukman Raimi*	55
4	Ethics in the research process *David Crowther*	63
5	Research methods in organization, management and management accounting: an evaluation of quantitative and qualitative approaches *Miriam Green*	76
6	Methodological and epistemological perspectives in the study of corporate social responsibility in Colombia *Duván Emilio Ramírez Ospina and José Fernando Muñoz Ospina*	94

PART II   QUANTITATIVE METHODS

7	Game theory as a research tool for sustainability *Shahla Seifi*	111
8	Key concerns in longitudinal study design *Rima Kalinauskaitė*	125
9	Sampling and sampling procedures in corporate social responsibility research *Habib Zaman Khan and Md. Rashidozzaman Khan*	139
10	Food deserts in British cities: comparing food access, obesity, and ethnicity in Leicester and Stoke on Trent *Hillary J. Shaw*	159

11 The application of statistical methods in CSR research 177
Christopher Boachie and George K. Amoako

12 Regression techniques and their application in the corporate social
responsibility domain: an overview 205
Sonali Bhattacharya, Madhvi Sethi, Abhishek Behl and V.G. Venkatesh

PART III QUALITATIVE METHODS

13 Analytic autoethnography as a tool to enhance reflection, reflexivity and
critical thinking in CSR research 231
Fernanda de Paiva Duarte

14 Insights regarding the applicability of semiotics to CSR communication
research 241
Kemi C. Yekini

15 Ethnographic research methods in CSR research: building theory out of
people's everyday life with materials, objects, practices, and
symbolic constructions 265
Linne Marie Lauesen

16 Interviews as an instrument to explore management motivation for corporate
social and environmental reporting 280
Homaira Semeen and Muhammad Azizul Islam

17 Participant observation as the data collection tool and its usage in the CSR
researches 293
Ilke Oruc

18 Application of correspondence analysis to determinants of human resources
disclosure 308
Esther Ortiz and José G. Clavel

19 The application of survey methodology in CSR research 328
Christopher Boachie

20 Content analysis method: a proposed scoring for quantitative and qualitative
disclosures 349
Juniati Gunawan and Kumalawati Abadi

21 Focus groups in social accounting as a stakeholder engagement tool 364
Sara Moggi

22 A phenomenological study of moral discourse, social justice and CSR 377
Julia J.A. Shaw

23 Social network analysis in CSR research 391
Duygu Türker

24	Theoretical storytelling as a meta-frame for all research methods in corporate social responsibility *Linne Marie Lauesen*	401

PART IV FUTURE RESEARCH AGENDA

25	Philosophical prolegomena to all future research in CSR *Nicholas Capaldi*	419
26	Beyond strategic CSR: the concept of responsibility as the foundation of ethics – political, technological and economic responsibility for the future of humanity *Jacob Dahl Rendtorff*	428
27	From positivism to social constructivism: an emerging trend for CSR researchers *Martin Samy and Fiona Robertson*	437

Index 463

Contributors

Kumalawati Abadi, SE, Ak, CA, MSi is a Lecturer in Accounting at Trisakti University, Jakarta-Indonesia. She graduated as best student from Master Degree in Trisakti University with the GPA 3.96/4. Her thesis is titled 'Guidance for Content Analysis Method: Concepts and Implementation'. She started her career as an auditor in Deloitte Touche Tohmatsu for three years and as practitioner, since 1999 she serves Danone AQUA and her last position is a Finance Operation Senior Manager. She is also actively involved in Indonesia Mengajar (Teaching for Indonesia) as a volunteer to motivate the younger generation in Indonesia. Her hobby is writing articles for the church, and currently she is completing an inspiring story book that will be published in the English and Indonesian languages.

George K. Amoako is a Senior Lecturer and Head of Marketing Department of Central Business School, Central University Ghana, an academic and a practising Chartered Marketer (CIM-UK). He was educated in Kwame Nkrumah University of Science and Technology in Kumasi, Ghana and at the University of Ghana and the London School of Marketing, UK. He obtained his PhD from London Metropolitan University, UK in January 2017. He has considerable research, teaching, consulting and practice experience in the application of marketing theory and principles to everyday marketing challenges and management and organizational issues. He has consulted for public sector and private organizations both in Ghana and the UK. He has a strong passion for branding, service quality and corporate social responsibility issues in the corporate world. George has published extensively in internationally peer-reviewed academic journals and presented many papers at international conferences in Africa, Europe and Australia.

Abhishek Behl is a full-time faculty member in Symbiosis Centre for Management and Human Resource Development, Symbiosis International University, Pune, India. He holds a PhD degree under Faculty of Management, Symbiosis International University. He undertakes corporate training in the areas of statistics and market research, and his research interests are in the empirical domain focusing on financial products and social responsibility in the microfinance area. His research interests envelop technology diffusion and sustainable policies. He has won the Junior Research Fellowship and was selected as the Emerald Research Scholar for Emerald Publishing House, UK.

Sonali Bhattacharya has been an Associate Professor at Symbiosis International University for the last ten years. Her research interests include applied probability, theatrical and applied statistics and cross-disciplinary studies. She has published more than 50 research papers in international journals. She is the Chief Editor of internationally indexed journal, *Drishtikon*.

Christopher Boachie is a lecturer at Central Business School, Central University Ghana, an academic and a practising Chartered Accountant (FCCA-UK) with specialization in corporate finance, international trade, social accounting and financial risk management.

He was educated in Kwame Nkrumah University of Science and Technology in Ghana, Technical University of Freiberg in Germany and the London School of Accountancy, UK. He is currently reading his PhD at Open University of Malaysia. He has considerable teaching, consulting and practice experience in the application of accountancy and finance theory and the financing of international trade and risk management. His professional focus is on corporate financial analysis, financial accounting and reporting, and he has a strong passion for financial risk management.

Nicholas Capaldi is a Legendre-Soulé Distinguished Chair in Business Ethics at Loyola University, New Orleans, USA and the Director of the National Center for Business Ethics. Previously, he has been a McFarlin Research Professor of Law at the University of Tulsa as well as professor at Colombia University, Queens College, City University of New York, the United States Military Academy at West Point, and the National University of Singapore. He obtained his PhD from Colombia University. His research interests are in public policy, political science, philosophy, law, religion and economy. He is the author of seven books, over 80 articles and has edited six anthologies. He is a member of the editorial board of six journals and served as editor of *Public Affairs Quarterly* and is thus an internationally recognized scholar in the fields of higher education, bio-ethics, business ethics, affirmative action, immigration, corporate social responsibility and free market ethics, as well as writing a John Stuart Mill biography and his involvement in the C-SPAN *Booknotes* television series.

José G. Clavel is a tenured Lecturer in the area of Applied Economics at the University of Murcia, Spain. A Doctor since 1997 with a thesis on the application of Correspondence Analysis and Classification and Regression Trees to bank customer segmentation, he has been visiting professor at the Ontario Institute for Studies in Education, Toronto, Canada, the Universitat Pompeu Fabra, Barcelona, Spain and the Indira Gandhi Institute of Development Research, Mumbai, India. His research is mainly oriented towards the application of multivariate techniques to the analysis of multivariate categorical data in fields that range from the International Accounting Standardisation to the Economy of Education.

Jane Claydon graduated with a PhD in Sociology from the University of Sussex in 2014. Her thesis investigates perceptions of blame and responsibility for consumer debt. The research focuses heavily on the concept of corporate social responsibility in assessing whether, and to what extent, consumer lending institutions can or should be blamed and be held responsible for increasing volumes of consumer debt in the UK and the US. Jane lives in Brighton with her husband and two children and has worked in the consumer credit sector for over ten years.

David Crowther is Professor of Corporate Social Responsibility at De Montfort University, UK, Research Professor at London School of Commerce and Chief Research Fellow at Lithuanian Institute of Agrarian Economics. His career includes many years as a general manager, consultant and accountant in a wide range of organizational settings before becoming an academic. He has published 50 books and more than 400 papers in journals in fields of organizational behaviour, knowledge management, environmentalism, corporate reporting and social accounting. He is a founding chair of the Social Responsibility Research Network, and founding editor of *Social Responsibility Journal* and an editorial board member of several other journals. He has organized many conferences and lectured in a variety of fields worldwide and acted as consultant to governments, politicians and businesses. His current research is into the effects of social responsibility and governance on sustainability.

Fernanda de Paiva Duarte has a PhD in Sociology and is an Adjunct Associate Professor at the School of Business, University of Western Sydney (UWS), Australia. Her research interests include corporate social responsibility, sustainability, organizational sociology, business ethics, leadership, qualitative methodology, and the scholarship of teaching and learning.

Miriam Green has a PhD in Organisation Studies, and is a senior lecturer at the Icon College of Technology and Management. Her research has focused on the representations of a major text about the management of innovation in mainstream management and management accounting scholarship. Her critique of such scholarship has centred on the need for complementing the dominance of objectivist, quantitative-based knowledge with subjectivist, qualitative approaches in order to produce inclusive, holistic and sustainable scholarship. She was awarded a doctorate from De Montfort University, UK in 2013, and has published several articles, mainly in *Social Responsibility Journal* and *Philosophy of Management*. She has co-authored a book with David Crowther, *Organisational Theory* (2004), and more recently has written chapters in books on corporate governance and on research methods. She is now interested in connections between mainstream management scholarship and neoliberal ideologies and practices.

Juniati Gunawan, PhD is a Director of Trisakti Sustainability Center (TSC), Trisakti University, Jakarta-Indonesia. She graduated with a PhD in Corporate Social Reporting from Edith Cowan University (ECU), Western Australia and specializes in sustainability reporting. She is a senior lecturer at Trisakti University, Jakarta, a guest lecturer and source person in national and overseas education institutions, a member of international journal editorial boards in social and environmental accounting, and social responsibility for Ebsco, Emerald and Cabell Publishing. As a practitioner, she serves on a number of organizations from various industries and on an expert committee for corporate social responsibility awards events in Indonesia. In 2016, she was also assigned to an expert committee for corporate social responsibility (CSR) under the Regional Representatives Council, Republic of Indonesia.

Muhammad Azizul Islam is Associate Professor of Accounting at the Queensland University of Technology in Brisbane, Australia. He is a Chartered Public Accountant, Australia. He has more than 15 years of teaching experience in Accounting in different universities and has published more than 40 peer-reviewed papers in journals and book chapters. Dr Azizul Islam's research interests include social and environmental disclosure and accountability. His work in the area of social and environmental disclosure appears in *Accounting, Auditing and Accountability Journal (AAAJ)*, *Accounting and Business Research Journal (ABR)*, *Critical Perspective on Accounting Journal (CPA)* and *Australian Accounting Review (AAR)*. Dr Azizul Islam's ongoing research projects include (but are not limited to) corporate social and environmental performance disclosure and accountability issues, and bribery and related accountability issues.

Rima Kalinauskaitė obtained her PhD at Kaunas University of Technology. During her doctoral studies, she spent half a year at the University of Konstanz preparing her doctoral project. In her thesis she analysed the interdependence between intergenerational relations and organizational climate. She discovered how organizational climate is affected by employees' age and how the manifestation of organizational climate depends on the sociodemographic (age, gender, education) structure of an organization and its subdivisions. Besides her sociological studies she holds an Advanced Master's in Higher Education Pedagogy from the University of Liege. Rima conducted a national longitudinal graduates' career and monitoring research project at MOSTA, the Research and Higher Education Monitoring and Analysis Centre. She has experience in conducting applied research and managing projects in the areas of organizations, management, social policy and education.

Habib Zaman Khan is Assistant Professor of Accounting, School of Information Systems & Accounting at University of Canberra, ACT, Australia. His research interests comprise corporate social responsibility and sustainability reporting in the banking sector, societal, political and cultural aspects of management control systems, multi-dimensional performance measurement systems and balanced scorecard (BSC) in service sectors and pro-environmental behaviour using behavioural theories and applying mixed methods of research design. He has published more than 25 articles in the peer-reviewed international journals. Among others, *Social Responsibility Journal*, *Environmental Education Research*, *Journal of Accounting in Emerging Economies*, *Corporate Control and Ownership*, *Tourism Analysis: An Interdisciplinary Tourism & Hospitality Journal*, *International Journal of Law and Management* and *Asia Pacific Management Accounting Journal* are the most notable. On top of journal publications, Dr Khan also published a chapter in the book series of Research in Accounting in Emerging Economies. Dr Khan is a Chartered Public Accountant, Australia.

Md. Rashidozzaman Khan is Assistant Professor at Dhaka Commerce College, Bangladesh, where he graduated with a Bachelor and Master's degree in Statistics, and an MSc in Information Technology (IT). Mr Khan has published many journal articles both at national and international level and is a co-author of statistics textbooks taught at the Higher School Certificate level in Bangladesh.

Linne Marie Lauesen graduated with a PhD in Organizational Governance and Corporate Social Responsibility from Copenhagen Business School in 2014. Her thesis investigates how water companies in Scandinavia, the UK, the US and South Africa work with and govern their role in society through the logic of corporate social responsibility. She has recently published the book *Sustainable Governance in Hybrid Organizations* (GOWER, now Routledge, 2015) and is co-editor with Professor David Crowther on the book *Accountability and Social Responsibility: International Perspectives* published by Emerald in 2016. Linne lives in Denmark with her husband and two children and has worked as a project manager in the water sector for 16 years. She has been a postdoctoral researcher at Copenhagen Business School and works as a project manager and business analyst in the Danish water company Waste & Water (Vang og Affald).

Sara Moggi is Assistant Professor in Accounting at the University of Verona and her research focuses on sustainability measurement and reporting. Her main stream of research examines sustainability reporting for stakeholders, taking these subjects as pivotal for evaluating and shaping the sustainable strategies of nonprofit organizations and firms in terms of social, economic and environmental performance. Her work has been published in the *International Journal of Public Administration, Nonprofit and Voluntary Sector Quarterly* and *Accounting History*.

Esther Ortiz is a tenured Lecturer in the area of Accounting and Finance in the University of Murcia, Spain. She finished her European PhD in 2001, and since then has been doing research in the fields of international accounting and capital markets. She is also interested in research about the relationship between profit and social responsibility for corporations around the world, and about corporate social practices and disclosure. She has collaborated in different research projects and stayed at various European universities, has presented papers at international congresses and published in several local and international journals and chapters in internationally edited books.

Ilke Oruc is an Assistant Professor at Trakya University, Faculty of Economics and Administrative Sciences, Edirne, Turkey. She obtained a Bachelor's degree from Abant Izzet Baysal University, Faculty of Economics and Administrative Sciences; a Master's degree from Trakya University, Department of Business Administration; her Doctorate degree from Anadolu University, Department of Business Administration; and her Post-doctorate from the University of South Africa (UNISA), Graduate School of Business Leadership. Her main research and interests are in gender, organizational behavior, corporate social responsibility, ethical behavior and management, and the sociology of work.

Duván Emilio Ramírez Ospina has a PhD in Business Administration and a Master's degree in Human Resources Management. He is an economist and teaches other courses in marketing and is a Dean of the Accounting Science, Economics and Administration Faculty of Manizales University. He has management experience of different kinds of organizations and is a Master's and PhD Professor at various universities and is an organizational issues researcher. His research interests include social responsibility, sustainable development, family business and agency theory. He has published books, book chapters and articles for a number of national and international science journals on diverse subjects.

José Fernando Muñoz Ospina holds a degree in Business Administration and a Master's degree in Environment and Sustainable Development. He is a PhD candidate in Sustainable Development from Manizales University. He is a professor at the Master's programme at Manizales University, and has been a researcher at the Research Center in Environment and Development CIMAD for ten years. His research interests include business organizations and sustainable development. He has been a presenter at different academic events at the national and international level. Currently, Professor Muñoz serves as the Director of the Business Administration programme at Manizales University.

Lukman Raimi is a Senior Lecturer and Coordinator Training at the Centre for Entrepreneurship Development, Yaba College of Technology, Lagos, Nigeria. He holds a Bachelor's degree (Hons) in Economics, Obafemi Awolowo University, Nigeria; a Master's degree in Economics, University of Lagos; and a Master's degree in Industrial Relations and Personnel Management, University of Lagos. Presently, he holds a PhD in Entrepreneurship and Corporate Social Responsibility from De Montfort University, Leicester, UK. He is also a full member of the American Economic Association (AEA), a member of the British Academy of Management (BAM), a full member of the Nigerian Institute of Management (NIM), a fellow of the African Association of Entrepreneurs Nigeria (AAEN), and a member of Emerald Literati Scholars and a full member of the American Association of International Researchers (AAIR). His teaching and research interests include: entrepreneurship, development economics, corporate governance and corporate social responsibility.

Jacob Dahl Rendtorff is a senior Associate Professor of Responsibility, Ethics and Legitimacy of Corporations at the Department of Communication, Business and Information Technologies at Roskilde University, Denmark. He has a background in research in responsibility and ethics, business ethics, bioethics, political theory and philosophy of law. Rendtorff received his Mag. art. (1993) and PhD (1999) at the University of Copenhagen, Denmark. In April 2010 he also received a Doctoral degree (Habilitation) in administration and social sciences (Dr. scient. adm.) from Roskilde University. He also has degrees in philosophy and political science from the University of Paris and Freie Universität, Berlin. Since 1994 he has been visiting professor at the University of Utrecht (1994), Max Planck Institut, Freiburg, Germany (1995), and the Catholic University of Rome (1996). Furthermore, he has been visiting professor at the Center for Business Ethics, Bentley College, Boston, the Markkula Center for Applied Ethics, Santa Clara University and the Consortium for Organizational Research (SCANCOR) at Stanford University (2001). In 2004 he visited the Centre for Ethics and Economics at the University of Louvain, Belgium and in 2011 he was visiting professor at Université France-Comté, and at Bard College, USA. He has given more than 150 international lectures and presentations at different universities and conferences around the world. Rendtorff has written more than 12 books, and he has also co-edited more than ten books on issues of ethics and social theory, and also on topics of existentialism and hermeneutics, French philosophy, and bioethics as well as philosophy of law.

Fiona Robertson, BA, MA (distinction), CA is a Chartered Accountant and a member of the Institute of Chartered Accountants of Scotland (ICAS) Corporate Reporting Committee and chairs the Leeds Beckett IR Steering Group. She is currently finalizing a PhD focused on Integrated Reporting and works as a part-time lecturer at Leeds Beckett University. She specializes in qualitative research and has published articles based on perceptions of integrated reporting in the UK. Previously she has over 20 years of experience working in a number of senior financial positions in the UK and multinational organizations.

Martin Samy was a Professor of CSR and Effectiveness Measurement at Leeds Business School. He managed students based in Nigeria, Mauritius and the United Arab Emirates in their Doctor of Philosophy studies. Prior to being an academic, Martin has had commercial experience as a financial manager of corporations in Singapore and Australia. He was an associate member of the Certified Practising Accountant, Australia, and member of the Australian College of Educators. He has been recognised in the *Marquis Who's Who in the World* in 2007 publication for his research in establishing a Quality Effectiveness Instrument. He actively researches and publishes both nationally and internationally. His research interests are Corporate Social Responsibility and Financial Performance research globally, where he has undertaken studies in Australia, United Kingdom, Indonesia, Bangladesh and Nigeria. He has published in international journals such as the *Corporation Reputation Review*, *Journal of Global Responsibility*, *Sustainability Accounting, Management and Policy Journal* and *Journal of Accounting & Organisational Change*.

Shahla Seifi is a research fellow at the University of Derby, UK, where she is completing her PhD. She holds a BSc in Applied Physics from Azad University, Iran, an MSc in Industrial Engineering from the University of Science and Technology, Iran and an MSc in Engineering from the University of Applied Science and Technology of Iran Industry, Iran. She has worked for almost 20 years as a senior manager at the Research Institute, Institute of Standards and Industrial Research of Iran (ISIRI) before moving to the UK. Her research interests are especially in the areas of the role of industrial engineering in facilitating sustainable development, factors involved in the development of responsible economic and financial performance, factors affecting corporate sustainability, governance in the global market, the implications of organizational activity upon the wider stakeholder environment, and the application of game theory to sustainability problems. Shahla is Conferences Chair of the Social Responsibility Research Network and on the Editorial Advisory Board of several journals. She lives in Derby, UK, with her loving husband David Crowther.

Homaira Semeen is undertaking a PhD in the School of Accountancy of Queensland University of Technology (QUT). She holds a Master's degree in Business Research from QUT, a Master's in Business Administration (MBA) from the University of Dhaka and a Bachelor of Business Administration (BBA) from the University of Dhaka. She has more than two years of teaching experience at university level. Homaira Semeen researches on social and environmental accounting and related management control systems. Her research work is published in *Social and Environmental Accountability Journal* (SEAJ), Journal of the Faculty of Business Studies, Jahangirnagar University and *Independent Business Review*.

Madhvi Sethi is an Associate Professor at Symbiosis Institute of Business Management, Bengaluru in the area of finance. She has a doctorate in finance and obtained her postdoctoral fellowship from the Indian School of Business, Hyderabad. Starting her full-time teaching career with XLRI – Xavier School of Management, Jamshedpur, she has been in academia for the last 11 years. During this tenure, she has undertaken teaching, research and management development program assignments. She has published several research papers in the field of corporate finance. She also co-authored a book titled *Indian Business Groups: Strategy and Performance* (Cambridge University Press, 2015). Three of her co-authored cases won her accolades in the ISB-Ivey case competition, leading to publications by Ivey Publishing and Harvard Business Publishing.

Hillary J. Shaw is Director of Research and Visiting Research Fellow at the London School of Commerce; having previously held posts at the universities of Southampton and Leeds, and also at Audencia Nantes School of Management in France. He is also Director of Shaw Food Solutions: www.fooddeserts.org. His doctorate, awarded by the University of Leeds in 2004, addresses the economics, geography and sociology of food consumer choice and obesity, particularly the dynamics and evolution of the food desert phenomenon. Current areas of research are sustainable economic development, corporate social responsibility and the integration of global and local food systems. The author of many journal articles, book chapters and reports, Hillary's recent book, *The Consuming Geographies of Food: Diet, Food Deserts and Obesity* (Routledge, 2014), explicates the development of the current global food system and discusses how sustainable and accessible political and economic structures for feeding the future global population of ten billion can be achieved. He is currently completing a further monograph, *Corporate Social Responsibility and the Global Food Chain* (Routledge, forthcoming 2017) which explores corporate social responsibility in relation to the food retailing industry.

Julia J.A. Shaw completed her doctoral thesis on Kant's metaphysics and moral judgement at Lancaster University. She has since held posts at Aston University and Université de Nantes, and is currently Reader in Law and Social Justice and Head of Research Students at the Faculty of Business and Law, De Montfort University, Leicester, UK. Julia is an Associate Editor of the *Social Responsibility Journal*, Guest Editor of *Contemporary Issues in Law* and the *Liverpool Law Review: A Journal of Contemporary Legal and Social Policy Issues*. She is currently an External Examiner for the universities of Buckingham and Southampton and a core member of the Centre for Urban Research on Austerity (CURA), the UK's only centre dedicated to urban austerity research. Her research spans the interdisciplinary fields of law, politics, public policy, sustainability, law and literature, philosophy, business ethics, and critical management theory; she has recently published a range of journal articles on law and aesthetics, legal semiotics and spatial justice. Julia is the author of *Jurisprudence* published by Pearson and now in its 3rd edition. She is completing a monograph for Routledge entitled *Law and the Passions: A Discrete History*, and is co-author of *Corporate Social Responsibility: Global Food Supply Chain*; both books to be published by Routledge in 2018.

Loreta Tauginienė is an Associate Professor in Management at Mykolas Romeris University. Lately, she engaged in European projects that focus on responsible research and innovation, and public engagement innovations. She has published some ten publications on the implementation of social responsibility from the perspective of the management of research performance, university social responsibility, stakeholder engagement and science in society. Loreta was given a Baltic University Programme Special Award for the Best PhD thesis in 2013 in the field of sustainability. Her research interests are academic ethics, academic integrity, research integrity, social responsibility of higher education institutions, public engagement, and responsible research and innovation.

Duygu Türker is an Associate Professor at the Department of Business Administration in Yasar University. She has a BA in Business Administration, Dokuz Eylul University, an MSc in Environmental Sciences, Ankara University, an MBA, Dokuz Eylul University, and she received her PhD from Dokuz Eylul University in Public Administration. She has been involved in various projects as researcher or administrator. Her research interests include corporate social responsibility, business ethics, interorganizational relations and entrepreneurship.

V.G. Venkatesh is currently a full-time doctoral candidate at Waikato Management School, University of Waikato, Hamilton, New Zealand. His background is a blend of academia and global industry. His areas of interest are supply chain management, procurement and global logistics. He has published many practice-oriented research papers in reputable journals. He is an invited speaker for many industrial forums and acts as the reviewer for many top-level journals. Besides his research work, he is actively involved in the post-graduate teaching and industry programmes.

Kemi C. Yekini's many years of experience in professional practice and industry has largely driven her teaching and research interest(s), which can be grouped around accountability and transparency in corporate disclosure practices. Kemi has developed a broad approach to examining corporate social responsibility (CSR) and sustainability reporting and other narrative company disclosures, to assess the accountability to these issues of the large multinationals. She interprets CSR to encompass many aspects of social and environmental interactions and has a particular interest in understanding a firm's interaction with its corporate and extended environment through high-quality disclosures. Her research interests encompass CSR communication, sustainability and accountability, auditing, corporate governance and forensic accounting. She currently supervises doctoral students within these research areas. Kemi is the Editor of the Accounting and Finance Occasional Paper Series of De Montfort University and a member of the Centre for Research into Organisational Governance (CROG) and the Corporate Social Responsibility Network.

Vilma Žydžiūnaitė is a Professor at Vytautas Magnus University, with a background in nursing and education sciences. She has received two PhDs – in Education (from Kaunas University of Technology, Kaunas, Lithuania) and in Nursing (from Tampere University, Tampere, Finland). For over 16 years she has been involved in qualitative and multidisciplinary research activities and projects. Vilma has published over 150 original articles, five monographs and six books on qualitative research methodology such as manuals for students, research studies and handbooks. She is the Head of the School of Social Researcher, Kaunas, Lithuania. Recently Vilma also provided original/authorship methodological workshops on qualitative research methodology for researchers, scientists and PhD students who represent almost all Lithuanian higher education institutions. Her research areas relate to higher education; research in self-directed and self-managed learning and competence development; qualitative research in social and health sciences; multidisciplinary and multiprofessional research; and leadership and ethical dilemmas.

Introduction
David Crowther and Linne Marie Lauesen

REASONS FOR RESEARCH

We all have some form of intellectual curiosity which causes us to seek to find out things. In our world this is known as research and for academics has become an essential part of our career development and even of our promotion. So we undertake research both because we want to and because we need to; naturally we research topics which are of interest or concern to us and we want our research to be as strong as possible. So the design of a research project is an essential part of undertaking research, as is choosing appropriate methods for investigation and analysis.

The methods of research are probably fairly well known and are mostly common to all research in the business and management areas as well as to all research in social sciences. Some things are, however, more suited to research in the area of corporate social responsibility (CSR), and we focus in this book upon these and ways to make best use of available methods.

This leads to the perennial problem of defining what we mean when we talk about CSR. People have spent a long time defining what this is and there are probably as many definitions as there are researchers. Some too have tried to make a clear distinction between CSR and corporate responsibility or corporate governance or sustainability. Some have focused on the history of such research and suggested changes over time. Some have also seized upon the word corporate to assume that this is a field which only considers corporations rather than other forms of organisation. Here, we have taken the opposite view and deliberately avoided defining the field. Instead we will simply state that if you think your research is about CSR – or indeed any of the other terms – then it is and the contents of this book are relevant to you. This may seem a grandiose claim, but we expect to justify it through the course of the book.

As in many other spheres of human endeavour, research provides a key basis for developing knowledge. In the physical sciences, we have long relied on and used research as a way of helping to define and refine knowledge in their subject areas. It is only comparatively recently that the social scientist has begun to use research for the same purpose. Certainly, research in business and management is one of the newest fields of research – with CSR being a new area within this field. In this introductory chapter we examine the background to, and the development of, business and management research, tracing the different approaches to such research, the purposes of the research and some of the particular problems and issues to which research in this area gives rise before moving on to consider the particular aspects of research into CSR and its allied topics. In the process we shall also examine the main traditions and approaches to conducting research in general including what is referred to as the different 'philosophies' of research.

THEORETICAL ANTECEDENTS TO RESEARCH: EPISTEMOLOGICAL AND ONTOLOGICAL ORIENTATIONS

Business and management research raises both theoretical and practical problems, which are not encountered in research into the physical sciences and even the social sciences. Contemporary research in this area contains certain theoretical strands and antecedents that serve to shape and inform how such research is conducted. Before we look at the different approaches to contemporary research, we need to consider what some of these key theoretical antecedents to management research practice are, and in particular, the different approaches to theory development and testing in the research process. We start by examining two of the earliest approaches which centre primarily on the development of knowledge and theory but which, in turn, have helped shape approaches to research. These two early approaches are the epistemological and ontological schools of thought. Both of these schools of thought date back to the Greek philosophers.

The Epistemological Orientation

Gilbert (1993) suggests that in this approach to developing knowledge and theories, theories are built on the basis of gaining knowledge of the world. An epistemological approach organises and explains knowledge in the form of theories. For example, an epistemological approach to a theory of leadership might be based on exploring what we can observe about effective leadership in the real world. By developing our knowledge of effective leadership in this way we might observe that effective leadership seems to be associated with the possession of certain traits or characteristics on the part of the leader. This knowledge can then be used to form theories of leadership based on the possession of certain traits and their relationship to effective leadership. As we shall see later in this chapter and in several of the chapters that follow, much research and theory building in the social sciences uses the epistemological approach of building knowledge. Admittedly, there are many critics of the limitations of the epistemological approach to developing knowledge (Feyerabend 1975, Cook and Campbell 1979). As Easterby-Smith et al. (2002) suggest, however, this orientation to building theories and knowledge can, and does, result in several approaches or methodologies to the generation of such knowledge. This means that there is little doubt that the epistemological school of thought has resulted in a powerful and enduring legacy when it comes to the development of theory and the practice of business and management research.

The Ontological Orientation

This approach to the development of theories is based on suggestions about the 'nature of phenomena' (Gilbert 1993). For example, an ontological approach to developing theories of leadership would consist of developing views on, for example, the nature of effective leadership with or without reference or an attempt to relate these views to a knowledge base. In fact, this represents a very simplified description of what is in fact a variety of ontological approaches in the physical and social sciences. For example, we have the so-called 'critical realism' ontology such as that of, say, Bhaskar (1989) compared to, say, the 'interpretative' ontological approach suggested by Sayer (2000). For our purposes at this stage and as you will probably recognise, we have now identified the main distinguishing difference between epistemological and ontological orientations. Specifically, that respectively they represent an empirical versus a conceptual approach to theory building and research and as such are indeed different orientations. As already mentioned, we shall see in some of our methodologies and approaches to management research that both epistemological and ontological orientations survive to influence and shape the nature of contemporary management research.

DEDUCTIVE VERSUS INDUCTIVE RESEARCH

From our two earliest schools of thought regarding theory development and knowledge building have developed two equally important, but also in their own ways equally contrasting, alternative schools of thought with regard to the methodology of theory and knowledge building – namely deductive versus inductive research methods. In fact, these methods of research derive from two alternative methods of thinking (Graziano and Raulin 2004). The differences between these alternative approaches to research are explained below.

Deductive Research

Deductive research develops theories or hypotheses and then tests out these theories or hypotheses through empirical observation. It is essentially a set of techniques for applying theories in the real world in order to test and assess their validity. Essentially the process of deductive research is as Saunders et al. point out 'the development of a theory that is subjected to a rigorous test' (2003, 2005 p. 124). Deductive research is the most widely used research approach in the natural sciences but in our area deductive and inductive research approaches are probably equally used. The process of deductive research can be described as shown in Figure I.1.

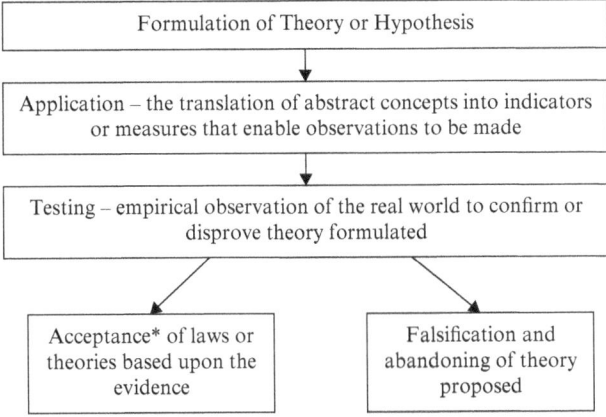

Note: * Acceptance means that such laws are not yet falsified rather than correct.

Figure I.1   The process of deduction

Others, such as Robson (2002), add another stage to this process namely that of modifying the theory in the light of findings, but the key steps in deductive research are now explained.

Theory/hypothesis formulation
The first step in deductive research is the generation of theories or hypotheses. These can be generated in a number of ways: for example, the researcher might simply have an idea based on, say, previous experience which he/she wants to test out or, for example, the theory or hypothesis to be tested might stem from a literature search bringing together the ideas of others. Yet other sources of theories or hypotheses are those that stem from the desire to work out a solution to a specific problem. You will appreciate that this source of theories or hypotheses is particularly important and relevant in the context of this book as many projects start with a specific set of problems or issues that the research is designed to address ultimately with a view to making recommendations to resolving the problem or issues. The deductive research method, therefore, is particularly appropriate and relevant to this type of research. Because of this, much deductive research can be considered as falling into the category of what is often referred to as applied research. We shall be considering the nature and process of such research in more detail in the subsequent chapters. In addition, we shall be considering the generation of theories and hypotheses for testing in later chapters when research design is considered in more detail.

Application
Having formulated theories or hypotheses, the next stage in the deductive research process is to operationalise these. Essentially, this is the process whereby the concepts in our theories or hypotheses are defined in such a way that they can be measured through empirical observation. As Burns (2000) points out, operational definition is necessary to eliminate confusion in meaning and communication. This means, for example, ensuring that we have defined precisely what is to be measured or observed and how this measurement or observation will be carried out. For example, if our hypothesis is along the lines that, say, 'personality traits' are associated with 'effective leadership', then we need to ensure that we have defined and can measure 'personality traits' and what constitutes 'effective leadership'. It is important to stress that the process of operationalising theories or hypotheses can be difficult as we are often dealing with abstract concepts which, of themselves, are difficult to measure. These, and other aspects of operationalising theories or hypotheses, are considered in more detail in later chapters.

Empirical observation – data collection
This stage in the process of deductive research is concerned with the process of measurement and observation such that we can eventually, in the next stage of the process, decide whether our theory or hypotheses can be supported or rejected. This stage of the deductive research process involves identifying and deciding between alternative techniques and approaches for measuring our operationalised concepts. It also includes the selection and design of the research methodologies to be used including, for example, any sampling plan, research instruments, and methods of analysing and interpreting empirical observations and measurements. In many ways, this stage of the deductive research process encompasses much of the activities that will be required to be planned and undertaken

in conducting the research and as such several of the chapters that follow are essentially concerned with the design and application of this stage.

Once we have completed this stage in the deductive process then we can move to the final stage of deciding the extent to which our theory or hypothesis has been falsified and the extent to which parts, if any, of our theory or hypotheses remains as not yet falsified. We refer to this as the falsification and discarding stage.

Falsification and discarding theory
At first, it may seem strange that the aim of the deductive process is to assess the extent to which a theory or hypothesis can be falsified and hence should be discarded. Surely, one might think, the process should be aimed at proving rather than refuting our hypotheses or theories. As you will appreciate, the idea that the outcome should be falsification and discarding of theories and hypotheses stems from the ideas of Karl Popper (1967) in what is often referred to as his maxim of falsification. Simply stated, this maxim is based on the premise that the researcher should aim to refute rather than verify their theories or hypotheses. He argued that no theory can ever be proven but only ever falsified – just as the sighting of one black swan would disprove the theory that all swans are white, whereas discovering millions of white swans over centuries would never prove the theory which would be disproved by a single example. To the extent that the empirical observations made in the previous step in the process of deductive research do not support our theory or hypothesis, then these observations can be said to falsify and may lead us to discard all or part of our theory or hypothesis. This is the bottom right-hand box in Figure I.1. That part of our theory or hypothesis which is not falsified through our observations and measurements of the empirical world does not prove our theory as such but rather allows those parts to remain as yet unfalsified theories or hypotheses. This is the bottom left-hand box in Figure I.1. Clearly, the falsification approach to testing of theory and hypotheses leads to possibly very different approaches to research design, methodology, and techniques of testing theories and hypotheses than where we are using a verification approach. For example, how we state hypotheses or theories for testing is very different with a falsification as opposed to a verification approach. Again, we shall see this when we discuss hypothesis setting and testing in later chapters.

These, then, are the main steps in the process of deductive research. It is a fact that this approach to research represents the main, and some would say, the only justifiable, method of research in the natural sciences. There are those who, in addition, suggest that this is the only truly 'scientific' approach to developing knowledge and therefore should also be the only approach that is used in the social sciences.

However, applying the deductive method in the social as opposed to the natural sciences is not without its problems. For example, measurement can be more problematical. Unlike the natural sciences, research is difficult to control and particularly the factors that can affect research outcomes, that is, the experimental method so widely used in the natural sciences is difficult. Again we shall consider some of these problems of the deductive methods of research and research techniques in later chapters but it is partly because of some of the problems and criticisms of the deductive approach to research that our second and alternative approach to research and research methods is almost exactly the reverse of deduction. This is of course known as inductive research.

Inductive Research

As has already been indicated, inductive research is essentially the opposite of the process found in deductive research. In this approach the researcher develops hypotheses and theories with a view to explaining empirical observations of the real world. These empirical observations can be based on many factors, even for example, they can simply be based on personal experience. Consider your own experiences in this respect. What have you observed best motivates you, or other people, in work organisations? Do you have any ideas on this? If so, you could develop your own explanations and theories about what you have observed through personal experience. Alternatively, theories might be developed to explain observed data and information, for example, the researcher might develop theories based on observed patterns of labour turnover. All sorts and types of information and data can be used to develop theories in inductive research. In fact, in the context of this book, when considering management research in general and CSR-based research in particular, the inductive research approach can be the more appropriate approach to research compared to the deductive method just outlined. Perhaps the greatest strength of inductive research is its flexibility. This research approach does not require the establishment of a-priori theories or hypotheses. On the contrary, we can build our theories based on our observations thereby allowing a problem or issue to be studied or approached in several possible different ways with alternative explanations of what is going on. It is particularly suited to the study of human behaviour, including of course behaviour in organisations. Inductive research also enables more flexibility in research design including aspects such as sample size and type of data.

It is apparent, therefore, that inductive research and investigation begins from description or observation and then moves towards explanation. This approach, then, is initially concerned with observations that then lead to the development of a hypothesis and theories in order to explain those particular observations. In this context, we should note that in many research projects the management researcher, and the consultant researcher in particular, might be required to investigate ideas that stem initially from the observation or more specifically the occurrence of practical and observable issues and problems. The researcher may then be required or called in to investigate these issues and problems in order to develop theories to first explain, and then perhaps solve, these issues and problems. As already stated, the inductive approach to conducting management research, therefore, can be particularly appropriate to research in the area of CSR. Indeed, we shall see when discussing some of the different approaches to, and techniques of, such research that some of the most powerful techniques of management research and consultancy use the inductive approach. The inductive approach is also better suited to the use and interpretation of qualitative data, whereas the deductive method, with its emphasis on measurement, often requires, and can only utilise, quantitative data. Given that such research and certainly management problems can often involve both qualitative and quantitative aspects, more often than not effective management research often requires a combination of inductive and deductive methods. We may, for example, begin a research project using inductive methods and approaches, by say, first observing and measuring a phenomenon or problem that we wish to explore. This in turn can lead us to develop theories that we can then test using the deductive methods and approach.

NOMOTHETIC VERSUS IDEOGRAPHIC RESEARCH

The contrast between inductive and deductive research methods has given rise to two alternative categories of research methods. Burrell and Morgan (1979) have referred to these alternatives as the nomothetic versus ideographic methodologies. In fact, these two methodologies are best thought of as the extremes of a continuum of research methods but as Burns (2000, p. 3) points out, each of these alternatives 'has profound implications for the way in which research is conducted'.

Nomothetic methods are most appropriate to the deductive approach to research in as much as they include the more highly structured research methodologies which can be replicated and controlled, and which focus on generating quantitative data with a view to explaining causal relationships. Perhaps the best examples of nomothetic research methodologies are those that are based on controlled laboratory experimentation. As such, they are obviously better suited to research in the natural sciences. Ideographic research methodologies, on the other hand, are much less structured and are focused more on the explanation and understanding of phenomena with much more emphasis on qualitative data. As such, the ideographic methods are better suited to the inductive research approach and in some ways are better suited to research in the social sciences including, of course, management research. Amongst the best examples of the ideographic research techniques are those of the previously referred to action research and the related research approach of ethnography, both of which are explained in more detail in later chapters.

Both nomothetic and ideographic methodologies can be used in our research, and again will often be used in combination. In addition, specific techniques of research within both methodologies often cut across and combine nomothetic and ideographic approaches. The characteristics of nomothetic and ideographic methods are considered in later chapters when we consider the selection and use of alternative research methodologies.

So far in this introductory chapter we have examined the main theoretical antecedents to the process of and practice of research in general in both the physical and social sciences – but particularly in the business and management area of the social sciences – including some of the main alternative research methodologies. It is important for us to understand these as they serve to shape and direct contemporary research practices including the practice of research in the area of CSR. As such, we have briefly explored some of the implications of these antecedents and major methodological approaches for the process of management research. Now, however, we need to focus more specifically on the nature and issues of management research in general and of CSR research in particular. We shall start the next part of this chapter, therefore, by discussing three main types of research in management, followed by an overview of the management research process. Then we move on to consider research in the CSR area specifically. Together, these will serve to set the framework for much of what follows in later chapters.

TYPES OF MANAGEMENT RESEARCH

Although there is overlap between them, it is possible to identify or categorise three different types of management research with regard to the primary focus or objective of the research.

Theory Building Research

First, there is that research which is primarily aimed at developing management theories, and by so doing, improving our understanding and knowledge of the management process. You will now recognise that this type of management research is essentially inductive in nature. For example, it seeks to develop theories based on, say, observations, experience, intuition and so on. Much academic research in management is of this nature.

Theory Testing Research

Secondly, there is that research which is primarily aimed at testing out theories of management. Again, as we have already seen, more often than not this testing involves the process of empirical observations and measurements. This makes us able to arrive at the decision as to whether or not to reject a hypothesis or theory; what parts of it can be rejected and thereby which part can remain as not yet falsified. Again, much academic research in management falls into this category.

Problem Centred/Practical Research

Our third type of research in management is that which is primarily aimed not at building or generating new theories, or adding to knowledge through the testing of theories or hypotheses. Rather, this type of research is primarily aimed at investigating a practical problem, question or issue in a specific organisation or management context with a view to resolving the problem and subsequently making recommendations for courses of action. The primary focus of such research, then, is not academic or knowledge building for its own sake, but rather is aimed at investigating and proposing solutions to real life management problems. This is not to say that this type of research does not potentially add to the body of theory and knowledge about management and indeed some of the most significant contributions to our knowledge and understanding in this area have stemmed from what was essentially problem centred consultancy type research. The so-called 'Hawthorne Experiments' at the General Electric Company, USA, are good examples (these experiments are explained in fuller detail in Chapter 17). Having said this, for the most part, in the past with consultancy type research any contributions to theory or knowledge building along the way have been more of a bonus than a primary aim. It is contended here, however, that this is changing. Increasingly, it is being recognised that consultancy type research, even if it is still primarily problem/application centred, can at the same time be used for theory building and theory testing and hence for knowledge building. As already mentioned, there are plenty of examples of consultancy type research making substantial contributions in this way. In this book, we continue this tradition, but in so doing, strive to bring even closer together and combine the applied consultancy type research approach with more academic type research that is so often the prime focus of most undergraduate and graduate projects and dissertations. In so doing, it is important to emphasise that this means that a variety of research methods and approaches may need to be combined for a particular project according to the circumstances. This is what Gill and Johnson (1997) refer to as 'methodological pluralism' by which they mean that there is no one best research method or approach, but rather 'many methods contingent on the issue being studied'.

The reason for stressing this increased emphasis on combining the different research approaches is because almost every user of this book will be actually undertaking a research project or dissertation as part of their academic working environment. Clearly there are different types of management research according to nature, purpose and context. However, it is useful to describe in broad terms the overall CSR-based management research process which can now be introduced.

AN OVERVIEW OF THE CSR-BASED MANAGEMENT RESEARCH PROCESS

As you will appreciate, the term management research encompasses a wide variety of approaches and types but certainly includes CSR research in all its various forms. It is perhaps, therefore, problematical to propose an outline or model of the process of management research that fits or reflects all these possible approaches and types. However, we share the view of Gill and Johnson (op. cit.), who suggest that despite the potential problems of proposing an overview of the research sequence, such an overview, although admittedly idealised, serves to help understand and appreciate the research process, including where the actual research process detracts from this idealised version. Using a framework similar to that proposed by Howard and Sharp (1983), however, we can identify that the stages in the research sequence are as follows:

- Identification of a general topic or field of research
- Selection within this field of specific research topic
- Deciding upon research methodology to be adopted
- Formulation of research plan
- Data collection
- Analysis of data collected
- Interpretation of the analysis within the context of the research topic
- Presentation of findings.

Probably we all recognise, but certainly it is worth emphasising, that rarely, if ever, is the process of research as smooth as suggested in the sequence above. More often, the process is messy and frustrating with the stages overlapping and often having to be revisited in an iterative manner as the research progresses. All too often there are cases when the research process does not progress at all with what initially appeared to be 'exciting' and 'feasible' research projects but has become problematic. For a variety of reasons, many turn out to be 'non-starters'.

Conducting any type of research project can be messy and frustrating. Some of these problems and issues are common to all types of social research. For example, unlike the natural sciences, in social science research, we have the problem of trying to apply some of the processes and methodologies in settings or situations which are difficult and sometimes impossible to control. Unlike the physicist or chemist, the social sciences researcher does not have the benefit of a 'laboratory' in which to conduct his/her research. Similarly, quantification and hence statistical analysis and verification can be more problematical in social sciences research. Additionally, within this field research there are particular problems and issues which are related to the particular types or methodologies which we tend to employ. For example, methodologies such as action research or ethnography give rise to certain special issues and problems only associated with these particular methodologies. These are of course covered in subsequent chapters.

Conducting CSR research can give rise to ethical problems: ethical issues in research encompass a set of mores and values for conducting and using research and the researcher must be careful not to violate these. The conduct of research therefore must conform to a set of ethical codes or values. A problem here, however, is as Wells (1994) points out that what is considered ethical – and therefore unethical – behaviour can vary from situation to situation; from researcher to researcher; and from culture to culture. This is something which will be returned to in a later chapter but it is important here to recognise the particular problems from international research. It is also important to recognise that all universities and most professional and funding bodies all have codes of conduct which must be adhered to. This can be problematic if your collaborator is from another institution in another country with different expectations. It is important, therefore, that ethical issues are a part of your research plan.

A perennial problem to researchers is that of access. As you will understand, access encompasses initial permission to enter an organisation, and this is what Gummesson (2000) refers to as 'physical access'. Obviously, without such permission, much research is virtually impossible. In addition to this initial access/permission we also have the issue of access to information and people as part of the research design. For example, the researcher and organisation have to consider and agree what information the researcher will have access to, and on what basis, and who the researcher will be allowed access to and what parts of the organisation the researcher can seek information from as part of the research. This of course raises the issue of confidentiality – another important issue which will be returned to. Obviously, access needs to be negotiated and agreed between researcher and the researched, but overall should be such as to ensure that the research objectives can be met. In practice, limitations or problems in access often result in modifications to initial research objectives and programmes.

Where the research involves, or cuts across, different cultures, such as when the research encompasses, say, different geographical divisions in a multinational organisation, there can be particular problems of methodology and interpretation. Even where the research is confined to one country, internal organisational culture too can be an issue in planning and conducting management consultancy based research projects. Because this type of research is conducted directly within an organisational environment the researcher must be careful to ensure that, for example, the research approach, techniques of data collection and so on are appropriate to organisational systems and procedures.

Much CSR research can be problematic because a number of stakeholders have an interest and possibly influence in the research. The most obvious stakeholder with an interest in the research, or certainly the research results and recommendations, is of course the organisation in which the research is being conducted. Clearly, the organisation may seek to influence the nature of the research, how it is conducted, the objectives and so on.[1] In addition, where the research is also the basis for a thesis there are also academic stakeholders – just as there increasingly is when we are driven to publish our findings in particular outlets. These stakeholders also have an interest in how research is conducted and the objectives and so on. This stakeholder group may have a fundamentally different perspective on these matters and will certainly often have a different set of criteria for judging how effective the research has been. This means that the researcher must often resolve any potential conflicts which stem from trying to meet potentially conflicting aims of different parties. In some cases, this may result in two different reports being produced, one for the organisation and its management, and one for the academic environment.

Conducting Research

In order to understand both the process and nature of our CSR research it is necessary to understand some of the theoretical antecedents to research in general. The researcher naturally needs to appreciate some of the major alternative schools of thought or models of research. Of particular relevance and importance in this context are the epistemological versus ontological orientations in research, the nature and differences between deductive and inductive research, and the comparison between nomothetic and ideographic research approaches. CSR research encompasses several different types and forms of research which can primarily be distinguished with regard to the objectives or purpose, and hence the outcomes of the research activities. Such research, therefore, encompasses both theoretical and applied research.

Having considered business and management research generally, as a subset of social science, we need to turn our attention to CSR research in all its various forms. After all this book is a handbook of research methods in this area! One way to start is to consider what has been published in this area. Many journals have published articles on CSR or on some aspect of this field but the number of journals dedicated to this area are limited. Some new ones are starting as this book is published but very few have any extensive pedigree. One exception which is well established is *Social Responsibility Journal*, published by Emerald Group. This journal is not just concerned with this field of research but is also the official journal of the Social Responsibility Research Network. Its activities are therefore worthy of consideration.

Perspectives from the Social Responsibility Research Network

The origin of the Social Responsibility Research Network can be traced to 2003 (Seifi and Crowther 2012) and was an outcome of an event organised by Professor David Crowther and hosted at London Metropolitan University. This international event attracted 150 participants from around the world and raised many important issues ranging from business ethics and social reporting to implications for biodiversity and sustainable construction, reflecting the interdisciplinary nature of the backgrounds and expertise of the participants. The success of the event led to a variety of international collaborative projects and to a number of publications.

The Network[2] itself was formed during 2004 and has become an established organisation which currently has over 850 members located all over the world. One of the prime purposes of the Network is to bring together people interested in the various aspects of social responsibility and to facilitate collaborative research. We believe that discussion and debate amongst interested people from different backgrounds and different parts of the world – and who very often work alone in their own location – will enrich the debate and lead towards developments in our understanding of some of the important issues facing the world today. Membership is open to anyone who has a perspective on any aspect of this important issue. This includes academics, researchers, business people, non-governmental organisation managers, government officials and politicians, consultants and scholars – and all groups are represented within the membership.

As a consequence of the focus upon the facilitation of a collaborative research agenda the prime focus of the Network has been upon both its annual conference – held at a different location around the world each year – and its publishing. Thus the official journal of the Network is *Social Responsibility Journal*, founded as an academic journal to publish work by members and others in this important and growing area. The journal is now in its fourteenth year and continues to grow in strength and reputation. The Network also publishes books within the series Developments in Corporate Governance and Responsibility, which currently publishes two books per year.

This background information is essential to explain the rationale for this analysis of the current state of research in the area of social responsibility and to look at some areas which are currently under-researched. In doing this we intend to explore the current agenda of research and to propose its development into new areas.

It is important at the outset of this analysis to state what we mean by the social responsibility research. This is interpreted in its broadest sense as being any aspect of the broad social responsibility agenda and covers the whole range of social, environmental, cultural and philanthropic aspects of corporate and organisational behaviour. It also extends into the very important areas of sustainability and sustainable development. Another significant area which falls within our definition is that of governance, which we regard as an integral aspect of social responsibility. It can be seen, therefore, that we adopt a very wide definition of social responsibility and this is reflected in the topics which have been presented at our conferences and published in our various journals and books. Naturally, we recognise that the topics being investigated have changed in the decade during which we have been in existence and we both welcome this and note it as an indication of the development and maturing of the field of social responsibility. We are only concerned with present and future lines of research and we have therefore conducted our analysis on the most recent papers in the journal (including those accepted but not yet published) and the most recent two conferences. We feel that this is sufficient to give an understanding of the topics which are of current concern as far as social responsibility research is concerned. From this some interesting findings are revealed.

There are a number of issues which are of current concern to businesses and to people (Crowther and Seifi 2011) and which comprise a current and future agenda for research. Broadly speaking they can be considered to be issues concerning the environment, human rights protection and governance. We can examine each in turn.

Environmental Issues

The changes to the climate around the world is apparent to most people and is being manifest in such extreme weather as excessive rain or snow, droughts, heatwaves and hurricanes which have been affecting many parts of the world. Possibly even some earthquakes are related to climate change. Global warming and climate change, its most noticeable effect, is a subject of discussion all over the world and it is generally, although by no means universally, accepted that global warming is taking place and therefore that climate change will continue to happen. Opinion is divided, however, as to whether the climate change which has taken place can be reversed or not. Some think that it cannot be reversed. Thus according to Lovelock (2006) climate change is inevitable with its consequences upon the environment and therefore upon human life and economic activity. Although there are many factors which are contributing to the global warming which is taking place it is clear that commercial and economic activity plays a significant part in this global warming. Indeed, many people talk about 'greenhouse gases', with carbon dioxide being the main one, as a direct consequence of economic activity. Consequently, many people see the reduction in the emission of such gases as being fundamental to any attempt to combat climate change.

Another factor which is of concern to people in general is that of their ecological footprint – the amount of physical area of the earth needed to provide for each person. Ecological footprint analysis compares human demand on nature with the biosphere's ability to regenerate resources and provide services. It does this by assessing the biologically productive land and marine area required to produce the resources a population consumes and absorb the corresponding waste, using prevailing technology. This approach can also be applied to an activity such as the manufacturing of a product or driving of a car. A possibly more fashionable term at the moment, however, is that of carbon footprinting.[3] General concern has been expressed worldwide and this has led to the Kyoto Protocol.[4] The Kyoto Protocol defines legally binding targets and timetables for cutting the greenhouse gas emissions of industrialised countries that ratified the protocol.[5]

Although scientific opinion has more or less reached a consensus that global warming is taking place and therefore that climate change is happening, there are still a considerable number of sceptics and people who deny that it is happening.[6] There are others who argue that the human contribution to global warming is negligible: they argue, therefore, that it is useless or even harmful to concentrate on individual contributions.

In many parts of the world water is becoming a serious problem. Irrigation has led to serious problems in such parts of the world as California while in Uzbekistan it has led to the shrinking of the Aral Sea to a fraction of its previous size. And many rivers, in all parts of the world, have so much water extracted from them that they no longer reach the sea. At the same time millions of people do not have access to safe drinking water. And countries are entering into disputes with each other for access to water that they share between them. Indeed, access to water is forecast to become a major source of conflict in the 21st century. Another issue concerning water is the question of virtual water and the Royal Academy of Engineering (UK) has documented (2010) that countries such as the UK are using water from developing countries where it is in short supply by embedding it in the products purchased from such countries.

It is fairly obvious that the resources of the planet are finite and this is a limiting factor to growth and development. The depletion of the resources of the planet, however, is one of the actors which has helped create the current interest in sustainability. Of particular concern are the extractive industries and such materials as aluminium are becoming in short supply. In the UK the mineral resources such as tin and lead have been fully extracted long ago and the thriving industries based around them are long gone. As other resources – such as coal – are extracted in total then the companies based upon them disappear, as do the jobs in those industries. This is an obvious source of concern for people.

Of particular concern is the extinguishing of supplies of oil, because much economic activity is only possible because of energy created by the use of oil. Indeed, many would argue that the wars in the Middle East,[7] particularly the problems in Iraq and Iran, are caused by oil shortages, actual or impending, and the problems thereby caused, rather than by any concern for political issues. Most people have now heard of Hubbert's Peak[8] and engaged with the debate as to whether or not it has been reached (Deffeyes 2004, Bower 2009). Certainly, it has in parts of the world such as the North Sea, but it is less certain if it has been reached for the world as a whole. Indeed, the creation of techniques for extracting fuel from shale beds has postponed the urgency of considering the arrival of Hubbert's Peak, although most people do not seem to realise that it is a relatively short-term postponement of about 25 years.[9] Nevertheless, the whole crux of sustainability – and sustainable development – is based upon the need for energy and there are insufficient alternative sources of energy to compensate for the elimination of oil as a source of fuel. Consequently, resource depletion, real or imagined, and particularly energy resources, is one of the most significant causes of the current interest in sustainability.

Human Rights Issues

Another matter which has become prominent is a concern with the supply chain of a business; in other words, with what is happening in other companies which that company does business with – their suppliers and the suppliers of their suppliers. In particular people are concerned with the exploitation of people in developing countries, especially the question of child labour but also such things as sweat shops.

So no longer is it acceptable for a company to say that the conditions under which their suppliers operate is outside of their control and so they are not responsible. Customers have said that this is not acceptable and have called companies to account. And there have recently been a number of high profile retail companies which have held their hands up to acknowledge problems and then taken very public steps to change this.

Interestingly the popularity of companies increases after they have admitted problems and taken steps to correct these problems. In doing this they are thereby showing both that honesty is the best practice and also that customers are reasonable. The evidence suggests that individual customers are understanding and that they do not expect perfection but do expect honesty and transparency. Moreover, they also expect companies to make efforts to change their behaviour and to try to solve their CSR problems.

Companies themselves have also changed. No longer are they concerned with greenwashing – the pretence of socially responsible behaviour through artful reporting. Now companies are taking CSR much more seriously not just because they understand that it is a key to business success and can give them a strategic advantage, but also because people in those organisations care about social responsibility. Sadly, however, examples of poor practice, such as Volkswagen's cheating of emission testing, continue to be uncovered.

So it would be reasonable to claim that the growing importance of CSR and sustainable development is being driven by individuals who care – but those individuals are not just customers, they are also employees, managers, owners and investors of a company.

So companies are partly reacting to external pressures and partly leading the development of responsible behaviour and reporting.

Problems of Governance

The 2008 financial and economic crisis and its aftermath have shown that there are failures in governance and problems with the market system. In the main these have been depicted as representative of systemic failures of the market system and the lax application of systems of governance and regulation. Thus many people are arguing for improved systems to combat this – although little change has been manifest (see Lauesen 2013, 2016). Naturally many people have discussed these failures and the consequent problems and will continue to do so in the future. It is not of course the first such crisis, and the market economy has been proceeding on a course of boom and bust for the last 20 years which is not dissimilar to that of the sixties and seventies which the neo-conservatives claimed to have stopped. The main differences are that recent cycles are driven by the financial markets rather than economics and in the era of globalisation no country is immune from contagion and the effects felt in other countries.

Thus we need to consider alternatives and spend a short time considering governance – and in the context of this book its relationship to CSR. All systems of governance are concerned primarily with managing the governing of associations and therefore with political authority, institutions and, ultimately, control. Governance in this particular sense denotes formal political institutions that aim to coordinate and control interdependent social relations and that have the ability to enforce decisions. Increasingly, however, in a globalised world, the concept of governance is being used to describe the regulation of interdependent relations in the absence of overarching political authority, such as in the international system. Thus global governance can be considered as the management of global processes in the absence of a form of global government. There are some international bodies which seek to address these issues and prominent amongst these are the United Nations and the World Trade Organization. Each of these has met with mixed success in instituting some form of governance in international relations but are part of a recognition of the problem and an attempt to address worldwide problems that go beyond the capacity of individual states to solve.

Global governance is not of course the same thing as world government: indeed, it can be argued that such a system would not actually be necessary if there was such a thing as a world government. Currently, however, the various state governments have a legitimate monopoly on the use of force – on the power of enforcement. Global governance therefore refers to the political interaction that is required to solve problems that affect more than one state or region when there is no power of enforcing compliance. Improved global problem-solving need not of course require the establishing of more powerful formal global institutions, but it would involve the creation of a consensus on norms and practices to be applied.

Steps are of course underway to establish these norms and one example that is currently being established is the creation and improvement of global accountability mechanisms. In this respect, for example, the United Nations Global Compact[10] – described as the world's largest voluntary corporate responsibility initiative – brings together companies, national and international agencies, trades unions and other labour organisations and various organs of civil society in order to support universal environmental protection, human rights and social principles. Participation is entirely voluntary,[11] and there is no enforcement of the principles by an outside regulatory body. Companies adhere to these practices both because they make economic sense, and because their stakeholders, including their shareholders (most individuals and institutional investors), are concerned with these issues and this provides a mechanism whereby they can monitor the compliance of companies easily. Mechanisms such as the Global Compact can improve the ability of individuals and local communities to hold companies accountable.

Organisational and Regional Studies

It has been customary to consider SMEs (small and medium-sized enterprises) as a separate category of organisations when investigating and analysing business activities. Thus any organisation with less than 250 employees is considered to be an SME while an organisation with more than 250 employees would be classified as large. This division is a convenient method of classification but it does create several problems and ignores some situations. Thus this division ignores cultural differences: for example, an organisation with 250 employees would not be considered particularly large in China but would be considered very large indeed in most sub-Saharan African countries. This division also ignores sectoral differences: service industries such as retailing or catering tend to employ many people and 250 employees would be quite a small organisation in these sectors but would be very big for a specialist manufacturing company. Similarly, the asset base of a company will vary greatly both according to industrial sector and according to country in which the company is based. And of course sales of €50 million is much more in some countries than in others. Nevertheless, this division between SMEs and large companies has been universally adopted as a basis for investigation and analysis despite these problems. This has led to a duplication of research between different sizes of organisation without too much consideration of whether or not there are differences in CSR according to size. Equally there has been an increase in studies of different regions with unspoken assumptions that there are differences in different regions or between developed countries and developing countries and undeveloped countries. Such research has increased the body of knowledge that exists without necessarily increasing our understanding.

One implication of this arbitrary division is that there is a difference in the characteristics of companies due to their size. This may well be true – a company with ten employees will most probably be different from a company with 1000 employees. Equally, however, a company with 200 employees – and therefore classified as an SME – is more likely to be similar to a company in the same sector with 500 employees – and therefore classified as large – than it is with a company with five employees in the same or even a different sector. Thus we can see that there is an element of artificiality in this definition of SME. Nevertheless, attention seems to have moved from a concern with large organisations – and primarily multinational companies – to an increasing concern with SMEs for investigation and analysis of CSR activity; indeed this has been the focus of this book. In this chapter, however, we are not treating SMEs as a homogenous sector; instead we are focusing our attention on those medium-sized enterprises which are on the cusp and could easily become classified as large in the near future.

Such firms are relatively small in number and comprise considerably less than 1 per cent of the total SME population. In the main they differ from very large companies in that they are national rather than multinational organisations. Moreover, they tend to be single site organisations rather than having multiple sites – although exceptions can be found to all of these generalisations. In the main they are different from small organisations and are certainly different from the micro-organisations which comprise around 98 per cent of this sector. They all have websites and have highly developed performance management and reporting systems, our starting point for analysis.

As socially responsible behaviour has moved up the agenda of corporate activity most corporations can be seen to be becoming more active in the reporting of their activities in this respect. On corporate websites this is very evident and is becoming more evident also in the annual reporting of these organisations. For many, however, this is represented by a separate CSR report rather than the embedding of this activity in the annual report itself (Crowther 2002). If socially responsible behaviour is being undertaken within organisations, then it seems appropriate that these organisations should report it and increased disclosure in this respect is to be expected. It has been suggested by Schaltegger et al. (1996) that one of the driving forces in the development of social and environmental accounting was the need to placate, through the production of appropriate information, those members of society who could be classified as environmental activists. They further suggest that such accounting information developed for this purpose has now been adopted into the repertoire of organisational accounting and forms an important part of the internal management control information of the organisation.

Of course it is equally true that, in the current environment, corporations have an incentive to present their activity as socially responsible whether or not they are particularly addressing this kind of activity. In this case such reporting becomes little more than window dressing rather than a reporting of activity. The purpose of this chapter is to explore the extent to which either of these motives apply.

An examination of the external reporting of organisations does, however, demonstrate an increasing recognition of the need to include environmental information and an increasing number of annual reports of companies include some information in this respect. This trend is gathering momentum as more organisations perceive the importance of providing such information to external stakeholders. It has been suggested, however (Till and Symes 1999), that the inclusion of such information does not demonstrate an increasing concern with the environment but rather some benefits to the company itself. One trend which is also apparent, however, is the tendency of companies to produce separate environmental reports. In this context such reports, which will be considered later in this chapter, are generally termed environmental reports although in reality they include both reporting upon environmental impact and upon social impact. Thus the terms social accounting and environmental accounting tend to have been conflated within the practice of corporate reporting and the two terms used interchangeably for the form of performance measurement and reporting which recognises and reports upon the effects of the organisation's actions upon its external environment.

While these reports tend to contain much more detailed environmental information than is contained in the annual report the implication of this trend is that such information is required by a separate constituency of stakeholders than the information contained in the annual report. This suggests an impression, therefore, that environmental information is not necessary for the owners and investors in a business but is needed by other stakeholders. This therefore leads to a further suggestion that organisations view environmental issues as separate from the economic performance of the business rather than as integral to it. This conflicts with some of the arguments and findings considered above, which suggest the need for the integration of environmental and economic performance within the accounting needs of a business for the sake of continuing future performance. It does, however, highlight the problematic nature of environmental accounting and some of the problems associated with environmental impact measurement which have been considered.

These concerns have led to the general opinion that there is something different about environmental information which deserves reporting in its own right rather than being subsumed within the general corporate reporting and lost in the organisation-centric norm of corporate reporting. This opinion is based upon a recognition, as described by Butler et al. (1992, p.60), that:

> The environment (which is a free resource to individual businesses) is increasingly being turned into a factor that does carry costs. Primarily as a result of requirements imposed by current or probable future government regulation on pollution control, but also to some extent because of the wider concern of the public, who can affect a business's profitability by their behaviour as consumers, employees, and investors, there is a financial impact that needs to be accounted for.

These kinds of argument support the practice of corporate reporting in suggesting a general agreement that environmental accounting is distinct from traditional accounting.

Stakeholder Perspectives

Alongside this recognition that corporations are accountable to their stakeholders has come a development of the principles upon which this demonstration of accountability should be based. Inevitably this is predicated in accounting as a mechanism by which such action can be measured and reported. In generic terms this has come to be called either social or environmental accounting. The objective of environmental accounting is to measure the effects of the actions of the organisation upon the environment and to report upon those effects. In other words, the objective is to incorporate the effect of the activities of the firm upon externalities and to view the firm as a network which extends beyond just the internal environment to include the whole environment (see Crowther 2002). In this view of the organisation the accounting for the firm does not stop at the organisational boundary but extends beyond to include not just the business environment in which it operates but also the whole social environment. Environmental accounting therefore adds a new dimension to the role of accounting for an organisation because of its emphasis upon accounting for external effects of the organisation's activities. In doing so this provides a recognition that the organisation is an integral part of society, rather than a self-contained entity which has only an indirect relationship with society at large. This self-containment has been the traditional view taken by an organisation as far as their relationship with society at large is concerned, with interaction being only by means of resource acquisition and sales of finished products or services. Recognition of this closely intertwined relationship of mutual interdependency between the organisation and society at large, when reflected in the accounting of the organisation, can help bring about a closer, and possibly more harmonious, relationship between the organisation and society. Given that the managers and workers of an organisation are also stakeholders in that society in other capacities, such as consumers, citizens and inhabitants, this reinforces the mutual interdependency.

While few would argue with the claim that a business is an entity insofar as it is perceived to act as a whole towards the fulfilment of the particular objectives which it has, it is in reality a composite entity which consists of an association of individuals each working towards a commonality of shared purpose. The actuality is different to this in that the common purpose is often not clearly identified and articulated and that the individuals are not necessarily working totally towards that common purpose, particularly when this purpose conflicts with or diverges from their individual motivations and objectives. This is particularly apparent when these individuals are considered within the context of the stakeholder community (Aras and Crowther 2009) because the different stakeholder groupings have different desires and different motivations, which are often in conflict with those of other stakeholders (Aras and Crowther 2007). These conflicts need to be resolved in some fashion in order for the business to function and it is obvious that, as businesses do actually function, they end up being resolved by some means.

Just as the functioning of an organisation, however, can be seen to be a composite of its various constituents, so too does this reflect upon the performance of the business and the multiple facets of that performance (Crowther 2002). It is clear that the determination of good performance is dependent upon the perspective from which that performance is being considered and that what one stakeholder grouping might consider to be good performance may very well be considered by another grouping to be poor performance (Child 1984). The evaluation of performance, therefore, for a business depends not just upon the identification of adequate means of measuring that performance but also upon the determination of what good performance actually consists of. Just as the determination of standards of performance depends upon the perspective from which it is being evaluated, so too does the measurement of that performance, which needs suitably relevant measures to evaluate performance, not absolutely as this has no meaning, but within the context in which it is being evaluated. From an external perspective, therefore, a very different evaluation of performance might arise.

Within the legal systems of the UK, the US and most Western countries the managers of a business have a fiduciary duty to the owners of that business. This duty to shareholders is 'more general and proactive' than the regulatory or contractual responsibilities to other groups (Marens and Wicks 1999, Goodpaster 1991). These more general duties have also been used as a justification of the appropriateness of shareholder theories of the firm. The purpose and meaning of fiduciary duty were considered by Marens and Wicks (1999), who suggest that in actual fact this duty does not limit managers to a very narrow shareholder approach. They argue that the purpose of the fiduciary duty was originally designed to prevent managers undertaking expenditures that benefited themselves (Berle and Means 1933). Further Marens and Wicks (1999) suggest that fiduciary duties simply require that the fiduciary has an honest and open relationship with the shareholder and does not gain illegitimately from their office. Therefore the tension between fiduciary responsibility and the responsibility to other stakeholder groups, the so-called stakeholder paradox (Goodpaster 1991), is not as apparent as is often assumed. Further support for this argument is provided from the US courts. When shareholders have challenged management's actions as being too generous to other stakeholder groups then the court has 'almost always' upheld the right of management to manage. Management's justification or defence has often been on rational business performance grounds, such as efficiency or productivity, and the accuracy of such claims is difficult to prove. As such, Marens and Wicks (1999, p. 281) suggest that 'virtually any act that does not financially threaten the survival of the business could be construed as in the long-term best interest of shareholders'.

Thus agency theory argues that managers merely act as custodians of the organisation and its operational activities and places upon them the burden of managing in the best interest of the owners of that business. According to agency theory all other stakeholders of the business are largely irrelevant and if they benefit from the business then this is coincidental to the activities of management in running the business to serve shareholders. This focus upon shareholders alone as the intended beneficiaries of a business has been questioned considerably from many perspectives, which argue that it is either not the way in which a business is actually run or that it is a view which does not meet the needs of society in general. Conversely stakeholder theory argues that there are a whole variety of stakeholders involved in the organisation and each deserves some return for their involvement. According to stakeholder theory, therefore, benefit is maximised if the business is operated by its management on behalf of all stakeholders and returns are divided appropriately amongst those stakeholders, in some way which is acceptable to all. Unfortunately, a mechanism for dividing returns amongst all stakeholders which has universal acceptance does not exist, and stakeholder theory is significantly lacking in suggestions in this respect. Nevertheless, this theory has some acceptance and is based upon the premise that operating a business in this manner achieves as one of its outcomes the maximisation of returns to shareholders, as part of the process of maximising returns to all other stakeholders. This maximisation of returns is achieved in the long run through the optimisation of performance for the business to achieve maximal returns to all stakeholders. Consequently, the role of management is to optimise the long-term performance of the business in order to achieve this end and thereby reward all stakeholders, including themselves as one stakeholder community, appropriately.

These two theories can be regarded as competing explanations of the operations of a firm which lead to different operational foci and to different implications for the measurement and reporting of performance. It is significant, however, that both theories have one feature in common. This is that the management of the firm is believed to be acting on behalf of others, either shareholders or stakeholders more generally. They do so, not because they are the kind of people who behave altruistically, but because they are rewarded appropriately and much effort is therefore devoted to the creation of reward schemes which motivate these managers to achieve the desired ends. Similarly, much literature is devoted to the consideration of the effects of reward schemes on managerial behaviour (see, for example, Briers and Hirst 1990, Child 1974, 1975, Coates et al. 1993, Fitzgerald et al. 1991) and suggestions for improvement.

ANALYSIS OF CURRENT RESEARCH

If we look at current trends in research by investigating what is published in the leading journals then we see a number of themes in addition to those already discussed. One that is increasing in importance is that of corruption, its consequences and what can be done to reduce it. Implicit within this is a concern for transparency which includes matters such as reporting, information and communication through media and internet and anything which leads to stakeholders and society knowledge on social responsibility of a special activity. Transparency, as a principle, means that the external impact of the actions of the organisation can be ascertained from that organisation's reporting and pertinent facts are not disguised within that reporting. Thus all the effects of the actions of the organisation, including external impacts, should be apparent to all from using the information provided by the organisation's reporting mechanisms. Transparency is of particular importance to external users of such information as these users lack the background details and knowledge available to internal users of such information. Transparency therefore can be seen to be a part of the process of recognition of responsibility on the part of the organisation for the external effects of its actions and equally part of the process of transferring power to external stakeholders. It is a principle which is related to disclosure and disclosure has been a core issue for social responsibility research for many years. Arguably the concern is shifting somewhat though from multinational corporations (MNCs) to small and medium enterprises (SMEs) and from developed to developing countries. Nevertheless, it still remains the main research topic.

Another topic of importance has been organisational. In part this is a concern with social responsibility in different organisational structures. Organisations of any kind and with any structure have been under attention but especially people have started to show particular interest in publicly owned enterprises (POEs) and in SMEs, alongside a continuing interest in multinational companies. Two relevant issues inside this category have been those of privatisation and organisational structure. We know of course that multinational companies in particular have recently received a great deal of attention considering the issues related to labour and human rights. These too are an issue for research.

Other topics of concern include sustainability and sustainable development; the terms have different meanings but are often used interchangeably. Sustainability is the substrate for any objective for any organisation (Seifi and Crowther 2011); so first it should exist and continue to exist and then should decide how to exist, whether to be socially responsible or not and where to have a concern for contributing to sustainable development or not. So people have shown interest in sustainability as a general awareness on global needs for countries who care for sustainable resource use; through sustainable purchasing decisions, sustainable production, sustainable consumption and in other words, an interest in sustainable development. We have witnessed academic papers on this topic.

Finance is something that has been either knowingly or unknowingly neglected in social responsibility research. But finance – or at least profit – is the main purpose for the existence of any organisation whether socially responsible or socially irresponsible. It is the sustainability of an organisation that matters at first priority and it all depends on finance and economy at the initial steps. The classical theoreticians believed that the main responsibility of a company is to undertake its own professional work. On the other hand, it was another way of telling the basic philosophy: the main objective of a company is to make money. As the main objective of a socially responsible organisation is to contribute to sustainable development and as economy is one of the pillars of sustainable development, therefore we conclude that neglecting finance is equal to neglecting sustainable development.

STRUCTURE OF THIS BOOK

As we have seen, there are many aspects to research in the area of CSR, and many topics which are relevant. This means inevitably that there are many approaches to researching these topics and many epistemological paradigms which can be – and are – applied. As we stated earlier, we have made no attempt to define the subject area as all definitions are acceptable to some. Equally we have made no attempt to define suitable research methods and have deliberately attempted to be inclusive in the belief that some aspects of this book will be useful to everyone.

Thus the book is organised into four parts. The first part we have titled Methodology Planning. In this part are chapters that are concerned with various aspects of planning the research project and dealing with such things as secondary data and with ethics in the research process. These are chapters which are relevant to all of us regardless of our project and regardless of our ontological stance. This part is followed by a part dealing with Quantitative Methods, which contains chapters considering a wide variety of quantitative methods which have all been used to research CSR. Following this is a part dealing with Qualitative Methods, again containing chapters dealing with a variety of qualitative methods which have also been used to research in the area of CSR. The methods selected to discuss in the chapters in these two parts are not exhaustive as there are other methods which can be, and have been, used but they do represent the vast majority of approaches to research which have been taken by those undertaking research into CSR. Although, as researchers, each of us has preferences about which methods we prefer to use, this has not influenced our decisions concerning what methods to include. For us every method which is available and has something to contribute to increase our understanding is an appropriate method and so we have sought to include consideration of all methods. Realistically this has needed to be limited to all the major methods plus some of the less common ones which give added insight.

One of the problems with considering published research is that there is always an historic element to it. This is inevitable as publications must always be about research that has already been undertaken. Moreover, there is a currency to publications, which means they remain relevant and useful for some years after the research originally took place. This is of course completely fine, but leaves us with a problem in that we do not know what topics are considered important for the research which is currently being undertaken and which will be undertaken in the very near future. Additionally, it does not tell us anything about the research methods which are currently considered to be useful, especially if they are new and have not been used before. With this in mind we have included a final section in the book to address this Future Research Agenda. In this part we have invited some prominent and experienced researchers to contribute. We have given them an open brief to consider what they think might become important in future CSR research. Unsurprisingly, these make for some interesting reading.

NOTES

1. This is an argument against the funding of research, where there is a tendency to 'find' what the funder expects. This is a problem with the physical sciences also, where medical research has been allegedly warped to favour the funders or where defence funding has affected the way investigations are conducted. In CSR research one of the problems is that the ontological stance of the researchers tends to favour the non-organisational stakeholders and be 'biased' for this reason.
2. See the Network website – www.socialresponsibility.biz – for further details of the Network, its history and its activities.
3. This conveniently obfuscates the problem. Carbon dioxide is not the only greenhouse gas and is not the most problematic but focusing on it means that carbon monoxide from the motor vehicle industry can be ignored as well as methane from the dairy industry. These industries are also a cause of significant other environmental problems.
4. This was agreed in 1997 and came into effect in 2005.
5. In late 2007 Australia ratified the protocol, leaving only one large developed country which has not done so. This country is, however, the USA, probably the largest producer of such greenhouse gases.
6. The European consensus is by no means worldwide in this respect.
7. And most probably any other parts of the world also – it would be instructive to correlate the presence of oil with conflicts.
8. In 1956 M. King Hubbert developed a model of oil production which showed that when the midpoint of oil reserves was reached then future production would slow down and less would be available. Although originally developed for US oil production it has been shown to be equally valid globally. This midpoint is known as Hubbert's Peak and has arrived or soon will arrive, at that point oil supplies start to get less with obvious implications in an environment in which demand continues to increase.
9. Many people continue to think that new technological developments will continue to solve the problems which are being created.
10. See www.unglobalcompact.org.
11. Voluntary but easier for some than others – the developed world is privileged again!

REFERENCES

Aras, G. and D. Crowther (2007), 'Is the global economy sustainable?', in Stephen Barber (ed.), *The Geopolitics of the City*, London: Forum Press, pp. 165–194.
Aras, Güler and David Crowther (2009), *The Durable Corporation: Strategies for Sustainable Development*, Aldershot, UK: Gower.
Berle, Adolph Augustus and Gardiner G. Coit Means (1933), *The Modern Corporation and Private Property*, New York: Commerce Clearing House.
Bhaskar, Roy (1989), *Reclaiming Reality: A Critical Introduction to Contemporary Philosophy*, London: Verso.
Bower, Tom (2009), *The Squeeze: Oil, Money and Greed in the Twenty-First Century*, London/UK: HarperCollins.
Briers, M. and M. Hirst (1990), 'The role of budgetary information in performance evaluation', *Accounting, Organizations and Society*, **15** (4), 373–398.
Burns, Robert B. (2000), *Introduction to Research Methods*, 4th edn, London: Sage Publications.
Burrell, Gibson and Gareth Morgan (1979), *Sociological Paradigms and Organisational Analysis: Elements of the Sociology of Corporate Life*, London: Heinemann.
Butler, D., C. Frost and R. Macve (1992), 'Environmental reporting', in Leonard C.L. Skerratt and David J. Tonkins (eds), *A Guide to UK Reporting Practice for Accountancy Students*, London: Wiley, pp. 47–78.
Child, J. (1974), 'Managerial and organisational factors associated with company performance: part 1', *Journal of Management Studies*, **11**, 73–189.
Child, J. (1975), 'Managerial and organisational factors associated with company performance: part 2', *Journal of Management Studies*, **12**, 12–27.
Child, John (1984), *Organisation: A Guide to Problems and Practice*, London: Harper and Row.

Coates, Jeffrey B., Edward W. Davis, Stephen G. Longden, Ralph J. Stacey and Clive Emmanuel (1993), *Corporate Performance Evaluation in Multinationals*, London: CIMA.
Cook, T. and D.T. Campbell (1979), 'Popper and falsificationalism' in Clive Seale (ed.), *Social Research Methods: A Reader*, London: Routledge.
Crowther, David (2002), *A Social Critique of Corporate Reporting*, Aldershot/UK: Ashgate.
Crowther, D. and S. Seifi (2011), 'The future of corporate social responsibility', in Maria A. Costa and Maria J. Santos (eds), *Empresas, Empresarios e Responsabilidade Social*, CES, Lisbon.
Deffeyes, K.S. (2004), 'Hubbert's Peak: the impending world oil shortage', *American Journal of Physics*, **72** (1), 126–127.
Easterby-Smith, Mark, Richard Thorpe and Andy Lowe (2002), *Management Research: An Introduction*, 2nd edn, London: Sage Publications.
Feyerabend, P. (1975), 'Against method', in Clive Seale (ed.), *Social Research Methods: A Reader*, London: Routledge, pp. 195–198.
Fitzgerald, Lillian, Robert Johnston, Stan Brignall, Rhian Silvestro and Chris Voss (1991), *Performance Measurement in Service Businesses*, London: CIMA.
Gilbert, Nigel (ed.) (1993), *Researching Social Life*, London: Sage Publications.
Gill, John and Phil Johnson (1997), *Research Methods for Managers*, 2nd edn, London: Paul Chapman Publishing.
Goodpaster, K.E. (1991), 'Business ethics and stakeholder analysis', *Business Ethics Quarterly*, **1** (1), 53–73.
Graziano, Anthony M. and Michael L. Raulin (2004), *Research Methods: A Process of Inquiry*, 5th edn, Boston/USA: Pearson Education Group.
Gummesson, Evert (2000), *Qualitative Methods in Management Research*, 2nd edn, Thousand Oakes, CA: Sage Publications.
Howard, Keith and John A. Sharp (1983), *The Management of a Student Research Project*, Aldershot/UK: Gower.
Lauesen, L.M. (2013), 'CSR in the aftermath of the financial crisis', *Social Responsibility Journal*, **9** (4), 641–663.
Lauesen, L.M. (2016), 'The landscape and scale of social and sustainable finance', in Othmar M. Lehner (ed.), *Routledge Handbook of Social and Sustainable Finance*, London: Routledge, Taylor and Francis Group, pp. 5–16.
Lovelock, James (2006), *The Revenge of Gaia*, Harmondsworth/UK: Penguin.
Marens, R. and A. Wicks (1999), 'Getting real: stakeholder theory, managerial practice, and the general irrelevance of fiduciary duties owed to shareholders', *Business Ethics Quarterly*, **9** (2), 273–293.
Popper, Karl R. (1967), *Conjectures and Refutations*, London: Routledge.
Robson, Colin (2002), *Real World Research*, 2nd edn, Oxford/UK: Blackwell.
Royal Academy of Engineering (2010), *Global Water Security: An Engineering Approach*, London: Royal Academy of Engineering.
Saunders, Mark, Philip Lewis and Adrian Thornhill (2003/2005), *Research Methods for Business Students*, 3rd/5th edns, Harlow/UK: Pearson Education.
Sayer, Andrew (2000), *Realism and Social Science*, London: Sage Publications.
Schaltegger, S., K. Muller and H. Hindrichsen (1996), *Corporate Environmental Accounting*, Chichester: John Wiley and Sons.
Seifi, S. and D. Crowther (2011), 'Disclosing the jargon of sustainability', *Social Responsibility Review*, **3**, 31–37.
Seifi, S. and D. Crowther (2012), 'Research on social responsibility strategies and governance: perspectives from the Social Responsibility Research Network', in Patricia A. Ashley and David Crowther (eds), *Territories of Social Responsibility: Opening the Policy Agenda*, Farnham: Gower, pp. 17–28.
Till, C.A. and C.F. Symes (1999), 'Environmental disclosure by Australian mining companies: environmental conscience or commercial reality?', *Accounting Forum*, 28 (3), 137–154.
Wells, P.E. (1994), 'Ethics in business and management research', in V.J. Wass and P.E. Wells (eds), *Principles and Practice in Business Management Research*, Aldershot: Dartmouth, pp. 277–297.

PART I

METHODOLOGY PLANNING

David Crowther and Linne Marie Lauesen

All research requires planning at the outset and the best projects tend to be those that are well planned – even more than those which are well executed. We start this book, therefore, with a section dealing with research planning as well as other general issues which need to be considered both before the research starts and often also continually as the project continues towards completion. The overall design is obviously important and we include some chapters dealing with differing choices which are available. We also include chapters dealing with the various perennial debates about meta-research and about qualitative versus quantitative issues. Ethics also is an important topic which merits a chapter in this section. It is important to understand that we take no view about the respective merits of differing approaches – although as individuals we have our own preferences. Instead we present options and debates in the belief that research is better if it is well planned and based upon informed choices made by the researcher.

With this in mind Vilma Žydžiūnaitė and Loreta Tauginienė begin our journey introducing the grounded theory (GT) methodology seen from three different perspectives: Barney Glaser's classic approach which emphasises abstract conceptualisations of time, place and people; Anselm Strauss and Juliet M. Corbin's structured approach aiming at the generation of a pragmatic theory of action; and Kathy Charmaz's constructivist approach, where the theory is not discovered, but constructed by the researcher as a result of his/her interactions with participants within the field. This chapter also introduces applied thematic analysis, as its main idea refers to GT. Each approach discloses strengths and limitations of GT, and gives guidelines for constructing GT research designs with the focus on corporate social responsibility (CSR). The reader will find here all the necessary information about the data analysis, coding, memoing, sorting and writing in each GT approach. Finally, Žydžiūnaitė and Tauginienė discuss some specifications, presentations and interpretations of their findings to inspire the CSR researcher to reflect on constructing the theoretical assumptions and establishing an original GT from the empirical data.

In the second chapter, Jane Claydon invites us into the realm of mixed methods for researching CSR. Her research investigates debtors' and debt collectors' (of a multinational credit card company) perceptions of responsibility and blame for consumer debt by using a number of research methods: qualitative in-depth interviews, focus groups and quantitative online surveys. Using a mixed methods approach was advantageous for a number of reasons. Using a number of methods ensures that the researcher can enjoy the qualities of several different research methods. Further, using different methods enables the researcher to recognise and assess the validity and reliability of a single research method when comparing it against another. Jane Claydon outlines the strengths, shortcomings, representativeness and validity of the aforementioned research methods, along with the sampling strategy used by the author as a CSR researcher. Her chapter is aimed at early career researchers in the field of CSR to provide them with an overview of using a mixed methods approach in CSR research and, specifically, a more detailed insight into the methods of interviewing, focus groups and surveys, using the author's research as a case study.

In the following chapter, Lukman Raimi explains meta-study as a relevant analytical tool for studying emerging issues in the field of CSR driven by heterogeneous and conflicting research findings. When viewed as a methodological approach in CSR research, a meta-study has four sequential and reinforcing stages, namely: meta-method, meta-theory, meta-data analysis and meta-synthesis. The purpose of Lukman Raimi's chapter is to discuss meta-study as a useful technique for research, its stages and justifications for adopting a meta-study in CSR research. She discusses the steps involved in conducting CSR research using meta-study, and shows how meta-study gives deeper, reliable and richer outcomes compared with an individual research finding. The implications of the chapter discussed in the conclusion is that the insights gained from meta-study serve as legitimate sources of knowledge for researchers in the field of CSR for synthesising findings from both qualitative and quantitative research in the field of CSR.

Whenever we are conducting research it is impossible not to be concerned with the ethical dimension of what we are doing. This is important for us as researchers not just for our own concerns but also because, by the nature of the topic which we are researching, we are concerned with the organisation and people involved in the research and their ethics and behaviour. In the next chapter, therefore, David Crowther considers the important question of ethics. In this chapter he deals with what ethics is and why it is important, arguing that the nature of CSR research makes ethics more central to the research. After consideration of various ethical philosophies and ethics within the context of corporate behaviour he then emphasises the need to deal with ethical dilemmas which we all tend to face during the research process – such issues as confidentiality – as well as conforming to the ethical guidelines and policies of our own organisation and gaining the ethical approval necessary to undertake our research.

The following chapter by Miriam Green explores the differences, debates and decisions among academics about the respective value of quantitative and qualitative methods, which originally arose in the US and the UK, and as research methodologies now span the world. Miriam explores the controversies as well as the advantages and legitimacy of either quantitative or qualitative research methods over the years. In her chapter she puts forward definitions of each research method; to outline their main features; discuss their applications in the management area; examine their advantages and disadvantages and outline the critiques regarding each method and whether they are 'commensurable' with each other or not.

The final chapter in this section follows up on Miriam Green's discussion when Duván and José Ospina discuss the implication of epistemological and methodological perspectives on CSR, giving us concrete examples from Colombia. Their chapter is the result of their investigating 'Role and Behavior of Corporate Organizations in the Context of Sustainability' and of the reflection of that line of research in the Department of

Doctoral Studies of Human and Social and Sustainable Development of the University of Manizales, Colombia. Its construction is part of the analysis of methodologies and processes adapted to different sectors in the field of CSR in Colombia, and thus addresses many of the themes from the scientific articles and published documents, including master's and doctoral work from Colombia. The observed works make use of qualitative, quantitative, mixed and triangulation methodologies, and the authors note that these methodologies are oriented towards the understanding and explanation of principles defined in the areas of government business organisations to cope with the social, economic and environmental factors, the reconfiguration of values that guide the conduct of corporations, the definition of management and production strategies for the solution of systemic organisational problems, and the redefining of certain corporate practices with the purpose of increasing the cohesion and legitimacy between the corporation and society.

1. Grounded theory in corporate social responsibility research
Vilma Žydžiūnaitė and Loreta Tauginienė

INTRODUCTION

Grounded theory (GT) is a qualitative methodology, which derives its name from the practice of generating theory from research, which is grounded in data (Babchuk 1997). Three GT methodologies have evolved, namely B.G. Glaser's classic, A.L. Strauss and J. Corbin's structured, and K. Charmaz's (1983, 2005, 2006, 2014) social constructivist methodology.

The thematic analysis based on GT is usually called applied thematic analysis (ATA) (Braun and Clarke 2006). As GT is designed to construct theories that are grounded in the empirical data themselves (Guest et al. 2012) this aspect is also reflected in ATA because its process also consists of reading transcripts, identifying and comparing themes, and building theoretical models (Boyatzis 1998).

CLASSIC GROUNDED THEORY

In this classic version of GT, developed by Glaser and Strauss (1967), the comparative analysis is a kind of strategy to generate analytic units of any size, ranging from small to large and from micro (individual), and meso (organizational) to macro (regional, national or worldwide) levels. The purpose of the comparative analysis is to obtain evidence from facts, that is, the conceptual category or its property is generated from one or more facts, and the concept from one fact. The concept is plainly a relevant theoretical abstraction about a certain area studied (Glaser and Strauss 2008, p. 23). Facts tend to be more susceptible to change while the concept itself remains steady. Arguably, concepts have meanings that can be revised from time to time as research purposes evolve (Figure 1.1).

Comparing Incidents

At the stage of comparing incidents, a researcher should code each incident in the data into as many categories as possible. Usually, coding refers to noting categories on margins, cards, or some other way. In the constant comparative analysis, the corporate social responsibility (CSR) researcher compares new emerging categories with already established categories in the same and different groups. This way of comparison leads to the generation of theoretical properties of the category. Here, a researcher may reveal two kinds of categories: (1) constructed by him/herself; and (2) abstracted from the language in the data.

```
                                                    Writing the theory
                                                   ┌─────────────────
                                                   │         4
                                  Delimiting the theory
                                 ┌─────────────────┘
                                 │        3
            Integrating categories
            and their properties
           ┌───────────────────┘
           │         
Comparing incidents
applicable to each       2
category
──────────┘

        1
```

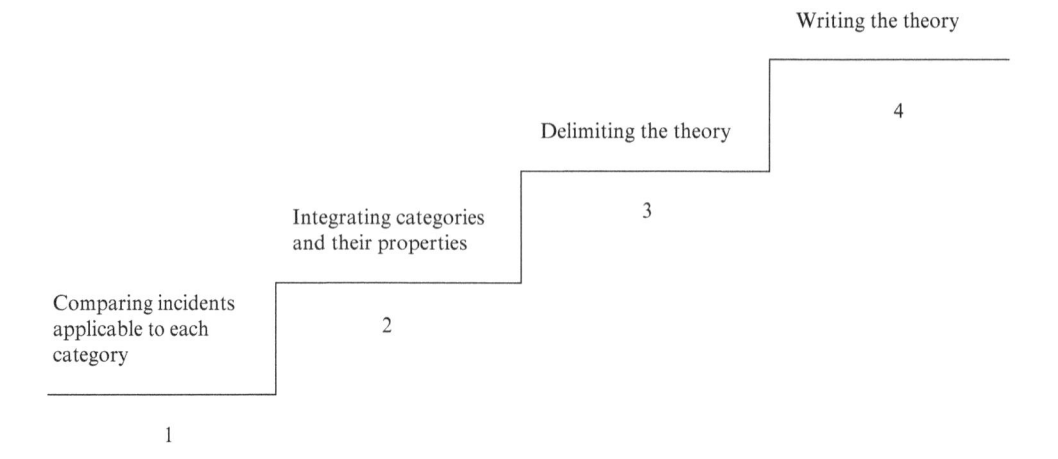

Figure 1.1 Stages of comparative analysis

Integrating Categories

At the stage of integrating categories and their properties, the coding continues. The constant comparative units change; comparison of incident with incident moves to the level of comparison of incident with properties of the category to those that came out at the first stage. At this stage an approach of integrative strategy occurs. For example, by joint coding and analysis, a researcher accumulates a large number of the *in vivo* patterns of integration in the data themselves. Extra questions provide a guide to filling gaps and extending theory.

Delimiting the Theory

At the stage of delimiting the theory, two levels emerge: solidification of theory and reduction of categories. Here, the theoretical saturation is important. In theoretical saturation the CSR researcher continues sampling and analyses data until no new data appear, and all concepts in the theory are well developed. Concepts and linkages between the concepts that form the theory are verified, and no additional data are needed. All of the conceptual boundaries are marked, and allied concepts have been identified and delineated. Negative cases must have been identified, verified, saturated, and incorporated into the GT scheme (Morse 2004).

Writing Theory

At the stage of writing theory, a researcher possesses coded data, a myriad of memos, and a theory. The foundation of the content is based on the discussions in his/her memos behind the categories.

The classic GT is considered as generating theory as a process that is continuously under development due to new categories being evolved, because such theory imparts the social interactions and their structural context. Thus, comparative analysis can be used for the purpose of two kinds of theories: substantive and formal.

Substantive theory
Substantive theory is developed for empirical areas, for example, within organizations, specific relations such as investigating employee engagement in fair trade companies or investigating perceptions of equity analysts on CSR, or exploring the perceptions of managers working in corporations with developed CSR programmes. In substantive theory a researcher does not generate the theory directly from the data. A substantive theory must first be formulated with the purpose of seeing which of the diverse formal theories is probably applicable to uphold additional substantive formulations.

Formal theory
Formal theory is developed for conceptual areas, for example, deviant behaviour, or status congruency. Formal theory can be based on one-area and multi-area; it combines many kinds of substantive areas that vary, for example, by numbers of groups represented, different hierarchical level, and interaction. One example would be to create a framework for social responsibility auditing. Formal theory requires more guidance than substantive theory due to a greater level of abstraction.

Elements such as conceptual categories and the conceptual properties of the GT are generated by comparative analysis, and are interrelated (see Figure 1.2).

Both categories and properties vary in the degree of conceptual abstraction. Lower level categories emerge during the early phases of data collection. Higher level conceptualizations, notably conceptual properties of the categories, emerge during the joint data collection, coding, and analysis. Then, the concepts should hold an analytic character, that is, be fairly generalized to nominate characteristics of concrete entities, not the entities themselves. Further, the concepts should be sensitizing, that is, giving a meaning, assisted by suitable illustrations that help to perceive the reference in terms of one's own experience.

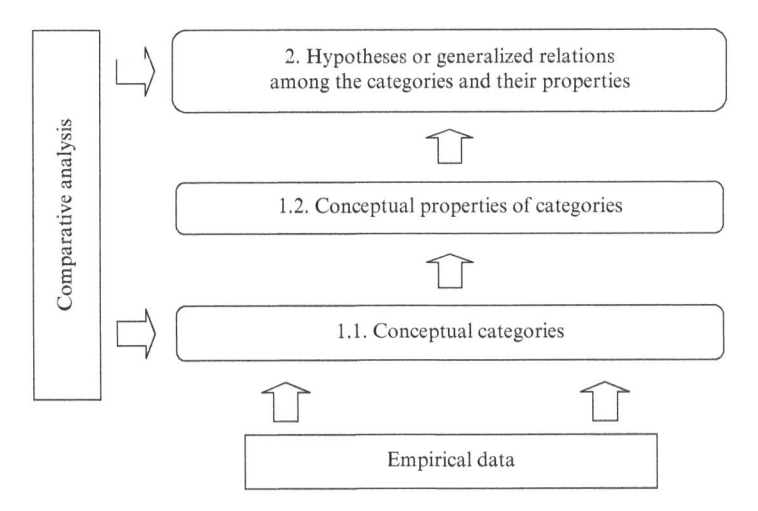

Figure 1.2 Elements of the theory

The classic GT consists of two phases (Hernandez 2009):

1. 'Open coding' is where the data are split into substantive codes or *in vivo* codes as interviews and field notes. Data are coded line by line, incident by incident with the purpose to look for similarities and differences in the expectation of finding out what the core category is.
2. 'Selective coding' is determined by the saturation of all categories through theoretical sampling. Here, substantive codes are tied in a substantive theory.

These coding processes are not isolated and are performed simultaneously.

The application of the classic GT necessitates developing the theory with four interrelated properties (Glaser and Strauss 2008, p. 237): (1) fits the substantive area in which it will be used; (2) is understandable to those concerned with this area; (3) is sufficiently general to be applicable to diverse daily situations within the substantive area; (4) allows the user partial control over the structure and process of daily situations as they change through time.

Glaser and Strauss (2008) suggest limiting the reading of conceptual literature before generating the GT. The authors argue that similarities and convergences with the literature can be established after the emergence of categories.

STRUCTURED GROUNDED THEORY

The GT approach, particularly the way Strauss and Corbin (also known as Straussian GT) developed it, consists of a set of steps of which careful execution is thought to 'guarantee' a good theory as the outcome (Borgatti 1996). GT evolves during research, and it does this through continuous interplay between analysis and data collection.

Data sources in GT are interviews and observations (transcripts and field notes) and written materials (for example, documents, CSR reports, books, newsletters, diaries, letters, websites). The researcher begins with the preliminary observations that are related to the first steps of GT research. Then, research participants (could be from individuals, groups, or institutions) are selected regarding their relationships with the phenomenon or concept they represent. Research ideas are grasped through theoretical sampling, coding, and constant comparison of the qualitative data, which are at the core of GT methodology. A research question should take the form of identifying the phenomenon to be studied and what is known about the subjects, participants, or 'actors', and their socially constructed realities (Strauss and Corbin 1998). The CSR researcher is committed to providing some important insights into the realities of cultural participants and seems to be relatively more concerned with producing a detailed description of the cultural scene (Babchuk 1997).

The central feature of this analytic approach is the constant comparative method (Glaser and Strauss 1967). Hence, at the heart of GT analysis the coding process is threefold (Glaser and Strauss 1967, 2008).

Open Coding

Open coding is the initial, exploratory, and interpretive 'analytic process through which concepts are identified and their properties and dimensions are discovered in the data' (Strauss and Corbin 1990, p. 101). It is the part of the analysis concerned with identifying, naming, categorizing, and describing phenomena found in the text.

Essentially, each line, sentence, and paragraph is meticulously read in search of the answer to the repeated questions 'What is this about? What is being referenced here?' (Borgatti 1996). In open coding the CSR researcher writes memos about the conceptual and theoretical ideas that emerge during the course of analysis (Walker and Myrick 2006). It involves the breaking down, analysis, comparison, and categorization of qualitative data. Here, events are labelled and grouped together through constant comparison to form categories (Babchuk 1997).

Development of dimensions regarding the category's properties (for example, the dimension 'from small to large' for the property of height) is the main task. To develop a category, and the relationships among categories, the researcher must develop the category in terms of its properties and the dimensions of the properties (Walker and Myrick 2006). These labels ((sub)categories) refer to things like individuals, institutions, social activities, events, communication, and so on. They are the nouns and verbs of a conceptual world. Part of the analytic process is to identify the more general categories of which these things are instances, such as institutions, work activities, social relations, and social outcomes (Borgatti 1996).

Axial Coding

Axial coding is focused on formulations of the emerging subcategories and categories, and the delineation of hypothetical relationships (Babchuk 1997) between them. The aim of this phase is 'making connections between a category and its subcategory' (Strauss and Corbin 1990, p. 97).

In such connections the coding paradigm is applied with the focus on the following aspects (Corbin and Strauss 1990; Strauss and Corbin 1998): situations and/or conditions in which the phenomenon occurs; actions and/or interactions of people in response to what is happening in actual situations; consequences or outcomes of action(s) and/ or inaction. In this phase, the researcher develops an understanding about categories in terms of other categories, and the subcategories of which these categories consist. The researcher here delineates and extricates relationships on which the axis of the category is being focused (Strauss 1987).

The GT methodological frame in axial coding consists of the following elements (Borgatti 1996):

1. 'Phenomenon' is the concept that holds the codes together; outcome of interest of the subject.
2. 'Causal conditions' are the set of events that are premises or causes and their properties (features) for the phenomenon to occur; conditions influence actions or strategies.
3. 'Context' means the specific locations and/or values of causal conditions that are called moderating variables.

4. 'Intervening conditions' are mediating variables that are related to the context and consequences.
5. 'Action strategies' are purposeful activities that are performed by actors regarding the research phenomenon and intervening conditions.
6. 'Consequences' are outcomes of strategies (or methods) used in a certain context.

Selective Coding

Selective coding is the process by which categories are related to the core category ultimately becoming the basis for the GT (Babchuk 1997). It is the process of choosing one category to be the core category, and relating all other categories to that category. The essential idea is to develop a single storyline around which everything else is draped. There is a belief that such a core concept always exists (Borgatti 1996).

Strauss and Corbin (1998) see it as the 'process of integrating and refining the theory' (p. 143). The CSR researcher selects a core category and then relates all other categories to the core as well as to the other categories (Walker and Myrick 2006). In this phase categories are developed, their relationships with dimensions are generalized, integration of codes at more abstract level of analysis is performed, and the conditional matrix is provided (Strauss 1987; Strauss and Corbin 1990, 1998; Corbin and Strauss 2008).

The matrix is 'an analytic device to help the analyst keep track of the interplay of conditions, consequences and (inter)actions and to trace their paths of connectivity' (Corbin and Strauss 1996, p. 199). The researcher by using the matrix is able to locate an interaction that appears repeatedly in the data and then trace the linkages from this through the micro and macro conditions that might influence it (Strauss and Corbin 1994). This allows the CSR researcher to reconstruct the original data in such a way that their broader context becomes apparent (Mills et al. 2006). Used as a tool, based on the emergence of subcategories and categories, the content of the matrix, where conditions and outcomes/consequences are incorporated, can add conceptual value to constructing GT.

In the coding process, logic diagrams such as flowcharts are used. When undertaking higher levels of analysis, researchers use both the conditional/consequential matrix and integrative diagramming, illustrating the complex interplay between the different levels of conditions (Strauss 1987; Strauss and Corbin 1990, 1998).

Memos are important in every analytical phase of GT. Memos are short documents that the CSR researcher writes to him/herself while proceeding through the analysis of a corpus of data (Borgatti 1996). There are three types of memos: field notes (researcher's reflections on the GT process at every analytical step, personal views, observations, etc.); code notes (creation of a codebook with the descriptions and reflective discussions on their content); and theoretical notes (where the researcher relates codes to the literature, and develops theoretical implications). When researchers write and sort memos, they are engaged in a critical process that allows new ideas to emerge and the connection of ideas, leading to a theory that intricately explains the phenomenon under study (Dillon 2012).

CONSTRUCTIVIST GROUNDED THEORY

The constructivist GT focuses on interpretive understandings of meanings, and this version of GT is equal to multiple social realities (Charmaz 2011). For example, exploring leadership styles and motivations of corporate leaders in line with their chosen CSR activities, where multiple social realities are perceived.

GT coding is inductive, comparative, interactive, and iterative and then deductive; encompasses a close coding of statements, actions, events, and documents; decomposes the data into components or properties; and qualifies actions (Charmaz 2012). Charmaz (2011, 2012, 2014) distinguishes several phases of GT coding: initial, focused, axial, and theoretical coding.

Initial Coding

Initial coding refers to the close data analysis. Spontaneity is the main tenet which helps a researcher to remain open throughout this phase of coding. Here, all details are important, that is, word-by-word coding (works well for short-term documents, for example, internet data), line-by-line coding (works well for interviews, observations, ethnographies), incident-by-incident coding (works well for observations to identify properties of emerging concepts). Engaging in line-by-line coding (labelling each line of data) helps a researcher to reconsider the next interviews. There *in vivo* codes contribute to the preservation of one's meanings of views and actions.

For example, at organizational or collective levels of analysis, *in vivo* codes indicate assumptions, actions, and imperatives that embrace action. For instance, examining the complexities which surround decision-making about mining communities, and the challenges faced to foster their sustainability after mining – this example points to looking for role, responsibilities, and actions of the state in relation to these communities. To pick out the advantages of initial coding, it is noteworthy to ensure that careful initial coding fulfils the fit and relevance that are considered to be the main criteria for data analysis.

Focused Coding

Focused coding enables a researcher to separate, sort, and synthesize piles of data. Here, a researcher begins to synthesize and explain larger segments of data.

Axial Coding

Axial coding aims at relating categories with subcategories. In this sense, a category consists of specific properties and dimensions. It means that this coding contributes to more extensive insight to the emerging ideas of the researcher.

Theoretical Coding

Theoretical coding emphasizes the guidance to reconsider the codes selected during the focused coding. The theoretical codes help to figure out possible relationships between categories. Hence, a researcher may be precise and clear as long as theoretical codes fit the CSR researcher's data and substantive analysis.

The codes should be formulated in gerunds (the noun forms of verbs), as these forms support building actions into codes. Charmaz (2011) argues that using gerunds stimulates theoretical sensitivity.

Interpreting the Codes

After coding, the researcher starts the memo-writing that is performed before writing the first draft of a report. The constant comparison of codes with memo-writing allows the researcher to 'specify the conditions under which the process arises, persists, or changes' (Charmaz 2012, p. 9). Charmaz (2014) advises the use of simple language and straightforward ideas to make theory readable, and to avoid using unexpected definitions and assertions, as they steal readers' attention.

Charmaz (2011) considers the GT to be interpretive, contrary to the definition of how Glaser defines what the theory is, who emphasizes the positivism. The interpretive character of GT manifests in understanding and, in contrast to Glaserian GT, not in explanation and prediction. Hence, interpretive theorizing may induce 'network analysis with the tools to bring meanings into view' (Charmaz 2011, p. 129). The interaction is an essential component of constructivist GT, and, accordingly, the theory depends on the view of the researcher.

Charmaz (2011) highlights the flexibility of guidelines in the GT, and stays away from strict methodological rules.

APPLIED THEMATIC ANALYSIS

Applied thematic analysis (ATA) is a method for identifying, analysing, and reporting patterns (themes) within the data (Daily 2001). A theme represents a level of patterned response or meaning from the data that is related to the research questions at hand. A theme does not necessarily mean the frequency at which a theme occurs, but in terms of space within each data item and across the data set. The potential data analysis pitfalls occur when researchers use the research question to code instead of creating codes and fail to provide adequate examples from the data. Eventually, themes need to provide an accurate understanding of the 'big picture' (Braun and Clarke 2006).

ATA comprises a bit of everything – grounded theory, positivism, interpretivism, and phenomenology – synthesized into one methodological framework (Guest et al. 2012). ATA is not restricted to building theory, but its primary goal is to describe and understand how people feel, think, and behave within a particular context relative to a specific research question (Guest et al. 2012); and the core topic of an ATA can be social and cultural phenomena (Braun and Clarke 2006).

Phases of Applied Thematic Analysis

The phases of ATA are the following (Braun and Clarke 2006):

Reading
Reading and re-reading data is done in order for the analyst to become familiar with what the data entail, paying specific attention at patterns that occur. The outcome is the preliminary 'start' of codes and detailed notes.

Initial coding
Afterwards, the analyst will generate the initial codes by documenting where and how patterns occur. This happens through data reduction where the researcher collapses data into labels and creates categories. Here, the researcher makes inferences about what the codes mean. The outcome is the comprehensive codes of how data answer the research question.

Combining codes into themes
Combining codes into overarching themes that accurately depict the data is where the researcher describes what the themes mean (even if the theme does not seem to 'fit') and what is missing from the analysis. The result is the list of candidate themes for further analysis.

Theme analysis
Now the analyst will look at how themes support the data and the overarching theoretical perspective. If the analysis seems incomplete, the researcher needs to go back and find what is missing.

The outcome is coherent recognition of how themes are patterned to tell an accurate story about the data. Defining what each theme is, which aspects of data are being captured, and what is interesting about the themes. The result is a comprehensive analysis of what themes contribute to understanding the data. Deciding which themes make meaningful contributions to understanding what is going on within the data. The researcher goes back to the sample at hand to see if his/her description is an accurate representation. The outcome is a description of results.

Stages of Data Coding

ATA suggests the following stages of data coding:

Developing the code manual
The code manual serves as a data management tool for organizing segments of similar or related text to assist in interpretation (Crabtree and Miller 1999). The use of a template provides a clear trail of evidence for the credibility of the study (Fereday and Muir-Cochrane 2006). The codes could be identified by the following components (Boyatzis 1998): (1) the code label or name; (2) the definition of what the theme concerns; (3) a description of how to know when the theme occurs.

Testing the reliability of the code
An essential step in the development of a useful framework for analysis is to determine the applicability of the code to the raw information (Crabtree and Miller 1999).

Summarizing data and identifying initial themes
The process of paraphrasing or summarizing each piece of data involves reading, listening to, and summarizing the raw data (Fereday and Muir-Cochrane 2006).

Applying template of codes and additional coding
The researcher applies the codes from the codebook to the text with the intent of identifying meaningful units of text (Crabtree and Miller 1999). During the coding of transcripts, inductive codes are assigned to segments of data that described a new theme observed in the text (Boyatzis 1998). These additional codes are either separate from the predetermined codes or they expand a code from the manual.

Connecting codes and identifying themes
Connecting the codes and identifying themes is the process of discovering themes and patterns in the data (Crabtree and Miller 1999). It is the process of connecting the codes and identifying themes across the sets of data, clustering under headings that directly relate to the research questions.

Similarities and differences between separate groups of data could emerge at this stage, indicating areas of consensus in response to the research questions and areas of potential conflict. Themes within each data group are also beginning to cluster, with differences identified between the responses of groups with varying characteristics, for example, demographics.

Corroborating and legitimating coded themes
The previous stages must be closely scrutinized to ensure that the clustered themes are representative of the initial data analysis and assigned codes. The interaction of text, codes, and themes in the study involves several iterations before the analysis proceeds to an interpretive phase in which the units are connected into an explanatory framework consistent with the text. Themes are then further clustered and assigned succinct phrases to describe the meaning that underpinned the theme (Fereday and Muir-Cochrane 2006).

CONSTRUCTING THE GROUNDED THEORY

GT construction 'entails the practical activity of engaging the world and of constructing abstract understandings about and within it' (Charmaz 2006, p. 128). The researcher should choose one of the versions of GT methodology, because the author/s of every version treat/s the understanding about GT construction differently:

1. Glaser's (1978, 1992, 2001, 2011) understanding is related to the indicator-concept approach. For him theoretical categories are variables and the theoretical statements should be context-free.
2. Strauss and Corbin (1998) focus on relationships among concepts the framework consists of and that is used to explain the research phenomenon.
3. Charmaz (1983, 2005, 2006, 2014) accentuates that GT is emergent and indeterminant, and emphasizes social life as a process and multiple realities in which values and facts are related.

The construction of GT is based on analytical procedures that involve two processes (Walker and Myrick 2006): (1) the researcher codes all data and then systematically analyses codes to prove a proposition; and (2) the researcher inspects the data (without engagement into coding data) for properties of categories, uses memos to track the analysis, and develops theoretical ideas.

The CSR researcher should be attentive because every GT version incorporates different consequences of analytical phases, which are inseparable from coding procedures.

Open Coding

For Glaser (1978) this is the initial stage of comparative analysis and the first part of substantive coding. There is no quick fix or preconceived framework to follow. Only patience, persistence, and going over and over the data using constant comparison will lead to emergent categories and their properties (Glaser 1978). Open coding is complete when the researcher begins to see the possibility of a theory that can embrace all of the data. Then, within the larger context of the data developed in open coding, it is appropriate to delimit one's coding efforts and begin selectively coding for a core variable (Walker and Myrick 2006).

From the first phase of data analysis the theoretical sensitivity is attained through the researcher's immersion in the data, comparisons, memos, and codes (Glaser 1992). The theoretical codes are available in the third phase of the analysis, and these are applied regarding the emerging essences in the data because the text 'speaks for itself' to the researcher. Strauss and Corbin (1990, 1998) argue that theoretical sensitivity is achieved through the use of specific analytic tools, including questioning; analysis of a word, phrases, or sentences; the flip-flop technique; making close-in and far-out comparisons and so on.

For Charmaz (2006) the first phase is the initial coding in which the researcher is open to the data and tries to see actions in each part or segment of it, but does not apply pre-existing categories to the data. She recommends paying attention to the words, which reflect action, and to 'code the data as actions . . . [t]he openness of initial coding should spark your thinking and allow new ideas to emerge' (p. 48). In this phase, the researcher may see or find the areas where needed data are lacking.

For the researcher it is useful to ask him/herself such questions as: 'How can I define the processes at issue in the data? How does the process develop and how, why, and when does it change and in what situations or contexts? What are the consequences of the process? Who are participants in this process and how does the research participant act in this process?' In coding, the researcher must fulfil two criteria for completing a GT analysis, namely fit (the researcher constructs codes from empirical data and develops them into categories, which highlight the research participants' experiences), and relevance (the researcher's constructed analytic framework interprets what is happening in the process and shows relationships among implicit processes and structures explicitly) (Charmaz 2011).

Focused Coding

This phase is only in the constructivist GT version. Here, the researcher is focused on the synthesis and explanation of larger parts of qualitative data. Focused coding means that the researcher uses 'most significant codes to sift through large amounts of data' (Charmaz 2006, p. 57). In this phase, the researcher determines the adequacy of the created codes in initial coding and decides about initial codes, which are valuable from an analytic point of view in order to categorize the qualitative data completely (Charmaz 2014). In this phase, events, interactions that the researcher did not grasp in initial coding, are important.

Axial Coding

Axial coding is a key step in the Straussian version but missing from the Glaserian one. In the Strauss and Corbin (1998) version the theoretical sampling and coding are keys to relate various concepts together into a theory that addresses the research questions (Dillon 2012). For Charmaz (2006, 2014) the axial coding means the same paradigm as for Strauss and Corbin (1998), where the categories and subcategories are interrelated and participants' statements are grouped according to three methodological components such as conditions, (inter)actions, and consequences.

Selective Coding

The researcher integrates the qualitative data around a core category and constructs the theory. For Glaser (1992) this coding is the second phase (the second part of the substantive coding), in which the codes are developed selectively around a core category. Selective coding integrates all the interpretive work of analysis. The principal objective here is to explain the storyline with the central phenomenon at the heart (Scott 2004).

Theoretical Coding

Theoretical coding for Glaser (1978) is the process in which theoretical codes are used to conceptualize through relating the substantive codes to each other and integrating these into the substantive theory. Theoretical codes are 'conceptual connectors' that develop relationships between categories and their properties (Glaser 1992, p. 38). Constant comparative coding describes the method of constant comparison that imbues both open and theoretical coding.

For Charmaz (2011, 2012) theoretical codes specify possible relationships between categories. According to Charmaz (2014) the researcher must check the created codes through the following questions: How does the coding reflect the described experience? Are the connections between the qualitative data and the created codes evidence based? Do these codes help to understand what indicates the data? Is it possible to explicate what is happening in every segment of data with these codes? Is it possible to interpret adequately the concrete segments of qualitative data without created codes? What codes to add to the data and what is the understanding of the researcher about the phenomenon?

INTERPRETING (CONCEPTUALIZING) THE DATA IN GROUNDED THEORY

Interpretations must include the perspectives and voices of the people whom we study. Interpretations are sought for understanding the actions of individual or collective actors being studied. Yet, those who use GT procedures accept responsibility for their interpretive roles. They do not believe that it is sufficient merely to report or give voice to the viewpoints of the people, groups, or organizations studied (Corbin and Strauss 2008; Strauss and Corbin 1990; Strauss 1987).

More focused reading only occurs when emergent theory is sufficiently developed to allow the literature to be used as additional data (Heath and Cowley 2004). In interpretation (or conceptualization) of GT, researchers are interested in patterns of action(s) and interaction(s) between and among a variety of social units, their changes and relationships with contexts, situations, and conditions that could be internal and/or external (Strauss 1987).

The Researcher's Role as Interpreter

When the researcher performs the analytical phases, this signifies an interpretation (conceptualization) of what occurs under certain conditions: with movement forward, downward, up and down, going one way then another – all depending on analytically specified conditions (Strauss and Corbin 1990, 1994).

Research participants authentically and originally interpret their own and others' actions, and these interpretations should be incorporated in the researcher's interpretations (or conceptualizations). Then, the researcher must learn from participants' interpretations and be attentive to *in vivo* used language, words that reflect the researcher participants' concerns regarding the phenomenon under research. GT methodology fosters the researcher to review and revise his/her own interpretations (conceptualizations) at every step of the GT development (Strauss and Corbin 1990, 1994; Strauss 1987).

The GT should be specified by the researcher. Researchers interpret (conceptualize) GT by theoretical memoing, which includes development of schemas with notes and maps during analytical phases (Dillon 2012). Only the researcher's expertise in its specificity makes it possible to present a situation or context to a GT and ask oneself what the outcome could be. Then, the researcher should collect a set of situations (contexts), which represent different contexts bearing different expectations. Only in such a rich research-based context will the researcher be able to combine different theories and to see opportunities to provide meaningful interpretation (conceptualization).

Literature Review

What about the literature review in GT interpretations? Glaser and Strauss (1967) recommend delaying the literature review until the completion of the qualitative data analysis. The authors note that literature review before data analysis may influence the researcher's thoughts and views, and the original analyses and interpretations will be postponed or 'disappear' all together. Then the GT will not be constructed, created, and interpreted as original research work, but as 'received theory' (Charmaz 2005), where the theoretical ideas of others will lead, rather than the researcher's original ideas.

After analysis the researcher must find the most significant works of other authors in relation to what the researcher addressed in his/her developed GT (Charmaz 2014). Engaging literature goes beyond sections of research reports; then the inclusion of a literature review involves the researcher's self-empowerment to clarify his/her ideas, make comparisons by showing how and where this concrete GT fits or extends relevant literature, and the points of divergence and convergence (Charmaz 2006).

REFERENCES

Babchuk, Wayne A. (1997), 'Glaser or Strauss? Grounded theory and adult education', in *Midwest Research-to-Practice Conference in Adult, Continuing and Community Education*, Michigan State University, East Lansing, Michigan, 15–17 October 1997, available at http://www.anrecs.msu.edu/research/gradpr96.htm (accessed 19 September 2014).
Borgatti, Steve (1996), 'Introduction to grounded theory', http://www.analytictech.com/mb870/introtogt.htm (accessed 21 September 2014).
Boyatzis, Richard E. (1998), *Transforming Qualitative Information: Thematic Analysis and Code Development*, Thousand Oaks, California: Sage.
Braun, Virginia and Victoria Clarke (2006), 'Using thematic analysis in psychology', *Qualitative Research in Psychology*, 3 (2), 77–101.
Charmaz, Kathy (1983), 'The grounded theory', in R. Emerson (ed.), *Contemporary Field Research*, Boston, MA: Little, Brown, pp. 109–126.
Charmaz, Kathy (2005), 'Grounded theory in the 21st century: applications for advancing social justice studies', in Norman K. Denzin and Yvonna S. Lincoln (eds), *Handbook of Qualitative Research*, Los Angeles, CA: Sage, pp. 507–535.
Charmaz, Kathy (2006), *Constructing Grounded Theory: A Practical Guide through Qualitative Analysis*, Los Angeles, CA: Sage.
Charmaz, Kathy (2011), *Constructing Grounded Theory: A Practical Guide through Qualitative Analysis*, London: Sage.
Charmaz, Kathy (2012), 'The power and potential of grounded theory', *Medical Sociology Online*, 6 (3), 2–15, available at http://www.medicalsociologyonline.org/resources/Vol6Iss3/MSo-600x_The-Power-and-Potential-Grounded-Theory_Charmaz.pdf (accessed 16 April 2014).
Charmaz, Kathy (2014), *Constructing Grounded Theory*, Los Angeles, CA: Sage.
Corbin, J.M. and A.L. Strauss (1990), 'Grounded theory research: procedures, canons, and evaluative criteria', *Qualitative Sociology*, 13 (1), 2–21.
Corbin, Juliet M. and Anselm L. Strauss (1996), 'Analytic ordering for theoretical purpose', *Qualitative Inquiry*, 2 (2), 139–150.
Corbin, Juliet M. and Anselm L. Strauss (2008), *Basics of Qualitative Research: Techniques and Procedures for Developing Grounded Theory*, Thousand Oaks, California: Sage.
Crabtree, Benjamin F. and William L. Miller (1999), 'A template approach to text analysis: developing and using codebooks', in Benjamin F. Crabtree and William L. Miller (eds), *Doing Qualitative Research*, Newbury Park, CA: Sage, pp. 163–177.
Daily, Gretchen C. (2001), 'Management objectives for the protection of ecosystem services', *Environmental Science & Policy*, 3 (2000), 333–339.
Dillon, Deborah R. (2012), 'Grounded theory and qualitative research', in *The Encyclopedia of Applied Linguistics*, available at http://www.tc.umn.edu/~dillon/CI%208148%20Qual%20Research/Session%2013/Dillon%20PDF%20Grounded%20Theory%202012.pdf (accessed 21 September 2014).
Fereday, Jennifer and Eimear Muir-Cochrane (2006), 'Demonstrating rigor using thematic analysis: a hybrid approach of inductive and deductive coding and theme development', *International Journal of Qualitative Methods*, 5 (1), 1–11.
Glaser, Barney G. (1978), *Theoretical Sensitivity*, Mill Valley, CA: Sociology Press.
Glaser, Barney G. (1992), *Basics of Grounded Theory*, Mill Valley, CA: Sociology Press.
Glaser, Barney G. (2001), *The Grounded Theory Perspective: Conceptualization Contrasted with Description*, Mill Valley, CA: Sociology Press.
Glaser, Barney G. (2011), *Getting out of the Data: Grounded Theory Conceptualization*, California: Sociology Press.

Glaser, Barney G. and Anselm L. Strauss (1967), *The Discovery of Grounded Theory: Strategies for Qualitative Research*, Chicago: Aldine.
Glaser, Barney G. and Anselm L. Strauss (2008), *The Discovery of Grounded Theory: Strategies for Qualitative Research*, New Brunswick, London: Aldine Transaction.
Guest, Greg, Kelly M. MacQueen and Emily E. Namey (2012), *Applied Thematic Analysis*, London: Sage.
Heath, Helen and Sarah Cowley (2004), 'Developing a grounded theory approach: a comparison of Glaser and Strauss', *International Journal of Nursing Studies*, **41** (2), 141–150.
Hernandez, Cheri Ann (2009), 'Theoretical coding in grounded theory methodology', *The Grounded Theory Review*, **8** (3), 51–66, available at http://groundedtheoryreview.com/2009/11/30/theoretical-coding-in-grounded-theory-methodology/ (accessed 20 October 2014).
Mills, Jane, Ann Bonner and Karen Francis (2006), 'The development of constructivist grounded theory', *International Journal of Qualitative Methods*, **5** (1), Article 3, available at https://www.ualberta.ca/~iiqm/backissues/5_1/PDF/MILLS.PDF (accessed 16 April 2014).
Morse, Janice (2004), 'Theoretical saturation', in Michael S. Lewis-Beck, Alan E. Bryman and Tim Futing Liao (eds), *Encyclopedia of Social Science Research Methods*, Thousand Oaks, CA: Sage, pp. 1123–1124.
Scott, Karen Wilson (2004), 'Relating categories in grounded theory analysis: using a conditional relationship guide and reflective coding matrix', *The Qualitative Report*, **9** (1), 113–126, available at http://www.nova.edu/ssss/QR/QR9-1/wilsonscott.pdf (accessed 4 October 2014).
Strauss, Anselm L. (1987), *Qualitative Analysis for Social Scientists*, New York: Cambridge University Press.
Strauss, Anselm L. and Juliet M. Corbin (1990), *Basics of Qualitative Research: Grounded Theory Procedures and Techniques*, Newbury Park, CA: Sage.
Strauss, Anselm L. and Juliet M. Corbin (1994), 'Grounded theory methodology: an overview', in Norman K. Denzin and Yvonna S. Lincoln (eds), *Handbook of Qualitative Research*, Thousand Oaks, CA: Sage, pp. 285–295.
Strauss, Anselm L. and Juliet M. Corbin (1998), *Basics of Qualitative Research: Grounded Theory Procedures and Techniques*, Newbury Park, London: Sage.
Walker, Diane and Florence Myrick (2006), 'Grounded theory: an exploration of process and procedure', *Qualitative Health Research*, **16** (4), 547–559.

2. Using a mixed methods approach for corporate social responsibility research
Jane Claydon

INTRODUCTION

This chapter focuses on the benefits of using a mixed methods approach when researching Corporate Social Responsibility (CSR). My PhD research investigated debtors' and debt collectors' perceptions of responsibility and blame for consumer debt, assessing who the respondents perceived to be to blame for increasing levels of debt in the UK.

The research revealed that, firstly, the majority of debtor respondents perceived that their consumer credit use was to supplement their low income, which contradicted previous stereotypes of debtors as reckless spendthrifts and, instead, proposed they are agentic rational decision makers. Secondly, debtors were negatively perceived and treated by their creditors (debt collectors) in that they were stigmatized and labelled as deviant. This occurred during the debtors' social interaction with debt collectors during the debt collection process. In line with the labelling theory of deviance, this societal reaction then led to self-labelling by the debtors, who expressed feelings of shame. Thirdly, therefore, both the debtors and debt collectors primarily blamed the debtor stakeholder group as responsible for increasing levels of consumer debt, although the debtors also placed some of the blame on the creditors for acting unethically in their lending practices, namely by lending irresponsibly to debtors without an accurate assessment of the affordability of the loan.

I shall argue in this chapter that using a mixed methods approach ensures the CSR researcher can enjoy the qualities of several different research methods. Further, using different methods enables the researcher to recognize and assess the validity and reliability of a single research method when comparing it against another. This chapter will outline to the reader the strengths, shortcomings, representativeness and validity of the aforementioned research methods, along with the sampling strategy used by the author as a CSR researcher.

Firstly, I provide a rationale for using a mixed methods approach, highlighting the benefits it can bring to academic research and the ways in which it was beneficial to my research on consumer debt, by comparing the participants' responses from the different methods used. Secondly, I explain how epistemological considerations regarding my position as an interpretivist researcher are important in understanding the methodological approach taken. Lastly, I explore the three methods used for my research (online surveys, in-depth interviews, and focus groups) by firstly providing an explanation of the definition and composition of the research method, assessing the aims and strengths and drawing out any issues regarding sampling, representativeness and validity.

USING A MIXED METHODS APPROACH

It could be considered that I used a mixed methods approach in two ways: firstly, by adopting both quantitative and qualitative research methods; and, secondly, by adopting two different qualitative methods, focus groups and interviews. However, as mentioned earlier, the rationale for adopting a quantitative method to support my two qualitative methods was primarily strategic. As already discussed, I used the online surveys as a recruitment process for the debtor interviewees. Thus, the definition of 'mixed methods' for the purpose of my research and this chapter shall focus on the use of two qualitative methods; focus groups and in-depth, semi-structured interviews.

Michell (1999) highlights the benefits of adopting a mixed methods approach when using focus groups to research social phenomena. She outlines the ways in which her secondary school children respondents formed a consensus towards pre-existing public knowledge of particular social issues. Michell points out '[f]ocus groups were thus a rich and productive way of gaining access to well-rehearsed "public knowledge" and highlighting the way in which social exchange reinforced such hierarchies' (1999, p. 36). However, whilst some members dominated the group discussions and ensured their voices were heard, the voices of other more passive group members were silenced (p. 37).

Though it is the role of the moderator to ensure that all participants have a chance to express themselves (Morgan 1996, p. 140), this is not always achievable, particularly with more vulnerable respondents. Michell, then, explains the way in which the voices 'in interview, revealed feelings and personal information which helped to develop an understanding of bullying and victimisation' (1999, p. 37).

Morgan (1996) corroborates that adopting a mixed method approach in qualitative social research is beneficial, particularly by combining individual interviews with focus groups as it results in the 'greater depth of the former and the greater breadth of the latter' (1996, p. 134). The original driver for my choice to combine focus groups and interviews for some of the debt collector respondents was for the purpose of validity; that is, to ensure that the individual's opinions and attitudes expressed in the focus group were consistent with the attitudes and opinions expressed in the one-to-one interview.

However, it is apparent that not only did this comparison reveal the validity of the research but also reveals how groups refer to pre-existing social perceptions and stereotypes of certain other social groups and issues. This is evidenced in my own research, whereby the respondents formed a consensus that the individual debtor has primary responsibility for their own indebtedness, yet did not always express this opinion within the individual interviews. This is demonstrated by the responses below from Rob (debt collector), firstly within the focus group and then within the individual interview.

> [Focus group response:]
> I think the credit card company has some responsibility but I think ultimately the responsibility should lie with the individuals. I think that although people say they've been given a bad deal I think ultimately it really does lie with the individuals.
> [Individual interview response:]
> I think it's kind of a lack of education as opposed to people, I just think people just aren't aware, there's just not enough information. I think people just aren't aware they can get themselves into that much trouble. And I think it's that that's the problem. So, to say that the individual isn't responsible because they think it's all going to be OK, I can see an argument for that . . .

So, yeah, I can see the argument saying that someone shouldn't be sort of blamed if they get themselves out there.

This suggests groups form a consensus on certain social issues, which is reflected by the wider pre-existing social perceptions around the issues, rather than being reflective of their own attitudes and opinions. This is likely a result of attitudes becoming more extreme after group discussion (Morgan 1996, p. 140).

Michell (1999) asserted that the primary reason for the difference in responses from focus groups and interviews was the difference in levels of confidentiality or privacy and awareness of peer feedback respondents had with each research setting (1999, p. 37). Further, the interviews were important for Michell to obtain the full picture of the research respondent's experiences, as there were several more reticent respondents who did not voice their opinions in the focus groups (p. 40).

Reflecting on my focus groups, there was generally an equal level of participation from each of the respondents. I achieved this by purposefully selecting respondents who were of equal experience and seniority levels (i.e. they were all senior representatives). This lowered the risk that some of the respondents in the group would perceive themselves to be the minority and thus become reticent.

Additionally, Michell observed the way in which respondents would talk about their family and social relationships exclusively in the interview environment (p. 36). This was certainly true for one of my respondents, Jim, who talked about wider society in the focus group, however, during the one-to-one interview made several references to his own family and friends' situations with debt.

Silverman (2005) further highlights the importance of adopting a mixed method approach in relation to the dangers he perceives with using interviews as the sole method in social research. His argument centres on the critique of interviews that the narrative of the interviewee is not necessarily an accurate reflection of their lived experiences (2005, p. 239).

Having said that, I have outlined above that the actual experience of the debtor is in many ways less important than the debtor's perception of their experiences and indebted socio-economic situation, a position informed by the phenomenological nature of my research.

EPISTEMOLOGICAL CONSIDERATIONS: INTERPRETIVISM

The epistemological position that a researcher takes before conducting research is key to understanding the researcher's motivations and preconceptions of the social world they are about to study. Epistemology poses the question of what should be regarded as acceptable knowledge in a discipline and, more specifically, whether there is a universal social 'truth' that exists which can be revealed and explained (Bryman 2008, p. 13).

I have adopted an interpretivist position, which asserts that social facts and truths are not considered things in themselves or universal and the social world can be assessed upon subjective observation and interpretation of human behaviour (Petrunik 1980, p. 216). Therefore, my data will provide accounts of narrative constructions and self-presentation rather than realist direct descriptive accounts of the facts behind their indebtedness. It is important to note here that my interest is in subjective interpretations but, of course, this is not the only possible approach for social science.

Individuals are social actors; their positionality is fluid and their sense of self is constantly influenced and changed by their social environment. Individuals construct their understanding of their social world by reacting to it in a cyclical process where social interaction determines understanding and vice versa. This extends to social research, as 'all research is interpretive, and reality is being constructed at every stage of a research process' (Maitland-Gholson and Ettinger 1994, p. 18).

My research did not aim to reveal universal social truths about debt in order to assign indebted individuals into one category or another of a certain type of debtor. Rather, it aimed to explore social perceptions of debt and indebtedness. Furthermore, as an interpretivist it is important to adopt a reflexive research approach by making constant assessments about the ways in which the researcher made decisions during the research process, which ultimately affects the direction and content of the research (Maitland-Gholson and Ettinger 1994, p. 27). This chapter will unveil the ways in which my reflexivity and reflectivity was achieved throughout the research process.

Interpretivist research aims to recognize the way in which social actors provide accounts of events that are examples of 'unanticipated or untoward behaviour' (Scott et al. 1968, p. 46). These accounts are an attempt of the social actor to justify, excuse or blame others for such actions. Though they provide strategies to avoid such accounts in a research environment, these accounts in my own research provide useful insight into the understanding debtors have of societal attitudes towards debt in the way that they seek to justify, excuse or blame others for their indebted situation.

Reflecting on my research, some of the respondents explained their indebtedness was due to external factors outside of their influence, for example life course events rather than internally attributing it to their own spending patterns. Further, analysing people's understanding and perceptions of why they are in debt is more interesting and relevant to my sociological investigation than asserting these self-perceptions are an accurate account of why people are in debt.

METHODS USED

Not only are the issues of pre-understanding and researcher effect important to consider reflexively when undertaking insider research, but also the appropriateness of the methods used is a key consideration (Costley et al. 2010, p. 81). I shall now provide such a discussion of the research methods used in terms of their structure, benefits to the research and sampling strategy used.

Online Surveys

Definition and composition

The online survey I conducted was primarily used as a recruitment technique for the debtor interview respondents, although the data from the survey was used as evidence of respondents' perceptions within several of the chapters in my PhD thesis. It is, therefore, important to briefly address the type of survey that I adopted and the other benefits it offered my research.

Respondents (debtors) were recruited by posting the survey on the National Debtline

48 *Handbook of research methods in corporate social responsibility*

website. With over 400,000 site visitors in 2009,[1] the National Debtline is the UK's most widely used debt advice website. I obtained access to posting the survey on this site through a contact at the Money Advice Trust, the charity which runs the National Debtline website, whom I met whilst networking at a Money Advice Group conference in London in 2008. The survey obtained a total of 195 respondents. I adopted an online self-completion survey rather than choosing to conduct the survey face to face with respondents.

Aims and strengths
There are a number of benefits to this method, primarily in that it is cheaper and quicker to administer and more convenient for the respondents but also in that it lacks interviewer presence, which can often detrimentally affect responses (Bryman 2008, pp. 217–218). This was particularly pertinent for the sensitive nature of the topic being researched (i.e. personal debt).

Lastly, four of the online survey respondents also chose to partake in an online qualitative questionnaire, which provided more valuable qualitative information about the debtors' reasons for indebtedness and relationship with their creditors.

Sampling, representativeness and validity
An important consideration is that the self-completion survey method often results in a lower response rate than if conducted with the researcher present (Bryman 2008, p. 219). This has a detrimental effect on the representativeness of these surveys in that they have increased bias, 'unless it can be proven that those who do not participate do not differ from those who do' (ibid.).

Despite this, I was satisfied with the number of responses I received from the survey (195) and this is largely due to the fact that the survey was posted on the National Debtline website. Further, it is important to again note here that the surveys were primarily conducted in order to recruit participants for the in-depth interviews, although, as already mentioned, the data generated was used within the PhD thesis.

Focus Groups

Definition and composition
For the focus groups, the respondents were debt collector staff and recruited via confidential email invitations. I held three focus groups with a total of 12 respondents; the first session had five respondents, the second session had four respondents and the final session had three respondents. A more comprehensive discussion of the sampling strategy adopted is outlined below.

According to Greenbaum (1998), there are three types of focus groups: (1) full group, consisting of eight to ten people and lasting 90 to 120 minutes; (2) mini-group, of the same time as a full group but with four to six people; and (3) a telephone group, for which the focus group is conducted via a conference call (p. 1–2). From this definition, it is apparent that my focus groups can be categorized as mini-groups, as they consisted of three to five respondents and the sessions ran from 60 to 90 minutes each.

The advantage of adopting the mini-group approach is that it allows the researcher to obtain more information from each individual (p. 3), which enables empowerment of the respondents, a key characteristic of the focus group method (Barbour and Kitzinger 1999, pp. 18–19).

Regarding the number of focus groups to be held, it is essential to conduct more than one to observe patterns in behaviour and to ensure the results are valid (Knodel 1993, p. 42). Yet, on a practical level there are important practical considerations, such as the time and resources the researcher has to conduct, transcribe and perform analysis on the sessions (p. 41). As a part-time self-funded researcher, my access to both time and resource was limited, thus I conducted three focus groups.

Focus groups should comprise of participants with 'control characteristics' (Knodel 1993, p. 37) of homogeneity as they are able to provide 'the highest quality discussion' (Greenbaum 1998, p. 2) by 'debating a set of questions' (Barbour and Kitzinger 1999, p. 4). As people are most likely to have already shared experiences and have discussed the topical issues being addressed in the focus group, many social science researchers prefer to work with 'naturally-occurring' pre-existing groups (p. 9).

This was the rationale for my focus groups, as those I deemed to be qualified for participating in a discussion about the lending practices of a credit card company were debt collectors who had knowledge of typical credit card company practices and shared experience in dealing with debtors. Each of these different types of focus groups featured a moderator who 'functions as the leader of the discussion and stimulates discussion among the participants, saying as little as possible during the group' (Greenbaum 1998, p. 2). I conformed to the role of researcher as moderator without power or influence (Krueger and Casey 2000, p. 9) in that my voice was silenced as much as possible by asking just three leading questions, allowing the respondent to discuss freely.

Minimal moderation was achieved by the use of visual discussion aids to stimulate conversation (Bruseberg and McDonagh 2003, p. 31). I created a collage of images for the focus groups relating to debt and credit to help initiate conversation around the issues at the heart of the research questions. Specifically, the collage comprised of images showing debtors locked in chains, credit cards posed as bait in the middle of animal traps and sharks dressed in business suits, all of which depicted consumer credit and debt as problematic in an attempt to provoke the respondents into expressing their attitudes on the topic. However, this approach could be critiqued in that showing images to respondents potentially places ideas in their heads and therefore influences their responses.

Aims and strengths
Primarily, the role of the focus group is to explore attitudes and experiences around particular subjects and to observe the way in which such attitudes are constructed and expressed through the interaction that takes place during the session (Barbour and Kitzinger 1999). Exploration of debt collectors' attitudes towards debtors was certainly one of the key aims of the research, thus the focus group method most suited the research aims.

Focus groups have an advantage over individual interviews in that the group can build upon the topic of discussion themselves, often without much prompting from the researcher (Langford and McDonagh 2003, p. 3). This results in the possibility of the conversation going in a direction which is far less predictable and more interesting. Morgan (1996) asserts 'the real strength of the focus group is not simply in exploring what people have to say, but in providing insights into the sources of complex behaviours and motivations' (p. 139) via the 'group effect' (ibid.).

This was especially pertinent for my own research in assessing how the workplace culture of debt collection was reflected in the attitudes and perceptions of debtors expressed during the focus groups. Further, the focus group researcher is able to ask participants to compare their experiences, which eliminates the need to collate individual data and speculate about why attitudes differ (ibid.). The discovery of differing opinions may not have been possible if I had analysed the individual interview transcripts separately.

Lastly, Morgan asserts that there are promising new uses for focus groups. The most notable of these involves researchers who are more actively engaged with the participants and their concerns (p. 149). Regarding the use of focus groups for my own research, this certainly fits with Morgan's vision, as my status as insider researcher allowed me to engage more with the respondents and listen to their concerns with credibility and interest.

Sampling, representativeness and validity

The sampling strategy I adopted for the focus group method was not statistically representative as this is not the aim of most focus group research (Barbour and Kitzinger 1999, p. 17). Rather, the appropriate number of respondents and groups depends on the research question, ensuring that the sampling strategy is topic specific by comprising the group of homogenous individuals who have knowledge on the issue being discussed (Morgan 1996, p. 143).

I adopted a purposive (Bryman 2008, p. 458) qualitative sampling strategy for the focus groups in that I chose research participants who had the most knowledge and experience of the issue being discussed. Respondents were chosen based on two key characteristics: tenure in the role and subject matter expertise. Both of these factors resulted in the respondents having most knowledge and experience with the issues being discussed in the focus group, which enabled a fuller and richer discussion revealing the attitudes of debt collectors towards the debtors.

In-Depth Interviews

Definition and composition

Interviews were conducted with both groups of respondents (debtors and debt collectors); the strategies and recruitment strategies for this have already been explained above. Of the 195 survey respondents, in-depth semi-structured investigative interviews, lasting between 40 and 80 minutes, were conducted with a total of ten respondents who volunteered to take part via the survey.

The interviews with the debt collectors were held with three of the focus respondents approximately one year after the focus groups were held. A further interview was conducted with Vince Cable who, at the time of this writing, is the UK government's Business Secretary but, at the time of being interviewed in 2009, was the Shadow Chancellor for the Liberal Democrat party. Vince Cable was specifically recruited as an expert informant as, shortly before the commencement of this research, his book *The Storm*, which provided insight into the subprime and global financial crises, was published and received wide critical acclaim. Between the years of 2006 and 2009 during which time the Global Financial Crisis and subsequent recession hit the UK, Cable was considered by many politicians and journalists to be a key spokesperson on the events, given his background as an economist, both in a corporate and academic context. However, as stated earlier in the thesis, he shall not be considered as a respondent as he does not represent any of the stakeholder groups at the focus of this research.

Silverman (2005) observes that the increased use of the interview method in social research may mirror its increased popularity in everyday culture, suggesting we live in 'what might be called an interview society in which interviews seem central to making sense of our lives' (2005, p. 111). However, it is for this reason that Silverman advises it is essential to question whether interviews can really help in addressing the topic of the researcher, rather than the researcher adopting the method simply because of the 'prominence of interviews in the media' (p. 48).

Typically, then, interviews are a method for collecting qualitative data relating to research questions that are exploratory in nature and aim to ask how- and why-questions. The interviewee's, not the researcher's, point of view is the aim of the investigation of the qualitative data (Bryman 2008, p. 192). Interviews can be either: structured, with a reasonably large number of direct questions that the researcher will ask; semi-structured, with a small number of leading questions that the researcher will ask; or unstructured, where the researcher may either ask the interviewee to provide a biography or the researcher will ask questions that have not been predetermined but are dependent on the interviewee's response and are more conversational in nature (p. 437).

Further, interviews can vary in duration, ranging from in-depth interviews, which can last several hours and explore several social issues, to shorter interviews of 30 minutes or less duration, which focus on a few key thematic social issues.

My research aimed to understand two key socio-economic issues for the debtor group: debtors' perceptions of credit and debt; and debtors' perceptions of and relationships with their creditors. Essentially, the interviews asked the debtors 'about their identity' as debtors (Silverman 2005, p. 59). Thus, my interviews were aiming to investigate quite a specific set of social issues (Bryman 2008, p. 196) of which the debtors had experience.

Further, although a brief overview of the socio-economic and socio-cultural background was provided from each of the debtors to place their indebted situation in a wider social context to assess implications for social mobility, I was not aiming to obtain a full biography of the debtors or to explore every social relationship they ever had. For these reasons, I chose to conduct semi-structured, in-depth interviews of approximately one-hour duration with nine questions, as an interview guide (p. 438). The questions were designed to encourage interviewees to express their opinions and share their experiences, even if this account telling led to off-topic rambling (p. 437) in a direction that I did not expect.

Lastly, logistical considerations are important when discussing the research design, particularly in light of the fact that the interviews I conducted with the debtors were telephone interviews, rather than face to face. The reasons for choosing to do so were both practical and methodological. Practically, it was not possible for me to travel all over the country to meet the interviewees from a time and cost perspective. Methodologically, social researchers have recognized that telephone interviewing can be more appropriate for more sensitive topics, such as personal debt, 'since interviewees may be less distressed about answering when the interviewer is not physically present' (p. 456).

Aims and strengths

Many social researchers have recognized that interviews are the most preferred method within social science research (Silverman 2005, Bryman 2008). One of the main advantages for the use of qualitative interviews is when aiming for a reconstruction of events in the research participant's life, which cannot easily be achieved through other methods (Bryman 2008, p. 440).

This was a particular requirement of my own research in that I wanted the debtors to recall their specific experiences with getting into debt and the relationships with their creditors. This type of account is too lengthy to be captured in an online survey or focus group, where individuals are often battling for their voices to be heard.

Roulston (2010) highlights the way in which high quality interviews can be an effective and data-rich method in qualitative research. Such quality can be assured using six criteria whereby interviews: are characterized by the 'spontaneous, rich, specific and relevant answers from the interviewee' (2010, p. 202); contain significantly more dialogue from the respondent than the researcher; demonstrate the researcher following up to clarify the meanings of answers where necessary; are, to a large extent, interpreted throughout the interview; contain moments where the interviewer verifies their interpretation of the respondent's answer during the interview itself; and are self-communicating in that they require little explanation (Kvale 1996, p. 145).

Reflecting on my research, the interviews I conducted with both sets of respondents met the criteria outlined above. It was evident from the transcripts that the respondents, particularly the debtors, produced a large amount of content-rich data. Additionally, during the often hour-long interviews there were very few pauses or points where I would have to interject in order to provoke a response and the respondents had significantly more input than me.

Further, where necessary I followed up with the respondents for clarification on the meaning of answers. Yet, there was little requirement for me to do so for either group (i.e. debtors and debt collectors), as my insider knowledge on the areas discussed meant that I was almost always aware of the language and terms being referred to. The only instances where such clarification occurred were in instances where a respondent's answer may have been interpreted in multiple ways and so validation of the interpretation was performed during the interview.

Sampling, representativeness and validity

The recruitment process for the focus group debt collector respondents differed to the debtor interviews, as the debt collectors were chosen based on their employment tenure. It is important to note that in relation to the number of debtor respondents who completed the online survey (195), the number who opted to take part in the interview (10) was relatively low in comparison. Yet, this small number of interviews still produced a large amount of qualitative quality-rich data.

Regarding validity, ensuring the credibility of interviews by evidencing the source and procedure for obtaining the information 'has been important for qualitative inquirers' (Roulston 2010, p. 201). Briggs (1986) has asserted the importance of the researcher asking questions in ways that might be understood by participants (1986, p. 25).

For the interviews conducted with the debt collectors this was a relatively easy task as my insider status enabled me to have the knowledge and experience on the topic being discussed, which informed the questions to be asked of the participants. Knowing the right questions to ask the debtors during the interviews was more difficult, as I had no previous connection with them. However, again my extensive knowledge and experience of the consumer credit sector enabled me to ask questions that I knew would be relevant to the debtors' experiences with debt and their creditors.

Further, the research process must be reflexive, by conducting an analysis of interviewing procedures and data and adopting a multiple method approach for data generation (p. 101). Reflexivity during my research was ensured by reading thoroughly on the literature around the interview method before, during and after the interviews had been conducted for the purpose of preparation and analysis. This links into the importance of analysing interview data as 'meta-communicative events' (Roulston 2010, p. 201), which was achieved by reflecting on and communicating to the reader about how I communicated to the respondents, in order to analyse the data obtained from the interviews and ensure their validity and credibility.

In terms of representativeness, 80 per cent of the debtor respondents were women, suggesting the sample was not representative of the general population. Yet, women are more likely to obtain higher volumes of consumer debt, seek debt advice and 'disclose personal problems' (Hayes 2010, p. 287). Therefore, it may have actually been more representative of the target population. Further, important to note is how my own gender affected those respondents who chose whether to take part in the research or not.

Silverman (2005) notes that 'where the researcher was the same gender as the informant, people were far more likely to discuss their sexual interests' (2005, p. 264). Though this evidence related to research conducted on sexuality, which has very obvious relevance to issues of gender, this would have affected my own research as debt is as sensitive, if not more so, than sex (Burton 2008, p. 32).

Research conducted on a US audience concluded that Americans will talk about sex before credit card debt. Therefore, as a female, it is perhaps not surprising and even inevitable and unavoidable that my research respondents were primarily female, even though I approached many male survey respondents who declined being interviewed. As debt is such a taboo subject, making it difficult to research (p. 31), this makes this research project even more valuable in contributing to the knowledge on debt in society.

CONCLUSION

As with any research method, there are benefits as well as obstacles. This chapter has outlined the aims, strengths, validity and representativeness of three key research methods, online surveys, in-depth interviews and focus groups, all of which are fit for CSR research. However, there are many more methods that would be useful for CSR research, depending on the researcher's epistemological position.

The main argument in this chapter is that using more than one different method and adopting a mixed methods approach greatly benefits the research for a number of reasons, primarily in that it allows for the generation of richer data and ensures validity of the research data, by enabling the researcher to compare responses from different methods.

NOTE

1. www.nationaldebtline.co.uk.

REFERENCES

Barbour, Rosaline and Jenny Kitzinger (eds) (1999), *Developing Focus Group Research*, London: Sage.
Briggs, Charles (1986), *Learning How to Ask: A Sociolinguistic Appraisal of the Role of the Interview in Social Science Research*, Cambridge: Cambridge University Press.
Bruseberg, A. and D. McDonagh (2003), 'Organising and conducting a focus group: the logistics', in Joe Langford and Deana McDonagh (eds), *Focus Groups: Supporting Effective Product Development*, London: Taylor and Francis, pp. 19–46.
Bryman, Alan (2008), *Social Research Methods* (3rd edition), Oxford: Oxford University Press.
Burton, Dawn (2008), *Credit and Consumer Society*, London: Routledge.
Cable, Vince (2009), *The Storm,* London: Atlantic Books.
Costley, Carol, Geoffrey Elliott and Paul Gibbs (2010), *Doing Work Based Research*, London: Sage.
Greenbaum, Thomas (1998), *The Handbook for Focus Group Research* (2nd edition), London: Sage.
Hayes, T. (2010), 'Labelling and the adoption of a deviant status', *Deviant Behaviour*, 31 (3), 274–302.
Knodel, J. (1993), 'The design and analysis of focus group studies', in David L. Morgan (ed.), *Successful Focus Groups: Advancing the State of the Art*, California: Sage, pp. 35–50.
Krueger, Richard A. and Mary Anne Casey (2000), *Focus Groups: A Practical Guide for Applied Research* (3rd edition), Thousand Oaks CA: Sage.
Kvale, Steiner (1996), *InterViews: An Introduction to Qualitative Research Interviewing*, Thousand Oaks CA: Sage.
Langford, Joe and Deana McDonagh (eds) (2003), *Focus Groups: Supporting Effective Product Development*, London: Taylor and Francis.
Maitland-Gholson, J. and L.F. Ettinger (1994), 'Interpretive decision making in research', *Studies in Art Education*, 36 (1), 18–27.
Michell, L. (1999), 'Focus groups and interviews: telling how it is; telling how it feels', in Jenny Kitzinger and Rosaline Barbour (eds), *Developing Focus Group Research: Politics, Theory and Practice*, London: Thousand Oaks, pp. 36–46.
Morgan, D.L. (1996), 'Focus groups', *Annual Review of Sociology*, 22(1), 129–152.
Petrunik, M. (1980), 'The rise and fall of "labelling theory": the construction and destruction of a sociological strawman', *The Canadian Journal of Sociology*, 5 (3), 213–233.
Roulston, K. (2010), 'Considering quality in qualitative interviewing', *Qualitative Research*, 10 (2), 199–228.
Scott, M.B., M. Stanford and S.M. Lyman (1968), 'Accounts', *American Sociological Review*, 33 (1), 46–62.
Silverman, David (2005), *Doing Qualitative Research*, London: Sage.

3. Imperative of meta-study for research in the field of corporate social responsibility and emerging issues in corporate governance
Lukman Raimi

INTRODUCTION

Meta-study is an integrative analytical tool in the field of medicine, psychology and management for fortifying, reinforcing and re-explaining the relationships among variables of interest to researchers (Beatty et al. 2011; Denyer and Tranfield 2006; Voils et al. 2008). The reason for using meta-study in a number of qualitative, quantitative and mixed research studies is to reshape, re-explain and transform the accumulated findings made by a number of researchers from different studies into a more concrete and legitimate body of knowledge (Paterson et al. 2001).

The quality of integrated findings from a meta-study is largely dependent on the thoroughness of data extraction sourced from diverse studies. Therefore, extraction of findings should be based on fairness and objectivity at the phase of literature gathering/accumulation, as no finding/result should be excluded on the pretext of quality at this preliminary phase; rather the value of extracted findings/results from previous studies are determined during the phase of synthesis of findings or meta-summary (Pawson 2006a, 2006b).

In theory and practice, a meta-study has four sequential and reinforcing stages, namely: meta-method, meta-theory, meta-data analysis and meta-synthesis. Each stage has its uniqueness and application in academic research. The meta-study, unlike a single study, is useful for identifying patterns, sources of divergence in results/findings of previous research, as well as integrating these results/findings gathered from multiple studies (Rothman et al. 2008; Rhoades et al. 2001; Walker et al. 2008).

In view of the discussion above, the purpose of this chapter is to discuss and justify the imperative of meta-study for research in the fields of corporate social responsibility (CSR) and corporate governance (CG) because of heterogeneous theoretical perspectives and conflicting empirical findings in previous studies across the two fields. Conceptually, the term CSR is viewed as voluntary obligations of corporations designed to improve the social, ethical, governance, economic, labour and environmental wellness of the host communities where they operate, as corporate citizens (Kotler and Lee 2005; Visser 2008). CG on the other hand describes the transactional relationship between the owners of corporations (as principals) and the managers (as agents) based on clear terms of engagement and governance structure (Hill and Jones 1992; Jensen and Meckling 1976; Ryan and Schneider 2003; Connelly et al. 2010). Both concepts have been extensively discussed, but the theoretical and empirical findings have been inconclusive. To harmonize the conflicting and overlapping findings from a number of empirical and exploratory studies in the field of CSR, the application of meta-study is imperative and relevant.

Over the years, the meta-study as an analytical technique has attracted modest application in a number of CSR and CG studies. For instance, Frooman (1999) utilized a meta-study to provide empirical justification for the presumption that social involvement has the plausibility of increasing shareholder wealth. Integrating findings from 27 previous studies, the study found that socially irresponsible and illicit behaviour has a negative effect on shareholder wealth (in other words, when a corporation becomes irresponsible and irresponsive to the expectations of society, their stockholders' wealth decreases). The meta-analysis therefore established that corporations must be socially responsible to promote the shareholders' interests.

Disturbed by the conflicting theoretical perspectives and empirical findings in CG studies, Rhoades et al. (2001) utilized the meta-study to harmonize the seeming contradictions in the relationship between board leadership structure and organizational performance, drawing together 22 independent samples across 5,751 companies. The meta-study revealed that independent leadership structure significantly influenced organizational performance. However, an earlier meta-analysis of 131 samples ($N = 20,620$) established a non-zero positive relationship between board of directors' size and firm performance; the finding is significant because it provided a consensus about the direction of that relationship which was absent in previous studies with conflicting findings.

Besides, Orlitzky et al. (2003) carried out a meta-study by reviewing 52 studies on CSR with a combined sample size of 33,878 observations. The finding indicated that different dimensions of CSR pay off, and in fact establish a significant relationship with regards to corporate social performance (CSP) and corporate financial performance (CFP) or what is often styled CSP-CFP synergy (Orlitzky et al. 2003). Another meta-study summarized the findings from 29 studies on the achievement effects of school reform after implementation of intervention programmes in such schools for a minimum of five years. The findings indicated that the impoverished schools where the comprehensive school reform had been implemented manifested strong achievement effects and positive benefits (Borman et al. 2003).

Furthermore, Margolis et al. (2007) investigated the relationship between CSP and CFP using a meta-analytical approach by examining 251 previous studies. It was found that the overall effect of CSP and CFP is positive but marginal (mean $r = 0.13$, median $r = 0.09$, weighted $r = 0.11$). The conclusion is that there is slight evidence of a CSP-CFP link. This aligned with the findings of Orlitzky et al. (2003), carried out four years earlier.

In another research, Aguinis and Glavas (2012) provided sound understanding of CSR from a meta-analytical perspective. From a review of 588 journal articles and 102 books, they found that CSR actions and policies have both internal and external effects/outcomes on stakeholders. Secondly, CSR outcomes have contingency effects, that is, they affect people, place, price and profile-based moderator variables. The study justified the need to employ different theoretical perspectives by researchers in studying and understanding CSR at three levels of analysis (institutional, organizational and individual levels).

From the preliminary discourse, meta-study is useful for bridging the substantive knowledge gaps in the fields of CSR and emerging issues in CG. There are four parts in this book chapter: the first part presents an introduction to meta-study; the second discusses meta-study and its four stages extensively; and the third part explains the choice of materials and methods. The last part concludes with research implication and gaps filled.

Imperative of meta-study and issues in corporate governance 57

META-STUDY IN ACADEMIC RESEARCH

In the fields of sciences, social sciences and management, scholars employ meta-study as a meta-summary to synthesize diverse findings from qualitative and quantitative descriptive research works, but the conceptual and methodological issues raised have not been completely resolved (Sandelowski et al. 2007). A meta-study is a distinct analytical technique for making new in-depth meaning from research by integrating the findings from diverse individual studies on a particular subject (Edwards et al. 2010). In practice, it is a systematic process identifying new insights/results from research. The steps could be shorter or longer. Doucouliagos and Paldam (2010) adopted a two-step process in their meta-study, namely: (1) identification of the degree of interaction among the terms/concepts/variables being studied; and (2) identification of determinants, which causes differences in results in previous studies. However, Feld and Heckemeyer (2011) followed three systematic steps in their meta-study on Tax-Foreign Direct Investment relationships. First, they aggregated the most recent studies and publications that have not been used in previous meta-analyses. Furthermore, they applied the meta-regression estimators for identifying the most suitable data from selected studies to be included in the meta-study. Lastly, they generated new results/insights that provide sound explanation and clarification on taxation-FDI relationships.

As a methodological issue, meta-study cuts across the three dominant research methods – quantitative observational studies, qualitative studies and mixed methods studies (Pawson 2006a, 2006b). These important features of meta-study need to be exploited for enriching, promoting and fortifying outcomes of CSR research.

To promote the calls for wider application in CSR research, it is important to mention that there are four stages in a complete meta-study, namely: (1) meta-method; (2) meta-theory; (3) meta-data analysis; and (4) meta-synthesis. These four stages are mutually reinforcing (and could be a stand-alone step) as depicted in Figure 3.1; one stage leads to the other until the terminal stage called meta-synthesis. Meta-synthesis is considered a 'richer, deeper and more multifaceted way of theorising about a phenomenon' being investigated by the researcher (Paterson et al. 2001, p. 119).

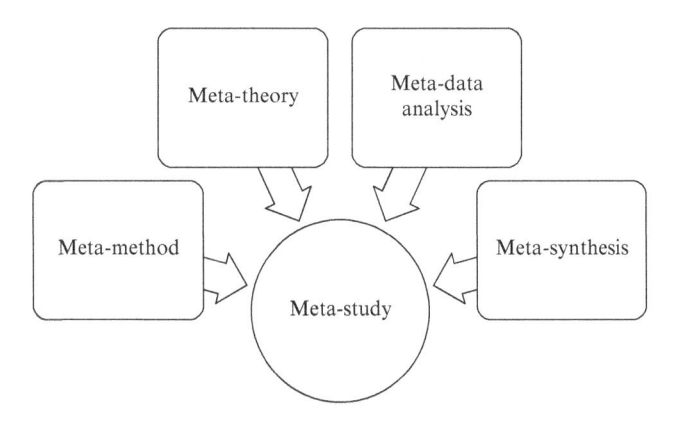

Source: Adapted from the analysis of Paterson et al. (2001).

Figure 3.1 Four stages of meta-study

Meta-Method

This is a critical analysis of the theory, methods and findings from previous research and the synthesis of these insights into new ways of thinking about a phenomenon. Meta-method entails combining several research methods such as: quantitative, qualitative and mixed methods (Saunders et al. 2012). For the qualitative research method, it is understood as understanding social interactions by collecting open-ended responses from people using interviews, observations, field notes and personal reflections on the basis of which new hypotheses and theory are generated. However, meta-method in the quantitative research method examines cause-effect relationships and tests hypotheses for the purpose of making predictions on the subject of enquiry. The mixed methods are hybrid methods that combine the strengths of qualitative and quantitative methods for fortification, triangulation and enhancement of research outcomes (Denscombe 2010; Saunders et al. 2012).

Meta-Theory

This is a critical and in-depth review of existing theoretical frameworks or issues in order to provide direction to research and researchers. The term meta-theory refers to a theory or theories that emerged from research in a particular field of academic study (Neufeld 1995). In a field of study with theory deficiency, meta-theory strengthens such a field by helping to develop relevant theories in order to provide explanations to findings. In any discipline where meta-theory is not embraced and applied, such field would leave unanswered several questions as well as reflecting serious limitations with regards to theorizing contemporary issues and problems. The import of the various explanations is that a meta-theory helps fortify old or new theory thereby providing direction for researchers and their research works. Researchers find meta-theory relevant because of the benefits it offers, apart from those mentioned above by Neufeld (1995). The first benefit of meta-theory is that it provides researchers with better and more robust understanding of socio-behavioural issues like why human beings think in a particular direction, and why researchers should explore alternative thought processes in finding explanations for contending issues in research. Secondly, meta-theory provides researchers with 'social, political and philosophical' clues for justifying their 'theoretical claims' which are limited by time and space (Paterson et al. 2001, p. 108).

Meta-Analysis

The credit for conceptualizing meta-analysis goes to Gene Glass, who coined the term 'meta-analysis' in 1976 as a novel form of statistical analysis for integrating heterogeneous findings thereby making sound meaning from a large collection of analyses arising from individual studies. Thereafter, several books and articles emerged discussing meta-analysis and its merits for research across fields (O'Rourke 2007). In the field of CSR, meta-analysis was found useful because of the growing number of conflicting research evidences on the relationships between CSR and financial performance metrics, which encouraged scholars to develop a formal statistical tool for synthesizing the varied evidences on the relationship between CSR and financial performance (Griffin and Mahon 1997; Roman et al. 1999; Margolis and Walsh 2003; Orlitzky et al. 2003).

Meta-analysis presents itself as a useful statistical technique for integrating conflicting evidences and synthesizing their findings beyond mere qualitative comparison of previous results (Allouche and Laroche 2005). The use of meta-analysis for harmonizing evidences arising from CSR research has continued to grow in leaps. It is preferred as more reliable because of its generalizable conclusions by drawing its premises from several related findings (Orlitzky et al. 2003). Meta-analysis can also be described as a 'comprehensive review of all known studies' or a technique that allows 'the researchers to summarize quantitatively all information about' the findings from several research works focusing on the same phenomenon (Borman et al. 2003; Jackson and Schuler 1985).

In explicating the process of a meta-analysis, Shachar (2008) identified ten steps, namely: defining the domain of research; criteria for including studies in the review; determining the type of effect size to use; searching for relevant studies; study database and selection of final set of relevant studies; data extraction and coding; determining the individual and overall effect sizes across studies; homogeneity and bias analyses; presenting the results; and qualitative interpretation of effect size (Shachar 2008). However, Field and Gillett (2010) compressed the process of conducting a meta-analysis into five, namely: selecting articles, developing inclusion criteria, calculating effect sizes, conducting the actual analysis and estimating the effects of publication bias (Field and Gillett 2010). It is important to submit that a meta-analysis is effective in establishing the most consistent and reliable relationship between two variables from multiple studies. Unlike a single study with an inconclusive relationship, a meta-analysis demonstrates the existence of a relationship, but cannot isolate the causative factor or the cause of the connection (Dalton et al. 1999).

Meta-Synthesis

This refers to the method of connecting findings from mixed or multiple research methods. It is a technique for integrating from different studies with interrelated intents for the purpose of generating new insights and understanding from such qualitative studies. Unlike a meta-analysis which is aggregative with a focus on quantitative studies, the meta-synthesis is interpretive and focused on qualitative studies (Walsh and Downe 2005). With regards to synthesizing data and/or results from the qualitative and quantitative research methods, the literature identified three major methods of integrating and synthesizing research results, namely: (1) merging of data/results; (2) connecting data/results; and (3) embedding of data/results (Driscoll et al. 2007; Creswell and Clark 2011). Creswell and Clark (2007, p. 7) assert:

> It is not enough to simply collect and analyze quantitative and qualitative data; they need to be 'mixed' in some way so that together they form a more complete picture of the problem than they do when standing alone.

The significance of a meta-synthesis is to enhance comparative analysis of findings arising from different independent studies.

MATERIALS AND METHOD

This book chapter adopted the qualitative research method while relying on previous journal articles as sources of data on meta-study. From the search engine, a request for articles on meta-study generated over 45 journal articles and diverse books. The sourced materials were systematically previewed on the basis of their suitability and relevance to the fields of CSR and emerging issues in CG. At the end of the preview, most relevant papers were finally selected and reviewed (that is, a purposive sampling technique was applied). The method of analysis found most appropriate was qualitative meta-analysis. It could therefore be stated that the qualitative meta-analysis was adopted for reviewing the literature to elicit evidences/facts and synthesizing them and bringing out new interpretations which bridge the gap between theory and practice (Denyer and Tranfield 2006). It is also an interpretative process of integrating results from many studies (Walsh and Downe 2005).

CONCLUSION/IMPLICATIONS

This book chapter sets out to make a case for the adoption of meta-study on the ground that it is a relevant analytical tool for studying emerging issues in the fields of CSR and CG where previous studies reflect heterogeneous theoretical perspectives and conflicting empirical findings. Meta-study is described as a methodological approach with application in qualitative, quantitative and mixed methods research. In theory and practice, a complete meta-study has four reinforcing stages, namely: meta-method, meta-theory, meta-data analysis and meta-synthesis. The implication of the book chapter is that meta-study has emerged as a legitimate source of knowledge for researchers and policymakers as it provides a better way of synthesizing and harmonizing different findings from one-off studies from qualitative research, quantitative research and mixed methods research in the fields of CSR and CG. It gives an evidence-based solution or weight of evidence to inconclusive research findings.

REFERENCES

Aguinis, H., and Glavas, A. (2012), 'What we know and don't know about corporate social responsibility a review and research agenda', *Journal of Management*, **38** (4), 932–968.

Allouche, J., and P. Laroche (2005), 'A meta-analytical investigation of the relationship between corporate social and financial performance', *Revue de gestion des ressources humaines*, **57**, 1–18. Accessed August, 2014, at https://hal.archives-ouvertes.fr/file/index/docid/923906/filename/CSR_and_CFP_a_meta_analysis_RGRH_2005.pdf.

Beatty, P., I. Reay, S. Dick and J. Miller (2011), 'Consumer trust in e-commerce web sites: a meta-study', *ACM Computing Surveys* (CSUR), **43** (3), 14.

Borman, G.D., G.M. Hewes, L.T. Overman and S. Brown (2003), 'Comprehensive school reform and achievement: a meta-analysis', *Review of Educational Research*, **73** (2), 125–230.

Connelly, B.L., L. Tihanyi, S.T. Certo and M.A. Hitt (2010), 'Marching to the beat of different drummers: the influence of institutional owners on competitive actions', *Academy of Management Journal*, **53** (4), 723–742.

Creswell, John W., and Vicki L. Plano Clark (2007), *Designing and Conducting Mixed Methods Research*, Thousand Oaks, CA: Sage.

Creswell, John W., and Vicki L. Plano Clark (2011), *Designing and Conducting Mixed Methods Research* (2nd ed.), Thousand Oaks, CA: Sage.

Dalton, D.R., C.M. Daily, J.L. Johnson and A.E. Ellstrand (1999), 'Number of directors and financial performance: a meta-analysis', *Academy of Management Journal*, **42** (6), 674–686.
Denscombe, M. (2010), *The Good Research Guide: For Small-Scale Social Research Projects*, United Kingdom: McGraw-Hill International.
Denyer, D., and D. Tranfield (2006), 'Using qualitative research synthesis to build an actionable knowledge base', *Management Decision*, **44** (2), 213–227.
Doucouliagos, H., and M. Paldam (2010), 'Conditional aid effectiveness: a meta–study', *Journal of International Development*, **22** (4), 391–410.
Driscoll, D.L., A. Appiah-Yeboah, P. Salib and D.J. Rupert (2007), 'Merging qualitative and quantitative data in mixed methods research: how to and why not', *Ecological and Environmental Anthropology*, (University of Georgia), **3** (1), 18–28.
Edwards, A.D., P. Brocklehurst, A.J. Gunn, H. Halliday, E. Juszczak, M. Levene, et al. (2010), 'Neurological outcomes at 18 months of age after moderate hypothermia for perinatal hypoxic ischaemic encephalopathy: synthesis and meta-analysis of trial data'. *BMJ*, **340**, c363.
Feld, L.P., and J.H. Heckemeyer (2011), 'FDI and taxation: a meta–study', *Journal of Economic Surveys*, **25** (2), 233–272.
Field, A.P., and R. Gillett (2010), 'How to do a meta–analysis', *British Journal of Mathematical and Statistical Psychology*, **63** (3), 665–694.
Frooman, J. (1999), 'Stakeholder influence strategies', *Academy of Management Review*, **24** (2), 91–115.
Griffin, J.J., and J.F. Mahon (1997), 'The corporate social performance and corporate financial performance debate twenty-five years of incomparable research', *Business and Society*, **36** (1), 5–31.
Haidich, A.B. (2010), 'Meta-analysis in medical research. Hippokratia', *Quarterly Medical Journal*, **14** (1), 29–37.
Hill, C.W.L., and T.M. Jones (1992), 'Stakeholder-agency theory', *Journal of Management Studies*, **29** (2), 131–154.
Jackson, S.E., and R.S. Schuler (1985), 'A meta-analysis and conceptual critique of research on role ambiguity and role conflict in work settings', *Organizational Behavior and Human Decision Processes*, **36** (1), 16–78.
Jensen, M.C., and W.H. Meckling (1976), 'Theory of the firm: managerial behavior, agency costs, and ownership structure', *Journal of Financial Economics*, **3**, 305–360.
Kotler, Philip, and Nancy Lee (2005), *Corporate Social Responsibility: Doing the Most Good for your Company and your Cause*, Hoboken, NJ: Wiley.
Margolis, J.D., and J.P. Walsh (2003), 'Misery loves companies: rethinking social initiatives by business', *Administrative Science Quarterly*, **48**, 268–305.
Margolis, J.D., H.A. Elfenbein and J.P. Walsh (2007), 'Does it pay to be good? A meta-analysis and redirection of research on the relationship between corporate social and financial performance', accessed 2 August 2016 at http://s3.amazonaws.com/academia.edu.documents/4323317/walsh__jim_does_it_pay_to_be_good.pdf?AWSAccessKeyId=AKIAJ56TQJRTWSMTNPEA&Expires=1470134465&Signature=s1PixLs%2FsRoD8FYmnzchqqPErCY%3D&response-content-disposition=inline%3B%20filename%3DDoes_it_pay_to_be_good_A_meta-analysis_a.pdf.
Neufeld, Mark A. (1995), *The Restructuring of International Relations Theory*, New York: Cambridge University Press.
Orlitzky, M., F.L. Schmidt and S.L Rynes (2003), 'Corporate social and financial performance: a meta-analysis', *Organization Studies*, **24** (3), 403–441.
O'Rourke, K. (2007), 'An historical perspective on meta-analysis: dealing quantitatively with varying study results', *Journal of the Royal Society of Medicine*, **100** (12), 579–582.
Paterson, Barbara L., Sally E. Thorne, Connie Canam and Carol Jellings (2001), *Meta-study of Qualitative Health Research: A Practical Guide to Meta-analysis and Meta-synthesis*, vol. 3, Thousand Oaks, CA: Sage.
Pawson, R. (2006a), 'Digging for nuggets: how "bad" research can yield "good" evidence', *International Journal of Social Research Methodology*, **9** (2), 127–142.
Pawson, Ray (2006b), *Evidence-based Policy: A Realist Perspective*, London: Sage Publications.
Rhoades, D.L., P.L. Rechner and C. Sundaramurthy (2001), 'A meta–analysis of board leadership structure and financial performance: are "two heads better than one"?', *Corporate Governance: An International Review*, **9** (4), 311–319.
Roman, R.M., S. Haybor and B.R. Agle (1999), 'The relationship between social and financial performance', *Business and Society*, **38** (1), 109–126.
Rothman, Kenneth J., Sander Greenland and Timothy L. Lash (eds) (2008), *Modern Epidemiology*, 3rd ed., Boston/Toronto: Lippincott Williams and Wilkins.
Ryan, L.V., and M. Schneider (2003), 'Institutional investor power and heterogeneity: implications for agency and stakeholder theories', *Business Society*, **42** (4), 398–429.
Sandelowski, M., J. Barroso and C.I. Voils (2007), 'Using qualitative metasummary to synthesize qualitative and quantitative descriptive findings', *Research in Nursing and Health*, **30** (1), 99–111.

Saunders, Mark, Phillip Lewis and Adrian Thornhill (eds) (2012), *Research Methods for Business Students*, Edinburgh Gate, Harlow, England: Pearson Education Limited.
Shachar, M. (2008), 'Meta-analysis: the preferred method of choice for the assessment of distance learning quality factors', *The International Review of Research in Open and Distance Learning*, **9** (3), ISSN 1492-3831. Accessed 27 May 2016 at http://www.irrodl.org/index.php/irrodl/article/view/493/1147.
Visser, W. (2008), 'Corporate social responsibility in developing countries', in A. Crane Andrew, Abagail McWilliams, Dirk Matten, Jeremy Moon and Donald Siegel (eds), *The Oxford Handbook of Corporate Social Responsibility*, Oxford: Oxford University Press, pp. 473–479.
Voils, C.I., M. Sandelowski, J. Barroso and V. Hasselblad (2008), 'Making sense of qualitative and quantitative findings in mixed research synthesis studies', *Field Methods*, **20** (1), 3–25.
Walker, E., A.V. Hernandez and M.W. Kattan (2008), 'Meta-analysis: its strengths and limitations', *Cleveland Clinic Journal of Medicine*, **75** (6), 431–439.
Walsh, D., and S. Downe (2005), 'Meta–synthesis method for qualitative research: a literature review', *Journal of Advanced Nursing*, **50** (2), 204–211.

4. Ethics in the research process
David Crowther

INTRODUCTION

Whenever we are conducting research it is impossible not to be concerned with the ethical dimension of what we are doing. This is important for us as researchers not just for our own concerns but also because, by the nature of the topic which we are researching,[1] we are concerned with the organisation and people involved in the research and their ethics and behaviour. This is inevitable when we consider research in the area of corporate social responsibility (CSR). Most institutions with which we are involved (as researchers, academics or students) have an ethical policy which guides their approach to research and to which we must comply. Additionally, most professional organisations have an ethical code and we must comply with these too when relevant. Also most organisations which award research grants have an ethical policy which we must comply with if we are to receive the grant. So we are bound by ethics whether we know this or not and it is obviously important to abide by such codes as infringing them can be problematic. We will discuss such codes and policies later in the chapter but first we will start with a brief discussion of what ethics is and how it might concern us in the research environment.

MANAGERS AND BUSINESS ETHICS

Business ethics is a subject of considerable importance to any organisation and such things as accounting information have often been accused of providing an excuse for unethical behaviour. Indeed, this accusation has been extended to accountants and business managers generally who have been accused of behaving unethically in their search for profits to the exclusion of all else. The unethical ways in which accounting information has been used have been described in detail by Smith (1992) who describes the way in which new accounting techniques have been created with the sole purpose of boosting reported profits. These techniques have become known as creative accounting and have been the subject of much media attention. Smith's book, *Accounting for Growth*, makes interesting reading for any prospective business manager. Previously Buckminster Fuller (1991) had shown how successive governments changed the rules to favour large companies.

Other writers have, however, been concerned with highlighting the value of ethical behaviour and have claimed that this actually leads to better business performance. Thus McCoy (1985) considers that ethics need to be at the core of business behaviour and that effective business management is based upon ethical behaviour. He claims that this recognition, and acting accordingly, actually increases the performance of a business. The UK accounting bodies are also concerned with business ethics and all have a stance in this matter, and have incorporated a requirement for ethical behaviour into their codes of conduct. The subject of ethical behaviour amongst businesses has also had an effect upon auditing practice and upon the financial reporting of businesses.

Any manager operating in a business environment needs to be aware of the importance of ethical behaviour. Equally (s)he will experience conflicts, in attempting to behave ethically, between different alternative courses of action, and may find conflicts between the firm's objectives[2] and his/her own personal motivation and objectives. No ready solution to these conflicts is available but a manager should be aware that research has shown that ethical behaviour leads to better performance in the longer term, and so should be encouraged to act accordingly.

THE 'WHAT' AND 'WHY' OF ETHICS

Ethics shows a corporation how to behave properly in all their business and operations. However, business ethics is characterised by conflicts of interests. Businesses attempt to maximise profits as a primary goal on one hand while they face issues of social responsibility and social service on the other. Ethics is the set of rules prescribing what is good or evil, or what is right or wrong for people. In other words, ethics is the values that form the basis of human relations, and the quality and essence of being morally good or evil, or right or wrong. Business ethics means honesty, confidence, respect and fair acting in all circumstances. However, such values as honesty, respect and confidence are rather general concepts without definite boundaries. Ethics can also be defined as overall fundamental principles and practices for improving the level of wellbeing of humanity.

Ethics is the natural and structural process of acting in line with moral judgements, standards and rules. Being a concrete and subjective concept, 'business ethics' can be discussed with differing approaches and in varying degrees of importance in different fields. Indeed, it is highly difficult to define ethics and identify its limits and criteria. Accordingly, there are difficulties in discussing this concept in literature as it is ubiquitous in business life, at the business level, and in human life. According to what, how, how much and for whom ethics is or should be is an important question. It is not always easy to find answers to these questions (Crowther 2004).

A business which does not respect ethical criteria and fails to improve them will disrupt its integrity and unity, that is, its capacity to achieve its goal, and lead to internal or external conflicts. Business ethics is the honest, respectful and fair conduct by a business and its representatives in all of its relations (Crowther 1996). An important question concerning the role of ethics in business is the question of why businesses should and do engage in ethical practices. Some authors, notably Milton Friedman (1962), would strongly deny that a business has a fiduciary responsibility to any group but the firm's stockholders.

To initiate corporate giving, for example, would be a fiduciary breach of management[3] in Friedman's opinion as an agent for a principal is neither legally nor morally permitted to give away or 'waste' the principal's capital (Joyner and Payne 2002). Milton Friedman also argued that 'there is only one social responsibility of business – use its resources and engage in activities designed to increase its profits so long as it . . . engages in open and free competition without deception and fraud' (Friedman 1962, p. 12).

However, ethical behaviour and ethical business has effects not only on stakeholders and shareholders, but also on the entire economy. We believe that when we act ethically in the business decision-making process this will ensure more effective and productive utilisation of economic resources.

ETHICAL PHILOSOPHIES

One component of the change to a concern with social responsibility and accountability has been the recognition (or reinstatement) of the importance of ethics in organisational activity and behaviour. In part this can be considered to be a recognition of the changing societal environment of the present time and in part a recognition of the problems brought about through corporate activity taken without any account of ethical implications. Amongst such activity can be seen the many examples of pollution (for example, Union Carbide at Bhopal, India or the Exxon Valdez oil spill) and greed (such as the Enron incident). These have caused a rethinking of the role of ethics in organisation theory.

Ethics is, however, a problematical area as there is no absolute agreement as to what constitutes ethical (or unethical) behaviour. For each of us there is a need to consider our own ethical position as a starting point because that will affect our own view of ethical behaviour. The opposition provided by deontological ethics and teleological ethics (regarding the link between actions and outcomes) (see below), and by ethical relativism and ethical objectivism (regarding the universality of a given set of ethical principles) represents key areas of debate and contention in the philosophy of ethics. This provides a starting point for our consideration of ethics.

Deontological Ethics

According to deontologists certain actions are right or wrong in themselves and so there are absolute ethical standards which need to be upheld. The problems with this position are concerned with how we know which acts are wrong and how we distinguish between a wrong act and an omission. Philosophers such as Nagel (1961) argue that there is an underlying notion of right which constrains our actions, although this might be overridden in certain circumstances. Thus, there may be an absolute moral constraint against killing someone, which in time of war can be overridden.

Teleological Ethics

Teleological theory distinguishes between 'the right' and 'the good', with 'the right' encompassing those actions which maximise 'the good'. Thus it is outcomes which determine what is right, rather than the inputs (i.e. our actions), in terms of ethical standards. This is the viewpoint which is promoted by Rawls (1971) in his *A Theory of Justice*. Under this perspective, one's duty is to promote certain ends, and the principles of right and wrong organise and direct our efforts towards these ends.

Utilitarianism

This is often interpreted as the greatest good of the greatest number but in actual fact just means the greatest good even if only a small number benefit. Utilitarianism is based upon the premise that outcomes are all that matter in determining what is good and that the way in which a society achieves its ultimate good is through each person pursuing his/her own self-interest. The philosophy states that the aggregation of all these self-interests will automatically lead to the maximum good for society at large. Some utilitarians have amended this theory to suggest that there is a role for government in mediating between these individual actions to allow for the fact that some needs can best be met communally.

Ethical Relativism

Relativism is the denial that there are certain universal truths. Thus, ethical relativism posits that there are no universally valid moral principles. Ethical relativism may be further subdivided into: 'conventionalism', which argues that a given set of ethics or moral principles are only valid within a given culture at a particular time; and 'subjectivism', that sees individual choice as the key determinant of the validity of moral principles.

According to the 'conventional' ethical relativism it is the mores and standards of a society which define what is moral behaviour and ethical standards are set, not absolutely, but according to the dictates of a given society at a given time. Thus if we conform to the standards of our society then we are behaving ethically. We can see, however, that ethical standards change over time within one society and vary from one society to another; thus the attitudes and practices of the 19th century are different to our own as are the standards of other countries.

A further problem with this view of ethics is that of how we decide upon the societal ethics which we seek to conform to. Thus there are the standards of society at large, the standards of our chosen profession and the standards of the peer group to which we belong. For example, the standards of society at large tend to be enshrined within the laws of that society. But how many of us rigorously abide by the speed limits of this country?

Different groupings within society tend to have different moral standards of acceptable behaviour and we have a tendency to behave differently at different times and when we are with different groups of people. Equally when we travel to a foreign country we tend to take with us the ethical standards of our own country rather than changing to the different standards of the country which we are visiting. Thus it becomes very difficult to hold to a position of ethical relativism because of the difficulty of determining the grouping to which we are seeking to conform.

Ethical Objectivism

This philosophical position is in direct opposition to ethical relativism; it asserts that although moral principles may differ between cultures, some moral principles have universal validity whether or not they are universally recognised. There are two key variants of ethical objectivism: 'strong' and 'weak'. Strong ethical objectivism or 'absolutism' argues that there is one true moral system. Weak ethical objectivism holds that there is a 'core morality' of universally valid moral principles, but also accepts an indeterminate area where relativism is accepted.

There is no single theory of ethics because there is no single view about what is ethical. Each of us can identify ethical and unethical behaviour but only contextually in relation to our own beliefs. We can see therefore that each of these theories of ethics is problematical and that there is no overarching principle which determines either what is ethical or what is not. Nevertheless a concern with ethics has been introduced explicitly into organisation theory and strategy in recent years. This has led to an increased interest in CSR.

CORPORATE BEHAVIOUR

Corporate behaviour is important for company success both financially and concerning the relationship between corporate and business interests (stakeholders). We cannot define corporate behaviour without an ethical and CSR base in order to refer to that behavioural aspect. Corporate behaviour involves legal rules, ethical codes of conduct and social responsibility principles. In other words, corporate behaviour is based on all of these components and involves law, ethics and CSR. It is important to recognise also that this behaviour must be ethical but must also be seen to be ethical – perceptions are very important.

Corporate behaviour has effects not only on stakeholders and shareholders but also on the entire economy. When a corporation acts ethically and socially responsibly in its business decisions and strategic planning then that corporation will be more sustainable. As we have seen socially responsible corporate behaviour is increasingly seen as essential to the long-term survival of companies.

CSR, ETHICS AND CORPORATE BEHAVIOUR

Carroll (1979, p. 500) describes CSR in these terms: 'the social responsibility of business encompasses the economic, legal, ethical, and discretionary expectations that society has of organizations at a given point in time'. Later Whetten et al. (2002, p. 374) defined CSR as 'societal expectations of corporate behaviour; a behaviour that is alleged by a stakeholder to be expected by society or morally required and is therefore justifiably demanded of a business'. After the first definition, the CSR definition on the one hand expanded and covered more corporate behaviour and stakeholder expectation. On the other hand, some broad terms – especially society – have been narrowed to stakeholders.

Corporate behaviour towards the stakeholders is becoming a much more important concept in every definition. Corporate behaviour is an important concept because it has to be ethical, legal and responsible behaviour for organisations, stakeholders and society. This aspect of corporate behaviour has more benefit for society also and so that is why it is more related to ethics and CSR. There have of course been many examples of unethical behaviour and probably the best known is the Enron debacle (see Cruver 2002). But the global financial crisis of 2008 onwards was caused at least in part by unethical behaviour. So the importance of ethics in corporate behaviour can clearly be seen.

To be a socially responsible corporation, a company must be more than a legal and ethical person also. CSR is not always a legal necessity; increasingly it is an obligation. However, a company has to be socially responsible even though it is not a legal obligation (Seifi and Crowther 2014) – which is one of the most important characteristics of CSR. These provide the platform upon which social responsibility is built.

ETHICS IN THE RESEARCH PROCESS

We have seen the importance of ethics in corporate behaviour and now we need to turn our attention to ethics in research and our own ethics as researchers. There are a number of issues which need to be considered in planning and undertaking our research.

Confidentiality

Probably the most important issue is that of confidentiality. It is often accepted that confidentiality needs to be offered to all potential interviewees and often to associated data and documents. This is not necessarily the case as it depends upon the scenario where and when the research is undertaken. If there is any danger that the person being interviewed may suffer depending upon what is said, then confidentiality should certainly be offered. This may also help interviewees to be more forthcoming and disclose information which they would not otherwise disclose; hence the interview can be more productive if confidentiality is guaranteed. Sometimes people do not mind if their views are disclosed. Nevertheless, it is important to have such a discussion before any interview is commenced and it is important to abide by the wishes of the interviewee.

If confidentiality is guaranteed to someone then this guarantee must be respected. What this means is that anything which is told to you or given to you cannot be used in your research (or any other purpose) in such a way that the person who told you can be identified or the source be attributed. But we all want to source our research data and want to present it in such a way that weight is added to it because of the source of the information. This is understandable and permissible but we need to be careful how we do this. It is not really sufficient to say 'an anonymous source told me . . .' as this tells us nothing about the weight which should be given to that source. Equally it is not sufficient to say 'the Chief Accountant of XYZ Company . . .' as this identifies the source. But it might be acceptable to say 'a senior manager in XYZ Company . . .' or 'a Chief Accountant in one of the firms involved . . .' depending upon the nature of the interview group. In other circumstances it might be necessary to say 'Interviewee A' or 'Interviewee B' to ensure anonymity. In general, you should give as much detail as possible of the source while making absolutely certain that the person cannot be identified. Anonymity is of paramount importance as far as confidentiality is concerned – and this applies equally to documents if necessary.

Consent

Before commencing an interview, it is important to obtain the consent of the interviewee and to ensure that they understand that you are interviewing for the purpose of collecting data for your research rather than just engaging in some general conversation. This understanding itself may shape the nature of the interview or the way in which disclosure is framed or undertaken. This will make the research richer because of the nature of the data and may lead to understandings which would not otherwise be derived from the data collection. It is quite normal that you will choose to record an interview and this is helpful to gain the greatest benefit from the data given during that interview. It is necessary, however, to explain that you will record the interview and to gain the consent of the interviewee. Often people are hesitant about being recorded during the interview but after some reassurance that it is just a record for your research most people will accept this and generally forget very quickly that they are being recorded. But occasionally someone will refuse to be recorded and you must accept this refusal and make use of handwritten notes as your record. It is not acceptable (and quite possibly not even legal) to go ahead and record someone without their knowledge even though we all possess technology such as smart phones which make this an easy thing to do. Respecting the interviewee's wishes in this respect is paramount.

It is equally important that consent is secured to use any documents or other data which you may be given or may discover during your research. Often this consent may be implicit in the agreement for data collection but must nevertheless be obtained if the situation is unclear.

Transparency of Purpose

In 1961, Stanley Milgram conducted a famous experiment (Milgram 1963) in which people believed that they were giving electric shocks to others to such an extent that they were lethal shocks. In 1973, Philip Zimbardo and colleagues conducted the famous Stanford Prison experiment (Hanley et al. 1973). In both of these experiments (and much other research undertaken at that time) the subjects did not know the purpose of the experiments and did not know the purpose of the research. Such an approach to research would not be considered acceptable today and would not be allowed at our establishments unless the purpose of the research was made clear and informed consent to participate had been obtained from all involved. In other words, when we undertake research we must make it clear to all involved that we are undertaking research and exactly what the purpose of that research is. This way we can ensure that we are obtaining the agreement of the participants to the research we are actually undertaking. You might think that this makes the research environment more difficult and makes certain kinds of research – especially experimental research – virtually impossible. In fact this is not so and it just means that we must take more care in the design of our research. When we have done so then the research is likely to be stronger and the results more certain and more verifiable.

Replicability

One important aspect of research is its replicability; indeed, it has been described by Simons (2014) as the cornerstone of science. Replicability means that other researchers must be able to understand how you have conducted your research and therefore be able to repeat your research under similar conditions. This is important in order to make findings verifiable but also in order to enable your research to be extended into other areas. Research in similar areas often produces differing results. This does not mean that some findings are invalid or open to doubt; often it simply means that the research is conducted under different conditions and therefore one set of research is not a replication of the other but merely differing research in a similar context. Enabling replication means describing in the write-up of your research all the conditions under which it was conducted. This means paying especial attention to the conditions under which research amongst your subjects (if relevant) was undertaken. Times change and what was considered acceptable in one period might well be unacceptable at a later time. For example, the research conducted by Milgram and by Zimbardo would no longer be considered acceptable and therefore would not be replicated now. This is why ethical approval (see a later section) needs to be sought for all intended research.

Disclosure of Findings

Obviously when the research is written up then the main results are disclosed to everyone but the question of disclosure has several aspects. One issue that often arises is whether information that is revealed during the course of the study should be disclosed, either to participants or third parties. This is of particular concern if the research data is confidential in nature and disclosure is of concern to the participants. Generally speaking, it must be made clear to participants that disclosure will take place in the context of the academic work being undertaken – and if necessary the wording can be agreed with major participants prior to publication. There can also be agreement not to disclose the findings prior to a certain date or other suitable milestone. Other disclosure must be by agreement.

Other circumstances in which disclosure of findings become a significant and ethical issue include:

- Incidental findings of technical or medical investigations:
    - Initially it may seem that participants should always be informed about issues found in the research but this needs to be balanced against their autonomy (right not to be given findings if they do not wish to be). Implications for family members or partners may also need to be taken into account. An important consideration is whether the researcher is qualified to interpret the results and the further support that is available for the participant. A further consideration is if the researcher is passing on information about a potentially serious medical condition and whether the researcher has the expertise to do this. For medical issues there may be an impact on the participant's insurance or future employability as a result of the findings and these must also be considered at the planning stages of the research.
- Participants expressing the intent to harm themselves or others:
    - An issue of importance is the measure that has been used to obtain the information. If the results of a questionnaire have suggested intent to harm the self or others, then the question arises as to how robust the measure used can be considered to be clinically. The researcher can be considered to have a duty of care to pass this information on to a third party but the point at which this should occur may not always be clear. Probably the researcher should discuss their intent to pass the information on to third parties with participants when the situation arises, providing this is feasible and the safety of the researcher will not be compromised.
- When illegal activities by participants are revealed:
    - The issue of disclosure is obviously more complex in the area of illegal activities. In general, there is no legal obligation to report an offence (except in certain terrorism and money laundering cases), but careful consideration needs to be given by the researcher and probably legal advice should be sought.

- If unethical practices are revealed:
  - If staff working at organisations, where the research is being carried out, reveal unethical practices (or even unsafe practices) this should generally be disclosed but there are a number of issues that need to be considered. These include why internal processes of reporting have not been used, consequences which might be disadvantageous to the participant (from whistle-blowing), and whether the person is disgruntled and making mischief amongst others.

The issue is complex and whether to disclose needs to be considered on a case-by-case basis for each research project. Advice from senior or experienced researchers is often useful in these cases.

OPPORTUNITIES FOR FURTHER WORK OR POSSIBILITY OF LITIGATION

When a researcher enters an organisation they are generally perceived to be a person with expertise in the area being researched. Organisations may just let a person enter the organisation and undertake research for sheer altruism but this is increasingly unusual. Instead the organisation expects to get some benefit from the research being undertaken. Some of this is naturally from the findings of the research and their applicability but there can be other benefits. It is not uncommon for an organisation to expect some extra work from the researcher and a report which is specific to their needs rather than the academic needs of the researcher. Thus the researcher needs to make it clear what the outcome of the research needs to be from his/her own perspective, and issues of confidentiality might be important here if the research involves several competing organisations. Equally the organisation will make it clear what outcomes they expect from allowing the researcher to enter the organisation and undertake their research. This might involve adapting the research report to meet the needs of the researched organisation as well as the academic needs of the researcher. In extreme cases this might involve the researcher writing two reports – one for academic reasons and the other to meet the needs of the organisation. This is of course a matter for negotiation between the researcher and the organisation but it is important to remain aware of one's own needs in this respect. It is important to remember that the researcher is perceived to be a person with considerable expertise and this in itself might lead to further work within the organisation. This further work may take the form of another research project. It may also take the form of some paid consulting work. It has even been known to take the form of a research project funded by a body such as the EU. It is important therefore to focus upon the current research project but to also be mindful that future possibilities might be an outcome from this.

Conversely it is also important to keep in mind that things may go wrong in the project. This might simply mean there is no useable research, but the most extreme example is that the researcher is subject to legal action. This is very unusual but has certainly happened in past research. To safeguard against this then the understanding and application of ethical practice is very important. Of particular importance in this context is complete agreement about issues such as confidentiality and the disclosure of findings.

Loyalty

Loyalty is of importance when considering ethics in the research process. In the first place each of us owes loyalty to ourselves and so should do nothing which compromises our own ethics values. Bearing in mind that ethics values differ from one person to another then this can be a source of conflict but each of us owes loyalty to ourself and this should not be breached. Equally most readers of this will be people undertaking research within an academic environment and we therefore owe some loyalty to the academy and seek to maintain academic integrity and perceived impartiality. After all academic standards are important and all of our published research has been subject to peer review so we need to be careful not to compromise this. Additionally, for some readers an academic organisation will be an employer and we owe a duty to our employers. In addition to all of these expectations many of us are also members of professional bodies and all professional bodies have codes of conduct and ethical codes. As a professional we have a duty towards maintaining the ethical standards of the profession.

It can be seen therefore that we have a number of requirements for loyalty towards ourselves and differing organisations. Normally there is no problem as these requirements do not conflict with each other. Sometimes they do, however, and need to be resolved in a way which is satisfactory – to us at the very least. Thus it is necessary sometimes to view these different ethical requirements in a hierarchical manner and decide which is most important to us. In the long term I think everyone would agree that our own ethical standards take precedence over all others – although it is often possible to view our own standards more flexibly in the light of circumstances. Other standards are less flexible and occasionally we need to decide which takes precedence. Certainly I have been in the position where I have refused to do something expected of me by my employers because it breached the ethical code of my profession. Fortunately my employers accepted this as a valid reason and there were no adverse consequences; others might not be so fortunate!

CODES OF ETHICS

It is very common nowadays for all organisations to have codes of ethical behaviour which they expect employees to adhere to. Most large organisation have such a code[4] and certainly all universities have a code of ethics. All professional bodies also have a code of ethics and expect their members to adhere to that code. For example, the Chartered Association of Business Schools (with the British Academy of Management and The Higher Education Academy (UK))[5] have published a set of ethical guidelines for researchers which considers the following categories:

1. Integrity, honesty and transparency in scholarship
2. Integrity, honesty and transparency in learning
3. Respect for persons and prevention of harm
4. Authorship and respect for intellectual property
5. Consent
6. Protecting privacy, ensuring confidentiality and maintaining anonymity
7. Declaring professional and personal affiliations and sources of funding and support

8. Avoiding misleading, misreporting, misunderstanding and unjustified deception
9. Governance, management and administration.

In the UK there is also an Association for Research Ethics[6] which aims to promote good practice in research. It is also clear that within a university setting all research must be approved by the appropriate university ethics committee.

University Ethics Committee

All universities have such an ethics committee and they may have subsidiary committees for faculties, schools or colleges to which the work is delegated. This committee is responsible for all matters concerned with research ethics and integrity and to ensure that all research is conducted according to the appropriate ethical, legal and professional frameworks and standards for that particular context of research. In general, it can be taken to mean that all research undertaken by staff or by visiting researchers or by students must be approved in the correct way before that research commences. Having said that, these committees recognise that many of us are governed by the ethical codes of professional bodies and take steps to ensure that there is no conflict – usually by allowing professional codes to take precedence. This is important in all research but particularly in the contexts of medical research and of psychology research.[7] Thus research needs ethical approval before it is sanctioned and the way this is done is via the ethical approval form. Generally speaking, research which has been sanctioned correctly can be taken to be covered by the university's public liability insurance but not covered if not sanctioned. It is therefore important to get that sanction for self-protection if for no other reason.

The Ethical Approval Form

All universities have precise rules concerning which research needs ethical approval. Some require approval for all research but often it is restricted to research involving human beings in any way.[8] Some require all students to get such approval but others restrict this to research students. It is important to know therefore what the requirements are at your own university. This is also important if the research is being conducted by people from more than one institution and what their respective requirements are.

The committee approves the research (or refuses it or seeks further information) based upon the information contained on the ethical approval form.[9] The design and contents are obviously specific to each institution but require the same basic information:

- Names of the researchers involved, including any from outside the organisation
- Nature of the research to be undertaken
- Composition of the population to be researched or sample to be investigated
- Timescale of the research
- A consideration of what ethical issues might arise and how they will be dealt with
- Details of how the findings will be disseminated.

Research in the area of CSR often needs ethical approval because of the involvement of people in the research but mostly it is of an uncontroversial nature and does not therefore

74   *Handbook of research methods in corporate social responsibility*

cause any approval. Before sanction is sought, however, it is important to consider all the issues mentioned in this chapter as well as the facets specific to the particular research and its context. Completing the form and obtaining sanction provides an opportunity to think through the issues involved in the research and is beneficial for this reason alone.

ETHICAL DILEMMAS

Although most research is conducted in a straightforward and uncontroversial manner the question of ethics arises more often than we might think. Indeed, it is probable that almost all of us will be faced with an ethical dilemma concerning the research at some point during our lives. Often – but by no means always – this involves the questions of confidentiality or informed consent at some point during the research. For example, it is not unknown that circumstances change and a subject wishes to withdraw consent. Alternatively access to an organisation might be changed or even withdrawn. Such changes will of course affect future research but may also affect the viability of using data from research already conducted. Essentially the researcher is faced with a dilemma and the effect of this is that there is no certainty as to the correct action to take. We each, when faced with such a dilemma, need to arrive at a resolution which is acceptable to us and hopefully to the other parties involved. There are no clear-cut answers to such ethical dilemmas but thinking through the issues outlined in this chapter prior to the commencement of the project will help to minimise the possibility of such a dilemma occurring.

CONCLUSIONS

It can be seen that ethics are much more central to the research process than we might think. This is probably more true of research in aspects of corporate social responsibility than it is for much research in the business and management area because of the nature of our topic. Good planning before the commencement of the research can help to minimise the issues which might arise but they can never be fully anticipated or controlled. Nevertheless, this is a topic which shows that good planning is very important. It is a truism to state that good planning results in good research; we all recognise this but are often careless or rushed in our approach to research planning, being too eager to get on with collecting data. The issues discussed surrounding ethics belie this and show how good planning can help greatly in ensuring a successful outcome. For many reasons therefore ethics is an issue which is central to the research process.

NOTES

1. Probably it is not possible to separate CSR and ethics within any organisational setting.
2. See, for example, Crowther (2004) for a discussion of the objectives of the firm – which tend to be much broader than the often assumed profit maximisation.
3. Although in the UK donations to charity is a recognised expenditure listed separately in company accounts.
4. Even an organisation such as Enron had a code of ethics. In the introduction Kenneth Lay, Chairman and

Chief Executive, stated that 'We want to be proud of Enron and to know that it enjoys a reputation for fairness and honesty and that it is respected.'
5. charteredabs.org/wp. . ./2015/. . ./Ethics-Guide-2015-Advice-and-Guidance.
6. www.arec.org.uk.
7. The Stanford Prison Experiment conducted by Zimbardo et al. breached their own ethical standards, not least because of lack of informed consent. Such experimentation would be severely sanctioned today.
8. This may well be extended to include research involving human tissue or research involving sentient animals – each institution has a precise specification of its own requirements.
9. Or whatever it is named.

REFERENCES

Buckminster Fuller, Richard (1991), *Critical Path*, New York: St Martin's Press.
Carroll, A.B. (1979), 'A three-dimensional conceptual model of corporate social performance', *Academy of Management Review*, **4**, 497–505.
Crowther, David (1996), *Management Accounting for Business*, Cheltenham/UK: Stanley Thornes.
Crowther, David (2004), *Managing Finance: A Socially Responsible Approach*, Oxford/UK: Elsevier.
Cruver, Brian (2002), *Enron: Anatomy of Greed*, London: Arrow.
Friedman, Milton (1962), *Capitalism and Freedom*, Chicago: University of Chicago Press.
Hanley, C., W.C. Banks and P.G. Zimbardo (1973), 'A study of prisoners and guards in a simulated prison', *Naval Research Review*, **30**, 4–17.
Joyner, B.E. and D. Payne (2002), 'Evolution and implementation: a study of values, business ethics and corporate social responsibility', *Journal of Business Ethics*, **41**, 297–311.
McCoy, Charles S. (1985), *Management of Values: The Ethical Difference in Corporate Policy and Performance*, Marshfield, Mass.: Pitman.
Milgram, S. (1963), 'Behavioral study of obedience', *Journal of Abnormal and Social Psychology*, **67**, 371–378.
Nagel, Ernest (1961), *The Structure of Science: Problems in the Logic of Scientific Explanation*, New York: Hackett Publishing.
Rawls, John (1971), *A Theory of Justice*, New York: Belknap.
Seifi, S. and D. Crowther (2014), 'Business ethics in society', in Roshima Said, David Crowther and Azlan Amran (eds), *Ethics, Governance and Corporate Crime. Challenges and Consequences*, Bingley. Emerald, 253–267.
Simons, D.J. (2014), 'The value of direct replication', *Perspectives on Psychological Science*, **9** (1), 76–80.
Smith, Terry (1992), *Accounting for Growth*, London: Century Business.
Whetten, D.A., G. Rands and P. Godfrey (2002), 'What are the responsibilities of business to society?', in Andrew M. Pettigrew, Howard Thomas and Richard Whittington (eds), *Handbook of Strategy and Management*, London: Sage, 373–408.

5. Research methods in organization, management and management accounting: an evaluation of quantitative and qualitative approaches
Miriam Green

INTRODUCTION

Differences and decisions among academics about the respective value of quantitative and qualitative methods in the organization, management and management accounting fields, and in the social sciences more generally, have had far-reaching consequences on what has counted as legitimate scholarship and been supported by the academy (scholars and universities) and also sometimes wider influences such as by governments. These debates arose originally in the US and the UK, and the resulting practices in research methodology now span a much wider field – in countries and institutions all over the world that value and emulate Anglo-Saxon (UK and US) approaches.

There has been much controversy as to the advantages and legitimacy of either quantitative or qualitative research methods over the years. There have also been differences as to whether one can combine quantitative with qualitative methods, or whether the two approaches are 'incommensurable'. It is proposed in this chapter to put forward definitions of each research method; to outline their main features; discuss their applications in the management area; examine their advantages and disadvantages and outline the critiques regarding each method and whether they are 'commensurable' with each other or not.

Examples from research papers in the management accounting area using different approaches will be discussed showing the advantages and disadvantages for the research of quantitative (Simons 1987) and qualitative approaches (Chenhall and Euske 2007).

The last part of the chapter involves a discussion as to the preponderance of quantitative research methods in mainstream management scholarship (although there is also a significant number of management scholars using qualitative or mixed research methods). Claims for the legitimacy of quantitative over qualitative approaches because of the scientific methods used in the former are examined in the light of what has been written by prominent historians of science such as Kuhn (1970) and Feyerabend (1993) and by social theorists, for example Bourdieu (1990). Ultimately an argument is made for commensurability, complementarity and inclusiveness wherever possible.

DEFINITIONS

Quantitative Ontologies, Epistemologies and Methodologies

Differences in quantitative and qualitative approaches are conceptualized in terms of ontology (what is real in the world) and epistemology (what counts as knowledge and therefore worth studying) and methodology (how one is going to find out the necessary knowledge). Quantitative ontologies assume that there is a reality 'out there' which must be found and added to by scholars in the various fields they are researching so that our knowledge of reality can be added to and the picture made fuller, rather like a jigsaw puzzle. Moreover, that reality exists independently of researchers – their attitudes, understandings and actions should in no way influence the truth or situation that exists. The knowledge that is produced must be free from all value judgements and moral overtones. This has been called an 'objectivist' approach.

Among the staunchest supporters of this view have been 'positivist' (and also 'neo-positivist') schools of thought, and among those the most extreme ideas came from a school of thought in the 1920s and 1930s known as the 'Vienna Circle' or the logical positivists. They were eminent philosophers, scientists and mathematicians who regarded true knowledge as achievable only through elements observed through our sense data or through a formal logic. All knowledge had to be verifiable through experience, and other information such as theory, deduction or moral judgements were regarded as invalid knowledge (Turner 2001; Uebel 2010; Bell and Willmott 2015).

Given that knowledge is regarded as based on a reality that is not dependent on or influenced by researchers, it follows that the methods used have also to be free of human influence or moral 'interference'. What have been considered to be free of human factors are science and the methods used in scientific inquiry. Logical positivists advocated sampling, scaling and statistical analysis as the basis for producing value-free knowledge (Turner 2001). Their vision of the natural sciences was to establish laws from observation and experiment in order to be able to predict and have technical mastery (McMullin 2010). They advocated also that sociology in order to be regarded as a science has to use scientific research methods (Halfpenny 2001). This has been followed not only by a particular branch of sociology, but has been adopted by scholars in other social sciences including in management and management accounting, as seen below. Kincaid (2010) has given strong counter-arguments particularly of the difficulties in producing value-free research regarding the social sciences generally. This is supported later with examples.

Quantitative methods are simple to define: they use quantification – statistical, numerical, mathematical or computational techniques – in order to describe, analyse and evaluate what is being researched. Research is often carried out through surveys, such as questionnaires. The questions are often 'closed' requiring 'yes/no' answers or plotting on a chart from 'strongly agree' to 'strongly disagree' often using numbers to indicate this.[1] The results of such research are often presented visually in the form of tables, graphs or charts. Another feature with closed questions is that surveys can be sent out to large numbers of people and information obtained from a sizeable sample of the population or, in management studies, of organizations or the managers or employees in them.

However, it would be misleading to attribute such methods and particularly visual representations such as graphs being methods used exclusively in quantitative research. They could easily also be used in qualitative research. Indeed, some people, for example the eminent organization scholar Derek Pugh (2014), have argued against conceptualizing quantitative and qualitative research methods as necessarily separate from each other. Notwithstanding this view, what has become important in the debates about quantitative as against qualitative research are the differences that have been associated with quantitative and qualitative research methods.

Examples from management accounting research will be discussed below, outlining these research methods and exploring their strengths and weaknesses in terms of the type of knowledge produced.

Qualitative Ontologies, Epistemologies and Methodologies

Qualitative research is normally associated with 'interpretive' or 'subjectivist' approaches. These are umbrella concepts for various schools of research including phenomenology, hermeneutics, symbolic interactionism and ethnomethodology. According to Hatch and Yanow (2003) these were developed to refute and replace logical positivism. And they continue to counter later neo-positivist approaches (Lather and St. Pierre 2013). Subjectivist approaches are quite different in important respects from objectivist approaches. Scholars adopting subjectivist approaches view the social world quite differently. They do not accept that it can be studied in the same way as the natural or physical world. They do not see an objective reality 'out there' regarding the social world.

Rather, they see knowledge of that world as created by people, and that one can only arrive at legitimate knowledge about the social world by first studying and understanding the human subjects who inhabit that world – how they understand the world and how they make sense of their situations. Then one can understand people's actions, which play an important part in shaping that external reality which objectivist scholars have regarded as fixed and uninfluenced by human agency (Halfpenny 2001). Of course people can ascribe different meanings to a situation, and so the researcher has to take into account these different understandings stemming from people's different consciousness and experience and interpret them, rather than simply transmit them (Hatch and Yanow 2003).

Researchers adopting subjectivist approaches regard legitimate knowledge as intimately bound up with people's interpretations of their situations, which are likely to influence how they behave and what actions they are likely to get involved in. Their research methods adopted include studying people's own understandings of their situations and the meanings they give to them (Hatch and Yanow 2003). As Lather and St. Pierre more recently have put it: 'We surely bring . . . the knowing subject with us, and that human is . . . at the centre of . . . all . . . quantitative inquiry' (Lather and St. Pierre 2013, p. 630).

This leads to research that is very different from quantitative research and usually involves more in-depth investigations such as participant observation and interviews where respondents are given time to express their own views rather than answering predetermined questions (Halfpenny 2001). The aim is 'to tell it like it really is out there in rich, thick descriptions' (Lather and St. Pierre 2013, p. 630).

The researcher too is seen as having a different role from that of being a neutral observer. Rather she is regarded as also being involved in the 'meaning-making' of the reality that her respondents are engaged with. Her background, knowledge and experience can influence the knowledge produced. Because of this, and in the interests of valid knowledge, she has to be reflective about her own role as well as those of her participants (Hatch and Yanow 2003, p. 67).

APPLICATIONS IN MANAGEMENT AND MANAGEMENT ACCOUNTING SCHOLARSHIP

Because the disciplines of management and management accounting are dealing with human beings at least as much as with systems and techniques, one might have thought that research approaches in these areas would incline towards subjectivist ideas and methodologies. However, this has not proved to be the case. There is a similar dialectic[2] which has constructed sharp dichotomies between objectivist and subjectivist scholarship also in these fields. Mainstream scholarship (prevalent in most textbooks in management and management accounting, and in most research publications in highly rated academic journals) is largely concerned with positive-quantitative research and with objective features such as structure rather than with organization members acting within those structures (Bell and Willmott 2015; Green 2012).

The subjects which have been the focus of much mainstream research include topics based on the 'natural laws of science' played out through concepts such as efficiency, effectiveness, rationalization and structural adjustment (Clegg 2002, pp. 430–431). Subjects researched in an objectivist framework include environmental conditions, organization size and structure – all regarded as objective and not subject to human influence.

A major organization theorist, Lex Donaldson, has, over the years, asserted ideas such as 'the key to the explanation of organizational structure does not lie in the consciousness of the organizational inhabitants' (Donaldson 1996, p. 172). Rather, it depended on an appropriate structure for the organization, which should be governed by factors such as the organization's size, its type of technology and the stability or volatility of its environment (Donaldson 1996; Westwood and Clegg 2003). For an in-depth justification of positivism in the social sciences by Donaldson himself, it is worth looking at his 'position statement' on the subject (Donaldson 2003).

Following on from the choice of an objectivist ontology, the research methods used have also been largely objectivist. Many management and management accounting researchers have aimed at developing a scientific methodology, using quantitative and analytic methods similar to those used in the natural sciences (Palmer 2006; Hogler and Gross 2009). Often these take the form initially of surveys and questionnaires, which are then analysed using quantitative and statistical techniques such as those advocated by positivist scholars. The subjects chosen, in order to achieve the aims of an objectivist ontology using quantitative and statistical methods, have been focussed, for example, on formal structures with regularities such as behavioural regularities measured within a particular space and time, and the causal relationships between variables (Marsden 2005; Bell and Willmott 2015). Some researchers have tried to measure the flexibility or rigidity of organizational systems through questionnaires which have then been analysed by different statistical methods. Simons' (1987) research, discussed below, is one of the detailed case studies used as an example of this particular scholarly approach, an approach still popularly employed to the present day.

The importance of this type of scholarship extends far beyond it being merely one of a variety of possible methods of research. Because it is the main approach practised by a majority of established scholars in the field, and is regarded by different position-holders in the academy such as administrative heads and journal editors as the superior method of scholarship, it has served to draw even more scholars into using objectivist approaches.

More than that, it has influenced what counts as knowledge in that area. It has given legitimacy to what is researched and what counts as knowledge – the subjects selected and the frameworks within which they are studied (Marsden 2005).

Thus subjectivist topics such as a study of employees in organizations, their interpretations of events and processes, their attitudes to these and their actions (or resistance) in response have largely been ignored by researchers using an objectivist framework. As mentioned earlier, these topics have been regarded as 'unscientific' because they are not neutral, are subject to human influences such as attitudes and emotions which are not objective and cannot be studied using mathematical techniques to analyse the data. Such research would not be based on observable and measurable factors and therefore would not be regarded as objective – the standard for positivist ideas and much mainstream scholarship.

What would also be excluded from mainstream management scholarship are issues to do with power, politics and control (Marsden 2005). Although these can easily be dismissed as being subjective, non-neutral and very much governed by human activity, it will be claimed later that these are important factors in understanding organizations and organizational processes as they play a part in determining what happens in them. Similarly, subjectivist approaches will also be critiqued from the point of view of what is lacking in them and how the knowledge produced using such approaches could be supplemented.

SCIENTIFIC KNOWLEDGE

Before considering the advantages and disadvantages of these two main approaches, some time will be spent looking at the underlying premise about what scientific approaches are and their enactment in mainstream management scholarship. As mentioned above, scientific approaches have been regarded as value-free, needing to be verified by observable elements acquired through sense data (or experience), and analysed using mathematical and statistical techniques (Turner 2001). One example is sociology. According to Neurath, one of the leading members of the Vienna Circle, in order for sociology to be accepted as a 'science', it had to engage in scientific methods of inquiry. This meant finding regularities between observable features, and establishing laws with the aim eventually of connecting all laws into a unified science. There was no place for the consideration of social factors, nor ideas (Halfpenny 2001). In this scheme there was also no place for theory or the logic of deduction (Turner 2001).

However, what constitutes science and scientific inquiry is not necessarily as straightforward as the above description implies. There has been a debate among scholars as to what counts as science and scientific research with reference both to the natural and to the social sciences. A much broader picture has been given of science by various philosophers, social theorists and historians of science. Some of their definitions of science have contradicted notions that science is only about observable phenomena; has to be executed only through methods involving experiment and observation; or that it is the onus upon researchers to find regularities and rules in the phenomena they are studying.

Kuhn, in what has become a famous book on scientific revolutions, defined science as 'any field in which progress is marked' (Kuhn 1970, p. 162). Kuhn (1970) and the philosopher Feyerabend (1993) both argued that science was not about steadily increasing the sum total of knowledge about the universe; rather there were new discoveries that provoked new questions, new ways of looking at the world, and, importantly, new methods of handling data – new research techniques. Feyerabend emphasized that science needed to be 'adaptable and inventive, not a rigid imitator of "established" behavioural patterns' (Feyerabend 1993, p. 159). These claims caused much debate in their time and have had a lasting effect on what is considered to be science and scientific method (Bird 2010).

These ideas oppose the belief that scientific research is about finding and fitting together more and more pieces of the jigsaw puzzle of reality. Rather there are different, sometimes conflicting views of how things are, and this requires new ways of thinking and researching. These ideas also challenge the view that research into and knowledge of the social sciences have to be conceptualized and studied in a certain way. This unlocks the constraints that have been placed on this area of knowledge in order to qualify for the label 'scientific'.

The challenges do not end there. The assertion that scientific work requires quantitative and statistical analysis has also been disputed. Kuhn did not mention the necessity for this kind of analysis. In fact he regarded quantitative and qualitative methods not as contradictory opposites, but as being interdependent and together aiding new scientific discoveries. An example he gave was of qualitative work being done first to surmise new laws which then were substantiated later through quantitative methods:

> so general and so close is the relation between qualitative paradigm and quantitative law that, since Galileo, such laws have often been correctly guessed with the aid of a paradigm years before apparatus could be designed for their experimental determination. (Kuhn 1970, p. 29)

Feyerabend supported the view that qualitative methods were at times important in scientific work. He gave the example of celestial mechanics, which although being 'one of the apparently most quantitative of all sciences', was found by scientists to be more easily studied using qualitative (topological) methods (Feyerabend 1993, p. 2).

And finally, one of the strongest arguments put by social scientists for their preference for quantitative over qualitative methods – the claim that science was value-free, uninfluenced by social values and by human consciousness – has also been contested by Kuhn, among others. He argued that scientists in any group were much influenced by the ideas of their scientific community, which played an important part in determining their activities: the type of science practised; which paradigm to use; which problems merited investigation; the validity of the solutions suggested; and in general what counted and what did not count as scientific achievement (Kuhn 1970).

The most important claim to value-free research, perhaps, the claim that the scientific researcher, unlike her qualitative counterpart, is not biased but neutral in her work, has been contradicted by Hanson, a philosopher of science. Hanson has argued that a scientific observer, just like a qualitative researcher, can influence the results of an experiment because of her background knowledge and assumptions (Hanson 1965). He argued that even the simplest observations were based on theoretical assumptions (Arabatzis 2010). Hanson himself gave the example of two astronomers who would understand the same data in different ways because of their different research interests and therefore see the same thing differently. Tycho Brahe and Kepler watching the same dawn would interpret it either as the sun moving above the horizon, or the earth rotating away to reveal the sun. They presented these different explanations not because the data were different, but because their theories of celestial bodies and their movement varied (Hanson 1965).

SCIENTIFIC KNOWLEDGE AS APPLIED IN SOCIAL SCIENCE RESEARCH

There have also been critiques of what have been regarded as scientific methods in social science research. Bourdieu (1990) took the view that although research in the social sciences might look scientific, it was usually only a question of the external appearance of the research. If one looked at the research more closely it often did not conform to the standards practised in the natural sciences. His comments are relevant for models practised in management and management accounting research. These models can be based on hypotheses that are then proved or disproved using various, usually quantitative, techniques. (See below for detailed analyses of an example of this type of management accounting research.) Bourdieu's view of scientific method was broader and more open than simply being an examination of previously suggested hypotheses. Bourdieu stipulated the necessity for much more work than what was commonly done in objectivist social science research in order to achieve the steady development of ideas which could then transform one's understanding of the subject studied:

> scientific practice . . . [requires] the long effort . . . which little by little leads to the *conversion* of one's whole view of action and the social world that is presupposed by 'observation' of facts that are totally new because they were totally invisible to the previous view . . . (Bourdieu 1990, p. 16) [emphasis original]

Bourdieu drives the point home that much social science research 'looked the part' in terms of showing quantitative and statistical techniques but lacked the depth of scientific investigation:

> The mania for methodology or the thirst for the latest refinements of componential analysis, graph theory, or matrix calculus assume the same ostentatious function as recourse to prestigious labels or fascinated attachment to the instruments – questionnaires or computers – most likely to symbolise the specificity of the craft and its scientific quality. (Bourdieu et al. 1991, pp. 70–71)

Bourdieu called this procedure 'scientificity' rather than science, as it did not meet the criteria of what might be regarded as scientific. Much sociological research, according to Bourdieu, fell into this category rather than having the empirical rigour to qualify for scientific legitimacy. It lacked a painstaking 'construction of the object' to be studied. Scientific research was not about a 'socially sanctioned epistemology', but about continual correction and reconstruction with presuppositions about the research consciously examined (Krais 1991, pp. 252, 253).

CHALLENGES TO MAINSTREAM TRADITIONAL OBJECTIVIST RESEARCH

These ideas put into question many convictions about what constitutes valid, scientific research. If one accepts the above arguments as to what is legitimate scientific work, then many of the assumptions previously made do not stand scrutiny. It is not necessary for research which is based only on quantitative or statistical analyses to be regarded as scientifically valid. Crucially, some of the divisions put up by objectivist scholars between legitimate objectivist research and non-legitimate qualitative work fall down as, according to the claims made by the eminent philosopher and historians of science mentioned above, the problems with qualitative research and researchers can apply equally well to scholars researching in the natural sciences.

Firstly, the types of scientific methods that are valid are broad and, according to Feyerabend's example, include qualitative research. The frequent criticism levied against qualitative researchers not producing value-free work is countered by similar situations arising in research into the natural sciences. Kuhn had argued for the importance of scientists' communities' decisions and judgements about what constituted valid scientific knowledge, and Hanson had showed how the astronomers Brahe's and Kepler's predilections about the sun and the earth respectively had influenced their very different interpretations and explanations of the dawn.

This opens up the possibility and legitimacy of new types of research methodologies for those seeking to legitimate their work by using scientific methods, and at the same time should close down criticisms against subjectivities in qualitative research. Importantly it also poses new questions about how to assess whether research methods are valid, be they quantitative, qualitative or a mix of both. From Bourdieu's comments, the 'object of inquiry' must be investigated to see whether the research methods used are truly investigative, opening up the possibility of new knowledge being discovered, rather than simply testing hypotheses already envisioned.

Moreover, as is claimed and demonstrated below, researchers in the management and management accounting fields having intended to do objectivist research, without justifying it possibly because they had not realized it, have been subjective in some of the decisions they have taken. Examples of subjectivities can be present in the object of inquiry, the choice of respondents and the questions posed in their surveys – all major aspects of research methodology, and having a huge influence on the results produced.

PROBLEMS WITH SUBJECTIVIST RESEARCH

Because subjectivity has been demonstrated to be present in scientific research, as shown by the example of the eminent astronomers given by Hanson, this does not mean that there are no problems to be concerned about regarding subjectivity. Firstly, researchers using subjectivist just as those using objectivist methods need to be aware of the criteria used when constructing an analysis.[3] It may be that qualitative researchers have been aware of this as a problem for much longer as subjectivities are more obvious when it is people who are the respondents for the researcher's data. The researcher is in a position to influence how her subjects respond to the questions and issues raised in an interview, and the respondents, as well as possibly trying to please the researcher and tell her what she wants to hear, may also be influenced by their own backgrounds, values, experiences and intentions regarding the research – their 'situatedness' (Sarbin and Kitsuse 1994; Green 2013; Bell and Willmott 2015). Researchers also, as claimed by Garfinkel (1967, cited in Miller 1997), are responsible for the framing of their research and so should be aware of their input regarding the knowledge produced.

As a result there has been much discussion around the need for researchers to be reflective in their research, and to be aware of the influence they may have on the people they are observing, interviewing or using other methods that involve them even more closely with their subjects, such as action research.[4] Most books on qualitative research methods contain guidance on how researchers should exercise reflexivity, as it is considered of such importance in producing valid research and knowledge. Miller (1997), in a book edited by Silverman (who developed the concept of action research), pointed out that the concept of reflexivity is important because our language about social realities is intricately linked to how we see these realities. Or as Garfinkel (1967) put it, reflexivity is connected with the way we portray reality as this does more than describing those realities – it constitutes them (Garfinkel 1967, cited in Miller 1997).

Seale (1999) argued that because data can be constructed by the researcher through pre-existing values and theories, she should use procedures to eliminate the influence of her personal perspectives. In any case she should also make it clear to the reader what those perspectives are. Then readers would be in a better position to judge for themselves the extent to which the researcher's own values and background have influenced the knowledge she has produced (Cain and Finch 1981, cited in Seale 1999). The author could also lay an 'audit trail' – the documentation of data, methods and decisions made during the process of research and writing the final script (Lincoln and Guba 1985, cited in Seale 1999, p. 45).

More recently Lather and St. Pierre have put it in these terms:

> entanglement [by the researcher in her research] makes . . . humanist qualitative research problematic . . . how do we determine the 'object of our knowledge' – the 'problem' we want to study . . . Can we discount ourselves from the mangle somehow (Self) and then carefully discount some other small piece of the mangle (Other) long enough to study it? (Lather and St. Pierre 2013, p. 630)

As outlined above, researchers who regard themselves as objectivist might in fact have made subjective choices in their research, and their work would benefit from reflective practice, regarding, for example, the results of their choice of subject, their survey questions and their selection of respondents. As indicated below, if a researcher, when investigating management systems, uses only senior managers as her source of data, this has implications not only for the type of information she is likely to receive, but also for her assumptions about how organizations operate and who in an organization has knowledge about that organization.

A problem mentioned earlier which is more likely to be of concern in qualitative research, is sole reliance on people's subjective understandings of their situations. What is likely to be ignored is the underlying structure, be it societal or organizational or both. Such structures may have as strong an influence on people as factors more visible to them and more in their control. The structural focus of many objectivist researchers in management and management accounting may here prove a useful and complementary addition to more subjectivist research.

A further problem with qualitative research is the limited number of respondents a researcher can use. In-depth explorations into how people interpret their situations and explain their actions of necessity involves a much smaller number of people than a survey can. Acquiring rich data through in-depth investigations involves much lengthier interviews than the surveys and questionnaires used by objectivist researchers. These have the advantage of being able to get data from much larger numbers of people in or outside organizations.

Having explored both advantages and disadvantages of quantitative (used in the main by objectivist researchers) and qualitative methods (used largely by subjectivist researchers), and having hinted at the advantages both would gain from considering each other's methods and conceptual frameworks, the remainder of this chapter consists of examples of the two main types of research, together with a critique very much along the lines of the arguments stated above.

OBJECTIVIST RESEARCH IN THE MANAGEMENT ACCOUNTING FIELD

Simons (1987)

Simons is a well-respected management accounting researcher who has written several articles in some of the most highly rated journals spanning interrelationships between organization studies and management accounting. Simons is one of the many researchers in this field who has aspired to using scientific methods in order to find regularities or 'laws' about organizations. His work is important enough to be regarded as among the 'important research efforts ... in the examination of the use of managerial accounting systems' (Covaleski et al. 1996, p. 7). His methods are still relevant, as they continue to be used extensively in mainstream management and management accounting research.

Simons was interested in testing the organizational 'model' of two 'contingency theorists', Burns and Stalker (1961; 1966; 1994). These writers concluded from their research that organizations should adapt their structures to be respectively hierarchical in stable environmental conditions and flexible in more changeable situations. The environmental conditions that Burns and Stalker were most concerned with were the market and technology. In order to test out their ideas Simons conducted research into a number of companies. He first took great care to identify which companies were situated in stable conditions and which found themselves in an unstable environment. Simons' research framework was based on Burns and Stalker's thesis as he established hypotheses that there would be correlations between an organization's control system and the stability or otherwise of its environment. Simons hypothesized that in stable conditions organizations would have more formal, hierarchical procedures and in more changeable situations organizations would have more flexible systems (Simons 1987).

Simons' approach is consonant with the ontological and epistemological characteristics of objectivism, outlined earlier. What he regarded as ontologically real were organizational structures or control systems, excluding the subjectivities and influences of human beings. Simons acknowledged that he had excluded informal structures from his research. His comment on this was 'excluded (somewhat arbitrarily) from this analysis are informal control mechanisms such as social and cultural control' (Simons 1987, p. 358) [brackets original].

Yet informal structures would be dealing with human groupings, intentions and actions, sometimes in contradiction with formal managerial policies and strategies and, as argued below, would be of additional value to the knowledge Simons was seeking about organizational systems.

In keeping with this objectivist approach, Simons' research methodology supports a form of scientific research. He first did qualitative work through lengthy interviews with senior managers in the companies he was researching in order to establish whether the company was in a stable or changing situation, and to get ideas for his questionnaire, designed to investigate the control systems in the firms he was researching. Simons also was rigorous in that he consulted other research work in similar areas and carried out further checks to establish the applicability of his questions for his respondents and to avoid ambiguities with regard to those questions.

All in all Simons asked 33 questions, with answers based on a seven-point Likert-type scale. (This is a scale indicating levels of agreement or disagreement with the question.) The questions asked were about the rigidity or flexibility of control systems, echoing Burns and Stalker's model of hierarchical structures being appropriate for organizations in stable conditions, and flexibility being necessary for companies facing rapid change (Burns and Stalker 1961; 1966; 1994).

Simons' questionnaires were completed by the senior managers of 76 companies. These questionnaires were then analysed by Simons using statistical techniques, which he again painstakingly justified from examples of similar research done by other management accounting scholars (Simons 1987). Such research fits what has been classified as scientific research by Chua (1986) and Panozzo (1997), also management accounting scholars. Their characterization of what constitutes scientific research includes large-scale surveys, empirical evidence through the collection of quantitative data, testing generalizable connections and the use of statistical methods for analysis. The focus of Simons' research on organization systems justifies claims that his work was objectivist, dealing with matters outside the influence of subjective human influences and actions.

Critique of Simons' (1987) Work

Despite Simons' rigorous and painstaking efforts to determine which in his sample of organizations were in a stable situation and which were facing rapid change, and despite the care he took over the questions in his survey, there are aspects of this research (and indeed of many others') that can be queried. The critique here of Simons' 1987 research paper is centred firstly on the fact that, despite its scientific format, there are subjective elements in his work, as is the case in other objectivist research in management, management accounting and in the other social sciences. And second, the decision to interview only senior managers is questioned in terms of the assumption that they would have enough knowledge about the control systems in their organizations, about both the formal systems and any deviations from these systems, in order to have conclusive and complete information as to what the actual control processes were in the organizations they researched.

Subjective Aspects

Any subjective aspects found would not of course by definition detract from the value of the research. If one accepts the broader interpretations of what constitutes scientific work, neither would this in itself detract from its claim to be scientific. The subjective aspects of the work, it is argued here, are firstly in the choice of the subject studied. If one intentionally took a direct subjectivist approach as many qualitative researchers do, one might not limit oneself solely to structural factors as Simons did, but might also study employees' opinions about their organizations' structures, and significantly about their potential and actual influence over how their organizational control systems worked in practice.

Linked to this is Simons' choice of respondent. He interviewed and surveyed only senior managers, which, one can argue, is a subjective choice, again ignoring other employees' views. It is possible that any employees interviewed might corroborate their senior manager's analysis of the organization's control system, but on the other hand, as elaborated below, they might have provided different information from their managers. Inclusion of employees other than managers could serve to deepen and strengthen the validity of Simons' analysis, because of a wider range of knowledge from which to draw. Finally, the questions asked, despite the care Simons took to establish relevance from his extended interviews, were ultimately subjective – they were in the end his judgement on what were suitable questions. This is not necessarily a criticism of his questions; rather a demonstration that such research unavoidably has subjective aspects.

Implications of Subjective Aspects

These subjectivist elements are significant: they affect the type and range of knowledge produced. Through not extending the research to including employees as respondents and also through not considering other than structural factors in what influences organization control processes has resulted in absences in the range of knowledge that could have been acquired. Though Simons, in using senior managers as his respondents, probably gained important information about their organizations, such knowledge was necessarily limited largely to the managers' perceptions and opinions about their organizations' control systems. These may have differed in important respects from the views of others in their organizations and also from the actual processes in operation in their organizations.

There is also the problem, as mentioned above, with respondents. While they may have been telling the truth as they saw fit (in itself also subjective), they may also have been modifying their real opinions for a number of reasons. It may be that they were telling Simons what they thought he wanted to hear, or they may have had reasons of their own – for example to show that everything was going according to plan, that their strategies had been successful and that there were no difficulties or failures in the system. See Vansina (1965) for an account of similar problems faced by social anthropologists during the colonial period. And as already mentioned, such research excluded information about the attitudes and potential influences on the control system of employees at all levels in the organizations below that of the senior executive. To get a fuller and perhaps more accurate picture of these systems, Simons would have had to interview subordinates at different levels in their organizations.

Research has been done showing that senior managers do not always have full knowledge of what happens further down in their organizations. Preston (1986) found in the large organization he researched a lack of communication between the managing director and production manager on the one hand and the subordinate factory managers on the other. The latter had developed their own informal connections in order to acquire and pass on information. This risked the increased possibility of inaccurate and conflicting information and the construction of different definitions of the same situation in the organization. Preston in fact recommended that informal systems be taken into account as this would improve the communications in organizations that were up to then limited by relying only on formal systems. Of course this applies equally to researchers wanting to find out about organizations and organizational processes – reliance solely on formal systems and on senior managers also risks limiting the amount and variety of information available to researchers.

This weakness is compounded if researchers use only one or a small number of managers from each organization, which is what Simons did for the first stage of his research, and probably also for his final questionnaire. Van der Stede et al. (2005) found that the information from research using a single or very few respondents in an organization weakened the validity of the scholarship, as one individual could not represent everyone's views in an organization, and of course, might be vulnerable to subjective bias:

> subjective measures of performance are likely to be less reliable as measures of higher-level performance . . . especially when they are obtained from only one respondent who is . . . far removed from it. (Van der Stede et al. 2005, p. 676)

Limitations of Survey Methods

Another point about Simons' otherwise excellent and important research is concerning the questions. Closed questions in any survey are liable to be limited because of their generality and inability to elicit specific information about the organization researched. In Simons' research, the managers surveyed were required to plot on the Likert-type scale the extent to which each control mechanism was rigid and tightly administered, or had flexibility. To give an example, one of the questions required the respondents to answer on this scale of 1 to 7 the extent to which 'Internal audit groups in checking financial information systems and reports' were used in their organizations (Simons 1987, p. 373).

The limitations of this, as with all questionnaires that are comprised of closed rather than open questions, is that the informants' understandings of their organizations have to fit into pre-defined questions and ranges. This does not provide for the expression of more subtle differences in organizations from the questions already determined by the researcher, and also does not allow for information about detailed differences between organizations. Some scholars have suggested that the questions asked in surveys can tell us more about the researcher and what she values and considers important than what is being researched and what the respondents' thoughts and feelings are (Stainton Rogers 1995). Chia put the same idea in terms of the researcher 'forming, framing and delimiting' her research and the knowledge produced from it (Chia 1996, p. 213).

Chua, harkening back to Feyerabend's critique of a narrow view of science, has more recently bemoaned the fact that mainstream accounting has continued to be positivist into the twenty-first century:

our few 'top' journals continue to be refuges for forms of positivism, so that accounting research appears trapped in a time capsule chained to a philosophy of the early 1900s. While debates about science range fiercely throughout other social sciences, we appear to be immune (or blind) to the issues . . . For as Feyerabend (1993) noted long ago, labelling only a narrow set of methods as science may in fact lead to 'bad' science.

It is argued below for the desirability of the positive aspects of objectivist research such as Simons' to be combined with the positive aspects of subjective research, so that the results found are richer in subject matter and analysis and provide knowledge that deals with more rounded pictures of organizations and organizational processes. This is important for research, for teaching and for allowing practitioners, not least managers, a fuller picture of what is really happening in their organizations.

BROADER RESEARCH IN THE MANAGEMENT ACCOUNTING FIELD

Not all research in management accounting, just as in management studies, is wholly objectivist. There are examples in management accounting intended to bridge the gap between objectivist and subjectivist scholarship. Brown and Brignall (2007), for example, suggested complementary approaches to accounting issues, where mathematical techniques would be adopted for accounting relationships and qualitative research for human and organizational aspects of research projects. They themselves followed this through by publishing research which used a triangulated methodology[5] through a dual method, mixed paradigm[6] approach. Another management accounting scholar, Modell (2009), also supported mixed method research, emphasizing the long history of management accounting research in which both quantitative and qualitative methods were used in combination.

Chenhall and Euske (2007)

An example of a qualitative management accounting research paper is Chenhall and Euske's (2007) research on how people in organizations facing organizational change perceived their situation and what actions they took. Unlike Simons' research, Chenhall and Euske paid attention to the actual processes involved in their organizations' change strategies, showing the complexities and consequences of the effects of managerial strategies on humans and human interactions in organizations.

Chenhall and Euske (2007) researched two military establishments which were in the process of changing from professional to more management-oriented cultures. As well as internal change, the context in which these policies were made – external pressures, local initiatives, levels of structural autonomy and employee attitudes to these changes – were taken into account. Their research was also diachronic, taking place over a long period. In one organization the research was continued for 11 years, in the second for 9 years. Their research methods were varied, including direct observation at both formal and informal meetings, the study of administrative processes, archival studies, semi-structured interviews and discussions with key participants about how the changes were progressing. They aimed at 'integrating the technical approach to MCS [management control systems] with a behavioral approach that focuses on how individual users respond to MCS facilitated change' (Chenhall and Euske 2007, p. 608).

One can already see the difference with the objectivist research outlined above. Their focus was on people in their organizations rather than being only about systems, and their research methods were also much more people-oriented. Their justification for this type of research was that in order to understand the technical aspects of change it was appropriate to adopt a 'rich' approach, in order to acquire information about: the extent of the integration between change initiatives and the people at whom they were directed; the relationship between the organization and environmental change; issues regarding changes in the organization's culture; why certain changes were more successful than others; and the actual work processes (Chenhall and Euske 2007, p. 635, passim).

Such detailed investigations resulted in their finding out that different issues arose at different points of the change process, requiring different strategies for each stage. The timing and pacing of changes therefore needed to be compatible. Their research also showed, unlike Simons', that social factors such as the extent of socialization between senior managers and more junior staff influenced the change process, as did the degree of engagement of the future users of the systems, and the level of trust in their working relationships with colleagues. Co-ordination between different systems, managers and trainers was important. Interestingly, autonomy at local levels from the centre worked well at some stages of the change process and less well at others. And support from senior management was crucial to the success of the whole process (Chenhall and Euske 2007).

Critique of Chenhall and Euske's (2007) Work

Rather than looking only at structural change as a recommendation for a successful change strategy, Chenhall and Euske's research provided knowledge into the responses of people at various levels in the organizations to the change initiatives, the successes and failures during the change process and the reasons for them. This rich research produced knowledge about the structures actually (rather than only theoretically) in use, and the ways in which people negotiated these systems to their own advantage. The data Chenhall and Euske provided was more informative about actual social processes, the successes and failures of organizational change and the role played by human subjectivities in these than would data only about structural issues.

Limitations of Qualitative Research Methods

Chenhall and Euske's research did not use the surveys or statistical analyses common to objectivist research. This may have been a weakness as their research methods were time-consuming and they had to limit their research to a small number of organizations – in their case only two. Just as Simons' research might have been complemented by using subjectivist research methods and reflective practices about his methods, so Chenhall and Euske's research might be complemented by the addition of surveys. These could be distributed to a much larger number of organizations and if the questions were designed to produce numerical answers, as for example on a Likert scale, the results could be arrived at more quickly by using statistical techniques. Simons, in using such research methods, managed to get data from 76 organizations as compared with Chenhall and Euske's two.

A second weakness in using only subjectivist research is losing explanations around the structural factors that may be instrumental in influencing change. This is not necessarily a criticism of Chenhall and Euske's work, but is a criticism of subjectivist research which ignores structural factors. It is important, as has been argued in this chapter, to know about people's interpretations of what is happening to them in organizations and, following on from this, the reasons for their actions. However, as outlined above, some of the influences on their actions may be to do with structural issues in their organizations or in the wider society, which they may be unaware of, and therefore not include in the information they present to researchers.

CONCLUSION

One might put a case for complementary research as advocated by Brown and Brignall (2007), perhaps using the data acquired from qualitative research methods to be the basis for the design of a questionnaire that would reach many more organizations and people. The idea of using a rich methodology in combination with more limited survey questions encourages the possibility of commensurability between objectivist and subjectivist scholarship using both quantitative and qualitative methods. Such research methods with their corresponding ontologies and epistemologies would have the advantages of framing organizational issues more broadly, encompassing a much wider range of knowledge about both structures and people, than the narrower foci of either objectivist or subjectivist scholarship. This richer knowledge would be more practical and helpful for managers, practitioners and of course also students. More inclusive knowledge using a range of methodological approaches would produce knowledge about organizations, organizational processes and the people working within and influencing them that would be more legitimate, more practical and ultimately more sustainable.

NOTES

1. Closed questions are those requiring a 'yes/no' answer or one where the answer is plotted on a scale, as in Simons' (1987) research. In either case the respondent is limited to a set of answers from which she must choose. Open questions allow the respondent freedom to answer the question in her own way.
2. A method of argument or exposition that systematically weighs contradictory facts or ideas with a view to the resolution of their real or apparent contradictions (TheFreeDictionary.com).
3. This statement was made about reflexive ethnography, a subjectivist research methodology (Denzin and Lincoln 1998).
4. Action research includes many traditions. Its important characteristics have been described as being participative, grounded in experience and action oriented. This includes face-to-face inquiry with others into areas of mutual interest and concern (Reason and Bradbury 2001).
5. Triangulation refers to the use of more than one approach to the investigation of a research question in order to enhance confidence in the results of any research (www.referenceworld.com/sage/socialscience/triangulation.pdf).
6. A paradigm is a way of seeing the world and therefore of what counts as knowledge and how to research it – a particular ontology, epistemology and methodology.

REFERENCES

Arabatzis, T. (2010), 'Experiment', in Stathis Psillos and Martin Curd (eds), *The Routledge Companion to Philosophy of Science*, London: Routledge, pp. 159–170.
Bell, E. and H. Willmott (2015), 'Editors' introduction: Qualitative research – themes and prospects', in Emma Bell and Hugh Willmott (eds), *Qualitative Research in Business and Management*, vol. 1, Classical and Contemporary Studies, Los Angeles: Sage, pp. xxi–liv.
Bird, A. (2010), 'The historical turn in the philosophy of science', in Stathis Psillos and Martin Curd (eds), *The Routledge Companion to Philosophy of Science*, London: Routledge, pp. 67–77.
Bourdieu, Pierre (1990), *The Logic of Practice*, trans. Richard Nice, Stanford: Stanford University Press.
Bourdieu, P., J.-C. Chamboredon and J.-C. Passeron (1991), in Beate Krais (ed.), *The Craft of Sociology: Epistemological Preliminaries*, trans. Richard Nice, Berlin: Walter de Gruyter.
Brown, R. and S. Brignall (2007), 'Reflections on the use of a dual-methodology research design to evaluate accounting and management practice in UK university central administrative services', *Management Accounting Research*, **18** (1), 32–48.
Burns, Tom and George Macpherson Stalker (1961), *The Management of Innovation*, London: Tavistock Publications.
Burns, Tom and George Macpherson Stalker (1966), *The Management of Innovation*, 2nd ed., London: Tavistock Publications.
Burns, Tom and George Macpherson Stalker (1994), *The Management of Innovation*, 3rd ed., Oxford: Oxford University Press.
Cain, M. and J. Finch (1981), 'Towards a rehabilitation of data', in Philip Abrams, Rosemary Deem, Janet Finch and Paul Rock (eds), *Practice and Progress: British Sociology 1950–1980*, London: George Allen and Unwin, pp. 105–119.
Chenhall, R.H. and K.J. Euske (2007), 'The role of management control systems in planned organizational change: an analysis of two organizations', *Accounting, Organizations and Society*, **32** (7), 601–637.
Chia, Robert (1996), *Organizational Analysis as Deconstructive Practice*, Berlin: Walter de Gruyter.
Chua, W.F. (1986), 'Radical developments in accounting thought', *The Accounting Review*, **lxi** (4), 601–632.
Clegg, S.R. (2002), 'Lives in the balance: a comment on Hinings and Greenwood's "Disconnects and consequences in organization theory?"', *Administrative Science Quarterly*, **47** (3), 428–441.
Covaleski, M.A., M.W. Dirsmith and S. Samuel (1996), 'Managerial accounting research: the contributions of organizational and sociological theories', *Journal of Management Accounting Research*, **8** (1), 1–35.
Denzin, Norman K. and Yvonna S. Lincoln (1998), *Collecting and Interpreting Qualitative Materials*, Thousand Oaks, CA: Sage.
Donaldson, L. (2003), 'Position statement for positivism' in Robert Westwood and Stewart Clegg (eds), *Debating Organization: Point-Counterpoint in Organization Studies*, Malden: Blackwell, pp. 116–127.
Donaldson, Lex (1996), *For Positivist Organization Theory: Proving the Hard Core*, London: Sage.
Feyerabend, Paul (1993), *Against Method*, 3rd ed., London: Verso.
Garfinkel, Harold (1967), *Studies in Ethnomethodology*, Englewood Cliffs, NJ: Prentice Hall.
Green, M. (2012), 'Objectivism in management knowledge: an example of Bourdieu's "mutilation"?', *Social Responsibility Journal*, **8** (4), 495–510.
Green, M. (2013), 'What counts as knowledge? Parameters of validity for the meaning and representation of a contingency theory in the organization, management and management accounting literature', unpublished PhD thesis, De Montfort University.
Halfpenny, P. (2001), 'Positivism in the twentieth century', in George Ritzer and Barry Smart (eds), *Handbook of Social Theory*, London: Sage, pp. 371–385.
Hanson, N.R. (1965), *Patterns of Discovery: An Inquiry into the Conceptual Foundations of Science*, Cambridge: Cambridge University Press.
Hatch, M.J. and D. Yanow (2003), 'Organization theory as interpretive science', in Harimidos Tsoukas and Christian Knudsen (eds), *The Oxford Handbook of Organization Theory*, Oxford: Oxford University Press, pp. 63–87.
Hogler, R. and M.A. Gross (2009), 'Journal rankings and academic research', *Management Communication Quarterly*, **20** (10), *Management Communication Quarterly OnlineFirst*, 2 June 2009, doi:10.1177/089335419 (accessed 10 January 2013).
Kincaid, H. (2010), 'Social sciences', in Stathis Psillos and Martin Curd (eds), *The Routledge Companion to Philosophy of Science*, London: Routledge, pp. 594–604.
Krais, B. (1991), 'Meanwhile I have come to know all the diseases of sociological understanding', an interview with Pierre Bourdieu in Pierre Bourdieu, Jean-Claude Chamboredon and Jean-Claude Passeron, *The Craft of Sociology: Epistemological Preliminaries*, trans. Richard Nice, Berlin: Walter de Gruyter, pp. 247–259.
Kuhn, Thomas S. (1970), *The Structure of Scientific Revolutions*, 2nd ed., Chicago, IL: Chicago University Press.

Lather, P. and E.A. St. Pierre (2013), 'Introduction: Post-qualitative research', *International Journal of Qualitative Studies in Education*, **26** (6), 629–633.

Lincoln, Yvonna S. and Egon Guba (1985), *Naturalistic Enquiry*, Beverly Hills, CA: Sage.

Marsden, R. (2005), 'The politics of organizational analysis', in Christopher Grey and Hugh Willmott (eds), *Critical Management Studies: A Reader*, Oxford: Oxford University Press, pp. 132–164.

McMullin, E. (2010), 'The virtues of a good theory', in Stathis Psillos and Martin Curd (eds), *The Routledge Companion to Philosophy of Science*, London: Routledge, pp. 498–508.

Miller, G. (1997), 'Building bridges: the possibility of analytic dialogue between ethnography, conversation analysis and Foucault', in David Silverman (ed.), *Qualitative Research: Theory, Method and Practice*, London: Sage, pp. 24–44.

Modell, S. (2009), 'In defence of triangulation: a critical realist approach to mixed methods research in management accounting', *Management Accounting Research*, **20** (3), 208–221.

Palmer, D. (2006), 'Taking stock of the criteria we use to evaluate one another's work: *ASQ* 50 years out', *Administrative Science Quarterly*, **51** (4), 535–559.

Panozzo, F. (1997), 'The making of the good academic accountant', *Accounting, Organizations and Society*, **22** (5), 447–480.

Preston, A. (1986), 'Interactions and arrangements in the process of informing', *Accounting, Organizations and Society*, **11** (6), 521–540.

Pugh, Derek S. (2014), 'Interview with Professor Derek S. Pugh', 6th December.

Reason, P. and H. Bradbury (2001), 'Preface', in Peter Reason and Hilary Bradbury (eds), *Handbook of Action Research: Participative Inquiry and Practice*, London: Sage, pp. xxiii–xxxi.

Sarbin, T.R. and J.I. Kitsuse (1994), 'A prologue to constructing the social', in Theodore R. Sarbin and John I. Kitsuse (eds), *Constructing the Social*, London: Sage, pp. 1–18.

Seale, Clive (1999), *The Quality of Qualitative Research*, London: Sage.

Simons, R. (1987), 'Accounting control systems and business strategy: an empirical analysis', *Accounting Organizations and Society*, **12** (4), 357–374.

Stainton Rogers, R. (1995), 'Q methodology', in Jonathan A. Smith, Rom Harre and Luk Van Langenhove (eds), *Rethinking Methods in Psychology*, London: Sage, pp. 178–192.

Turner, J.H. (2001), 'The origins of positivism: the contributions of Auguste Comte and Herbert Spencer', in George Ritzer and Barry Smart (eds), *Handbook of Social Theory*, London: Sage, pp. 30–42.

Uebel, T. (2010), 'Logical empiricism', in Stathis Psillos and Martin Curd (eds), *The Routledge Companion to Philosophy of Science*, London: Routledge, pp. 78–90.

Vansina, Jan (1965), *Oral Tradition: A Study in Historical Methodology*, trans. Hope M. Wright, London: Routledge and Kegan Paul.

Van der Stede, W.A., Young, M.S. and Chen, C.X. (2005), 'Assessing the quality of evidence in empirical management accounting research: the case of survey studies', *Accounting, Organizations and Society*, **30** (7), 655–684.

Westwood, R. and S. Clegg (2003), 'The discourse of organization studies: dissensus, politics and paradigms', in Robert Westwood and Stewart Clegg (eds), *Debating Organization: Point-Counterpoint in Organization Studies*, Malden: Blackwell, pp. 1–42.

6. Methodological and epistemological perspectives in the study of corporate social responsibility in Colombia

Duván Emilio Ramírez Ospina and José Fernando Muñoz Ospina

INTRODUCTION

The current chapter is the result of the investigation 'Role and behavior of corporate organizations in the context of sustainability' and of the reflection of that line of research in the Department of Doctoral Studies of Human and Social and Sustainable Development of the University of Manizales, Colombia. Its construction is part of the analysis of methodologies and processes adapted to different sectors in the field of corporate social responsibility (CSR) in Colombia. Thus, it addresses many of the themes from the Master's and Doctoral theses from different citizens and universities in Colombia. It also takes into account many different scientific articles and published documents from Colombian authors, especially aimed at fulfilling degree requirements for Master's and Doctorate programs at different universities both from Colombia and other countries.

In the first part of the chapter, we will discuss the assumptions and nature of the realities that are studied within the context of CSR in Colombia. In this section we indicate what research in CSR is of particular interest to the different Colombian researchers at the root of the diverse theoretical concepts that have been developed in the last few decades. Also, we will observe what socio-environmental and economic problems are determined by the existence and development of corporate organizations. This has been studied since the conceptualization of CSR, which emerges as a paradigm that encourages business management practices and behaviors that are guided by the need for legitimacy and validity criteria on the stage of social value judgment behaviors.

In this first part of the chapter we will indicate that the notion of CSR has been understood on the part of Colombian researchers as the integral result of entrepreneurial action into the economic, environmental, and social environments, and furthermore, that businesses are directly interdependent with social realities, and from this, that businesses take certain elements of their decision-making based on the different expectations from different interest groups and stakeholders. In the same sense, we can assume that these corporate behaviors are the basis for the definition of social justice for many different social groups and deal with the legitimacy or illegitimacy of corporate behavior.

The second part of the chapter deals with the study of methodological approaches used for the research of CSR on the part of the Colombian researchers. We find that the approach to CSR has two perspectives. In the first, we observe the academic reflection of the review concepts within the context of CSR, generally breaking up the review around the historical and conceptual evolution of the concept and how the changes in the concept of CSR have influenced the different ways of studying and in the diffusion of the concept. As much from the academic perspective as from the practical, what has been brought to the establishment are theoretical ties between CSR and other concepts such as sustainable development, corporate strategy, management, marketing, and territorial development.

In the second, we observe that the research perspective of CSR affects the analysis of certain corporate practices, and as such, considers that these studies have been guided by the subjectivity of corporate leaders and therefore has been observed by different corporate instruments such as in-depth interviews, surveys, polls, focus groups, observation, qualitative research with a focus on ethnographic results, case studies, and primary data collected directly from the researchers.

Also we will present research reports that were developed through secondary data, making use of methods such as content analysis, source surveys from corporate reports, surrendered reports from accounts from state organizations, and press documents published in magazines and specialized publications.

Finally, we will present the conclusions of how CSR research is done in Colombia. With this research we hope to contribute to the discussion about different methodological approaches used in different parts of the world in order to investigate around this theme, which has become of great importance in recent years, not just for research, but also for practical purposes.

ASSUMPTIONS AND NATURE OF THE REALITIES OF CORPORATE SOCIAL RESPONSIBILITY STUDIED IN COLOMBIA

Business organizations, in all their forms and types, constitute the central axis of modern society. In this way, the corporation, understood in a general way, is a human creation with the end goal of achieving a connection between human work and the availability of resources both natural and material. In this dynamic of work, the concept of the corporation emerges from multiple dimensions such as the economic, the social, and the environmental, as understanding that we live in constant interaction with social and natural networks with the overall goal of sustainability and mutual survival.

In this order of ideas, the corporation can be considered as the mark on which human beings can create all of their intended work. It is fundamental to the social context of a region and to the environmental context that arises from and is supported by these behaviors and productions. In this sense, the actions of a corporation intervene in the function of the social and environmental contexts in order to satisfy the needs, wishes, and ambitions of human beings.

From their initial conception, organizations were understood as being a technical mechanism designed and configured by human beings to be used as a way of transforming society and nature. For Fisher (2010), 'mechanisms that are properly technical, are those that are invented, produced, and used as a means of transforming the things of the world' (p. 9).

Based on this perspective, the corporation is a fundamental axis in the mentality of evolution, elevating itself as the way upon which society can base its progressive processes.

The corporation exists as a framework of transactions and exchanges between society and nature. That said, it corresponds to its own rationality that can make sense of its conduct and actions.

In this scenario, different reflections about socioeconomic and environmental phenomena have emerged that should be understood and taken care of by the corporations in order to give answer to these necessary and interdependent relationships between the developmental processes of countries and their organizations. These days, it is evident that these relationships have been suffering transformations and have configured a much more complex scenario, where the creative contributions of the business units are fundamental to the achievement of those objectives determined by a global influence of social and productive direction (Muñoz 2011).

In accordance with what is stated above, the study of CSR has risen to be of particular interest for various Colombian researchers and is at the root of many diverse theoretical concepts that have been developed in the last few decades. Lately, the socio-environmental and economic problems that determine the development of corporate organizations have been studied from the perspective of CSR which arises from the paradigm question that brings about differing managerial behaviors and practices that are oriented towards the necessity of obtaining legitimacy and validation on the stage of social value judgment behavior.

The research on issues of CSR in Colombia has been done since the first integral investigations into these corporate organizations from different units of analysis seeking to define the concept or shared sense of what is CSR. In the same way, the studies have tried to make clear the actions of firms considering their socially responsible work. In this perspective the frame of these studies of CSR in Colombia, have been formed to be just as empirical reality as the imaginary and senses that are constructed by the people who maintain multiple relationships, both direct and indirect, with these corporate organizations.

The products from different Colombian researchers that are brought to the attention of the people who are responsible for CSR within the corporate organizations are focused specifically on delineating the fundamentals of thought and the distinct actions of organizations within the context of social, economic, cultural, and political institutional problems that derive from the development of their own results. In this way, they are focused on understanding the form that arises from the evolution and institutionalization of the principle ideas that frame the natural configuration of the organizational entity.

Within the frame of the previous considerations, the studies about CSR arise from the interest in defining the ideas that are supported by the be and do from different organizational contexts. At the root of this, it is inferred that the interest in studying these organizations, within the conception of their responsibilities, has its genesis in the configuration of their thought structures in relation to the coexistence and the role that they occupy in society and in the process of development. That is to say, that the studies are framed within the definition of their 'role' that these organizations should take up and put into practice in order to better serve the economic, environmental, and social needs that are demanded by the complex realities that coexist between the people.

On the path towards the achievement of objectives, of the different researches developed by Colombian researchers, it refers to the understanding of CSR as a multifaceted, interdisciplinary, systematic, and dynamic reality that permits addressing these objectives from diverse components, that in a natural way, it forms the organization as a dynamic and complex structure. In this respect, they try to provide representations of the phenomenon and sense of CSR in different symbolic, natural, and institutionalized scenarios.

In effect, assuming that CSR acts as a sense of purpose, a process, and a result, the research about the mentioned theme brings out the manifestation of the responsible behaviors of the organizations and has its roots within the taken positions or within the convictions of the organizations bringing to light their contributions to the human condition. That is to say, to help and support the satisfaction of the necessities of preservation and improvement of the environment where taking resources has an impact and from the necessity to maintain the competitive structure of the economic system and from the necessity of promoting the progress and wellbeing of society.

In this same scope of understanding, the incorporation of a sense of purpose in CSR takes a reactive and proactive position within the frame of an organization. From the reactive point of view, it is understood that organizations establish a systematic modification of productive logics, and contractual and social relationships that have been deleterious to the environment and to society in general. From the proactive point of view, it puts the organizations on the vanguard of the new order of relationships that should be established in the long term in order to serve all of the social groups that interact in order to survive and develop within the context that is determined by the moral necessity and from the contribution of wellbeing of the community.

As a way of understanding the rise and construction of the analysis entities with which the various Colombian researchers have sought to explain the phenomenon of CSR, in this work they made use of the basic organization outline put forth by Bédard (2004). The author puts forth that all of the organizations in order to survive and develop create a framework within the three basic functions. 'The organization is completely organic in that all of the specialized units and activities concur with the three large base functions which are: production and creation, protection and security, and government and general interest groups' (p. 91).

According to the author, these are not exclusive functions of the organization but rather that they are omnipresent and encompassing in the individual, in society, collectively, and in each of the base functions they contribute to a specific objective within the framework of the organization.

> Production and creation are in search of the material and physical wellbeing of each member, for the evaluation of the natural resources and of the human capital. Defense and protection serves in order to maintain order and peace between human relations that are at the base of socialization. Government and general interest groups whose end goals are to elicit a sense of shared roots, ideals, and ideas with the value chain and community of stake holders. (p. 105)

From the described concept of the organization and the relationship that emerges from the research about CSR in Colombia, it is inferred that the three basic functions are derived from the departments and from the sense of responsibility that a corporate organization should assume within their determined context.

In the same form, it is assumed that the organization within its framework of the three base functions acts according to the demands that are conferred upon the organization by society and the context to which it pertains. In this, they should act in order to maintain the processes of reconstruction while acting within the values and principles that society deems important. And so arises the notion of the corporate organization as an actor of fundamental importance within the aspects of social living and the development of a community. It is summarized in Aktouf (2001) when he states: 'Corporations today have reached a time of such importance, direct and indirect, in the life of human beings that we cannot abstain from thinking about the role that they occupy in relation to every aspect of our lives' (p. 70).

In agreement with the previous statement, the notion of CSR is understood in the research scenarios of Colombia as the integral result of corporate action and economic, environmental, and social factors. The corporate organization is directly interdependent with the realities of society, and from them, takes elements that guide their behavior and answer to the expectations from their different social interest groups and stakeholders. Similarly, they assume that these corporate behaviors are fundamental to these different social groups in order to define the values of social justice, legitimacy, or illegitimacy of corporate behavior.

Based on our partial or integral observations of the corporate reality, we found that the Colombian researchers understand that CSR is a product of the philosophical convictions that give way to reality and the generation of ideas that guide action. It is the definition of a system of values and the moral arena of the organization within the relationships between the social-system and eco-system; the creation of a rationality sustained by a dialogue of learning that creates methods and procedures in search of socially responsible action; and based on the three previous aspects, the guidance of corporate practices in accordance with socioeconomic and environmental realities.

Therefore, it can be affirmed that the research about CSR in Colombia puts corporate practices in a critical scenario that gives rise to much questioning and the search for systematic observation about how corporate organizations construct, deconstruct, and reconstruct their principles, values, and practices that are fundamental for the productive function, the structural formation of the government, of the face of responsibility, and that are derived from their actions within a given environment.

In the productive scenario, the corporation studies and understands that the logic of creations and corporate products have been only slightly preoccupied by the balance of socio-ecological factors where the predominant vision was the generation of goods and services while being indifferent to the environmental and social impacts. In this sense, the productive function of the corporation seen from the perspective of CSR delves into how a corporation incorporates their know-how, skills, and creative abilities into the arena of common wellbeing for the current and future generations.

The research that analyses the functioning aspects of the structural conformation of a corporation in relation to CSR has a focus on the corporation and their notions related to society where it is assumed that the corporation takes fundamentals or elements that permit the configuration of a consequential corporate skill from the processes of change and transformation of society. In relation to this, the research is oriented towards the comprehension of the sense of interdependency and of the structural mechanisms that lead the corporation oriented towards the contribution to the common good of the territories where they coexist.

The studies that have a focus on the function of the governing of the corporation from the perspective of CSR look to generate scenarios that rationally explain and understand the way in which the interior of the corporation, from the thoughts and actions of the directors, generates a system of representations. That, which is understood as the shared purpose of all of the members of the organization and creates an identity and a culture that begins to address the necessity of defining the principles of management, the values that give legitimacy to the actions, and the logic that validates the processes, products, results, and behaviors of the corporation and also, the systematic revision of the practices that correspond to social, economic, and environmental problems within the territory in which the corporation operates.

METHODOLOGICAL FOCUSES ON THE STUDY OF CSR IN COLOMBIA

In the reviewed works, you can observe that the approach to CSR in Colombia has two perspectives. On one side, you can see the academic reflection around the concept and its relation to the context, generally parting from the revisions about the historic evolution of the concept and how this has influenced the forms of studying the diffusion of the concept as much as from the academic perspective as from the practical. This is what has been brought to the establishment from theoretical ties between CSR and other concepts such as sustainable development, strategic management, human management, marketing, and territorial development. This tendency is observed in authors such as Raufflet (2010); Azuero, Melo, and García (2011); Cuervo (2009); Duque, Cardona, and Rendón (2013); and D'Amato (2013).

On the other hand, analysis from these practices has been greatly affected. These studies have been guided by the subjectivity of the corporate leaders since the observation while making use of different instruments such as surveys, in-depth interviews, panel discussions, focus groups, observation, qualitative investigation with a focus on ethnography, and case studies. These types of data being collected directly by the researchers.

Also, we find that works are developed through secondary data by making use of methods such as content analysis, using source data from corporate reports, rendition processes from accounts that were handled by the state, press releases, and public documents published in specialized journals. Some of the authors that use such methods are Saavedra (2011); Calderón, Álvarez, and Naranjo (2011); Raufflet (2010); Atehortúa (2008); Duque, Cardona, and Rendón (2013); and Rueda and Uribe (2011).

The research done by Lozano (2012) is a type of qualitative research intending to reach a holistic description. He addresses CSR activities, corporate behavior from the region focused on CSR practices, and micro, small, and medium agricultural companies from the southwest region of Cauca, Colombia. The research method of the case allowed him to learn and analyse the causes, advantages and disadvantages, and impacts of social responsibility among those same micro, small, and medium companies. The methodological focus was based fundamentally on descriptive facts of the object of study within the situations, through the technique of direct observation and using semi-structured interviews accompanied by a bibliographical review and analysis of the appropriate conceptual references that allowed for the application of the previous case studies.

The method of the case study used in the research allowed for in-depth research of certain important aspects of CSR. For example, the incorporation of qualitative data that describes and enables a better understanding of the studied phenomenon. It was adopted as an instrument or guide for semi-structured interviews, in which the interviewee responds to various options but with the possibility of talking openly with respect to the question. This instrument was used by the administrators for the interviews of the previously selected micro, small, and medium companies from each of the four municipalities that pertain to the southwestern region of Valle del Cauca in Colombia: Palmira, Candelaria, Florida, and Pradera.

Also we observed reflections from different theoretical perspectives from works such as Cuervo (2009), in a work done as a partial requirement for the title of Magister in Social Politics of the University of Javeriana of Colombia. It starts with the idea of a qualitative research method utilizing the intertextuality in the form of construction and presentation of new speeches, considering the inclusive negotiations as the key to the work. This permits the construction of a proposal born from ethical, economic, social, and political analysis in order to obtain a view that is oriented towards the achievement of personal and collective wellbeing while recognizing the multi-sector cooperation as an ideal way to provide alternatives of reflection and interaction for the social policy in Colombia.

Cuervo (2009) continues by signaling the importance of generating alternatives for reflection and interaction that allow for the possibility of a rise of spaces of social development in Colombia by way of explanatory types of qualitative studies using technical methodologies such as non-participatory observation and semi-structured interviews as the principle ways to revise documentation that allowed for the two phases of identification and construction of the study and also the initial conceptualization.

The previous being established as a process of analysis and syntheses starting with the intertextual revision of more than 100 bibliographical resources, looking to address the social reality from a normative perspective and offer through an ethical perspective of wellbeing a socially responsible alternative for the social policy in Colombia.

In this way, Cuervo (2009) tries to present from his interpretation a new space of thought and a new way of action that, through cooperation, allows for new options about discussion about the contribution by the private corporation to the social development of Colombia, with the true value of the included solutions provided by the market and the challenges and limitations on the Colombian territory to achieve cooperation between different social actors.

On the other hand, Mejía (2011) in a thesis as a requirement to obtain the title of Doctor of Administration of the University EAFIT of Colombia, address the support of the critical theory of the construction of the concept of social responsibility, looking for a proposal of a critical alternative for CSR, new perspectives and formulations that allowed the orientation and better understanding of the significance of CSR from a humanism view.

Cuervo (2009) poses a relationship between two seemingly incommunicable worlds, Social Policy and Inclusive Business. The latter when addressed from a social responsibility perspective, where CSR is presented as a means for action requiring multiple changes in mentalities and governments' imagination. Then, business and civil society have potential to do an effective articulated effort of shared responsibility.

Mejía (2011) used a non-mathematical design of interpretation putting forward the purpose of discovering concepts and relationships in the raw data and later organizing them into a theoretical explanatory outline, starting with the deductive categorizing and then later showing a research of deductive analytics.

This research was developed in three different studies:

1. The study of conceptualization of social responsibility and the critical theory. It was used to create a deconstruction of the traditional vision of social responsibility and the formulation of a critical paradigm starting with the revision of literature.
2. Empirical study which was done by way of in-depth interviews with 42 different large corporations from the city of Barranquilla (Colombia) using a simple random spot check. Also, by way of confirmation and refutation of the obtained data, making a point to compare them with the results of the interviews, they did a non-participatory observation of the practices and events being completed by five of the corporations.
3. These observations were converted in a triangulation mechanism that makes up part of the technical validity of the results of the doctoral thesis and with this process tried to understand the coherency within the corporate dialogue and their practices.

The theoretical study was done on the basis of social responsibility starting with the critical theory making contrast to the theoretical construction of the organizational practices that are supporting the empirical basis.

Another work put forward by Solarte (2009) titled 'Violence and institution' supports the ethics of social responsibility. It was put forward for the title of Doctor in Philosophy of the University of Javeriana, working with the problem of social responsibility starting with the theory of social systems understood as systems that are self-regulating through the violence that is proposed by Rene Girard. In order to think philosophically of this problem, the concepts of mimesis and sacrifices from Girard were confronted with the theories of civil society and recognized by Hegel with which he arrived at the proposal of responsibility within the concrete life of the people, which allowed for the deconstruction of the pretentions of the civic ethic and utilitarianism and the usual tools for thinking of CSR.

The research finished with a critical reading and the proposal of the understanding of CSR with their stakeholders bringing up the question of responsibility towards an alternative that is only possible from the perspective of the victims. They did this under a sense of self-unconditional gratitude of the renouncing of violence as a condition to redirect the role of the corporation as a medium for the concrete life of the people and the environment.

On the other hand, patrimonial responsibility arose from the state regulation that made an emphasis on the telecommunications sector and as the result of the work done by Muñoz (2013) as a partial requirement to obtain the title of Magister of Administrative Law from the University of the Rosario (Colombia). These works look to respond to the warranties that the legal regime offered as extra-contractual responsibility in order to protect the rights of those affected by the action of the regulation, those which made an approximation of different relevant topics to frame the patrimonial responsibility of the State. By their actions or omissions, they can generate damages to people that are not obligated to tolerate it, and by their breach of the parameters or guidelines of the regulators or by way of failure in the service of the public, their ignorance comes from the legitimate trust and from application of those rules.

Starting from regulations and a selection of cases and national and international doctrines we show the tendencies in the application of the paternal responsibility of the regulating state and as such, the difficulties that arise from these situations. The liberating framework will influence the conception of control, tending towards a large margin of maneuvers at the national authorities in relation to complex activities (Muñoz 2013).

Lastly, we present a synopsis of important cases in Colombia with an emphasis on the telecommunications sector. They are about paternal responsibility outside of state contracts. Also we show some relevant cases within the context of contractual responsibility.

The first addresses the paternal responsibility of the regulating state and keeping in mind the fundamental aspects of responsibility and the regulation to respond to the following question: Can the it be omitted by the regulator if wrongful facts generate damages to the state or to a person that is not obligated to tolerate them? (Muñoz 2013).

It is about a type of documentary style research that addresses the methodology of the case and tries to establish a connection between paternal responsibility of the state that is eminently public and the predictable responsibility of the concessionary regulator that is within the framework of civil responsibility and what that brings to the argument about inherent paternal consequences to the changes within the regulator. In this sense, the regulating authorities have tried to find a way to fuse these two connections or on the contrary those consequences that are brought about by the disconnection between the two.

From the perspective of CSR as a competitive strategy, Rincón (2012), in a work done as a requirement for the Master's in Administration of Health from the University of Rosario (Colombia), researched the theory, concepts, and actions that contribute to a socially responsible style of management. In its development he took the ISO 26000 as the theoretical base practices, and from the methodological point of view, he adapted a diagnostic instrument and applied to the parts of the corporation that interested him and tried to measure current socially responsible practices.

Additionally he analysed the value chain of the company and tried to look for possible actions in order to strengthen the strategy of CSR as a function of total accumulated value. With these elements he proposed some lines of action in order to follow the model of Socially Responsible Management that is vital for the long-term continuity of a corporation. Rincón's study (2012) was about a type of qualitative study that described the effects coming from the presented circumstances about the theme of CSR within the organization 'Care for Your Health SAS'.

The objective of the study was to accomplish a specified search of the characteristics of their social contribution in order to later arrive at an analysis and a conclusion of the problem. He tried to describe, measure, and evaluate whether the social intervention brought about an aggregate value for the company to positively affect their competitive strategy. Additionally, with the objective of broadening the evaluation and identifying the relevant points in regards to start-ups, he did an internal and external situational analysis (Rincón 2012).

Medina and Vargas (2013), in a study titled 'Globalization, financial capitalism and corporate social responsibility: structural tensions', address the study of the harmful effects of financial capitalism on globalization and how these have led to changes within social equilibrium and economics, especially those that they considered particularly related to the conceptual arguments such as those that have brought to attention the corporations and businesses within the context of CSR.

However, the model was constructed around the accumulation of capital and benefits that have created a symbiotic relationship between those that act as a resource and the end of their own existence taking place within the structural tensions that cancel the alternatives of having sustainable and socially responsible practices at the same time.

In a work elaborated by way of documentary revision the authors looked over the origin and evolution of the concepts of globalization, financial capitalism, and social responsibility from secondary sources in order to analyse if those elements constituted the concepts and had a relationship between them that allowed the consideration of social responsibility as an effective part of the previously stated problems.

As a result of the research performed by Medina and Vargas (2013), they identified four structural tensions that contributed to the comprehension and the exacerbation of the stated problems in spite of the large forces that are being put out by countries, governments, and corporations. These four tensions are:

1. The duty of the state to guarantee rights to the citizens within their own territory versus the existing dependency of large economic groups and capital agents with both public and private origin whether they are national or transnational.
2. The duty of the economic system to offer equal opportunity based on jobs and profits versus a model of the creation of wealth and a wealthy portion of the population with speculation and risk.
3. Equal property rights for all citizens within democratic models versus the concentration of resources within a minority of the population.
4. The duty of the corporation within the economic model and the ethical obligation to assume CSR practices. They conclude that it is necessary to continue working on the comprehension of these phenomena in order to advance the construction and redefinition of more effect and effective practices.

Botero (2010) published a work with the clear intention of questioning in order to later understand the study 'CSR of the construction sector of Colombia' from the perspective of the actors. He tries to understand from different perspectives how the labor conditions of the workers in the construction sector are affected by differing policies within the CSR practices or their companies.

With this in mind, the fieldwork he was doing propitiated dialogic relationships between the researcher and the stakeholders. He directly addressed the actors that he found and discovered two extremes: those who assume the responsibility of performing the CSR and using the company practices to realize those goals and then those who are affected by the said responsibilities and practices.

In this order of ideas, without losing sight of the research problem, they were looking to select two different groups of participants for their interviews. These interviews would be about the announcements and CSR practices within the construction sector of Colombia and they selected their participants based on this knowledge, the two groups being the business owners and the employees and they chose to address these groups through semi-structured open interviews (Botero 2010).

CONCLUSION

The analysis from the methodological and epistemological perspectives in the field of CSR in Colombia found that the view of reality within this sector circumscribes the territory of multiple disciplines in both direct and indirect ways. In this sense, the study of these themes implies a recognition and acceptance that the explanations for these realities are built of many different interdisciplinary scenarios and that these realities converge from different perspectives of representation and explanations that are generated by the diverse focus of analysis, but that in this configuration of facts and phenomena form both social and organizational implications.

The business practices nurture the majority of empirical studies of CSR in Colombia and they implicate that the research in this field is guided by the subjectivity of each business owner. The actions of the business leader are sometimes seen as social responsibility as a way of relating with the demands of the market more than an ethical compromise that arises from their own values. This form of addressing this field of study limits the possibility of planting new alternative forms of thought in order to better the current practices of organizations in this aspect.

In the analysis of the research of CSR in Colombia they observed two perspectives. First, that of the studies that participate in a conceptualization in order to establish a relationship with the context, generally starting with historical revision and their influence from both the practical and the academic perspective. This has generated joint theories between CSR and other concepts such as sustainable development, corporate strategy, human management, marketing, and territorial development.

Secondly, it has affected research that begins with the practices of business owners. These works were oriented by the subjectivity of the business owners and each time comes as a source of direct observable information of their behavior in regards to CSR. They can make use of different instruments like polls, surveys, interviews, panel questionnaires, focus groups, observations, and the like. Qualitative data focused on ethnography and other such resources are made use of as primary data.

It results in an interesting highlight that in some works is the notion that CSR has been understood on the part of the Colombian researchers as the result of integrated action of business owners within the economic, social, and environmental contexts, and that there is a direct interdependence with the social groups and the corporation. From there we can take these elements and configure their behavior and look for answers to the expectations of different interest groups. In the same way, we assume that their behaviors are fundamental for different social groups to be able to define their own visions of justice and their ability to criticize and the actions of business owners as legitimate or illegitimate.

We do not find work that addresses the study of the concept of CSR in Colombia from the perspective of the interest groups that are the object of the actions and practices of CSR. In this way, it is not the sole subjectivity of the business owner that guides the study of these themes. In this order of ideas we are able to mark such themes for future investigation of social responsibility from the perspective of the beneficiaries of its application.

Although we observed some studies that addressed social responsibility from the critical standpoint, it is important to highlight that these works were very underdeveloped. This indicates that the process of observation is limited from these perspectives and that this implicates a lack of thought on alternatives for the models of social responsibility within the context of Colombia and Latin America. We reduced the analysis to the interpretation from theoretical perspectives that occur around the world and that are established as accepted practices. In this way we can leave behind a new research topic that allows for a view from a critical and objective stand point.

In this way, a critical analysis of the nature and moral condition of these CSR practices and the focus on the theory of CSR in Colombia, we can bring about a search of alternative theories that can give account to the many forms and processes that should be in agreement with the vision of many different actors and from a multilateral perspective rather than from the singular vision of the business owner.

We were able to observe deficiencies in the support of the theory in order to realize the reality of the Colombian perspective of such CSR practices. The large part of these models is imported and, therefore, it is necessary to advance the process of construction and deconstruction of some theoretical models that correspond with the personal dynamics of Colombian society.

These observed works allowed for the affirmation of CSR practices in Colombia that are limited to large and medium size corporations, and indicate that the thick of the business activity of the country is conformed to micro and small size business that do not have a clear or explicit vision of what CSR means and how they can achieve improvement within this field.

REFERENCES

Aktouf, O. (2001), *La administración: entre tradición y renovación*, Cali Colombia: Artes Gráficas del Valle.

Atehortúa, F. (2008), 'Responsabilidad Social Empresarial: Entre la Ética Discursica y la Racionalidad Técnica', *Revista Escuela de Administración de Negocioas*, **62**, January–April, 125–139.

Azuero, R.A., J.M. Melo and M. García (2011), 'Una Presentación de la Región Socialmente Responsable del Norte del Cauca', *Cuadernos de Administración*, **27** (45), 109–121.

Bédard, R. (2004), 'Los Fundamentos del Pensamiento y las Prácticas Administrativas: La Trilogía Administrativa', Medellín: *AD-MINISTER Universidad EAFIT*, **4**, January–June, 80–108.

Botero, L.F. (2010), *La noción de responsabilidad social empresarial y sus prácticas empresariales en la construcción en Medellín y Bogotá: Una mirada desde la condición laboral del trabajador del sector*, Tesis para optar el título de Magister en Administración, Universidad EAFIT, Medellín, Colombia.

Calderon, G., C. Álvarez and J. Naranjo (2011), 'Papel de la Gestión Humana en el cumplimiento de la Responsabilidad Social Empresarial', *Estudios Gerenciales*, **27** (118), January–March, 163–188.

Cuervo, A. (2009), *Una mirada ética y del bienestar a los negocios inclusivos*, Tesis para optar el título de Magister en Política Social, Pontificia Universidad Javeriana, Bogotá, Colombia.

D'Amato, G. (2013), 'Tendencias Académicas en el Estudio de la Responsabilidad Social Corporativa y Asuntos del Desarrollo en America Latina', *Cuadernos de Administración*, **29** (49), January–June, 86–94.

Duque, Y., M. Cardona and J. Rendón (2013), 'La Responsabilidad Social Empresarial: Teorías, indices, estándares y certificaciones', *Cuadernos de Administración*, **29** (50), July–December, 196–206.

Fisher, J. (2010), *El Hombre y la Técnica: Hacia una filosofía política de la ciencia y la tecnología*, México: Universidad Nacional Autónoma de México.

Lozano, E. (2012), *Comportamientos Socialmente Responsables en las Pymes Agrícolas del Sur Oriente del Valle del Cauca: Un Estudio de Casos*, Tesis para optar el título de Magister en Administración, Universidad Nacional de Colombia, sede Manizales, Manizales, Colombia.

Medina, L.C. and L.M.S. Vargas (2013), *Globalización, Capitalismo Financiero y Responsabilidad Social Empreasrial: Tensiones Estructurales*, Tesis para optar al título de magister en Dirección y Gerencia de Empresas, Colegio Mayor de Nuestra Señora del Rosario, Bogotá, Colombia.

Mejía, C. (2011), *Los aportes de la teoría crítica a la construcción del concepto de responsabilidad social: Contrastación en prácticas empresariales de Barranquilla*, Tesis para obtener el grado de Doctor en Administración, Universidad EAFIT, Medellín, Colombia.

Muñoz, A. (2013), *La responsabilidad patrimonial del estado reguladro (Enfasis en el sector de las telecomunicaciones*, Tesis para optar al título de magister en Derecho Administrativo, Universidad del Rosario, Bogotá, Colombia.

Muñoz, J.F. (2011), *Concepción Emergente del Rol y Comportamiento de las Organizaciones Empresariales en el Contexto de la Sostenibilidad a partir de los Principios del Desarrollo Sostenible y los Aportes Epistemológicos de Renée Bedard*, Tesis para optar el título de Magister en Desarrollo Sostenible y Medio Ambiente, Universidad de Manizales, Manizales.

Raufflet, E. (2010), 'Responsabilidad Corporativa y Desarrollo Sostenible: Una perspectiva historica y conceptual', *Cuadernos de Administración*, **26** (43), 23–32.

Rincón, L.D.C. (2012), *Identificación de la responsabilidad social corporativo como estrategia de la IPS cuidarte tu salud SAS durante el año 2012*, Tesis para optar al título de Magister en Administración en Salud, Universidad del Rosario, Bogotá, Colombia.

Rueda, G. and M. Uribe (2011), 'Aportes de la Información Contable a una Responsabilidad Empresarial Acorde con las Necesidades de la Sociedad: Una Mirada Crítica', *Cuadernos de Administración*, **24** (43), July–December, 241–260.

Saavedra, M. (2011), 'La Responsabilidad Social Empresarial y las Finanzas', *Cuadernos de Administración*, **27** (46), July–December, 39–54.

Solarte, R.M.R. (2009), *Violencia e Institución: Aportes para una ética de la responsabilidad social*, Tesis para optar al título de Doctor en Filosofía, Pontificia Universidad Javeriana, Bogotá, Colombia.

PART II

QUANTITATIVE METHODS

David Crowther and Linne Marie Lauesen

Most research focuses upon a single methodology for its investigative process and these fall into the two categories of quantitative research or qualitative research. In this section we focus upon quantitative methodologies. Naturally we have chapters considering the most prevalent forms of quantitative research and analysis but we have deliberately chosen to also include chapters on more unusual forms of analysis which have been used by some of the contributors. In doing so we believe that we are opening up more and different options to our readers in the belief that this will help make CSR research stronger by the use of a greater number of methodologies. Again we make no comments about which methods are the best – all work well within appropriate contexts and it is for the reader, as individual researcher, to consider the options available and to make an informed choice.

We start this section, therefore, with one of the less common forms of analysis and in the first chapter Shahla Seifi takes us into the field of game theory. Game theory provides a method of formulating a business situation in terms of strategies – the strategy of the decision maker and the strategy of his/her opponent – and in terms of outcomes. Each player in the game selects and executes those strategies which he/she believes will result in 'winning the game', that is will result in the most favourable outcome to the problem situation. In determining this strategy for winning each player makes use of both deductive and inductive logic and attempts quantification of the outcomes, Shahla Seifi explains. She defines and distinguishes between when there is only one decision maker (decision theory) having the main purpose to maximise utility before making a decision and when a factory or company affects the external environment by its decision, such as when a firm is considering the launch of a new product, increasing its prices, or commencing a marketing campaign. Then, Shahla Seifi explains, it demands much more than decision theory since a firm is not separated from its rivals and the external atmosphere. So more than decision theory is necessary to deal with factory decision making. Here is actually where game theory matters.

In the next chapter Rima Kalinauskaitė introduces us to longitudinal research, when phenomena under investigation in any organisation are inherent in changes at individual and organisational levels. Longitudinal research design is typically used to draw up changes during a defined period. This is especially useful when gathering information on the knowledge, skills, opinions, attitudes and behaviours of individuals that develop across the lifespan or change due to environmental factors in an organisation. Longitudinal surveys can be conducted in prospective and retrospective ways, and could be either quantitative or qualitative depending on the kind of method used to collect data with the same respondents twice or more. The importance of longitudinal study is in understanding organisations as a way of providing data on the mechanisms and processes through which changes are created. Issues related to CSR can be measured as 'in' (examining the behaviour of individuals inside an organisation) and 'on' (examining how an organisation is seen from outside) levels. This chapter outlines the definition and distinctive features of longitudinal study: intervals and periodicity between waves; advantages and challenges in designing longitudinal studies; and methodological aspects of cohort studies in organisations.

The following contribution from Habib Zaman Khan and Md. Rashidozzaman Khan continues with describing sampling methods and sampling procedures in the field of CSR research. Their chapter starts with an overview of sampling and population, necessity of sampling in particular for the survey based quantitative research method, and the sampling frame. Hereafter, the chapter outlines types of sampling, advantages and disadvantages of different sampling techniques, and discusses sampling errors, sampling units, how to determine sample size, together with discussion of errors in sampling (e.g., random sampling and non-sampling errors) in survey based research design. Discussions of appropriate sample design together with recent trends of sampling techniques (internet and web based sampling), and some challenges of internet sampling are also mentioned. The chapter ends by suggesting that a thorough understanding of sampling procedures is a key aspect of studies in both business and the field of CSR research. Several suggestions are made for future CSR researchers when considering sampling both for quantitative and qualitative research design. This chapter is a valuable reference for researchers and students in particular who are interested in understanding sampling and sampling procedures in their future CSR research.

The next contribution also considers one of the less usual methodologies which the author has used extensively. In this chapter Hillary J. Shaw takes us further into the field of food deserts as a special issue of CSR. His chapter critically examines the socio-economic factors affecting diet, health and obesity in two major British cities. Diet is not merely a private issue but has significant health and financial implications due to the rapidly rising medical costs of obesity, in the UK and elsewhere. A co-ordinated approach, involving government, corporations, SMEs and the local community, is fundamental to tackling the health issues raised by 'food deserts'. Social responsibility, not the exclusive pursuit of private profit alone, is crucial. Multiple food access related factors are explored in relation to how they affect quality of diet and therefore increase or decrease a person's chance of being obese. Hillary J. Shaw uses a quantitative approach involving partial correlations using data from neighbourhood statistics to explicate the effect of social, spatial, demographic and economic factors on nutrition. Ethnicity is significant to diet, both through cultural and economic mediation of consumption and through the provision of ethnic-minority oriented grocery shops in certain areas. His comparison of obesity levels in Leicester and Stoke on Trent suggests that Stoke on Trent offers easier access to lower-priced food than does Leicester, due to its polycentric urban structure, which gives better access to local shops and markets for its less affluent citizens.

Thereafter, Christopher Boachie and George K. Amoako continue by explaining how statistical methods represents that body of methods by which characteristics of a population are inferred through observations made in a representative sample from that population. Since scientists rarely observe entire populations, sampling and statistical inference are essential. The chapter examines specifically the role of statistical methods in CSR research. Statistical methods are designed to detect and measure relationships and effects in situations where results cannot be identically replicated because of natural variability in the measurements of interest. They are generally used as an intermediate step between anecdotal evidence and the determination of causal explanations. Statistical methods play a major role in making appropriate conclusions from those studies. Statistical methods most often play an important role in the discovery phase. These methods are an intermediate step between the anecdotal evidence or theoretical speculations that lead to discovery research, and the justification phase of the research process in which elaborated theories and comprehensive understanding are established. This chapter seeks to review the current status of statistical methods and their influences on financial CSR research. The study used secondary data on statistical research methods and a survey of published articles on CSR.

The final chapter in this section is contributed by Sonali Bhattacharya, Madhvi Sethi, Abhishek Behl and V.G. Venkatesh who round off the path of quantitative methodologies in explaining regression analysis. Regression analysis is one of the most frequently used tools in market research. In its simplest form, regression analysis allows researchers to analyse relationships between one or more independent and one dependent variable. In CSR applications, the dependent variable is usually the outcome we care about (e.g., beneficiaries), while the independent variables are the instruments one has to achieve those outcomes with (e.g., economic and legal responsibility). Knowing about the relative strength of effects is useful for companies as it may help answer questions on certain observed factors such as societal or environmental factors. Most importantly, regression analysis will help to compare the effects of variables measured on different scales. Regression analysis can also help make predictions which are precise and can be used to study the dynamics of a company in future. A CSR team can thus plan strategies and allocate funds for proper and effective output. Similarly, different CSR research works used regression analysis for the various objectives. In the current CSR research domain, it is important to understand the fundamentals of regression analysis and various techniques along with their applications. The chapter also discusses various advanced techniques and their applications in the CSR domain. It would lead the researchers to diligently choose those relevant variant techniques in the research.

7. Game theory as a research tool for sustainability
Shahla Seifi

INTRODUCTION

Even now, when hearing the name of 'Game theory', the first thing which may occur to one's mind might be a card game, and this is not unreasonable. In fact, Game theory was originally devised to raise the chance of winning in card games. Card players were presumably clever mathematicians. Today, Game theory is considered as a branch of applied mathematics. Game theory did not really exist as a unique field until John von Neumann published a paper in 1928 which 'attempts to mathematically capture behaviour in strategic situations, or games, in which an individual's success in making choices depends on the choices of others' (Myerson 1991, p.1). In any decision-making process, there is always a factor of risk associated which needs to be treated appropriately to optimize the expected result. Researchers throughout the years have sought for the ways to gain such an optimization. Mathematical methods like Bayes theorem and risk analysis are all utilized to evaluate and optimize results. But when the problem is of a strategic nature then it is Game theory which always leads the way.

The purpose of Game theory is to enable someone to set out the various options and to analyse the outcomes. In doing so it does not quantify the solutions of the various options so much as to assign probabilities to them and therefore enables the researcher to identify options and their likelihood of success. It is for this reason that it has been adopted by political and military strategists as a tool to assist their decision-making. It has also been adopted by businesses as a strategic tool to assist in analysing not just their decisions but the possible reactions of competitors and this is one of its benefits – to take into account that business decisions are not made in a static environment[1] but are in a dynamic environment. In this chapter, I show that the theory is not just a tool for strategists but also can be used to assist researchers.

Although such techniques as risk analysis can be useful tools for making operational and strategic decisions, when it comes to making strategic decisions the most useful tool is Game theory. This is particularly helpful when deciding about production and marketing decisions because, just as in making many management decisions, it is important to recognize that the decision is not made in isolation and that the effects of the decision cannot be realistically quantified as if that decision is made in isolation. This is particularly true when the external environment is affected by the decision, such as when a firm is considering the launch of a new product, a change to its prices, or the conduct of an advertising campaign. In such circumstances it is not sufficient to consider how the decision might affect the firm itself or how it might be received by its customers. It is also necessary to recognize that the firm's competitors will be affected by the decision and may very well decide to respond to the actions of the firm. In such a situation the firm and its decision makers can be regarded as either in competition with another firm and its decision makers or in conflict, and the generic term to describe this kind of situation is that of a game and Game theory can help to model this kind of situation (Crowther 2004) and therefore improve the decisions which are made.

In games the participants are competitors and the success of one is usually at the expense of the other, such as when one firm gains a market share through the use of an advertising campaign at the expense of the other firms in the industry. For the purposes of Game theory in such a situation the number of players can very often be simplified to two players – the firm and the competition, with all competitors being regarded as a single player. It is possible to model the actions and reactions of all competitors separately through Game theory but this makes the mathematics very complicated, often without significantly changing the analysis. In this chapter therefore we shall consider the theory in the context of just two players.

Game theory provides a method of formulating a business situation in terms of strategies – the strategy of the decision maker and the strategy of his/her opponent – and in terms of outcomes. Each player in the game selects and executes those strategies which (s)he believes will result in 'winning the game', that is, will result in the most favourable outcome to the problem situation. In determining this strategy for winning each player makes use of both deductive and inductive logic and attempts quantification of the outcomes.

The simplest situation when dealing with a problem is when there is only one decision maker. This is usually called decision theory. The main purpose here is to maximize utility before making a decision. Decision theory can be viewed as a theory of one person games, or a game of a single player against nature (Levine 1998). However, when the case refers to a factory or a company, it is by no means a discrete entity which can be treated as a black box. This is particularly true when the external environment is affected by the decision, such as when a firm is considering the launch of a new product, or increasing its prices, or commencing a marketing campaign (Crowther 1996). So it demands much more than a decision theory since a firm is not separated from its rivals and the external atmosphere. So more than a decision theory is necessary to deal with factory decision-making. Here is where Game theory actually matters.

HISTORY AND IMPACT OF GAME THEORY

The earliest example of a formal Game-theoretic analysis is the study of a duopoly by Antoine Cournot in 1838. The mathematician Emile Borel suggested a formal theory of games in 1921, which was furthered by the mathematician John von Neumann in 1928 in a 'theory of parlor games'. Game theory was established as a field in its own right after the 1944 publication of the definitive book, *Theory of Games and Economic Behavior* by von Neumann and the economist Oskar Morgenstern. This book provided much of the basic terminology and problem setup that is still in use today.

In 1950, John Nash[2] (Nash 1950) demonstrated that finite games always have an equilibrium point, at which all players choose actions which are best for them given their opponents' choices. This central concept of non-cooperative Game theory has been a focal point of analysis since then. In the 1950s and 1960s, Game theory was broadened theoretically and applied to problems of war and politics. Since the 1970s, it has driven a revolution in economic theory. Additionally, it has found applications in sociology and psychology, and established links with evolution and biology. Game theory received special attention in 1994 with the awarding of the Nobel prize in Economics to Nash, John Harsanyi, and Reinhard Selten.

At the end of the 1990s, a high-profile application of Game theory was in the design of auctions. Prominent Game theorists have been involved in the design of auctions for allocating rights to the use of bands of the electromagnetic spectrum to the mobile telecommunications industry, for example. Most of these auctions were designed with the goal of allocating these resources more efficiently than traditional governmental practices, and additionally raised billions of dollars in the western world – the United States and Europe.

RISK FACTORS

In any decision-making process, there is always a factor of risk associated which needs to be treated appropriately to optimize the expected result. In the case of energy utilization in domestic appliances for instance there are different decision makers and their choices are of vital importance for the welfare of the environment on the whole. One decision maker is the manufacturer who wishes to maximize its profit. In a globalized economy, the manufacturer is facing up to a quite strong pressure through a global market and international standards. The other main decision maker is the customer who desires to acquire a cost-effective appliance. In the modern world an informed customer has more than a basic need of lower immediate cost as s/he is aware of long term costs due to rational choices. The government on the whole has several concerns. One is to protect the resources so less energy consumption is desired, also the government wishes to keep the wheels of industry running, so energy labelling should bear a reasonable cost to the manufacturer. Also the government has an external prestige that should be promoted by protecting the environment and respecting the international concerns.

There are different parties involved in the decision-making process for sustainable production, sustainable consumption and sustainable governance. In order to understand this, it is necessary to first start with a review of the background of decision-making processes before deciding what to choose for this special case.

The other way to deal with decisions is through a strategy using Game theory. Dietz and Zhao (2011) describe Game theory as one of the most powerful tools for making sense of common problems like climate change. Although originally devised to raise the chance of winning in card games, Game theory, as a branch of applied mathematics, attempts to mathematically capture behaviour in strategic situations, or games, in which an individual's success in making choices depends on the choices of others (Myerson 1991). Turocy and Stengel (2001) define Game theory as 'the formal study of decision-making where several players must make choices that potentially affect the interests of the other players' (p. 2).

There are several types of game incorporated in the theory, such as symmetric and asymmetric, zero-sum and non-zero-sum, simultaneous and sequential, perfect information and non-perfect information, infinitely long game, discrete and continuous, one-player and many-player, and meta-games. Some authors have categorized different sorts of game as other theories. For example, Levine (1998) describes mechanism design theory as differing from Game theory in that Game theory takes the rules of the game as given, while mechanism design theory asks about the consequences of different types of rules. However, there are several ways to present the game, for instance, extensive, normal, characteristic function, and partition function. Game theory as a branch of applied mathematics has so far been used in different fields such as politics, biology, physics, economics and business, computer science, and philosophy. Now it is appropriate to explain the above mentioned terms.

CLASSIFYING GAMES

There are several types of game included within Game theory, such as symmetric and asymmetric, zero-sum and non-zero-sum, simultaneous and sequential, perfect information and non-perfect information, infinitely long game, discrete and continuous, one-player, and many-player. These definitions are important for the development of the model and so it is worth spending time explaining them.

Symmetric versus Asymmetric Games

Symmetry means that (Turocy and Stengel 2001) the game stays the same when the players exchange positions. Probably the most famous model for such a situation is known as the Prisoner's Dilemma, in which dividing the matrix by the diagonal will lead to two equal halves with the same payoffs. So the halves are symmetrical (see Figure 7.1).

An asymmetric game as a single strategy is not dependent upon other strategies or theories. The most commonly studied asymmetric games are games where there are not identical outcomes for the two parties, which is a general reflection of strategic decision-making and therefore attracts the most interest, such as in Figure 7.2.

	E	F
E	1, 2	0, 0
F	0, 0	1, 2

Figure 7.1   An example of a symmetric game

	G	H
G	3, 2	0, 1
H	0, 0	1, 2

Figure 7.2   An example of an asymmetric game

Zero-Sum versus Non-Zero-Sum Games

Consider sharing a pizza for two people. When one person takes more slices the other person will always have only what remains, which is less although the whole is only the same one pizza. This is a zero-sum game. A game is said to be zero-sum (Turocy and Stengel 2001) if, for any outcome, the sum of the payoffs to all players is zero. The *Merriam-Webster Dictionary*[3] defines a zero-sum game as a kind of game in which one player's gain corresponds to the other player's loss. It can be concluded that the players' interests are diametrically opposed. Whenever the total value can be changed to an increasing amount then whatever one has is a non-zero-sum game. And it is important to note that a majority of theoreticians, like Wright (2001), consider that societies are becoming increasingly non-zero-sum by becoming more complex, specialized, and interdependent. There is, however, an innate assumption that in a non-zero-sum game then the decisions made by the players can increase the total size of the payoffs as well as distributing them differently.

In an interview in December 2000, Bill Clinton[4] noted that:

> The more complex societies get and the more complex the networks of interdependence within and beyond community and national borders get, the more people are forced in their own interests to find non-zero-sum solutions. That is, win-win solutions instead of win-lose solutions Because we find as our interdependence increases that, on the whole, we do better when other people do better as well – so we have to find ways that we can all win, we have to accommodate each other.

Simultaneous versus Sequential Games

Simultaneous game implies either a game in which participants move simultaneously or when they do not move simultaneously with the condition that they are not aware of the earlier players' choice when choosing their own strategy. An example of a simultaneous game is the Prisoner's Dilemma. Hughes (2011) defines a sequential game as one in which the players take alternate turns to take their actions. An example of a sequential game is chess. The players know each other's movements sequentially so they can decide on their own using such information. It can be claimed that a simultaneous game is a fair one in that none of the players have any advantage, but in the sequential, the second player has an advantage over the other one.

Perfect versus Non-Perfect Games

Turocy and Stengel (2001) believe that when at any point in time only one player makes a move so that s/he knows the actions previously taken by all other players, the game is said to have perfect information. As the *Dictionary of Game Theory Terms*[5] denotes, a sequential game is a game of imperfect information if a player is uncertain about the exact actions taken by other players up to that point. Chess is a good example of a perfect game whereas the Prisoner's Dilemma can be denoted as an imperfect one.

There is a similar but different definition worthy of mention here. This is complete information. In complete information, the player is aware of the strategies and payoffs of the other players but not necessarily his/her actions. Another term used commonly

116 *Handbook of research methods in corporate social responsibility*

in games is infinitely long game. Actually an infinitely long game is usually followed by pure mathematicians rather than other experts who deal with real problems.[6] The former tend to develop a game for infinitely long actions, with the winner decided after all those actions are completed. So it can be gathered that an infinitely long game is a kind of game with an indefinite time horizon, in other words a game in which players act as though there will always be a tomorrow (Eatwell et al. 1987).[7]

Discrete versus Continuous Games

By a discrete game it is meant that the plays, number of players, outcomes, and so on are finite. Therefore, it can be claimed that most games are of discrete nature. In a discrete game the player chooses from a finite set of pure strategies (Wikipedia[8]). As an extension of the discrete game, a continuous game is one which includes more general sets of pure strategies which may be uncountably infinite (Wikipedia[9]).

One-Player versus Many-Player Games

As defined before, when the player is only one person then this is called a case of decision theory instead of Game theory. Anytime the number of players exceeds one, then the stage of Game theory starts. In fact, the object of studying in Game theory is the game, which is a formal model of an interactive situation (Turocy and Stengel 2001). When a game consists of an arbitrary, but finite, number of players then it is called an n-person game (Luce and Raiffa 1957).

IMPORTANCE OF GAME THEORY FOR CORPORATE SOCIAL RESPONSIBILITY

After this introduction to the definitions of games, it is important to work out why Game theory is important for research into corporate social responsibility. In order to do so I will take an example of dealing with the consumption of resources in the form of raw materials. In other words, I attempt here to make use of Game theory to define a roadmap to preserve the earth and to motivate countries and businesses to take responsible actions. One significant aspect of raw material consumption is concerned with the consumption of energy. Earlier in this discussion, the diverse and sometimes opposing tendencies of three major stakeholders, namely consumers or customers, manufacturers or suppliers, and the governments were summarized. It was pointed out that there are likes and dislikes about following energy plans for each stakeholder. The objective to implement a Game theory is to make the major stakeholders in different countries have a balanced participation to develop sustainability strategies and participate in programmes to lower their energy consumption and act responsibly towards energy conservation and therefore towards combating global warming for their own self-preservation, without depending on other countries to take the lead.

> Getting self-interested and often distrustful nations to co-operate is a major obstacle to addressing the climate problem. So far, international agreements have not had much impact on the

trajectory of emissions or the concentration of greenhouse gases in the atmosphere. (Dietz and Zhao 2011, p. 15671)

Taking the case of the atmosphere, and applying Game theory, it can clearly be seen that if one nation bears the costs of reducing greenhouse gas (GHG) emissions[10] but other nations do not act, the reductions in risk from climate change will not be very substantial, as no single nation can have much effect.

> Additionally, if other nations do not co-operate, my nation will have borne all of the costs of emissions reductions but will not see less risk from climate change. Conversely, if other nations reduce emissions but my nation does not, we receive the benefits of reduced risk without the costs of emissions reductions. The result could be the classic tragedy of the commons in which each nation has incentive to free ride and undertake little or no reduction in emission, and thus, all nations bear substantial risks as the climate warms . . . If we assume that each nation will act rationally in its own self-interest, then the path to reducing climate change risk is to design a set of rules for emissions that countries will agree to because they find the rules beneficial, explain Dietz and Zhao 2011 (p. 15671).

A major international step in the direction of reducing GHG emissions was the Kyoto Protocol.[11] The Kyoto Protocol prescribes three mechanisms that enable developed countries with quantified emission limitation and reduction commitments to acquire GHG reduction credits. These mechanisms are the Clean Development Mechanism (CDM), Joint Implementation (JI), and International Emission Trading (IET). Under CDM, a developed country can take up a GHG reduction project activity in a developing country where the cost of GHG reduction project activities is usually much lower. The developed country would be given credits for meeting its emission reduction targets, while the developing country would receive the capital and clean technology to implement the project.

In JI, a developed country with a relatively high cost of domestic GHG reduction would set up a project in another developed country that has a relatively low cost, such that the CO_2 emission of the project is counted within a country that has a surplus. Under IET, countries can trade in international carbon markets. Countries with a shortage in carbon credits can buy from countries with surplus credits. The process of buying and selling of carbon credits is known as 'carbon trading'.[12] Trading of carbon credits occurs through Certified Emission Reductions (CERs). A CER is a certificate issued by the authorized body (CDM Executive body) to the approved projects that have reduced GHG emissions in a calendar year.

While punishments for not meeting GHG emissions targets are important, the scientists point to how such punishments can prove costly. Dietz and Zhao (2011, p. 15672) note:

> First, nations may choose not to participate if they feel that they will be punished. The substantial uncertainty about some aspects of climate change may make nations leery of committing to binding targets for emissions and punishments for missing those targets. Therefore, punishments, although essential for generating compliance, can also lead to pressure to not participate or change an agreement and thus, obviate its benefits.

118 *Handbook of research methods in corporate social responsibility*

Linear Compensation Proposition

A development of the standard model is the linear compensation proposition, or LinC as Dietz and Zhao term it, which is a mechanism or type of social psychology model for helping to coerce countries to act on climate change, rather than solely punishing them. According to Pfeiffer and Velthuis (2005), linear compensation would mean that punishments for not meeting climate change targets could be 'adjusted' when compared to how other nations are meeting their sustainability goals.

According to Dietz and Zhao (2011, p. 15672),

> Under LinC, if a nation does not meet its reduction target, it does indeed face a punishment – a penalty in the form of an increased target for next year. However, unlike the Kyoto Protocol where the punishment is a fixed multiplier of 1.3 times the shortfall, the LinC punishment is adjusted relative to the performance of other nations. If most other nations also failed to meet their targets (that is, if the average of underperformance is substantially greater than zero), the punishment for each nation is less. In fact, it is proportional to how much below average performance a nation falls. Nations are punished most for being far from the norm of how other nations performed rather than being judged on an absolute basis.

They add (p. 15672):

> Therefore, LinC is an effective way of dealing with our uncertainty about how difficult it will be to reduce emissions. Furthermore, it is well-established in social psychology that descriptive norms – information about how one is doing relative to others in one's peer group – are an exceptionally powerful influence on behaviour.

'A key feature of linear compensation is that if a nation fails to meet its treaty obligations, other nations punish it by reducing their own abatement', said Zhao in *Science Daily*.[13] 'So each nation has leverage: its own abatement helps make other nations abate more. This is the beauty of the linear compensation mechanism.'

The Dominance Strategy

A dominant strategy (commonly called simply dominance) occurs when one strategy is better than another strategy for one player, no matter how that player's opponents may play. Many simple games can be solved using dominance.[14] When a player tries to choose the 'best' strategy among a multitude of options, that player may compare two strategies A and B to see which one is better.

If a strictly dominant strategy exists for one player in a game, that player will play that strategy in each of the game's Nash equilibria but if both players have a strictly dominant strategy, the game has only one unique Nash equilibrium. However, that equilibrium is not necessarily Pareto optimal[15] as there may be non-equilibrium outcomes of the game that would be better for both players. The classic game used to illustrate this is the Prisoner's Dilemma. Strictly dominated strategies cannot be a part of a Nash equilibrium, and as such, it is irrational for any player to play them. On the other hand, weakly dominated strategies may be part of Nash equilibria.

Since all players are assumed to be rational, they make choices which result in the outcome they prefer most, no matter what their opponents do. In the extreme case, a player may have two strategies A and B so that, given any combination of strategies of the other

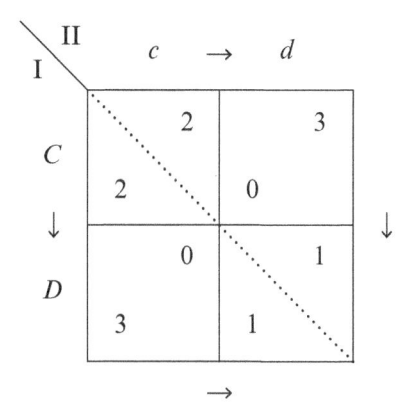

Figure 7.3 The Prisoner's Dilemma game

players, the outcome resulting from A is better than the outcome resulting from B. Then strategy A is said to dominate strategy B. A rational player will never choose to play a dominated strategy. In some games, examination of which strategies are dominated results in the conclusion that rational players could only ever choose one of their strategies for all rounds.

The most common game used to illustrate this point is known as the Prisoner's Dilemma. The Prisoner's Dilemma is a game in strategic form between two players. Each player has two strategies, called 'cooperate' and 'defect', which are labelled C and D for player I and c and d for player II, respectively. (For simpler identification, upper case letters are used for strategies of player I and lower case letters for player II.)

Figure 7.3 shows the resulting payoffs in this game. Player I chooses a row, either C or D, and simultaneously player II chooses one of the columns c or d. The strategy combination (C, c) has payoff 2 for each player, and the combination (D, d) gives each player payoff 1. The combination (C, d) results in payoff 0 for player I and 3 for player II, and when (D, c) is played, player I gets 3 and player II gets 0.

Any two-player game in strategic form can be described by a table like the one in Figure 7.3, with rows representing the strategies of player I and columns those of player II. (A player may have more than two strategies.) Each strategy combination defines a payoff pair, like (3, 0) for (D, c), which is given in the respective table entry. Each cell of the table shows the payoff to player I at the (lower) left, and the payoff to player II at the (right) top. These staggered payoffs, according to Thomas Schelling (1960), also make transparent when, as here, the game is symmetric between the two players. Symmetry means that the game stays the same when the players are exchanged, corresponding to a reflection along the diagonal in Figure 7.4. Note that in the strategic form, there is no order between player I and II since they act simultaneously (that is, without knowing the other's action), which makes the symmetry possible.

In the Prisoner's Dilemma game, 'defect' is a strategy that dominates 'cooperate'. Strategy D of player I dominates C since if player II chooses c, then player I's payoff is 3 when choosing D and 2 when choosing C; if player II chooses d, then player I receives 1 for D as opposed to 0 for C. Hence, D is indeed always better and dominates C. In the same way, strategy d dominates c for player II.

	c	d
C	1, 2	0, 0
D	0, 0	1, 2

Figure 7.4 The symmetrical game

No rational player will choose a dominated strategy since the player will always be better off when changing to the strategy that dominates it. The unique outcome in this game, as recommended to utility-maximizing players, is therefore (D, d) with payoffs (1, 1). Somewhat paradoxically, this is less than the payoff (2, 2) that would be achieved when the players chose (C, c).

The story behind the name 'Prisoner's Dilemma' is that of two prisoners held suspected of a serious crime. There is no judicial evidence for this crime except if one of the prisoners testifies against the other. If one of them testifies, he will be rewarded with immunity from prosecution (payoff 3), whereas the other will serve a long prison sentence (payoff 0). If both testify, their punishment will be less severe (payoff 1 for each). However, if they both 'cooperate' with each other by not testifying at all, they will only be imprisoned briefly, for example for illegal weapons possession (payoff 2 for each). The 'defection' from that mutually beneficial outcome is to testify, which gives a higher payoff no matter what the other prisoner does, with a resulting lower payoff to both. This constitutes their 'dilemma'.

The Prisoner's Dilemma game arises in various contexts where individual 'defections' at the expense of others lead to overall less desirable outcomes. Examples include arms races, litigation instead of settlement, environmental pollution, or cut-price marketing, where the resulting outcome is detrimental for the players. Its Game-theoretic justification on individual grounds is sometimes taken as a case for treaties and laws, which enforce cooperation.

Game theorists have tried to tackle the obvious 'inefficiency' of the outcome of the Prisoner's Dilemma game. For example, the game is fundamentally changed by playing it more than once. In such a repeated game, patterns of cooperation can be established as rational behaviour when players' fear of punishment in the future outweighs their gain from defecting today. Economists have never, however, treated it as an infinite game, as the analysis is considerably different.

Quality Choice

The principle of elimination of dominated strategies may be applied iteratively as a development of the game. Suppose player I is an internet service provider and player II a potential customer. They consider entering into a contract of service provision for a period of time. The provider can, for himself, decide between two levels of quality of service, High or Low. High-quality service is more costly to provide, and some of the cost is independent of whether the contract is signed or not. The level of service cannot be put verifiably into the contract. High-quality service is more valuable than low-quality service

	Buy	Don't buy
High	2, 2	0, 1
Low	3, 0	1, 1

Figure 7.5 High-low quality game

to the customer, in fact so much so that the customer would prefer not to buy the service if (s)he knew that the quality was low. His/her choices are to buy or not to buy the service.

Figure 7.5 gives possible payoffs that describe this situation. The customer prefers to buy if player I provides high-quality service, and not to buy otherwise. Regardless of whether the customer chooses to buy or not, the provider always prefers to provide the low-quality service. Therefore, the strategy Low dominates the strategy High for player I.

Now, since player II believes player I is rational, (s)he realizes that player I always prefers Low, and so (s)he anticipates low-quality service as the provider's choice. Then (s)he prefers not to buy (giving him/her a payoff of 1) to buy (payoff 0). Therefore, the rationality of both players leads to the conclusion that the provider will implement low-quality service and, as a result, the contract will not be signed.

This game is very similar to the Prisoner's Dilemma in Figure 7.3. In actual fact, it differs only by a single payoff, namely payoff 1 (rather than 3) to player II in the top right cell in the table. This reverses the top arrow from right to left, and makes the preference of player II dependent on the action of player I. (The game is also no longer symmetrical.) Player II does not have a dominating strategy. However, player I still does, so that the resulting outcome, seen in Figure 7.5, is still unique. Another way of obtaining this outcome is the successive elimination of dominated strategies: first, High is eliminated, and in the resulting smaller game where player I has only the single strategy Low available, player II's strategy buy is dominated and also removed.

As in the Prisoner's Dilemma, the individually rational outcome is worse for both players than another outcome, namely the strategy combination (High, buy) where high-quality service is provided and the customer signs the contract. However, that outcome is not credible, since the provider would be tempted to renege and provide only the low-quality service.

The Nash Equilibrium

In the previous examples, consideration of dominating strategies alone yielded precise advice to the players on how to play the game. In many games, however, there are no dominated strategies, and so these considerations are not enough to rule out any outcomes or to provide more specific advice on how to play the game.

The central concept of Nash equilibrium is much more general. A Nash equilibrium recommends a strategy to each player that the player cannot improve upon unilaterally, that is, given that the other players follow the recommendation. Since the other players are also rational, it is reasonable for each player to expect his opponents to follow the recommendation as well. This therefore provides a basis for the assumptions underpinning all games, namely the rationality of decision-making. This is important to consider in the developments made later in the thesis.

CRITIQUING GAME THEORY

Game theory was originally developed as an application to assist governments – and especially their military aspects – in strategic decision-making, and proved very effective in this purpose. It was subsequently adopted by businesses to aid their strategic decision-making by taking into account the possible responses of their competitors. It has proved equally effective as an application in the business arena. It has also been applied in various other arenas such as social anthropology where outcomes are not clear-cut and straightforward. Considering all the facts mentioned above therefore it is possible to see how to implement such a novel mathematics tool to investigate a recent matter of international concern, such as sustainable materials consumption.

Although risk analysis can be a useful tool, when it comes to making strategic decisions it is generally accepted that the most useful tool is Game theory. This is particularly helpful when deciding about materials consumption because just as in making many engineering and management decisions it is important to recognize that the decision is not made in isolation and that the effects of the decision cannot be realistically quantified as if that decision is made in isolation. This is particularly true when the external environment is affected by the decision. In such circumstances it is not sufficient to consider how the decision might affect the firm itself or how it might be received by its customers. It is also necessary to recognize that the firm's competitors will be affected by the decision and may very well decide to respond to the actions of the firm. In such a situation the firm and its decision makers can be regarded as either in competition with another firm and its decision makers or in conflict, and the generic term to describe this kind of situation is that of a game and Game theory can help to model this kind of situation (Crowther 2004) and therefore improve the decisions which are made.

Nevertheless, despite its suitability, it must be recognized that there are some limitations which affect its utility and mean that some developments are necessary to increase its usefulness. Some time has been spent in explaining that there are several types of Game theory such as symmetric and asymmetric, zero-sum and non-zero-sum, simultaneous and sequential, perfect information and non-perfect information, infinitely long game, discrete and continuous, one-player, and many-player. Although these are all relevant, the logic of the argument in this thesis is that there are only two possible strategies – competition and collaboration – and in a simple game the best result is always obtained by competition. But when there is a continuous series of games the best result is always obtained by adopting the strategy used last by the other side. This only works for a zero-sum game.

If the game is not zero-sum then the best result for everyone is obtained by collaboration rather than by competition.[16] But it is always possible for one person to make a short term gain by competition. This, however, is the limit of Game theory: either it is a zero-sum game or it is an open game where the total rewards can be increased. It is argued in this thesis that this is flawed because it does not represent the modern condition of the world. At present the environmental situation means that the available resources are shrinking because of the depletion of many natural resources. Thus the resources of the planet are shrinking as they become used and there are no more available for future economic development.[17] So it is necessary to extract the best use from shrinking resources – this is the essence of sustainability. The game is not zero-sum or increasing – so new mathematics is required. For the new game which reflects the modern world and the availability of resources then there is a non-zero-sum game where the total resources are actually shrinking. This is an extension of the game and requires a new strategy for playing in this environment. From this it is possible to prove that the only way to get the best outcome in this new environment is through collaboration. So sustainability (and of course sustainable development) requires collaboration – competition no longer works.

CONCLUSION

As has been shown, Game theory is useful for modelling situations and dynamic environments. This is why it has proved so useful as a business decision tool. For a researcher its utility is also in the modelling of situations. In doing so it enables the researcher to understand a situation and the actions taken by the players. It is thus a different form of analysis which provides explanations rather than conclusions. As such it is a powerful research tool which is different from the others which are normally used.

NOTES

1. Such as in a chess game – my move, your move, etc.
2. John Nash won the Nobel prize for his work and is known from the film *A Beautiful Mind*. Actually it is interesting to note that von Neumann really created Game theory but did so before the Nobel prize in economics was established, but since then more Nobel prizes have been awarded for contributions to Game theory than to any other branch of economics.
3. www.merriam-webster.com, accessed 21 June 2016.
4. https://placesjournal.org/article/non-zero-sum/, accessed 4 June 2016.
5. gametheory.net, accessed 3 June 2016.
6. Economists almost always assume that the game has a finite number of iterations, presumably because this makes the analysis easier even if it is less of a reflection of the real world. This is one of the problems with economic analysis.
7. This of course reflects business behaviour as business decisions are always (almost) made based upon the going concern principle.
8. https://en.wikipedia.org/wiki/Strategy_%28game_theory%29, accessed 4 June 2016.
9. Op cit.
10. Greenhouse gases are gases that trap heat in the Earth's atmosphere. The main greenhouse gases defined within the context of the Kyoto Protocol include: carbon dioxide (CO_2), methane (CH_4), nitrous oxide (N_2O), and industrial gases such as hydrofluorocarbons (HFCs), perfluorocarbons (PFCs) and sulphur hexafluoride (SF_6). Though GHG covers six gases, CO_2 is a major component accounting for around 55 per cent of it, which explains why GHG accounting is mostly referred to as carbon accounting.
11. The United Nations Framework Convention on Climate Change (UNFCCC) was first agreed in 1992 by most developed countries and was designed to impose limits on GHG emissions and thus minimize the adverse effects of climate change. The third session of the Conference of the parties to the UNFCCC took place in Kyoto, Japan in December 1997, resulting in the Kyoto Protocol. The Kyoto agreement became legally binding on 16 February 2005 when 132 signatory countries agreed to strive to decrease CO_2 emissions accounting for an estimated 55 per cent of global GHG emissions. The Kyoto Protocol proposed division of the total participating countries into two groups namely Annex I (developed) countries and non-Annex I (developing) countries as a measure for global climate protection. Since developed countries are discharging a very high proportion of GHGs, this working agreement of the signatories commits

developed countries to reduce their collective emissions of six GHGs by at least 5.2 per cent of 1990 levels by the end of 2012. This can be done with huge cost affecting their growth rate or the same is possible at a low cost if routed through developing countries as the ultimate object is to stabilize GHG emissions globally. The developing countries did not need to reduce their GHG emissions for that time. Since the lapse of the protocol, however, negotiations have run into difficulties as three major countries – USA, China and India – and three major polluters have indicated that they will not agree to anything limiting their production of CO_2. Obviously they have not used Game theory to understand the problem!

12. What is traded in 'carbon trading' is not actual carbon, but the right to emit CO_2. The basic unit is one metric ton of CO_2 per year. Other greenhouse gases are traded as carbon equivalents.
13. https://www.sciencedaily.com/releases/2011/09/110912152858.htm, accessed 21 June 2016.
14. The opposite is known as intrasensitivity and occurs in games where one strategy may be better or worse than another strategy for one player, depending on how the player's opponents may play.
15. Pareto optimality is a condition under which the state of economic efficiency means that no one can be made better off even by making someone worse off.
16. Strictly speaking the argument is that for the best outcomes a party should always adopt the strategy adopted by the other party in the last round. In a continuing series of games this leads to collaboration by default without the need to agree to collaborate.
17. The economic system under which nations operate means of course that an individual firm can acquire additional resources through outbidding its competitors for the use of these resources. This naturally increases the cost of production and gives an imperative towards minimizing the need to bid competitively for additional resources, but this nevertheless remains an option. But for the world economic system this is no longer an option so an alternative must be sought to enable development to take place. These two factors both tend towards the need to use available resources as effectively as possible.

REFERENCES

Crowther, David (1996), *Management Accounting for Business*, Cheltenham: Stanley Thornes.
Crowther, David (2004), *Managing Finance: A Socially Responsible Approach*, London: Elsevier.
Dietz, T. and J. Zhao (2011), 'Paths to climate cooperation', *Proceedings of the National Academy of Sciences*, **108** (32), 15671–15672.
Eatwell, John, Murray Milgate and Peter Newman (eds) (1987), *The New Palgrave: A Dictionary of Economics*, vol. 2, Macmillan: London, pp. 460–482.
Hughes, Barry (2011), 'Simultaneous and sequential games', available at http://www.gametheorystrategies.com/2011/09/15/simultaneous-and-sequential-games/, accessed 15 September 2011.
Levine, David K. (1998), 'Modeling altruism and spitefulness in experiments', *Review of Economic Dynamics*, **1**, 593–622.
Luce, Robert D. and Howard Raiffa (1957), *Games and Decisions: Introduction and Critical Survey*, New York: Wiley.
Myerson, Roger B. (1991), *Game Theory: Analysis of Conflict*, Cambridge, MA: Harvard University Press.
Nash, John F. (1950), 'The bargaining problem', *Econometrica*, **18**, 155–162.
Nash, John F. (1951), 'Non-cooperative games', *Annals of Mathematics*, **54**, 286–295.
Neumann, J. von (1928), 'On the theory of games of strategy', in Albert W. Tucker and Robert D. Luce (eds), *Contributions to the Theory of Games*, Princeton, NJ: Princeton University Press, pp. 13–42.
Neumann, John von and Oskar Morgenstern (1944), *Theory of Games and Economic Behaviour*, Princeton, NJ: Princeton University Press.
Pfeiffer, T. and L. Velthuis (2005), 'On the optimality of linear contracts to induce goal-congruent investment behavior', *Applied Economics Letters*, **12**, 207–211.
Schelling, T.C. (1960), *The Strategy of Conflict*, Cambridge, MA: Harvard University Press.
Turocy, T.L. and B. von Stengel (2001), 'Game theory', CDAM Research Report, LSE-CDAM-2001-09, available at http://www.cdam.lse.ac.uk/Reports/Files/cdam-2001-09.pdf, accessed 2 June 2016.
Wright, Robert (2001), *Nonzero: History, Evolution & Human Cooperation – The Logic of Human Destiny*, New York: Abacus.

8. Key concerns in longitudinal study design
Rima Kalinauskaitė

INTRODUCTION

In terms of phenomena under investigation in any organization, many of them are inherent in changes at individual and organizational levels. Longitudinal research design is typically used to draw up changes during a defined period. This is especially useful when gathering information on the knowledge, skills, opinions, attitudes, and behaviours of individuals that develop across the lifespan or change due to environmental factors in an organization. Longitudinal surveys can be conducted in prospective and retrospective ways, and could be either quantitative or qualitative depending on the kind of method used to collect data with the same respondents twice or more. The importance of longitudinal study is in understanding organizations as a way of providing data on the mechanisms and processes through which changes are created. Issues related to CSR can be measured as 'in' (examining the behaviour of individuals inside an organization) and 'on' (examining how an organization is seen from outside) levels.

This chapter outlines the definition and distinctive features of longitudinal study: intervals and periodicity between waves; advantages and challenges in designing longitudinal studies; and methodological aspects of cohort studies in organizations.

CONCEPT AND DEFINITION

Longitudinal survey design is used in social science research to study processes, changes, and causal relationships. A general and common definition of longitudinal study is that the same people or other units are surveyed on two or more occasions over time (de Vaus 2002; Johnson 1995; Lynn 2009; Petersen 2004; Piquero and Carmichael 2005; Sikkel and Hoogendoorn 2008; Steel 2005; Wagenaar 2005). 'Surveyed' on this occasion could be applied less directly – if we interviewed just once but gathered retrospective data (now and at some period before), such data could be called longitudinal. In general 'longitudinal' is applicable rather to a data structure than to a separate social method – any of the social methods (quantitative or qualitative) could be in this term longitudinal (if it is applied to the same respondents twice or more). In addition, experimental research involving before and after research can be classified as a longitudinal study because it contains temporal measuring points.

The history of collecting longitudinal data goes back 300 years, but the idea of using such data for research purposes developed in the last decades of the last century, especially in the field of sociology (Ruspini 2002; Menard 1991). Most of the longitudinal studies began after the First World War but were criticized for lack of representativeness and problems of dropout. Actually collecting repeated data periodically from the same individuals was common practice long before the term 'panel' began to be used by scientists. Paul F. Lazarsfeld introduced the concept of panel in the 1940s (Ruspini 2002). He suggested that repeated interviews with the same subjects but at different points in time might be able to reveal whether listening to a particular radio advert was the cause or the effect of any purchase made of a specific product. Longitudinal surveys became popular in the 1980s because of the development of new methodological and computational techniques (multilevel models, mixed models, hierarchical linier models, and others) for repeated measurement data. The people participating in repeated interviews were known as panel members, and the sample is called a panel: the whole procedure has become widely known as panel technique (Boudon 1993).

There are different definitions used as synonyms for longitudinal study, and different approaches of different authors to what longitudinal data involves. Panel studies, repeated measures, time series, and cohort studies share the same or a closely similar definition. Researchers across disciplines have used different terms to describe the design of the longitudinal studies (Lavrakas 2008): econometrics makes use of 'panel' or 'time series' data; psychologists use 'repeated measures'; and sociologists use 'longitudinal' and more often 'panel'. Some researchers describe the panel survey as a type of longitudinal study (Rasinski 2005), while others see a longitudinal survey as a form of panel survey (Steel 2005). More often in scientific literature longitudinal and panel studies are used as synonyms (Aldridge and Levine 2001; Johnson 1995; Jennings 2005; Sikkel and Hoogendoorn 2008; Steel 2005). Trend studies (repeated cross-sectional studies) that use respondents from the same population each time, but not necessarily the same respondents, could also be described as longitudinal design. It is possible to combine data from several different studies of the same population in order to show a trend. But the most 'truly longitudinal' studies are those which gather information about the same individuals or units (Hassett and Paavilainen-Mäntymäki 2013; Ruspini 2002).

THE LENGTH AND PERIODICITY OF INTERVALS

The length of a longitudinal study, number of data collection periods, and duration between data collections vary across designs, and depend on research objectives. The same people are repeatedly examined over a period of time, which can range from a few days to many years, depending upon the objectives of a study (Abrahamson 1983). Zaheer et al. (1999) conceptualized five timescales in organizational theory, which are not related to specific length but rather to research purpose – they are existence, observation, recording, aggregating, and validity intervals. For example, the existence interval is the time needed for phenomena to occur. There is no one appropriate time period for all researches and only abstract suggestions for periodicity of intervals. In literature, the 'period' in longitudinal research is defined as an 'appropriate' (Marsh 1982), 'extended' or 'relatively long' period of time (Lavrakas 2008). What is considered 'appropriate' or 'relatively long' depends on the subject and the issues addressed. Studies of newcomers' experience of adaptation may continue from a few months up to a few years, while studies of organizational culture may continue for decades. When observation intervals are regular it is clear that research is conducted perhaps in the last month of each year. However, in longitudinal data it is clear whether a change occurred between two panel dates, but not the exact date when it happened (Petersen 2004). It is possible to have unequal period intervals, especially when we want to measure psychological issues and experiences;

perhaps within one week, one month or two months after, and so on. For example, when measuring impact on employees' training the manager may ask respondents to complete a questionnaire at the end of the course to evaluate what they learned, and then may decide six months later to ask the same respondents the same or similar questions to see whether the course had a lasting impact. Such a design provides data that allow an analysis of the short- and long-term effects (Dillman 2009).

A panel study is usually constructed at 'regular intervals' for short-term longitudinal study, usually of one to five years' duration (Johnson 1995; Petersen 2004). Cohort studies examine the same units for longer periods of time, from 5 to 25 years or longer (Vitalari and Venkatesh 1991). Sample members are then re-interviewed, sometimes at fixed intervals and at other times to track the effects of some important event (Rasinski 2005), for example, changes in chief executive officer (CEO) management, or restructuring.

In any analysis of change there is the question of how many times different periods must be compared. The more it is likely to have fluctuations of observable phenomena, the greater the number of time periods needing to be sampled. To some extent, the desirable periodicity depends on how quickly the phenomena under study are expected to change. Distinct time points where data are collected in a survey are sometimes called waves (Steel 2005). In general, more waves are always better (Singer and Willett 2003) and at least three different time periods should ordinarily be compared (Abrahamson 1983; Singer and Willett 2003), because it is always problematic to infer change without examining at least three points in time. The periodicity can be no shorter than the time needed to collect response rate. If intervals of survey are planned longer than is desirable, it is possible to ask respondents retrospective questions as well. If the change is to be measured only over a relatively short time (weeks or months), a retrospective design may be appropriate for data concerning events or behaviour (Ruspini 2002).

PURPOSE AND ADVANTAGES OF LONGITUDINAL DESIGN IN ORGANIZATIONS

Social processes have become increasingly complex. Such external factors as economic, social, political, and cultural and market conditions stimulate and engage corporations in CSR. To analyse this complexity, longitudinal data are needed. Mainly, it is necessary to discover cause-and-effect relationships between variables. Longitudinal research designs have many significant advantages, including revealing change in a dependent variable (e.g., attitude, perception, behaviour, employment, mobility, and retention) and predicting the long-term effects of change on a particular outcome (Lavrakas 2008).

Longitudinal design is powerful for many organizational phenomena that cannot be studied experimentally. Longitudinal design became more attractive over recent decades in helping researchers discover different CSR-related aspects: the effect of ethical signals on recruitment outcomes (DeGrassi 2012); the ethics of organizations (Kaptein 2010); CSR themes by magazine advertisers (Lill et al. 1986); frames of environmental responsibility (Bortree et al. 2013); and the effects of CSR on customer relationships (Lacey and Kennett-Hensel 2010). Advantages of longitudinal studies refer to cause-and-effect relationships, as well as to facilitating evaluation of individual changes, organizational changes, and changes in work practices.

Change

The main purpose of longitudinal study is to enable estimates of changes at the individual or organizational level. This is especially useful when gathering information on the knowledge, skills, opinions, attitudes, and behaviours of individuals that change across their lifespan or due to environmental factors in an organization. Psychologists and social scientists study trends across generations. The purpose of longitudinal research studies in organizations is to gather and analyse quantitative or qualitative data, or both, on 'growth, change and development over time' (Lavrakas 2008, p. 439). The use of longitudinal methods is fundamental to understand the dynamics of organizational change, to develop and test theories of organizational adaptation, change, innovation, and redesign (Huber and Van de Ven 1995).

The longitudinal research design is typically used to pattern change during a time period or to control for unobserved explanatory variables (Dillman 2009; Petersen 2004; Solga 2001). In this sense, longitudinal research enables researchers to get close to causal explanations, which are usually attainable only with experiments (Johnson 1995).

One of the most difficult problems that can be associated with panel designs is differentiating between changes that are attributable to a life cycle, or maturation, and those which reflect fundamental social change. As the people in a sample become older, they may become more conservative in their attitudes (Menard 1991). Thus, a long-term panel study might observe that the sample of people had become more conservative, but it would be inappropriate to conclude that these results indicated a pervasive change that influenced an entire society. It is possible to recognize this distinction, but it is quite difficult to conclude that changes are due to life cycles and maturation (Abrahamson 1983). Longitudinal research allows the researcher to model time as an independent variable. Whereas theories often explicitly state the importance of time (e.g., in employee socialization or leadership development), longitudinal data actually allow the use of time as a research variable. Longitudinal data can provide information about how processes remain stable or change over time, for example, effects on company image and reputation, market development, and competitiveness. Change is typically measured in terms of chronological time or age (individual or company, or CSR performance).

As variables are qualitative or quantitative, changes may also be qualitative and quantitative. Qualitative change typically measures a 'characteristic' of a data unit, like 'which category' or 'what type', often as a 'yes' and 'no' dichotomy. For example, measurement of a company's ethical responsibility could involve the existence of such qualitative variables as corporate governance codes, codes of ethics, or CSR reports. Quantitative change, in contrast, is measured numerically as the difference between an individual's (unit's) 'scores' or 'ranks' on a characteristic at two waves; for example, market responses after CSR-related events, relationship between environmental and economic performance, repurchase rates, reputation indices and rankings, or the number of positive media reports.

A longitudinal survey permits analysis not only for change at the aggregate level (net change) but of changes at the individual level (gross change) (Bynner 2005; Ruspini 2002; Sikkel and Hoogendoorn 2008; Steel 2005). Analysis of gross change is perhaps one of the most common objectives of longitudinal surveys. Repeated cross-sectional surveys can be used to estimate net change. They enable one to monitor the effects of change on a population's macro-level characteristics – 'net effects', for example, month-to-month change in the reputation of a company in the media. Hence, only a longitudinal survey can help to identify what group was affected by change and why. While cross-sectional data only allow investigation of differences between individuals, a longitudinal study can examine change within individuals as well as variation between them. To study change we generally need to study over time. It is very difficult to establish causality in a cross-sectional study because for this purpose we need to see that change in one variable results in change in another. Repeated data with the same respondents enables investigation of changes in individuals within the population as well – 'gross effects'. The same sample interviewed twice is always a more sensitive measurement of change than two separate samples of the same population (cross-sectional survey).

Cause-and-Effect Relationships

Cross-sectional research measures phenomena at one point in time, while longitudinal research measures the same variables at a minimum of two different time periods (Hassett and Paavilainen-Mäntymäki 2013) so they can be compared. In cross-sectional research, there is no way to state whether a relationship existing between two variables will remain the same or will change with time. All studies of trends or changes in opinions require repeated studies. Longitudinal studies are well suited to examining issues of change (or stability) over time and find out what caused it.

In line with cause-and-effect relationships, generally, longitudinal research studies are based on the fact that the 'knowledge, skills, attitudes, perceptions, and behaviours of individual subjects usually develop, grow and change in essential ways over a period of time' (Lavrakas 2008). For example, after introducing new policies into an organization, it is possible to measure how they affect that company's employees.

Cross-sectional design can show only association between organizational phenomena, and only longitudinal design allows interpretation of data's causal relationship. This limitation could be solved using longitudinal data to show the causality. For example, in measuring the influence of CSR on employees' commitment or causality it is better to use not cross-sectional but longitudinal data. Another example refers to the impact of CSR on the firm's financial performance that could be measured by correlation, which shows a positive or negative (or none) relationship. However, longitudinal data enable stronger causal interpretations and allow the researcher to eliminate a number of competing explanations for effects observed. For example, explaining whether financial performance increased due to advertising to the target audience or was influenced by CSR practices, what elements of population had changed their mind and why, and whether all groups of population were influenced by CSR and so on.

Longitudinal surveys in organizations can help to discover different issues – work stressors, social stressors at work, work-related social support, job content variables (Zapf et al. 1996), changes in organizational structure, causal mechanisms, organizational adaptation, group decision support, organizational restructuring, and so on. According to Kimberly (cited in Vitalari and Venkatesh 1991) longitudinal analyses can be carried out 'on' and 'in' organizations. Analyses conducted 'on' organizations focus on organizational macro issues, as on the organization and its structure, performance, strategy, and environment as well as on interrelationships between organizations (e.g., interorganizational systems, interlocking directorates, how customers perceive the company, or how CSR policies increase the company's attractiveness for potential employees (applications per vacancy, hiring rate), or company reputation). Studies 'in' organizations examine the behaviour of individuals (e.g., with regard to job satisfaction, decision-making performance, how CSR is perceived by company employees and how it influences employees' motivation and retention) or work groups (e.g., cooperative work, job redesign, employee turnover, fluctuation rate, and absenteeism). Most longitudinal research 'in' organizations is usually run within a single organization and longitudinal research 'on' organizations is rare because the study of macro-organizational variables is complicated by measurement problems and cost.

DIFFICULTIES ASSOCIATED WITH LONGITUDINAL DESIGN

Longitudinal surveys are conducted in many fields (medicine, economy, psychology, sociology); however, application in organizational research is complicated due to high cost and to being time consuming. In addition, employees move from one job to another and it makes it difficult to track former respondents for subsequent measurement. Disadvantages of longitudinal studies are associated with the length of time it takes to conduct the research, the cost of sustaining the study over time, and the potential for participants to drop out in the course of the study.

Longitudinal surveys are often undertaken to measure changes in perceptions and behaviours over time. One of the unique challenges in such surveys is asking the same questions during multiple periods of data collection and examining the differences (Dillman 2009). In longitudinal surveys, questions are often asked to examine how a specific event affected people's lives or attitudes. Sometimes they are used simply to understand how time has affected them. In order to measure change accurately it is therefore critical that respondents be presented with the exact same question stimulus each time a measurement is made. It is very important to ensure that the exact same question was asked in both surveys, because question wording can have a substantial effect on survey results measuring attitudes.

Attrition and Missing Data

The major difficulty in longitudinal research is maintaining the original sample. People lose interest, move, or leave the organization. This causes decreasing of sample size and with it the validity of conclusions drawn from the data. Sample attrition means the decrease in the size of the panel from one wave to the next. This is a common problem because respondents may not be available for many reasons. One possible reason is that some individuals are not available for some of the data collection time to provide responses (holidays, days off, business trips). Another reason is that some subjects might drop out from the study at any time point by leaving or retiring from the organization: that is attrition. Attrition is common in longitudinal designs, so data for some participants are often incomplete. Big or intensive samples' mortality (attrition) can be another reason for having incomplete longitudinal data to make valid conclusions about change. This is particularly true if the survey is lengthy in time, for example, for years or decades. In addition, some may refuse to continue to participate in the research because they get tired of answering questions, especially the same questions every time.

The response rate at any single wave of a longitudinal survey may be sufficient, but the difference in the number of respondents from the first to, say, the fifth wave can be quite big (Lynn 2009). If substantial numbers of people initially included in a panel are gone, for any reason, by the end of the study, then the data cannot be meaningfully interpreted (Abrahamson 1983). Organizations may use different ways to motivate employees and induce them to participate in a survey and further interviews.

Anonymity

Researchers in an organization may face other problems – anonymity issues. Even when research is conducted only once the respondent may not agree to participate, or leave some answers empty because of the possibility of attribution. For example, if there is only one woman in a department she might not be willing to tick a gender box because it is easy to detect who filled in the questionnaire. Employees may not want to participate simply because they are not willing to participate in talking about such sensitive topics as evaluating company policies and position on CSR, or evaluating managers' performance, or questions about job satisfaction. Research in an organization always concerns the personal situation of individuals and not every employee would be willing to share this information with others. Thus, a person may refuse to participate at all in providing such private information as performance indices. Longitudinal study in this case is even more complicated. In longitudinal study, the same participants must be contacted by email, phone, or face-to-face interview at least twice, so they must be identified. In this case, the longitudinal method is not anonymous. Knowing that it is mandatory to provide at least one item of such contact information makes it more difficult to expect participation and sincere answers even in the first interview, because respondents may be reluctant to answer questions that they feel are sensitive or invasive. It is necessary to guarantee confidentiality and anonymity of data and to exclude sensitive topics.

Cost

Longitudinal studies are often quite expensive because they require conducting the survey at least twice and sustaining the survey between and during waves. In addition, during the study a huge amount of data is generated and must be managed and analysed by researchers or practitioners which is time-consuming and costly. New technology has made longitudinal studies cheaper with the possibility of emailing and providing a link for respondents to complete an online questionnaire. Yet, because of time and cost limits, longitudinal studies often have only a small group of subjects, which makes it difficult to apply the results to a larger population. Organizations may use survey results for their own practical reasons and decisions, with no obligation to have representative samples. In some cases, repeated surveys with the same respondents are simpler and more cost-effective to conduct than to select a new sample for each study (Das et al. 2011), especially in organizations where change of personnel is low.

Weaknesses of Retrospective Study

A retrospective mode is not suitable for attitudes or beliefs but can be used for behaviour and events analysis, and it is appropriate and worthwhile in analysing documents (such as employment records, annual reports, management initiative documentation). For example, Tengblad and Ohlsson (2010) analysed CEO letters in the annual reports for a period of transformational change. This longitudinal study revealed the change in discourse from a national view toward an international and individualistic view of social responsibility. If we talk not about documented data but about remembering past data and events, the retrospective design introduces serious concerns over recall errors (Piquero and Carmichael 2005; Marsden and Wright 2010). Memory always opens the possibility that a person will reinterpret the past in the light of the present. Subjective measures such as expectations, intentions, attitudes and reasons for making particular choices, and respondents' ability to recall even quite major events, can be prone to recall error (Lynn 2009; Marsh 1982). Respondents can misremember the past and become confused about recalling time periods (de Vaus 2002).

For recall data, higher frequency waves are likely to produce higher quality data. The optimal frequency will depend on the nature of the information to be recalled. For indicators of current circumstances, where the intention is to identify changes in circumstances, the optimum frequency will depend on the rate of true change (Lynn 2009). If waves are rare the important changes might be missed, but if they are too frequent, then the data collection (which is expensive) is less useful.

Another disadvantage is that retrospective data are also determined by the amount of data which can be collected on one occasion. In prospective longitudinal studies (where the study takes a single sample or group and follows it up with repeated data collections over time) it is possible to ask research questions in smaller portions.

Panel Conditioning

Panel conditioning is another disadvantage of longitudinal study. The term refers to the tendency for respondents to answer survey questions differently because of their participation in previous surveys. There are two ways in which conditioning can take place: the way in which respondents change their minds and the way they change their actual behaviour because of their participation in the survey (Dillman 2009; Ruspini 2002). This problem is even more apparent in organizations because, unlike public research where respondents do not know each other and have little opportunity to discuss interviews, the respondents in organizations have more opportunities to talk over and discuss research during formal or informal meetings at work. Surveys about organizations are usually closely related to the employees' everyday life, and research conducted in an organization raises a need to discuss those topics with colleagues. For example, questions in a survey about going to work by public transport or bicycle may raise later discussion and change opinions. Even more it may change respondents' behaviour to use public transport instead of using their own car. Generally speaking it is good to achieve changes in attitudes on issues of sustainability especially when it is a concern of the company's CSR policy, but it presents difficulties for researchers. Panel conditioning refers to the possibility that survey responses given by a person who has already taken part in the survey previously may differ from the responses that the person would have given for the first time (Lynn 2009). In other words, the response may be conditioned by the previous experience of taking part in the survey.

Questions asked in the first wave of the panel may lead respondents to think about the issue. Because it is now better known to the respondent and may give rise to further thinking and discussion, attitudes may be more likely to change. It may be a problem in any research but it is mostly problematic in a panel design (Abrahamson 1983).

For example, a two-wave survey of what forms of CSR are implemented might find that more different forms appear at the second wave. This might reflect a genuine increase but it could also be affected by panel conditioning. This could happen because the first wave interview made some sample members aware of possible CSR forms, which they then started to use in their organizations. Hence, there was a genuine increase in the extent of the activity, but only amongst sample members – not amongst the population as a whole. The behaviour of the sample members has been conditioned by the experience of the first interview.

Alternatively, the experience of the first interviews may have affected the way in which some sample members respond to the questions in the second interview, even if nothing changed in their organizations. Perhaps in the first interview they might discover that reporting no activity of a particular type led to them being asked a series of questions about why they did not participate in that activity. People become experienced interviewees. In this regard, to make the second interview shorter, or to avoid embarrassing questions, they now report that they have participated in this particular activity. In this case, the reporting of the sample members has been conditioned by the experience of the first interview (Das et al. 2011; Lynn 2009). They may report 'no change' since the previous interview so as to avoid detailed questioning on changes that have in fact occurred.

COHORT STUDIES

A panel may include a sample deliberately selected to represent a diverse population, or it can consist solely of people who possess a particular characteristic that is relevant to the objectives of a study – a specific cohort. A cohort is any subgroup of population defined by a demographic attribute, such as age or gender, for which the members of the group are followed up individually across time (Bynner 2005; Newbold 2005). These individuals usually share a certain condition, for example, birth year, year of retirement, or are employees who have joined the organization one year ago (Piquero and Carmichael 2005; Sikkel and Hoogendoorn 2008). This focus is due to the fact that the point where people initially enter the labour force is a critical consideration. For example, Catlin and Maupin (2004) found out that new recruits tend toward an idealistic ethical dimension more than employees of one year's standing. It means that the time someone enters the organization can make significant differences in their ethical orientation.

High-level jobs in the labour force may be expanding or contracting. The size of entry cohorts may be increasing or decreasing, resulting in greater or lesser amounts of competition for jobs. Studies of cohorts often follow specific subpopulations throughout their lives. Age cohorts are identified with groups of a particular age; birth cohorts are defined as people born at a particular time. Birth cohorts often are defined in terms of five to ten year periods, such as those born between 1970–75 or 1940–50. There are also social class cohorts, cohorts defined by social situation or health condition, and so on. 'Cohort' as a non-scientific term is more familiar under the sense of 'generations', but 'generation' may involve different meanings – length of time, parent-child relationship, or historical period – and if it is not defined with time bounds it might be difficult to distinguish one generation from another.

To be born at a specific time determines some features of all of one generation. Cohort studies in terms of generations are common in organizations – there are different issues discussed by scientists about generational differences that influence many organizational phenomena.

There are publicly used common names applied to different generations, and used in organizational research – for example, baby boomers, X, Y, Z generations – which differ from each other by different values, and different styles of collaboration, leadership, preferred communication, and so on. For example, Lynne and Joiner (2014) studying CSR values of Millennial business students found out that values (particularly environmental concerns) are not front-of-mind in Millennial students' job choice decisions.

The cohort is an important sociological concept, especially in the study of social change. Because each new cohort experiences its society in its own way under unique historical conditions, it contributes to social change by reinterpreting cultural values, beliefs, and attitudes and adjusting to structural constraints. A cohort that grows up during times of economic depression, for example, may be expected to develop quite different values about hard work and the importance of saving than will a cohort growing up during times of economic prosperity and consumer values (Johnson 1995).

A cohort panel can be considered as a specific form of panel study. In line with cohort design, social change can be studied from three viewpoints: age, period, and generation (Menard 1991; Ruspini 2002). 'Age effects' are those attributable to the ageing process. Data collected at a particular time point in a cohort study may be a product of the age of the individual concerned; that is, associated with changes in age. 'Period effects' are those attributable to events in the historical period during which the study is conducted (e.g., recession, economic crisis, political climate). Those events affect all generations equally and simultaneously (Ruspini 2002). 'Cohort or generation effects' are associated with the time when the individual was born, and concern all events that one generation experienced and another generation did not (Ruspini 2002). These effects are explained by similarities amongst individuals, for example, the 'baby boomer' generation experienced more competition for jobs when entering the labour market. Cohorts with a smaller birth rate as a whole experience a less competitive environment and more favourable life changes in terms of occupational and economic attainment (Hakim 2000). All three types of effect overlap.

Panel and cohort designs differ in their outcomes. Panel study enables a distinction between age effects (the impact of the ageing process on individuals) and cohort effects (effects due to being born at a similar time), because its members will have been born at different times. A cohort study can distinguish only ageing effects, since all members of the sample have been born at more or less the same time (Bryman 2012).

To control for cohort effects it is necessary to include several additional cohorts in the study. Cohort studies are common in organizational and management research – different generations have different values and what is important to one generation may not be the concern of another. McGlone et al. (2011) in their research revealed that Millennials who rated working for a company that incorporates CSR as an important policy component reported more volunteerism than non-Millennials. Millennials (or generation Y) are traditionally thought to care less about pay, and more about flexible working, travel opportunities, and CSR. Generational values affect how people perceive organizations and make preferences between one job and another job. Hence, incorporating CSR into an organization's strategic plan may affect the company's attractiveness to a particular generation.

Talking about 'in' organization research – managers implement different approaches in how to cope with employees of particular generations. For example, it is helpful to know features of each generation and apply different methods for motivation, preference to work in a team or independently, and ways of communication.

Cohort studies are always culturally determined, as in every country generations may differ accordingly to economic, political, or cultural circumstances (Abrahamson 1983). Important changes may be occurring in people's initial opportunities. Data from only one age cohort representing a certain generation may not be generalizable to other cohorts raised and living under different social and physical environmental conditions (Ruspini 2002). This makes cohort studies by age complicated in a multicultural organizational environment. In this case, the attribute associated with organization may help, for example, to form the cohort of which a feature is the year when an employee joins the organization. In the case of a longitudinal design, it is not important to collect data from the same respondents but it is necessary that all the respondents belong to the cohort being studied. Longitudinal cohort study enables the observation of properties at aggregate level rather than at individual level and is the main distinction of cohort analysis from ordinary longitudinal analysis.

THE APPLICATION OF LONGITUDINAL RESEARCH DESIGN IN CSR

Most research in CSR, and in organizations in general, has so far been cross-sectional in design, allowing for only a static understanding of results. However, longitudinal research design is essential to show whether a concept changes or not over time. For example, D. Mazutis (2013), in her dissertation about the relationship between executive orientation and corporate social strategy, used a longitudinal approach to discover how the concepts of corporate social responsibility, corporate citizenship, and business sustainability have evolved over time, as societal expectations and managerial interpretations may also change. However, the dissertator applied archival method (examining the corporate social strategies of firms over 19 years) which nonetheless only indirectly tested the relationships between executive orientation and corporate social strategy; hence it was noted as a limitation of the research. Tang et al.'s study (2012), with longitudinal data collected from 130 firms from 1995 to 2007, revealed that firms benefit more when they adopt a CSR engagement strategy that is consistent, involves related dimensions of CSR, and begins with aspects of CSR that are more internal to the firm. Another longitudinal data analysis using archive data was performed by Oikonomou et al. (2012), and focused on the wealth-protective effects of socially responsible firms' behaviour by examining the association between corporate social performance and financial risk for an extensive panel data sample of 500 companies between the years 1992 and 2009. They found that CSR is negatively weakly related to systematic company risk, and that corporate social irresponsibility is positively and strongly related to financial risk.

Analysing and using documents (data and text) for longitudinal study purposes is relatively low cost and affords possibly larger sample size compared with organizing and conducting interviews; however, it is more complicated to draw outcomes on how and why the changes occurred. For example, content analysis of advertisements of three weekly German magazines of 2002–07 showed (Mogele and Tropp 2010) that the share of CSR print advertisements has increased significantly (about four times) during the period, and that the companies increasingly link their ecological and social commitment with product advertising. But it is more complicated to explain why it happened, due to public communication pressure, global tendencies or changes of education programmes, or social-cultural context. Lacey and Kennett-Hensel analysing how CSR performance impacts customer relationships over time (interviewing respondents twice) found that firms which had engaged CSR initiatives built trusting and committed customer relationships and helped forge desirable customer behaviour. The study revealed that CSR had a strengthening effect on customer relationships. However, as longitudinal study faces attrition it requires larger samples sizes at the beginning.

Archival method is more cost-effective than interviewing, can include long periods, and has broad application in an organizational environment (many processes are usually documented or retrieved). However, such data are limited by causal conclusions, and not all the concepts of interest could be found registered in an organization's archive (e.g., CSR in an organization's strategy and board minutes is more likely to be collected, but not employees' perception of it). Those examples show that either a qualitative or quantitative longitudinal approach could be applied in CSR research where there is a concern to measure a change or dynamics. In addition, the use of longitudinal data (both prospective and retrospective) can ensure a more complete approach to empirical research.

CONCLUSION

Longitudinal study is a research method in which the same respondents are surveyed at least twice. The study makes comparisons over time, which helps identifying change and clarifies the causal status. For example, to discover whether or not, or how, CSR policies influenced employee loyalty, and what caused the biggest influence, it is essential to survey the same respondents at least twice. The benefit of such a study is that changes (if any) can be analysed at both the group (organization or team) and the individual level. The number of data collection periods and time between data collections may vary across designs, and depend on research objectives. The study might last from a few months to a few years, or even decades.

The main disadvantage of longitudinal study is panel attrition. People lose interest, move, or leave the organization. This causes a decrease of initial sample size and reduces useable data, which makes results no longer representative. The deciding factor in choosing longitudinal study may be the amount of time for the study, budget, and, most important, the purpose and nature of the research.

REFERENCES

Abrahamson, Mark (1983), *Social Research Methods*, Englewood Cliffs, NJ: Prentice-Hall.
Aldridge, Alan and Ken Levine (2001), *Surveying the Social World: Principles and Practice in Survey Research*, Buckingham: Open University Press.
Bortree, Sevick Denise, Lee Ahern, Alexandra Nutter Smith and Xue Dou (2013), 'Framing environmental responsibility: 30 years of CSR messages in National Geographic Magazine', *Public Relations Review*, **39** (5), 491–496.
Boudon, Raymond (ed.) (1993), *Paul Felix Lazarsfeld: On Social Research and its Language*, Chicago, IL: University of Chicago Press.
Bryman, Alan (2012), *Social Research Methods*, 4th edition, Oxford: Oxford University Press.
Bynner, John (2005), 'Longitudinal cohort designs', in Kimberly Kempf-Leonard (editor-in-chief), *Encyclopedia of Social Measurement*, vol. 2, Amsterdam: Elsevier Academic Press, pp. 591–599.
Catlin, Dennis W. and James R. Maupin (2004), 'A two cohort study of the ethical orientations of state police officers', *Policing: An International Journal of Police Strategies & Management*, **27** (3), 289–301.
Das, Marcel, Peter Ester and Lars Kaczmirek (eds) (2011), *Social and Behavioral Research and the Internet: Advances in Applied Methods and Research Strategies*, London: Routledge.
De Vaus, David (2002), *Surveys in Social Research*, London: Routledge.
DeGrassi, Sandra W. (2012), 'Go, stop, yield: the effect of ethical signals on recruitment outcomes', *Journal of Leadership, Accountability & Ethics*, **9** (4), 30–43.
Dillman, Don A. (2009), 'Some consequences of survey mode changes in longitudinal surveys', in Peter Lynn (ed.), *Methodology of Longitudinal Surveys*, Chichester, UK: John Wiley & Sons.
Hakim, Catherine (2000), *Research Design: Successful Designs for Social and Economic Research*, London: Routledge.
Hassett, E. Melanie and Eriikka Paavilainen-Mäntymäki (2013), 'Longitudinal research in organizations: an introduction', in Melanie E. Hassett and Eriikka Paavilainen-Mäntymäki (eds), *Handbook of Longitudinal Research Methods in Organisation and Business Studies*, Cheltenham, UK and Northampton, MA, USA: Edward Elgar Publishing, pp. 1–22.
Huber, George P. and Andrew H. Van de Ven (1995), *Longitudinal Field Research Methods: Studying Processes of Organizational Change*, London: SAGE Publications.
Jennings, Gayle R. (2005), 'Business, social science research methods used in', in Kimberly Kempf-Leonard (editor-in-chief), *Encyclopedia of Social Measurement*, vol. 1, Amsterdam: Elsevier Academic Press, pp. 219–230.
Johnson, Allan G. (1995), *The Blackwell Dictionary of Sociology: A User's Guide to Sociological Language*, Malden, MA: Blackwell Publishers.
Kaptein, Muel (2010), 'The ethics of organizations: a longitudinal study of the U.S. working population', *Journal of Business Ethics*, **92** (4), 601–618.
Lacey, Russell and Pamela Kennett-Hensel (2010), 'Longitudinal effects of corporate social responsibility on customer relationships', *Journal of Business Ethics*, **97** (4), 581–597.
Lavrakas, Paul J. (ed.) (2008), *Encyclopedia of Survey Research Methods*, Thousand Oaks, CA: SAGE Publications.
Lill, David, Charles Gross and Robin Peterson (1986), 'The inclusion of social-responsibility themes by magazine advertisers: a longitudinal study', *Journal of Advertising*, **15** (2), 35–41.
Lynn, Peter (2009), 'Methods for longitudinal surveys', in Peter Lynn (ed.), *Methodology of Longitudinal Surveys*, Chichester, UK: John Wiley & Sons.
Lynne, Leveson and Therese A. Joiner (2014), 'Exploring corporate social responsibility values of millennial job-seeking students', *Education + Training*, **56** (1), 21–34.
Marsden, Peter V. and James D. Wright (2010), *Handbook of Survey Research*, London: Emerald Group Publishing Limited.
Marsh, Catherine (1982), *The Survey Method: The Contribution of Surveys to Sociological Explanation*, London: Allen & Unwin.
Mazutis, Daina D. (2013), 'The CEO effect: a longitudinal, multilevel analysis of the relationship between executive orientation and corporate social strategy', *Business & Society*, **52** (4), 631–648.
McGlone, Teresa, Judith Winters Spain and Vernon McGlone (2011), 'Corporate social responsibility and the Millennials', *Journal of Education for Business*, **86** (4), 195–200.
Menard, W. Scott (1991), *Longitudinal Research*, Newbury Park, CA: SAGE Publications.
Mogele, Bastian and Joerg Tropp (2010), 'The emergence of CSR as an advertising topic: a longitudinal study of German CSR advertisements', *Journal of Marketing Communications*, **16** (3), 163–181.
Newbold, Bruce K. (2005), 'Dynamic migration modeling', in Kimberly Kempf-Leonard (editor-in-chief), *Encyclopedia of Social Measurement*, vol. 1, Amsterdam: Elsevier Academic Press, pp. 705–714.

Oikonomou, Ioannis, Chris Brooks and Stephen Pavelin (2012), 'The impact of corporate social performance on financial risk and utility: a longitudinal analysis', *Financial Management*, **41** (1), 483–515.
Petersen, Trond (2004), 'Analyzing panel data: fixed- and random-effects models', in Melissa Hardy and Alan Bryman (eds), *Handbook of Data Analysis*, London: SAGE Publications, pp. 332–346.
Piquero, Alex R. and Stephanie Carmichael (2005), 'Attrition, mortality, and exposure time', in Kimberly Kempf-Leonard (editor-in-chief), *Encyclopedia of Social Measurement*, vol. 3, Amsterdam: Elsevier Academic Press, pp. 97–101.
Rasinski, Kenneth A. (2005), 'Surveys', in Kimberly Kempf-Leonard (editor-in-chief), *Encyclopedia of Social Measurement*, vol. 3, Amsterdam: Elsevier Academic Press, pp. 733–747.
Ruspini, Elisabetta (2002), *Introduction to Longitudinal Research*, London: Routledge.
Sikkel, Dirk and Adriaan Hoogendoorn (2008), 'Panel surveys', in D. Edith de Leeuw, Joop J. Hox and Don A. Dillman (eds), *International Handbook of Survey Methodology*, New York: Lawrence Erlbaum Associates, pp. 479–498.
Singer, Judith D. and John B. Willett (2003), *Applied Longitudinal Data Analysis: Modeling Change and Event Occurrence*, New York: Oxford University Press.
Solga, Heike (2001), 'Longitudinal surveys and the study of occupational mobility: panel and retrospective design in comparison', *Quality & Quantity*, **35** (3), 291–309.
Steel, David G. (2005), 'Time sampling', in Kimberly Kempf-Leonard (editor-in-chief), *Encyclopedia of Social Measurement*, vol. 3, Amsterdam: Elsevier Academic Press, pp. 823–828.
Tang, Zhi, Clyde Eiríkur Hull and Sandra Rothenberg (2012), 'How corporate social responsibility engagement strategy moderates the CSR-financial performance relationship', *Journal of Management Studies*, **49** (7), 1274–1303.
Tengblad, Stefan and Claes Ohlsson (2010), 'The framing of corporate social responsibility and the globalization of national business systems: a longitudinal case study', *Journal of Business Ethics*, **93** (4), 653–669.
Vitalari, P. Nicholas and Alladi Venkatesh (1991), 'Longitudinal surveys in information systems research: an examination of issues, methods, and applications', in Kenneth L. Kraemer (ed.), *The Information Systems Challenge: Survey Research Methods*, Cambridge, MA: Harvard University Press, pp. 115–144.
Wagenaar, Theodore C. (2005), 'Survey design', in Kimberly Kempf-Leonard (editor-in-chief), *Encyclopedia of Social Measurement*, vol. 3, Amsterdam: Elsevier Academic Press, pp. 715–721.
Zaheer, Srilata, Stuart Albert and Akbar Zaheer (1999), 'Time scales and organizational theory', *Academy of Management Review*, **24** (4), 725–741.
Zapf, Dieter, Christian Dormann and Michael Frese (1996), 'Longitudinal studies in organizational stress research: a review of the literature with reference to methodological issues', *Journal of Occupational Health Psychology*, **1** (2), 145–169.

9. Sampling and sampling procedures in corporate social responsibility research
Habib Zaman Khan and Md. Rashidozzaman Khan

INTRODUCTION

Sampling is a common part of everyday life. As a customer, when you go into local grocers' to buy rice, you pick up a little rice from the display pots, look at the rice, and touch a few grains to get a sense of the quality and freshness before deciding whether to buy. When you think of buying a car, you visit a car showroom to see different models of car and take a short test drive. Taking the decision of purchasing rice based on initial touching and looking at, or buying a car on the basis of one showroom visit, may not be precise and scientific sampling, but at a personal level, it is a practical sampling experience for you. As a matter of fact, if measuring every item in a population is impractical, difficult, and costly, we naturally take a sample.

Although sampling is commonly used in various activities of daily life, these types of sampling are rarely considered as a scientific approach. For academic researchers, the processes of sampling are not a straightforward task. Sampling is a fundamental feature of business research including research on corporate social responsibility (CSR), which calls for profound assessment and discussion.

Furthermore, statistical application is mainly related with the collection, presentation of data, and analysis and interpretation of information. In a research project, after research models are developed, primary data collection is an important step. Most statistical analysis methods are based on the fact of the randomization (i.e. representation of sampling) used in data collection. It is therefore essential to acquire the knowledge on sampling before learning the statistical analysis. This chapter explains the character of sampling and ways to determine the suitable sample design with a particular focus on CSR research.

Overview of Sampling and Population

Population
A population is the complete set of all items of interest for an investigator in a specified space and time. Population size is denoted by 'N'. Examples include all registered voters in a country such as Bangladesh or Australia, or the total number of stars in the sky.

Sample
A sample is a subset or representative part of a population which has all the characteristics of that population. It provides the fact that conclusions from the sample may be extended to that about the whole population. The number of elements selected for a sample is known as the 'sample size', denoted by 'n'. For example, to investigate certain

characteristics of all 1000 postgraduate students (e.g., understanding pro-environmental behavior of students) of a university, 100 students are selected to collect necessary data. These 100 students constitute a sample of the population of postgraduate students ($n = 100$).

Sampling
The methods for selecting a sample from a population are known as sampling. In practice, a sample will be drawn from a list of population elements that often differs somewhat from the defined target population.

Sampling frame
A list of elements from which the sample may be drawn is called a sampling frame. The sampling frame is also called 'working population' because units will eventually provide units involved in analysis. An example of a sampling frame would be a list of all members of the Australian Teachers Association. A sampling frame should always be made up to date and free from errors of omission, inaccuracy, and non-existence and duplication of sampling units (for a review of different aspects of sampling frames, please see Seal (1962), and Singh (1983).

Sampling unit
This refers to an element or unit containing the elements that are available for selection at some stage of the sampling process. Before selecting the sample, the population must be divided into parts which are distinct, unambiguous, and non-overlapping so that every element of the population belongs to one and only one sampling unit. Examples: all businessmen in a city, all garments workers of Dhaka city, or all environmental activists in Sydney.

Parameter
A parameter is a specific characteristic of a population. The unknown constants or any function of them that appear in a mathematical specification of a population are known as parameters. For a normal population, unknown mean (μ) and variance (σ^2) are parameters.

Statistic
A statistic is a specific characteristic of a sample. Any function of a sample is known as a statistic. σx, $\bar{x}$, s, s^2, r, and b are examples of statistics which are used to test a hypothesis about population. The sample mean, below, is a function of sample observations, and is a statistic.

$$\bar{X} = \frac{\sum X_i}{n} \tag{9.1}$$

Census
The total count of all units of the population for a certain characteristic is known as 'complete enumeration', also termed as 'census survey'. Examples: population census or agricultural census.

Sample survey
When a part of the population is selected and examined, it is called a 'sample survey'.

Pilot survey
Small-scale surveys are sometimes conducted in order to get quick primary information before an actual sample survey or census is carried out. Such type of survey is known as a 'pilot survey'.

Why Sampling?

In practice, it is not often realistic to collect data from an entire population (universe). Rarely, researchers would have either enough time or money to gather information from everyone or everywhere in a population. The goal of sampling is therefore to find a representative sample (or subset) of that population. There are several advantages of sampling over census. Firstly, the costs of sampling are much lower than that of census. For example, if a government department wants to take public opinions from a particular community, one-third of the population is large enough to declare what the government wants to know. It is not meaningful to spend more time and money to interview the entire population in that community.

Secondly, it is argued that the quality of a study is often better with sampling data than with census data (Deming 1960; Cooper and Emory 1995; Cochran 1953). Deming (1960) suggested that sampling possesses the possibility of better interviewing (testing), more thorough investigation of missing, wrong, or suspicious information, better supervision, and better processing than that of complete coverage. Indeed, factors such as interviewer mistakes, tabulation errors, and other non-sampling errors may be influential during a census because of the greater volume of work. But in a sample, increased level of accuracy may sometimes be achievable because experienced researchers have opportunities to more closely supervise and monitor the fieldwork and tabulation of data. Thirdly, sampling can save time. The speed of implementation reduces the time between the recognition of a need for information and the availability of that information.

TYPES OF SAMPLING

There are three types of sampling:

1. Probability sampling
2. Non-probability sampling
3. Mixed sampling.

Probability Sampling

In probability sampling, every unit in the population has a chance (greater than zero) to be selected in the sample. Probability samples are of five types, such as simple random sampling (SRS), systematic sampling, stratified sampling, cluster sampling, and multi-stage

142 *Handbook of research methods in corporate social responsibility*

area sampling. The probability sampling process relies on randomness; therefore it is free from the bias associated with the non-probability sampling procedures. However, in non-probability sampling, the chance of any particular unit of the population is not known. That is, the selection of sampling units in non-probability sampling is subjective and arbitrary, above all, subject to researchers' choice.

There are four types of non-probability sampling. These are convenience sampling, judgement sampling, quota sampling, and snowball sampling. Past studies mentioned that non-probability sampling has some demerits. For example, no appropriate statistical tools are available in the literature for measuring non-sampling errors from a non-probability sampling. Therefore, projecting the data beyond the sample is not appropriate at all (Zikmund 2008). However, there are certain situations where non-probability sampling techniques are more appropriate than probability sampling techniques for the purpose of achieving the researcher's research objectives. The next sub-sections discuss the various types of probability and non-probability sampling techniques in detail.

Simple random sampling (SRS)
Simple random sampling (SRS) is a sampling technique that ensures each element in the population will have an equivalent prospect of being selected in the sample. It is a scientific sampling method based on probability theory. In this method each population unit has the same probability of being included in the sample. Examples include selecting the winning raffle tickets from a large container at a picnic party. If the raffle tickets are comprehensively stirred, each ticket will have an equal chance of being included. SRS is most suitable when a population is small, homogeneous, and readily available. Such a sampling technique provides for the greatest number of possible samples by assigning a number to each unit in the sampling frame. If the unit selected in any draw is not replaced in the population before making the next draw, it is known as 'simple random sampling without replacement' and if the selected unit is replaced back before making the next draw, then the sampling is called 'simple random sampling with replacement'.

Systematic sampling
Systematic sampling is a sampling technique in which only the first unit is selected with the help of a random number and the rest would be selected automatically according to some pre-designed pattern. Specifically, it is a sampling procedure in which a starting point is selected by a random process and then every nth number on the list is selected. Suppose N units of the population are numbered from 1 to N in some order. Let $N = nk$, where n is the sample size and k is an integer, and a random number less than or equal to k be selected and every kth unit thereafter. Such a procedure is termed as systematic sampling. If the serial number of the selected first sample unit is i ($i \leq k$), the next units of the sample will be $i + k, i + 2k, \ldots, i + (n - 1)k$. Example:

Population = 100 food stores
Sample desired = 20 food stores
a. Number of population = 100, sample size = 20. Therefore, number of sample = 100/20 = 5.
    Draw a random number 1–5.
b. Sample every Xth store (see Table 9.1).

Table 9.1 Example of systematic sampling

Sample	Numbered stores					
1	1,	6,	11,	16,	21, …	96,
2	2,	7,	12,	17,	22, …	97,
3	3,	8,	13,	18,	23, …	98,
4	4,	9,	14,	19,	24, …	99,
5	5,	10,	15,	20,	25, …	100

Assume that you chose the 3rd store, then the rest of the stores will be selected following the pattern of 8th, 13th, 18th, … and so on because the kth number in this example is every 5th store. It is not purely a random sampling because all the samples are not equally probable of being selected. There are some advantages of this method. For example, systematic sampling is easy to draw and often easier to exclude in the field. Similarly, it has control over fieldwork, permits concurrent listing and sampling, and greatly reduces cost. However, there are some disadvantages of this method too. Systematic sampling is less representative because it has a chance of increasing the variance when there is either hidden periodicity in the population or a periodic movement of the data. As argued by Zikmund (2008), the problem of periodicity occurs when arrangements of items in the lists are not random in character. For example, if a researcher wants to collect information on CSR expenditure from a company, and collect information every seventh day, it would provide an inaccurate sample because information on CSR expenditure based only on one day of the week (perhaps Friday or Monday) would be selected.

The systematic sampling is extensively used in manufacturing industries for statistical quality control of their products. It has wide applications in market research as well. For example, every 20th departing customer at a checkout counter in a superstore may be asked for his or her opinion on the taste, color, or texture of an organic food item.

Stratified sampling

Stratified sampling is a sampling plan in which the population is divided into several non-overlapping and exhaustive strata on the basis of some known characteristics of the population. These characteristics could be several administrative divisions of the country, ecological zones, rural-urban residence, and so on. Under this sampling, units within the strata are homogeneous but between strata they are heterogeneous. Here selection of a random sample is carried out from each stratum. The main objective of stratification is to give a better cross-section of the population so as to gain a higher degree of relative precision.

In stratified sampling, the population of N units is sub-divided into k sub-populations called strata, the ith sub-population having N_i units ($i = 1, 2, …, k$). These sub-populations are non-overlapping so that they comprise the whole population such that:

$$N_1 + N_2 + … + N_k = N \tag{9.2}$$

A sample is drawn from each stratum independently, the sample size within the ith stratum being n_i ($i = 1, 2, …, k$) such that:

144   *Handbook of research methods in corporate social responsibility*

$$n_1 + n_2 + \ldots + n_k = n \tag{9.3}$$

At the time of designing stratified sampling, three key issues have to be adequately taken into consideration. Firstly, the bases of stratification, that is, what characteristics should be used to sub-divide the population into strata? Secondly, the number of strata, that is, how many strata should be constructed and what stratum boundaries should be used? Thirdly, sample sizes within strata, that is, how many observations should be taken in each stratum?

To exemplify, if researchers want to know attitudes towards buying environmentally friendly products in a community, they can sub-divide the total community (population) into groups based on age, profession, geographical region, religion, income, and so on. It is likely that the attitude towards purchasing behavior of environmentally friendly products will differ between different locations, for example, people living in rural areas might have a more positive attitude on purchasing environmental friendly products than people living in the urban areas, assuming that the population are sub-divided based on geographical region. Furthermore, behavior of the people in the same areas will be similar (homogeneous). Therefore the strata (geographical groups) are externally heterogeneous and internally homogeneous.

Allocation of sample size in different strata

A good allocation is one where maximum precision is obtained with minimum resources, or to minimize the variance for a fixed budget, thus making effective use of the available resources. The allocation of the sample to different strata is done based on three factors. These include stratum size, variability within the stratum, and cost in taking observations per sampling unit in the stratum (Levin and Rubin 2001). There are four methods to allocate sample size to different strata. These are:

1. Equal allocation
2. Proportional allocation
3. Optimum allocation
4. Neyman allocation.

Example: Once strata have been established, the question becomes, 'How big a sample must be drawn from each?' Consider a situation where a survey of a two-stratum population is to be carried out (see Table 9.2).

Let us assume that the total sample size is 500.

Equal allocation: Sampling the same size or number of items in each stratum is termed as equal allocation. In this example, the overall sampling fraction is:

Table 9.2   Two-stratum population

Stratum	Number of items in stratum
A	10,000
B	90,000

$$\frac{\text{Sample size}}{\text{No. of stratum}} = \frac{500}{2} = 250 \qquad (9.4)$$

Thus, this method of allocation would result in: stratum A = 250 and stratum B = 250.

Proportional allocation: The most common approach would be to sample the same proportion of items in each stratum, which is termed as proportional allocation. In this example, the overall sampling fraction is:

$$\frac{\text{Sample size}}{\text{Population size}} = \frac{500}{100{,}000} = 0.005 \qquad (9.5)$$

Thus, under this method, allocation would result in: stratum A (10,000 × 0.005) = 50 and stratum B (90,000 × 0.005) = 450.

Optimum allocation: In situations where the standard deviations of the strata are known it may be advantageous to make a disproportionate allocation. Optimum allocation minimizes the standard error of the estimated mean by ensuring that more respondents are assigned to the stratum within which there is greatest variation. Suppose that the individuals assigned to stratum A were more varied with respect to their opinions than those assigned to stratum B, then more sample units will be drawn from stratum A.

Neyman allocation: When the unit costs of strata are all equal, the cost element of the optimum allocation can be cancelled out. This special case is known as Neyman allocation. That is, in the above example if the cost per observation is fixed in each stratum (say $5), then it is the Neyman allocation.

Advantages and disadvantages of stratified sampling
Stratified sampling provides less variability than random sampling. Characteristics of each sub-group can be estimated and comparisons can be made. The cost per observation in the survey may be reduced by stratification. When separate estimates for population parameters for each sub-population within an overall population are required, stratification is the preferable method. Stratification makes it possible to use different sampling designs in different strata. It is also most effective in handling heterogeneous populations such as data on wages of industrial workers, amount of rainfall, and so on. This method has some limitations as well. For example, it requires accurate information of the proportion of the population in each stratum. Otherwise it might be costly to prepare. Every chance of faulty classification will increase the variability. There is a need of previous experience. Furthermore, it is not possible to apply sampling if sizes of the different strata are unknown.

Cluster sampling
Cluster sampling is a sampling technique which consists in forming suitable clusters of elements and surveying all the elements in a sample of clusters selected according to an appropriate sampling scheme. In cluster sampling the sampling unit is a cluster. It is an economically efficient sampling technique in which the primary sampling unit is not the individual element in the population but a large cluster of elements. Cluster sampling is classified as a probability sampling technique because of either the random selection of clusters or the random selection of elements within each cluster.

To illustrate, for estimating the milk production in a city, different areas, such as different suburbs, can be taken as clusters, which consist of elements such as households. In order to save time and expenditure researchers can choose some suburbs/villages as clusters from the city council and take all households belonging to the suburbs/villages and surveying them. Such procedure of estimating the milk production in a city is called cluster sampling.

A large number of small clusters is better, all other things being equal, than a small number of large clusters. The lower cost of cluster sampling often outweighs the disadvantages of statistical inefficiency. In short, cluster sampling tends to offer greater reliability for a given cost rather than greater reliability for a given sample size. Ideally a cluster should be as heterogeneous as the population itself – a mirror image of the population. That is, clusters are internally heterogeneous and externally homogeneous as much as possible. Consider a researcher who aims to conduct 500 personal interviews with consumers scattered throughout the country, travel costs are likely to be enormous because the amount of time spent traveling will be substantially greater than the time spent in the interviewing process, cluster sampling may be used to represent the country. The key shortcomings of this sample are that if the clusters are not homogeneous among themselves, the sample may not be representative of the population.

Difference between stratified and clusters sampling
Although strata and clusters are both subsets of the population, they differ in several ways. For example, all strata are represented in the sample; but only a subset of clusters is represented in the sample. With stratified sampling, the best survey results occur when elements within strata are internally homogeneous. However, with cluster sampling, the best results occur when elements within clusters are internally heterogeneous (Zikmund 2008). Clustering, often done on the basis of geographical location, is subject to complete listing or records, and thus requires lower cost. On the other hand, stratification is done on the basis of some characteristics of the population, is subject to sampling, and therefore is costlier. Stratified sampling gives more efficient results than cluster sampling.

Multi-stage sampling
As the name implies, this method of sampling is carried out in several stages. The data are regarded as being made up of the first stage sampling units, which are, in turn, made up of second stage sampling units, which are made up of third stage sampling units, and so on. For example, to collect data for understanding an individual's intention to become involved in community activities, a state may be divided into a number of different districts (which will constitute first stage sampling units) and a certain number of districts might be selected by the method of random sampling. Then these districts may be divided into different villages. From the districts selected earlier, we might select some council or *thanas* as sub-areas of a district, again using random sampling. *Thanas* might then be divided into different villages; villages might be divided into different suburbs (*mohallas*), suburbs into households, and so on. The process of random selection, in this case, will be repeated in each stage.

Multi-stage sampling is used frequently when a complete list of all members of the population does not exist and is inappropriate. Moreover, by avoiding the use of all sample units in all selected clusters, multi-stage sampling avoids the large and perhaps unnecessary costs associated with traditional cluster sampling. This type of sampling technique is suitable particularly when researchers conduct a nationwide survey.

Non-Probability Sampling

Convenience sampling
Convenience sampling (also known as opportunity, accidental, or haphazard sampling) is a type of non-probability sampling which involves the sample being drawn from that part of the population which is near to hand. Field workers have the freedom to choose whomever they find. In other words, in convenience sampling, a sample is obtained by selecting convenient or suitable units from the population. The primary objective of such sampling is to collect samples at a lower cost. This type of sampling is most useful for a pilot testing phase.

While a convenience sample has no control to ensure precision, this method is quite frequently used, especially in market research and public opinion surveys. If the interviewer has to conduct a survey at a shopping center early in the morning on a particular day in a particular community, the people that he/she could interview would be limited to those people passing the center at that particular time, which may not represent the views of other members of the community in such an area, if the survey is to be carried out at different times of the day and several times per week. On the eve of nationwide elections, television channels can take public opinion and interview people that are on the street to get a quick response.

Judgement sampling
Judgement sampling (also known as purposive sampling or expert choice) is one type of non-probability sampling in which individuals are selected who are considered to be most representative of the population as a whole. It is called judgement sampling because choice of the individual units depends entirely on the researchers' decision. Researchers select samples that satisfy their specific purposes, even if samples are not fully representative. The consumer price index (CPI) is based on a judgement sample of market-basket items, housing costs, and other selected goods and services expected to reflect a representative sample of items consumed by most citizens.

In attempts to forecast election results, political and sampling experts judge which small voting districts approximate overall state results from previous election years; then these areas are selected as the sampling units known as judgement sampling. Of course, the assumption is that the past voting records of these districts are still representative of the political behavior of the state's population. This is used primarily when there are a limited number of people that have expertise in the area being researched.

Quota sampling
Under quota sampling, the population is first divided into mutually exclusive sub-groups similar to what is done in stratified sampling. Then judgement is used to select subjects or units from each segment based on a specified proportion. For example, in a country if it is known that one-third of the population lives in urban areas and two-thirds in rural areas, the sample can be selected purposively from urban and rural areas in the same proportion. A total of 300 respondents would mean 100 urban residents and 200 rural residents would

be included in the study. In quota sampling, the selection of the sample is non-random. Interviewers might be tempted to interview those who look most helpful. The problem is that these samples may be biased because not everybody gets a chance of selection (Levin and Rubin 2001). Rather, it is likely that people who are easily available will be included for interview. This random element is the greatest weakness and quota versus probability has been a matter of controversy for many years. Nevertheless, such sampling approach is popular because of lower costs, convenience, and so on.

Snowball sampling
Under snowball sampling, initial respondents are selected following the probability method, but later respondents are selected based on referral of initial respondents. That is, in snowball sampling, respondents initially chosen for the sample are used as informers to locate other respondents having the necessary characteristics to make them eligible for the sample through a referral network. This type of sampling approach is very much suitable if a population is rare. Consequently, referral is required from the individuals who were initially interviewed. Snowball sampling has been particularly useful to study drug cultures, heroin addiction, teenage gang activities, and so on. For example, a researcher wants to study teenage crimes in a particular city. The researcher would interview one teenage criminal, and would request him/her for the name of other teenage criminals. This sampling technique is clearly less expensive and suitable for rare samples.

Mixed Sampling

In the mixed sampling process probability sampling or random sampling are done at some stages and some non-probability methods are followed at other stages. In systematic sampling at first we draw the first element at random (with probability) and then other elements are drawn systematically (without probability). Mixed sampling has no classification. It may also be named hybrid sampling. For example, let us consider that a bank will pay 200 scholarships for the undergraduate and/or postgraduate students all over the country as part of its community activities. The bank may first select 40 universities using any probability sampling (SRS, stratified, cluster sampling, etc.) and request the heads of those selected universities to select and inform about five eligible students for scholarship. Institute heads then may use any non-probability sampling (convenient, judgement, snowball sampling, etc.) to select the desired five students as sampling units.

SAMPLING ERRORS, SAMPLE SIZE IN SURVEY-BASED RESEARCH DESIGN

Several potential sources of sampling errors can affect a research design. A good research design attempts to control the various sources of errors. Error is the variation between the true mean value in the population of the variable of interest and the observed mean value obtained in the research. Total error is composed of random sampling error and non-sampling error.

Sampling Errors

These are errors that arise due to the fact that a sample is being studied while inference is being made about the whole of the population. It is generally not possible to eliminate these errors completely because a sample is never a perfect representation of the population. Such errors are of two types, that is, biased errors and unbiased errors. Biased errors are those that occur due to any type of activity that favors a specific method of samples techniques selection. Unbiased errors occur unintentionally.

Sources of sampling errors

Rejection of certain items: sometimes it happens that the sample has been selected keeping the requirements in view but the researchers reject certain units which have been sampled on the grounds that they are extreme or atypical. Furthermore, researchers may modify the sample frame before the sampling takes place. For example, collection of information from the viewers who were on the spot of a bus accident case but omitting the interview of the bus driver himself.

Substitution: it may happen that the researcher resorts to substitution. For example, in a budget enquiry if researchers are required to visit a certain household, they may substitute that household with another household either because the members of the original household are not available or, if available, do not cooperate with the investigator. Or because it is difficult to reach that household on account of transportation problems. Such substitution induces bias in the study and affects the results adversely.

Non-response: non-response introduces bias if respondents who reply belong to the same stratum or differ significantly from the people who do not reply.

Presence of a selective factor: bias can also arise if a selective factor is present. It happens when respondents do not give a reply to a particular question in the questionnaire.

Faulty formulation and biased information: any bias in formulating the research problem, choosing the sampling frame, error in measurement of constructs, poorly designed questionnaire, and so on can cause an error in the final data analysis. Such biases have a more adverse effect in a sample study than a census study because the size of a sample is usually much smaller than the size of a population.

Bias due to a wrong estimation method: sometimes bias occurs due to a faulty estimation method. Such biases can be easily avoided if proper care is taken in choosing the method of analysis. This can be ensured by employing skilled and trained research team members to do the job.

Reducing Sampling Errors

The easiest method of reducing the sampling error is to increase the size of the sample. There is an inverse relationship between the sampling error and the sample size shown in Table 9.3.

Presenting the above data on graph paper, the graph shown in Figure 9.1 is depicted.

The figure below shows that when the size of the sample is very small, sampling error is very large. As the sample size increases, the sampling error decreases. Thus, when a sample survey becomes a census, sampling error becomes zero.

Table 9.3 Comparison of sample size and sampling errors

Sample size	100	200	300	400	500	600	800	1000	1200	1500	2000	2500	3000	4000	5000
%-error (95% CI)	4.4	3.1	2.5	2.2	2	1.8	1.5	1.4	1.3	1.1	0.96	0.87	0.79	0.69	0.62

Note: CI – confidence interval.

Source: Malhotra (2000), p. 376.

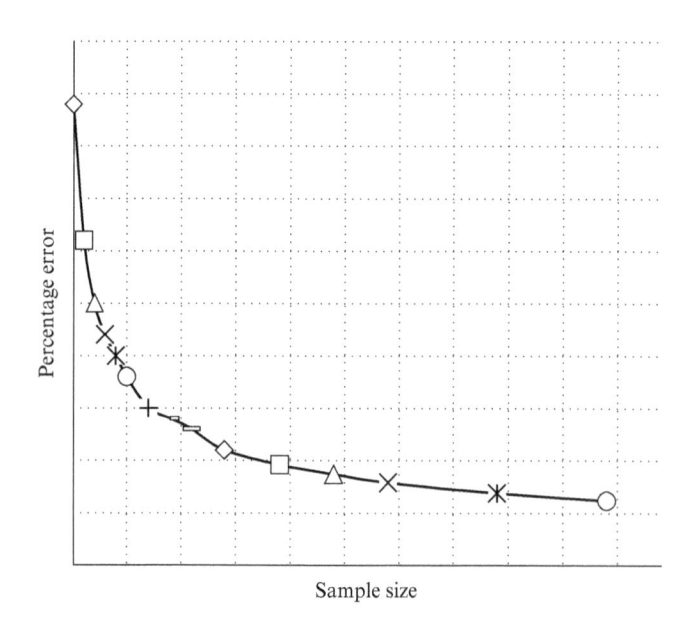

Figure 9.1 Comparison of sample size and sampling errors

Non-Sampling Errors

Errors that occur in acquiring, recording, or tabulating statistical data are known as non-sampling errors. Such errors can exist in a sample enquiry as well as a census enquiry. Non-response to a survey by respondents is a good example of non-sampling error. To exemplify, to sanction some funds for the poor and talented students, suppose a university authority wants to collect information from the selected students as sample units. Students may hide their guardian's income, or his/her age to cover the age limits. This causes non-sampling errors.

Sources of non-sampling errors

In academic research, researchers experience non-sample errors as a result of many factors. These include faulty definitions of the population or the statistical units, faulty formulation of the questionnaire, faulty methods of conducting interviews such as asking 'sensitive' questions, lack of trained and skilled investigators to carry out the survey, bias of the investigators, non-response or incomplete response to the questionnaire, and so on. Incomplete response occurs when the respondent does not provide information on certain questions. Sometimes the respondent might furnish wrong information to safeguard his/her interest or show off his/her wealth, social status, and so on.

Calculation of Sample Size

In the literature, there have not been any short-cut methods of determining the sample size. Past researchers proposed sample sizes for different types of research, given in Table 9.4.

The appropriate sample size for a particular application depends on many factors, including the following:

1. Cost considerations (e.g., maximum budget, desire to minimize cost).
2. Administrative concerns (e.g., complexity of the design, research deadlines).
3. Minimum acceptable level of precision.
4. Confidence level.
5. Variability within the population or sub-population (e.g., stratum, cluster) of interest.
6. Sampling method.

Estimation of sample size (n) for estimating population mean

For estimating the population mean when the population size is large, the sample size is $n = z^2\sigma^2/D^2$ where n = sample size; σ^2 = population variance; D = margin of error; z = critical value. That is, critical value of 5 per cent and 1 per cent level of significance are 1.96 and 2.58 respectively.

If the population size is not large, then modify the sample size as:

Table 9.4 Sample sizes used in market research studies

Types of study	Minimum size	Typical range
Problem identification research	500	1000–2500
Problem solving research	200	300–500
Product tests	200	300–500
Testing different studies	200	300–500
Different commercial ad test	150	200–300
Testing market audits	10 stores	10–20 stores
Focus groups	6 groups	10–15 groups

Source: Malhotra (2000), pp. 332–333.

$$n^* = \frac{n}{1 + \frac{n}{N}} \qquad (9.6)$$

where N = size of population.

Estimation of sample size (n) for estimating population proportion
If P is a population proportion and p is its corresponding proportion in the sample, then:

$$n = \frac{Z^2 pq}{D^2} \qquad (9.7)$$

where n = sample size
   z = with the standard normal deviate (z at 5% = 1.96 and z at 1% = 2.58)
   p = proportion of target population
   $q = 1 - p$
   D = level of accuracy precision level, usually it is taken at 5%
or the margin of error.

If p is unknown then consider $p = 0.5$ which maximizes the distribution:

$$n = \frac{z^2 \times 0.5 \times 0.5}{D^2} \qquad (9.8)$$

If the population is less than 10,000 then n should be adjusted by the finite population correction factor:

$$n_f = \frac{n}{1 + \frac{n}{N}} \qquad (9.9)$$

Estimation of sample size using sample size calculator
The calculator shown in Table 9.5 can be used for determining the minimum sample size for a given range of error. For example, if an investigator assumes acceptable sampling errors are 2 per cent at a 95 per cent confidence interval, sample size would be 500. Similarly, if the researcher wants to calculate the sample size to estimate at 50 per cent confidence interval within 5 per cent sampling error, the answer would be 400.

APPROPRIATE SAMPLE DESIGN TOGETHER WITH RECENT TRENDS OF SAMPLING TECHNIQUES AND THE CHALLENGES OF INTERNET SAMPLING

When designing an appropriate sample, a number of factors will have an influential role. These include degree of accuracy, availability of resources, time frame of research projects, advance knowledge of the population, nationwide versus local research projects, necessity of types of statistical analysis to be done, and so on (Zikmund 2008).

Table 9.5 Sample size calculation for a given level of significance (confidence interval) with a given percentage of sampling errors

Sig. level (Confidence interval) \ Sample size	100	200	300	400	500	600	800	1000	1200	1500	2000	2500	3000	4000	5000
5% (95%)	4.4	3.1	2.5	2.2	2.0	1.8	1.5	1.4	1.3	1.1	0.96	0.87	0.79	0.69	0.62
10% (90%)	6.0	4.3	3.5	3.0	2.7	2.5	2.1	1.9	1.7	1.6	1.3	1.2	1.1	0.95	0.85
15% (85%)	7.1	5.1	4.1	3.6	3.2	2.9	2.5	2.3	2.1	1.9	1.6	1.4	1.3	1.1	1.0
20% (80%)	8.0	5.7	4.6	4.0	3.6	3.3	2.8	2.5	2.3	2.1	1.8	1.6	1.4	1.3	1.1
25% (75%)	8.7	6.1	5.0	4.3	3.9	3.6	3.0	2.8	2.5	2.3	1.9	1.7	1.6	1.4	1.2
30% (70%)	9.2	6.5	5.3	4.6	4.1	3.8	3.2	2.9	2.7	2.4	2.0	1.8	1.7	1.4	1.3
35% (65%)	9.5	6.8	5.5	4.8	4.3	3.9	3.3	3.1	2.8	2.5	2.1	1.9	1.7	1.5	1.4
40% (60%)	9.8	7.0	5.7	4.9	4.4	4.0	3.4	3.1	2.8	2.5	2.2	2.0	1.8	1.5	1.4
45% (55%)	9.9	7.0	5.8	5.0	4.5	4.1	3.5	3.2	2.9	2.6	2.2	2.0	1.8	1.6	1.4
50% (50%)	10.0	7.1	5.8	5.0	4.5	4.1	3.5	3.2	2.9	2.6	2.2	2.0	1.8	1.6	1.4

Source: Malhotra (2000), p. 376.

Recent Trends of Sampling Techniques (Internet and Web-Based Sampling), and Some Challenges of Internet Sampling

Nowadays, researchers are interested in collecting data using internet and websites. Consequently online, internet surveys have gained immense popularity. This sub-section discusses various types of internet-based sampling techniques.

Types of internet-based surveys

Fricker (2008) classifies the most common types of internet-based surveys (shown in Table 9.6) based on probability or non-probability sampling methods and which internet-based survey mode or modes apply or are most generally used. For example, although it is realistic to conduct an entertainment poll by e-mail, virtually all such polls are conducted using web-based surveys.

Surveys using a list-based sampling frame

Sampling for 'internet-based surveys using a list-based sampling frame' can be conducted in a similar manner to that which one would consider for a traditional survey using a sampling frame. In this regard, SRS is easy to implement and requires merely contact information (generally an e-mail address for an internet-based survey) for each unit in the sampling frame. Although only contact information is required to complete the survey, having as much additional demographic and other information about each unit in the sampling frame is desirable to assess (and perhaps adjust for) non-response effects.

While internet-based surveys using list-based sampling frames can be conducted either

Table 9.6   Different types of internet-based sampling techniques

Sampling method	Web	e-mail
Probability-based		
Surveys using a list-based sampling frame	√	√
Surveys using non-list-based random sampling	√	√
Intercept (pop-up) surveys	√	
Mixed mode surveys with internet-based option	√	√
Pre-recruited panel surveys	√	√
Non-probability-based		
Entertainment polls	√	
Unrestricted self-selected surveys	√	
Surveys using 'harvested' e-mail lists (and data)	√	√
Surveys using volunteer (opt-in) panels	√	

Source: Fricker (2008).

via the web or by e-mail, the invitations to take part in the surveys are generally made by means of e-mail. However, given that e-mail lists of general populations are not readily available at all times, this survey approach is most applicable to large homogeneous groups for which a sampling frame with e-mail addresses can be assembled (e.g., universities, government organizations, large corporations, and so on).

In more complicated sampling schemes, such as stratified sampling, auxiliary information about each unit, such as membership of the relevant strata, must be available and linked to the unit's contact information. Multi-stage and cluster sampling schemes are impossible to implement for internet-based surveys for a few reasons. First, to implement without having to contact respondents will likely require significant auxiliary data available as part of the sampling frame, which is unlikely to be available except in the case of specialized populations. Second, if contact is required, then the researchers are likely to have to resort to the telephone or mail in order to ensure sufficient coverage and response rates are achieved.

Surveys using non-list-based random sampling
Non-list-based random sampling methods allow for the selection of a probability-based sample without the need to actually specify a sampling frame. With traditional surveys, random digit dialing (RDD) is a non-list-based random sampling method that is used mainly for telephone surveys. There is no equivalent of RDD for internet-based surveys. For example, it is not possible to generate random e-mail addresses. Hence, internet-based surveys requiring non-list-based random sampling depend on contacting potential respondents via some traditional means such as RDD (Fricker 2008).

However, communicating with respondents by means of a traditional medium involves additional complications and costs. For example, researchers must either screen potential respondents to ensure they have internet access or field a survey with multiple response modes. Surveys with multiple response modes introduce further complications, both in terms of fielding complexity and possible mode effects.

Intercept surveys

Intercept surveys on the web frequently use systematic sampling for every nth visitor to a website or web page (Fricker 2008). These surveys are mostly applicable in research projects such as customer satisfaction surveys or marketing surveys. Fricker (2008) mentioned that this type of systematic sampling can provide information that is generalizable to particular populations, such as those that visit particular websites/pages. Furthermore, the surveys can be restricted to only those with certain IP (internet protocol) addresses, allowing one to target more specific populations of inference than just all visitors to a website/page (Fricker 2008). However, a potential issue with this type of survey is non-response.

Pre-recruited panel surveys

In general, pre-recruited panel surveys are conducted among groups of individuals who have given their consent previously (therefore are named as 'pre-recruited') to take part in a series of surveys. Respondents are compensated with small financial incentives for their time. For internet-based surveys requiring probability samples, these respondents have to be pre-recruited by some means. Very often, their consent to take part in the survey is confirmed by telephone or postal mail. Pre-recruited panel surveys that use probabilistic sampling such as knowledge networks can be a smart option for researchers who desire to field an internet-based survey (see Pineau and Dennis (2004) for further analysis). However, pre-recruited panels have some drawbacks too. In particular, researchers should be aware that long-term panel participants may respond differently to surveys and survey questions (Fricker 2008).

Entertainment polls

Internet-based entertainment polls are 'surveys' conducted purely for their entertainment value. In the internet-based territory, they largely consist of websites where site visitors can respond to one or more surveys that are posted where anyone can complete without restriction. The telephone equivalent of these types of polls is the certain digit numbers (e.g., number 900) to call-in poll those advertised on various television shows where viewers can vote for their favorite contestant or character while watching TV shows.

Surveys using 'harvested e-mail lists'

'Harvested e-mail lists' are those collected somehow from the web, either automatically or manually, that are posted on websites. Sometimes it is also deliberately managed from individuals browsing the web. Many commercial organizations such as 'e-mail brokers' sell the lists of e-mail addresses or access to lists of e-mail addresses (just Google 'buy e-mail list'). Researchers can also gather various lists of e-mail addresses directly from the web. For example, anyone can create the detailed lists of Yahoo e-mail address holders by name or geographic area by means of the Yahoo search engine!

Sampling technique used in harvested e-mail lists are non-probability samples because they are based on a convenience sample of e-mail addresses which are often an aggregation of addresses collected. Researchers in this regard argued that the effectiveness of sending unsolicited surveys to a list of purchased or otherwise managed list of e-mail addresses is dubious and uncertain (Fricker 2008). Because many of those potential respondents on the e-mail list are likely to be selected either without their knowledge or

156 *Handbook of research methods in corporate social responsibility*

they may have unintentionally agreed by failing to uncheck a box when they signed up for something else, it is not therefore unusual that response rates under such survey will be very low. Besides, an unsolicited survey basically creates not only spam but also is unethical, even prohibited in some parts of the world.

Unrestricted self-selected surveys
Unrestricted self-selected surveys are surveys that are open to the general public who wish to take part. They may just be posted on a website so that anyone browsing through that page may choose to take the survey. Sometimes, the public may be promoted to participate via website banners or other internet-based advertisements, or they may be publicized in traditional print and broadcast media. Similar to entertainment polls, unrestricted self-selected surveys are based on convenience sampling technique. As such, the results cannot be generalized to a larger population (Fricker 2008).

Volunteer (opt-in) panels
Volunteer (opt-in) panels are similar in concept to the pre-recruited panels with one exception. For example, in volunteer panels the participants are not recruited. Rather, they offer to participate voluntarily, perhaps after coming across a solicitation on a website (Fricker 2008).

SUGGESTIONS AND CONCLUSIONS FOR SELECTING SAMPLES IN CSR RESEARCH

In this chapter, we discuss the selection of sample procedures for a researcher who wants to study the social responsibility field. The sampling design process or selection of samples includes several steps. These steps are closely related and relevant to all aspects of any research project, which are shown sequentially in the diagram in Figure 9.2.

At first, researchers need to define the population or target population, which is the collection of elements or objects that possess the information sought by the researcher. The target population should be defined in terms of elements, sampling units, extent, and time. Then researchers need to select a sampling frame. As stated earlier, a sampling frame is the representation of the elements of the target population. It consists of a list or set of directions for identifying the target population. Examples are a telephone book or city directory.

As a third step, researchers will select sampling techniques. Selecting a sampling technique involves several broader decisions. For example, the researcher must decide whether to use a traditional sampling approach, or to sample with or without replacement. The most important decision about the choice of sampling technique is whether to use probability or non-probability sampling (discussed in the previous sections).

After selecting the sampling techniques, researchers will define the procedure of selecting the sample units from the sampling frame. Subsequently, researchers will focus on determination of sample size. As discussed earlier, the number of elements to be included in a study is the sample size. Determination of sample size is complex and involves several qualitative and quantitative considerations. Quantitative consideration includes the application of some statistical techniques to determine the sample size (discussed previously).

```
┌─────────────────────────────────────────────────────────────────────────────┐
│                            Define a population                              │
└─────────────────────────────────────────────────────────────────────────────┘
                                      ⇩
┌─────────────────────────────────────────────────────────────────────────────┐
│                           Select a sample frame                             │
└─────────────────────────────────────────────────────────────────────────────┘
                                      ⇩
┌─────────────────────────────────────────────────────────────────────────────┐
│   Determine whether a probability or non-probability sampling technique     │
│                              will be chosen                                 │
└─────────────────────────────────────────────────────────────────────────────┘
                                      ⇩
┌─────────────────────────────────────────────────────────────────────────────┐
│        Plan a procedure for selecting sampling units from sample techniques │
└─────────────────────────────────────────────────────────────────────────────┘
                                      ⇩
┌─────────────────────────────────────────────────────────────────────────────┐
│                           Determine sample size                             │
└─────────────────────────────────────────────────────────────────────────────┘
                                      ⇩
┌─────────────────────────────────────────────────────────────────────────────┐
│                       Determine actual sampling units                       │
└─────────────────────────────────────────────────────────────────────────────┘
                                      ⇩
┌─────────────────────────────────────────────────────────────────────────────┐
│                            Conduct fieldwork                                │
└─────────────────────────────────────────────────────────────────────────────┘
```

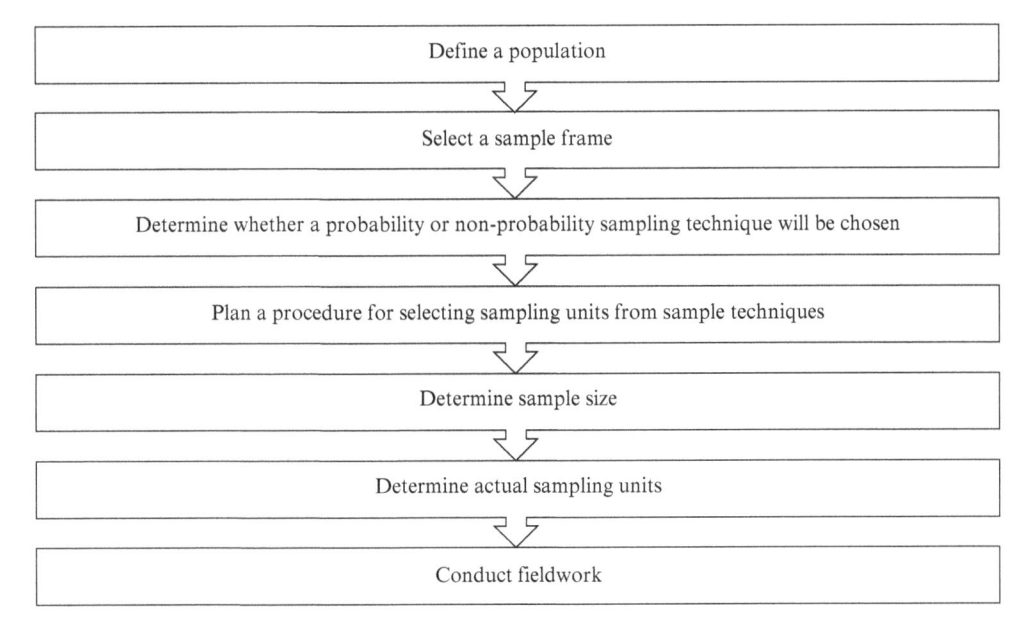

Source: Zikmund (2008).

Figure 9.2 Stages in the selection of a sample

In the qualitative consideration, a few factors are taken into consideration. For example, the importance of the decision, the nature of the research, number of variables, nature of the data analysis, sample size used in similar previous studies, incidence rate, completion rate, and resource constraints.

Following determination of sample size, researchers need to specify the actual sampling units. That is, from which and how many sample units will be selected. Finally, researchers need to execute the sampling process with respect to the population; sampling frame, sampling unit, sampling technique, and sample size are to be implemented in the fieldwork level.

The above-mentioned steps are illustrated in the following example. Suppose a telephone survey will be conducted for the Sydney Department of Tourism to gain an understanding of in-state residents' travel behavior. Households will be screened to locate family members with a working telephone number and having four qualifications such as age 25 or more, living in Sydney at least eight months of the year, having lived in Sydney for at least the last three years, having a valid driving license.

To obtain a representative sample of qualified respondents, the steps in the sampling design process are:

1. Target population: adults meeting the four qualifications in a household with a working telephone number in the city of Sydney during the survey period.
2. Sampling frame: computer program for generating random telephone numbers.
3. Sampling technique: the target population was geographically stratified into four

regions such as North, Central, West, and South Sydney. In such a case, stratified sampling would be followed.
4. Sample size: determined by the above explained technique.
5. Sampling unit: working telephone numbers.
6. Execution: allocate the sample among strata; select a member of the household meeting the qualifications and other interpretation about the population and conduct the field study.

BIBLIOGRAPHY

Cochran, William (1953), *Sampling Techniques*, New York: John Wiley & Sons, Inc.
Cooper, Donald R. and C. William Emory (1995), *Business Research Methods*, 5th edn, New York: Richard D. Irwin, Inc.
Deming, Edward (1960), *Sample Design in Business Research*, New York: John Wiley & Sons.
Fricker, R.D. (2008), 'Sampling methods for web and e-mail surveys', in N. Fielding, R.M. Lee and G. Blank (eds), *The SAGE Handbook of Online Research Methods*, Los Angeles, CA: Sage, pp. 195–216.
Levin, R. and D. Rubin (2001), *Statistics for Management*, 7th edn, New Delhi: Prentice-Hall, India.
Malhotra, N. K. (2000), *Marketing Research*, 3rd edn, USA: Prentice Hall International Editions.
Parimal, Mukhopadhyay (1998), *Theory and Methods of Survey Sampling*, New Delhi: Prentice-Hall, India.
Pineau, V. and J. Dennis (2004), 'Methodology for probability-based recruitment for a web enabled panel', dated 21 November, accessed 21 November 2014 at www.knowledgenetworks.com/ganp/reviewer-info.html.
Seal, K.C. (1962), 'Use of outdated frames in large scale sample surveys', *Calcutta Statistics Association Bulletin*, **11**, 12–26.
Singh, R. (1983), 'On the use of incomplete frames in sample survey', *Biomedical Journal*, **25**, 545–549.
Zikmund, William (2008), *Business Research Method*, 7th edn, USA: South-Western College Pub.

10. Food deserts in British cities: comparing food access, obesity, and ethnicity in Leicester and Stoke on Trent
Hillary J. Shaw

INTRODUCTION

This chapter critically examines the socio-economic factors affecting diet, health and obesity in two major British cities. Diet is not merely a private issue but has significant health and financial implications due to the rapidly rising medical costs of obesity, in the UK and elsewhere. A coordinated approach, involving government, corporations, small to medium-sized enterprises (SMEs) and the local community is fundamental to tackling the health issues raised by 'food deserts'. Social responsibility, not the exclusive pursuit of private profit alone, is crucial. Multiple food access-related factors are explored in relation to how they affect quality of diet and therefore increase or decrease a person's chance of being obese. A quantitative approach involving partial correlations using data from the UK Government socio-economic database website Neighbourhood Statistics is used to explicate the effect of social, spatial, demographic and economic factors on nutrition. Ethnicity is significant to diet, both through cultural and economic mediation of consumption and through the provision of ethnic-minority oriented grocery shops in certain areas. Comparison of obesity levels in Leicester and Stoke on Trent suggests that Stoke on Trent offers easier access to lower-priced food than does Leicester, due to its polycentric urban structure, which gives better access to local shops and markets for its less affluent citizens.

WHAT ARE 'FOOD DESERTS'?

An explanation of key terms is an important starting point for any research conducted in the field. In this case, the phrase 'food desert' was first coined by a respondent in Glasgow, during a survey by the Low Income Project Team (LIPT) in 1996, as a local resident communicated their perception of the poor quality of the food retailers in the area, the lack of fresh produce on their shelves, and the high cost of healthy foodstuffs where they were sold locally (Cummins and Macintyre 2002). Difficulties of physical access to grocery shops, for some sections of the population, had been recognized as a problem back in the 1970s when the Women's Institute began research into widows left stranded in English villages with no car. Rural trains and buses had been cut back as car ownership grew, rural settlements became commuter dormitories, and local independent stores were beginning to close as the supermarket concept crossed the Atlantic from America to Britain.

The LIPT described food deserts as 'areas of relative exclusion where people experience physical and economic barriers to accessing healthy food' (Reisig and Hobbiss 2000,

p. 138). The election of New Labour in Britain in 1997 brought a new focus on urban deprivation, and studies of food access in other cities began. Without any formal definition ever being made, the concept of 'food deserts' has come to generally signify residential areas, urban or rural, with the following attributes (Shaw 2014, p. 106).

Green Stores

'Green stores' are shops selling items that would count towards the 'Five-a-Day' dietary guidelines. Many such green stores have closed, and the remaining retailers sell mainly processed ready meals, takeaways, frozen or tinned food. Although tinned vegetables are better, dietarily, than none at all, they tend to be higher in sugar or salt, and may be lower in vitamin content. Meanwhile frozen fruit and vegetables can be good nutritionally but it is hard for the consumer to spot signs of ageing and vitamin decay; local convenience stores also often have a rather limited range of these, especially the higher-nutrient vegetables such as broccoli and blueberries.

Retailers

Retailers in food desert areas are often independent stores and therefore charge higher prices than supermarkets. Since 1994 the supermarkets have been opening local branches, such as Tesco Express, but these charge more than full-scale supermarkets, which tend to be located away from poorer residential areas and are car-access focused. Fresh produce is frequently costlier than processed or takeaway food, the 'health premium', and this premium has widened across the UK from 18 per cent over unhealthy food in 1988 to 48 per cent in 2007.

In less affluent areas the UK health premium has widened over the same period from 20 per cent to 58 per cent (*Food Magazine* 2008), as meals like burgers have become 'ridiculously cheap', to quote a Birmingham nutritionist. Healthier food can be bought cheaply in markets; this is discussed below.

Residents Affected

Residents affected by food deserts tend to be low income, and therefore lack private motor transport. Lack of private transport makes accessing distant cheaper supermarkets problematical in several ways. What is a maximum acceptable walking distance to shops (and back with shopping) will vary from person to person; in 2000 Beverley Hughes, UK Government Minister, suggested 500 metres. Some poor rural dwellers will walk much further, but older or disabled consumers, or those with children, might not manage even this distance, and sickness is more prevalent amongst those on low income.

Other obstacles such as hills or busy roads can reduce the mobility of pensioners or mothers with children. Beyond walking access, the car-less must resort to buses, which are expensive, difficult to carry multiple bags of shopping on, may not go near everyone's home, and involve long stands in the cold, not good for the elderly. Fresh fruit and vegetables are not only more expensive per calorie; they are also heavier per calorie. For a family of four, the 'five-a-day' rule would probably entail one extra shopping trip a week, at a cost of circa £3.00, to carry the extra five bags of shopping required (Shaw 2014, p. 114), which is a big slice of income or Jobseeker's Allowance for the low paid or unemployed, who unlike pensioners get no bus travel concessions. Some consumers have developed coping strategies, to facilitate cheaper transport of shopping from distant supermarkets, for example walking out and sharing a taxi back with shoppers from other households, but this level of community co-operation does not exist in all deprived areas.

Consequences

Although there are malnourished people in Britain, people who do not consume enough micronutrients (vitamins and minerals) for good health, there are very few undernourished people. Even in food deserts, people do not starve; the opposite in fact, they often consume too many calories, from food with high levels of sugar and fat, leading to obesity. Obesity is not just damaging to the individual; it carries high costs for society, through the diseases it causes. Cheap food is also often high in salt. Consuming excess levels of fat, salt and sugar predisposes, via obesity, towards a wide range of diseases, including arthritis (from overloaded joints), asthma, cancer, cardiovascular problems (ranging from heart attacks to clogged arteries and strokes), diabetes (which itself predisposes towards blindness and amputations), gallstones, gout, osteoporosis (unhealthy diets may be low in micronutrients such as calcium) and psychiatric problems (low self-esteem from being obese, which itself may push people into extra 'comfort' eating, of sugary fatty foods). Sleep apnoea, another side effect of obesity, leads to daytime tiredness, predisposing to car accidents and injuries from machinery operations. The multiple morbidities from obesity may age the body so that a 40-year-old obese person has the body of a 55-year-old from a less obese population (Hulsegge et al. 2013).

SOCIAL ISSUES ARISING FROM FOOD DESERTS AND POOR DIET

When New Labour was elected in Britain in 1997 they had a further problem to tackle; the rise in adult obesity, from 6 per cent in 1980 to nearly 25 per cent by 2010 and predicted to be 40 per cent by 2025 (Butland et al. 2007, p. 6). The increase in obesity since the 1970s, a phenomenon observed in many developed countries, costs the UK economy in excess of £20 billion so it is not surprising that a considerable body of research has been undertaken on why many consumers persist with unhealthy diets, and the best approaches to rectifying such poor eating habits. Growing one's own food, eating fresh fruit and vegetables, and reducing intake of convenience food and fast food are major themes in the Department of Health report, *Healthy Lives, Healthy People* (Department of Health 2010).

UK Government reports, at a national as well as a city-wide scale, have implicated a range of socio-economic factors moderating the diet of individuals and families. White et al. (2004) stated that 'less healthy diets were associated with social disadvantage, having poorer dietary knowledge and spending less on food'. Butland et al. (2007, p. 84) presents a wide range of factors, environmental, physiological, psychological and sociological, that may have positive or negative feedback effects on obesity. The Low Income Diet and Nutrition Survey (Nelson et al. 2007, p. 44) implicated lifestyle and knowledge factors in poor diet, for the less affluent, but stated 'access to cooking facilities and shops did not seem to be a limiting factor in terms of food consumption or nutrient intake'. The presence of multiple independent shops and even small supermarkets in densely populated less affluent areas, often with significant ethnic-minority communities, is a confounding factor when attempting to correlate distance to shops with obesity. In contrast, very affluent areas, for example parts of Hampstead in London or Sutton Coldfield in Birmingham, have large areas entirely free of any shops, and very little evidence of dietary deprivation either. However, some older residents in these affluent areas may face difficulties with accessing groceries, if they have no Internet, are disabled, and there is, as is often the case, no bus service in these wealthier areas.

The effect of distance to retailers selling healthy foodstuffs has been investigated by a number of researchers. Guy proposed a link between poor access to healthy food and poor diet in Cardiff and Leeds (Guy et al. 2004), whilst Wrigley et al. (2002) notes connections between diet and physical access to high-quality supermarket retailing in several UK cities, including Birmingham (Castle Vale), Leeds (Seacroft) and Manchester (Hulme). Ethnicity has also been linked to quality of diet; recent migrants are frequently poor, on low earnings, and faced with an unfamiliar and often culturally inappropriate selection of foods (Shaw 2009). Ethnic communities are often slow to change their dietary habits so such issues persist amongst second and third generation migrants. Therefore research into the impact of ethnicity on consumption of a healthy diet must cope with a wide range of interrelating factors. Donkin et al. (1999) found that whilst physical access for Gujarati Hindus in Wembley, London, was good, financial access was poor because food at independent small shops selling Gujarati foods was expensive. The UK situation contrasts with findings in the USA, where researchers have discovered that ethnic minorities, especially Black Africans, tend to live in deprived areas that are physically further from retailers selling healthy food, and this distance combines with poverty to predispose towards obesity. Gallagher found the worst access to food and highest obesity was in the deprived southwest of Chicago (Gallagher 2006). Zenk et al. (2005a) reported a similar situation prevailing in Detroit; Zenk et al. (2005b) also found that as the educational attainment and the wealth of Black African households rose, so did their propensity to eat a healthy diet. Lee and Hyunwoo (2009), and Sparks et al. (2011) also find that lower income is a significant factor in promoting a poor diet.

Understanding the relationship between food deserts, diet and obesity therefore encompasses a wide range of social factors, including economics, education, ethnicity, housing, psychology, retail geography and transport. In the remainder of this chapter the social characteristics of two contrasting UK cities are compared to explore the statistical relationships between obesity and their demographic composition.

LEICESTER AND STOKE ON TRENT: DEMOGRAPHIC AND GEOGRAPHIC CHARACTERISTICS

Leicester and Stoke on Trent are both medium-sized industrial cities located in the Midlands region of the UK. However, these cities differ greatly in the ethnic composition of their populations. Leicester is very racially diverse and has been pinpointed as the first city in Britain where White people were predicted to become a minority 'soon after 2011' (Finney and Simpson 2009). In the 2001 Census, 63.9 per cent of the population of

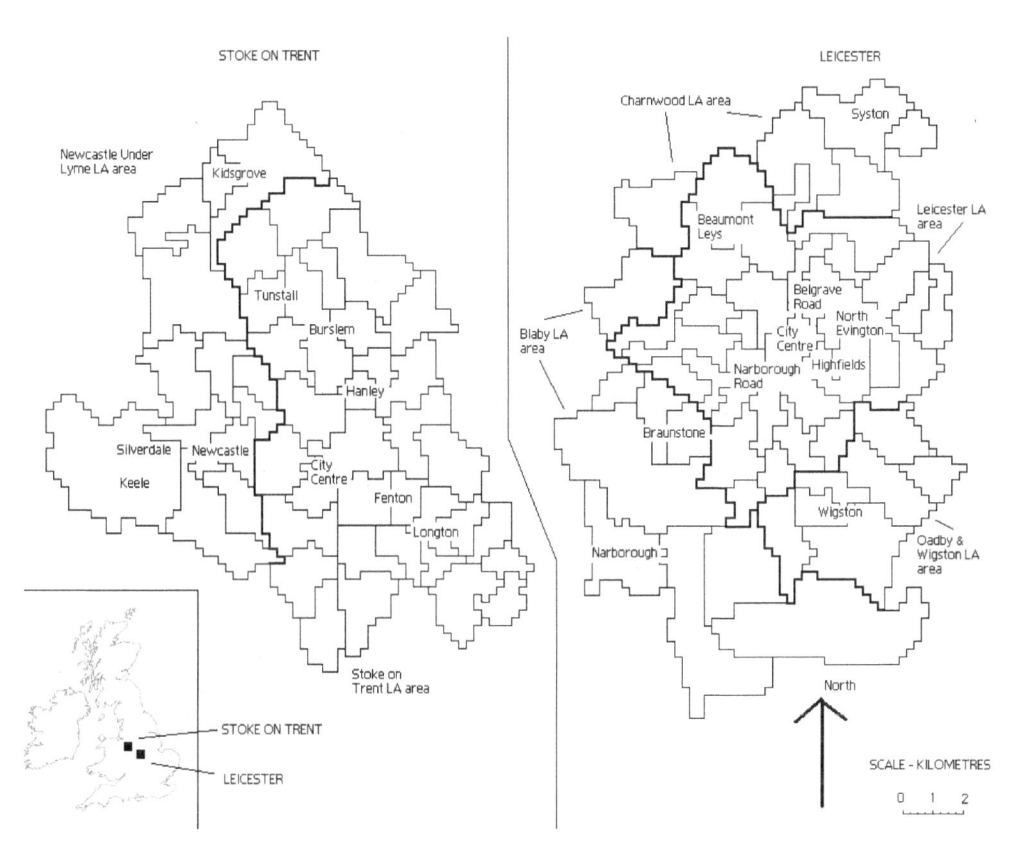

Note: Middle Level Super Output Areas (MLSOAs) are statistical areal units of population circa 7,000 used on the UK Government's Neighbourhood Statistics website.

Figure 10.1 Maps for Leicester and Stoke on Trent, showing MLSOA boundaries and place names mentioned in text

Leicester (292,000) described themselves as White; in Stoke on Trent (240,000) the figure was 94.8 per cent (Office for National Statistics 2009). Across the areas studied here (see map above, Figure 10.1), the percentage of the population who were Asian was 21.29 per cent in Leicester and its suburbs, but only 3.07 per cent in Stoke and its suburbs.

Cordy and Robson (1985) wrote that the Belgrave Road area, north of Leicester city centre, had changed from no Asian shops in 1969 to having 179 Asian shops; 76 per cent of shops along the Belgrave Road. Highfields, east of the centre, was also noted as an ethnic-retail centre. Today Leicester also has a third centre of ethnic-minority shopping, the Narborough Road, southwest of the centre.

Belgrave Road caters mainly for an Indian/Hindu population, Highfields for Pakistanis/Muslims, and the Narborough Road is more mixed, with Indian/Hindu retailers, together with some Pakistani/Muslim and East European/Kurdish shops. In 1985 Cordy found that the Belgrave Road comprised mainly comparison goods retailers, with convenience goods sold in the hinterland behind the main shop frontages, and that Asian households

164 *Handbook of research methods in corporate social responsibility*

still bought most food at Leicester's city centre market. In 2010 the market still operated, but the Asian superstores had arrived; for example Pak Foods had two stores in the North Evington area of Leicester. Pak Foods also has a store in Stoke on Trent, but there are far fewer signs of an Asian population, for example ethnic-minority food stores or non-Christian places of worship, than in the similarly sized city of Leicester. Figure 10.2, map 1, shows the MLSOAs with the highest and lowest percentage of Asian people in Leicester and Stoke.

Leicester is more varied racially, but in terms of urban form Stoke on Trent has a

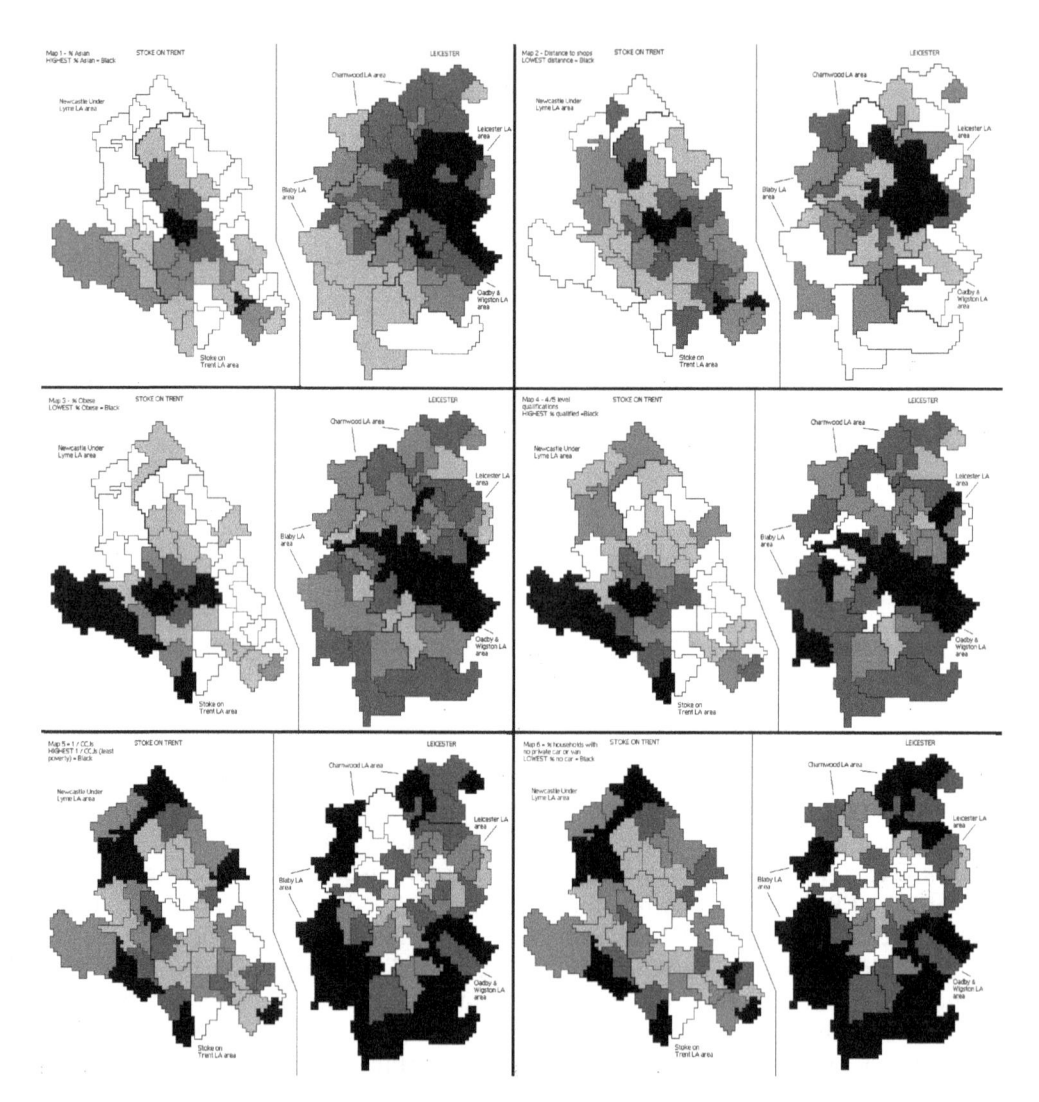

Note: Grey shading is by quintile, with darker colours showing higher ethnicity, or socio-economic characteristics expected to produce lower obesity rates, for example higher car ownership.

Figure 10.2 Selected MLSOA characteristics for Leicester and Stoke on Trent

more diverse structure. Leicester is a standalone monocentric city, in contrast Stoke on Trent has a dispersed, polycentric, urban structure, with historic urban cores at Burslem, Fenton, Longton, Silverdale and Tunstall. Figure 10.2, map 2, shows the MLSOAs in the two cities with highest and lowest average distances between homes and FFV (fresh fruit and vegetable) shops. These older districts, shaded black on the map, correspond to the densely built-up terraced housing areas; the polycentric nature of Stoke contrasts with the single core of Leicester. These inner areas have fewer supermarkets such as Tesco and Sainsbury, and more independent 'corner shops'. Street markets, cheaply priced, are often found in these areas, for example at Longton. The geography of race and poverty is therefore very different in Leicester and Stoke on Trent.

In Stoke, the poorer areas are mainly White and are dispersed across the conurbation, tending towards the older urban districts scattered across the presently built-up area. In Leicester the less affluent White areas are in the outer council housing (local government owned housing) districts of Beaumont Leys and Braunstone. The less affluent Asian areas occur in Leicester in inner (western) Highfields, with the more affluent Asian area in outer (eastern) Highfields; in Stoke the less affluent Asians live in inner city areas such as Stoke and Burslem. Poverty is closely linked with poor diet and obesity, but consumption of a healthy diet can be facilitated by the proximity of healthy food outlets, making access easier for car-less households. One might therefore expect (less affluent) Asians to enjoy a healthier diet with lower obesity rates in Leicester, where this community has a substantial Asian-oriented number of FFV shops, compared to the Asians in Stoke who lack this retail provision. Figure 10.2, maps 3–6, show selected socio-economic characteristics for Leicester and Stoke. The next section now analyses the statistical data from Neighbourhood Statistics, to ascertain whether this pattern of Asian healthy eating and obesity holds true.

METHODOLOGY

In 2009–10 I visited all grocery retail outlets in Leicester and Stoke on Trent to ascertain whether they stocked ten or more kinds of FFV. The mapped area was then divided into 250 times 250 metre squares. The squares were categorized according to whether they contained a FFV retailer or not. The Euclidean distance of all residential areas to their nearest FFV retailer was then calculated. Actual travel from house to retailer must be according to the street pattern, not following a straight line, but White et al. (2004) and Donkin et al. (1999) consistently suggest a ratio of Euclidean to street-pattern distance of around 1:1.2.

The boundaries of the 105 Middle Level Super Output Areas (MLSOA) covering the urban agglomerations of Leicester and Stoke on Trent were downloaded from the Office for National Statistics website and the 250 metre squares allocated to each MLSOA. An average shop-to-residence distance can now be calculated for each MLSOA, and compared with socio-economic data and figures on obesity and FFV consumption for each MLSOA from Neighbourhood Statistics.

Limitations to this Methodology

By fitting the MLSOA boundaries to a 250 metre grid, the Modifiable Areal Unit Problem (MAUP) emerges; we cannot be certain that the demographic composition of the altered MLSOA remains similar to the original spatial unit. However, this MAUP issue only affects data dependent on shop distance; correlations between MLSOA-based obesity figures and socio-economic data remain true. In the event, shop distance did not emerge as the primary indicator of poor diet (educational attainment was the primary factor), so the overall results of this research are not invalidated by this MAUP issue.

Furthermore, correlations do not indicate causality. If A correlates with B, this does not prove whether A causes B, B causes A, both are caused by variable C, or the relationship is random to a particular dataset and further data will produce regression to the mean. However, in some cases the direction of causality can be intuited. Being unqualified is more likely to promote obesity than vice versa. Third or confounding variables are likely, especially when dealing with linked factors such as Asian, age, distance to shops, and poverty. These confounding variables may, however, be disentangled using partial correlations as described below.

Finally, the results only apply to two cities. However, the factors which emerged as affecting diet and obesity in each city (e.g. distance to shops, access to private transport, low income, level of education, ethnicity) were congruent with other UK cities such as Birmingham, and these factors have been shown to affect obesity rates in a wide range of developed countries, including Canada, France, Italy, Spain and the USA (Shaw 2012). This study extends that research by comparing two typical UK cities, with very different demographics, it is likely that similar results would appear if two other such cities had been chosen.

RESULTS: CORRELATIONS

Health Related

OBESITY = % adults who are obese
5+ FFV = % adults who consume 5 or more portions of fruit or vegetables daily
LLTILL = Limiting Long-term Illness

Geographical/Access Related

SHOPDIST = Average distance home to FFV retailer
CARE50+ = % adults who give 50 hours or more care per week

Demography Related

%ASIAN = % of population of Asian origin
%WHITE = % of population of White origin
AGE75+ = % population aged 75 or more

Wealth Related

4/5 QUAL = % of adults qualified to university degree level or equivalent
NO QUAL = % adults with no qualifications
INACT = % adults who are economically inactive
NOCAR = % households without access to a private car or van
1/CCJs = Number of county court judgments per head of population of MLSOA[1]
%ABclass = % households who are in social class A or B
POVERTY = % of households defined as being in poverty
SBLTU = % adults on state benefits and long-term unemployed
CTAXHB = % households receiving Council Tax Benefit or Housing Benefit
CBEN = % households receiving Child Benefit

Table 10.1 below gives the correlations between obesity, consumption of five or more portions of FFV daily, and other socio-demographic variables for the 105 MLSOA areas of Stoke on Trent and Leicester; aggregated for both cities, and separately.

Table 10.1 suggests that the main influence on both obesity and on eating FFV is attaining a university degree level qualification; since earnings, wealth, and social class are closely interlinked it is not surprising that social class AB is also significant to diet. Access-related factors such as distance to shops or not having a car are much less significant;

Table 10.1 Correlations between obesity, consumption of five or more portions of FFV daily, and selected socio-economic indicators

Indicator	Obesity S and L	Obesity S	Obesity L	5+ FFV S and L	5+ FFV S	5+ FFV L
5+ FFV	−0.741	−0.823	−0.685	NA	NA	NA
SHOPDIST	+0.070	−0.070	+0.074	+0.308	+0.339	+0.364
CARE50	+0.672	+0.622	+0.550	−0.776	−0.701	−0.801
LLTILL	+0.547	+0.378	+0.258	−0.634	−0.608	−0.658
NGH	+0.530	+0.410	+0.252	−0.720	−0.675	−0.761
%ASIAN	−0.356	−0.247	−0.146	+0.059	+0.176	−0.127
%WHITE	+0.270	−0.159	+0.058	+0.061	+0.236	+0.245
AGE75+	+0.102	−0.034	+0.026	−0.040	−0.144	+0.091
4/5 QUAL	−0.892	−0.878	−0.938	+0.868	+0.919	+0.833
INACT	−0.047	−0.166	−0.153	−0.235	+0.016	−0.359
NO QUAL	+0.732	+0.728	+0.659	−0.909	−0.841	−0.940
NOCAR	+0.143	+0.173	+0.092	−0.687	−0.616	−0.734
1/CCJs	−0.242	−0.375	−0.109	+0.676	+0.671	+0.681
%ABclass	−0.646	−0.618	−0.624	+0.930	+0.844	+0.959
POVERTY	+0.024	+0.366	+0.299	−0.537	−0.661	−0.766
SBLTU	+0.496	+0.344	+0.456	−0.737	−0.612	−0.778
CTAXHB	+0.313	+0.330	+0.271	−0.764	−0.684	−0.807
1+Room	−0.059	+0.224	+0.139	−0.314	−0.333	−0.488
CBEN	+0.240	+0.517	+0.482	−0.298	−0.231	−0.462

Notes: Top row, S = Stoke on Trent, L = Leicester.

however, the factors of caring for another for 50+ hours a week, not being in good health, and having a limiting long-term illness, all of which limit travel to shops, are more relevant to obesity and diet.

Factors directly related to poverty, such as the number of county court judgments, or the number of households in poverty or on state benefits, appear less significant to obesity, although they do seem (negatively) related to consumption of FFV. Being older, which has been found to be positively correlated with healthy diet by some researchers, did not appear significant here. However, increased age, although associated with greater food knowledge, concerns about health, and more time to cook if retired, also brings reduced mobility, loss of ability to drive, being bereaved and so living alone, and possibly greater risk of poverty (Meneely et al. 2009), all of which tend to reduce the quality of diet.

Regarding ethnicity, Table 10.1 suggests that Asians are slightly less likely to be obese in Stoke on Trent than in Leicester. This seems counter-intuitive since Asians in Leicester have good access to Asian-oriented retail areas, whereas Stoke lacks such areas. Since obesity is strongly negatively correlated with being educated to degree level and with being of social class AB, one might expect, then, that Asians in Stoke experience less poverty than do those in Leicester.

In fact, Table 10.2 indicates that the correlation between a range of poverty indicators and being Asian is similar in both cities. Moreover, Stoke scores worse on these poverty indicators than does Leicester; suggesting that the overall population of Stoke, and along with it, its Asian component, is more prone to poverty than the population, and Asian

Table 10.2 Correlations between percentage of ASIAN and poverty indicators for Stoke on Trent and Leicester, and average level of poverty indicators across Stoke on Trent and Leicester

Indicator	Asian Stoke correlation	Asian Leicester correlation	Average Stoke	Average Leicester
1/CCJs	−0.252	−0.176	38.42*	45.45*
%ABclass	−0.123	−0.181	13.00%	17.38%
CTAXHB	+0.212	+0.184	11.48%	10.00%
CARE50+	+0.015	+0.161	3.57%	2.71%
4/5 QUAL	−0.004	+0.131	8.25%	12.22%
POVERTY	+0.397	+0.597	21.79%	30.52%
SBLTU	+0.021	−0.049	15.57%	13.78%
NOCAR	+0.241	+0.223	30.34%	28.45%
INACT	+0.293	+0.479	39.25%	35.96%
CBEN	−0.019	+0.473	28.94%	32.82%
NO QUAL	+0.061	+0.283	30.37%	25.53%
SHOPDIST**	−0.339	−0.497	1.59	1.46
OBESITY	−0.247	−0.146	30.0%	25.1%
5+ FFV	+0.176	−0.127	21.3%	24.2%

Notes: Grey-shaded cells indicate the city with greater poverty.
* People per CCJ – a higher figure suggests less poverty.
** A derived measure of average household to FFV shop distance; 1 unit = ca. 300 metres actual travel distance.

population, of Leicester. So the Asian population of Stoke is doubly disadvantaged regarding diet, compared to Asians in Leicester; worse access to culturally Asian foodstuffs, and poorer. Table 10.2 also suggests Asians in Stoke are slightly further from all grocery shops than are Asians in Leicester, and that average house to shop distances are slightly further for all households in Stoke compared to Leicester. This raises the question of what accounts for the lower associations with obesity, and higher propensity to consume 5+ FFV, of Asians in Stoke compared to those in Leicester.

By using partial correlations to create transects across each city, not spatial transects from east to west but social transects from affluent to poor, more detail emerges as to how various socio-demographic factors work towards or against promoting a healthy diet.

Partial Correlations as Social Transects

Although Table 10.1 gives rather low correlations across the whole of Leicester and Stoke on Trent for many socio-demographic indicators and obesity, these correlations become more significant if one disaggregates these cities into high and low qualification areas, or high and low unemployment areas. Often the correlation even changes sign when moving from one area to another, giving a low correlation overall, but masking significant effects in certain social area types. Partial correlations were calculated by shaving off, for example, the least qualified decile, the least qualified two deciles, and so on, continuing this process of shaving the next lowest qualified decile until only the two highest qualified deciles were left in the analysis. The analysis was then performed the other way, shaving off the most qualified decile, the two most qualified deciles and so on until only the two least qualified deciles were left. This methodology transforms a single correlation between two variables (level of qualifications and prevalence of obesity) into a 'transect' across the city from most to least per cent qualified areas.

Taking partial correlations revealed major shifts in correlations between the sociodemographic variables and obesity. Besides the substantial changes in correlation value and even sign referred to above, there were also major differences in correlation values between Leicester and Stoke. For example, the correlations between OBESITY and %ASIAN for Leicester and Stoke are −0.146 and −0.247 respectively. However, for the 40 per cent of MLSOAs where households are furthest from FFV shops, the correlations become considerably more negative, at −0.473 and −0.774 respectively. For the 40 per cent of MLSOAs where households are closest to FFV shops, the correlations are +0.060 and −0.343 respectively. The pan-cities correlation therefore hides a trend of increasing positive association between OBESITY and %ASIAN as one moves from areas far from FFV shops to areas closer to these shops, in Leicester.

For Stoke on Trent the tendency is also for areas distant from FFV shops to have negative correlations between OBESITY and %ASIAN, but for areas closer to FFV shops the association between OBESITY and %ASIAN remains negative, unlike Leicester. Furthermore the propensity of Asians to consume 5+ FFV daily rises in areas of Stoke that are close to shops, whereas in Leicester the propensity of Asians to consume 5+ FFV daily steadily falls as one moves towards areas close to FFV shops. This raises several questions: why do Asians in areas closer to FFV shops appear at greater risk of obesity, and why do Asians living close to FFV shops in Leicester, with its many Asian-oriented shops, appear at greater risk of obesity, and poor diet, than Asians living close to shops in Stoke?

Data Narratives: Diet and Obesity in Leicester and Stoke on Trent

The partial correlation lines for OBESITY and %ASIAN as moderated by SHOPDIST, described in the previous paragraph, are shown in Figure 10.3; graph A line 1 = Leicester, graph A line 2 = Stoke; Right Hand Side (RHS) = closest to shops. Lines 3 and 4 show the correlations between FFV and %ASIAN as moderated by SHOPDIST, for Leicester and Stoke respectively; RHS = closest to shops. From these lines one can derive a 'data narrative'; a verbal analysis of the statistical shifts in relationships between OBESITY and other socio-economic indicators seen as one moves across a transect. Other such data narratives derived from the transects are examined in this section.

In Leicester and Stoke, Asians appear more likely to be obese in areas with a higher %ASIAN. In similar manner to the transect between %ASIAN and OBESITY as moderated by SHOPDIST, Asians in areas of Stoke with a higher %ASIAN have higher FFV consumptions than Asians in corresponding areas of Leicester. A socio-economic basis for this is suggested by the correlations between %ASIAN, OBESITY and FFV as moderated by the variable 'Never Worked or Long-term Unemployed' (NWLTU). In higher unemployment areas, Asians in Leicester are more prone to obesity than Asians in corresponding areas of Stoke; in lower unemployment areas this is reversed, with Asians in Stoke in these low unemployment areas being more prone to obesity than those in Leicester. The differences in correlations OBESITY–%ASIAN when transecting from high to low unemployment areas are not large; they fall from around -0.05 to -0.31 when going from high unemployment to low unemployment areas of Leicester, and rise from -0.35 to -0.25 for this transect in Stoke (a more positive correlation means more propensity to be obese). For FFV consumption, the differences are more marked, and show FFV consumption falling from $+0.5$ correlation with %ASIAN to -0.1 correlation (graph 2, line 2) as one moves to higher employment areas of Stoke, but level (graph 2, line 1) as one moves towards such areas in Leicester (RHS = higher employment).

Summing up: the Asians in stereotypically 'inner city' areas of Stoke (densely populated, many small independent grocers, fewer supermarkets, higher unemployment) appear better off regarding diet than Asians in similar districts of Leicester; this is despite the greater presence of Asian-oriented shops in such areas of Leicester compared to Stoke.

A similar economic difference between Leicester and Stoke emerged in the correlation between OBESITY and LLTILL (Limiting Long Term Illness) when transecting across POVERTY. LLTILL is closely linked to poverty (Equality Commission 2006). In Leicester, the correlation between OBESITY and LLTILL changed from $+0.45$ in areas with many households in poverty (graph 3, line 1) to -0.25 in areas with few households in poverty; in Stoke (graph 3, line 2) the correlation figure barely changed across this transect (RHS = fewer households in poverty). Again it appears that poverty in Leicester has a much more negative effect on diet and obesity than it does in Stoke. For the long-term unemployed, in Leicester most areas see a negative correlation with FFV (graph 3, line 3), but this correlation tends to be less negative in areas of higher employment; in Stoke the opposite pattern occurs (graph 3, line 4), with a negative correlation between FFV and NWLTU except in areas of high unemployment, where it becomes strongly positive (RHS = high employment).

The correlation of NWLTU with OBESITY overall is very marginally positive for

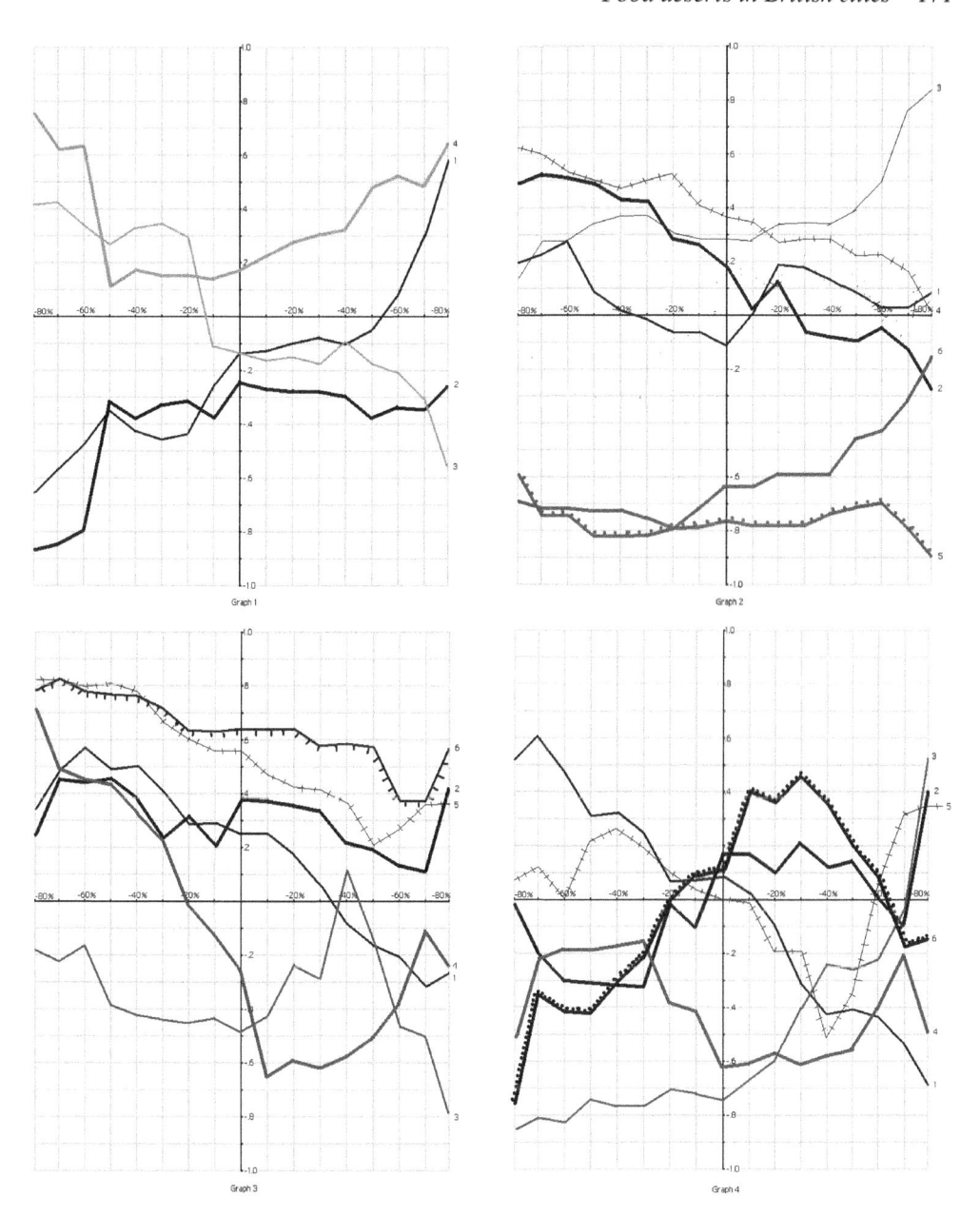

Note: For explanation of graphs, see text. Vertical axis for all graphs is correlation, −1.0 to +1.0. Horizontal axis represents per cent of MLSOAs shaved from sample to create the transect.

Figure 10.3 Partial correlation transects for Leicester and Stoke on Trent

Leicester (+0.006) and Stoke (+0.122) overall. However, when transecting from high NWLTU to low NWLTU areas in Leicester, the lowest NWLTU areas show a negative correlation between NWLTU and OBESITY of about −0.4. The opposite occurs in Stoke where lower NWLTU areas produce a more positive correlation with OBESITY, of around +0.3; the higher NWLTU areas show a negative correlation with OBESITY of around −0.4 (graph 4, line 5 = Leicester, graph 4, line 6 = Stoke; RHS = areas with lower NWLTU). Also in Stoke, but not in Leicester, being NWLTU has a positive correlation with FFV consumption in areas of higher unemployment.

Summing up: the poverty indicators are associated with higher obesity and lower FFV consumption in Leicester, especially when people in poverty live in poorer areas. However, being poor in Stoke, and living in a less affluent area, could be associated with a positive effect on diet and obesity.

Indicators of ease of access to FFV shops also support the suggestion that in Stoke lower levels of household wealth in a less affluent area might not have the deleterious effects on diet that are evident in Leicester. Households with no car in Stoke are slightly more likely to be obese in affluent areas than in areas where more households are in poverty; households with no car in Leicester are considerably less likely to be obese in affluent areas compared to areas with more households in poverty (graph 4, line 1 = Leicester, graph 4, line 2 = Stoke; RHS = areas with lower per cent of households in poverty). Households with no car in Leicester, in less affluent areas, are strongly negatively correlated with consumption of 5+ FFV; similar households in less well-off parts of Stoke are very weakly negatively correlated with consumption of 5+ FFV (graph 4, line 3 = Leicester, graph 4, line 4 = Stoke; RHS = areas with lower per cent of households in poverty). The correlation between OBESITY and POVERTY, transected across SHOPDIST, indicates that individuals in poorer households in Leicester are more likely to be obese if they live close to FFV shops than far from them, whereas in Stoke it is the poorer households, living closer to FFV shops, who are less likely to contain obese persons (graph 2; line 3 = Leicester, line 4 = Stoke; RHS = closer to FFV shops). Regarding FFV consumption, people in poor households in Leicester are unlikely to consume 5+ FFV whatever distance they live from the shops, but in Stoke such individuals are more likely to consume 5+ FFV if they live close to FFV shops (graph 2; line 5 = Leicester, line 6 = Stoke; RHS = closer to FFV shops).

Summing up: poorer households (those in poverty, those without access to private transport) tend to eat more FFV and contain less obese individuals when, in Leicester, they live in more affluent areas, and areas more remote from FFV shops. However, the opposite applies in Stoke; here households with no car experience a better diet in areas of greater poverty, and households in poverty eat more healthily when domiciled in areas closer to FFV shops.

Other statistical analysis showed relatively small differences in obesity or FFV consumption, either between Leicester and Stoke or across a socio-economic transect. The strongest (negative) association with OBESITY was shown by 4/5 QUALS (university level or equivalent qualifications); correlations in excess of −0.9 were derived across most transects in all variables measured. CARE50+ showed a moderately positive (0.6–0.7) correlation with OBESITY with little change across most transects plotted. The largest variation occurred when CARE50+ was transected across NOCAR. Here, there was a decline in positive correlation with OBESITY, from +0.7 to around +0.3, as one moved towards areas where most households had private transport (graph 3; line 5 = Leicester, line 6 = Stoke; RHS = more households have cars). This decline in correlation value was more marked in Leicester, suggesting that any access or time problems (to accessing FFV) caused by devoting 50 or more hours a week to being a carer were more alleviated by having access to a car in Leicester than they were in Stoke. In other words, Stoke households with time or money constraints have better access to shops without need of a car than do the equivalent households in Leicester. This would agree with the indications discussed earlier that less affluent households in poor areas in Stoke manage to eat more healthily than do the equivalent in Leicester.

There is a well-known description of many affluent Western consumers as 'cash-rich-time-poor'. The concept of 'food time', the time it takes to access food retailers, bring the food back home, and prepare it, might be ranked as a fourth dimension of food accessibility; the other three being food cost, food knowledge, and physical accessibility of food retailers. A decade ago Professor Rathje of the University of Arizona reported on how busy professionals would buy the healthy fresh food they knew they should eat, but also purchase ready meals as a back-up, in case they had insufficient time to cook (Brockes 2002). Inevitably the fast food was always chosen, and the fresh food would go bad and be thrown away, a phenomenon Rathje called the 'fast lane syndrome'. Low-paid workers can also be 'time-poor', because of having to work long hours, overtime, to accumulate enough pay. Poverty often co-exists with employment (Jackson and Bussell 2003, p. 13). At both ends of the pay spectrum, being employed may militate against healthy eating. Inglis et al. (2005, p. 34) and Hamlett et al. (2008, p. 99) have noted how low wages can mean both partners working, and consequently being too tired to cook fresh food even if they do have the time; post-work tiredness also deters travel to a distant FFV shop, meaning a local takeaway may be patronized instead. Butland et al. (2007, p. 38) shows a positive relationship between hours worked and propensity to be obese, at least for annual work hours of between 1,300 and 1,900; over this range of hours the average male obesity rate rises from 8 per cent to 22 per cent.

For those on low wages, the extra income from being in employment is scarcely adequate to make any improvement in diet when set against the 'time-penalty' for being in work. According to Directgov.uk figures (2012), a household with two children and no adults in work will receive a total income of £432 in Benefits. If one household member works 35 hours a week on the minimum wage (£6.08/hour in 2012), the total household income will be £504 (both figures are after accommodation costs). With work-related costs such as commuting, this extra £72 a week will not go far in paying for travel to supermarkets or to buy more nutritious food. If a typical 2-adult, 2-child household in a less affluent area moved from an unhealthy to a healthy diet, their food bill could rise from £80 a week (Nelson et al. 2007, p. 165) to £131.40, based on the 58 per cent premium estimated by the *Food Magazine* (2008) for healthy food in poorer areas. Long hours of unpaid work such as full-time informal caring can also deter healthy eating, as measured here in the variable CARE50+.

These time and food effects will likely operate equally in Leicester and Stoke, but there is a further time effect that may give Stoke consumers an advantage compared to Leicester. When the low paid or unemployed want to buy food cheaply, from local street markets, the time of day they go can be crucial. The optimum time to obtain good value food may be early in the morning when the market has just opened, to get the best bargains, or mid-afternoon when most street markets are closing down and stallholders reduce prices markedly. Leicester, a monocentric city, has inner city areas with a dense network of small FFV shops, but only near the city centre; it has some smaller suburban centres but also large lower social status areas such as Beaumont Leys and Braunstone where distances to the nearest FFV shop can be considerable. By contrast Stoke is more polycentric, with the original 'Five Pottery Towns' retaining their identity within the conurbation as town and market centres with many small independent FFV shops. The quality of the walk to the shops is also significant. In Salt Lake County, USA, Smith et al. (2008) found that the easier it is to walk from one's neighbourhood to the shops the lower the local obesity rate will be, so that inner city neighbourhoods close to local shops may have a healthier diet than outer suburban areas of American cities where busy roads and lack of shaded sidewalks makes walking unattractive, where a car is vital to access distant supermarkets. In Leicester the out-of-town FFV retailers will be mainly large supermarkets, surrounded by extensive car parks, close to main roads or by-passes, unattractive to walk to; in Stoke the less affluent, the car-less, may just have to walk along a few streets to reach a local independent FFV retailer. The same effect of poorer households managing to eat more healthily, if they are in a less affluent area with many smaller retailers, was noted in Birmingham, UK (Shaw 2012).

CONCLUSION: COMMUNITY AND GOVERNMENT INITIATIVES TO IMPROVE FOOD ACCESS

In the UK, legal intervention has been used to support the disadvantaged consumer, for example the less mobile, and urban planning regulation has been concerned with retail provision in the UK (Shaw 2015, p. 7). The laissez-faire planning attitude of the 19th century has given way to the planned city of the 20th century (Davis 1966, p. 300). The results for Leicester and Stoke on Trent suggest that good quality local retailing (small, easily accessible, good quality FFV retailers, along with sustainable street markets) is most significant in improving the diet of less affluent consumers, especially the unemployed, those most likely to suffer obesity. The task of urban planners and health workers may be to ensure that the food retail environment is appropriate in terms of finance and time. Promoting healthy but labour-intensive recipes that involve purchasing ingredients hard to come by in less affluent areas may simply increase health inequalities (Butland et al. 2007, pp. 65–66). Ethnicity appears to be less of a determinant of diet, in Leicester and Stoke on Trent, than economic and time opportunities; Hamlett et al. (2008, p. 100) found that ethnic minorities may in fact be quite flexible as to what ethnic orientation of grocery shop they use, so long as the foods they find in these shops conform to desired tastes and required cultural or religious stipulations.

Interventions in the 'food environment' – which includes the accessible grocery retail environment as well as lifestyle, attitudes towards, and knowledge of, nutrition and food preparation – need to be culturally appropriate; as dietary improvement messages that are too generalist 'may conflict with cultural beliefs for many immigrants, minority, and low-income populations' (Winham 2009, p. 64). The research results for Leicester and Stoke on Trent suggest that time is a major part of this food culture. Rather than providing good quality but remote supermarkets to serve deprived areas, supporting and preserving small local stores that sell FFVs would have a significant impact on diet and obesity. To reduce obesity amongst the poor in cities like Leicester, a less corporatist and more community-oriented solution would be more effective (Shaw and Shaw 2016, p. 41). Rather than a top-down approach based on what large retailers would like to do, a bottom-up approach based on what assistance is necessary for smaller agents, such as independent shops and market stallholders, would be more appropriate, culturally and economically. This change in policy direction would almost certainly shift the funding burden away from the private sector towards the public purse, but would ultimately produce a financial return to the government in terms of reduced public health costs for dietary-related illnesses.

NOTE

1. CCJs are awarded when a debtor defaults on a loan, so are a proxy indicator for poverty. So 1/CCJs means fewer CCJs per head, so suggests less poverty.

REFERENCES

Brockes, E. (2002), 'On the bins', *The Guardian*, 20 May 2002, accessed 2 May 2015 at http://www.guardian.co.uk/society/2002/may/20/localgovernment.g2.

Butland, B., S. Jebb, P. Kopelman, K. McPherson, S. Thomas, J. Mardell and V. Parry (2007), *Foresight: Tackling Obesities – Future Choices*, 2nd ed., UK Government report.

Cordy, T. and F. Robson (1985), 'Amazing growth of ethnic shopping', *Town & Country Planning*, Issue 54, p. 225.

Cummins, S. and S. Macintyre (2002), 'A systematic study of an urban foodscape: the price and availability of food in greater Glasgow', *Urban Studies*, **39** (11), 2115–2130.

Davis, Dorothy (1966), *A History of Shopping*, London, UK: Routledge and Keegan.

Department of Health (2010), *Healthy Lives, Healthy People*, UK Government report.

Directgov.uk (2012), UK Government website, accessed 30 April 2015 at www.direct.gov.uk.

Donkin, A., E. Dowler, S. Stevenson and S. Turner (1999), 'Mapping access to food at a local level', *British Food Journal*, **101** (7), 554–564.

Equality Commission (2006), *Census 2001: Limiting Long-term Illness in Northern Ireland*, published by UK Government.

Finney, Nissa and Ludi Simpson (2009), *Sleepwalking to Segregation? Challenging Myths about Race and Migration*, Cambridge, UK: Polity Press.

Food Magazine (2008), *Healthy Food Costs More*, January/March, Issue 80, p. 6.

Gallagher, Mari (2006), *Examining the Impact of Food Deserts on Public Health in Chicago*, report published by Mari Gallagher Research and Consulting Group, Chicago, IL, USA.

Guy, C., G. Clarke and H. Eyre (2004), 'Food retail change and the growth of food deserts: a case study of Cardiff', *International Journal of Retail and Distribution Management*, **32** (2), 72–88.

Hamlett, J., A. Bailey, A. Alexander and G. Shaw (2008), 'Ethnicity and consumption: South Asian food shopping patterns in Britain 1947–75', *Journal of Consumer Culture*, **8** (1), 91–116.

Hulsegge, G., H. Susan, J. Pivavet, A. Blokstra, A. Nooyens, A. Spijkerman, Y. van der Schouw, H. Smit and W. Vershuren (2013), 'Today's adult generations are less healthy than their predecessors: generation shifts in metabolic risk factors – the Doetinchem Cohort Study', *European Journal of Preventive Cardiology*, published online 10 April 2013, doi: 10.1177/2047487313485512.

Inglis, V., K. Ball and D. Crawford (2005), 'Why do women of low socio-economic status have poorer dietary behaviour than women of higher socio-economic status? A qualitative exploration', *Appetite*, **45** (3), 334–343.

Jackson, Teresa and Trish Bussell (2003), *A Healthy Diet: Accessible to All?*, report published by the Dudley Food Network on behalf of Dudley Health Authority and Dudley Metropolitan Borough Council.

Lee, G. and L. Hyunwoo (2009), 'A spatial statistical approach to indentifying areas with poor access to grocery foods in the City of Buffalo, New York', *Urban Studies*, **46** (7), 1299–1315.

Meneely, L., A. Burns and C. Strugnell (2009), 'Age associated changes in older consumers' retail behaviour', *International Journal of Retail & Distribution Management*, **37** (12), 1041–1056.

Nelson, Michael, Bob Erens, Beverley Bates, Susan Church and Tracy Boshier (2007), 'Low income diet and nutrition survey', Food Standards Agency, Norwich, UK, Office for National Statistics, UK Government website, accessed 2 May 2015 at www.neighbourhood.stastics.gov.uk/dissemination.

Office for National Statistics (2009), accessed 1 March 2015 at www.neighbourhood.statistics.gov.uk.

Reisig, V. and A. Hobbiss (2000), 'Food deserts and how to tackle them: a study of one city's approach', *Health Education Journal*, Issue 59, 137–149.

Shaw, H.J. (2009), 'Identifying and overcoming barriers to healthy eating faced by ethnic minorities in the United Kingdom', in Adam Lindgreen and Martin Hingley (eds), *The New Cultures of Food*, Surrey, UK: Gower, pp. 21–36.

Shaw, H.J. (2012), 'Food access diet and health in the UK: an empirical study of Birmingham', *British Food Journal*, **114** (4), pp. 598–616.

Shaw, H.J. (2014), *The Consuming Geographies of Food: Diet, Food Deserts and Obesity*, London, UK: Routledge.

Shaw, J.J.A. (2015), 'Compassion and the criminal justice system: stumbling along towards a jurisprudence of love and forgiveness', *International Journal of Law in Context*, **11** (1), 1–17.

Shaw, J.J.A. and H.J. Shaw (2016), 'Mapping the technologies of spatial (in)justice in the Anthropocene', *Information and Communications Technology Law*, **25** (1), 32–49.

Smith, K., B. Brown, I. Yamada, L. Kowaleski-Jones, C. Zick and J. Fan (2008), 'Walkability and body mass index, density, design, and new diversity measures', *American Journal of Preventive Medicine*, **35** (3), 237–244.

Sparks, A., N. Bania and L. Leete (2011), 'Comparative approaches to measuring food access in urban areas: the case of Portland, Oregon', *Urban Studies*, **48** (8), 1715–1737.

White, Martin, Jane Bunting, Liz Williams, Simon Raybould, Ashley Adamson and John Mathers (2004), *Do 'Food Deserts' Exist? A Multi-level, Geographical Analysis of the Relationship between Retail Food Access, Socio-economic Position and Dietary Intake*, Food Standards Agency report, February 2004, accessed 14 March 2015 at http://www.ncl.ac.uk/ihs/assets/pdfs/fsareport.pdf.

Winham, D.M. (2009), 'Culturally tailored foods and cardiovascular disease prevention', *American Journal of Medicine*, **3** (1), 64–8.

Wrigley, N., C. Guy and M. Lowe (2002), 'Urban regeneration, social inclusion, and large store development: the Seacroft development in context', *Urban Studies*, **39** (11), 2101–2114.

Zenk, S., A. Schulz, B. Israel, S. James, S. Bao and M. Wilson (2005a), 'Neighbourhood racial composition, neighbourhood poverty, and the spatial accessibility of supermarkets in metropolitan Detroit', *American Journal of Public Health*, **95** (4), 660–667.

Zenk, S., A. Schulz, T. Horris-Neely, R. Campbell, N. Holmes, G. Watkins and R. Nwankwo (2005b), 'Fruit and vegetable intake in African Americans', *American Journal of Preventive Medicine*, **29** (1), 1–9.

11. The application of statistical methods in CSR research
Christopher Boachie and George K. Amoako

INTRODUCTION

Statistics represents that body of methods by which characteristics of a population are inferred through observations made in a representative sample from that population. Since scientists rarely observe entire populations, sampling and statistical inference are essential. The purpose of the chapter was to examine the role of statistical methods in corporate social responsibility (CSR) research. Statistical methods are designed to detect and measure relationships and effects in situations where results cannot be identically replicated because of natural variability in the measurements of interest. They are generally used as an intermediate step between anecdotal evidence and the determination of causal explanations. Statistical methods play a major role in making appropriate conclusions from those studies.

Statistical methods most often play an important role in the discovery phase. These methods are an intermediate step between the anecdotal evidence or theoretical speculations that lead to discovery research, and the justification phase of the research process in which elaborated theories and comprehensive understanding are established. This chapter seeks to review the current status of statistical methods and their influences on financial CSR research. The study used secondary data on statistical research methods and a survey of published articles on CSR. The key findings of the study were how statistical methods are applied in CSR research.

Statistical Methods in Corporate Social Responsibility Research

Statistical methods are widely used in CSR research. There is a vast amount of supporting theory, practical tips, examples of good practice, and so on, to support these methods. However, some fundamental aspects of the way statistical approaches are typically used sometimes seem problematic – even in studies published in respected journals whose reviewing process ensures that the obvious pitfalls are avoided.

Statistics can be called that body of analytical and computational methods by which characteristics of a population are inferred through observations made in a representative sample from that population (Curwin and Slater, 2006). Since scientists rarely observe entire populations, sampling and statistical inference are essential. Although the objective of statistical methods are to make the process of scientific research as efficient and productive as possible, many CSR researchers and engineers have inadequate training in experimental design and in the proper selection of statistical analyses for experimentally acquired data. Gill (1978) opined that statistical analysis too often has meant the manipulation of ambiguous data by means of dubious methods to solve a problem that has not been defined.

The purpose of this chapter is to provide readers with various statistical methods to be employed in CSR research. However, the chapter excludes hypothesis testing and regression analysis since full chapters will be dedicated to both statistical methods.

STATISTICS IN RESEARCH

The role of statistics in research is to function as a tool in designing research, analysing its data, and drawing conclusions therefrom. Most research studies result in a large volume of raw data, which must be suitably reduced so that the same can be read easily and can be used for further analysis.

Clearly, the science of statistics cannot be ignored by any research worker, even though he or she may not have occasion to use statistical methods in all their details and ramifications.

Classification and tabulation achieve this objective to some extent, but we have to go a step further and develop certain indices or measures to summarize the collected/classified data. Only after this can we adopt the process of generalization from small groups (i.e., samples) to population. In fact, there are two major areas of statistics viz., descriptive statistics and inferential statistics. Descriptive statistics concern the development of certain indices from the raw data, whereas inferential statistics concern with the process of generalization. Inferential statistics are also known as sampling statistics and are mainly concerned with two major types of problems: (1) the estimation of population parameters; and (2) the testing of statistical hypotheses.

The important statistical measures that are used to summarize the CSR research data are:

1. Measures of central tendency or statistical averages;
2. Measures of dispersion;
3. Measures of asymmetry (skewedness);
4. Measures of relationship; and
5. Other measures.

Among the measures of central tendency, the three most important ones are the arithmetic average or mean, median and mode. Geometric mean and harmonic mean are also sometimes used. From among the measures of dispersion, variance, and its square root – the standard deviation – are the most often used measures. Other measures such as mean deviation, range, and so on are also used. For comparison purposes, we use mostly the coefficient of standard deviation or the coefficient of variation.

In respect of the measures of skewness and kurtosis, we mostly use the first measure of skewness based on mean and mode or on mean and median. Other measures of skewness, based on quartiles or on the methods of moments, are also used sometimes. Kurtosis is also used to measure the peakedness of the curve of the frequency distribution.

Among the measures of relationship, Karl Pearson's coefficient of correlation is the frequently used measure in the case of statistics of variables, whereas Yule's coefficient of association is used in the case of statistics of attributes (Manly, 2005). Multiple correlation coefficient, partial correlation coefficient, and regression analysis are important measures often used by a researcher. Index numbers, analysis of time series, and coefficient of contingency are other measures that may be used by a researcher as well, depending upon the nature of the problem under study.

The entrance of human beings into and departure from this world are recorded as statistical events. Birth and death, marriage and divorce, the school attendance of our children, the crops grown by farmers, the number of miles flown by commercial planes, the hours of our labour, the output of manufacturing plants, the acres of wood demanded for paper, the hours of sunshine, the inches of snowfall – all such events and activities are recorded somehow and somewhere. Myriads of such experiences and events affecting the daily lives of roundly two billion human beings lie behind the statistical data condensed in volumes, published and unpublished. In reverse, we are daily translating into their real meaning statistical data obtained from newspapers, radio reports, lectures, books, and conversations.

The public is constantly exposed to statistical data occurring in advertisements, in arguments, and in the distribution of information. If something is said to have been statistically proved, opposition is supposed to become quiescent. Everywhere the ordinary citizen needs some ability to distinguish between what is truth and what is falsehood. In a democracy statistical methods are employed where public opinions are used in the settlement of public problems and contribute toward the growth of public opinion. The ability to use and scrutinize data, to look beneath the surface of things and to discern relations between reality of given data, affords an important safeguard against the dangers of omnipresent propaganda. The practice of applying certain statistical methods, however simple they may be, is a critical social need for all.

The most important and undisputed use of statistics in daily life is connected with all the activities of political, social, and commercial institutions, which determine the economic and cultural life of a nation. In the realm of policy, it is the function of statistics to measure the importance of various problems and to place them in a proper perspective. In many branches of government factual data already are governing policy to a great extent. For instance, the decision to build a number of new schools and to engage more teachers implies legislative measures, which are based on statistical investigations of the school-leaving age, the rising birth rate, the increase of population through migration, and other factors. Problems in the economic, industrial, and social fields, such as increase or decrease of employment, shortage of houses, expansion or contraction of existing plants, decrease or increase of crime – these and thousands of others should be solved statistically before political action can be considered.

The whole structure of the national budget depends on the sound appraisal of the relationship between potential sources of revenue and planned expenditure. Local authorities need statistical information for the districts they serve; national agencies need it for the country; the organization of the United Nations needs it for the world. It is essential that governmental agencies be prepared to make the fullest possible use of modern statistical methods. The public is entitled to the benefit that may be derived from the progress in research. Old methods are often wasteful or have been found unreliable. One should expect that government, the foremost user of statistics on a large scale, should pioneer in the application of modern statistical methods.

The urge to apply modern statistical developments seems to be greater where an immediate personal advantage is involved in commercial life. The next section looks at data measuring scales.

SCALES OF DATA

The values of a variable define the scale or level of measurement used to study the variable. Before one can advance very far in the field of data analysis one needs to distinguish the different kinds of numbers with which one is working with. Variables differ in how well they can be measured, that is, in how much measurable information their measurement scale can provide. Different measurement scales allow for different levels of exactness, depending upon the characteristics of the variables being measured. There is obviously some measurement error involved in every measurement, which determines the amount of information that we can obtain. Another factor that determines the amount of information that can be provided by a variable is its type of measurement scale. This takes us to the commonly reported issue of scales or levels of data, and four are identified, each of which, in the order given below, subsumes its predecessor.

Nominal Variables

Nominal variables allow for only qualitative classification. That is, they can be measured only in terms of whether the individual items belong to some distinctively different categories, but we cannot quantify or even rank order those categories. This scale measures data by name only. For example, all we can say is that two individuals are different in terms of a certain variable (e.g., they are of different race), but we cannot say which one has more of the quality represented by the variable. Typical examples of nominal variables are gender, race, colour, city, marital status, and so forth.

The nominal scale simply denotes categories: '1' means such-and-such a category, '2' means another and so on; for example, '1' might denote females, '2' might denote males. The categories are mutually exclusive and have no numerical meaning. For example, consider numbers on a football shirt: we cannot say that the player wearing number '4' is twice as anything as a player wearing a number '2', nor half as anything as a player wearing a number '8'; the number '4' simply identifies a category, and, indeed, nominal data are frequently termed categorical data. The data classify, but have no order. Nominal data include items such as divorced, married, separated, subject taught, type of school, socio-economic status. Nominal data denote discrete variables; entirely separate categories.

Ordinal Variables

Ordinal variables allow us to rank in order the items we measure in terms of which has less and which has more of the quality represented by the variable, but still they do not allow us to say how much more. A typical example of an ordinal variable is the socio-economic status of families. For example, we know that upper-middle is higher than middle but we cannot say that it is, for example, 18 percent higher. Also, this very distinction between nominal, ordinal, and interval scales itself represents a good example of an ordinal variable. For example, we can say that nominal measurement provides less information than ordinal measurement, but we cannot say how much less or how this difference compares to the difference between ordinal and interval scales.

The ordinal scale not only classifies but also introduces an order into the data. These might be rating scales where, for example, 'strongly agree' is stronger than 'agree', or 'a very great deal' is stronger than 'very little'. It is possible to place items in an order, weakest to strongest, smallest to biggest, lowest to highest, least to most, and so on, but there is still an absence of a metric – a measure using calibrated or equal intervals. Therefore, one cannot assume that the distance between each point of the scale is equal, i.e. the distance between 'very little' and 'a little' may not be the same as the distance between 'a lot' and 'a very great deal' on a rating scale. One could not say, for example, that in a 5-point rating scale (1 = strongly disagree; 2 = disagree; 3 = neither agree nor disagree; 4 = agree; 5 = strongly agree) point 4 is in twice as much agreement as point 2, or that point 1 is in five times more disagreement than point 5. However, one could place them in an order: 'not at all', 'very little', 'a little', 'quite a lot', 'a very great deal', or 'strongly disagree', 'disagree', 'neither agree nor disagree', 'agree', 'strongly agree', that is, it is possible to rank the data according to rules of 'lesser than' or 'greater than', in relation to whatever the value is included on the rating scale. Ordinal data include items such as rating scales and Likert scales, and are frequently used in asking for opinions and attitudes.

Interval Variables

Interval variables allow us not only to rank in order the items that are measured, but also to quantify and compare the sizes of differences between them. For example, temperature, as measured in degrees Fahrenheit or Celsius, constitutes an interval scale. We can say that a temperature of 40 degrees is higher than a temperature of 30 degrees, and that an increase from 20 to 40 degrees is twice as much as an increase from 30 to 40 degrees. However, interval scale variables do not have an absolute zero. If the temperatures in Accra and Berlin are 30° C and 15° C respectively, we cannot say that it is twice as hot in Accra as it is in Berlin. This is simply because it would not be the case if these temperatures were measured in degrees Fahrenheit: 86° F and 59° F respectively. The interval scale introduces a metric – a regular and equal interval between each data point – as well as keeping the features of the previous two scales, classification and order. This lets us know precisely how far apart are the individuals, the objects, or the events that form the focus of our inquiry. In fact, twice as hot as 50° F is 68° F ((\{50 − 32\} × 2) + 32).

Let us give another example. Many IQ (intelligent quotient) tests commence their scoring at point 70, that is, the lowest score possible is 70. We cannot say that a person with an IQ of 150 has twice the measured intelligence as a person with an IQ of 75 because the starting point is 70; a person with an IQ of 150 has twice the measured intelligence as a person with an IQ of 110, as one has to subtract the initial starting point of 70 (\{150 − 70\} ÷ 2). In practice, the interval scale is rarely used, and the statistics that one can use with this scale are, to all extents and purposes, the same as for the fourth scale, which is the ratio scale.

Ratio Variables

Ratio variables are very similar to interval variables; in addition to all the properties of interval variables, they feature an identifiable absolute zero point, thus they allow for statements such as x is two times more than y. Typical examples of ratio scales are measures of time or space. For example, as the Kelvin temperature scale is a ratio scale, not only can we say that a temperature of 200 degrees is higher than one of 100 degrees; we can correctly state that it is twice as high. Interval scales do not have the ratio property. Most statistical data analysis procedures do not distinguish between the interval and ratio properties of the measurement scales. Height is also a ratio scale variable since, if a person is twice as tall as another, he/she will remain so, irrespective of the units used (centimetres, inches, etc.).

This enables the researcher to determine proportions easily – 'twice as many as', 'half as many as', 'three times the amount of', and so on. Because there is an absolute zero, all of the arithmetical processes of addition, subtraction, multiplication, and division are possible. Measures of distance, money in the bank, population, time spent on homework, years teaching, income, Celsius temperature, marks on a test, and so on are all ratio measures as they are capable of having a 'true' zero quantity. If I have 1000 dollars in the bank, then it is twice as much as if I had 500 dollars in the bank; if I score 90 percent in an examination then it is twice as many as if I had scored 45 percent. The opportunity to use ratios and all four arithmetical processes renders this the most powerful level of data. Interval and ratio data are continuous variables that can take on any value within a particular, given range. They typically use more powerful statistics than nominal and ordinal data.

Summing Up

The delineation of these four scales of data is important, as the consideration of which statistical test to use is dependent on the scale of data: it is incorrect to apply statistics which can only be used at a higher scale of data to data at a lower scale. For example, one should not apply averages (means) to nominal data, nor use t-tests and analysis of variances for ordinal data. Which statistical tests can be used with which data are set out clearly later. To close this section, we record Cohen, Manion, and Morrison's (2013, p. 127) view that the scale of measurement is not inherent to a particular variable, but something that researchers bestow on it based on our theories of that variable. It is a belief we hold about a variable. What is being suggested here, is that we have to justify classifying a variable as nominal, ordinal, interval, or ratio, and not just assume that it is self-evident.

DESCRIPTIVE AND INFERENTIAL STATISTICS

Descriptive Statistics

Descriptive statistics are tabular, graphical, and numerical methods by which essential features of a sample can be described. Although these same methods can be used to describe entire populations, they are more often applied to samples in order to capture population characteristics by inference.

We will differentiate between two main types of data samples: qualitative data samples and quantitative data samples. Qualitative data arises when the characteristic being observed is not measurable. A typical case is the 'success' or 'failure' of a particular test. For example, to test the effect of a drug in a clinical trial setting, the experimenter may define two possible outcomes for each patient: either the drug was effective in treating the patient, or the drug was not effective. In the case of two possible outcomes, any sample of size 'n' can be represented as a sequence of n nominal outcome $x1, x2, \ldots, xn$ that can assume either the value 'success' or 'failure'.

By contrast, quantitative data arise when the characteristics being observed can be described by numbers. Discrete quantitative data is countable whereas continuous data may assume any value, apart from any precision constraint imposed by the measuring instrument. Discrete quantitative data may be obtained by counting the number of each possible outcome from a qualitative data sample. Examples of discrete data may be the number of subjects sensitive to the effect of a drug (number of 'success' and number of 'failure'). Examples of continuous data are weight, height, pressure, and survival time. Thus, any quantitative data sample of size n may be represented as a sequence of n numbers $x1, x2, \ldots, xn$ and sample statistics are functions of these numbers.

Discrete data may be pre-processed using frequency tables and represented using histograms. This is best illustrated by an example. For discrete data, consider a survey in which 1000 patients fill in a questionnaire for assessing the quality of a hearing aid device. Each patient has to rank product satisfaction from 0 to 5, each rank being associated with a detailed description of hearing quality.

If you have a large set of data, then descriptive statistics provides graphical and numerical (e.g. summary tables, means, quartiles) ways to make sense of the data. The branch of statistics devoted to the exploration, summary, and presentation of data is called descriptive statistics. This will include, for example:

- Mode:
  - The most frequently occurring value. If several values share the greatest frequency of occurrence, each of them is a mode.
- Mean:
  - It is a measure of central tendency, the arithmetic average, the sum divided by the number of cases.
- Median:
  - The value above and below which half of the cases fall, the 50th percentile. If there is an even number of cases, the median is the average of the two middle cases when they are sorted in ascending or descending order. The median is a measure of central tendency not sensitive to outlying values, unlike the mean, which can be affected by a few extremely high or low values.
- Minimum and maximum:
  - The smallest and largest numeric variable. It scores the range that is, the distance between the highest and the lowest scores.
- Standard deviation:
  - It is a measure of dispersion around the mean. In a normal distribution, 68 percent of cases fall within one standard deviation of the mean and 95 percent of cases fall within two standard deviations. For example, if the mean age is 45, with a standard deviation of 10, 95 percent of the cases would be between 25 and 65 in a normal distribution.
- Variance:
  - A measure of dispersion around the mean, equal to the sum of squared deviations from the mean divided by one less than the number of cases. The variance is measured in units that are the square of those of the variable itself.

184 *Handbook of research methods in corporate social responsibility*

- Standard error of the mean:
  - A measure of how much the value of the mean may vary from sample to sample taken from the same distribution. It can be used to roughly compare the observed mean to a hypothesized value (i.e., you can conclude the two values are different if the ratio of the difference to the standard error is less than −2 or greater than +2).
- Skewness:
  - If the distribution (or 'shape') of a variable is not symmetrical about the median or the mean it is said to be skewed. The distribution has positive skewness if the tail of high values is longer than the tail of low values, and negative skewness if the reverse is true.
- Kurtosis:
  - A measure of the extent to which observations cluster around a central point. For a normal distribution, the value of the kurtosis statistic is zero. Positive kurtosis indicates that, relative to a normal distribution, the observations are more clustered about the centre of the distribution and have thinner tails until the extreme values of the distribution, at which point the tails of the leptokurtic distribution are thicker relative to a normal distribution. Negative kurtosis indicates that, relative to a normal distribution, the observations cluster less and have thicker tails until the extreme values of the distribution, at which point the tails of the platykurtic distribution are thinner relative to a normal distribution.

Such statistics make no inferences or predictions; they simply report what has been found, in a variety of ways.

Inferential Statistics

Inferential statistics, by contrast, strive to make inferences and predictions based on the data gathered (Rencher, 2002). These will include, for example, hypothesis testing, correlations, regression and multiple regression, difference testing (e.g. t-tests and analysis of variance, factor analysis, and structural equation modelling). Sometimes simple frequencies and descriptive statistics may speak for themselves, and the careful portrayal of descriptive data may be important. However, often it is the inferential statistics that are more valuable for researchers, and typically these are more powerful. These inferential statistics such as hypothesis testing and regression analysis will be dealt with in other chapters.

Tables 11.1 and 11.2 show the descriptive statistics for both dependent and independent variables.

The data shown in Table 11.1 illustrates the perceived influence of CSR disclosures on revenue can be ranked as (1), followed by the perceived influence of CSR information on return on equity (0.1409), whereas return on asset (0.0592) can be ranked as (3).

Table 11.2 presents descriptive statistics for all the variables of interest. The average indexes illustrate higher disclosure on consumer information (mean = 0.382), employee information (mean = 0.358), and community information (mean = 0.255) and less disclosure on environmental information (mean = 0.216).

Table 11.1 Perceived influence of corporate social responsibility disclosures on revenue

Dependent Variables	Min	Max	Median	Mean	Std. D	Skewness	Kurtosis
Return on Asset	0.0007	0.3702	0.0204	0.0592	0.0853	2.26	5.085
Return on Equity	0.0007	0.78	0.102	0.1409	0.1514	2.295	7.567
Revenue	0.034m	1303.05m	39.89m	185.04m	318.84m	2.377	5.309

Notes: Std. D = the standard deviation; m = million.

Table 11.2 Descriptive statistics for all variables of interest

Independent Variables	Min	Max	Median	Mean	Std. D	Skewness	Kurtosis
Environment Disclosure	0.0	1.0	0.14	0.21675	0.2563	1.435	1.354
Consumer Disclosure	0.0	1.0	0.25	0.3825	0.2033	0.804	1.153
Community Disclosure	0.0	0.8	0.2	0.255	0.2218	0.843	0.197
Employee Disclosure	0.11	0.56	0.33	0.3582	0.1174	−0.477	−0.217

The descriptive statistics (skewness and kurtosis) for the dependent and independent variables shown in Table 11.2 indicate that the overall disclosure index and all dependent variables are normally distributed (both skewedness and kurtosis coefficients are not significantly different from zero at the 0.05 level of significance) except return on asset, return on equity, and revenues.

The application of descriptive statistics analysis to CSR can be further highlighted by the study of Sun (2012) wherein he examined the association between corporate social responsibility and financial performance. Samples were selected by downloading KLD data, including the seven major areas and six controversial issues, during the period from 1999 to 2009. KLD represents Kinder, Lydenberg, and Domini which is a database on CSR performance. The KLD sample consists of 24,283 firm-year observations. CompuStat was used to obtain financial statement data, which include total assets, total liabilities, net value of property, plant and equipment (PPE), gross value of PPE, operating income, depreciation and amortization, and total net sales. A descriptive statistic was used to describe the independent variable in the regression analysis. Results revealed a significant and positive association between CSR and financial performance. In addition, it finds that the age of long-term assets is highly correlated with CSR.

PARAMETRIC AND NON-PARAMETRIC DATA

Before choosing a statistical test to apply to your data you should address the issue of whether your data are parametric or not. A parametric test is a statistical test, which requires the distribution of the population to be specified. Thus, parametric inferential methods assume that the distribution of the variables being assessed belongs to some form of known probability distribution. Parametric data assume knowledge of the characteristics of the population, in order for inferences to be able to be made securely. They often assume a normal, Gaussian curve of distribution, as in reading scores, for example Cohen, Manion and Morrison (2013, p. 128), who suggest that normal distributions are actually rare in psychology.

In contrast, a non-parametric test, also known as distribution free test, does not require the distribution to be specified prior to the research. This family of tests does not require the assumption on the distribution. Most commonly, non-parametric tests rank the outcome variable from low to high and then analyse the ranks rather than the actual observation.

In practice this distinction means this: nominal and ordinal data are considered to be non-parametric, while interval and ratio data are considered to be parametric data. The distinction, as for the four scales of data, is important, as the consideration of which statistical test to use is dependent on the kinds of data. It is incorrect to apply parametric statistics to non-parametric data, although it is possible to apply non-parametric statistics to parametric data – it is not widely done, however, as the statistics are usually less powerful. Non-parametric data are often derived from questionnaires and surveys, though these can also gain parametric data, while parametric data tend to be derived from experiments and tests (e.g. examination scores).

Choosing the right test will contribute to the validity of the research findings. Improper use of statistical tests will not only cause the validity of the test results to be questioned and do little justification to the research, but at times it can be a serious error especially if the results have major implications (e.g., if these are used in policy formulation on CSR). Parametric tests have greater statistical power compared to their non-parametric equivalent. However, it is not all the time that parametric tests are the best tests to use; a parametric test should be used if the researcher is sure that the data are sampled from a population that follows a pre-defined distribution (e.g. a normal distribution). On the other hand, a non-parametric test should be used if: (1) the outcome is a rank (e.g. rank order of the test scores); (2) no assumption is made on the population distribution; and (3) there are outliers.

Exploratory Data Analysis: Frequencies, Percentages, and Cross-Tabulations

This is a form of analysis, which is responsive to the data being presented, and is most closely concerned with seeing what the data themselves suggest, akin to a detective following a line of evidence. The data are usually descriptive.

Here much is made of visual techniques of data presentation. Hence frequencies and percentages, and forms of graphical presentation are often used. A host of graphical forms of data presentation are available in software packages, including, for example:

- Frequency and percentage tables
- Bar charts (for nominal and ordinal data)
- Histograms (for continuous – interval and ratio – data)
- Line graphs
- Pie charts
- High and low charts
- Scatterplots

- Stem and leaf displays
- Box plots (box and whisker plots).

With most of these forms of data display there are various permutations of the ways in which data are displayed within the type of chart or graph chosen. While graphs and charts may look appealing, it is often the case that they tell the reader no more than could be seen in a simple table of figures, which take up less space in a report. Pie charts, bar charts, and histograms are particularly prone to this problem, and the data in them could be placed more succinctly into tables. Clearly the issue of fitness for audience is important here: some readers may find charts more accessible and able to be understood than tables of figures, and this is important. Other charts and graphs can add greater value than tables, for example, line graphs, box plots, and scatterplots with regression lines, and we would suggest that these are helpful. Here is not the place to debate the strengths and weaknesses of each type, although there are some guides here:

- Bar charts are useful for presenting categorical and discrete data, highest and lowest. Avoid using a third dimension (e.g. depth) in a graph when it is unnecessary; a third dimension to a graph must provide additional information.
- Histograms are useful for presenting continuous data.
- Line graphs are useful for showing trends, particularly in continuous data, for one or more variables at a time.
- Multiple line graphs are useful for showing trends in continuous data on several variables in the same graph.
- Pie charts and bar charts are useful for showing proportions.
- Interdependence can be shown through cross-tabulations (discussed below).
- Box plots are useful for showing the distribution of values for several variables in a single chart, together with their range and medians.
- Stacked bar charts are useful for showing the frequencies of different groups within a specific variable for two or more variables in the same chart.
- Scatterplots are useful for showing the relationship between two variables or several sets of two or more variables on the same chart.

At a simple level one can present data in terms of frequencies and percentages (a piece of datum about a course evaluation). The table below presents an example of frequencies and percentages on a training course evaluation. Participants were asked to assess the level

Table 11.3 Frequencies and percentages for a course evaluation

		Frequency	Percentage
Valid:	Not at all	24	12.6
	Very little	49	25.7
	A little	98	51.3
	Quite a lot	16	8.4
	A very great deal	4	2.1
Total:		191	100.0

188 *Handbook of research methods in corporate social responsibility*

of difficulty of the course by selecting 'not at all', 'very little', 'a little', 'quite a lot 'and 'a very great deal'. One hundred and ninety-one participants completed the item.

- Most respondents thought that the course was 'a little' too hard (with a response number of 98, i.e. 51.3 percent); the modal score is that category or score which is given by the highest number of respondents.
- The results were skewed, with only 10.5 percent being in the categories 'quite a lot' and 'a very great deal'.
- More people thought that the course was 'not at all' too hard than thought that the course was 'quite a lot' or 'a very great deal' too hard.
- Overall the course appears to have been slightly too difficult but not much more.

A unique study has been undertaken to evaluate the corporate social performance of Islamic financial institutions by Sairally (2013). The study takes up a case study specific to Islamic finance. It involved the application of exploratory data analysis to assess the respondents' view on the practical field of Islamic banking and finance. Recent debates on the evolution of the practice of Islamic finance highlighted the profit and economic efficiency motives of Islamic financial services rather than their concern for socio-economic equity and welfare. The findings revealed that the majority of the Islamic financial practitioners believed in attributing an integrated social role to Islamic financial services. However, the practices of the Islamic financial services reflected a more limited approach to CSR. Most of the Islamic financial services were observed to be focused on meeting their legal, economic, and Sharia's responsibilities, that is, were concerned with the goals of profit maximization and for their transactions to meet Sharia's compliance. CSR was practised as a peripheral activity by the Islamic financial services as opposed to being an integral, well-thought-out and deliberate policy decision of management.

CROSS-TABULATION AND THE CHI-SQUARE STATISTIC

Cross-tabulation is one of the most frequently used methods of analysis for questionnaire data. It enables us to examine the relationship between categorical variables in greater detail than simple frequencies for individual variables (Zikmund, Babin, Carr and Griffin, 2010). In this chapter we will see how to do this in SPSS (Statistical Package for Social Sciences) and also apply a statistical analysis associated with cross-tabulation – known as chi-square (pronounced 'key square').

Cross-Tabulating Data in the Questionnaire

The cross-tabulations procedure forms two-way and multi-way tables and provides a variety of tests and measures of association for two-way tables. The structure of the table and whether categories are ordered determine what test or measure to use.

Cross-tabulation statistics and measures of association are computed for two-way tables only. If you specify a row, a column, and a layer factor (control variable), the cross-tabulations procedure forms one panel of associated statistics and measures for each value of the layer factor (or a combination of values for two or more control variables). For

Table 11.4 Contingency table

		Poor	Below average	Average	Above average	Excellent	Total
Male	Count	7	20	26	4	5	62
	% of total	3.5%	10.0%	13.0%	2.0%	2.5%	31.0%
Female	Count	19	38	73	7	1	138
	% of total	9.5%	19.0%	36.5%	3.5%	0.5%	69.0%
Total	Count	26	58	99	11	6	200
	% of total	13.0%	29.0%	49.5%	5.5%	3.0%	100.0%

example, if 'gender' is a layer factor for a table of 'married' (yes, no) against 'life' (is life exciting, routine, or dull), the results for a two-way table for the females are computed separately from those for the males and printed as panels following one another.

Table 11.4 shows that, of the total sample, nearly three times more females (36.5 percent) than males (13.0 percent) thought that the quality of accommodation was 'average' or 'below average'. Deductions can be made in terms of both percentages and absolute numbers on both female and male voting pattern.

However, one also has to observe that the size of the two subsamples was uneven. Around three-quarters of the sample were female (69.0 percent) and around one-quarter (31.0 percent) was male. There are two ways to overcome the problem of uneven subsample sizes. One is to adjust the sample, in this case by multiplying up the subsample of males by an exact figure in order to make the two subsamples the same size (138/62 = 2.23). Another way is to examine the data by each row rather than by the overall totals, that is, to examine the proportion of males voting such and such, and, separately, the proportion of females voting for the same categories of the variable.

The Chi-Square Statistical Test

Chi-square (represented as χ^2) applies a statistical test to cross-tabulation by comparing the actual 'observed' frequencies in each cell of tables with expected frequencies. Expected frequencies are those we would expect if data were 'randomly distributed'.

It may help at this point to think of the four cells in the cross-tabulation table as buckets. Now imagine a lottery machine designed to pump balls into each of the buckets through four pipes – one leading into each bucket. If the distribution of balls by the lottery machine is truly random, then we would expect a similar number of balls in each bucket. Thus, if the lottery machine was set up to distribute 200 balls we would expect roughly 50 balls in each of the four buckets. So, using the hypothetical data in Table 11.4 we can see that there is no difference across male/female patients. The actual observed counts match the expected counts.

The expected result is based on a statistical process discussed below. The chi-square statistic addresses the notion of statistical significance, itself based on notions of probability. Here is not the place to go into the mathematics of the test, not least because computer packages automatically calculate the results. That said, the formula for calculating chi-square is:

$$\chi^2 = \sum \frac{(O-E)^2}{E} \qquad (11.1)$$

where
O = observed frequencies
E = expected frequencies
$\sum$ = the sum of

In the hypothetical example above, say that the computer package (SPSS) tells us that the significance level is 0.016, that is, the distribution of the data is not simply due to chance. We recall that the conventionally accepted minimum level of significance is usually 0.05, and the significance level of our data here is smaller than that, that is, it is statistically significant. Hence we can suggest that the difference between the voting of the males and females is statistically significant and not just due to chance, that is, there is a meaningful difference between the two groups. Hence the null hypothesis is not supported and the alternative hypothesis, that there is a statistically significant difference between the voting of the two groups, is supported.

One can report the results of the chi-square test thus, for example: when the chi-square statistic is calculated for the distribution of males and females on their liking for CSR activities, a statistically significant difference may be found between the males and the females: ($\chi^2 = 14.51$, $df = 2$, $p = 0.01$).

The chi-square statistic is usually used with nominal data, and our example illustrates this. For a chi-square statistic, data are set into a contingency made up of horizontal rows and columns.

Statistical Significance

In discussing the outcomes of the chi-square analysis we have introduced an important concept – that of statistical significance. There is a convention in research that we may accept a 5 percent (written as 0.05 which is 5 in 100, or 1 in 20) probability of accepting that there is a significant difference if it were true that there was really no difference (a false positive). In actual fact, the chi-square test has calculated that the odds are 1 in 100 (0.01) that this distribution of scores in the four cells could occur by chance.

The problem being that we have to strike a balance. The lower you set your criteria for significance, the more likely you are to conclude with a false positive – concluding that there *is* a significant difference when there is not in reality – in our counselling example, arguing for a male and a female counsellor to cater for patient preferences when further research with a larger sample would show that there really is not a preference for a same-sex counsellor. But conversely, if you set your threshold for significance too high, you are more likely to conclude with a false negative – saying there is no difference when there actually is. In statistics books these are known as Type I (false-positive) and Type II (false-negative) errors.

This also raises the issue of 'power' and 'effect size'. Imagine two experiments. The first aims to test the effects of a drug on humans, which is known to be highly noxious through laboratory and animal experiments. What sample size would you need? Well, if we expect that the effect is going to be particularly distinctive – vomiting, convulsions, and so forth – then we would hope not very many.

Hopefully, after say five people taking the drug and another five taking a placebo, we would have some pretty strong data comparing the two conditions. But imagine a second experiment, which is using a questionnaire to measure levels of anxiety before and after counselling. The researchers think that counselling will reduce the levels of anxiety for most patients, but possibly not by that much, and for some patients their levels of anxiety may rise as they confront their issues. So the effect that we were expecting is not particularly distinctive in this case – and therefore we would need a much larger sample to avoid concluding with a false negative. This is the basis of 'power calculations' where, basically, the smaller the effect size, the larger the sample size needed.

Unfortunately, then, there is no simple answer to the question, 'How large a sample do I need?' since it depends on the particular research you are conducting, the outcome measures you are using, and the size of the effect you might be expecting. As a general rule of thumb, you should be aiming for as large a sample as possible (to detect differences if they do exist), but not continuing the recruitment beyond that which is required to determine any effects you are investigating. Otherwise you will be wasting your time and your patients' time, which, furthermore, may be regarded as unethical particularly where there may be adverse effects – as in the example of testing a noxious drug.

In practice, there are often limitations in terms of time, resources, and the available sample. For example, if there are only 30 referrals to a counselling service during the year, and you need to evaluate the service after a year, then that is your sample. Alternatively, if this is deemed to be too small a sample for your purposes (to provide meaningful results) then you would have to extend the recruitment period until you achieved a larger sample.

SPECIAL STATISTIC FOR RESEARCH

In addition to the traditional statistical techniques that are used for data analysis, several special mathematical procedures have been developed to help evaluate and interpret research results. Most of these special techniques address questions concerning measurement procedures, specifically the reliability of measurements. One way of ensuring that measurement error is kept to a minimum is to determine properties of the measure that give us confidence that it is doing its job properly. The first property is 'validity', which is whether an instrument actually measures what it sets out to measure. The second is 'reliability', which is whether an instrument can be interpreted consistently across different situations. Reliability refers to the stability or consistency of measurements. Specifically, reliability means that when the same individuals are measured under the same conditions, you should obtain nearly identical measurements.

Notice that reliability refers to the relationship between two sets of measurements. Often, the relationship is measured by computing a correlation. However, there are situations where a simple correlation may not be completely appropriate. To deal with these special situations, researchers have developed several techniques that produce a correction or an adjustment to the correlation. In this section, we examine four statistical techniques for adjusting or correcting measures of reliability: the Spearman–Brown formula, the Kuder–Richardson formula 20, Cronbach's coefficient alpha, and Cohen's kappa.

The Spearman–Brown Formula

When a single variable is measured with a test that consists of multiple items it is common to evaluate the internal consistency of the test by computing a measure of split-half reliability. The concept behind split-half reliability is that all the different items on the test measure the same variable and, therefore, the measurement obtained from each individual item should be related to every other item. Specifically, if you split the test in half, then the score obtained from one-half of the test should be related to the score obtained from the other half.

There are a number of ways to split a test in half. For a 20-item test, for example, you could compute one score for the first ten items and a second score for the last ten items. Alternatively, you could compute one score for the odd-numbered items and a second score for the even-numbered items. In any case, you obtain two scores for each participant, and you can compute a correlation to measure the degree of relationship between the scores. The higher the correlation, the better the split-half reliability.

Although computing a correlation appears to be a straightforward method for measuring the relationship between two halves of a test, this technique has problems. In particular, the two split-half scores obtained for each participant are based on only half of the test items. In general, the score obtained from half of a test is less reliable than the score obtained from the full test. With a smaller number of items, there is a greater chance for error or chance to distort the participant's score. Therefore, a measure of split-half reliability (based on half the test) tends to underestimate the true reliability of the full test. A number of procedures have been developed to correct those problems, but the most commonly used technique is the Spearman–Brown formula. The formula adjusts the simple correlation between halves as follows:

$$\text{Spearman–Brown, } R = \frac{2r}{1+r} \tag{11.2}$$

where r is the simple correlation between the two halves of the test.

For a test consisting of 20 items, for example, each participant receives two scores with each score based on ten items. If the split-half correlation between the two scores was $r = 0.80$, then the corrected correlation from the Spearman–Brown formula would be:

$$R = \frac{2(0.8)}{1+0.8} = \frac{1.60}{1.80} = 0.89 \tag{11.3}$$

Notice that the effect of the correction is to increase the size of the correlation.

The Kuder–Richardson Formula 20

As we noted earlier, there are many different ways to split a test in half to obtain the two scores necessary to calculate a split-half reliability. Depending on how the test is split, you are likely to obtain different measures of reliability. To deal with this problem, Kuder and Richardson (1937) developed a formula that estimates the average of all the possible ways to split a test in half. The formula is the 20th and the best one they tried and is, therefore, called the Kuder–Richardson formula 20 (often shortened to K–R 20).

The Kuder–Richardson formula 20 is limited to tests in which each item has only two possible answers such as true/false, agree/disagree, or yes/no, and the score is the total, summed over all the items. The Kuder–Richardson measure of reliability is obtained by:

$$\text{K-R 20} = (n/n\text{-}1)(SD^2 - \Sigma pq)/SD^2 \tag{11.4}$$

where
The letter 'n' represents the number of items on the test.
SD is the standard deviation for the set of test scores.
For each item, p is the proportion of the participants whose response is coded 0.
For each item, q is the proportion of the participants whose response is coded 1 (note that $p + q = 1$ for each item).
Σpq is the sum of the p times q products for all items.

The Kuder–Richardson formula 20 produces values ranging from 0 to 1.00, with a higher value indicating a higher degree of internal consistency or reliability.

Cronbach's Alpha

One limitation of the Kuder–Richardson formula 20 is that it can only be used for tests in which each item has only two response alternatives. Cronbach (1951) developed a modification of the K–R 20 formula that can be used when test items have more than two alternatives such as a Likert scale that has five response choices. Cronbach's alpha has a structure similar to the K–R 20 formula and is computed as follows:

$$\text{Cronbach's alpha} = n/n\text{-}1\,(SD^2 - \Sigma\text{variance})/SD^2 \tag{11.5}$$

The elements in Cronbach's formula are identical to the elements in the K–R 20 formula except for Σvariance. To compute this new Cronbach's alpha, first calculate the variance of the scores for each item separately. With 20 participants, for example, you would compute the variance for the 20 scores obtained for item 1, and the variance for the 20 scores on item 2, and so on. Then sum the variance across all the test items.

Like the K–R 20 formula, Cronbach's alpha is intended to measure split-half reliability by estimating the average correlation that would be obtained by considering every possible way to split the test in half. Also, like the K–R 20 formula, Cronbach's alpha produces values between 0 and 1.00, with a higher value indicating a higher degree of internal consistency or reliability.

A yield of alpha coefficient of 0.97, is very high. The alpha coefficients are set out in a table. According to Bryman and Cramer (1990) the following guidelines can be used for the split-half coefficient and the alpha coefficient:

> 0.90   very highly reliable
0.80–0.90   highly reliable
0.70–0.79   reliable
0.60–0.69   marginally/minimally reliable
< 0.60   unacceptably low reliability

Bryman and Cramer (1990, p. 71) suggest that the reliability level is acceptable at 0.8, although others suggest that it is acceptable if it is 0.67 or above.

Cohen's Kappa

When measurements are obtained by behavioural observation, it is customary to evaluate the measurement procedure by determining inter-rater reliability. Inter-rater reliability is the degree of agreement between two observers who have independently observed and recorded behaviours at the same time. The simplest technique for determining inter-rater reliability is to compute the percentage of agreement as follows:

$$\text{Percent agreement} = \frac{\text{Number of observations in agreement}}{\text{Total number of observations}} * 100 \quad (11.6)$$

For example, if two observers agree on 46 out of 50 observations, their percent agreement is $(46/50)100 = 92\%$.

The problem with a simple measure of percent agreement is that the value obtained can be inflated by chance. That is, the two observers may record the same observation simply by chance. As an extreme example, consider two observers who are supposed to be watching the same child but, by mistake, are actually watching two different children. Even though the two observers are watching different children, it is possible that, from time to time, they will still record the same behaviours. Thus, the two observers will agree, but their agreement is just chance.

'Cohen's kappa' is a measure of agreement that attempts to correct for chance (Cohen, 1960). Cohen's kappa is computed as follows:

$$\text{Cohen's kappa} = \frac{PA - PC}{1 - PC} \quad (11.7)$$

The elements in the formula are defined as follows:
PA is the observed percent agreement.
PC is the percent agreement expected from chance.
Assume the data recorded observations of two observers watching a child over 25 observation periods. For every observation period, each observer records yes or no indicating whether or not an example of aggressive behaviour was observed. The number of agreements is obtained by counting the number of periods in which both observers record the same observation. Assume there are 21 agreements out of the 25 observation periods. Thus, the percent agreement is

$$PA = 21/25 = 84\% \quad (11.8)$$

To determine the percentage agreement expected from chance (PC), we must call on a basic law of probability. The law states: given two separate events, A and B, with the probability of A equal to p and the probability of B equal to q, then the probability of A and B occurring together is equal to the product of p and q.

VALIDITY

Validity refers to whether an instrument measures what it was designed to measure. The basic question behind the concept of validity is whether an indicator measures what we say or believe it does. This may be quite a basic question if the subject matter of the indicator is visible and readily understood, but the practicalities can be more complex in mundane, but sensitive, areas such as measurement of household income.

Validity takes us into issues of what different people understand words to mean, during the development of the indicator and its use. It is good practice to try a variety of approaches with a wide range of relevant people, and carefully compare the interpretations, behaviours, and attitudes revealed, to make sure there are no major discrepancies of understanding. The processes of comparison and reflection, then the redevelopment of definitions, approaches, and research instruments, may all be encompassed in what is sometimes called triangulation – using the results of different approaches to synthesize robust, clear, and easily interpreted results. Survey instrument or indicator validity is a discussion topic, not a statistical measure, but two themes with which statistical survey analysts regularly need to engage are the following.

Criterion and Content Validity

Criterion validity is whether the instrument is measuring what it claims to measure (does your lecturers' helpfulness rating scale actually measure lecturers' helpfulness?). In an ideal world, you could assess this by relating scores on your measure to real-world observations.

For example, we could take an objective measure of how helpful lecturers were and compare these observations to students' ratings on ratemyprofessor.com. This is often impractical and, of course, with attitudes you might not be interested in the reality so much as the person's perception of reality. With self-report measures/questionnaires one can also assess the degree to which individual items represent the construct being measured, and cover the full range of the construct, that is, 'content validity'. Validity is a necessary but not sufficient condition of a measure. Content validity looks at the extent to which the questions in a survey, and the weights the results are given in a set of indicators, serve to cover in a balanced way the important facets of the notion the indicator is supposed to represent.

Criterion validity can look at how the observed values of the indicator tie up with something readily measurable that they should relate to. Its aim is to validate a new indicator by reference to something better established, for example, to validate a prediction retrospectively against the actual outcome. If we measure an indicator of 'intention to participate' or 'likelihood of participating' beforehand, then for the same individuals later ascertain whether they did participate, we can check the accuracy of the stated intentions, and hence the degree of reliance that can in future be placed on the indicator.

As a statistical exercise, criterion validation has to be done through sensible analyses of good-quality data. If the reason for developing the indicator is that there is no satisfactory way of establishing a criterion measure, criterion validity is not a sensible approach.

Factor Analysis

Factor analysis attempts to identify underlying variables, or 'factors', that explain the pattern of correlations within a set of observed variables. It is often used in data reduction to identify a small number of factors that explain most of the variance that is observed in a much larger number of manifest variables. Factor analysis can also be used to generate hypotheses regarding causal mechanisms or to screen variables for subsequent analysis. An example is to identify collinearity prior to performing a linear regression analysis.

For example, what underlying attitudes lead people to respond to the questions on a political survey as they do? Examining the correlations among the survey items reveals that there is significant overlap among various subgroups of items – questions about taxes tend to correlate with each other, questions about military issues correlate with each other, and so on. With factor analysis, you can investigate the number of underlying factors and, in many cases, identify what the factors represent conceptually. Additionally, you can compute factor scores for each respondent, which can then be used in subsequent analyses. For example, you might build a logistic regression model to predict voting behaviour based on factor scores.

DATA

The variables should be quantitative at the 'interval' or 'ratio' level. Categorical data (such as religion or country of origin) are not suitable for factor analysis. Data for which Pearson correlation coefficients can sensibly be calculated should be suitable for factor analysis.

Assumptions

The data should have a bivariate normal distribution for each pair of variables, and observations should be independent. The factor analysis model specifies that variables are determined by common factors (the factors estimated by the model) and unique factors (which do not overlap between observed variables); the computed estimates are based on the assumption that all unique factors are uncorrelated with each other and with the common factors.

Examples from the Corporate Social Responsibility Literature

An empirical study was conducted by Chen and Wang (2011) in China in order to find the relationship between CSR and financial performance in Chinese companies. On the whole, considering time lag and cause and effect factors, the authors explored the relationships between CSR and corporate financial performance (CFP) with data in 2007 and 2008 from investigation. With factor analysis, the authors divided CSR into six factors (employees, customers, community, preponderant stakeholders, partners, and managing diversity). In 2007, the data analysis results showed that CSR could be divided into seven factors (employees, customers, community, preponderant stakeholders, partners, managing diversity, and operators). Both results were very similar. Through descriptive statistics the authors found that almost half of the surveying companies (46.5 percent) were in the manufacturing and information industry. The authors used various methods to test reliability and validity of the survey design. For structured problems described by a Likert 5-scales table, the authors used Cronbach's values to evaluate internal consistency, reflecting the reliability of survey design. They implemented pilot and formal surveys based upon repeated modification. Besides, the authors involved numerous discussions with enterprise senior executives. So their analysis has considerable content validity. To ensure this study embodied constructing validity, before factor analysis, they did the KMO (Kaiser–Meyer–Olkin) test and Bartlett Test of Sphericity to decide whether the parameters were appropriate for factor analysis. They processed data through factor analysis, relative analysis, and multi-regression. The data analysis indicated that there were significant and reciprocal relationships between homophonous CSR and CFP in Chinese enterprises. In addition, the postponement influence between CSR and CFP was significant as well, while the variances between CSR and CFP were significant and positive. H1 to H5 were basically tested and verified.

Another empirical study was conducted by Aras, Aybars and Kutlu (2010), where the authors investigated the relationship between CSR and firm financial performance. The main part of the authors' research paper was based upon an exploration of the relationship between CSR and financial performance in developing countries. The authors did this by investigating the Istanbul Stock Exchange (ISE) 100 index companies and their social responsibility policy and financial indicators. The authors tested for reliability and validity of the data used.

The problem of reliability exists for content analysis just like any quantitative technique. The disagreement between the coders distorts the significance of the analysis. Three types of reliability have been defined by Krippendorff: stability, reproducibility, and accuracy. Stability, which is the weakest form of reliability, is measured as the degree that a coder reaches the same results while analysing the data over time. Reproducibility, which is a stronger form of reliability than stability, measures the repeatability of the data by multiple coders. The strongest form of reliability is named as accuracy and it measures the performance of coding against the performance of a method that has been applied by experts and regarded as being correct.

In Aras, Aybars and Kutlu's study, the annual reports were read by two coders who are academicians familiar with social and environmental disclosure research. In order to capture the degree of stability of the data, the annual reports that have been read once by a coder were read a second time after two weeks. It was seen that no significant difference existed between the two readings. To analyse the degree of reproducibility, the two coders read the annual reports independently applying the same set of dimensions and decision rules for coding. Again, no significant difference was noted between the two coders. To achieve accuracy, Hackston and Milne's (1996) coding approach, which has been cited by many academic studies, was undertaken. The authors also used descriptive statistics for the measures of size, profitability, risk, research and development intensity, and CSR.

CLUSTER ANALYSIS

Cluster analysis is a major technique for classifying a 'mountain' of information into manageable meaningful piles (Everitt, Landau and Leese, 2001). It is a data reduction tool that creates subgroups that are more manageable than the individual datum. Like factor analysis, it examines the full complement of inter-relationships between variables. Both cluster analysis and discriminant analysis are concerned with classification. However, the latter requires prior knowledge of membership of each cluster in order to classify new cases. In cluster analysis there is no prior knowledge about which elements belong to which clusters.

Clustering occurs in almost every aspect of daily life. A factory's Health and Safety Committee may be regarded as a cluster of people. Supermarkets display items of similar nature, such as types of meat or vegetables, in the same or nearby locations. Biologists have to organize the different species of animals before a meaningful description of the differences between animals is possible. In medicine, the clustering of symptoms and diseases leads to taxonomies of illnesses. In the field of business, clusters of consumer segments are often sought for successful marketing strategies.

A cluster is a group of relatively homogeneous cases or observations. Cluster analysis (CA) is an exploratory data analysis tool for organizing observed data (e.g. people, things, events, brands, companies) into meaningful taxonomies, groups, or clusters, based on combinations of IV's, which maximizes the similarity of cases within each cluster while maximizing the dissimilarity between groups that are initially unknown (Wright and Simon, 2003). CA is the statistical method of partitioning a sample into homogeneous classes to produce an operational classification.

Extension Chapters on Advanced Techniques

Using CA, a customer 'type' can represent a homogeneous market segment. Identifying their particular needs in that market allows products to be designed with greater precision and direct appeal within the segment. Targeting specific segments is cheaper and more accurate than broad-scale marketing. Customers respond better to segment marketing which addresses their specific needs, leading to increased market share and customer retention. This is valuable, for example, in banking, insurance, and tourism markets. Imagine four clusters or market segments in the vacation travel industry. They are:

1. The elite – they want top level service and expect to be pampered;
2. The escapists – they want to get away and just relax;
3. The educationalist – they want to see new things, go to museums, have a safari, or experience new cultures; and
4. The sports person – they want the golf course, tennis court, surfing, deep-sea fishing, climbing, and so on.

Different brochures and advertising is required for each of these.

Brand image analysis, or defining product 'types' by customer perceptions, allows a company to see where its products are positioned in the market relative to those of its competitors. This type of modelling is valuable for branding new products or identifying possible gaps in the market. Clustering supermarket products by linked purchasing patterns can be used to plan store layouts, maximizing spontaneous purchasing opportunities (Wright and Simon, 2003).

Banking institutions have used hierarchical CA to develop a typology of customers, for two purposes, as follows: (1) to retain the loyalty of members by designing the best possible new financial products to meet the needs of different groups (clusters), that is, new product opportunities; and (2) to capture more market share by identifying which existing services are most profitable for which type of customer and improve market penetration.

Assuming a major bank completed a CA on a representative sample of its members, according to 16 variables chosen to reflect the characteristics of their financial transaction patterns. From this analysis, 30 types of members were identified. The results were useful for marketing, enabling the bank to focus on products which had the best financial performance; reduce direct mailing costs and increase response rates by targeting product promotions at those customer types most likely to respond; and consequently, to achieve better branding and customer retention. This facilitated a differential direct advertising of services and products to the various clusters that differed inter alia by age, income, risk taking levels, and self-perceived financial needs. In this way, the bank could retain and win the business of more profitable customers at lower cost.

Cluster analysis, like factor analysis, makes no distinction between dependent and independent variables. The entire set of interdependent relationships is examined. CA is the obverse of factor analysis. Whereas factor analysis reduces the number of variables by grouping them into a smaller set of factors, CA reduces the number of observations or cases by grouping them into a smaller set of clusters.

The Technique of Cluster Analysis

Because one does not usually know the number of groups or clusters that will emerge in a sample and because we want an optimum solution, a two-stage sequence of analysis occurs as follows:

1. We carry out a 'hierarchical cluster analysis' using Ward's (1963) method applying 'squared Euclidean distance' as the distance or similarity measure. This helps to determine the optimum number of clusters we should work with.
2. The next stage is to rerun the hierarchical cluster analysis with our selected number of clusters, which enables us to allocate every case in our sample to a particular cluster. There are a variety of clustering procedures of which hierarchical cluster analysis is the major one.

Hierarchical Cluster Analysis

This is the major statistical method for finding relatively homogeneous clusters of cases based on measured characteristics. It starts with each case as a separate cluster, that is, there are as many clusters as cases, and then combines the clusters sequentially, reducing the number of clusters at each step until only one cluster is left. The clustering method uses the dissimilarities or distances between objects when forming the clusters. The SPSS programme calculates 'distances' between data points in terms of the specified variables. A hierarchical tree diagram, called a dendrogram on SPSS, can be produced to show the linkage points. The clusters are linked at increasing levels of dissimilarity. The actual measure of dissimilarity depends on the measure used, for example, see Figure 11.1.

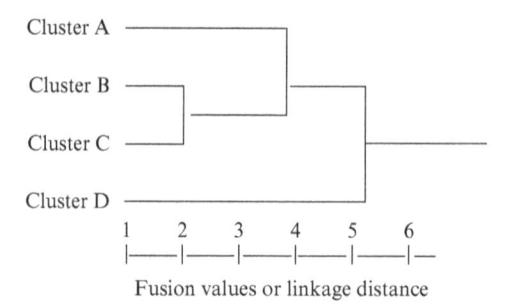

```
                Cluster A  ─────────────┐
                                        │
                Cluster B  ──────┐      │
                                 ├──────┤
                Cluster C  ──────┘      │
                                        │
                Cluster D  ─────────────┴────────
                           1   2   3   4   5   6
                           |───|───|───|───|───|─
                           Fusion values or linkage distance
```

Figure 11.1 Dendrogram on SPSS

This example (Figure 11.1) illustrates clusters B and C being combined at the fusion value of 2, and BC with A at 4. The fusion values or linkage distances are calculated by SPSS. The goal of the clustering algorithm is to join objects together into successively larger clusters, using some measure of similarity or distance. At the left of the dendrogram we begin with each object or case in a class by itself (in our example above there are only four cases). In very small steps, we 'relax' our criterion as to what is and is not unique. Put another way, we lower our threshold regarding the decision when to declare two or more objects to be members of the same cluster.

As a result, we link more and more objects together and amalgamate larger and larger clusters of increasingly dissimilar elements. Finally, all objects are joined together as one cluster. In these plots, the horizontal axis denotes the fusion or linkage distance. For each node in the graph (where a new cluster is formed) we can read off the criterion distance at which the respective elements were linked together into a new single cluster. As a general process, clustering can be summarized as follows:

- The distance is calculated between all initial clusters. In most analyses, initial clusters will be made up of individual cases.
- Then the two most similar clusters are fused and distances recalculated.
- Step 2 is repeated until all cases are eventually in one cluster.

Distance Measures

Distance can be measured in a variety of ways. There are distances that are Euclidean (can be measured with a 'ruler') and there are other distances based on similarity. For example, in terms of kilometre distance (a Euclidean distance) Perth, Australia is closer to Jakarta, Indonesia, than it is to Sydney, Australia. However, if distance is measured in terms of the cities' characteristics, Perth is closer to Sydney (e.g. both on a big river estuary, straddling both sides of the river, with surfing beaches, and both English speaking, etc.). A number of distance measures are available within SPSS. The squared Euclidean distance is the most used one.

Squared Euclidean Distance

The most straightforward and generally accepted way of computing distances between objects in a multi-dimensional space is to compute Euclidean distances, an extension of Pythagoras' theorem. If we had a two- or three-dimensional space, this measure is the actual geometric distance between objects in the space (i.e. as if measured with a ruler). In a univariate example, the Euclidean distance between two values is the arithmetic difference, that is, value 1 – value 2. In the bivariate case, the minimum distance is the hypotenuse of a triangle formed from the points, as in Pythagoras' theory. Although difficult to visualize, an extension of the Pythagoras' theorem will also give the distance between two points in n-dimensional space. The squared Euclidean distance is used more often than the simple Euclidean distance in order to place progressively greater weight on objects that are further apart. Euclidean (and squared Euclidean) distances are usually computed from raw data, and not from standardized data.

Having selected how we will measure distance, we must now choose the clustering algorithm, that is, the rules that govern between which points distances are measured to determine cluster membership. There are many methods available, the criteria used differ and hence different classifications may be obtained for the same data. This is important since it tells us that, although CA may provide an objective method for the clustering of cases, there can be subjectivity in the choice of method. SPSS provides five clustering algorithms, the most commonly used one being Ward's method.

Ward's Method

This method is distinct from other methods because it uses an analysis of variance approach to evaluate the distances between clusters. In general, this method is very efficient. Cluster membership is assessed by calculating the total sum of squared deviations from the mean of a cluster. The criterion for fusion is that it should produce the smallest possible increase in the error sum of squares.

K-Means Clustering

This method of clustering is very different from the hierarchical clustering and Ward method, which are applied when there is no prior knowledge of how many clusters there may be or what they are characterized by. K-means clustering is used when you already have hypotheses concerning the number of clusters in your cases or variables. You may want to 'tell' the computer to form exactly three clusters that are to be as distinct as possible. This is the type of research question that can be addressed by the k-means clustering algorithm. In general, the k-means method will produce the exact k different clusters demanded of greatest possible distinction.

Very frequently, both the hierarchical and the k-means techniques are used successively. The former (Ward's method) is used to get some sense of the possible number of clusters and the way they merge as seen from the dendrogram. Then the clustering is rerun with only a chosen optimum number in which to place all the cases (k-means clustering).

One of the biggest problems with CA is identifying the optimum number of clusters. As the fusion process continues, increasingly dissimilar clusters must be fused, that is, the classification becomes increasingly artificial. Deciding upon the optimum number of clusters is largely subjective, although looking at a dendrogram may help. Clusters are interpreted solely in terms of the variables included in them. Clusters should also contain at least four elements. Once we drop to three or two elements it ceases to be meaningful.

Example

A keep fit gym consisting of a group of employees wants to determine the best grouping of their customers with regard to the type of fitness work programmes they want in order to facilitate timetabling and staffing by specially qualified staff. A hierarchical analysis is run and three major clusters stand out on the dendrogram between everyone being initially in a separate cluster and the final cluster after conducting the hierarchical analysis. This is then quantified using a k-means CA with three clusters, which reveals that the means of different measures of physical fitness measures do indeed produce the three clusters (i.e. customers in cluster 1 are high on measure 1, low on measure 2, etc.).

Interpretation of results

The cluster centroids produced by SPSS are essentially means of the cluster score for the elements of a cluster. Then one usually examines the means for each cluster on each dimension using ANOVA (analysis of variance) to assess how distinct our clusters are. Ideally, we would obtain significantly different means for most, if not all dimensions, used in the analysis. The magnitude of the F values performed on each dimension is an indication of how well the respective dimension discriminates between clusters. It is useful to create on SPSS a new variable on the data view file which indicates the cluster to which each case has been assigned. This cluster membership variable can be used in further analyses. Techniques for determining reliability and validity of clusters are as yet not developed. However, one could conduct CA using several different distance measures provided by SPSS and compare results. Alternatively, if the sample is large enough, it can be split in half with clustering performed on each and the results compared.

SPSS Activity – Conducting a Cluster Analysis

The initial step is determining how many groups exist. The SPSS hierarchical analysis actually calculates every possibility between everyone forming their own group (as many clusters as there are cases) and everyone belonging to the same group, giving a range in our dummy set of data of from 1 to 20 clusters.

How to proceed
1. Click on 'Analyse > Classify > Hierarchical Cluster';
2. Select 'Variables for the analysis' and transfer them to the 'Variables' box; and
3. Click on 'Plots' and select 'Dendrogram'.

Warning about Cluster Analysis

Cluster analysis has no mechanism for differentiating between relevant and irrelevant variables. Therefore, the choice of variables included in a CA must be underpinned by conceptual considerations. This is very important because the clusters formed can be very dependent on the variables included.

Non-Hierarchical or *K*-Means Clustering Methods

In these methods the desired number of clusters is specified in advance and the 'best' solution is chosen. The steps in such a method are as follows:

1. Choose initial cluster centres (essentially this is a set of observations that are far apart – each subject forms a cluster of one and its centre is the value of the variables for that subject);
2. Assign each subject to its 'nearest' cluster, defined in terms of the distance to the centroid;
3. Find the centroids of the clusters that have been formed;
4. Re-calculate the distance from each subject to each centroid and move observations that are not in the cluster that they are closest to; and
5. Continue until the centroids remain relatively stable.

Non-hierarchical cluster analysis tends to be used when large data sets are involved. It is sometimes preferred because it allows subjects to move from one cluster to another (this is not possible in hierarchical CA where a subject, once assigned, cannot move to a different cluster). Two disadvantages of non-hierarchical CA are: (1) it is often difficult to know how many clusters you are likely to have and therefore the analysis may have to be repeated several times; and (2) it can be very sensitive to the choice of initial cluster centres. Again, it may be worth trying different ones to see what impact this has. One possible strategy to adopt is to use a hierarchical approach initially to determine how many clusters there are in the data and then to use the cluster centres obtained from this as initial cluster centres in the non-hierarchical method.

CONCLUSION

Corporate social responsibility has attracted the attention of both businesses and policymakers. The aim of this chapter was to review the current status of statistical methods and their application in CSR research. The science of statistics cannot be ignored by any research worker. The important statistical measures that are used to summarize the CSR research data are measures of central tendency or statistical averages; measures of dispersion; measures of asymmetry; measures of relationship; and other measures. The values of the variable define the scale or level of measurement used to study the variable. Descriptive statistics are graphical and numerical methods by which essential features of a sample can be described. Inferential statistics make inferences and predictions based on the data gathered. With the introduction of new statistical methods, it is a challenging task for researchers to use specific methods, substantiate it, and interpret the result.

BIBLIOGRAPHY

Aras, G., A. Aybars and O. Kutlu (2010), 'Managing corporate performance', *International Journal of Productivity and Performance Management*, **59** (3), 229–254, doi.org/10.1108/17410401011023573.

Bryman, Alan and Duncan Cramer (1990), *Quantitative Data Analysis for Social Scientists*, London, UK: Routledge.

Chen, H. and X. Wang (2011), 'Corporate social responsibility and corporate financial performance in China: an empirical research from Chinese firms, corporate governance', *The International Journal of Business in Society*, **11** (4), 361–370, doi.org/10.1108/14720701111159217.

Cohen, J. (1960), 'A coefficient of agreement for nominal scale', *Educational and Psychological Measurement*, 20, 37–46.

Cohen, Louis, Lawrence Manion and Keith Morrison (2013), *Research Methods in Education*, 7th ed., New York, NY, USA: Routledge.

Cronbach, L. J. (1951), 'Coefficient alpha and the internal structure of tests', *Psychometrika*, 16, 297–334.

Curwin, Jon and Roger Slater (2006), *Quantitative Methods for Business Decision*, 5th ed., London, UK: Gray Thomson.

Everitt, Brian S., Sabine Landau and Morven Leese (2001), *Cluster Analysis*, 4th ed., London, UK: Arnold.

Gill, John L. (1978), *Design and Analysis of Experiments in the Animal and Medical Sciences*, Ames, IA USA: Iowa State University Press.

Gravetter, Frederick J. and Lori-Ann B. Forzano (2006), *Research Methods for the Behavioral Sciences*, 2nd ed., Belmont, CA, USA: Thomson Wadsworth.

Hackston, D. and Milne, M. J. (1996), 'Some determinants of social and environmental disclosures in New Zealand companies', *Accounting, Auditing and Accountability Journal*, **9** (1), 77–108.

Kuder, G.F. and M.W. Richardson (1937), 'The theory of the estimation of test reliability', *Psychometrika*, **2** (3), 151–160.

Manly, Brian F.J. (2005), *Multivariate Statistical Methods: A Primer*, 3rd ed., London, UK: Chapman and Hall.

Rencher, Alvin C. (2002), *Methods of Multivariate Analysis*, 2nd ed., London, UK: Wiley.

Sairally, B.S. (2013), 'Evaluating the corporate social performance of Islamic financial institutions: an empirical study', *International Journal of Islamic and Middle Eastern Finance and Management*, **6** (3), 238–260, doi.org/10.1108/IMEFM-02-2013-0026.

Sun, L. (2012), 'Further evidence on the association between corporate social responsibility and financial performance', *International Journal of Law and Management*, **54** (6), 472–484, doi.org/10.1108/17542431211281954.

Ward Jr, J. H. (1963), 'Hierarchical grouping to optimize an objective function', *Journal of the American Statistical Association*, **58** (301), 236–244.

Wright, G. W. and Simon, R. M. (2003), 'A random variance model for detection of differential gene expression in small microarray experiments', *Bioinformatics*, **19** (18), 2448–2455.

Zikmund, William G., Barry J. Babin, Jon C. Carr and Mitch Griffin (2010), *Business Research Methods*, 8th ed., Mason, OH, USA: South-Western Cengage Learning.

12. Regression techniques and their application in the corporate social responsibility domain: an overview

Sonali Bhattacharya, Madhvi Sethi, Abhishek Behl and V.G. Venkatesh

INTRODUCTION

Corporate social responsibility (CSR) has attracted a lot of academic attention in the recent years. CSR research studies can be categorized as theoretical and empirical (Salzmann et al. 2005). The theoretical studies are based on frameworks that aim to explain the nature of the relationship between different variables with CSR. For example, some studies refer to the relationship between social and financial performance. The frameworks differ in terms of the hypothesized causal sequence and the direction of the relationship. The empirical studies follow two lines of research: instrumental and descriptive. Instrumental studies aim to empirically test the relationships hypothesized in theoretical studies, and descriptive studies are intended to examine how companies and managers approach CSR in practice. In social sciences, regression has become a widespread tool for empirical analysis especially while investigating relationships between variables. While reviewing CSR literature, it has been found that the empirical studies involving quantitative analysis rely heavily on regression analysis. Therefore, it becomes imperative to understand the basic structure and form of regression analysis. Also, for understanding different applications of regression analysis in CSR research, it becomes essential to look at some of the past research works in CSR which have applied this approach. For future research in the field of CSR, it is essential to look at further scope of various regression techniques and their application.

In its simplest form, regression analysis investigates relationships between variables. It allows the researcher to analyse the relationship of one variable (independent variable) to the other variable (dependent variable). In CSR research applications, the dependent variable is usually the outcome we care about (e.g., beneficiaries), while the independent variables are the instruments we have to achieve those outcomes with (e.g., economic and legal responsibility). Different CSR research studies used the regression analysis for various objectives. Some researchers studied the relationship between CSR and financial performance (Anderson and Frankle 1980; Ingram and Frazier 1980; McGuire et al. 1988) using regression analysis. Stanwick and Stanwick (1998) examined the relationship between CSR and three variables namely financial performance of the organization, size of the organization and environmental performance of the organization.

Researchers have also used regression analysis in understanding the relationship between CSR and consumers' attributions and brand evaluations (Bhattacharya and Sen 2004; Klein and Dawar 2004; Vogel 2005). The studies in the past have tried to develop models around different domains of management including strategy, finance, marketing, human resources, operations and how CSR is an integral part of each one of them. The basic motivation behind the studies was to ascertain the relative strength of effects, which in turn would prove useful for companies to make decisions regarding CSR. These studies also helped answer questions relating to the type of factors such as societal or environmental factors which are significant for firms.

The past studies and their findings provide a roadmap for further research studies in the area especially when applying regression models. Not only can more factors be brought into the models but also a proper use of regression analysis might help to compare the effects of variables measured on different scales. One of the major advantages of using regression models in social sciences has been its ability to predict. Regression analysis helps in making predictions which are precise and can be used to study the dynamics of the company in future. This also provides the basis for its popularity at large. The strategic implications from such studies have been immense and have helped the firms plan their managerial actions for effective outputs. Using regression models provides a platform for a researcher to predict behaviour and this characteristic of regression can be used for future studies in CSR. The significance of regression analysis in understanding CSR and different variables associated with it is emerging as a field of research. This chapter therefore focuses on the basic framework of regression analysis, different techniques of regression analysis and how these have been applied in CSR research. The chapter is divided into three sections. The first section introduces regression analysis in its basic form, the second section describes the different kinds of regression models and the last section explores the application of regression models in CSR research.

BASIC REGRESSION CONCEPT IN SOCIAL SCIENCES

Many theoretical and applied questions in the sciences and arts focus on whether there is evidence of association between some presumed causal antecedents X and some consequent or outcome Y. A management scientist may be interested in knowing if rewarding performance at work increases employee satisfaction and reduces turnover (e.g., Judge et al. 2010), a medical practitioner may want to know if a therapeutic method is effective at reducing depression (e.g., Hofmann and Smits 2008), a behavioural scientist may want to experiment if playing violent video games or watching violent television makes people aggressive (e.g., Anderson and Bushman 2001; Anderson et al. 2010), a market researcher may be interested in finding if exposure to negative political advertisements turns people off from participating in the political process (e.g., Lau et al. 1999). All these scientific queries set forth to establish causal association between two variables based not on speculation but documented by data collected from authentic sources. Behaviour of a phenomena can be better understood in trying to answer queries on not only whether X affects Y, but also how X exerts its effect on Y, and when X affects Y and when it does not. The 'how' question relates to the underlying psychological, cognitive or biological process that causally links X to Y, whereas the 'when' question pertains to the boundary conditions of the causal association – under what circumstances, or for which types of people.

CORRELATION AND PREDICTION

The most popular method of quantifying association between two variables X and Y is 'Pearson's product moment correlation', more simply known as 'Pearson's r'. It can be used to quantify linear association between two quantitative variables, a quantitative and a dichotomous variable, as well as between two dichotomous variables. Mathematically, it can be given as:

$$r_{XY} = \frac{\sum_{i=1}^{n} Z_{X_i} Z_{Y_i}}{n} \qquad (12.1)$$

One interpretation of Pearson's correlation between two variables X and Y is that it provides an estimate as to how many times the standard deviations from the sample mean of Y a case is given the number of times the standard deviations from the sample mean the case is on X.

$$\widehat{Z_{Y_j}} = r_{XY} Z_{X_j} \qquad (12.2)$$

For example, in a study by Bhattacharya (2010) based on 161 nations the SPSS output of the correlation coefficients between the Developmental Well-being Index and the Spiritual Well-being Index is as given in Table 12.1. The corresponding scatter plot is given in Figure 12.1.

The correlation and prediction are closely connected concepts. If two variables are correlated with each other, then one should be able to use information about values of one of the pair of variables (X, Y) to estimate with at least some degree of accuracy the values on the other variable in the pair.

Table 12.1 Coefficients of correlation

		Developmental Well-being Index	Spiritual Well-being Index
Developmental Well-being Index	Correlation coefficient	1.000	0.131
	Sig. (2-tailed)	0.000	0.097
	N	168	161
Spiritual Well-being Index	Correlation coefficient	0.131	1.000
	Sig. (2-tailed)	0.097	0.000
	N	161	161

Source: Bhattacharya (2010). Originally published in *Journal of Human Values*, Vol. 16, No. 1. Copyright © 2010 Management Centre for Human Values, Indian Institute of Management, Calcutta. All rights reserved. Reproduced with the permission of the copyright holders and the publishers Sage Publications India Pvt. Ltd, New Delhi.

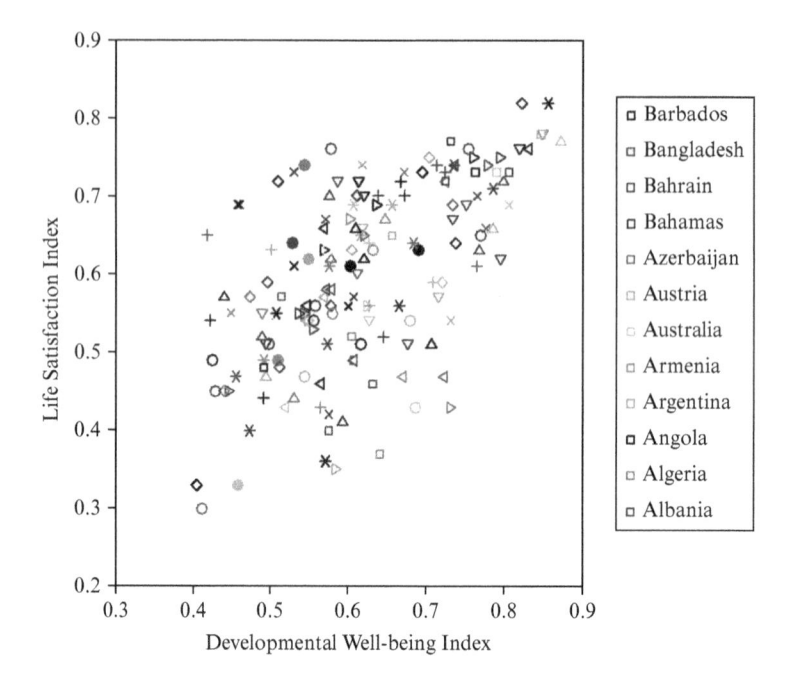

Source: Bhattacharya (2010). Originally published in *Journal of Human Values*, Vol. 16, No. 1. Copyright © 2010 Management Centre for Human Values, Indian Institute of Management, Calcutta. All rights reserved. Reproduced with the permission of the copyright holders and the publishers Sage Publications India Pvt. Ltd, New Delhi.

Figure 12.1 Scatter plot of Developmental Index and Life Satisfaction Index of Nations

THE SIMPLE LINEAR REGRESSION EQUATION AND ORDINARY LEAST SQUARE ESTIMATOR

A linear regression model is an equation that links one or more input variables (independent) to an output variable (dependent) by exploring information contained in the association between inputs and output. The input variables are often called 'predictor', 'independent' or 'explanatory' variables, whereas the output variable is called the 'criterion', 'outcome' or 'dependent' variable.

Many of the statistical procedures that scientists use can be represented in the form of a regression model, such as the independent group's t-test and analysis of variance. The objective of conducting a linear regression analysis is to estimate various parameters of the regression model such that the resulting equation yields estimations of the output variable from the input variable to a reasonable degree of accuracy with assumption of the linearity of associations between the input variables and the output variable. The information that comes from a regression model can be used to test hypotheses about degree and kind of linkage between the inputs to the output, and helps in determining which inputs should be retained for further study and which can possibly be ignored when attempting to explain variation in the output variable.

A simple linear regression model is simple, in that it contains only a single input variable. Expressed mathematically, the simple linear regression model is:

$$Yj = a + bXj + ej \qquad (12.3)$$

where Yj and Xj refer to case j's measurement on an outcome and input (predictor) variable, respectively, b is the regression coefficient or regression weight for predictor variable X, a is the regression intercept, and ej is the error in estimation of case j's value of Y from case j's value of X, and is also known as a residual. The process of estimating the parameters of such a model is referred to as regressing Y on X. The values of Xj and Yj can be taken from the data while performing analysis using a liner regression model. Our objective is to find the unknown constants a and b. Suppose we did know a and b. In that case, we could generate an estimate of Y from X with a variant of this model:

$$\hat{Y}_j = a + bX_j \qquad (12.4)$$

Where $\hat{Y}_j$ in this case is the predicted value of Y_j for given value of X_j
Substituting, $Y_j = \hat{Y}_j + e_j$
So that $e_j = Y_j - \hat{Y}_j$

Thus, the residual e_j is the difference between case jth estimated value for Y from the jth actual value of Y. Hence, if $e_j > 0$, it implies the estimator $\hat{Y}_j$ underestimates the actual value of Y_j and hence, if $e_j < 0$, it implies the estimator $\hat{Y}_j$ overestimates the actual value of Y_j.

For an ordinary least squares criterion, the researcher can only obtain one of the many possible pairs of a and b. Ordinary least squares (OLS) regression procedure minimizes the residual sum of squares (SS$_{residual}$), defined as:

$$SS_{residual} = \sum_{j=1}^{n} (Y_j - \hat{Y}_J)^2 \qquad (12.5)$$

SS$_{residual}$ cannot be negative (as the sum of squared values must be positive) and that if $Y_j = \hat{Y}_J$ for all n cases then SS$_{residual}$ = 0. The largest that SS$_{residual}$ could possibly be is the 'total sum of squares', defined as:

$$SS_{total} = \sum_{j=1}^{n} (Y_j - \overline{Y})^2 \qquad (12.6)$$

So OLS regression derives the values of a and b and produces the best fitting model of the data as defined by the least squares criterion – meaning that they make SS$_{residual}$ as small as it can have its value between 0 and SS$_{total}$.

MULTIPLE REGRESSION AND OLS

When there are multiple predictors, the researcher has an opportunity to look at multiple dimensions to arrive at predictive analysis of the dependent variable. The simple linear regression model can therefore be extended to the estimation of an outcome variable using more than one predictor variable. A multiple linear regression model with k predictor variables can be represented as:

$$Y_j = \alpha + b_1 X_{1j} + b_2 X_{2j} + \ldots + b_k X_{kj} + e_j \tag{12.7}$$

Eliminating the residuals, it can be represented as:

$$\hat{Y}_J = a + \sum_{j=1}^{k} b_j X_j \tag{12.8}$$

Using the OLS regression routine the intercept a and the k model containing k regression coefficients can be obtained. This minimizes $SS_{residual}$, $MS_{residual}$ and the standard error of estimate. It will also maximize R^2, the squared correlation between Y and $\hat{Y}$, which in multiple regression analysis is known as the coefficient of determination.

OLS regression exploits information contained in the associations between predictor variables and outcome when it derives the regression coefficients. Any linear association whatsoever between outcome (predicted variable) and predictor will generate a regression coefficient, whatsoever is the degree of association unless the association is absolutely zero, which rarely happens, and hence there is an increase in the coefficient of determination, the measure of fit, whenever a new predictor variable is added. In other words, the estimation is based on $SS_{residual}$, which can never go down on addition of variable, as adding a variable to a model will improve its fit relative to when it is absent. The exception would be if the unique association between a predictor and the outcome is exactly zero, in which case it will be given a regression weight of zero and $SS_{residual}$ will be the same whether the variable is in the model or not.

Interpretative focus in multiple regressions is typically directed squarely toward the regression coefficients in a multiple regression model rather than the intercept. This interpretation applies to the standardized regression coefficients, but the meaning of 'one unit' is different following standardization. If X_i and Y are both standardized (regardless of whether or not the other predictor variables are standardized), $\hat{b}_i$ is the estimated difference in standard deviations of Y between two cases that differ by one standard deviation of X_i but are equal on all other predictor variables in the model.

The standardized regression coefficients will be based on a model in which all X_i and Y variables are standardized. However, one can standardize only some of the predictor variables rather than all of them if one chooses them. This would have to be done before estimating the model. Once this is done and the model generated, the unstandardized regression coefficients rather than the standardized regression coefficients are interpreted. The unstandardized coefficients will be in standardized form for those predictor variables that were first standardized. To illustrate let us look at the SPSS output (Bhattacharya 2013) for predicting 'subjective well-being' of people of a nation (see Table 12.2).

Suppose the rate of urbanization increases by 5 percent, HDI increases by 10 units, and Freedom House Rule of Law decreases by 2 units, then subjective well-being increases by 5 units approximately, that is, increase (decrease) in 'subjective well-being' of people of a nation.

Table 12.2 SPSS output for predicting 'subjective well-being' of people of a nation

	Unstandardized Coefficients		Standardized Coefficients		
	B	Std. Error	Beta	T	Sig.
(Constant)	−0.330	0.111		−2.978	0.005
URBANRTE	0.147	0.017	1.135	8.540	0.000
HDI2010	0.443	0.075	0.695	5.907	0.000
FHROLAW	0.034	0.005	0.678	6.408	0.000

Notes: URBANRTE: Annual rate of urbanization (most recent estimate over 2005–2010 or 2010–2015) (CIA: The World Fact book).
HDI2010: Human Development Index, 2010 (UN Human Development Report).
FHROLAW: Freedom House Rule of Law score (0 to 16, lower is weaker rule of law).

Source: Bhattacharya (2013). Originally published in *Journal of Human Values*, Vol. 19, No. 1. Copyright © 2013 Management Centre for Human Values, Indian Institute of Management, Calcutta. All rights reserved. Reproduced with the permission of the copyright holders and the publishers Sage Publications India Pvt. Ltd, New Delhi.

Table 12.3 Recall ability of students

Model	Coefficients				
	Unstandardized Coefficients		Standardized Coefficients		
	B	Std. error	Beta	T	Sig.
(Constant)	−0.671	0.337		−1.991	0.052
Gender	0.417	0.208	0.259	2.007	0.051
Task	0.337	0.111	0.393	3.047	0.004

Source: Originally published in S. Bhattacharya et al. (2016), 'Relationship between self-regulated learning strategy and motivation of management students', *International Journal of Innovation and Learning*, **19** (2), 125–149. Reproduced with the permission of Inderscience Publishers.

REGRESSION WITH A DICHOTOMOUS PREDICTOR

In linear regression analysis, a predictor variable can also be a dichotomous variable. An example of a dichotomous variable would be whether a person is male or female, a person is employed or unemployed, and so on. No modifications are necessary to the mathematics when using a dichotomous variable as a predictor.

To illustrate let us try to interpret the following SPSS output (see Table 12.3) for predicting recall ability of students with task motivation and gender as predictors, where female was represented by 0 and male was represented as 1.

Male has higher recall ability than female. In fact, the average recall ability of female was found to be 4.52 and that of male was found to be 4.63. The regression coefficient of task motivation will thus be 0.417 + 0.337 (Gender). Hence the regression coefficient for task motivation for female is 0.417 and for male it is 0.754, which implies with unit increase of task motivation recall ability in female increases by 0.417 and for male it increases by 0.754 unit.

BINARY LOGISTIC REGRESSION: LOGIT AND PROBIT MODELS

Binary logistic regression is a type of regression analysis where the dependent variable is a dummy variable: coded 0 (did not vote) or 1 (did vote) or an individual is a victim of violence or not, etc.

If we use OLS when the predicted output variable is binary or dichotomous, then the model can be described as follows:

$$Y = \gamma + \varphi X + e \quad (12.9)$$

where $Y = (0, 1)$
Then the following problems may arise:

- The residual terms are heteroskedastic
- e is not normally distributed because Y takes on only two values.

So, both conditions contradict the assumptions underlying OLS. Further, the predicted probabilities can be greater than 1 or less than 0, which is against the basic assumptions of probability.

The binary logistic model attempts to solve this problem. The basic assumption of the model is: $\ln[p/(1-p)] = \alpha + \beta X + e$, $\ln[p/(1-p)]$ is the log odds ratio, or 'logit'–p is the probability that the event Y occurs, or the probability that the predicted variable Y takes the value 1. $P/(1-p)$ is the 'odds ratio' or the odds in favour of occurrence of the event Y. The model ensures probability p will always take a value between 0 and 1 and p can be estimated as: $p = 1/[1 + \exp(-\alpha - \beta X)]$.

If we let $\alpha + \beta X = 0$, then $p = 0.50$; if $\alpha + \beta X$ is asymptotically large, p approaches 1 and if $\alpha + \beta X$ gets really small, p approaches 0. The regression coefficient and the value of the constant are estimated using maximum likelihood estimation. The regression coefficient can be interpreted as follows:

Since $[p/(1-p)] = \exp(\alpha + \beta X)$, $\exp(\beta)$ is the effect of the independent variable on the 'odds ratio'.

Let us consider the following SPSS output (see Table 12.4) for determining the existence of domestic violence in India based on National family health survey in 2005 (see Bhattacharya and Bhattacharya 2014).

The Wald statistic for the β coefficient is: Wald $= [\beta/s.e._{(\beta)}]^2$ which is distributed chi-square with 1 degree of freedom. Also, see Table 12.5.

The model likelihood ratio (LR) statistic is:

$$LR[i] = -2[LL(\alpha) - LL(\alpha, \beta)] \quad (12.10)$$

Table 12.4 The existence of domestic violence in India based on National family health survey in 2005

		Estimate	Std. Error	Wald	Df	Sig.	95% Confidence Interval	
							Lower Bound	Upper Bound
Threshold		13.845	0.456	923.112	1	0	12.952	14.738
Age 5-year group		0.066	0.007	85.667	1	0	0.052	0.080
Number of control issues		0.556	0.007	5854.370	1	0	0.542	0.570
Highest educational level	No education	0.431	0.088	24.082	1	0	0.259	0.603
	Primary	0.461	0.089	27.000	1	0	0.287	0.635
	Secondary	0.345	0.082	17.493	1	0	0.183	0.506
	Higher	.	.	.	0	.	.	.
Household structure	Nuclear	−0.024	0.060	0.155	1	0.69	−0.142	0.095
	Non-nuclear	−0.126	0.061	4.275	1	0.04	−0.245	−0.007
	Not de jure resident	.	.	.	0	.	.	.
Type of caste or tribe	Scheduled caste	0.751	0.166	20.378	1	0	0.425	1.077
	Scheduled tribe	0.745	0.168	19.547	1	0	0.415	1.075
	Other backward class [OBC]	0.663	0.166	16.010	1	0	0.338	0.987
	None of them	0.560	0.166	11.349	1	0.001	0.234	0.886
	Don't know	.	.	.	0	.	.	.
Partner's education level	No education	−0.032	0.120	0.070	1	0.79	−0.267	0.204
	Primary	−0.022	0.121	0.033	1	0.86	−0.260	0.216
	Secondary	−0.131	0.120	1.183	1	0.28	−0.367	0.105
	Higher	−0.277	0.131	4.471	1	0.034	−0.535	−0.020
	Don't know	.	.	.	0	.	.	.
Type of place of residence	Urban	0.210	0.032	44.366	1	0	0.148	0.272
	Rural	.	.	.	0	.	.	.
Respondent currently work	No	−0.014	0.042	0.115	1	0.73	−0.097	0.068
	Yes	.	.	.	0	.	.	.
Wealth index	Poorest	0.545	0.055	97.228	1	0	0.437	0.653
	Poorer	0.572	0.052	119.999	1	0	0.469	0.674
	Middle	0.433	0.049	76.750	1	0	0.336	0.530
	Richer	0.256	0.046	30.940	1	0	0.166	0.346
	Richest	.	.	.	0	.	.	.

Table 12.4 (continued)

		Estimate	Std. Error	Wald	Df	Sig.	95% Confidence Interval	
							Lower Bound	Upper Bound
Partner's occupation	Did not work	0.055	0.404	0.019	1	0.89	−0.736	0.846
	Prof., Tech., Manag.*	−0.093	0.400	0.054	1	0.82	−0.878	0.692
	Clerical	−0.226	0.402	0.317	1	0.57	−1.014	0.562
	Sales	−0.172	0.398	0.187	1	0.67	−0.952	0.608
	Agri-employee	−0.271	0.397	0.468	1	0.49	−1.049	0.506
	Services	−0.147	0.399	0.135	1	0.71	−0.929	0.636
	Skilled and unskilled manual	−0.198	0.397	0.250	1	0.62	−0.976	0.579
	Don't know	.	.	.	0	.	.	.
Respondent's occupation	Not working	9.943	0.053	34749.593	1	0	9.838	10.048
	Prof., Tech., Manag.	10.038	0.103	9569.904	1	0	9.837	10.240
	Clerical	10.384	0.148	4921.160	1	0	10.090	10.670
	Sales	10.341	0.086	14327.914	1	0	10.172	10.510
	Agri-employee	10.270	0.041	63140.266	1	0	10.189	10.350
	Services	10.303	0.065	25165.757	1	0	10.176	10.430
	Skilled and unskilled manual	10.257	0.000	.	1	.	10.257	10.257
	Don't know	.	.	.	0	.	.	.

Notes: *Professor, Technical and Management professionals.

Source: Bhattacharya and Bhattacharya (2014).

Table 12.5 Log likelihood statistic

Model	−2 Log Likelihood (LL)	Chi-square	Df	Sig.
Intercept Only	52281.846			
Final	44099.565	8182.280	35	0.000

The LR statistic is distributed as chi-square with 'i' degrees of freedom, where 'i' is the number of independent variables. The model chi-square statistic helps to determine if the overall model is statistically significant. The SPSS output also generates the pseudo-R^2 statistic which is the McFadden's-R^2 statistic calculated as:

$$\text{McFadden's-}R^2 = 1 - [LL(\alpha, \beta)/LL(\alpha)]$$
$$= 1 - [-2LL(\alpha, \beta)/-2LL(\alpha)] \quad (12.11)$$

where the R^2 is a scalar measure which varies between 0 and (somewhat close to) 1 much like the R^2 in an OLS model. In our example, the model was found to be significant with pseudo-R^2 of 82 percent.

One can also find the 'percent correct predictions' statistic. It assumes that if the estimated $\hat{p}$ is greater than or equal to 0.5 then the event is expected to occur and not occur otherwise. By assigning these probabilities 0s and 1s and comparing these to the actual 0s and 1s, the percent correct Yes, percent correct No, and overall percent correct scores can also be calculated. Another type of binary regression model is the 'probit model'. In the probit model we consider an unobserved latent predicted variable: unobservable variable y^* which can take all values in $(-\infty, +\infty)$.

Underlying latent model:

$$y_i = \begin{cases} 1 & y_i^* > 0 \\ 0 & y_i^* \leq 0 \end{cases} \quad (12.12)$$

$$y_i^* = x_i' \beta + \varepsilon_i \quad (12.13)$$

$$P(y_i = 1|x) = P(y_i^* > 0|x) = P(x_i'\beta + \varepsilon_i > 0|x) = P(\varepsilon_i > -x_i'\beta|x) = 1 - F(x_i'\beta) \quad (12.14)$$
$$= \Phi(x_i'\beta)$$

Hence error terms are independently and normally distributed.

Interpretation of the Estimated Coefficients

Estimated coefficients do not quantify the influence of the predictor variables on the probability that the predicted variable takes on the value 1, rather estimated coefficients are parameters of the latent model. In the case of continuous predictor variables, say X_i, the regression coefficient can be interpreted as: if X_i increases by an infinitesimal amount, the probability for the predicted variable taking the value 1 rises by the regression coefficient β_i percentage. In the case of a dummy predictor variable, say X_j, the regression coefficient can be interpreted as: if the dummy variable changes value from 0 to 1, the probability for the predicted variable taking the value 1 rises by the regression coefficient β_j percentage.

The decision problem is similar to the t-test for testing significance of regression coefficients in OLS, wherein the probit test statistic follows a standard normal distribution. The z-value is equal to the estimated parameter divided by its standard error. Goodness-of-fit is tested by McFadden's pseudo R^2.

Likelihood ratio test

Comparison of the log likelihood functions of the unrestricted model ($\ln L_U$) and that of the restricted model ($\ln L_R$):

$$LR = -2\ln\lambda = -2(\ln L_R - \ln L_U) \tag{12.15}$$

is a distribution with degrees of freedom equal to the number of restrictions.

NON-LINEAR REGRESSION MODEL

A non-linear regression model is a regression model in which first order condition of least square estimators is a non-linear function of parameters. For example, if a phenomenon is increasing exponentially, a straight line cannot be fitted, instead one may require it to fit a curve and that is when we require a non-linear regression.

The non-linear regression model can be represented as $y_i = h(x_i, \beta) + \varepsilon_i$

Some of the assumptions made in the non-linear regression model are

1. $E[y_i|x_i] = h(x_i, \beta), i = 1, 2, ..., n$,
2. $E[\varepsilon_i h(x_i, \beta)] = 0$, the disturbance has zero mean.

The model has partial homoscedasticity and is non-autocorrelated.

$$E[\varepsilon_i^2 | h(x_j, \beta), j = 1, 2, ..., n] = 0 \tag{12.16}$$
$$E[\varepsilon_i \varepsilon_j | h(x_i, \beta), h(x_j, \beta) j = 1, 2, ..., n] = 0, i \neq j \tag{12.17}$$

The first and second order moments converge to finite population parameters. There is well-defined probability distribution function defining ε_i. An illustration of a non-linear regression model is as follows:

$$Y = Ae^{bx}u \tag{12.18}$$

This is a process which has continuous growth with a constant growth rate.

$$\ln(Y) = \ln(Ae^{bX}u) \tag{12.19}$$
$$\ln(Y) = \ln(A) + bX + \ln(u) \tag{12.20}$$

The regression coefficient can be interpreted as follows: if X increases by 1, Y is multiplied by e^b. In other words, as X increases by one unit Y will increase by 100b. So if b = 0.05 then Y will increase by 5 percent and becomes 1.05 Y.

PANEL DATA REGRESSION

Panel data represents repeated cross sectional data over different periods of time. It is also known as pooled data, micro panel data, longitudinal data, event history analysis or cohort analysis. Some of the relevant examples of panel data can be annual unemployment rates of each state over several years, quarterly sales of individual stores over several quarters, and so on. The basic form of panel regression model is of the type:

$$y_{it} = x'_{it} + z'_i \alpha + \varepsilon_{it} \qquad (12.21)$$

Where there are K regressors in x_{it}, not including error terms. The individual effect is $z'_i \alpha$, where z_i has a constant component and a vector component which comprise of a set of individual group of specific variables which may be observed or are latent.

The various cases of non-linear regression can be:

1. Pooled regression: if z_i only has a constant term, then OLS will give a consistent and efficient estimate of common α and slope vector β.
2. Fixed effects: if z_i is unobserved but correlated with x_{it}, then the least square estimator of β is biased and inconsistent.

   Then, $y_{it} = x'_{it} \beta + \alpha_i + \varepsilon_{it}$, where $\alpha_i = z'_i \alpha$ embodies all observable effects, may be considered as a group specific constant term which does not vary over time. There are three methods of estimation for fixed effect models:

   - 'n-1 binary regressors' OLS regression
   - 'Entity-demeaned' OLS regression
   - 'Changes' specification.

3. Random effects: if unobserved individual heterogeneity can be assumed to be uncorrelated with the endogenous variables then the model is formulated as:

Table 12.6 Difference between random and fixed effect

	Fixed Effect Model	Random Effect Model
Intercepts	Varying across groups and or times	Constant
Error Variances	Constant	Varying across groups and/or times
Slopes	Constant	Constant
Estimation	Least Square Dummy variable (LSDV)	Generalized Least Square (GLS)
Hypothesis Test	Instrumental F-test	Breusch–Pagan LM test

$$y_{it} = x'_{it}\beta + E[z'_i\alpha] + \{z'_i\alpha - E[z'_i\alpha]\} + \varepsilon_{it} \quad (12.22)$$
$$= x'_{it}\beta + \alpha + u_i + \varepsilon_{it}$$

This is a linear regression model with compound disturbance which can be estimated consistently and rather inefficiently by least square estimator.

To test whether a model has a fixed effect or a random effect, a Hausman test is conducted which tests whether error terms are correlated with the regressors. The difference between random effect and fixed effect can be summarized in Table 12.6.

4. Random parameters: the random effect model can be viewed as a regression model with random constant term, that is, the coefficients are assumed to be random. The model can be of the form:

$$y_{it} = x'_{it}(\beta + h_i) + (\alpha + u_i) + \varepsilon_{it} \quad (12.23)$$

Thus, h_i induces the variations in parameters between individuals, with some commonality in terms of mean.

STRUCTURAL EQUATION MODELS

Structural equation modelling (SEM) is a statistical methodology that takes a confirmatory (i.e., hypothesis-testing) approach to the analysis of a structural theory bearing on some phenomenon. It throws light on the causal relationship between interacting variables representing them through a series of structural equations that can be represented pictographically. The hypothesized model can then be tested statistically in a simultaneous analysis of the entire system of variables to determine the extent to which it is consistent with the data. If goodness-of-fit is adequate, the model is assumed to be plausible for a set of equations representing the interrelationship. Structural equation modelling, also known as simultaneous equation modelling or SEM, takes a confirmatory rather than an exploratory approach to the data analysis. Furthermore, by demanding that the pattern of intervariable relations be specified a priori, SEM lends itself well to the analysis of data for inferential purposes. Also, whereas traditional multivariate procedures are incapable of either assessing or correcting for measurement error of the explanatory variables, SEM provides explicit estimates of these error variance parameters. Indeed, alternative methods (e.g., those rooted in regression, or the general linear model) assume that error(s) in the explanatory (i.e., independent) variables is minimal to be ignored but may lead to serious consequences. SEM is the only method which provides easily manageable solutions to depict complex multivariate interrelationships between both observed and latent variables.

Given these highly desirable characteristics, SEM has become a popular tool for testing theories non-experimentally where experimentation is not feasible (Bentler 1980). In the behavioural sciences, researchers are often interested in studying theoretical constructs that cannot be observed directly. These abstract phenomena are termed latent variables, or factors. Examples of latent variables in psychology are self-concept, personality, commitment, job engagement and motivation; in sociology, powerlessness, trust, and so on;

in education, verbal ability and teacher expectancy; and in economics, capitalism and social class.

Because latent variables are not observed directly, it follows that they cannot be measured directly. Thus, the researcher must operationally define the latent variable of interest in terms of behaviour believed to represent it, which can be through study of literature or in consultation with experts. As such, the unobserved variable is linked to one that is observable, thereby making its measurement possible. Assessment of the behaviour, then, constitutes the direct measurement of an observed variable, as well as the indirect measurement of an unobserved variable (i.e., the underlying construct). Recording of observations may include self-report responses, scores on an achievement or psychometric test, scores on activity coded responses to interview questions, and the like. These measured scores (i.e., measurements) are termed observed or manifest variables. They serve as indicators of the underlying construct which they are presumed to represent.

Latent variables can be exogenous or endogenous. Exogenous latent variables are synonymous with independent variables; they 'cause' fluctuations in the values of other latent variables in the model. Changes in the values of exogenous variables are not explained by the model. Rather, they are considered to be influenced by other factors external to the model. Background variables such as gender, age and socioeconomic status are examples of such external factors. Endogenous latent variables are synonymous with dependent variables and, as such, are influenced by the exogenous variables in the model, either directly or indirectly. Fluctuation in the values of endogenous variables is said to be explained by the model because all latent variables that influence them are included in the model specification.

The relationship between observed and latent variables can be found through factor analysis. In using this approach to data analysis, the researcher examines the co-variation among a set of observed variables in order to gather information on their underlying latent constructs (i.e., factors). There are two basic types of factor analyses: exploratory factor analysis (EFA) and confirmatory factor analysis (CFA). EFA is designed for the situation where links between the observed and latent variables are unknown or uncertain. The analysis thus proceeds in an exploratory mode to determine how, and to what extent, the observed variables are linked to their underlying factors. CFA, on the other hand, is appropriately used when the researcher has some knowledge of the underlying latent variable structure. Based on knowledge of the theory, empirical research, or both, the researcher postulates relations between the observed measures and the underlying factors a priori and then tests this hypothesized structure statistically. The model is evaluated by statistical means to determine the adequacy of its goodness-of-fit to the sample data (Bollen 1989; Byrne 1998; Cheung and Rensvold 2002).

In contrast to the factor analytic model, the full latent variable (LV) model allows for the specification of regression structure among the latent variables. That is to say, the researcher can hypothesize the impact of one latent construct on another in the modelling of causal direction. This model is termed full (or complete) because it comprises both a measurement model and a structural model: the measurement model depicting the links between the LVs and their observed measures (i.e., the CFA model), and the structural model depicting the links among the LVs themselves. A full LV model that specifies direction of cause from one direction only is termed a recursive model; one that allows for interrelation between latent variables is called a reciprocal or feedback model. Expressed either diagrammatically or mathematically via a set of equations, such models explain how the observed and latent variables are related to one another. It is highly unlikely that a perfect fit will exist between the observed data and the hypothesized model, there will necessarily be a difference between the two; this differential is termed the residual. The model-fitting process can therefore be summarized as follows:

$$\text{Data} = \text{Model} + \text{Residual} \qquad (12.24)$$

Where 'data' represent score measurements related to the observed variables as derived from persons comprising the sample. 'Model' represents the hypothesized structure linking the observed variables to the LVs and, in some models, linking particular LVs to one another. 'Residual' represents the discrepancy between the hypothesized model and the observed data.

In the strictly confirmatory scenario, the researcher postulates a single model based on theory, collects the appropriate data and then tests the fit of the hypothesized model to the sample data. From the results of this test, the researcher either rejects or fails to reject the model; no further modifications to the model are made. In the alternative models case, the researcher proposes several alternative (i.e., competing) models, all of which are grounded in theory. Following analysis of a single set of empirical data, he or she selects one model as most appropriate in representing the sample data. Finally, the model-generating scenario represents the case where the researcher, having postulated and rejected a theoretically derived model on the basis of its poor fit to the sample data, proceeds in an exploratory (rather than confirmatory) fashion to modify and re-estimate the model, which is the most common out of the three situations.

Structural equation models are schematically portrayed using particular configurations of four geometric symbols – a circle (or ellipse): representing unobserved latent factors, a square (or rectangle): representing observed variables, a single-headed arrow: representing the impact of one variable on another, and a double-headed arrow: representing co-variances or correlations between pairs of variables. These symbols are also accompanied with

- Path coefficient for regression of an observed variable onto an unobserved LV (or factor)
- Path coefficient for regression of one factor onto another factor
- Measurement error associated with an observed variable
- Residual error in the prediction of an unobserved factor.

The path diagram is the schematic representation of a model. These are termed path diagrams because they provide a visual portrayal of relations which are assumed to hold among the variables under study. Regression equations represent the influence of one or more variables on another, and this influence, being symbolized by a single-headed arrow pointing from the variable of influence to the variable of interest, one can think of as each equation summarizing the impact of all relevant variables in the model (observed and unobserved) on one specific variable (observed or unobserved). Thus, one relatively simple approach to formulating these equations is to note each variable that has one or more arrows pointing toward it, and then record the summation of all such influences for each of these dependent variables. See Figure 12.2 for an example.

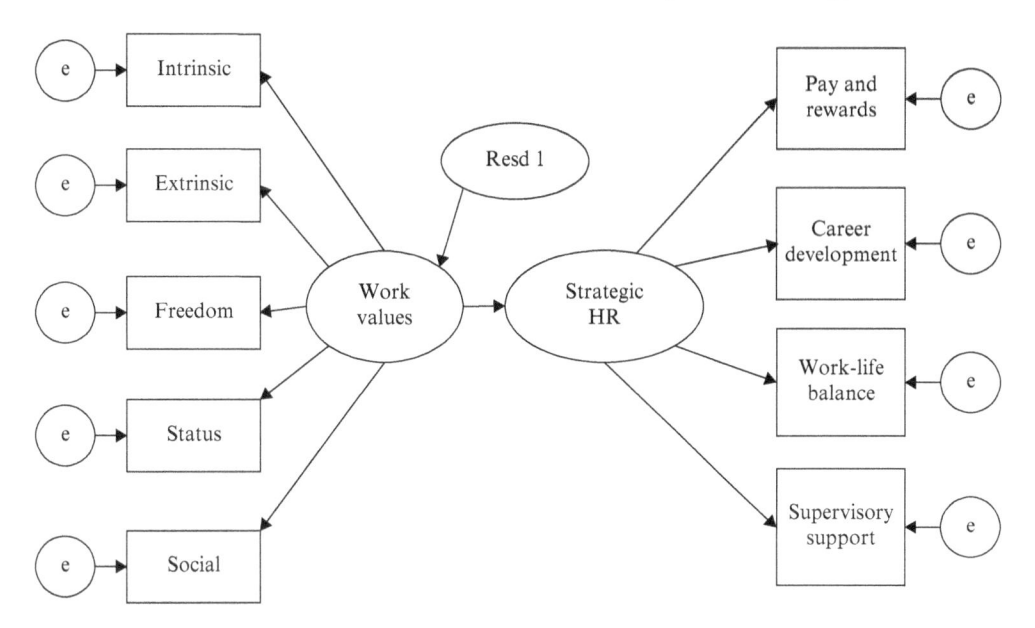

Figure 12.2   Path diagram

The set of equations can be written as:

Intrinsic = Work values + e1
Extrinsic = Work values + e2
Freedom = Work values + e3
Status = Work values + e4
Social = Work values + e5
Strategic HR = Work values + resd 1
Pay and rewards = SHP + e6
Career development = SHP + e7
Work-life balance = SHP + e8
Supervisory support = SHP + e9

These models need to be run through advanced software such as AMOS to establish the relationship. Interpretation of the AMOS model is a complex exercise (Anderson and Gerbing 1988; Hooper et al. 2008; Markus 2012). For any beginners, establishing the regression models are the first step and selection of the technique to study is highly relevant.

RECENT APPLICATIONS OF THE TECHNIQUES IN CSR RESEARCH

A regression analysis is applied for the following purposes: (1) to predict the value of the dependent variable for individuals for whom some information concerning the explanatory variables is available, (2) to compute the effect of some explanatory variable on the dependent variable. CSR activities are covered by many variables. These activities have the strong objective to connect firms and many stakeholders with those variables. Hence, regression analysis can be used depending upon the data types.

In recent years, the domain has taken on a new dimension by applying various measurement techniques which are of strategic importance. The field is growing exponentially with many variables. It leads to the analysis of the data in a much closer way using sophisticated techniques. It has been applied right from finding the relationship between financial performances with CSR to understanding the impact of the latent factors to CSR implementation. Some of the recent works have been listed below to refer to for applications of CSR.

A unique study has been undertaken to see the link between corporate social performance (CSP) and corporate financial performance (CFP) (Simpson and Kohers 2002). The study takes up a case study specific to the banking sector. It involved the application of ordinary least square regression analysis within which two regression equations have been estimated with CFP as dependent variables and the Community Reinvestment Act 1977 USA(CRA) which is used as a proxy for social performance. Finally, the results of the study support the hypothesis of the authors that the two variables move positively together.

The application of regression analysis to CSR can be further highlighted by the study of Brammer and Pavelin (2006) wherein they estimated a model of corporate reputation applied to a sample of a large number of firms. Here, in the paper, an OLS regression model of corporate reputation has been presented. The impact of corporate reputation is studied on social performance indicators which mainly comprise of community performance, environmental performance and employee performance. Finally, in the light of CSR the study concludes that the reputational effect of social performance is found to vary across and within sectors. Thus concluding that there needs to be a fit achieved among the type of CSP and the firm's stakeholder environment.

In a work by Husted and Allen (2007), CSR is studied from the point of view of creation of innovation, competitive advantage and value creation for the firms. This is studied using three strategic CSR variables. These are: visibility, appropriateness and voluntarism and with the application of hierarchical regression analysis. The conclusion drawn from the findings pointed out the need for managers to understand how CSR is similar to and different from other traditional corporate activities if they are looking at pursuing value creation through the channel of CSR.

Ringov and Zollo (2007) studied CSR through Socio-Institutional Perspective. The research set out to investigate the effect of the difference in the national cultures on the social and environmental performance of the countries. In this pertinent study, the dependent variable is the social and environmental performance of the firms as measured by 'intangible value assessment score' while the explanatory variables include power distance, individualism, masculinity and uncertainty avoidance. The analysis uses the pooled ordinary least square regression approach to test the hypothesis of the paper. The results thus obtained pointed out that cultural specificity plays a moderate yet an important role in determining the behaviour of corporations toward social and environmental concerns. Siegel and Vitaliano (2007) in an empirical study pointed out that information asymmetry in CSR are being imbedded in the differentiation strategy of a firm. The key empirical implications of these theories is that firms selling experience and credence goods are more likely to be following CSR compared to the rest. A specific type of regression model is designed for the study which is often estimated as binomial probit or logit modelling. Finally, the study concludes that the original hypothesis holds true though, and the degree of credence and the CSR level vary from one sector to another.

The relationship between CSR and the path dependent nature of firm stakeholders was established by a study undertaken by Barnett (2007). The paper develops a construct of stakeholder influence capacity to fill the gap and to be studied through regression analysis. This construct helps in explaining the reasons for varying effects of CSR on CFP across firms and time. The Stakeholder Influence Capacity (SIC) construct and the conceptual framework developed in this paper resulted in specifying a contingent model of the business case for CSR. The work concludes that the precise payoff for a particular CSR act for a particular firm at a particular point of time is not particularly predictable as it depends on various factors.

Another sector specific study in the sphere of CSR was undertaken by Inoue and Lee (2011) for the tourism sector mainly comprising of airlines, casinos, hotels and restaurants. The study was primarily aiming to disaggregate the CSR into five dimensions, that is: employee relations, product quality, community relations, environmental issues and diversity issues, while their impact was studied on the financial performance of the firms. The empirical analysis is undertaken using simple regression analysis specifically by using a dummy for years. The results indicated a positive relation between CSR and financial performance, but each dimension has a differential effect on the short-term and future profitability of the firms across sectors.

CONCLUSION

Corporate social responsibility is growing horizontally as well as vertically by linking various concepts in business operations. Regression techniques are very powerful in establishing the linkages between variables of interest. With the introduction of new techniques, it is a challenging task for any researcher to use a specific one and substantiate the selection of that technique. While variants of the statistical and quantitative techniques are creating complexity, it is mandatory for the researchers to keep abreast with the new techniques developed. More importantly, it is essential to know the application of the techniques; in which context to use it; how to select the right technique; how to use it, and how to interpret the results.

REFERENCES

Anderson, C.A. and B.J. Bushman (2001), 'Effects of violent video games on aggressive behaviour, aggressive cognition, aggressive affect, physiological arousal, and pro-social behaviour: a meta-analytic review of the scientific literature', *Psychological Science*, **12**(5), 353–359.

Anderson, C.A., A. Shibuya, N. Ihori, E.L. Swing, B.J. Bushman, A. Sakamoto and M. Saleem (2010), 'Violent video game effects on aggression, empathy, and pro-social behaviour in eastern and western countries: a meta-analytic review', *Psychological Bulletin*, **136**(2), 151–173.

Anderson, J. and A. Frankle (1980), 'Voluntary social reporting: an iso-beta portfolio analysis', *The Accounting Review*, **55** (3), 467–479.

Anderson, J.C. and D.W. Gerbing (1988), 'Structural equation modeling in practice: a review and recommended two-step approach', *Psychological Bulletin*, **103**(3), 411–423.

Barnett, M.L. (2007), 'Stakeholder influence capacity and the variability of financial returns to corporate social responsibility', *Academy of Management Review*, **32**(3), 794–816.

Bentler, P.M. (1980), 'Multivariate analysis behaviour problems: with latent variables–causal modelling', *Annual Review of Psychology*, **31**(1), 419–456.

Bhattacharya, S. (2010), 'Relationship between three indices of happiness material, mental and spiritual', *Journal of Human Values*, **16**(1), 87–125.

Bhattacharya, S. (2013), 'A global spiritual index: its predictors and relationship to crime', *Journal of Human Values*, **19**(1), 83–104.

Bhattacharya, S. and S. Bhattacharya (2014), 'Battered and shattered: where will they go for justice', *The Journal of Adult Protection*, **16**(4), 244–258.

Bhattacharya, C. and S. Sen (2004), 'Doing better at doing good: when, why and how consumers respond to corporate social initiatives', *California Management Review*, **47**(1), 9–24.

Bhattacharya, S., N. Neelam and D. Tanksale (2016), 'Relationship between self-regulated learning strategy and motivation of management students', *International Journal of Innovation and Learning*, **19**(2), 125–149.

Bollen, Kenneth A. (1989), *Structural Equations with Latent Variables*, New York: John Wiley and Sons.

Brammer, S.J. and S. Pavelin (2006), 'Corporate reputation and social performance: the importance of fit', *Journal of Management Studies*, **43**(3), 435–455.

Byrne, B.M. (1998), *Structural Equation Modeling with LISREL, PRELIS and SIMPLIS: Basic Concepts, Applications and Programming*, Mahwah, New Jersey: Lawrence Erlbaum Associates.

Cheung, G.W. and R.B. Rensvold (2002), 'Evaluating goodness-of-fit indexes for testing measurement invariance', *Structural Equation Modeling*, **9**(2), 233–255.

Factbook, C.I.A. (2010), The world factbook. See also: https://www.cia.gov/library/publications/the-world-factbook.

Hofmann, S.G. and J.A. Smits (2008), 'Cognitive-behavioural therapy for adult anxiety disorders: a meta-analysis of randomized placebo-controlled trials', *The Journal of Clinical Psychiatry*, **69**(4), 621–632.

Hooper, D., Coughlan, J., and Mullen, M. (2008), 'Structural equation modelling: Guidelines for determining model fit'. *Articles*, 2.

Husted, B.W. and D.B. Allen (2007), 'Strategic corporate social responsibility and value creation among large firms: lessons from the Spanish experience', *Long Range Planning*, **40**(6), 594–610.

Ingram, R. and K. Frazier (1980), 'Environmental performance and corporate disclosure', *Journal of Accounting Research*, **18**(2), 614–622.

Inoue, Y. and S. Lee (2011), 'Effects of different dimensions of corporate social responsibility on corporate financial performance in tourism-related industries', *Tourism Management*, **32**(4), 790–804.

Judge, T.A., R.F. Piccolo, N.P. Podsakoff, J.C. Shaw and B.L. Rich (2010), 'The relationship between pay and job satisfaction: a meta-analysis of the literature', *Journal of Vocational Behavior*, **77**(2), 157–167.

Klein, J. and N. Dawar (2004), 'Corporate social responsibility and consumers' attributions and brand evaluations in a product-harm crisis', *International Journal of Research in Marketing*, **21**(3), 203–217.

Lau, R.R., L. Sigelman, C. Heldman and P. Babbitt (1999), 'The effects of negative political advertisements: a meta-analytic assessment', *American Political Science Review*, **93**(4), 851–875.

Markus, K.A. (2012), 'Principles and practice of structural equation modeling by Rex B. Kline', *Structural Equation Modeling: A Multidisciplinary Journal*, **19**(3), 509–512.

McGuire, J., A. Sundgren and T. Schneeweiss (1988), 'Corporate social responsibility and firm financial performance', *Academy of Management Journal*, **31**(4), 854–872.

Ringov, D. and M. Zollo (2007), 'Corporate social responsibility from a socio-institutional perspective: the impact of national culture on corporate social performance', *Corporate Governance*, **7**(4), 476–485.

Salzmann, O., A. Ionescu-Somers and U. Steger (2005), 'The business case for corporate sustainability: literature review and research options', *European Management Journal*, **23**(1), 27–36.

Siegel, D.S. and D.F. Vitaliano (2007), 'An empirical analysis of the strategic use of corporate social responsibility', *Journal of Economics and Management Strategy*, **16**(3), 773–792.

Simpson, W.G. and T. Kohers (2002), 'The link between corporate social and financial performance: evidence from the banking industry', *Journal of Business Ethics*, **35**(2), 97–109.

Stanwick, P.A. and S.D. Stanwick (1998), 'The relationship between corporate social performance and organizational size', *Journal of Business Ethics*, **17**(2), 195–204.

Vogel, David (2005), *The Market for Virtue: The Potential and Limits of Corporate Social Responsibility*, Washington DC: Brookings Institution Press.

PART III

QUALITATIVE METHODS

David Crowther and Linne Marie Lauesen

It is likely that qualitative approaches to CSR research are more prevalent than quantitative approaches. Certainly there are more options and this section is therefore longer than the preceding section, and with a greater number of contributions. Qualitative research tends to give a richer picture by making more detailed use of a smaller data set. Perhaps these approaches appeal more to the ontologies of CSR researchers or perhaps there are just more methods to choose from. Again we have included the common methodologies as well as some other less usual ones which are available to use, and have been used by the authors of the chapters. And again we make no choice about method – all are equally valid in appropriate circumstances – and all options are available to the researcher.

This section opens with Fernanda de Paiva Duarte's chapter about autoethnography. In this chapter, she makes a case for analytic autoethnography as an effective qualitative tool to enhance reflection, reflexivity and critical thinking in research on CSR. Autoethnography is a constructive approach that encourages deep thinking patterns to unveil multiple layers of meaning in the research process. Fernanda de Paiva Duarte illustrates the usefulness of autoethnography in CSR research through a vignette that draws on her personal experiences and reflections during a fieldwork trip carried out a few years ago. The purpose of this project was to attain a better understanding of CSR discourses and practices in the Brazilian mining sector. Through the autoethnographic lens, she was able to delve beyond the 'official' view on CSR promoted by a large mining company to reveal alternative perspectives from non-corporate sources.

This is followed by a chapter outlining a methodology which is rarely used in CSR research, although used extensively in other disciplines. In this chapter Kemi C. Yekini contributes by explaining semiotics as a research method in the field of CSR, which in the last decade has hosted a debate that seems to have shifted from the question of whether to report on CSR activities to what should be the actual content of the reports. Fresh concerns are being expressed about the scope, quality and authenticity of the reports in this chapter. This could be born out of increased awareness and reporting of it in annual reports. Consequently, scholars have called it a 'linguistic turn' – that is, the idea of treating a phenomenon as a text and analysing it for its textual properties – in evaluating such disclosures. The argument is that corporate disclosures should be seen as polysemous texts or languages that are capable of being misinterpreted. In this way, firms will be inclined to give more consideration to the contents and hence quality of the reports. What is being interpreted is the language itself rather than the intended meaning of the author as each language involves particular interpretation uncommon to other languages and that such interpretation is interrelated with a variety of knowledge and experiences and hence is capable of influencing thoughts and perceptions in different ways. This chapter explores the use of a linguistic based theory and analytical tool – semiotics as a research methodology in evaluating the content and the quality of CSR reporting. The argument of this chapter is that given the narrative nature of CSR reports (CSRR), research into the content and quality of CSRR can be better achieved with a linguistic based framework.

In the next chapter Linne Marie Lauesen takes us into the realms of ethnographic methods as an umbrella framework containing several features such as observation techniques, interviews, document and audio/video performance analysis. She defines what is meant by ethnographic methods giving us a literature overview of the development of this field. Next, she takes us on a tour through the historic developments of ethnography and finalises by reviewing the contemporary CSR literature. She concludes her exploration of ethnography containing a multiple qualitative approach to the studies, which qualifies this method as the most ingenious version of in-depth studies making theory developments from rich data collection possible. The newer studies in the CSR literature show that ethnographic studies are used to get 'under the skin' of corporations and their interpretation and use (and misuse) of CSR. Most companies utilise the good motives of CSR for corporate branding, to obtain legitimacy and to form their identity as 'a good corporation' in the eyes of their stakeholders. However, these ethnographic studies show how corporations are not always aligned with the intentions of CSR, because their motives are typically steered by making profits primarily, in which CSR becomes a means to this end, which is not the purpose of CSR eventually.

This is followed by a chapter in which Homaira Semeen and Muhammad Azizul Islam make an in-depth analysis of interview techniques as an instrument to explore management motivation for corporate social and environmental reporting. Interview as a research method is crucial to understand the motivation behind the corporate social and environmental reporting practices. This chapter documents the use of the interview method within social and environmental accounting research and finds that using interviews as the procedure of securing knowledge in relation to motivation behind corporate social and environmental reporting is relatively new. The significance of the use of such a method to support social and environmental accounting research is also discussed in this chapter.

Following this Ilke Oruc continues with a chapter setting out her in-depth analysis of observation studies. This chapter focuses on the participant observation method as a data collection tool that will lead us into CSR research. She presents information for why and how we can use participant observation especially among these methods in our research. As many qualitative researchers highlight, observation is one of the activities that we realise mostly in our life; but we often do not think too much about how this can be accounted for in a systematic way or what inferences we make as a result of these observations. When we approach the issue in methodological terms, observation is a tool that can provide us with important data resources within the method that we determined as being based on the research problem. The participant observation method that we mostly emphasise constitutes one of the fundamental parts of the ethnographic method as an umbrella term. Even though the usages and method related to the CSR field have been explained in detail in Chapter 16, it is necessary to make explanations regarding the concepts of ethnography and organisational ethnography in terms of providing the integrity in the issues here.

Subsequently the contribution by Esther Ortiz and José G. Clavel gives us a detailed account of document analysis with in-depth examples of business reporting. Today global capital markets require an international consensus about disclosure requirements and other barriers to globalisation. Business reporting has improved during the years and we are witnessing a wide range of disclosure of non-financial information. Research methods used in CSR are conditioned by the characteristics of this information. It is necessary to use the right methods to develop conclusions in this field. This is why we used correspondence analysis to examine Annual Reports and Forms 20-F according to different generally accepted accounting practice (GAAP). We examined 84 Annual Reports and Forms 20-F prepared before the harmonisation to international financial reporting standards (IFRS) (for 1998 and 1999 of Spanish, German and British companies listed on the New York Stock Exchange (NYSE)). Correspondence Analysis has been useful to determine whether human resources disclosure policy depends on factors such as the firm's country, size, industry, listing status or audit company. The results show that there was a wide range of variety in this disclosure and that the country, size, industry and listing status shaped this policy, with the most important difference being the kind of report. This is just one clear example of the kind of research that can be applied in CSR and that can open up new methods in this field.

Following this, Christopher Boachie invites us into the world of survey methods. Typically, surveys gather data at a particular point in time with the intention of describing the nature of existing conditions, or identifying standards against which existing conditions can be compared, or determining the relationships that exist between specific events. Thus, surveys may vary in their levels of complexity from those that provide simple frequency counts to those that present relational analysis. The purpose of this chapter is to provide details on the application of surveys in CSR research. This chapter should be read in conjunction with the chapters on sampling, questionnaires, interviews and data analysis techniques. Many researchers reading this book will probably be studying for higher degrees within a fixed and maybe short time frame, which may render longitudinal study out of the question for them. Nevertheless, longitudinal study is an important type of research. More likely, researchers for higher degrees will find cross-sectional survey research appropriate, and it is widely used in higher degree research. This chapter defines the subject. It also discusses typical research objectives that may be accomplished with surveys and various advantages of the survey method. The chapter explains survey and data gathering techniques, ethical issues and the main potential errors that researchers must be careful to avoid. Finally, it presents the current applications of survey techniques in CSR research.

Then, Juniati Gunawan and Kumalawati Abadi show us how to use content analysis for CSR research in the next contribution. Their chapter develops a scoring guideline for conducting a content analysis of sustainability reports to reduce subjectivity, and secondly, to provide scoring numbers to improve the quality of the results. The guideline is applied by implementing every step of the new scoring numbers to examine sustainability reports, to evaluate whether or not the new proposed scoring measurement works appropriately in terms of scrutinising the quantity and quality information of the reports. Samples for analysis are selected from a population of six Indonesian mining companies.

These numbers are the majority of industrial companies which produce sustainability reports in 2009. Their findings show that the guideline developed in this study provides detailed steps and assists the coder in performing the scoring measurement process. In addition, this guideline also confirms that subjectivity can be reduced during the process. Further, detailed scoring numbers seem to be more applicable to evaluate the quality of reports and provide better analysis. The analysis results demonstrate that information of 'economic aspects' is the most disclosed information, while 'environment aspects' is the least disclosed in the companies' sustainability reports. Documentation of disclosed information in the reports is mostly positive and descriptive in nature, rather than negative and quantitative. Some suggestions to improve the writing in the context of sustainability reports are also provided.

In the next chapter Sara Moggi explores the focus group method, in the context of social accounting, as a stakeholder engagement tool. The social reporting process occurs in several phases that can include stakeholder engagement practice. When an organisation decides to follow this path, the inclusion of these subjects is a pivotal element to consider in the definition of both stakeholder map and the features of the subsequent social report. This research focuses on how stakeholders can be involved, through a focus group, at the start of the reporting process. The case of Sirio, an international nonprofit organisation with more than 2000 members, is considered in order to describe the features and management of focus groups as a stakeholder engagement tool in Sirio's social accounting process. This study also presents the strengths and potential weaknesses inherent in this research path, describing the steps that should be followed in the construction of a focus group and offering guidance on the behaviour that researchers must exhibit before and during group meetings. This research proves a valuable guide for researchers who decide to follow the reporting process as an external auditor or a person involved in the process itself.

Julia J.A. Shaw next introduces us to a phenomenological study of social justice and moral discourse moving us towards a reimagined CSR. Phenomenological inquiry constitutes a naturalistic method that aims to understand and clarify phenomena in context-specific settings. Not based on any particular conceptual framework or series of techniques, it is creatively informed by a broad range of liberal and humanistic disciplines such as philosophy, anthropology, sociology, politics, socio-legal theory, psychology and history. Defined as 'any kind of research that produces findings not arrived at by means of statistical procedures or other means of quantification', qualitative researchers engage in the intellectual pursuit of enlightenment and insight rather than causal determination and assured predictable outcomes. Arising from a post-positivist repudiation of a single or objective truth, focus is placed on the social meaning and experiences of individuals, communities and sub-cultures, and the significance of words and texts. In order to explore the concept of moral duty and CSR this chapter adopts a phenomenological mode of inquiry, which is useful for reimagining over-familiar problems and, importantly, provides a contextual and flexible interdisciplinary framework within which to investigate diverse perspectives and practices for generating knowledge.

This is followed with a chapter by Duygu Türker who takes us into social network analysis (SNA), which is a viable multidisciplinary method that has been frequently used to reveal the nature and structure of the relationship among different actors in a network or to analyse the network itself for a long time. This network perspective together with consideration of the relational aspects of phenomena can be particularly useful to conceptualise and analyse the social, economic or political structures of social units. Therefore, this social network perspective can also be used in the analysis of relational context of social responsibility and ethical issues. The purpose of the current study is to provide a viable understanding of the application of SNA for CSR literature. In doing so, this study first provides a conceptual framework of SNA and then briefly discusses its paradigmatic stance and methodological approach based on the relevant literature. In the second section, it is analysed whether and how SNA can address our CSR related research problems over three selected research mainstreams: as stakeholder management, collaborative social responsibility projects, and ethical conduct among employees.

Linne Marie Lauesen completes this section with her chapter on another method which is often used elsewhere and has obvious applications for research in CSR. As a method that has not been seen much in use in the last 15 years, Linne shows us how to frame our research in a narrative way regardless if it is based on a quantitative or qualitative research method. Using theoretical storytelling as a meta-frame for all research methods in CSR, we learn to analyse our own and others' writing styles by using the Narrative Arc. So what does it take to write a good overall theoretical story? She refers to editors and good academic writers in order to underpin her claim that all research can be improved by exercising good storytelling. Then, she presents some theoretical and practical ideas of how to write a good story. It does not matter whether it is a fictional story or a scientific/academic story – the tricks are the same. It is all based on the author having good data – either in terms of measures, good or enough respondents, interviews, observations, archival texts for the academic scholar, and similarly: a good plot for the fiction-writer. It is hard not to find one or more good stories within a good set of data acquired by sound research methodologies as those presented earlier in this volume. The main activity for creating such a story – fiction or 'real' – is to use the so-called 'Narrative Arc'. She presents this model and uses it for further analysis of two exemplars of writing for the reader to see that they have actually – consciously or unconsciously – been used in these accounts.

13. Analytic autoethnography as a tool to enhance reflection, reflexivity and critical thinking in CSR research
Fernanda de Paiva Duarte

INTRODUCTION

Autoethnography is a constructivist approach through which the researcher studies her or his own experience alongside that of participants. In contrast with positivist approaches that seek impartiality and objectivity, autoethnography embraces the researcher's values and beliefs to foster a deeper understanding of the phenomenon under study.

In this chapter, I propose to demonstrate the value of autoethnography in research projects exploring corporate social responsibility (CSR), in particular those focusing on companies that have a poor environmental and social track record. In projects of this kind there is often a possibility that the investigator will become part of the research process because of the effect they have on participants. Researchers might inadvertently become an 'audience' for 'corporate performances' (Goffman 1959) carried out by employees who act like gatekeepers of their company's image and reputation. Autoethnography is an ideal tool to understand these situations of impression management, as it unleashes higher order thinking skills such as reflection, reflexivity and critical thinking to make explicit the intricate web of elements in the research process: the researcher's own values; the corporate discourses of the company under study; the participants' values; the data produced by the research; the theoretical perspectives that inform the data analysis; and the academic narratives that will emerge from the data analysis. Autoethnography enables the researcher to probe beneath the surface of the 'official' discourse on CSR promoted by the gatekeepers, to unveil alternative points of view that are not acknowledged in the corporate performances. This method can produce a more holistic picture of the findings.

I will demonstrate the benefits of the autoethnographic method in CSR research through a vignette that draws on my personal experiences and reflections during a field-work project I carried out in Brazil a few years ago. The substantive purpose of this project was to examine the CSR practices of a large mining company, but my autoethnographic lens unearthed other interesting aspects of the phenomenon under investigation. For a better understanding of the autoethnographic approach used in my research, I draw on the model proposed by Anderson (2006) which highlights the analytic dimensions of autoethnography.

Before proceeding, it will be useful to define three concepts that inform autoethnographic analyses – 'reflection', 'reflexivity' and 'critical thinking'. 'Reflection' is a cognitive process with affective undertones, characterized by intense mindfulness of self 'either within or after experience' (Johns 2004, p. 3); this can lead to new understandings and perspectives that can considerably broaden the researcher's horizons. 'Reflexivity' is a state of 'critical subjectivity' through which the researcher reflects critically on or interrogates the self, taking into account the impacts that the self may have on the research participants, and on the research process itself (Guba and Lincoln 2005, p. 210). 'Critical thinking' is a skill that involves the ability to engage in reflexive and independent thinking to assess both explicit and implicit claims about a given phenomenon (Langsdorf 1988; Moon 2005). In other words, it involves the ability to make judgements and evaluations to identify and interrogate different points of view. In the specific context of CSR research, this process enables the researcher to distinguish between 'official' accounts of CSR practices promoted by the company, and 'divergent' perspectives that call into question the integrity of the 'official view' (Duarte 2010a, 2010b).

This chapter is structured as follows: the first section describes the key features of the autoethnographic approach; the second identifies the elements of analytic autoethnography that I borrow from Anderson (2006); the third discusses my own autoethnographic study and presents a vignette based on my fieldwork experience; and the fourth discusses the theoretical insights that emerged from the vignette.

AUTOETHNOGRAPHY

Autoethnography is a broad methodological category that encompasses a wide variety of practices, with different styles and emphases (Ellingson and Ellis 2008; Reed-Danahay 1997). While it commonly takes the form of autobiographic accounts that shed light on social phenomena (see, for example, Holman-Jones (2005), Humphreys (2005), Pelias (2003), and Sparkes (1996)), autoethnography can be used in other ways: it can function as an analytic tool to produce theoretical insights (Anderson 2006); it can be written as a performative practice (Denzin 2003); it can be used in film (Russell 1999); and it can be written also collaboratively (Allen-Collinson and Hockey 2001; Lapadat 2009). Nevertheless, as distinct as these autoethnographic practices may be, they share in common a 'lens' that views the researcher as an integral part of the research context.

The writing style in autoethnography is essentially autobiographical, displaying 'multiple layers of consciousness' (Ellis and Bochner 2000, p. 739) that connect personal experience to the research process. Autoethnographic texts are made evocative through literary techniques that render events more engaging and emotionally rich (Ellis et al. 2011). The idea is to lure the reader 'into the narrative' to enable them to 'experience an experience' (Ellis 1993, p. 711; Ellis and Bochner 2006). In contrast with positivist approaches premised on the existence of an objective reality 'out there', and on the assumption of the investigator as an impartial observer of this reality, autoethnography does not seek prediction and generalizability. It is concerned with lived experience; with meaning co-created by the researcher and participants.

From the perspective of some scholars, the highly subjective and confessional style of autoethnographic accounts can render this method problematic, as it has no claim to objectivity or impartiality. Delamont (2009, p. 2) has described autoethnography as a 'narcissistic' genre and 'an abrogation of the honourable trade of the scholar'; and autoethnographers have been accused of personal bias (Atkinson 1997; Gans 1999) and navel gazing (Madison 2006). However, my own experience with autoethnography has indicated that this approach can enhance the research process, as it encourages researchers to be more mindful of their own role and the relationships they form with the participants. As will be seen later, this is particularly relevant in the context of CSR research projects where the researcher's presence can influence the participants' behaviour.

In autoethnographic narratives the writer generally holds back on interpretation, 'asking the reader to emotionally "relive the events" recounted in the text' (Richardson 2000, p. 11). For example, Sparkes (1996) has produced a vivid account of a chronic back injury that ultimately shortened his career as an elite athlete; Holman-Jones (2005) has explored her own experience with infertility and adoption, in a study about cultural attitudes to these issues; Holt (2001) has recounted the hurdles he faced as a PhD student teaching for the first time at the university level; and Wall (2006) has reflected on the challenges she faced when she was learning how to write autoethnographic accounts. The type of autoethnography discussed in this chapter encourages analysis that will lead to deeper theoretical understanding of the research process itself. The section below examines the three key elements I borrow from Anderson's (2006) 'analytic autoethnography' framework, proposed as a counterpoint to the more evocative styles of autoethnography (Ellis 1997, 2004).

ANALYTIC AUTOETHNOGRAPHY

While autoethnographic accounts commonly privilege subjective descriptions of research experience aiming to create an emotional engagement with the reader, analytic autoethnography highlights deeper levels of reflection to produce theoretical insights on the phenomenon under study. For the purpose of this chapter, I borrow from Anderson (2006) three features of analytic autoethnography: (1) the researcher's visibility in the narrative; (2) the use of analytic reflection and reflexivity to make sense of personal experience; and (3) commitment to theoretical and/or methodological understandings of the object of inquiry. While these three elements are closely linked, they are examined separately below, for the sake of greater clarity.

Researcher's Visibility

In conventional ethnographic accounts the researcher is 'largely invisible – a hidden and yet seemingly omniscient presence' in the writings that emerge from fieldwork (Anderson 2006, p. 384). In analytic autoethnography, the researcher becomes a 'highly visible social actor within the written text' (Anderson 2006, p. 384), consciously exploring their personal engagement with the object of inquiry. The researcher's feelings and experiences are brought to life through field journals and notes written in the first person to document their personal reactions to fieldwork events (Lofland 1971).

Analytic Reflection and Reflexivity

Reflection is a core activity of analytic autoethnography because, by its very nature, this approach requires that the researcher be mindful of self during and following the research experience. Reflection can help identify patterns in the data that are not immediately obvious to the researcher, generating new insights.

Deeper levels of reflection produce reflexivity, which involves a conscious awareness of the self as an 'agent' in the research process – as 'both inquirer and respondent, as teacher and learner, as the one coming to know the self within the processes of research itself' (Guba and Lincoln 2005, p. 210). Reflexivity is manifested through the way researchers construct themselves socially while simultaneously constructing the phenomenon they investigate (Steier 1991). Reflexivity keeps the researcher aware of the impact that she or he may have on the people they research; the influence of her or his own identity on the writing process.

Commitment to Theoretical Understandings

Commitment to theoretical understandings is the feature that most clearly distinguishes analytic autoethnography from its more evocative counterparts. Analytic autoethnographers use the data they generate about themselves (in their fieldwork journal, for example) to gain insight and advance knowledge which will 'transcend the data' (Anderson 2006, p. 388). This is because analytic autoethnography contributes 'to a spiralling refinement, elaboration, extension and revision of theoretical understanding' (Anderson 2006, p. 388). This process will be further explored in the discussion of the autoethnographic vignette which will follow the methodological considerations below.

MY AUTOETHNOGRAPHY

My autoethnography is based on a six-week fieldwork project designed to promote a better understanding of CSR practices in a large Brazilian mining company (referred to in the vignette below as 'Ferrus'). Borrowing from Czarniawska (1997, p. 65), this short field trip can be described as a 'window study' in which I opened an 'arbitrary time window' to describe phenomena and events I could see through it – including my own participation in the research process.

In this study, I used purposive sampling, which means that my choice to investigate a mining company was not accidental: my interest in the mining sector stems from its historic association with environmental degradation and social impacts. The mining industry has faced criticism arising from poor social and environmental performance, whether real or perceived (Walker and Howard 2002), and mining companies are particularly conscious of their public image, reputation and legitimacy. They tend to promote a rhetoric of social justice and environmental protection, and to avoid public criticism, often provide comprehensive CSR programs to local communities. They also employ sophisticated public relations strategies to project a positive image for their stakeholders (Ching et al. 2014; Jenkins and Yakovleva 2006).

When I travelled to the field, I was not aware that these impression management strategies would affect my role as the researcher. It was only when I had sufficiently distanced myself from the fieldwork context after returning to Australia, that I realized that I had become an integral part of my research project. Therefore, what I discuss in this chapter can be described as a 'meta-autoethnography' (Duarte and Hodge 2007) that moves beyond my original aim to attain a better understanding of CSR practices in a Brazilian mining company. The aim of this meta-autoethnography is to understand why and how my presence impacted on my key informants and other participants in my research project; more specifically, how I was transformed into 'the audience' for a series of corporate performances that took place during my visits to the company.

My reflections on selected sections of my fieldwork journal produced the 'explicitly reflexive' vignette (Humphreys 2005, p. 852) examined below, which is informed by Goffman's (1959) classical formulations on 'impression management'.

VIGNETTE

Impression Management Performances for the 'Researcher-as-Audience'

A few months before I left for Brazil, I received an email from a Brazilian fellow academic confirming that he had organised access for me to conduct fieldwork research at Ferrus, a major mining company located in the outskirts of Belo Horizonte. All I had to do when I arrived there, he explained, was to ring Lucia (pseudonym), a middle-manager from Ferrus' CSR Division to arrange the visits to the company. I rang Lucia, and was reassured to find out she was warm and friendly, and showed willingness to help me. To my delight, she offered to become my key informant, and proposed an 'informal' meeting the following day. Encouraged by Lucia's helpfulness and efficiency, I agreed to meet her at Ferrus' head office at 10:00am the next day.

I was expecting just an informal chat over a cup of coffee in Lucia's office, but it was clear that she had other plans in mind. Looking professional and elegant in a well-tailored business suit, she greeted me warmly in the company's reception area, taking me straight up to the fourteenth floor of the building, where the boardroom was located. Without wasting time, she invited me to sit at the large mahogany table that dominated the room and announced that she was going to show me a special PowerPoint presentation with 'all I needed to know about CSR at Ferrus'. In a didactic, authoritative tone of voice, Lucia regaled me for one hour with a solid overview of the company's CSR strategy and initiatives, punctuated by catchy slogans ('Our aim is to create long-term stakeholder value'; 'People are our most important assets'); stylish graphs with optimistic forecasts ('By the end of next year, we'll be implementing another six CSR programs . . .'); and glossy photos of smiling employees and community members, celebrating Ferrus' CSR achievements. This presentation was designed to impress.

Following the presentation, Lucia gave me a folder labeled 'Dr. Fernanda Duarte's Visit to Ferrus', which contained a busy schedule of activities for the next two weeks. I got to know that I would be visiting the company's two main sites – a large iron ore mine, some 80 km from Belo Horizonte, and the export plant, located on the coast, some 500 km from the iron ore mine. For the first visit, I would be picked up at 8:00am the following morning by a company car. At the plant, I would be given a guided tour of the mine, followed by interviews with staff from the CSR Division, and members of local communities who had benefitted from CSR initiatives.

A similar schedule had been planned for the visit to the export plant, the following week: I would be picked up from the airport by a company car and taken to the plant to meet staff from Ferrus' CSR Division; I would be given a guided tour of the plant, and later would interview CSR staff and community members. 'You don't need to worry about a thing', said Lucia smugly, 'It's all taken care of!'

Reflecting later on the events of my first day in the field, I concluded that I wasn't happy about those unsolicited arrangements. While Lucia's expediency would save me a great deal of time (and indeed research funds!), I felt she was 'taking control' of my project instead of allowing me to run it my own way, at my own pace. I realized my role as researcher was shifting; I was no longer 'in control' but had been drawn into the research process in ways I had not foreseen. While I felt uncomfortable with the situation, I knew there was nothing I could do. 'Beggars can't be choosers', I wrote philosophically in my fieldwork journal that night.

The guided visits to Ferrus' mine and export plant went according to plan, although my discomfort with the situation persisted. While I had managed to gather massive amounts of data from the interviews and informal conversations with staff from the CSR Division, I had misgivings about the authenticity of the data collected. The information I received from the participants was consistently positive: excellent CSR initiatives, committed employees and happy local community members . . . 'Would this be really the case? Some serious critical thinking is in order', I wrote in my journal.

The first major insight that emerged from a critical appraisal of the situation was that the participants might be 'putting on an act' for me. They were portraying the company in a certain way that might not correspond to reality . . . It was at that point that I remembered Goffman's (1959) formulations on 'impression management' tactics, and revisited his book 'The Presentation of Self in Everyday Life'. I realized that something like a metamorphosis had occurred, where *the researcher had become an audience.* This happened in the boardroom as I watched Lucia's PowerPoint presentation on Ferrus' CSR achievements, becoming thus the spectator of one of the many corporate performances I was to witness during my fieldwork. The behaviour of Lucia and her associates could be explained in terms of impression management, or in Goffman's (1959, p.xi) words, 'the way in which the individual in ordinary work situations presents himself (sic) and his activity to others, the ways in which he guides and controls the impression they form of him'.

Once more, I cast my mind back to my first meeting with Lucia, concluding that she had 'presented herself' in a way that controlled my impression of the company. She promoted the 'official' view of CSR at Ferrus which was to be sustained throughout my visit. Lucia wanted to make sure the impressions I formed in relation to her employer, would be congruent with the positive perceptions that Ferrus' leaders wanted to convey to outsiders. This was done by controlling 'what was disclosed and how' (Bansal and Kistruck 2006, p.166) through corporate performances that projected an idealised image of the company's CSR activities; the kind of image that a mining company with a poor track record *needs* to project in order to maintain its legitimacy and license to operate.

The second insight that emerged from my reading of Goffman's work was that the corporate performances presented to me were confined to the 'front region' of the company – that is, a domain 'bounded to some degree by barriers to perception' (Goffman 1959, p.106). Within the front region, the researcher-as-audience could see and hear only what the performers wanted her to see and hear, based on a certain 'definition of the situation' (Goffman 1959, p.141) promoted by the gate-keepers. The front region thus existed in contradistinction to the 'back region' of the performative space (Goffman 1959, pp.112, 238) – a domain where unauthorised information thrived, away from the gaze of the audience. This domain was off limits to the researcher.

The existence of front and back regions of performance was also evident during my visits to the mine and the export plant. In both sites Lucia had arranged for a junior employee from the CSR Division to escort me everywhere for the duration of the visit ('Company policy', Lucia explained with a polite smile). While my corporate escorts turned out to be two affable young women, they were no doubt under strict instructions not to lose sight of me. Their role was to ensure that I remained in the front region of Ferrus' performances and did not venture into the mysterious realm of Ferrus' back regions. I realised that I was not allowed to wander around on my own, in case I witnessed activities or events that I was not meant to see ('Perhaps environmentally polluting activities or breaches of occupational health and safety regulations?', I speculated in my journal). My corporate escorts remained with me even during my lunch break. They took me to the company's refectory and made sure we shared the same table. They ensured there were no 'disruptions' (Goffman 1959, pp. 13, 67) to the authorised performances offered to the researcher-as-audience.

The third insight that emerged from my reflections was that impression management also involved control of the information imparted during the performances (Goffman 1959, p. 67). As Goffman (1959, p. 48) put it, an effective corporate performance will 'involve the over-communication of some facts and the under-communication of others'; it will also 'conceal or underplay' information that is incompatible with an idealised version of the company and its services. This point made sense when I considered that, in both company sites, the interviewees had been 'cherry-picked' by Lucia and her colleagues from the CSR Division. Most likely, these individuals had been chosen because the gate-keepers knew they could be trusted, and would not make negative comments about Ferrus' CSR performance. My original plan to have a plurality of views on CSR to enrich my research was discarded when I noticed the homogeneous character of the sample of participants chosen by the performers. At the mining site, the interviewees were all female aged between 30 and 40 years, who lived in the same village. All of them were involved in the same CSR project: a successful handicraft workshop that used recyclable materials to manufacture handbags, patchwork quilts and table cloths for tourists. Not surprisingly, these women gave glowing appraisals of Ferrus' CSR programs, emphasising the company's positive relationship with local communities. The women expressed deep gratitude to the CSR staff for their help and encouragement. Pushing my critical thinking further, I could not help but wonder whether these handpicked individuals were members of what Kapelus (2002, p. 282) described as 'local elites' – a group of conformist, compliant people approved by the company as its legitimate representatives; trustworthy individuals that would not 'disrupt' the flow of the corporate performances.

The above insight led to the realization that the official perspective imparted to me by the performers did not include dissident voices – the voices of people who had been negatively affected by the company's operations. I found out later through independent sources that these dissident voices existed, but had not been acknowledged in the authorised performances. Talking later to some fellow academics who had done research on Ferrus, I found out, for example, that parents of adolescent daughters in local communities were concerned about the sudden influx of 3,000 male workers (hired to build Ferrus mining plant) into their villages; there were also concerns about the health impacts of the fine black dust that was carried by the wind from the mining site. I was also told that some community leaders were indignant with the fact that Ferrus had made decisions that affected local communities without previous consultation with them. This information remained in the back regions of Ferris' performances.

238 *Handbook of research methods in corporate social responsibility*

After I returned to Australia, I continued to gather information from independent sources, exercising my critical thinking and reflexivity skills. The Internet was a valuable source of alternative perspectives that exposed the biases of the official perspective. I found independent reports on air pollution by dust and gases from Ferrus' export plant, and pollution of neighbouring water sources. I found media accounts of pollution fine evasions by Ferrus, and allegations of collusion between Ferrus and local government. I found a mining workers' union newsletter that denounced poor working conditions at Ferrus' plants and unacceptably low salaries for the miners. I was now in possession of knowledge that had been hidden from me in back regions of Ferrus' performances. Through reflection and critical thinking I was able to probe beneath the surface of the official view to obtain information that helped to construct a more holistic (and realistic) picture of CSR at Ferrus. I was now ready to produce a rich meta-autoethnography.

DISCUSSION

The above vignette illustrates the usefulness of the autoethnographic method in CSR research, and in particular the role of three higher order skills that drive the autoethnographic process: reflection, critical thinking and reflexivity. Reflection allowed me to remain mindful of 'the self' within and after the fieldwork experience, generating a number of unexpected insights (e.g., the researcher as part of the research process; the performative dimensions of CSR; the existence of official and divergent discourses on CSR). The subjectivity of reflexivity made me aware that my role in the project shifted at some point, given the effects of my presence on the participants. Critical thinking enabled me to question the validity of the official perspective on CSR at Ferrus promoted by the gatekeepers of the company, and to engage in reflexive and independent thinking to unearth alternative points of view. As an inherently reflexive approach, analytic autoethnography strengthened my voice and self-confidence, prompting unique insights that I would not have been able to achieve through more conventional methodological approaches.

The vignette also illustrates the three elements of Anderson's analytic autoethnography framework discussed earlier: textual visibility; analytic reflection and reflexivity; and commitment to theoretical understandings. Textual visibility is evident in the technique of writing in the first person, which shows me as the 'author' of the narrative. Reflection and reflexivity were extensively used in my autoethnography, creating opportunities to unveil hidden phenomena that were not immediately obvious to me.

Most importantly, the vignette demonstrates a commitment to theoretical understandings about CSR, reflected in my realization that Goffman's (1959) impression management concepts could adequately explain the unexpected events that took place during my fieldwork.

CONCLUSION

This chapter has explored the use of the autoethnographic approach in research on CSR in the mining sector. To this end, I presented a reflexive vignette that recounted how I became a component of my own research project as a result of my relationship with the participants. Given my inexperience at the time of that fieldwork, this role change came as a surprise, but. I now accept that this is bound to happen in CSR research, especially when the company under study has a poor environmental and social track record.

The use of higher order thinking skills implicit in the autoethnographic lens enables the researcher to interrogate 'commonsense' explanations in order to discover different points of view. Autoethnography is therefore a valuable qualitative method to foster a fuller, multi-faceted understanding of the complexities of CSR.

This chapter will be particularly useful for novice CSR researchers, as it provides theoretically informed knowledge about events and processes that can unexpectedly unfold in the field. Equipped with this knowledge, new researchers will feel more 'in control' of the fieldwork experience. Through their field notes new researchers will be able to map out more consciously the different layers of the research process, producing richer data analyses and new theoretical insights.

REFERENCES

Allen-Collinson, J. and Hockey, J. (2001), 'Runners' tales: autoethnography, injury and narrative', *Auto/Biography*, **4** (1–2), 95–106.
Anderson, L. (2006), 'Analytic autoethnography', *Journal of Contemporary Ethnography*, **35**, 373–395.
Atkinson, P. (1997), 'Narrative turn or blind alley?' *Qualitative Health Research*, **7**, 325–344.
Bansal, P. and G. Kistruck (2006), 'Seeing is (not) believing: managing the impressions of the firm's commitment to the natural environment', *Journal of Business Ethics*, **67** (2), 165–180.
Boyd, E.M. and A.W. Fales (1983), 'Reflective learning as key to learning from experience', *Journal of Humanistic Psychology*, **23** (2), 99–117.
Ching, M., C. Chan, J. Watson and D. Woodliff (2014), 'Corporate governance quality and CSR disclosures', *Journal of Business Ethics*, **125** (1), 59–73.
Czarniawska, Barbara (1997), *Narrating the Organization: Dramas of Institutional Identity*, Chicago: The University of Chicago Press.
Delamont, S. (2009), 'The only honest thing: autoethnography, reflexivity and small crises in fieldwork', *Ethnography and Education*, **4** (1), 51–63.
Denzin, Norman K. (2003), *Performance Ethnography Critical Pedagogy and the Politics of Culture*, University of Illinois, USA: Sage Publications.
Didion, Joan (2005), *The Year of Magical Thinking*, New York: A.A. Knop.
Duarte, F.P. (2010a), 'Corporate social responsibility in a Brazilian mining company: "official" and divergent narratives', *Social Responsibility Journal*, **6** (1), 4–17.
Duarte, F.P. (2010b), 'Social responsibility as organizational culture in a Brazilian mining company: a three-perspective narrative', *Journal of Organizational Culture, Communications and Conflict*, **14** (1), 13–32.
Duarte, F. and Hodge, B. (2007), 'Crossing paradigms: a meta-autoethnography of a fieldwork trip to Brazil', *Culture and Organization*, Special Issue on Auto-ethnography, **13** (3), 191–203.
Ellingson, L. and C. Ellis (2008), 'Autoethnography as constructionist project', in James A. Holstein and Jaber F. Gubrium (eds), *Handbook of Constructionist Research*, New York: Guilford Press, pp. 445–466.
Ellis, C. (1993), '"There are survivors": telling a story of a sudden death', *The Sociological Quarterly*, **34** (4), 711–730.
Ellis, C.S. (1997), 'Evocative autoethnography: writing emotionally about our lives', in William G. Tierney and Yvonna S. Lincoln (eds), *Representation and the Text: Re-framing the Narrative Voice*, Albany: State University of New York Press, pp. 115–142.
Ellis, C.S. (2004), *The Ethnographic I: A Methodological Novel about Autoethnography*, Walnut Creek, CA: Altamira Press.
Ellis, C.S. and A. Bochner (2000), 'Autoethnography, personal narrative, reflexivity: researcher as subject', in Norman Denzin and Yvonne Lincoln (eds), *Sage Handbook of Qualitative Research*, Thousand Oaks, CA: Sage (2nd edn.), pp. 733–768.
Ellis, C. and A.P. Bochner (2006), 'Analyzing analytic autoethnography: an autopsy', *Journal of Contemporary Ethnography*, **35** (4), 429–449.

Ellis, C.S. and L. Ellingson (2000), 'Qualitative methods', in Edgar Borgatta and Rhonda Montgomery (eds), *Encyclopedia of Sociology*, New York: Macmillan, pp. 2287–2296.
Ellis, C.S., T.E. Adams and A. Bochner (2011), 'Forum: qualitative social research', **12** (1), Art. 10, available at http://www.qualitative-research.net/index.php/fqs/article/view/1589/3095 (accessed 2 April 2014).
Freeman, R.E. and D.E. Reed (1983), 'Stockholders and shareholders: a new perspective on corporate governance', *California Management Review*, **25** (3), 93–104.
Gans, H.J. (1999), 'Participant observation: in the era of ethnography', *Journal of Contemporary Ethnography*, **28** (5), 540–548.
Geertz, Clifford (1973), *The Interpretation of Cultures: Selected Essays*, New York: Basic Books.
Goffman, Erving (1959), *The Presentation of Self in Everyday Life*, New York: Double Day & Company Inc.
Guba, E. and Y.S. Lincoln (2005), 'Paradigmatic controversies, contradictions, and emerging influences', in Norman K. Denzin and Yvonna S. Lincoln (eds), *Sage Handbook of Qualitative Research* (3rd ed.), Thousand Oaks, CA: Sage, pp. 191–215.
Holman-Jones, S. (2005), 'Autoethnography: making the personal political', in Denzin, N.K. and Lincoln, Y.S. (eds), *The Sage Handbook of Qualitative Research* (3rd ed.), Thousand Oaks, CA: Sage pp. 763–91.
Holt, N.L. (2001), 'Beyond technical reflection: demonstrating the modification of teaching behaviors using three levels of reflection', *Avante*, **7** (2), 66–76.
Humphreys, M. (2005), 'Getting personal: reflexivity and autoethnographic vignettes', *Qualitative Inquiry*, **11** (6), 840–860.
Jenkins, H. and N. Yakovleva (2006), 'Corporate social responsibility in the mining industry: exploring trends in social and environmental disclosure', *Journal of Cleaner Production*, **14** (3–4), 271–284.
Johns, Christopher (2004), *Becoming a Reflective Practitioner* (2nd ed.), Oxford, UK: Blackwell.
Kapelus, P. (2002), 'Mining, corporate social responsibility and the "community": the case of Rio Tinto, Richards Bay Minerals and the Mbonambi', *Journal of Business Ethics*, **39** (3), 275–296.
Langsdorf, L. (1988), 'Ethical and logical analysis as human science', *Human Studies*, **11** (1), 43–63.
Lapadat, J.C. (2009), 'Writing our way into shared understanding: collaborative autobiographical writing in the qualitative methods class', *Qualitative Inquiry*, **15** (6), 955–979.
Lofland, John (1971), *Analyzing Social Settings: A Guide to Qualitative Observation and Analysis*, Belmont, CA: Wadsworth.
Madison, D.S. (2006), 'The dialogic performative in critical ethnography', *Text and Performance Quarterly*, **26** (4), 320–324.
Moon, Jenny (2005), 'We seek it here . . . a new perspective on the elusive activity of critical thinking: a theoretical and practical approach', available at http://escalate.ac.uk/2041 (accessed 23 December 2014).
Pelias, R.J. (2003), 'The academic tourist: an autoethnography', *Qualitative Inquiry*, **9** (3), 369–73.
Reed-Danahay, D.E. (1997), 'Introduction', in Deborah E. Reed-Danahay (ed.), *Auto/Ethnography: Rewriting the Self and the Social*, Oxford: Berg, pp. 1–17.
Richardson, L. (2000), 'New writing practices in qualitative research', *Sociology of Sport Journal*, **17** (1), 5–20.
Russell, Catherine (1999), *Experimental Ethnography: The Work of Film in the Age of Video*, Durham, North Carolina: Duke University Press.
Sparkes, A.C. (1996), 'The fatal flaw: a narrative of the fragile body-self', *Qualitative Inquiry*, **2** (4), 463–494.
Steier, Frederick (1991), *Research and Reflexivity*, London: Sage.
Walker, J. and S. Howard (2002), *Finding the Way Forward: How Could Voluntary Action Move Mining Towards Sustainable Development?*, London: Environment Resources Management (ERM) in collaboration with the International Institute for Environment and Development and World Business Council for Sustainable Development.
Wall, S. (2006), 'An autoethnography on learning about autoethnography', *International Journal of Qualitative Methods*, **5** (2), available at http://www.ualberta.ca/~ijqm/ (accessed 23 December 2014).

14. Insights regarding the applicability of semiotics to CSR communication research
Kemi C. Yekini

INTRODUCTION

In the last decade, corporate social responsibility (CSR) debate seems to have shifted from the question of whether to report on CSR activities to what should be the actual content of the reports. Fresh concerns are being expressed about the scope, quality and authenticity of the reports. This could be borne out of increased awareness and reporting of it in annual reports. Consequently, scholars such as Davison (2007, 2011) and Macintosh and Baker (2002) have called for a 'linguistic turn' in evaluating such disclosures. The linguistic turn as defined in Macintosh and Baker (2002, p. 185) refers to 'the idea of treating the phenomena . . . as a text and analyzing it for its textual properties . . .' The argument is that corporate disclosures should be seen as polysemous texts or languages that are capable of being misinterpreted. In this way, firms will be inclined to give more consideration to the contents and hence quality of the reports. Davison (2011) argued that each language involves particular interpretation uncommon to other languages and that such interpretation is interrelated with a variety of knowledge and experiences and hence is capable of influencing thoughts and perceptions in different ways.

This chapter explores the use of a linguistic-based theory and analytical tool – Semiotics – as a research methodology in evaluating the content and the quality of CSR reporting. The argument of this chapter is that given the narrative nature of CSR reports (CSRR), research into the content and quality of CSRR can be better achieved with a linguistic-based framework.

Since the CSR communication research lacks a fundamental theoretical conception and methodology, researchers from a variety of disciplines have approached their work from their individual and often conflicting perspective. The result is that the last decade witnessed enormous and conflicting studies on the content of CSRR. Over the years the findings from the various studies have remained unintegrated and often pedestrian or overlapping. However, as debates have now moved from the question of whether to report on CSR activities to what should be the scope and quality of the reports, the importance of establishing a consensus and cardinal methodological base for the CSR communication research cannot be overemphasized. The debates on these issues (Beattie et al. 2004, Beretta and Bozzolan 2004, 2008, Botosan 2004, Yekini and Jallow 2012, Yekini et al. 2015), basically, centre on the best measure of CSRR generally, that is whether to measure CSRR in terms of its quantity or its quality and, if the latter, what should be the best measure for quality. Nevertheless, a variety of definitions and measurements of disclosure quality exists in the literature, while the debate centres on the best way of measuring disclosure quality.

Consequently various methods of measurement have been used in literature as a measure of disclosure quality, while some have used analyst ratings (Hasseldine et al.

2005, Toms 2002); others have constructed their own index (Beattie et al. 2004, Botosan 2004, Freedman and Stagliano 1992, 1995, 2008, Walden and Schwartz 1997). Beattie et al. (2004) categorized the different approaches used in literature into two, namely subjective analyst ratings studies and semi-objective studies. Studies adopting semi-objective approaches include thematic content analysis studies, readability studies, linguistic analysis studies and disclosure index studies (see Beattie et al. 2004, p. 208–213 for detailed review of these studies and approaches).

Furthermore in measuring the quality of CSRR some scholars (Gray et al. 1995, Guthrie and Parker 1990, Guthrie et al. 2004, Hackston and Milne 1996) included the 'quantity' of disclosure along with other criteria, such as 'location' and 'evidence', while some authors simply used 'quantity' alone as a proxy for 'quality'. These authors do not distinguish between the quantity and quality of disclosures, arguing that the quantity of information is capable of influencing the quality. On the other hand, some other scholars (Walden and Schwartz 1997, Freedman and Stagliano 1992, 1995, 2008, Toms 2002, Beattie et al. 2004, Hasseldine et al. 2005) distinguished between quality and quantity of disclosures arguing that quantity alone will not be an adequate measure of quality and that measuring the quality of disclosure is much more important than the quantity as the quality conveys the meaning and importance of the message.

To this end, Beattie et al. (2004) argued for the development of a comprehensive disclosure profile that could serve as a practical tool for measuring disclosure quality and suggested a four-dimensional framework for measuring quality, namely, the amount of disclosure spread across topics and three attributes of the information, namely, historical/forward-looking; financial/non-financial; and quantitative/non-quantitative, while describing the quality of narrative disclosures as a complex and 'multi-faceted concept' (p. 227). In addition, they introduced a computer-assisted methodology for the applicability of the framework. Arguably, however, while commending the holistic approach of Beattie et al. (2004), it is instructive to note that their approach, apart from the introduction of computer-assisted methodology, is not entirely different from previous methods of measuring CSRR quality documented in extant literature. For example, Guthrie and Parker (1990), Gray et al. (1995), Hackston and Milne (1996) and Guthrie et al. (2004) all included in their measurement of CSR information quality, the volume of disclosure spread across theme, the financial/non-financial and quantitative/non-quantitative attributes, while Walden and Schwartz (1997) and Freedman and Stagliano (1992, 1995, 2008) also considered the timing (i.e. historical/forward-looking attributes) in the construction of their index.

Accordingly, Botosan (2004) suggested that as there are no generally accepted frameworks of disclosure quality, researchers could employ the guidelines provided by the International Accounting Standards Board (IASB) and the Financial Accounting Standards Board (FASB), arguing that such guidelines give a better foundation for the development of a framework of disclosure quality. The IASB and FASB stated that information disclosed in annual reports can only be useful to economic decision makers if they possess the attributes of:

1. Understandability
2. Relevance
3. Reliability
4. Comparability.

To this end Botosan (2004) offered a definition of quality as follows:
Quality = f (understandability, relevance, reliability, comparability)
She opined that since this framework is produced by the standard-setters, it is reflective of a more generally accepted definition of disclosure quality. However, even if we accept Botosan's framework, the operationalization of these attributes becomes an issue as observed by Hooks and van Staden (2011), who, adopting Botosan's approach, found that although it was possible to assess the understandability, relevance and comparability of the information, the reliability was very difficult to assess. Consequently, while some studies have continued to raise fundamental questions as to the quality and authenticity of CSRR (Aras and Crowther 2009, Burritt and Schaltegger 2010, Cho et al. 2010, Yekini and Jallow 2012), others have examined this from the point of view of stakeholders' concerns, thus examining a cross-country and developing-economy comparison (De Villiers and van Staden 2010) and its relationship with accountability (Adams 2004, Cooper and Owen 2007), while other scholars have called for a literary approach to examining the reliability of the information (Aras and Crowther 2009, Bebbington et al. 2008, Crowther 2002, Davison 2011, Yekini and Jallow 2012, Yusoff and Lehman 2009). These scholars argued that to investigate the reliability and quality of disclosures of this nature, they should be subjected to textual analysis which is an active way of decoding the messages in the text by the reader. Bebbington et al. (2008, p. 353) therefore encourage CSR communication researchers that the 'focus on linguistic strategies, . . ., may be especially appealing if analysis of reporting moves towards examining discourses rather than quantitative measures of disclosure'. In this chapter, the author is therefore motivated to explore and develop a semiotic framework that is grounded in literary theoretical underpinnings for measuring the reliability and quality of CSRR.

Previous studies (Fiol 1989, Macintosh et al. 2000, Crowther 2002, Macintosh and Baker 2002, Yusoff and Lehman 2009, Davison 2011) have attempted the application of literary perspectives in their interpretation of corporate and CSR reports. Fiol (1989) examined the semiotics of chief executive officers' (CEOs') letters in annual reports and was able to establish that these letters revealed the link between organizational beliefs and strategic behaviour which has hitherto been very difficult to capture with conventional research methods. Macintosh et al. (2000) and Macintosh and Baker (2002) drew on radical semiotics and Baudrillard's orders-of-simulacra theory to investigate the reality of accounting information and concluded that a literary theory perspective gives a different view of the nature of accounting and accounting reports. Similarly, Yusoff and Lehman (2009) found semiotics very useful in 'making sense' (p. 241) of corporate reporting practices in their investigation and comparisons of corporate reporting practices in Malaysia and Australia. Also, Crowther (2002) investigated the binary opposition between corporate reporting and environmental reporting using the semiotic stage and found that corporate performance in both financial and environmental dimensions cannot be dissociated from one another. He found that a company performing well financially was found to be performing well in both dimensions, which appears contrary to the findings of studies adopting conventional research methods such as Hackston and Milne (1996), Ho and Wong (2001) and Hasseldine et al. (2005) who found no relationships between profitability and CSRR. In this chapter, we depart from others whose focus is on evaluating the intended meaning of the reports by viewing the reports from the standpoint of the audience/users.

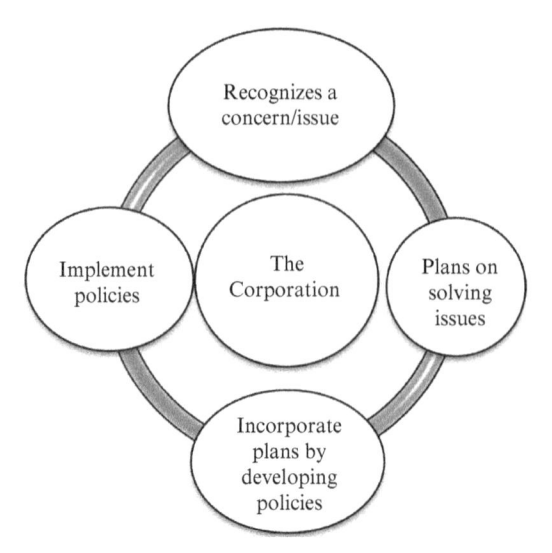

Figure 14.1   Corporation/society relationship – Preston and Post (1975 [2012]) and Preston (1975) perspective

Towards Developing a Theoretical Framework for CSRR-Quality Measure

We developed the CSRR-quality framework by employing both the Preston and Post (1975 [2012]), Preston (1975) and the Wood and Jones (1995) Firm/Society relationship models; see Figures 14.1 and 14.2 for representations of these models. Preston and Post (1975 [2012]), looking at it from the point of view of the organization, developed a framework for managing social issues. In the framework, they recognize the fact that corporations would: first, be aware and/or recognize a social issue (i.e. establish an expectation gap); secondly, the corporation plans on solving the issue and incorporate such plan into its corporate goal; thirdly, the corporation responds in terms of policy development, and finally implementation of the policy.

Wood and Jones (1995) on the other hand argued that the role of the society in the stakeholder system is first and foremost to set the expectation gap. It is this expectation gap that is being addressed by management through corporate actions and, consequently, corporate disclosures/reporting. Corporate reports such as CSRR are invariably seen as the language of business with which the firms communicate with society. This then enables society to evaluate the outcome of corporate actions in addition to experiencing the effect of corporate actions. Since CSR is regarded as a corporate action intended to meet the expectations of society, then its communication via CSRR or disclosures in annual reports will signal adherence to societal expectations. Therefore, as beneficiaries, society should be the best judge of the quality of such reports/disclosures.

Wood and Jones (1995) pointed out that in order to achieve a better understanding of the legitimization process, the question 'to whom does corporate social performance make a difference?' must first be answered (ibid., p. 241). They describe this as the missing link in understanding the overall relationship between corporations and society. Nevertheless,

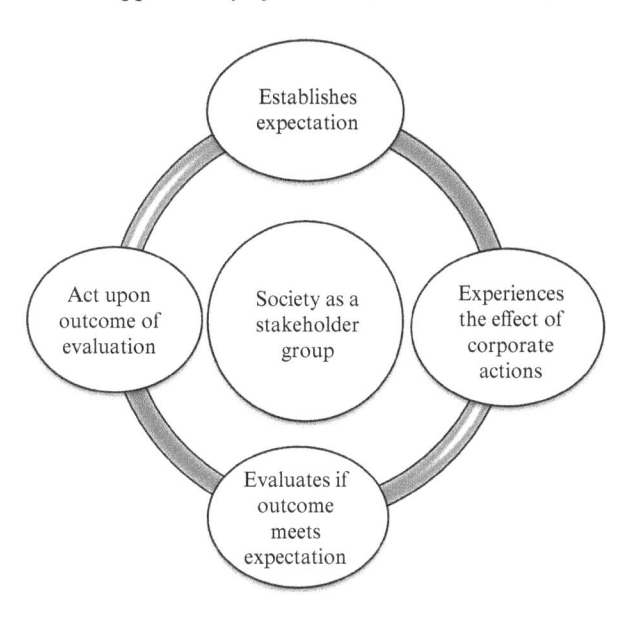

Figure 14.2 Corporation/society relationship – Wood and Jones (1995) perspective

they opined that understanding the CSRR phenomenon from a stakeholder theory perspective involves identifying the particular stakeholder group involved. They therefore proposed a corporation/stakeholder model, where multiple stakeholders' expectations, effects, evaluations and behaviours are well defined. This, they argued, would allow for a better understanding of how the relationship between the corporation and the stakeholder arises in the first place and what led to the expectation gap being addressed by management through disclosures. The knowledge of such a relationship would lend itself to the development of relevant measures of investigation while taking into consideration the role of the stakeholder in setting expectations, experiencing the effect and evaluating the outcome (ibid.). We conjecture that the Wood and Jones (1995) model, when applied in conjunction with the Preston and Post (1975 [2012]) model could form the basis for the application of the Greimas semiotics framework and, thus, help to define the components necessary to create a semiotic model for the evaluation of CSRR quality.

Following the Wood and Jones (1995) model, since society is responsible for setting the expectation gap, we argue that it should also be in a better position to evaluate whether or not the outcome of the corporate plans/actions (CSR activities) meets societal expectations. This is consistent with the viewpoints of Price and Shanks (2005) who argued that the users of data, CSR reports in this case, should constitute the final judge of the quality of such data/reports (Price and Shanks 2005). In other words, to unearth the reliability and quality of CSRR, we argue that the reports should be viewed and interpreted from the perspective of the audience (i.e. the society that sets the expectation gap in the first place) since they are in a better position to determine whether their expectation has been met. To this end, we incorporated the evaluative stage into our framework following the principles of the Greimasian canonical narrative schema (discussed later in this chapter). In the next section, we explore corporate reporting as a language capable of influencing the reader. This will give us further insights that would enable us to better understand the place of semiotics in the development of the CSRR-quality framework.

Corporate Reporting as Language of Business

The fact that language influences thinking and hence perception has been well argued by renowned scholars in the field of linguistics and psychologists such as Gumperz and Levinson (1996) and Lucy (1992, 1997). Lucy (1997) classified the manner in which language can influence perception into three parts: semiotic or semiology,[1] structural and functional.[2] Of particular interest to this chapter is the semiotic effect of language on perception. The argument is that when language is used in a particular way it may influence thinking and hence have an effect on perception (Lucy 1992, 1997).

Consequently Jain (1973) and Belkaoui (1978), drawing from the 'Sapir-Whorf Hypothesis'[3] (Belkaoui 1978, p. 97), in an attempt to address the communication problem between corporations and stakeholders, argued that as a language of business, information contained in corporate annual reports can be read or spoken like any other language. This followed the argument put forward by Sapir and Whorf that each language involves particular interpretation uncommon to other languages and that such interpretation is interrelated with a variety of knowledge and experiences and hence is capable of influencing thoughts and perceptions in different ways (Jain 1973, Belkaoui 1978, Gumperz and Levinson 1996).

As a language of business, scholars such as Jain (1973), Belkaoui (1978), Cooper and Puxty (1994), Macintosh et al. (2000), Macintosh and Baker (2002), Macintosh (2003) and McGoun et al. (2007) argued that corporate disclosures whether contained in annual reports, press releases, accounting magazines or even a separate CSR report and in whatever format, whether quantitative, narratives, images, graphs or in tables, all represent means of communication. They therefore emphasized the need for a 'linguistic turn' in drawing meanings from such disclosures, arguing that corporate disclosures should be seen as texts capable of being interpreted like any other language. Davison (2007, 2011) supported these views and argued that what is being interpreted is the language itself rather than the intended meaning of the author. Consequently, since as text, they have polysemous characteristics, Price and Shanks (2005) argued that 'information consumers (i.e. internal or external users of organisational data) are the final judge of quality' (Price and Shanks 2005, p. 659).

However, in an earlier study Jain (1973) argued that as languages represent phenomena in the real world so do corporate disclosures in the business world. Therefore, he described accounting rules as financial grammar and considered them as analogous to grammatical structure in linguistics and therefore examined their effect on the perception of the listeners (i.e. the readers/users) of such information. He found that accounting information affected decision-making. Similarly, Belkaoui (1978) argued that the lexical characteristics and grammatical rules of corporate disclosures will affect the linguistic and non-linguistic behaviour of users of the information. He argued that the use of accounting language in different ways by different users can affect its information content and therefore influence behaviour in different ways. Moreover, Macintosh and Baker (2002) illustrated that as the language of business, the claim that accounting information represents an objective reflection of reality may only be sustained when such information is investigated for its narrative qualities. Davison (2007, 2011) argued that researchers should employ linguistic-based theories such as semiotics in accounting and finance research, arguing that economic-based theories have lost power in predicting social phenomena.

In this chapter, we present a framework for measuring CSR information quality based on semiotic theory. Specifically, we adopt the Greimas semiotics approach. Semiotics as a well-established linguistic theory spanning over ten decades has been proved to be suitable for analysing sign related communications (Price and Shanks 2005). Hence it is apt as a theoretical framework for defining criteria to establish the reliability and quality of information. The aim of this chapter is to provide an approach for measuring the reliability and quality of CSRR that is both theoretically grounded and practical and that can serve as a basis for further research in CSRR research. The framework can also serve as a theoretical tool and procedure for measuring the quality of CSRR. Therefore, the focus of this chapter is on the use of the Greimas semiotics tools as a suitable theoretical technique for determining the criteria with which to measure CSR information quality. In the next section, we review semiotic theory: its origin, development and criticisms. This is followed by detailed discussion on the Greimas and Barthes semiotics. The section starts with a comparison of the Barthesian and the Greimasian semiotics, followed by detailed description of the processes involved with the development of the Greimas CSRR-quality semiotics framework.

SEMIOTICS AND THE SEMIOTIC THEORY

The Saussure Semiology[4] (Semiotics)

Semiotics[5] is, simply put, the study of signs and is based on semiotics theory. The foundation stone of semiotics was laid by Swiss linguist Ferdinand de Saussure (1857–1913) through his lecture 'Course in General Linguistics' published in 1916 after his death (Barthes and Duisit 1975). Semiology (as known by Saussure) actually developed out of linguistics, which is the scientific study of languages and has since expanded to conceptualize the general study of signs (Crystal 1987). Saussure described semiology as a science of signs encompassing any system of producing signs which constitute some form of signification. Such signs which could be in the form of behaviour, a pattern of doing things, an image, an object, a sound or even a name is usually intended as a form of 'signifier' or signal carrying many more messages than the written words (Barthes and Duisit 1975). Eco (1976) summed up that semiotics is concerned with anything that can be taken as a sign, including an act or behaviour by an individual or a corporation.

According to Saussure, the linguistic sign does not unite a thing and a name but rather a concept and the sound, image or gesture (Saussure 1983). For instance, the colour 'red' could mean much more than being just one of the primary colours, but could connote a range of apparently differing emotions. For example, it could denote anger, violence or war. It could also mean stop, danger or emergency. Better still, it could denote energy, strength or power as well as passion, desire or love. The meaning assigned to it at any point in time therefore depends on the circumstances surrounding its use, any other sign that goes with it, as well as the experience and knowledge of the interpreter. If we apply Saussure's model of a sign – the 'signifier' and the 'signified' – the colour 'red' represents

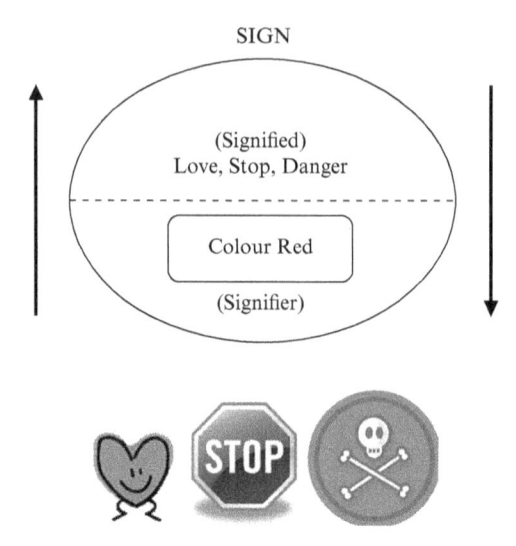

248 *Handbook of research methods in corporate social responsibility*

Source: Adapted from Chandler (2007).

Figure 14.3 Saussure's dyadic model of the sign

the 'signifier' while the concepts of 'love', 'stop' or 'danger' represent the 'signified' as shown diagrammatically above. In other words, the Saussure model divides a sign into two inseparable components – the 'signifier' and the 'signified' – while the relationship between the two is the signification.

The Peirce Semiotics

At about the same period as Saussure, an American philosopher, Charles Sanders Peirce (1839–1914), developed the theory of semiotics, which he defined as a doctrine of signs (Chandler 2007). To Peirce, a sign is anything which stands for something in some respect or capacity to somebody. Accordingly, Peirce considered a sign as having three elements: 'iconic', 'symbolic' and 'indexical'; as against the two components of Saussure's 'signifier' and 'signified'. 'Iconic' signs are those that bear close resemblance to the 'signifier'. For instance, a picture of a school building in support of a community involvement project disclosed in an annual report may be 'iconic', if the narrative also indicates educational support. However, the same picture may be seen as symbolic (i.e. used as a mere symbol of involvement in community activity) if no mention is made in the narrative that the company is actually involved with the building of a school. A sign is indexical if the signifier is usually associated with a particular signified; for example, smoke could be seen as signifying fire. Peirce argued that all social practices can be seen as signs ('representamen') which stand for something (its 'object') to somebody (its 'interpretant') in some respect or capacity (its 'ground') (Peirce 1931–58).

The triadic interactions of these terms, known as 'semiosis', refer to the process of signification which is quite different to the dyad relationship of Saussure's 'signifier' and 'signified'. Peirce's triadic model is usually represented by a triangle (see Figure 14.4) showing

```
                    Interpretant
                        /\
                       /  \
                      / SIGN \
                     /_____\
            Representamen      Object
             (Signifier)      (Signified)
```

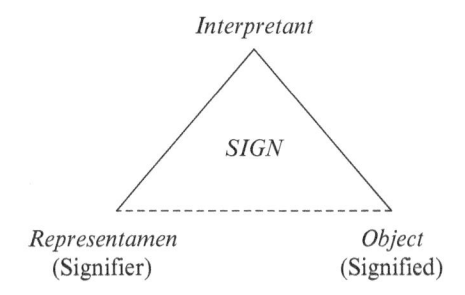

Source: Adapted from Chandler (2007).

Figure 14.4 Peirce's triadic model of the sign

the triad relationship (Chandler 2007). Peirce proposes various possible combinations of these triadic relationships depending on the type of sign and ends up with several classes of signs (Hawkes 2004). Arguably, therefore, Peirce's analysis appears to extend the work of Saussure by enumerating different types of signs, how they interact and what rules govern each set of signs to form signification. While Saussure's model made no reference to any external reality outside the sign system, but simply identified the hidden binary oppositions in the signs in order for signification to occur, Peirce's model made reference to an 'interpretant' or 'referent' which is beyond the sign and is a sign in itself (Chandler 2007), thus leading to a series of signs the collective presence of which constitutes signification. Therefore, in Peirce's model, signification is seen as a generative process (Floch 1988).

Further Developments in Semiotics

Since the death of these two founding theorists of semiotics, semiotics has undergone different stages of development; notable works among contemporary semioticians are Morris (1946), Jakobson (1942, 1960), Barthes (1967, 1972, 1975), Lévi-Strauss (1972), Eco (1976), Greimas (1983, 1987), Sebeok (1977, 1994) and Baudrillard (1988). Barthes introduced different orders of signification (Barthes and Duisit 1975). He refers to the first order signification as 'denotation', which simply refers to the iconic meaning of a sign in which the photograph of a new school building within a community system could simply mean a school or a place of learning. The second order signification, referred to as 'connotation', is when further interpretation is given to the photograph. Such connotation will normally be influenced by our knowledge of the financier of the school building as well as our experiences and knowledge of the ideological and political phenomenon within the community where the building is located. This is referred to as 'myth' by Barthes. However, taking into consideration the on-going debate on CSR and the current trend among corporations to be seen as socially responsible, a further meaning or myth may be activated from the photograph going by Barthes' mythological analysis. The photograph of a new school building within a community displayed on the front page of a CSR report or the annual report of a multinational company may connote a second order signifier, signifying that the multinational company is involved in community development or could be said to be socially responsible.

Semiotics is often used as a form of textual analysis. Text here could be in the form of words, images, gestures or sounds, recorded in a particular medium of communication which will be independent of both the sender and the receiver; the message could be in writing, audio or video recording or an image (Chandler 2007). Semioticians believe that an analogy can be drawn between languages and signs. In other words, signs in whatever form (gestures, sounds, pictures or television films) are like languages or texts that can be read like the written word, while the users of such texts are referred to as readers (Crystal 1987). Reading a text is an active way of decoding the messages in the text by the reader. In the same way, the reader of a sign can decode the signification of that sign within the repertoire offered by the sign (Fiske 1987).

Semiotics as a social science emphasizes the fact that social practices are expressed like languages. Hence, as languages are a structured system of symbolic representation developed out of culture, the meaning we give to any social practice is also developed out of our cultures and therefore has symbolic cultural meaning and values (Kristeva 1973). Billington (1991) asserted that all forms of social practice have the potential to mean something with the meaning finding its route from the codes used within a particular cultural environment. For example, in Eastern culture the refusal of a woman to wear the veil could signify refusal of Islamic laws and as such she stands the risk of being prosecuted under Islamic law, whereas in Western culture whether a woman wears the veil or not is a matter of choice and may either signify nothing or in the present times, if she is from an Eastern background, may signify fundamentalism. In other words, the codes used in the sign systems of different cultural settings express and support the social organization of those cultures. To this end the meaning we read to a sign cannot be independent of the ideological and political situation in existence (Billington 1991).

Accordingly, Saussure argued that for signs to be useful as a tool of communication, the sign system will have cultural meaning and values incorporated in it, that is, the value of a sign is culture-specific since it is developed out of culture. Therefore, the values of our culture are incorporated into the signs we use. In other words, the meaning given to a particular sign is a function of the reader's cultural knowledge and experience of the system within which the sign developed (Saussure 1983, Chandler 2007). Consequently, Saussure argued that signs can only give signification where they enjoy relational values. That is, the value attached to a sign is as a result of its relationship to other similar values and the fact that one event follows after another, otherwise signification would not exist (Berger 2005). Saussure refers to these relational values as syntagmatic and paradigmatic relations as we have them in the text of languages where one word would have to come after another for us to make a meaningful sound or statement.

Criticisms of Semiotics Theory

One of the popular criticisms of semiotics as a study of signs is that, as it concentrated mainly on the generation of meanings from signs, it totally ignored the quality of such signs (Berger 2005). Furthermore, it ignored the institutional frameworks, and the social, economic and the political context within which the sign was produced (Chandler 2007). It is only concerned with 'how' the sign generates meanings rather than answer the question: 'why' produce the sign in the first instance? (Slater 1997, p. 141). Accordingly, the structuralist semioticians are criticized for the way texts are related to their own structures. Buxton (1990) argued that text ought to be related to other things outside its own structures, while Chandler (2007) argued that since structures are not the causes of producing the sign, semioticians should not only be concerned with structural signification but also why signs are socially produced, while maintaining that the ontological arbitrariness between the signifier and the signified in the structural context may not apply in the social or political context. Furthermore, work on semiotics has centred on establishing its scope and fundamentals. Chomsky (1968) criticized the fundamental assumption of semiotics that all social practices are like written texts capable of being read and interpreted; while commenting on the work of Lévi-Strauss on the kinship systems, he argued that nothing was documented to show any resemblance to language in the study. Although Saussure's semiology is accepted as the starting point, both the Saussure and Peirce models have received criticism and have undergone various developmental stages (Jakobson 1960, Lévi-Strauss 1972, Barthes 1975, Greimas 1983).

Notwithstanding the criticism, semiotics has been applied to empirical studies by scholars in various fields basically testing the semiotic principles. However, while the early semioticians (Saussure 1983, Peirce 1931–58, Propp 1968, Barthes 1967) were more concerned with seeking deep structures beneath the surface of a phenomenon, modern semioticians (Greimas and Courtés 1982, Cooper and Puxty 1994, Macintosh and Baker 2002, Davison 2007, 2011, Crowther 2002, Yusoff and Lehman 2009) are more concerned with the use of signs to shed more light on specific social phenomenon (Chandler 2007).

Chandler (2007), emphasizing the importance of semiotics, asserted that semiotics is very useful if the task is to look beyond the content of the text. He pointed out that semiotics reveals the role of humans in the construction of reality and the fact that meaning is not 'transmitted' to humans through books, computers or media, but that humans are actively involved in the creation of meaning through a complex interplay of codes and conventions. He remarked that 'becoming aware of such codes is both inherently fascinating and intellectually empowering' (Chandler 2007, p. 11). He argued further that the study of signs helps to define reality as it is represented, since reality as presented in the social world may not be what it appears to be; accordingly, a particular representation may symbolically stand for something else. This echoes Belkaoui's (2004) argument, in his book on accounting theory, that a statement believed to be true or false should still be proven as true or false before it is accepted as the truth or as false. Similarly, Eco (1976) argued that to establish reality, one must be able to distinguish whether the sign is actually telling the truth or a lie about the phenomena, since anything that can be used to communicate the truth can also be used to communicate lies.

However, while semiotics as a method of analysis is well established in France and Italy, the drive for its use has only just begun in the UK and other countries (Berger 2005). For instance, its use in the UK may be traced to the work of the Centre for Contemporary Cultural Studies (CCCS) at the University of Birmingham between 1969 and 1979 (Chandler 2007). Similarly, semiotic principles and techniques have been scantly applied to management and social research generally; nevertheless, its use is gradually gaining ground. Although its application in management research has largely concentrated on marketing and corporate communication studies (Burgh-Woodman and Brace-Govan 2008, Corea 2005, Kameda 2005, Otubanjo and Melewar 2007), its use in management research is fast growing as studies on organizational behaviour (Hancock 2006), accountability and management research (Bell et al. 2002, Cooper et al. 2001, Fiol 1989,

Lindblom and Ruland 1997, Joutsenvirta and Usitalo 2010), accounting research studies (Cooper and Puxty 1994, Macintosh and Baker 2002, McGoun et al. 2007, Davison 2007, 2011) and in fact corporate social and environmental reporting studies (Crowther 2002, Yusoff and Lehman 2009) have all begun a skeletal adoption of its use.

GREIMAS SEMIOTICS

Greimas versus Barthesian Semiotics

As an emerging research technique, semiotics has developed into different strands depending on the sort of sign system being studied (Chandler 2007), while different schools of thought have also emerged (Propp 1968, Jakobson 1960, Greimas 1983, Lévi-Strauss 1972, Barthes 1975). However, these schools of thought are broadly grouped into the paradigmatic and the syntagmatic techniques, with the sign system being the distinguishing feature. Consequently, semioticians and those adopting semiotics as a technique of analysis have often analysed text according to the structural relationship inherent in the text using either syntagmatic or paradigmatic approaches.

A sign enjoys syntagmatic relations where signification occurs as a result of the sequence of events that made up the narrative or story, while in paradigmatic relations signification occurs as a result of the association of the sign with other signs within the narrative. Therefore, the Saussure model, discussed earlier, may be said to be paradigmatic in nature while the Peirce model is syntagmatic in nature. While the Saussure model emphasizes the natural language (that is, words) as the sign system, the Peirce model emphasizes the sequence of events in the narrative or groups of narratives as the sign system (Fiol 1989, Hawkes 2004).

Semioticians such as Lévi-Strauss (1972) and Barthes (1975) who are more concerned about the latent structure of the text rather than what happened in the text follows the paradigmatic schools of thought (Berger 2005). While semioticians such as Propp (1968) and Greimas (1983), who believe that the true meaning of a claim in a narrative can only be uncovered by identifying the pattern in which the components constituting the story are combined or structured employs the syntagmatic method of analysis. A general review of management and social research literature revealed that management and social researchers, most often, employed either the Greimas semiotics (Floch 1988, Fiol 1989, Sulkunen and Törrönen 1997, Joutsenvirta and Usitalo 2010) or the Barthes semiotics (Bell et al. 2002, Davison 2007, 2011). Accordingly, semioticians adopting the paradigmatic method are commonly referred to as the Barthesian semioticians, while those adopting the syntagmatic approach are commonly referred to as the Greimas semioticians. The Barthesian semioticians are more interested in the 'code through which the narrator's and the reader's presence can be detected within the narrative itself' (Barthes and Duisit 1975, p. 260) rather than the narrator's actions or motives or the effect the actions would have on the reader. Greimasian semioticians on the other hand defined signification as when the reader is able to uncover the truth inherent in the narrative by analysing the actions of the narrator using logical, temporal and semantic criteria (Greimas 1983). Hence Greimasian semioticians believe that the actions or motives of the subject in the narrative are more important than the words used in describing the actions. Consequently,

Greimas semiotic analysis is based on the 'doings' of the words in the texts rather than the meaning; hence the words are seen as 'actants' helping to describe the actions of the narrator (Hébert 2011).

It is instructive to note, that whatever the approach, the interrelationship between the author, the reader and the message itself forms the basis of all semiotic analysis. However, the question of whether the Greimas semiotics is superior over the Barthesian semiotics or vice versa is an empirical question that should best be answered through empirical analysis of both techniques. Therefore, since this is beyond the scope of this chapter, we focus our discussion on why the Greimas semiotics is more suitable in the development of the CSRR-quality framework. Since our focus is to develop a framework for measuring the content and the quality of CSRR, our interest is on the motive and actions of the narrator. This appears contrary to the views of the Barthes Semioticians; Barthes and Duisit (1975) argued that, once written, the author of the message as well as the motive of writing has no relevance in the interpretation of the message. Hence, the Barthesian semiotics is considered unsuitable for our purpose. Further justification for Greimas semiotics is inherent in our objective, which is to unravel the quality of CSRR and the truth inherent in the narratives. Syntagmatic analysis is particularly suitable for this purpose, because the disclosures are recorded corporate messages narrated in the form of folktales. They consist of stories that could be re-ordered in order to achieve a recurring structure, thereby reflecting the underlying values of the company and would be best interpreted as a whole (Propp 1968, Eco 1994).

Against this background therefore, since CSRR consists of stories narrated in the form of folktales about the involvement of the corporation with their community of operations, the Greimas semiotics analysis is considered the most suitable. This is because our objective, as previously discussed, is to develop a framework that could be used to establish the reliability and by extension the quality of the claims made by organizations (the narrator) about their social responsibility and community involvement activities. In other words, we are more interested in what actually happened in the story, which is consistent with the Greimas semiotics. This, however, is contrary to the objectives of the Barthesian semioticians who adopt a paradigmatic method of analysis. The Barthesian semioticians emphasize the functions of the words and their relationship to other words used in the narrative to form signification (Barthes and Duisit 1975). Greimas semiotics, on the other hand, is concerned with identifying the events (actions) within the narratives and how one event relates to another to form signification. Texts are analysed as a sequence of events forming a narrative thus revealing the reality or what actually happened in the story (Berger 2005).

Greimas CSRR-Quality Semiotic Framework

To develop our framework, we employed the Greimasian narrative semiotic method[6] (Greimas 1983, Greimas and Courtés 1982). The Greimasian narrative semiotic identifies the structural pattern in narratives and aims to clarify the necessary condition producing values through which reality may be perceived (Sulkunen and Törrönen 1997). The method looks beyond the sign itself into the system of signification in order to uncover the truth or falseness of the sign. A narrative, as defined by Propp (1968), is a 'set of interlocking signs whose meanings are determined by underlying rules that regulate how different units of text may be combined' (Propp 1968, cited in Fiol 1989, p. 279). Narratives take the form of a sequence of events, actions or experiences with different parts all put together as a meaningful whole (Feldman et al. 2004) and connected to a central purpose (Gilbert 2002), thus reflecting the underlying values of the narrator (Propp 1968, Eco 1994). Accordingly, narratives usually consist of a subject (the narrator or author), the object (the act or story being narrated) and the subject's competence/performance (ability to do/the act of doing) (Hébert 2011).

The narrative semiotics method is particularly suitable for CSRR research because CSRR are recorded corporate messages narrated in the form of folktales/stories in annual reports. The reports give specific details of the company's activities within its community of operation with the objective of reflecting the underlying values of a good corporate citizen to the readership of the reports. Therefore, the management (of corporations) is the 'subject' or 'author', the contents of CSRR is the 'object' or 'message', while the audience consists of investors, analysts and other users of CSR reports, who from time to time may need to read the content of CSRR to help inform their decision-making.

The Canonical Narrative Schema

In narrative semiotics, narratives are analysed as a series of schemas in which the semiotic act or story may be structured into components (Hébert 2011). The five components identified by the Greimasian canonical narrative schema are:

1. The action/idea – that is, the act itself
2. Competence – what is required to achieve the act, described in semiotics as 'wanting-to-do' or 'knowing-how-to-do'
3. Performance – the actualization of the action, that is, 'having-to-do' and 'being-able-to-do'
4. Manipulation – the compelling force, described in semiotics as 'causing-to-do'
5. Sanction or reward – that is, evaluation of performance for its quality.

This may be illustrated diagrammatically as shown in Figure 14.5.
Although in a typical analysis not all these components are used, the components could

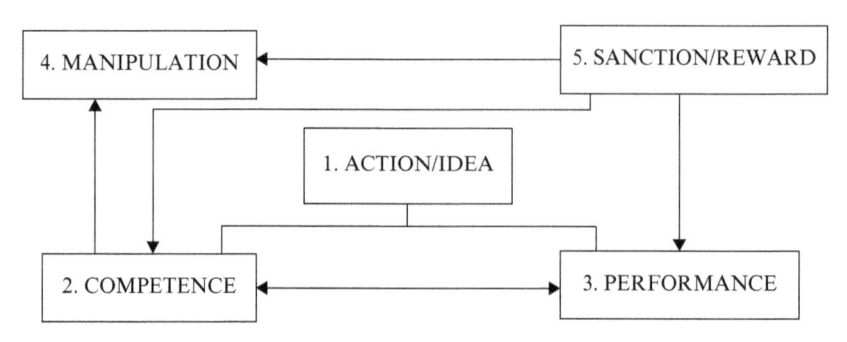

Source: Hébert (2011, p. 93).

Figure 14.5 The canonical narrative schema

at least provide the basis for a typology of discourse in a particular narrative analysis, depending on the trajectory of the texts and on what component is most emphasized in the narrative to be analysed (Courtés 1991, cited in Hébert 2011), or on what the researcher is interested in investigating. Moreover, the existence of one component ultimately leads to the logical presence of the other (Floch 1988). This confirms the fact that the structure of narratives is syntagmatic and is both temporal and spatial.

For instance, the 'idea' of getting involved in community development will usually be preceded by the 'manipulation' component – 'causing-to-do', that is, the corporation must have been compelled or motivated by something, say community need or the need to legitimize its operation, before deciding to get involved (i.e. 'competence' or 'wanting-to-do') in community development (i.e. 'performance'). In other words, the 'competence' and 'performance' components follow simultaneously, thus indicating that two components may be implicit in one. Hébert (2011) argued that the relationship between 'competence' and 'performance' is that of 'reciprocal presupposition', in which case 'competence' will necessarily mean 'performance' and whenever there is 'performance' this would have been preceded by 'competence' (Hébert 2011, p. 96). Furthermore, the 'performance' component is ultimately followed by the 'sanction' component, which is an evaluative component.

The Framework

To develop our framework, we employed a two-phased narrative analysis technique. The first phase involves the identification of the modality of the narratives based on the narrative schema discussed above. The second phase identify the cognitive perspective (Maddox 1989), developed into 'veridictory' positions using the semiotic square of 'veridiction' in order to determine the ontological status. However, before proceeding into the description of each process, it is imperative to discuss the creation of modality. The modality refers to the structure evaluating the state of affairs of the subject (Sulkunen and Törrönen 1997): that is, the 'being' and 'doing' of the subject of the narratives (Fiol 1989) and whether or not reality may be constructed.

Modality may be viewed from two perspectives: the morphological and the semantic. The morphological perspective views modality from the grammatical angle, that is, the interconnectivity and interdependence of the words used in the narrative (Sulkunen and Törrönen 1997), while the semantic approach views modality from the perspective of the content of the narrative and their signified (Hébert 2011). The semantic approach is considered relevant to our framework since the values imputed to a phenomenon by the components of the narrative schema enumerated above do not make up the meaning of the action itself, nor do the grammatical relationships of words reveal the reality of the phenomenon (Sulkunen and Törrönen 1997, Hébert 2011). Conversely, in the semantic plane of texts, values are imputed when the 'dialectics', that is, the tensions between the processes and the actors involved in them along with the logical sequencing of the content of the narratives, are subjected to modal evaluation known in semiotics as 'dialogics'. Modal evaluation is to determine whether the semiotic act can be said to be true or false (known as 'veridictory status') or whether the semiotic act can be situated in one of the three worlds of the semantic universe, that is: the actual world ('what is'), the counterfactual world ('what is not') or the possible world ('what could be'). This is known in semiotics as the ontological status, that is, relating to existence or ontology, hence the ontological status may be: real, unreal or possible/doubtful (Hébert 2011).

Consequently, to understand social reality, a semantic unit is usually formulated as a logical proposition and then evaluated on its veridictory and ontological status (Hébert 2011). For instance, the proposition (the sky is blue), may be assigned a true or false value (the veridictory status) which will then determine the world in which it should be situated (i.e. actual, counterfactual or the possible world). So if the proposition – 'the sky is blue' – is say true, then it is situated in the actual world and assigned an ontological status of 'real'. Conversely, if it is false or a combination of true and false, it might be situated in the counterfactual or the possible world. Furthermore, the components of the canonical narrative schema enumerated above suggested that to perform a semiotic act, an actor or narrator is not only motivated by something, but should also exhibit the desire and willingness to perform the act. In addition, the competence to perform and actual performance of the act must be evident before signification can occur. This may require the construction of several related modal structures and consequently different propositions with different degrees of certainty and, therefore, may pose some challenges in determining the semantic universe and hence the ontological status.

This is so, particularly for the semiotic of CSRR, because as previously discussed, the values we input to a sign could be influenced by our knowledge and experience of the system within which the sign developed as well as the ideological and political situation in existence (Kristeva 1973, Billington 1991). For example, as with CSRR, some studies (Toms 2002, Hasseldine et al. 2005, Yekini and Jallow 2012) have provided evidence that the production of the reports is reputation-management motivated. This knowledge, if not well guided, may influence the values we assign to the semiotic acts in the CSRR.

To solve this problem, Greimasian semioticians such as Floch (1988), Fiol (1989) and Sulkunen and Törrönen (1997) argued that the signification process should be generative in nature. First, it should begin with the formation of propositional discourse which develops from 'simple deep' semio-narrative structures, that is, exhibiting abstract articulation with little condition for signification and then progress to the formation of discourses developed from 'rich and complex discursive structures' (Sulkunen and Törrönen 1997, p. 51) which enriches signification by manifesting a distinct expression of reality.

Therefore, for the semiotic of CSRR, the generative process of signification requires a logical organization of modal structures such that the juxtaposition of a set of propositions should qualify them to be situated in the same semantic universe so as to generate signification. For instance, the semio-narrative structure may include simple utterances of 'being', that is, the corporation has knowledge of a specific need within their community of operation and therefore is motivated to a further utterance of 'doing', which could be supplying or meeting the specific need. These thus show a transformation from the state of 'being' to the state of 'doing' and thus form a rich and complex discursive structure (Sulkunen and Törrönen 1997).

Nevertheless, in order to achieve a logical and comprehensive taxonomy of discourses that would reveal the underlying value of corporations and thus allow for the construction of reality, we argue that a real act of corporate citizenship should not be a one-off event but should take into consideration future development. Hence the content of such narrative reports should not only be outward-looking, but also forward-looking (Crowther 2002). Forward-looking information, it has been argued, is capable of producing value-relevance information to the audience (Beretta and Bozzolan 2008). Consequently, in formulating our propositions, we put into perspective both the current and future semiotic act of social responsibility and community involvement, while taking into consideration how these might be articulated in the narratives. The propositions form the basis of the modal structure upon which narrative contents will be analysed. They describe the necessity or possibility of each phenomenon. Therefore, following from the Preston (1975) and Preston and Post (1975 [2012]) framework and the Wood and Jones (1995) model discussed earlier, the following propositions are typical examples that could be considered in analysing the text of CSRR using the Greimasian narrative semiotics method:

Proposition 1a
The written report on CSR shows evidence of corporations' concern or awareness of specific needs or issues identified within their community of operation – Manipulation component.

Proposition 1b
The written report on CSR shows evidence of the corporations meeting the specific needs of the community within their community of operation – Competence and Performance component.

Proposition 2a
The written report identifies future development targets – Manipulation component.

Proposition 2b
The written report considers future targets as a reflection of further CSR performance along with past performance – Competence components which will ultimately lead to future Performance.

It follows therefore that proposition (1b) follows logically from proposition (1a) and proposition (2b) follows logically from proposition (2a), essentially conceptualizing the components of the narrative schema discussed earlier: Manipulation or motivation (causing-to-do); Competence (wanting-to-do or knowing-how-to-do); and Performance (having-to-do or being-able-to-do). Therefore, for signification to occur proposition (1a) must be evident along with (1b) or at least implicit in one another. In addition, proposition (2a) must be evident along with (2b) or at least implicit in one another. Hence for the purpose of ontological classification the propositions are paired up such that the validity of each set of propositions is investigated under various world conditions by applying them to the contents of the CSR reports.

To apply the above propositions, we propose the following steps:

Phase 1
The first phase involved three steps:

- Step 1: This step is to identify the semiotic act or acts – how many stories are told in each report? Each topic represents a semiotic act of social responsibility, thus a unit of analysis.

- Step 2: This is to uncover the structural pattern of the narratives, that is, to identify the modality of each semiotic of CSR as discussed earlier.
- Step 3: This step is to examine each topic or unit of analysis by applying the four propositions above in order to determine the veridictory characteristics of each story, which is denoted by the meta-terms (being, not-being, seeming, not-seeming – see discussions in phase 2 and Figure 14.6 below). This is similar to examining whether or not a hypothesis was supported in a quantitative experiment.

Phase 2

This is the 'sanction' phase. In this phase, the outcome of step 3 above is subjected to further evaluation in order to examine the truth or falseness of the performance using the 'semiotic square of veridiction', also called the Veridictory Square. It is a type of semiotic square built on the oppositions 'being' and 'not-being' or 'seeming' and 'not-seeming' and was developed by Greimas and Courtés (1982). The Veridictory Square is used to examine the extent of truth/falseness in any semiotic act where truth or falseness is fundamental to the whole analysis (Hébert 2011).

Consequently, since quality lies in the truth and authenticity of the performance reported, we considered the use of the semiotic square of veridiction as very relevant to this framework. The square will be adopted in the construction of our framework in order to determine the 'sanction' components referred to in the semiotic schema above. It will be used in evaluating the reality, hence the reliability and quality of performance as claimed by the performing subject based on the characteristics of the features observed in the story from step 3 above. Basically, the main elements of the Veridictory Square are (Hébert 2011, pp. 51–52):

- The 'subject' – the narrator or author shown as 'S' on the square
- The 'object' – the act or performance shown as 'O' on the square
- The 'characteristics' observed in the object shown as 'C' on the square
- The Veridictory status, which could be true, false, illusory or secret depending on the combination of the meta-terms ('being', 'not-being', 'seeming' or 'not-seeming') assigned to it in Phase 1 (step 3), that is:
  - True ('being' + 'seeming'),
  - False ('not-being' + 'not-seeming'),
  - Illusory ('not-being' + 'seeming'), and
  - Secret ('being' + 'not-seeming').

This is illustrated diagrammatically in Figure 14.6.

In other words, the story narrated by subject S in time T is assessed on the basis of the propositions and awarded a sanction or reward by assigning the Veridictory status – true, false, illusory or secret – depending on the combination of the meta-terms (being, not-being, seeming or not-seeming) assigned to it. See Table 14.1 for a fuller description of the process.

In Table 14.1, we present an overview of the framework, illustrating how the components of the narrative schema Manipulation, Competence and Performance are conceptualized in the four propositions thus serving as a deep-structure schema. Similarly, the Sanction component is conceptualized in the Veridictory/Ontological evaluation.

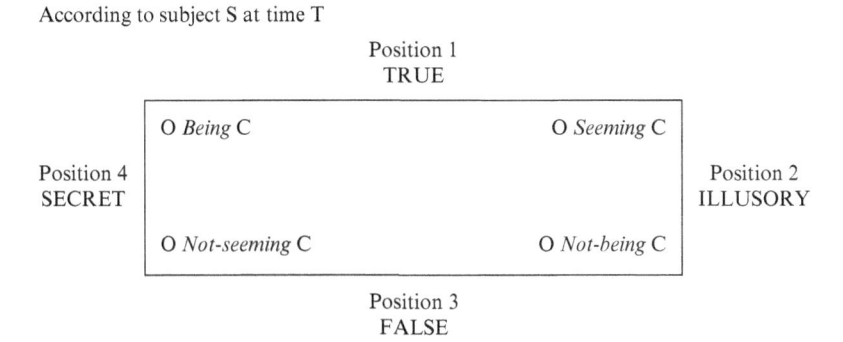

The applicability of semiotics to CSR communication research 259

According to subject S at time T

```
                         Position 1
                           TRUE
    ┌─────────────────────────────────────────────┐
    │  O Being C                      O Seeming C │
Position 4                                      Position 2
 SECRET                                          ILLUSORY
    │  O Not-seeming C            O Not-being C   │
    └─────────────────────────────────────────────┘
                         Position 3
                           FALSE
```

Source: Hébert (2011, p. 54).

Figure 14.6 The semiotic square of veridiction

Table 14.1 An overview of the Greimas CSRR-quality semiotic framework

Time	Unit of analysis	Procedure	Propositions	Veridictory status	Ontological status
T1	Specific aspect of CSR reports: e.g. health and safety, HR, community involvement etc.	Read each topic/unit of analysis and check for evidence of P1a–P2b	P1a: The written report on CSR shows evidence of corporations' concern or awareness of specific needs or issues identified within their community of operation.	Seeming/Being ⎫ ⎬ True ⎭	⎫ ⎪ ⎪ ⎬ Real/Certainty ⎪ ⎪ ⎭
			P1b: The written report on CSR shows evidence of the corporations meeting the specific needs of the community within their community of operation.	Being	
			P2a: The written report identifies future targets.	Seeming/Being ⎫ ⎬ True ⎭	
			P2b: The written report considers future targets as a reflection of further CSR performance along with past performance.	Being	

Therefore, to construct reality, we seek to find evidence of the juxtaposition of both current CSR performance and future performance targets in a particular story. It follows that a particular CSRR should necessarily embrace all four propositions for signification to occur. In view of this, the analysis is designed to find a distinct spatial description that allows for the coexistence of two pairs of complementary meta-terms[7] – 'being'/'seeming' or 'seeming'/'being' for the first set of propositions (1a and 1b) and 'being'/'seeming' or 'seeming'/'being' for the second set of propositions (2a and 2b) – such that the two pairs are awarded True Veridictory status as depicted in Table 14.1. This allows both pairs to be placed in the same semantic universe and thus awarded a common ontological status. Therefore, a story with veridictory status as depicted in Table 14.1 can be said to be a true reflection of CSR performance and thus be awarded an ontological status of 'real'.

However, a change in time, say T1 to T2, may bring about a change in the position depicted in Table 14.1. For instance, in a scenario where a change in time from T1 to T2 leads to proposition (P2a) in Table 14.1 being assigned a 'seeming' characteristic and (P2b) being assigned 'not-being', the position for this pair of propositions will move on the Veridictory Square to position 2 (Illusory). In this case, the ontological status of such a semiotic act will be doubtful as far as CSR performance signification is concerned, because if the first set of propositions is true and the second set is a lie (i.e. illusion), then it is not clear if this is a real act of CSR or just a one-off event. For instance, a community involvement story considered as a semiotic act may only acquire the full ontological status of 'real' (reality/certainty) when the Veridictory status of True is assigned to both pairs of propositions consistently through time.

SUMMARY AND CONCLUSION

In this chapter, we argue that reality might better be construed when the texts of CSRR are subjected to semiotic analysis. Therefore, given the folktale nature of the reports, we employ the Greimasian canonical narrative schema in developing a framework, while the semiotic square of veridiction is used as an evaluative tool in determining the ontological status of each semiotic act. We develop propositional discourses following ideologies from the works of Preston and Post (1975 [2012]), Preston (1975) and Wood and Jones (1995).

We distinguished between the Barthesian and Greimasian semioticians and clearly explained our standpoint and why we took a position for the Greimas semiotics. The Barthes semiotics employs a purely paradigmatic approach while the Greimas semiotics employs the syntagmatic approach. The paradigmatic approach considers the system of signification, while the syntagmatic approach considers the process of signification. Nonetheless, though our analysis centres on the syntagmatic approach to semiotic analysis we embrace a bit of the paradigmatic paradigm in our analysis. The paradigmatic aspect of our analysis can be seen in the use of the opposing meta-terms 'being', 'not-being' and 'seeming', 'not-seeming' which determines the Veridictory status assigned to each pair of propositions when applied to the semiotic acts. The syntagmatic aspect of the analysis is the complete arrangement of all components into propositional combination, the collective presence of which constitutes signification. We ensured objectivity in our analysis by ignoring the institutional frameworks, and the social, economic and/or the political context within which the CSRR might have been produced and focusing on how the CSRR as a semiotic sign can generate meanings from the perspective of the audience.

In our two-phase model, we address the ways in which each CSR activity reported can be examined based on evidence obtained from the organization's CSR reports in relation to: the organization's awareness of and concern for a need/an issue within their community of operation; the corporate action to actually meet the needs/issues identified; a demonstration of planned efforts for the future; and identifying links between past activities, present actions and future plans. We then assign values (veridictory status) to each evidence obtained to enable us to determine the semiotic reality of the narratives. The strength of the value assigned, whether true, false, illusory or secret, based on the meta-terms 'being', 'not-being' and 'seeming', 'not-seeming', determines our position.

For the purpose of quantitative research analysis such as regression and/or trend analysis, researchers can assign percentage values or scores to the veridictory status (true, false, illusory or secret) described above. This will produce a unique quality measure for measuring the quality of the content of CSRR. However, in addition to being a useful tool of analysis and measurement of quality, the framework is capable of guiding corporations in their CSR activities and reporting. It could also be useful to other stakeholders, particularly advocates and beneficiaries of CSR activities, such as the local community, to assess the reliability of corporations' claims to being socially responsible. The percentage value/scores can be used to facilitate trend analysis of the organization's CSR performance. Such analysis can be useful to both the organization and its stakeholders. While the former can use it to monitor its progress in CSR activities, the latter will be able to use it to make important economic and social decisions.

NOTES

1. The term semiotics is more widespread in English-speaking countries, while semiology is preferred by the French linguists. However, in this chapter the term semiotics has been used.
2. The functional use of language developed from the concept of functional fixation. This concept according to Jain (1973) states that once a person relates a meaning to a particular phenomenon or event through past experience, this meaning becomes fixed in his head and is related to subsequent phenomena or events irrespective of alternative meanings or causes of that event.
3. Also, known as the Linguistic Relativity Hypothesis. The hypothesis historically developed through the works and propositions of Edward Sapir (1884–1939) and Benjamin Lee Whorf (1897–1941). Although most of these works were not published, they later became the source of controversial debate among anthropologists, psychologists and linguists (Gumperz and Levinson 1996).
4. While Saussure refers to it as Semiology, Peirce refers to it as Semiotics.
5. Semiotics is associated with the structuralist philosophical standpoint. Structuralism is a 20th century philosophical school of thought and although it has its roots in interpretivism, while human beings are the central focus of the interpretivist, the structuralist decentres humans and rather focuses on the structures of which humans are seen as elements (Bryman 2008).
6. See the previous section for discussions on other schools of thought on semiotic analysis.
7. The complementarities of the 'being' and 'seeming' meta-terms can be explained from the point of view of the relational values they possess, for instance for a 'being' to exist, there must be a 'seeming' in operation, either at the beginning, midway or at the end, which may or may not match its 'being', in other words, according to Hébert (2011), '*being* is only an abstract reconstruction derived from *seeming*, which is the only accessible reality' (Hébert 2011, pp. 51–52).

REFERENCES

Adams, C.A. (2004), 'The ethical, social and environmental reporting-performance portrayal gap', *Accounting, Auditing & Accountability Journal*, **17** (5), 731–757.
Aras, G. and D. Crowther (2009), 'Corporate sustainability reporting: a study in disingenuity?', *Journal of Business Ethics*, **87** (S1), 279–288.
Barthes, Roland (1967), *Elements of Semiology*, trans. Annete Lavers and Colin Smith, London: Jonathan Cape.

Barthes, Roland (1972), *Mythologies*, trans. Annete Lavers, London: Jonathan Cape.
Barthes, Roland (1975), *The Pleasure of the Text*, trans. Richard Miller, New York: Hill and Wang.
Barthes, R. and L. Duisit (1975), 'An introduction to the structural analysis of narrative', *New Literary History*, **6** (2), 237–272.
Baudrillard, Jean (1988), *Selected Writings*, ed. Mark Poster, Cambridge: Polity Press.
Beattie, V., B. McInnes and S. Fearnley (2004), 'A methodology for analysing and evaluating narratives in annual reports: a comprehensive descriptive profile and metrics for disclosure quality attributes', *Accounting Forum*, **28** (3), 205–236.
Bebbington, J., C. Larrinaga-González and J.M. Moneva-Abadía (2008), 'Corporate social reporting and reputation risk management', *Accounting, Auditing & Accountability Journal*, **21** (3), 337–361.
Belkaoui, A. (1978), 'Linguistic relativity in accounting', *Accounting, Organizations & Society*, **3** (2), 97–104.
Belkaoui, Ahmed (2004), *Accounting Theory*, 5th ed., Cornwall, UK: Thomson Learning.
Bell, E., S. Taylor and R. Thorpe (2002), 'Organizational differentiation through badging: investors in people and the value of the sign', *Journal of Management Studies*, **39** (8), 1071–1085.
Beretta, S. and S. Bozzolan (2004), 'A framework for the analysis of firm risk communication', *The International Journal of Accounting*, **39** (3), 265–288.
Beretta, S. and S. Bozzolan (2008), 'Quality versus quantity: the case of forward-looking disclosure', *Journal of Accounting, Auditing & Finance*, **23** (3), 333–375.
Berger, Arthur Asa (2005), *Media Analysis Techniques*, 3rd ed., Thousand Oak, London: Sage, pp. 3–36.
Billington, Rosamund (1991), *Culture and Society: A Sociology of Culture*, London: Macmillan Education.
Botosan, C.A. (2004), 'Discussion of a framework for the analysis of firm risk communication', *The International Journal of Accounting*, **39** (3), 289–295.
Bryman, A. (2008), *Social Research Methods* (3rd ed.), New York: Oxford University Press. ISBN: 9780199202959.
Burgh-Woodman, H. De and J. Brace-Govan (2008), 'Jargon as imagining: Barthes' semiotics and excavating subcultural communication', *Qualitative Market Research: An International Journal*, **11** (1), 89–106.
Burritt, R.L. and S. Schaltegger (2010), 'Sustainability accounting and reporting: fad or trend?', *Accounting, Auditing & Accountability Journal*, **23** (7), 829–846.
Buxton, David (1990), *From 'The Avengers' to 'Miami Vice': Form and Ideology in Television Series*, Manchester: Manchester University Press.
Chandler, Daniel (2007), *Semiotics: The Basics*, London: Routledge.
Cho, C.H., R.W. Roberts and D.M. Patten (2010), 'The language of US corporate environmental disclosure', *Accounting, Organisations & Society*, **35** (4), 431–443.
Chomsky, Noam (1968), *Language and Mind*, New York: Harcourt, Brace and World.
Cooper, C. and A. Puxty (1994), 'Reading accounting writing', *Accounting, Organizations & Society*, **19** (2), 127–146.
Cooper, M., O. Dimitrov and P.R. Rau (2001), 'A rose.com by any other name', *The Journal of Finance*, **56** (6), 2371–2388.
Cooper, S.M. and D. Owen (2007), 'Corporate social reporting and stakeholder accountability: the missing link', *Accounting, Organizations & Society*, **32** (7–8), 649–667.
Corea, S. (2005), 'Refocusing systems analysis of organizations through a semiotic lens: interpretive framework and method', *Systemic Practice and Action Research*, **18** (4), 339–364.
Crowther, David (2002), *A Social Critique of Corporate Reporting: A Semiotic Analysis of Corporate Financial and Environmental Reporting*, Adlershot, England: Ashgate Publishing.
Crystal, David (1987), *The Cambridge Encyclopaedia of Language*, Cambridge: Cambridge University Press.
Davison, J. (2007), 'Photographs and accountability: cracking the codes of an NGO', *Accounting, Auditing & Accountability Journal*, **20** (1), 133–158.
Davison, J. (2011), 'Barthesian perspectives on accounting communication and visual images of professional accountancy', *Accounting, Auditing & Accountability Journal*, **24** (2), 250–283.
De Villiers, C. and C.J. van Staden (2010), 'Shareholders' requirements for corporate environmental disclosures: a cross-country comparison', *British Accounting Review*, **42** (4), 227–240.
Eco, Umberto (1976), *A Theory of Semiotics*, Bloomington, IN: University of Indiana Press.
Eco, Umberto (1994), *Apocalypse Postponed*, ed. by Robert Lumley, London, BFI/Bloomington: Indiana University Press.
Feldman, M.S., K. Sköldberg, R.N. Brown and D. Horner (2004), 'Making sense of stories: a rhetorical approach to narrative analysis', *Journal of Public Administration Research and Theory*, **14** (2), 147–170.
Fiol, C.M. (1989), 'A semiotic analysis of corporate language: organizational boundaries and joint venturing', *Administrative Science Quarterly*, New York University, **34** (2), 277–303.
Fiske, John (1987), *Television Culture*, London: Routledge, pp. 1–5.
Floch, J.-M. (1988), 'The contribution of structural semiotics to the design of a hypermarket', *International Journal of Research in Marketing*, **4**, 233–252.

Freedman, M. and A.J. Stagliano (1992), 'European unification, accounting harmonization, and social disclosures', *The International Journal of Accounting*, **27** (2), 112–122.
Freedman, M. and A.J. Stagliano (1995), 'Disclosure of environmental clean-up costs: the impact of the Superfund Act', *Advances in Public Interest Accounting*, **6**, 163–176.
Freedman, M. and A.J. Stagliano (2008), 'Environmental disclosures: electric utilities and Phase 2 of the Clean Air Act', *Critical Perspectives on Accounting*, **19** (4), 466–486.
Gilbert, K.R. (2002), 'Taking a narrative approach to grief research: finding meaning in stories', *Death Studies, Brunner-Routledge*, **26**, 223–239.
Gray, R., R. Kouhy and S. Lavers (1995), 'Constructing a research database of UK companies', *Accounting, Auditing & Accountability Journal*, **8** (2), 78–101.
Greimas, Algirdas Julius (1983), *Structural Semantics*, Lincoln, NB: University of Nebraska Press.
Greimas, Algirdas Julius (1987), *On Meaning: Selected Writings in Semiotic Theory*, London: Frances Pinter.
Greimas, Algirdas Julius and Joseph Courtés (1982), *Semiotics and Language: An Analytical Dictionary*, Bloomington: Indiana University Press.
Gumperz, John Joseph and Stephen Curtis Levinson (1996), *Rethinking Linguistic Relativity*, Cambridge: Cambridge University Press.
Guthrie, J. and L.D. Parker (1990), 'Corporate social disclosure practice: a comparative international analysis', *Advances in Public Interest Accounting*, **3**, 159–175.
Guthrie, J., R. Petty, K. Yongvanich and F. Ricceri (2004), 'Using content analysis as a research method to inquire into intellectual capital reporting', *Journal of Intellectual Capital*, **5** (2), 282–293.
Hackston, D. and M.J. Milne (1996), 'Some determinants of social and environmental disclosures in New Zealand companies', *Accounting, Auditing & Accountability Journal*, **9** (1), 77–108.
Hancock, P. (2006), 'The spatial and temporal mediation of social change', *Journal of Organizational Change Management*, **19** (5), 619–639.
Hasseldine, J., A.I.I. Salama and J.S.S. Toms (2005), 'Quantity versus quality: the impact of environmental disclosures on the reputations of UK Plcs', *The British Accounting Review*, **37** (2), 231–248.
Hawkes, Terence (2004), *Structuralism and Semiotics*, 2nd ed., New York: Routledge.
Hébert, Louis (2011), *Tools for Text and Image Analysis: An Introduction to Applied Semiotics*, trans. from the French version by Julie Tabler, version 3:2011, accessed 24 August 2011 at http://www.signosemio.com/documents/Louis-Hebert-Tools-for-Texts-and-Images.pdf.
Ho, S.S.M. and K.S. Wong (2001), 'A study of the relationship between corporate governance structures and the extent of voluntary disclosure', *Journal of International Accounting Auditing and Taxation*, **10** (2), 139–156.
Hooks, J. and C.J. van Staden (2011), 'Evaluating environmental disclosures: the relationship between quality and extent measures', *The British Accounting Review*, **43** (3), 200–213.
Jain, T.N. (1973), 'Alternative methods of accounting and decision making: a psycho-linguistic analysis', *Accounting Review*, **48** (1), 95–104.
Jakobson, R. (1942), 'The paleosiberian languages', *American Anthropologist*, **66** (6), 602–620.
Jakobson, Roman (1960), 'Closing Statement: Linguistics and Poetics', in *Style in Language*, ed. Thomas Sebeok, Cambridge, MA: M.I.T. Press, pp. 350–377.
Joutsenvirta, M. and L. Usitalo (2010), 'Cultural competences: an important resource in the industry–NGO dialog', *Journal of Business Ethics*, **91** (3), 379–390.
Kameda, N. (2005), 'A research paradigm for international business communication', *Corporate Communications: An International Journal*, **10** (2), 168–182.
Kristeva, J. (1973), 'The semiotic activity', *Screen*, **14** (1–2), 25–39.
Lévi-Strauss, Claude (1972), *Structural Anthropology*, trans. Claire Jacobson and Brooke Grundfest Schoepf, Harmondsworth: Penguin.
Lindblom, C.K. and R.G. Ruland (1997), 'Functionalist and conflict views of AICPA code of conduct: public interest vs. self interest', *Journal of Business Ethics*, **16** (1997), 573–582.
Lucy, John A. (1992), *Language Diversity and Thought: A Reformulation of the Linguistic Relativity Hypothesis*, Cambridge: Cambridge University Press.
Lucy, J.A. (1997), 'Linguistic relativity', *Annual Review of Anthropology*, **26** (1), 291–312.
Macintosh, N.B. (2003), 'From rationality to hyperreality: paradigm poker', *International Review of Financial Analysis*, **12** (4), 453–465.
Macintosh, N.B. and C.R. Baker (2002), 'A literary theory perspective on accounting: towards heteroglossic accounting reports', *Accounting, Auditing & Accountability Journal*, **15** (2), 184–222.
Macintosh, N.B., T. Shearer, D.B. Thornton and M. Welker (2000), 'Accounting as simulacrum and hyperreality: perspectives on income and capital', *Accounting, Organizations & Society*, **25** (1), 13–50.
Maddox, D. (1989), 'Veridiction, verification, verifactions: reflections on methodology', *New Literary History, Greimassian Semiotics*, **20** (3), 661–677.

McGoun, E.G., M.S. Bettner and M.P. Coyne (2007), 'Pedagogic metaphors and the nature of accounting signification', *Critical Perspectives on Accounting*, **18** (2), 213–230.

Morris, Charles W. (1946), *Signs, Language and Behaviour*, New York: Prentice-Hall.

Otubanjo, B.O. and T.C. Melewar (2007), 'Understanding the meaning of corporate identity: a conceptual and semiological approach', *Corporate Communications: An International Journal*, **12** (4), 414–432.

Peirce, Charles Sanders (1931–58), *Collected Writings*, 8 Vols, eds Charles Hartshorne, Paul Weiss and Arthur W. Burks, Cambridge, MA: Harvard University Press.

Preston, L.E. (1975), 'Corporation and society: the search for a paradigm', *Journal of Economic Literature*, **XIII** (June), 434–453.

Preston, Lee E. and James E. Post (1975), *Private Management and Public Policy: The Principle of Public Responsibilty*, Englewood Cliffs, New Jersey: Prentice Hall, reprinted in Stanford Business Classic Edition (2012), Stanford University Press, CA.

Price, R. and G. Shanks (2005), 'A semiotic information quality framework: development and comparative analysis', *Journal of Information Technology*, **20** (2), 88–102.

Propp, Vladimir I. (1968), *Morphology of the Folktale*, trans. Laurence Scott, 2nd ed., Austin: University of Texas Press.

Saussure, Ferdinand de (1983), *Course in General Linguistics*, trans. Roy Harris, London: Duckworth.

Sebeok, Thomas A. (1977), *A Perfusion of Signs*, Bloomington: Indiana University Press.

Sebeok, Thomas A. (1994), *An Introduction to Semiotics*, London: Pinter [an introduction to Thomas Sebeok].

Slater, D. (1997), *Consumer Culture and Modernity*, Cambridge: Polity Press.

Sulkunen, P. and J. Törrönen (1997), 'The production of values: the concept of modality in textual discourse analysis', *Semiotica*, **113** (1–2), 43–69.

Toms, J.S. (2002), 'Firm resources, quality signals and the determinants of corporate environmental reputation: some UK evidence', *The British Accounting Review*, **34** (3), 257–282.

Walden, W.D. and B.N. Schwartz (1997), 'Environmental disclosures and public policy pressure', *Journal of Accounting and Public Policy*, **16**, 125–154.

Wood, D.J. and R.E. Jones (1995), 'Stakeholder mismatching: a theoretical problem in empirical research on corporate social performance', *The International Journal of Organizational Analysis*, **3** (3), 229–267.

Yekini, K. and K. Jallow (2012), 'Corporate community involvement disclosures in annual report: a measure of corporate community development or a signal of CSR observance?', *Sustainability Accounting, Management and Policy Journal*, **3** (1), 7–32.

Yekini, K., I. Adelopo, P. Andrikopoulos and S. Yekini (2015), 'Impact of board independence on the quality of community disclosures in annual reports', *Accounting Forum*, **39** (4), 249–267.

Yusoff, H. and G. Lehman (2009), 'Corporate environmental reporting through the lens of semiotics', *Asian Review of Accounting*, **17** (3), 226–246.

15. Ethnographic research methods in CSR research: building theory out of people's everyday life with materials, objects, practices, and symbolic constructions

Linne Marie Lauesen

INTRODUCTION

This chapter is about how research in CSR is made using ethnographic methods. First, the background for doing ethnography as a general research method is presented followed by a review of the newer literature in CSR, which uses ethnographic research methods.

DEFINITION OF ETHNOGRAPHIC RESEARCH METHODS

What is ethnography anyway? Is it a methodology, field, or discipline? Many scholars have had this debate with each other, and somehow it still remains difficult to argue that it is only one thing, say, a methodology. In Ellis and Bochner's (1996) terminology, ethnography is 'what ethnographers *do*' (p. 16, italic in original), that is, a research methodology and not a discipline. They argue that it is an 'activity', because what researchers do is to 'inscribe patterns of cultural experience; they give perspective on life' (p. 16). Subsequently they mean the way that ethnographers interact with the research field by taking notes, photographs, collecting materials, describing the world they see, and then writing it up and drawing moral conclusions (p. 16). In short – ethnography is the search of 'meaning' that people devote to everyday life. Already here, it is implied that ethnography is more than just a research method: it also has a purpose – something to look for.

Obviously, not only ethnographers look for the meaning of life; scientists of all perspectives have more or less always been looking for the meaning of life. However, the ways and the means that scientists use for their search differ. Although Ellis and Bochner claim that there is a difference between looking for 'laws' (as natural scientists supposedly do) and looking for 'meaning' (as sociologists and humanists supposedly do) (p. 16), a question arises: is natural scientists' search for and understanding of (new) natural laws not the same as looking for the meaning of life eventually? My answer to this is that every scholar is looking for meaning, but their approaches to this search differ depending on the philosophy of science that they follow.

In the editorial and debates of the first volume of the *Journal of Organizational Ethnography* (2012), editors Matthew Brannan, Mike Rowe, and Frank Worthington argue that the purpose of ethnography is what Van Maanen (2009) suggested, to study and write about 'what it is like to be somebody else' (p. 16). Although this seems like a viable definition, it does not answer the question: what about being one's self? Is ethnography thereby excluding the field of autoethnography in one closed loop? Ellis and Bochner (1996) discussed this issue 16 years earlier, and concluded 'if auto-ethnography doesn't touch a world beyond the self of the writer, then there is no need to worry about its potentially profound impact on one's material existence' (Ellis and Bochner 1996, p. 24). Thus, autoethnography is not the same as self-indulgency, because the self is not free of connection to the world beyond it. See also Chapter 13, 'Analytic autoethnography as a tool to enhance reflection, reflexivity and critical thinking in CSR research' by Fernanda de Paiva Duarte, this volume, about autoethnography.

The editors of the *Journal of Organizational Ethnography* highlight Tony J. Watson's point that researchers should treat 'ethnography as much more than a research method' (Watson 2012, p. 16). By this, Watson suggests that ethnography is a 'genre' of social science writing,

> which draws upon the writer's close observation of and involvement with people in a particular social setting and relates the words spoken and the practices observed or experienced to the overall cultural framework within which they occurred. (Watson 2012, p. 16)

The above – although it indirectly includes autoethnography – distinguishes ethnography quite differently from generally qualitative inquiry, because it points out that in order to name it 'ethnography', the researcher should actually 'be there'. In other words – it equates it with participant observation studies as a main research method (besides interviewing) or 'tool', which can be discussed. How do we see digital ethnography as part of the above definition, if it is a request that the researcher should have 'been there'? Is it not down to the critique that ethnography has received in its early stages of anthropology that researchers' only trustworthiness consisted of their claim: 'I was there', somehow? Patrick Sullivan argues in the volume that certainly,

> publicly documents of organisations, those that outline policy or report on activities, are legitimate ethnographic subjects in themselves as they are an embodiment of the cultural practices of modernity, not simply one of its primary cultural artefacts. (Sullivan 2012, p. 53)

Many ethnographic studies apparently also include textual and visual analyses, and to include this 'third leg' (besides participant observation and interviewing) in an imaginative triangle included in ethnographic research methods, ethnography is 'a way of seeing and knowing', as Dwora Yanow (2012, p. 35) argues in the same volume. She defines ethnography as 'literally people writing' (p. 46) about what they see and come to know. This short definition appeals to multiple ways of doing ethnography, but it also has a shortfall of being specifically imprecise: every scholar writes. But every scholar does not do ethnography.

Thus, it is obvious that a thorough definition of ethnography is still being debated. Thus, a definition can be proposed as a conglomerate of the above, in order to guide this chapter, to be:

> Ethnography is a genre, which includes multiple methodologies aimed at studying the meaning of life and human activity to people grounded in rich data collections over an extended amount of time.

In the next section, the most used research tools will be examined, although it will not claim to be an exhaustive examination of all tools available for ethnography, since these tools are continuously evolving.

SUMMARY OF THE MAIN TOOLS TYPICALLY USED IN ETHNOGRAPHIC RESEARCH METHODS

Participant Observation

Contemporary ethnographic research methods often include participant observation studies, which are further demonstrated in Ilke Oruc's chapter (17, 'Participant observation as the data collection tool and its usage in the CSR researches') in this volume. Shortly, participant observation includes the researcher to be in situ in a social setting over a period of time, where he or she interacts with the people around and takes field notes, perhaps photographs or video films of occurring events, which is used as data for further analysis and 'writing up' (Van Maanen 2009, Watson 2012, Sullivan 2012, Yanow 2012).

Interviewing

Participant observation studies are often combined with interviews with people active in the social setting that the researcher is studying. The point of doing interviews is to get information in a specific area of interest, and most ethnographers use qualitative interviews with interview-guides or open interviews (see also Kvale and Brinkmann 2009, Spradley 1979, Denzin and Lincoln 2011). Interviewing as part of the data collecting in ethnographic research is further described in this volume in Homaira Semeen and M. Azizul Islam's chapter (16, 'Interviews as an instrument to explore management motivation for corporate social and environmental reporting').

Textual Analysis

Textual analysis mentioned here covers techniques from archival studies, document studies, web-studies, and similar studies, where the main point is to study published texts. Document analysis as part of the data collecting in ethnographic research is further described in this volume in Esther Ortiz and José G. Clavel's chapter (18, 'Application of correspondence analysis to determinants of human resources disclosure').

Visual and Artistic Analyses

Visual analysis covers analysing techniques of published images, photographing, video-making, documentaries, and films, whereas artistic analysis covers analysing techniques of various artistic performances such as musical events, dramas and theatre, art collections or exhibitions, and several other artistic events, which ethnographers may study (for an overview, see Lauesen 2016). Often these techniques alongside textual analysis involve an in-depth knowledge of the specific field in question including its history and particular genres and its particular analysis methodologies and traditions (for instance, the analyst's capability of nodes and rhythm reading in musical analysis), which are too extensive to set out in this chapter.

REVIEW OF ETHNOGRAPHY USED AS A RESEARCH METHOD

Studies of anthropology have for many decades shown how ethnographic methods can be used to study people, their culture, and their use of materials, physical objects, their (material) practices, and which symbolic constructions they use in their society or community. Often these studies use a combination of (participant) observation studies, interviews of members of the community or organization studies, and textual or document analysis. According to John Van Maanen, ethnography is the final product, which is based on fieldwork as the method in order to study culture as an overall purpose of ethnographic studies (Van Maanen 1988).

Regarding the ethnographic research method of fieldwork, it is often similar to participant observation, in which the researcher interacts with the social setting and takes field notes in order to describe what goes on in the setting about 'who or what is involved, when and where things happen, how they occur, and why—at least from the standpoint of participants—things happen as they do in particular situations' (Jorgensen 2003). Interviews are typically used to validate the observational study by asking the people that are researched of how they interpret what is going on (Spradley 1980). Finally, textual or document analysis is typically used for the researcher to get a meta-impression of the organizations' or community's communication and perception about itself and the rest of the world, for example its stakeholders through, for instance, content analysis (Altheide 1987).

Ethnographic research methods have been used since the birth of anthropology in the late 19th century, where the English-born Londoner and anthropologist, Sir Edward Burnett Tylor (1871), was among the first to study a people in so-called 'primitive cultures', as he termed it, in Mexico. Tylor came from a tradition where natural science and positivism were the approach used in early ethnographic studies. He used observation studies and analysed the minds and the materials the people in the community used, and from there defined their culture and its relation to materials and material practices (Kroeber and Kluckhohn 1952, Stocking 1966, p. 868). He used an evolutionist approach to claim that the primitive belief in spirits was similar to 'animism', imagining early humans as dominated by supernaturalism in order to understand natural phenomena such as thunder (Tylor 1871, p. 21). Thus, many contemporary social science ethnographers and anthropologists claim that early ethnography had a rather racist approach to ancient communities (see Denzin and Lincoln 2011).

Later, the Polish-English anthropologist Malinowski (1922) studied the people of the Kula Ring in Papua New Guinea, and its ritual of gifts exchange, also using observation studies, from which he described the role of materials as symbolically reflecting the cultural values of the Kula Ring (Ziegler 1990, Jones et al. 2013, p. 68). Explaining how the economic and social exchange was linked together in establishing the social order in tribal societies as a primer of commercial trade, Malinowski initiated the viability of materiality and value in modern ethnographic studies of foreign culture (Ziegler 1990, p. 142).

Ethnography, or observation studies, in the late 19th and early 20th centuries typically consisted of a researcher (mainly anthropologists) travelling to remote and detached communities from the modern world carrying their pen and notebook or writing machine and perhaps a camera, and they stayed and interacted in these communities for several years writing down what they saw and heard. When they came home, and sometimes also while they were present, they typically were obliged and of course motivated to 'write it all up' in books, reports, and letters to the fundraisers of the field of study (Van Maanen 1988). This was the way Colonist nations typically used anthropologists using ethnographic methods in their studies of the cultures existing in their colonies. The motives for the fundraisers of such quite expensive field trips have often been said to map out the territory of the ownership including the inhabitants and their cultures, and if this was for emperors, it could also be to find ways of how new trade routes could be established and the colonies could be utilized.

The ethnographic studies completed by anthropologists surely inspired the social sciences in other fields as well, and from America, the early Chicago School (e.g. Park 1915, Park et al. 1925, Thomas and Znaniecki 1918), we find many similar studies in other 'exotic' social settings than colonial habitats. The Chicago School researchers chose a more qualitative approach to their studies grounded in pragmatism (e.g. Peirce 1878) as the American philosophy of science for ethnography. These scholars studied 'urban ethnography' and focused on participant observation as the primary research methodology, but also interviews and surveys. This meant that the researchers socialized in odd milieus among the deviant, the criminals, the homeless, the gangs, and the opium addicts. Others studied organizations and bureaucracies such as medical professionals, schoolteachers, policemen, and business life (e.g. Van Maanen 1988). Despite the philosophical turnaround from natural science to pragmatism, the Chicago School scholars were still looking for 'facts', but also 'meaning' of human activity, which they found related to the social structures of regulation or community succession.[1] They studied the physical environment such as buildings, vegetation, availability and accessibility of food, and other materials for exchange such as money retrieved either through work or crime (Thomas and Znaniecki 1918, Park 1915, Park et al. 1925). But the new way of participating actively in the setting instead of presumed objectively observing, meant that these researchers came into radically different and sometimes dangerous environments, which they often were not prepared for. Van Maanen (1988) wrote vividly in *Tales of the Field* of his ride with the Police Academy Recruit Class during his six-month study of police attitude and socialization working in situ with the new recruits sitting armed on the back seat of their police car. One of the most famous incidents, Van Maanen experienced and wrote about during his research, was a situation where he was teamed up with only one policeman, and was asked to assist him with arrests, handcuffing, keeping a protective eye on dissidents, keeping logs, calling on the radio, and post himself on corners looking for criminals – that is, working as a 'shotgun-partner' (Van Maanen 1988, p. 90) although he had no police training at all. He had to immerse himself into the actual situation and act like those he studied the work of. From now on, being a participant means something really concrete and sometimes requires the researcher to step out of his or her role as an observer (only). You do what you study, and in return you get to know what you study.

In the period from the 1970s to the 1980s scholars of social psychology enlarged studies of ethnography into literature (texts), art, games, and music, which had an intrinsic meaning of expressing ideas and values transmitted to an audience or group members in a community (e.g. Blumer 1969, Becker and Geer 1970, Goffman 1974, Geertz 1973, Spradley 1979, 1980, Clifford 1988, Van Maanen 1988, Fine 1995). A famous game study is Clifford Geertz's study in 1958 of the illegal Balinese cockfights (Geertz 1973). Geertz travelled together with his wife, and they both experienced difficulties getting into the life of the Balinese. They felt like intruders, they were ignored, and could not get much out of their first days after arrival. However, ten days after, a cockfight was established to collect money to build a school. Suddenly, the armed police arrived, and chaos arose. The police asked for the village chief, who had been out of the village during the illegal event, and when Geertz could identify himself and his wife as legal researchers and confirm the village chief's story, things suddenly shifted for his research. Now he and his wife were treated as 'insiders' and could get access to the study they came for, and get lots of informants willing to share their stories about Balinese life.

The value of materials is in this period in high focus, and ethnographers look specifically for the meanings that things or events have for human action and how people modify these meanings through the process of social interaction (Blumer 1969, pp. 2, 4). This focus is also resembled in Schein's concept of 'organisational culture', in which materials and material practices can be understood as 'carriers of meaning': a way of transmitting ideas and values between people through 'cultural artefacts' (Schein 1985, 1990, p. 111).

In recent times, ethnography has as a research method evolved into the Digital Age and been used by social scientists to study the Internet (e.g. corporate texts), social media, texting (SMS, Twitter, blogs, etc.), consumerism (including online questionnaires), photo/video-documentary (visual ethnography), that is, modern globalism traced through the Web. Digital ethnography (also named online-, virtual-, cyber-, or Web 2.0-ethnography) is a new research field that has evolved especially in the social sciences during the last ten years. Some of the pitfalls, however, of using digital ethnography as the only research method, are that the media (mainly the Internet) divides respondents and researchers into those with access and those without. The digital divide expressed through digital ethnography includes problems related to race, gender, and economic resources for both responders and researchers (Murthy 2008). This, however, should not let researchers shy away from using digital ethnography, but as Murthy (2008) argues, it becomes more socially responsible when combined with physical ethnography. Nevertheless, digital ethnography seems to be the new way forward especially in studies of consumption and markets. Davis Masten and Tim Plowman (2003) suggest that the new ventures of digital media can enhance (especially young) people's (willingness to) participation in ethnographic studies. They propose that ethnographers should use digital and wireless communication as platforms for rethinking ethnographic principles, methodologies, and analysis in order to produce deep insights into people's lives and needs in an on-going world primarily based on such media, which people use in their everyday lives (Masten and Plowman 2003, pp. 75–76).

> [T]he pathways to information should include PCs, cell phones, Webcams, global positioning equipment, digital cameras, and a growing number of other technologies. Structured creatively for self-reporting, passive observation, and participant observation, these media can yield facts businesses can analyze to shape individual and strategic design decisions. (Masten and Plowman 2003, p. 75)

The new digital ventures within ethnography have a 'cousin' regarding self-reporting ethnography, also called autoethnography (see Ellis and Bochner 1996) or the New Ethnography (Goodall 2000). Autoethnography is a research method that – as digital ethnography – has been debated much and received critique for being narcissistic, but has emerged to be an acknowledged way to study. Autoethnography has been embraced, contested, and explored as a new ethnographical style in a response to the representation crisis of contemporary ethnography (Denzin 1989, Goodall 2000, Ellis and Bochner 1996). Academia has struggled with the acceptance of the account of blended fiction with faction in the autoethnographic attempt to represent stories of selves where authors reveal interpreted realities of their own lives. For instance, H. Lloyd Goodall, Jr.'s (2006) autobiography *A Need to Know: The Clandestine History of a CIA Family* investigates his own child- and adulthood living in a family where his father was a CIA agent for almost his entire career, which Goodall discovers late in life. He regrets that he first of all had to wait to publish his story till both his parents had passed away out of respect for them, however, he also regrets that he did not have the opportunity to receive answers to all the multiple questions he had about his father's job, his life, and their lives living as a clandestine family. Autoethnographic accounts thus can explore other ventures which traditional ethnography cannot, because respondents are rarely that intimate with the researcher so that they want to share their most inner-felt worries with others or even get them published.

All in all, ethnography as a research method allows materials, objects, practices, and symbolic constructions to be studied as meaning-carrying symbols for human values and interaction such as gift-giving, respect, trade, identity, legitimacy, communication, and practice in order to sustain life in many spheres from work to private life and business.

In the next, I will follow the leads from the above review of how ethnography as research methods have been used in general in sociology studies and carry it into the literature of corporate social responsibility in order to see as to whether these phenomena are applied or if new ways of using ethnography have emerged alongside this field.

REVIEW OF ETHNOGRAPHY USED AS A RESEARCH METHOD IN THE LITERATURE OF CORPORATE SOCIAL RESPONSIBILITY

Corporate social responsibility (CSR) can be hard to find a universal definition of, since the literature has developed myriads of more or less clear expressions of what CSR really is. One of the most precise definitions assembling many other definitions in a short sentence is Crowther and Aras' (2008) definition:

> The broadest definition of corporate social responsibility is concerned with what is – or should be – the relation between global corporations, governments of countries, and individual citizens. (Crowther and Aras 2008, p. 10)

This definition also covers some of the most imminent institutional concepts regarded by most governments as a way to understand CSR. For instance, the United Nations defines CSR as:

> Corporate Social Responsibility is a management concept whereby companies integrate social and environmental concerns in their business operations and interactions with their stakeholders. CSR is generally understood as being the way through which a company achieves a balance of economic, environmental and social imperatives ('Triple-Bottom-Line-Approach'), while at the same time addressing the expectations of shareholders and stakeholders. In this sense it is

important to draw a distinction between CSR, which can be a strategic business management concept, and charity, sponsorships or philanthropy. Even though the latter can also make a valuable contribution to poverty reduction, will directly enhance the reputation of a company and strengthen its brand, the concept of CSR clearly goes beyond that. (United Nations 2017)

All in all, the way corporations should be, according to Aras and Crowther and generally agreed by the members of the United Nations, is responsible in at least three ways – economic, environmental, and social – towards (all) their stakeholders. Thus many researchers in the field of CSR are specially focused on as to what degree corporations really are socially responsible, and for such studies, ethnographic research methods can help researchers go beyond corporations' seemingly nice wording on websites and find out the deeper layers of corporations' use (and misuse) of their claim of being socially responsible.

Ethnography is a research methodology, which is used especially in newer literature of CSR. A quick search on Google Scholar does not suggest the use of ethnographic approaches to CSR studies much before the 1990s. This may coincide with the evolution of CSR research in general, which began to rise from this decade too (see Lauesen 2013, p. 644). However, from the Millennium, more CSR studies have been conducted using ethnographic studies, but since ethnography as a methodology cannot be said to have declined in organizational nor community studies in general since the rise of anthropology in the 19th century, it can be assumed that many authors in CSR may have used other synonyms for similar studies, such as qualitative studies or organizational studies, instead of ethnography considering the obvious overlaps between wording. Even Howard Bowen (1953), R. Edward Freeman (1984), and Archie B. Carroll (1979) have used qualitative methodologies in their studies of organizations and CSR, but they often do not mention words like 'qualitative inquiry' nor 'ethnography' as their research methods even though it can be argued that they have used such methodologies as well – at least partly. Bowen wrote in the preface of the *Social Responsibilities of the Businessman* (1953, p. xvii–xviii):

> I have consulted widely and have drawn upon the opinions of many business leaders and scholars. I am deeply indebted to the numerous persons who have assisted directly in the project [of making this book] and to the many others who have left their imprint on it.

Surely, Bowen has somehow interviewed or collected 'opinions' and studied business leaders in order to write his famous volume. Similarly, Freeman (1984) states in the preface to *Strategic Management: A Stakeholder Approach*: 'I have talked, in both formal interviews and informally, to several thousand managers over the past five years . . .' (p.vii).

During the last 25 years, we see ethnographic research methods used in the literature of CSR in all areas from physical to digital ethnography. One of the seminal works in this period is David Crowther's *A Social Critique of Corporate Reporting*, where he used document analysis and semiotics to analyse web-based integrated reporting (Crowther 2012, 2nd ed.). David studied a range of business sectors in the late 1990s, published in the early years of the new Millennium as an early approach to what would now be termed digital ethnography as a way of doing mixed methods including a large part of qualitative research. Of course, in the 1990s not many companies had web-pages disclosing their corporate reporting; however, Crowther's study is one of the first, which may have included 'hard copies' as well as digital material, and certainly his semiotic approach to analysing corporate reports has since inspired newcomers on the scene of digital ethnography.

Ethnographic research methods in CSR research 273

Although the 'old' ethnographers might argue that digital ethnography is not ethnography because the researcher 'was not there', the methods involved in digital ethnography do not necessarily require the researcher to be located in the physical social setting. When researchers explore the Internet for relevant data for their study, they 'are' actually in the social setting they study: the Web. Texts such as corporate reports have been published on the Web for a wide audience to study. Such text cannot easily be hidden again because of the traces web-texts leave on the Internet. Thus, when corporations choose to publish their corporate reports on the Internet, they indirectly ask a wider audience to read these texts and to evaluate the corporations accordingly. The Web is a way for corporations to brand and legitimize their existence for a wide range of different stakeholders, and thus these corporations also take the risks of getting critiqued. Thus, document studies made on the Web can be said to be digital ethnographic fieldwork, because the social setting the researcher studies is not the physical setting of the corporations in question – it is the digital setting and the artefacts (corporate texts) and traces corporations leave about themselves on the Web.

Another study of CSR in corporate reporting was made by Markus Höllerer et al. (2013), who studied companies' use of images in CSR reports in Austria. They analysed more than 1,600 images using framing analysis and structural linguistics, and found that imageries of practice are just as well equipped to resonate symbolic representations using a rhetoric emphasizing the qualities of CSR and bridge the inconsistencies in the texts they accompany. Images bridge time, institutions, logics, appease ideational oppositions and reduce institutional complexities, and aid overcoming credibility gaps, the authors claim (Höllerer et al. 2013, pp. 139–140). However, this part especially has been discussed elsewhere, especially in the literature of accounting, where images in corporate reporting have been accused of blurring the facts and masking the lack of performance, or rather 'window-dressing' (see also Lauesen 2015, Crowther 2012).

In contemporary studies of CSR, where researchers use ethnographic research methods, we typically find longer studies conducted by PhD students. This seems natural, since the longitude of ethnography study especially if it focuses on the researcher being located as participant observer in a setting – requires more than a few months away from university. Most ethnographic studies of CSR involve one or more case studies, where the researcher typically is studying a business sector. Such studies are found in utilities such as oil (e.g. Billo 2012, 2015), gas, mining (see also Fernanda de Paiva Duarte's Chapter 13, this volume), and water (e.g. Lauesen 2014), but also in large business consortia from CSR in financial institutions (e.g. Kubo and Saka 2002), the fashion or garment industry (e.g. De Neve 2014), beverage (e.g. Christiansen and Lounsbury 2013), tourism (Bondy 2008), and other multinational settings.

Emily Ruth Billo (2012) studied CSR related to oil extraction by the Spanish-owned multinational oil company, Repsol-YPF, operating in the Ecuadorian Amazon region. She used ethnographic methods such as interviews, participant observation, and textual analysis of company and state documents to examine the social relationships produced through CSR programmes, and found that the relationships formed within CSR programmes enable on-going resource extraction. Her findings showed that the CSR programmes of the oil company were aimed 'to deflect blame for a company's operations, by providing development or infrastructural improvements in indigenous communities, including micro-credit projects, potable water systems, and electricity' (Billo 2015, p. 268).

Billo's ethnographic study allowed her to go beyond the CSR programme of a multinational oil company and realize that the company used CSR for their motive of mitigating blame from stakeholders on company operations. In this study we see how a company utilizes CSR as 'reputation management', but despite its efforts to blur the negative impact the company has on society by investing in local infrastructure and giving micro-credits, the company can hardly cover up the real problems it is responsible for.

A similar study was conducted by Geert De Neve, who conducted an ethnographic study during 2008–2009 on CSR in one of the largest knitwear garment clusters of Tiruppur, located in the western part of Tamil Nadu, South India (De Neve 2008). Tiruppur exports for the world market and employs more than 400,000 workers, and De Neve was present in participant observation studies and conducted interviews among workers and contractors. De Neve found that garment workers engage with different labour regimes and that some workers actively avoid employment in companies where Fordist[2] regimes prevail and CSR policies are implemented, because they are used to control the labour force and curtail its freedom and dignity at work. Similarly to Billo's, De Neve's ethnographic research showed how multinational companies exploit the nature of CSR as a cover-up for control and human rights violations. This is a clear example of corporations utilizing CSR as window-dressing, because in this setting the company does the opposite of the intentions within CSR. The study shows how ethnographic research methods can reveal documentation of corporate bad behaviour, which can be hard to find in corporate texts and outside the actual social setting. Had De Neve 'only' studied corporate texts, he might not have discovered the real corporate behaviour lying underneath its CSR policies, which suggests that Murthy's (2008) argument that combining physical and digital ethnography comes closer to the point in this particular setting is correct. De Neve could not have made his findings without being physically present in the garment industry.

Depending on the issues, other studies show that digital ethnography, as a stand-alone methodology, can be vital without the researcher doing a physical ethnography. For instance, Gabriela Coronado and Wayne Fallon (2011) studied corporate websites and used ethnographic analysis of hypertexts to map the relevant meanings of narratives of corporate communication: 'The mapping allows identification of the agents and events that represent the way organisations operate and the kind of relationships they establish' (Coronado and Fallon 2011, pp. 93–94).

The corporations and the stakeholders confirmed their CSR policies apparently to maintain their positive benefactor-recipient relations and to mask more complex tensions in their relationships, Coronado and Fallon found. If researchers are interested in corporate communication of CSR, it is not necessary for them to be physically present. The difference between Coronado and Fallon's as well as Crowther's studies and De Neve's is the scope of their research interests: Coronado and Fallon and Crowther were interested in analysing corporate texts per se, whereas De Neve was interested in corporate behaviour. Thus, different ethnographic approaches are necessary depending on the issue and scope of study. This is further developed in the next example.

Lærke Højgaard Christiansen (in Christiansen and Lounsbury 2013, pp. 199–232) studied the Carlsberg brewery with special focus on Carlsberg's work with their Responsible Drinking concept as part of its framing of CSR. Knowing that alcoholism and good marketing are two sides of the same coin, Carlsberg has tried to mitigate criticism of selling sweet drinks to young consumers leading to early alcoholism, drunk driving, and other critical behaviours or societal problems. For Christiansen to go beyond the corporate communication of Responsible Drinking, it was necessary for her to use participant observations at Carlsberg's Danish headquarters and subsidiaries from 2010 to 2012 and combine it with interviews of key employees from different departments (from production to marketing) and analyse various corporate documents. She found that the communication and CSR staff were intent on making the Responsible Drinking Guide Book in order to redefine the organizational identity across geographically dispersed subsidiaries (p. 213), bridging a socially responsible logic with the prevailing market logic. Such study of corporate logics often requires multiple ethnographic research methods, because studying corporate identity is about employees' and managements' perception of CSR.

This too I had realized (Lauesen 2015), when I studied CSR in seven water companies from Denmark on location, and further studied corporate texts of CSR from the Danish companies and compared them with similar companies from the United Kingdom, the United States, and South Africa during the years 2011–2013, in total 28 water companies. I used ethnographic research methods such as participant observation (in mainly one Danish water company, and partially in two more), interviews in all seven Danish companies, and web-based as well as physical studies of corporate documents from all 28 water companies. My study showed how water companies use a logic of CSR and frame it into existing institutional logics (Friedland and Alford 1991, Thornton et al. 2012). My work was mainly based on two and a half years of participant observation studies in the Danish water company Vand & Affald besides visits and interviewing the six other Danish water companies. The data material consisted of 50 interviews and meetings with managers and regulators of Danish water companies and a web-study of corporate reports from 2000–2013 of water companies from the UK, the US, and South Africa. My findings showed that employees in the water sector use materials, objects, material practices, and symbolic constructions as their way of finding a logic of CSR. The purpose of the CSR-logic in the water companies for the receiving subject/object (for instance stakeholders, but also concepts such as 'the environment', 'the climate', 'habitats') were fundamental for the water companies and the institutional logics they framed their CSR-logic with. Beyond this, I found that materials were constitutional for the CSR-logic of the water companies and thus their institutional logics, for instance that the water companies always referred to CSR in terms of the purpose of it using materials as a means to obtain legitimacy (for instance how the use of a certain material and installation technique was better for the environment than others). And that the material practices regarding the companies' work with CSR legitimize their use of institutional logics, for instance when companies highlight that they prefer trenchless technologies for pipe installations, because they emit less carbon dioxide to the air. Finally, I found that water companies use symbolic constructions related to CSR in order to justify the institutional logics in the water sector, exemplified in the water companies' justification of their legitimacy in being 'cost-recovery' or 'price-cap-controlled', which in the companies' perceptions makes them more accountable than fully for-profit companies, because profit is not their only or at least not their primary mission.

From the above examples, we see that ethnographic research methods are used in the CSR literature mainly in connection with particular case studies of companies which the researchers have gained access to. The use of ethnography as research method has in this field moved away from the typical societal studies in the first part of the 20th century, which of course can be explained by the link between CSR and business fields as case studies. However, we also find partial ethnographic methods used in archival/document studies of CSR related to policy studies (e.g. Buhmann 2014). Buhmann shows in her postdoctoral thesis that the discursive CSR normativity in the UN (through its Global Compact) and the EU (through its CSR Alliance) from 1999 to 2008 was based on legitimizing businesses through them being socially responsible towards society at large, but that the soft law and non-regulative characteristics of the power relations between global institutions and local corporations is making the purpose of legitimizing businesses rather hard:

> The analysis demonstrated that reflexive law offers a viable regulatory strategy for above-national public-private regulation of issues related to businesses' impact on society but that the procedural design of reflexive law forums is important in order to balance power disparities between participants for the process and output to be legitimate. (Buhmann 2014, p. 637)

Buhmann's thesis shows that the balance of how to regulate or at least evaluate as to what degree businesses are socially responsible had not yet been found, which means that the intentions of the UN and the EU are stated, but the means to evaluate or even regulate CSR, which Buhmann suggests is necessary to some degree (p. 637), is not in place, which makes intergovernmental CSR rather diluted (see also Lauesen 2013).

DISCUSSION AND CONCLUSION

Ethnographic research methods are typically used in research of businesses and their conduct of CSR mainly published in doctoral theses and to some degree in journals, however, it seems as if the way from thesis to journal paper has been hard for many students so far. Most ethnographic studies have been reported in book volumes, chapters, and rarely in academic journals. This may coincide with the spatial problem of writing up and presenting ethnography, which is much more voluminous than paper requirements. We also see that the typical CSR ethnographer studies company CSR in more business sectors or in companies in the same business sector, which suggests a limitation for ethnography as a research method to be anchored in single or fewer case studies.

Ethnographic research methods are splendid for in-depth studies of one or a few organizations for explorative and discursive studies suggesting new theory development; however, it would be an interesting approach to engage ethnographic studies with quantitative approaches in order to come further up the ladder of actually imposing that the findings from case studies can be found in more than one company/business sector (the studied one) – maybe even be statistically significant. This suggestion calls for a more mixed method study, but it also reveals the Achilles heel of most qualitative studies: that it can suggest new theory grounded on in-depth findings of a few examples, and if these findings should be verified or generalizable, it needs a quantitative (statistical, significant) doubling. Or, the ethnographer should search for the stand-alone example that proves others wrong (see e.g. Flyvbjerg 2006).

Despite the limitations of ethnographic studies in general, the imperative of ethnographic studies moves beyond single qualitative research methods such as interviewing and document studies: ethnography today contains a multiple qualitative approach making it possible for the researcher to make an even 'thicker description' (Geertz 1973) of the subjects, which qualifies this method as the most ingenious version of in-depth studies making theory developments from rich data collection possible.

The above examples of newer studies in the CSR literature shows that ethnographic studies are used to get 'under the skin' of corporations and their interpretation and use (and misuse) of CSR. Most companies utilize the good motives of CSR for corporate branding, to obtain legitimacy, and to form their identity according to be 'a good corporation' in the eyes of its stakeholders. However, these ethnographic studies show how corporations are not always aligned with the intentions of CSR, because their motives are typically steered by making profits primarily, in which CSR becomes a means to this end, which is not the purpose of CSR eventually.

NOTES

1. For example institutions like the family, school and church, policing, business, and political institutions, as well as groups of gang members controlling the flux of money and stimulant drugs in a certain concrete and bounded area to other competing groups.
2. Fordism refers to working conditions in industrialized, standardized mass production and mass consumption in the 20th century – especially before the focus on CSR and Sustainability had entered everyday organizational considerations. See also http://www.willamette.edu/~fthompso/MgmtCon/Fordism_&_Postfordism.html, accessed 2 April 2017.

REFERENCES

Altheide, David L. (1987), 'Reflections: Ethnographic content analysis', *Qualitative Sociology*, **10** (1), 65–77.
Becker, H.S. and B. Geer (1970), 'Participant observation and interviewing: a comparison', in George J. McCall and J. Lee Simmons (eds), *Issues in Participant Observation: A Text and Reader*, Reading, Mass: Addison-Wesley Publishing Co.
Billo, E. Ruth (2012), *Competing Sovereignties: Corporate Social Responsibility, Oil Extraction, and Indigenous Subjectivity in Ecuador*, PhD Thesis, Publication Number: AAT 3550318; ISBN: 9781267873682; Source: Dissertation Abstracts International, vol. 74-05(E), sect. A.
Billo, E.R. (2015), 'Sovereignty and subterranean resources: an institutional ethnography of Repsol's corporate social responsibility programs in Ecuador', *Geoforum*, **59**, 268–277.
Blumer, Herbert (1969), *Symbolic Interactionism: Perspective and Method*, California: University of California Press.
Bondy, K. (2008), 'The paradox of power in CSR: a case study on implementation', *Journal of Business Ethics*, **82** (2), 307–323.
Bowen, Howard (1953), *Social Responsibilities of the Businessman*, NY: Harper & Row.
Buhmann, Karin (2014), *Normative Discourses and Public-private Regulatory Strategies for Construction of CSR Normativity*, Roskilde, DK: Multivers.
Carroll, A.B. (1979), 'A three-dimensional conceptual model of corporate performance', *Academy of Management Review*, **4** (4), 497–505.
Christiansen, L.H. and M. Lounsbury (2013), 'Strange brew: bridging logics via institutional bricolage and the reconstitution of organizational identity', in Michael Lounsbury and Eva Boxenbaum (eds), *Research in the Sociology of Organizations*, **39** (A), Bingley, UK: Emerald Publishing Group, pp. 199–232.
Clifford, James (1988), *The Predicament of Culture: Twentieth-century Ethnography, Literature, and Art*, USA: Harvard University Press.
Coronado, G. and W. Fallon (2011), 'Using hypertext ethnography to understand corporate-stakeholder relations in CSR', *Social Responsibility Journal*, **7** (1), 87–103.
Crowther, David (2012), *A Social Critique of Corporate Reporting*, 2nd ed., Aldershot: Gower.
Crowther, David and Güler Aras (2008), *Corporate Social Responsibility*, Ventus Publishing ApS. Accessed

at Bookboon.com, http://bookboon.com/dk/defining-corporate-social-responsibility-ebook, 7 September 2015.

De Neve, G. (2008), 'Global garment chains, local labour activism: new challenges to trade union and NGO activism in the Tiruppur garment cluster, South India', in Geert De Neve, Peter Luetchford, Jeffrey Pratt and Donald C. Wood (eds), *Hidden Hands in the Market: Ethnographies of Fair Trade, Ethical Consumption, and Corporate Social Responsibility*, Research in Economic Anthropology, **28**, Bingley, UK: Emerald Group Publishing, pp. 213–240. ISBN 9781848550582.

De Neve, G. (2014), Entrapped Entrepreneurship: Labour contractors in the South Indian garment industry, *Modern Asian Studies*, **48** (5), 1302–1333.

Denzin, Norman K. (1989), *Interpretive Biography*, vol. 17, London: Sage.

Denzin, Norman K. and Yvonne S. Lincoln (eds) (2011), *The SAGE Handbook of Qualitative Research*, vol. 4, Thousand Oaks: Sage.

Ellis, Carolyn and Arthur P. Bochner (eds) (1996), *Composing Ethnography: Alternative Forms of Qualitative Writing*, Walnut Creek, CA: Altamira Press.

Fine, G.A. (ed.) (1995), *A Second Chicago School? The Development of a Postwar American Sociology*, Chicago: University of Chicago Press.

Flyvbjerg, B. (2006), 'Five misunderstandings about case-study research', *Qualitative Inquiry*, **12** (2), 219–245.

Freeman, R. Edward (1984), *Strategic Management: A Stakeholder Approach*, Boston: Pitman.

Friedland, R. and R.R. Alford (1991), 'Bringing society back in: symbols, practices and institutional contradictions', in Walther W. Powell and Paul J. DiMaggio (eds), *The New Institutionalism in Organizational Analysis*, Chicago: University of Chicago Press, pp. 232–266.

Geertz, Clifford (1973), *The Interpretation of Cultures: Selected Essays*, vol. 5019, New York: Basic Books.

Goffman, Erving (1974), *Frame Analysis: An Essay on the Organization of Experience*, USA: Harvard University Press.

Goodall, Jr., H. Lloyd (2000), *Writing the New Ethnography*, Walnut Creek, CA: AltaMira Press.

Goodall, Jr., H. Lloyd (2006), *A Need to Know. The Clandestine History of a CIA Family*, Walnut Creek, CA: Left Coast Press, Inc.

Höllerer, M.A., D. Jancsary, R.E. Meyer and O. Vettori (2013), 'Imageries of corporate social responsibility: visual recontextualization and field-level meaning', in Michael Lounsbury and Eva Boxenbaum (eds), *Research in the Sociology of Organizations*, **39** (B), Bingley, UK: Emerald Publishing Group, pp. 139–174.

Jones, C. Boxenbaum, E., Anthony, C. (2013), 'The immateriality of material practices in institutional logics', in E. Boenbaum and M. Lounsbury (eds), *Institutional Logics in Action, Part A*, Bingley: Emerald Group Publishing Ltd., pp. 51–75.

Jorgensen, Danny L. (2003), 'The methodology of participant observation', *Qualitative Approaches to Criminal Justice: Perspectives from the Field*, Thousand Oaks, CA: Sage Publications, pp. 17–26.

Kroeber, Alfred Louis and Clyde Kluckhohn (1952), 'Culture: a critical review of concepts and definitions', *Papers*, **47** (1), viii, 223. Cambridge, MA: Peabody Museum of Archaeology and Ethnology, Harvard University.

Kubo, I. and A. Saka (2002), 'An inquiry into the motivations of knowledge workers in the Japanese financial industry', *Journal of Knowledge Management*, **6** (3), 262–271.

Kvale, Steinar and Svend Brinkmann (2009), *Interviews: Learning the Craft of Qualitative Research Interviewing*, Thousand Oaks: Sage Publications, Inc.

Lauesen, L.M. (2013), 'Corporate social responsibility in the aftermath of the financial crisis', *Social Responsibility Journal*, **9** (4), 641–663.

Lauesen, Linne Marie (2014), Corporate Social Responsibility in the Water Sector: How Material Practices and their Symbolic and Physical Meanings Form a Colonising Logic, PhD thesis, PhD series, no. 6.2014, ISSN 0906-6934, ISBN (print) 9788793155121, ISBN (electronic) 9788793155138, Copenhagen: Copenhagen Business School.

Lauesen, Linne Marie (2015), *Sustainable Governance in Hybrid Organizations*, Finance, Governance and Sustainability: Challenges to Theory and Practice, series edited by: Professor Güler Aras, Yildiz Technical University, Istanbul, Turkey, Surrey, UK: Gower Publishing Limited.

Lauesen, L.M. (2016), 'The role of the (governance of the) arts in cultural sustainability: a case study of music', in David Crowther and Linne Marie Lauesen (eds), *Accountability and Social Responsibility: International Perspectives*, Developments in Corporate Governance and Responsibility, vol. 9, Bingley, West Yorkshire, UK: Emerald Group Publishing, pp. 49–74.

Malinowski, Bronislaw (1922), *Argonauts of the Western Pacific: An Account of Native Enterprise and Adventure in the Archipelagos of Melanesian New Guinea*, London: George Routledge and Sons.

Masten, D.L. and T.M. Plowman (2003), 'Digital ethnography: the next wave in understanding the consumer experience', *Design Management Journal*, **14** (2), 75–81.

Murthy, D. (2008), 'Digital ethnography: an examination of the use of new technologies for social research', *Sociology*, **42** (5), 837–855.

Park, R.E. (1915), 'The city: suggestions for the investigation of human behavior in the city environment', *The American Journal of Sociology*, **20** (5), 577–612.
Park, Robert E., Ernest W. Burgess and R.D. McKenzie (1925), *The City: Suggestions for the Study of Human Nature in the Urban Environment*, Chicago: University of Chicago Press.
Peirce, C.S. (1878/1992), 'How to make our ideas clear', in Nathan Houser and Christian Kloesel (eds), *The Essential Peirce*, vol.1, Bloomington IN: Indiana University Press, pp. 124–141.
Schein, E.H. (1985), 'How culture forms, develops, and changes', in R.H. Kilmann, M.J. Saxton and R. Serpa (eds.), *Gaining Control of the Corporate Culture*, San Francisco, CA: Jossey-Bass, pp. 17–43.
Schein, E.H. (1990), 'Organizational culture', *American Psychologist*, **45** (2), 109–119.
Spradley, James P. (1979), *The Ethnographic Interview*, Florida: Holt, Rinehart, and Winston.
Spradley, James P. (1980), *Participant Observation*, Florida: Holt, Rinehart, and Winston.
Stocking, G.W. (1966), 'Franz Boas and the culture concept in historical perspective', *American Anthropologist*, **68** (4), 867–882.
Sullivan, Patrick (2012), 'The personality of public documents: a case study in normalising Aboriginal risk', *Journal of Organizational Ethnography*, **1** (1), 52–61.
Thomas, William Isaac and Florian Znaniecki (1918), *The Polish Peasant in Europe and America*, vol. 1, New York: Alfred A. Knoff.
Thornton, P.H., W. Ocasio and M. Lounsbury (2012), *The Institutional Logics Perspective: A New Approach to Culture, Structure, and Process*, Oxford, UK: Oxford University Press on Demand.
Tylor, Edward Burnett (1871), *Primitive Culture: Researches into the Development of Mythology, Philosophy, Religion, Art, and Custom*, vol. 2, London: John Murray, Albemarle Street.
United Nations (2017), United Nations Industrial Development Organization, as found on http://www.unido.org/csr/o72054.html, accessed 2 April 2017.
Van Maanen, John (1988), *Tales of the Field: On Writing Ethnography*, Chicago: University of Chicago Press.
Van Maanen, John (2009), 'Ethnography then and now', *Qualitative Research in Organizations and Management: An International Journal*, **1** (1), 13–21.
Watson, Tony J. (2012), 'Making organisational ethnography', *Journal of Organizational Ethnogrphy*, **1** (1), 15–22.
Yanow, Dvora (2012), 'Organizational ethnography between toolbox and world-making', *Journal of Organizational Ethnography*, **1** (1), 31–42.
Ziegler, R. (1990), 'The Kula: social order, barter, and ceremonial exchange', in Michael Hecter, Karl-Dieter Opp and Reinhart Wippler (eds), *Social Institutions: Their Emergence, Maintenance, and Effects*, Berlin and New York: de Gruyter, pp. 141–168.

16. Interviews as an instrument to explore management motivation for corporate social and environmental reporting
Homaira Semeen and Muhammad Azizul Islam

INTRODUCTION

This chapter discusses interviews as an instrument to explore motivations for corporate social reporting from global perspectives. While interviewing is one of the widely used data collection methods in conducting qualitative research, the method is crucial to understand the depth of motivation behind the corporate social reporting. Using interviews as the procedure of securing knowledge is relatively new (Holstein and Gubrium 2001; Kvale 2007) but securing knowledge of the reasons for social and environmental reporting via the interview method is newer. Therefore, within social and environmental accounting (SEA) literature, the use of the interview method is also relatively new.

In terms of methodologies, where earlier reviews found less presence of empirical research in the field of SEA (Deegan and Soltys 2007; Gray 2002; Owen 2008), Parker (2011) has tracked some important changes in trends. His analysis depicted a pronounced preference of literature/commentary/historical based research over the 1988–2008 period. Among the other categories of methodologies, the presence of content analysis/statistical relationships, survey, case/field/action/ethnographic research were significant. The findings of Parker's (2011) study closely resembled the investigation on development in SEA research during the period of 2000 to 2006 conducted by Eugénio et al. (2010) especially in terms of the publication trends and topics of research interest in this field. However, in terms of research method Eugénio et al. (2010) observed extensive use of content analysis followed by questionnaire, interview, case studies, action research and ethnographies among the qualitative techniques. While existing research used different methods to document motivation for social reporting, this has largely overlooked the consideration of in-depth interviews as a method to understand the phenomena. Moreover, despite the importance of interview based study, there is limited research to understand the motivation for the social disclosures of companies operating globally. This chapter highlights the significance of interview methods in exploring social reporting from the global context.

The review of SEA research suggests that researchers in this field are increasingly relying on the qualitative interview method to explore social and environmental issues surrounding accounting and accountability. While SEA researchers are increasingly using interview to understand the motivation for social reporting, use of such method within the global context is still new. This chapter has brought out a discussion of motivation for social reporting by organizations operating globally.

The rest of the chapter is structured as follows. We begin with background of interview as a research method, followed by description of types and significance of interviews, highlighting situations where interviews can be used, discussion on the use of interviews in SEA, presenting a case where the interview is used to explain organizational social and environmental reporting practices and concluding remarks.

DEFINING INTERVIEW AS A RESEARCH METHOD

The interview is one of the widely used data collection methods in conducting qualitative research. From a general understanding, the interview is a face-to-face verbal exchange where a person attempts to elicit information or expression of opinion from another person (Maccoby and Maccoby 1954, p. 449). This general definition has been interpreted, expanded, modified by different schools of qualitative interview over the period of time (Brinkmann 2013). As human beings are linguistic creatures, all human research is conversational, that is, humans can be best understood in the context of the conversation (Brinkmann 2013). In identifying the circumstances of using interview Rubin and Rubin (2005) maintained that all kinds of research do not require interview to be conducted. According to them interviews, especially qualitative interviews, are primarily used by naturalistic researchers when the objective is to acquire explanations and descriptions of insights and experiences which would not be possible to be answered simply or briefly. Through observations from separate yet overlapping angles qualitative interview makes researchers more hesitant to leap to conclusions and therefore encourages more nuanced analysis (Rubin and Rubin 2005).

From a historical point of view, using interviews as the procedure of securing knowledge is relatively new (Holstein and Gubrium 2001; Kvale 2007). However, reviewing the history of interviewing, Platt (2001) noted that it is very difficult to derive a meaningful generalization about the development and changes in the interview process as it encompasses a vast range of different practices driven by methodological as well as socio-political motives. Maccoby and Maccoby (1954) traced the tradition of interviewing research from two trends: the clinical diagnosis and counselling and the psychological testing. In the field of academic research, interview became a dominant data collection method in sociology in the late 1950s (Fontana and Frey 2008). Since then, interviewing continued to be practiced along with the participant observation method.

The initial utilization of interview was more structured in implementing the quantifiable scientific rigor of survey research. At that time interview was thought to be an easy and straightforward approach. However, when the use of qualitative interviews became one of the basic methods of social science research, the technical, epistemological and cultural issues started to influence the key aspects of interview knowledge (Kvale 2007). In recent times, many scholars (Atkinson and Silverman 1997; Fontana 2002; Hertz 1997; Holstein and Gubrium 2003; Scheurich 1995) are of the opinion that interviewing is not a neutral exchange of asking questions and getting answers. As two or more people are involved in creating knowledge, the process is very much contextually bound (Holstein and Gubrium 2003). Scholars are now recognizing that language constructs rather than mirrors phenomena which makes the empirical work problematic (Alvesson 2003; Alvesson and Karreman 2000; Alvesson and Sköldberg 2000; Denzin and Lincoln 1994; Van Maanen 1995). The understanding that interviews are complex social events calls for emphasis on the reflexive approach to consider the variety of possible meanings in an open and self-critical way (Alvesson 2003).

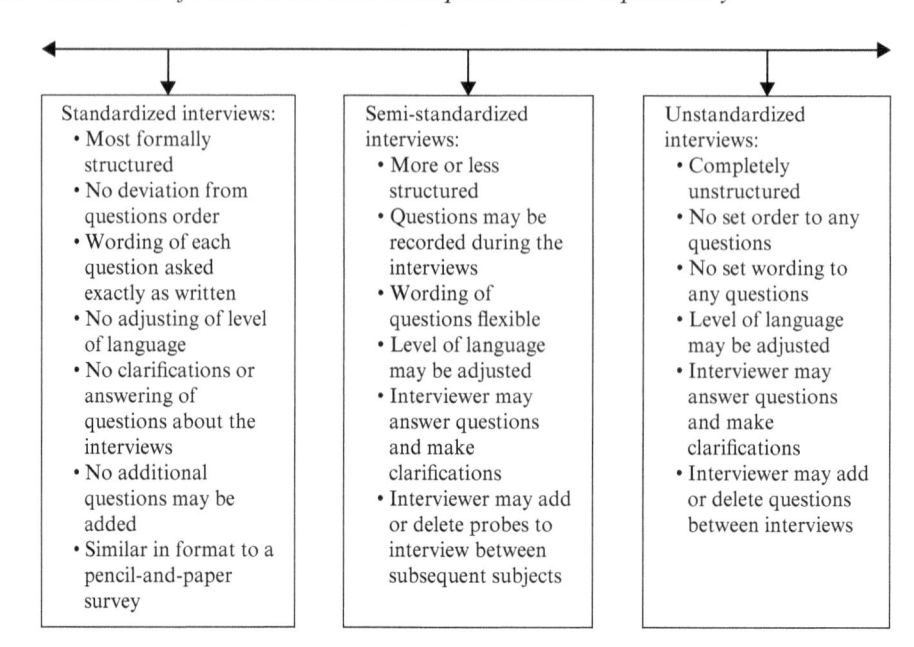

Standardized interviews:	Semi-standardized interviews:	Unstandardized interviews:
• Most formally structured • No deviation from questions order • Wording of each question asked exactly as written • No adjusting of level of language • No clarifications or answering of questions about the interviews • No additional questions may be added • Similar in format to a pencil-and-paper survey	• More or less structured • Questions may be recorded during the interviews • Wording of questions flexible • Level of language may be adjusted • Interviewer may answer questions and make clarifications • Interviewer may add or delete probes to interview between subsequent subjects	• Completely unstructured • No set order to any questions • No set wording to any questions • Level of language may be adjusted • Interviewer may answer questions and make clarifications • Interviewer may add or delete questions between interviews

Source: Adapted from Berg (2009).

Figure 16.1 *The continuum of interview structure*

TYPES OF INTERVIEWS AND THEIR SIGNIFICANCE

In general the use of interview is so extensive (less likely to be the case in accounting literature) that many scholars referred to this modern society as the 'interview society' (Atkinson and Silverman 1997; Fontana and Frey 2008; Silverman 2001). This extensive usage of interview gradually revealed the active nature of this process (Holstein and Gubrium 2003). Earlier, the interview was utilized from a conventional positivist point of view, assuming the respondent to be honest in his/her response (see Douglas (1985)). With the progress of qualitative research, scholars increasingly admitted that interviewing is a negotiated accomplishment, not a neutral exchange of asking questions and getting answers (Fontana and Frey 2008).

However, despite the challenges in asking questions and getting answers, interview is the most common method of human research. The continuum of this understanding endeavour ranges from standardized through semi-standardized to unstandardized forms (Figure 16.1) (Berg 2009). As mentioned earlier, interviews used in the earlier academic research were more in structured form, though the semi-structured and unstructured forms gradually took the form of qualitative interviewing, realizing the need for interaction of the interviewer with the people (Edwards and Holland 2013).

The structured form of interviewing assumed survey approaches. The structured interview follows the questionnaire format with a sequence of questions in which little flexibility is available to the researchers (Edwards and Holland 2013). The objective is to derive comparable information from a large sample and usually takes the positivist approach with a statistical approach to analyse data. Where it was hoped that nothing is left to chance in the structured form of research, in reality, this form of interview is subject to response effect or non-sampling errors and the interviewer effect (Fontana and Frey 2008).

Recognizing the need of making appropriate adjustments according to the respondents' differences, a considerable range of qualitative research has been conducted using semi-structured and unstructured forms of interviews. Semi-structured interview utilizes a prepared set of questions guided by identified themes in a consistent and systematic way and supports the conversations with probes to elicit an elaborated response (Dumay and Qu 2011). Semi-structured interview allows the interactional exchange of dialog, a fluid and flexible structure, and the recognition of contextually bound understanding created in the interactions (Edwards and Holland 2013). Extensive literature has documented that the semi-structured interview is preferable for the qualitative research because of its flexibility, accessibility and more importantly, its capability of understanding human behaviour (Alvesson and Deetz 2000; Dumay and Qu 2011; Edwards and Holland 2013). On the other end of the continuum, the interview could take a completely unstructured form. This form of interviews with an assumption that interviewers do not know the questions in advance and expect that real life events and complex social reality will be revealed by the participants from informal conversations (Dumay and Qu 2011). Through building rapport, the interviewer gets close to the reality of the interviewee (Alvesson and Deetz 2000). Accordingly, this form of interview can be aligned with the empathetic approach where the interviewer takes a more ethical stance to advocate and partner in the study and uses the result to pursue social policy in favour of the interviewee (Fontana and Frey 2008).

CIRCUMSTANCES WHERE INTERVIEW METHODS ARE USED

In most of the cases the objectives of qualitative interviewing is to derive interpretations from the conversation, not the fact or law (Warren 2001). It is based on a guided conversation where emphasis is placed on asking questions as well as listening to respondents' answers (Kvale 2007; Rubin and Rubin 2005; Warren 2001). The purpose is to gain a thick description of the social world to analyse for cultural patterns and themes (Warren 2001). This places qualitative interview in opposition to the questionnaire or survey interview which is loosely structured and open to what the interviewee feels is relevant and an important issue to be discussed within the research interest (Alvesson 2003). As opposed to positivist and neopositivist approaches, qualitative interview is more appropriate to address research problems under interpretive constructionist approaches (Rubin and Rubin 2005; Warren 2001). A number of philosophies such as critical, postmodern, feminist and constructionist paradigms assume that the research is about learning the contingent truth where the researchers' idea and personality affect the research (Rubin and Rubin 2005). As the qualitative interview relies more on understanding human experience, this method is more appropriate for the research under those paradigms.

This interviewing technique has long been used in ethnographic studies together with document analysis as the qualitative or interpretative method (Kvale 2007; Rubin and

Rubin 2005; Warren 2001). However, qualitative interviewing often received priorities from researchers, especially when the topics of interest are not focusing on a particular setting, but the objective is to establish a common pattern of themes from a particular category of respondents (Rubin and Rubin 2005; Warren 2001). Recognizing the fact that the interview is politically, socially and contextually bound, Fontana and Frey (2008) suggested understanding the interpretation of the interview in its specific context rather than its literal meaning. In their review of new trends in interviewing they identified that researchers are increasingly becoming interested in empathetic interviewing where the interaction with people elicits knowledge.

Using the breadth of focus and the subject of focus Rubin and Rubin (2005) grouped various types of qualitative interview that can be used. Furthermore, to describe the nature of the interview, Rubin and Rubin (2005) classified qualitative interviewing into cultural and topical interviews. Where cultural interview explores the ordinary, the routine, the shared history, the taken-for-granted norms and values, the rituals and the expected behaviour of a group of people, the topical interview explores what, when, how, why or with what consequences something happened. According to them, cultural interview allows flexibility of what is discussed in any conversation and involves more active listening than active questioning whereas in topical interview researchers are interested in a particular piece of information and use more directive and aggressive questions.

In relation to the design of qualitative interview, Kvale (2007) suggested an open-ended design as it is more about being attuned with the research environment than a survey research. However, Johnson (2001) identified that researchers should be conscious about the emotional cost of doing interviews because of their exploration and open-ended nature. In order to overcome the potential limitation of the design of qualitative interview research, Warren (2001) suggested using the relevant literature at the initial stage and emphasize the time, access and the researchers' concerns related to the meaning making causes more than the structured design. This could be ensured by taking an open stance, which would allow developing a meaning that may make previously designed questions irrelevant in light of the changes in contexts. Warren's opinion on designing qualitative research resembles Alvesson's (2003) proposition of reconceptualizing interview where he suggested adopting a reflexive theoretical framework to be adopted in interpreting interview results. Drawing upon Alvesson's (2003) proposition, Dumay and Qu (2011) argued that while structured interview takes the more neopositivist approach and unstructured interview takes the more romanticist approach, semi-structured interview takes the localist perspective to open up alternative understanding of the interview process and the account to provide additional insights.

USE OF INTERVIEWS IN SEA RESEARCH

Studies on social and environmental accounting (SEA) emerged as a substantial discipline in the mid-1960s (Gray 2002; Owen 2008). In response to the dissatisfaction with conventional accounting practices (Gray 2002) and the interest in exploring new forms of accounting with the potential of creating a fairer society were two core concerns that led to the development of this field (Bebbington 1997). According to Gray (2002),

> Social accounting can be usefully thought of as the universe of all possible accountings ... One dimension of social accounting is with the social and environmental consequences of conventional accounting ... but it is equally about (attempts at) mitigation of this and consequential change in accounting. (Gray 2002, p. 692)

Even though research in this field took a conservative and a managerialist stance at its initial stage (Owen 2008; Parker 2011), it has now become one of the mainstream fields of research. Reviewing the first 25 years of SEA literature, some prominent scholars (Bebbington 1997; Deegan and Soltys 2007; Gray 2002; Mathews 1997; Owen 2008) had identified skewed attention to social and environmental issues, limited scope to publish, absence of meta-theory, less engagement of researchers and practitioners and a dearth of empirical research. In response to the call of these scholars, researchers in this field made drastic improvements in all aspects (Eugénio et al. 2010; Parker 2011). Reviewing the progress of SEA literature over the last 40 years, Parker (2011) contended that SEA literature in the second half of its tenure duly addressed the call of the scholars by expanding its boundaries not only in terms of its scope and theoretical underpinning, but also in terms of research methodologies employed in investigating phenomena.

In terms of methodologies, where earlier review found less presence of empirical research in the field of SEA (Deegan and Soltys 2007; Gray 2002; Owen 2008), Parker (2011) has tracked some important changes in trends. His analysis depicted a pronounced preference of literature/commentary/historical based research over the 1988–2008 period. Among the other categories of methodologies, the presence of content analysis/statistical relationships, survey, case/field/action/ethnographic research were significant. The findings of Parker's (2011) study closely resembled the investigation on development in SEA research during the period of 2000 to 2006 conducted by Eugénio et al. (2010) especially in terms of the publication trends and topics of research interest in this field. However, in terms of research method Eugénio et al. (2010) observed extensive use of content analysis followed by questionnaire, interview, case studies, action research and ethnographies among the qualitative techniques.

Revisiting studies in the field of SEA used interviews as a technique of data collection method in major international journals, it can be observed that a good number of papers used interviews as the research method/methodologies. While a consistent presence of case study (both single and multiple), action research, ethnographic studies and mixed method research were observed, interview either solely and coupled with document analysis and/or observation has become more apparent in the last two to three years. Moreover, interview and interview with document analysis were more common as compared to other compositions of data collection methods. Some of the recent studies which used interviews as the research methods are as follows: Bouten and Everaert (2014), Edgley et al. (2014), Christ (2014), Solomon et al. (2013), Momin (2013), Beddewela and Herzig (2013), Sargiacomo et al. (2014), Taylor et al. (2014), Haigh and Shapiro (2012), Yang et al. (2014), Passetti et al. (2014).

These studies equally focused social and environmental issues as opposed to solely focusing on environmental with a broader range of focus covering extents of disclosures on social and environmental issues, managerial motivations and legitimizing efforts, aspects of social and environmental performance measurement, associated cultural and political issues, employees' perceptions and engagement in upholding social and environmental agendas, and so on. Furthermore, along with investigating the performance of the local and multinational corporations, NGOs (non-governmental organizations), public authorities and social alliances are gaining increased attention. To justify interview as the data collection method, researchers frequently referred to issues such as gaining deeper insights through communication, search for better explanation and interpretations, uncovering processes, understanding cultural background, share experiences, and so on. Interviews undertaken in these studies were mostly semi-structured in nature while a few in-depth/unstructured interviews can be observed with numbers of interviewees ranging from 8 to 20 (approximately). In many cases authors mentioned the term 'in depth semi structured' indicating that the format of semi-structured interview was followed to gain a deeper understanding of the phenomena. This trend can be compared with the suggestions of some scholars that semi-structured interviews are more suitable from functionalist and interpretivist perspectives as compared to unstructured and structured interviews (Arksey and Knight 1999; Dumay and Qu 2011; Keats 2000; Kvale 2007; Rubin and Rubin 2005).

Among other qualitative methodologies, a consistent presence of case studies, ethnographies, grounded theory approach and action research can be observed in SEA literature. Some research works with these methodologies are as follows: Spence and Rinaldi (2014), Saravanamuthu and Lehman (2013), Ranamagar et al. (2013), Bewley and Schneider (2013), Fraser (2012), Contrafatto (2014), Mitchell et al. (2012), Mir and Rahaman (2011), Cooper and Pearce (2011), Bessire and Onnée (2010), Jayasinghe and Wickramsinghe (2011).

While the range of focus and the topics of interest were similar to the interview method, case studies/ethnographies/grounded theory/action research provided researchers with the advantage of deeper engagement with the observed event and the participants. It is not surprising that most of the SEA research with these methodologies used the multiple data collection method (i.e. interview, document analysis, observations) as it is a requirement of these methodologies. While authors of these papers provided similar reasons for using interviews as mentioned before, they indicated the significance of triangulating data from different sources to achieve the rigor of the findings.

A number of SEA studies, however, have exclusively used interviews for data collections. For example, Spence and Rinaldi (2014), Saravanamuthu and Lehman (2013), Bryer (2011) and Jayasinghe and Wickramsinghe (2011) have used only interviews in their case studies/ethnographies. According to these authors, interviews were used for these studies with the objectives of unveiling relationships, allowing communication about shift in thinking process, drawing divergent experience, exploring processes rather than outcome, determining the specific field involved, recognizing and understanding complex phenomena, ascertaining the reasons of choices and the managerial perceptions about events that caused the choices. Even though semi-structured interviews were predominant in this research, some use of in-depth (e.g. Cooper and Pearce (2011), Jayasinghe and Wickramsinghe (2011)) was also found in these studies with a range of participants numbering between 6 and 30.

These observations indicate that in spite of the extensive use of interview in conducting qualitative empirical research, researchers in the field of SEA have not yet explored some of the advanced techniques of interviewing. The presence of focus group interviewing, convergent interviewing and critical incident techniques were insignificant. In conducting interviews, the semi-structured form has been used following some in-depth form of interview. Moreover the increasing proportion of 'in depth semi structured' (as mentioned by the authors) interviews is noticeable, which allowed researchers to acquire a deeper insight while using some specific questions to probe on a particular phenomenon.

A CASE OF USE OF INTERVIEW WITHIN THE GLOBAL CONTEXT OF CORPORATE SOCIAL AND ENVIRONMENTAL REPORTING

Islam and Deegan (2008) appears as an important interview based study that focused on motivation for social and environmental reporting practices of organizations that supply products to global companies. Islam and Deegan (2008) in particular used a combination of semi-structured in-depth interviews and annual report content analysis to explore motivation for social and environmental disclosure practices by a major industry body, this being Bangladesh Garment Manufacturers and Exporters Association (BGMEA) in Bangladesh. In-depth semi-structured interviews with 12 senior executives from BGMEA were undertaken to gather information about the types and degrees of social and environmental pressures exerted on BGMEA. An analysis of BGMEA's annual reports (1987–2005) was then performed to explore the link between the perceived pressures (and changes effected therein) and the social and environmental disclosure practices of BGMEA across the period of analysis.

Islam and Deegan (2008) conducted a total of 12 in-depth interviews with senior officials from BGMEA which were undertaken over a three-month period from November 2005 to January 2006. Interviews were deemed to be the best way to obtain information, from the managers' perspective, about the various pressures that were being exerted upon the industry. The research considered that given it was investigating the pressures that were being exerted on the industry, and how these pressures in turn influenced the decision by managers to disclose social responsibility information, then the most direct way to access the information was to interview senior managers within the focus organization.

The executives of BGMEA interviewed for Islam and Deegan (2008) were deemed to be aware of the various stakeholder pressures being exerted on BGMEA and its member organizations, and the strategies that BGMEA adopted to respond to various pressures and expectations. All interviews, except two, were tape-recorded with the consent of interviewees and were subsequently translated and transcribed. Two interviewees did not agree to tape-recorded interviews. In this context, interviews were conducted by intensive note-taking with the consent of interviewees. Translation and transcription were carefully scrutinized against the tape recordings and amendments made where necessary. All interviews were conducted in person. Interviews lasted between half an hour and one and a half hours. While an interview guide was utilized, interview questions were open-ended.

While interviews enabled the researchers to collect information that was not otherwise available and allowed the researchers to gain an insight into managers' perceptions of the pressures exerted on the industry, the interview responses could not be deemed to be reliable by any absolute measure. Responses would potentially be influenced by various factors, and the reliability of the respondents' recollections would be influenced by the willingness or ability to provide an accurate account of the past (which might in turn be influenced by various cognitive, cultural, political or organizational factors), the existence of reflexivity (i.e., giving the interviewer the information the respondent thinks the interviewer wants to hear), and so forth (Easterby-Smith et al. 1991).

CONCLUSION

The finding of this chapter shows that the interview method has significant promise for a deep understanding of the motivation for social and environmental disclosures practices by companies operating globally.

With the growing concerns that the interview cannot be lifted out of its context, postmodern interviews are increasingly adopting a more reflexive approach. It has now been widely acknowledged that the interviewer is not a neutral tool of inquiry. Recognizing the active role played by the interviewers, in the late 1980s researchers started to explore new and innovative forms of interviewing, such as polyphonic interview and interpretive interactionism (Fontana and Frey 2008). These new trends have been duly acknowledged by Holstein and Gubrium (2003). According to them, in this postmodern era of interviewing, researchers should not only consider the 'what' of the interview, but equally the 'how' of the interview. This means that researchers need to take into account the context, particular situation, nuances, manners and people involved in each interview that takes place (Fontana and Frey 2008).

In relation to the 'how' of the interviews, the exploration of different postmodern techniques is very limited in this field. Where semi-structured interviews duly received priority compared to structured and unstructured interviews, SEA researchers frequently termed their interview method as in-depth semi-structured interview, advocating that this method allowed them to get an in-depth understanding while keeping the structural facilities of the semi-structured interview. Different techniques of interviewing, such as convergent interviewing (Dick 1990), critical incident technique (Flanagan 1954; Gremler 2004; Grove and Fisk 1997), laddering technique (Holtzclaw 2012; Reynolds and Gutman 1988), internet interviewing (Fontana and Frey 2008; Mann and Stewart 2003), creative interviewing (Douglas 1985), active interviewing (Holstein and Gubrium 2003) and so on, have the potential to extend a deeper understanding. Exploiting these variations of interviewing techniques could help SEA researchers not only in terms of achieving the rigor of the study, but also exploring new aspects of social and environmental phenomena.

The information obtained from in-depth interviews with managers and relevant stakeholders appears to be the most effective way to gain deep insights into the motivations underlying the social and environmental reporting practices of global organizations. Despite this, the following limitations to the interview method need to be noted.

Limitations

Inherent in all research using interviews is the issue of reliability. While adopting interviews as the primary method of inquiry enabled this study to collect information that would not otherwise be available and to gain an insight into managers' and relevant stakeholders' perceptions, the interview responses cannot be deemed to be reliable by any absolute measure. Potentially, responses will be influenced by various factors, and the reliability of the respondents' recollections will be influenced by their willingness or ability to provide an accurate account of the past (which might in turn be influenced by various cognitive, cultural, political or organizational factors), the existence of reflexivity (that is, giving the interviewer the information the respondent thinks the interviewer wants to hear), and so forth (Easterby-Smith et al. 1991). Hence, as with most research that relies upon interviews as a main source of information, the results need to be considered in light of potential biases or inaccuracies in the responses.

During the coding process (for both primary and secondary data), interpretations and judgement by the researcher were required to categorize the data. Subjectivity was therefore unavoidable, which could lead to possible bias in the results. It seems likely that the researcher's prior expertise in relation to the specialized areas being investigated would be more satisfactory and productive than employing a research assistant to attempt a formalized 'coding' of the transcripts (Walker 1985). In this context, the coding process should be performed by the researcher himself/herself or an expert research assistant, who is closely supervised by an expert who has long-term local and global experience in the field of social and environmental accounting. Using this research expertise, adequate efforts should be undertaken to ensure consistency while conducting and coding interviews and categorizing secondary data such as annual reports or global media articles.

Another possible limitation is in relation to translating and transcribing the interviews conducted in different languages. The experience and knowledge of the researcher in terms of translating and transcribing interview data may raise concerns about interpretation issues. Marshall and Rossman (2006) argue that more concerns about interpretation issues are raised when someone other than the researcher performs the task. Hayes and Mattimoe (2004) suggest that the researchers should do the transcription themselves because an outside transcriber can type salient and material and irrelevant parts where the interviewee has rambled. They also suggest that if the researchers have a small number of interviews to transcribe, it may be better to do this task by themselves. Miles and Huberman (1994) argue that the coding process is dependent on the knowledge and skill of the transcriber. The researchers or their research assistants acting as translators as well as transcribers may cause limited concern over issues of interpretation, but instead offer the benefit of assembling the meaning in a consistent way throughout the study.

REFERENCES

Alvesson, M. (2003), 'Beyond neopositivists, romantics, and localists: a reflexive approach to interviews in organizational research', *The Academy of Management Review*, **28** (1), 13–33.

Alvesson, Mats and Stanley Deetz (2000), *Doing Critical Management Research*, Thousand Oaks, Calif; London: Sage Publications.

Alvesson, M. and D. Kärreman (2000), 'Varieties of discourse: on the study of organizations through discourse analysis', *Human Relations*, **53** (9), 1125–1149.

Alvesson, Mats and Kai Sköldberg (2000), *Reflexive Methodology: New Vistas for Qualitative Research*, London: Sage.

Arksey, Hilary and Peter Knight (1999), *Interviewing for Social Scientists*, Thousand Oaks, Calif, London: SAGE Publications Ltd.

Atkinson, P. and D. Silverman (1997), 'Kundera's Immortality: the interview society and the invention of the self', *Qualitative Inquiry*, **3** (3), 304–325.

Bebbington, J. (1997), 'Engagement, education and sustainability: a review essay on environmental accounting', *Accounting, Auditing and Accountability Journal*, **10** (3), 365–381.

Beddewela, E. and C. Herzig (2013), 'Corporate social reporting by MNCs' subsidiaries in Sri Lanka', *Accounting Forum*, **37** (2), 135–149.

Berg, Bruce L. (2009), *Qualitative Research Methods for the Social Sciences*, Boston: Allyn and Bacon.

Bessire, D. and S. Onnée (2010), 'Assessing corporate social performance: strategies of legitimation and conflicting ideologies', *Critical Perspectives on Accounting*, **21** (6), 445–467. doi: 10.1016/j.cpa.2010.01.015.

Bewley, K. and T. Schneider (2013), 'Triple bottom line accounting and energy-efficiency retrofits in the social-housing sector: a case study', *Accounting and the Public Interest*, **13** (1), 105–131. doi: 10.2308/apin-10359.

Bouten, L. and P. Everaert (2014), 'Social and environmental reporting in Belgium: "Pour vivre heureux, vivons caches"', *Critical Perspectives on Accounting*, 33 (2015): 24–43. doi: 10.1016/j.cpa.2014.10.002.

Brinkmann, Svend (2013), *Qualitative Interviewing*, Oxford, UK: Oxford University Press.

Bryer, A.R. (2011), 'Conscious practices and purposive action: a qualitative study of accounting and social change', *Critical Perspectives on Accounting*, **25** (2), 93–103. doi: 10.1016/j.cpa.2011.09.001.

Christ, K.L. (2014), 'Water management accounting and the wine supply chain: empirical evidence from Australia', *The British Accounting Review*, 46.4 (2014): 379–396. doi: 10.1016/j.bar.2014.10.003.

Contrafatto, M. (2014), 'The institutionalization of social and environmental reporting: an Italian narrative', *Accounting, Organizations and Society*, **39** (6), 414–432.

Cooper, S. and G. Pearce (2011), 'Climate change performance measurement, control and accountability in English local authority areas', *Accounting, Auditing and Accountability Journal*, **24** (8), 1097. doi: 10.1108/09513571111184779.

Deegan, C. and S. Soltys (2007), 'Social accounting research: an Australasian perspective', *Accounting Forum*, **31** (1), 73–89. doi: 10.1016/j.accfor.2006.11.001.

Denzin, N.K. and Y.S. Lincoln (1994), 'Introduction: entering the field of qualitative research', in Norman K. Denzin and Yvonne S. Lincoln (eds), *Handbook of Qualitative Research*, Thousand Oaks, Calif: Sage Publications, pp.1–16.

Dick, Robert (1990), *Convergent Interviewing*, Chapel Hill, Qld: Interchange.

Douglas, Jack D. (1985), *Creative Interviewing*, vol. 159, Beverly Hills: Sage Publications.

Dumay, J. and S.Q. Qu (2011), 'The qualitative research interview', *Qualitative Research in Accounting and Management*, **8** (3), 238–264. doi: 10.1108/11766091111162070.

Easterby-Smith, Mark, Richard Thorpe and Andy Lowe (1991), *Management Research: An Introduction*, London: Sage Publications.

Edgley, C., M.J. Jones and J. Atkins (2014), 'The adoption of the materiality concept in social and environmental reporting assurance: a field study approach', *The British Accounting Review*, **47** (1), 1–18. doi: 10.1016/j.bar.2014.11.001.

Edwards, Rosalind and Janet Holland (2013), *What is Qualitative Interviewing?*, London: Bloomsbury Academic.

Eugénio, T., I.C. Lourenço and A.I. Morais (2010), 'Recent developments in social and environmental accounting research', *Social Responsibility Journal*, **6** (2), 286–305. doi: 10.1108/17471111011051775.

Flanagan, J.C. (1954), 'The critical incident technique', *Psychological Bulletin*, **51** (4), 327–358. doi: 10.1037/h0061470.

Fontana, A. (2002), 'Postmodern trends in interviewing', in James A. Holstein and Jaber F. Gubrium (eds), *Handbook of Interview Research: Context and Method*, (1st ed.), Thousand Oaks, Calif: SAGE Publication, pp.161–175.

Fontana, A. and J.H. Frey (2008), 'The interview: from neutral stance to political involvement', in Norman K. Denzin and Yvonne S. Lincoln (eds), *Collecting and Interpreting Qualitative Materials*, (3rd ed.), Los Angeles: Sage Publications, pp.115–160.

Fraser, M. (2012), '"Fleshing out" an engagement with a social accounting technology', *Accounting, Auditing and Accountability Journal*, **25** (3), 508–534. doi: 10.1108/09513571211209626.

Gray, R. (2002), 'The social accounting project and accounting organizations and society privileging engagement, imaginings, new accountings and pragmatism over critique?', *Accounting, Organizations and Society*, **27** (7), 687–708. doi: 10.1016/S0361-3682(00)00003-9.

Gremler, D.D. (2004), 'The critical incident technique in service research', *Journal of Service Research*, **7** (1), 65–89. doi: 10.1177/1094670504266138.

Grove, S.J. and R.P. Fisk (1997), 'The impact of other customers on service experiences: a critical incident examination of "getting along"', *Journal of Retailing*, **73** (1), 63–85. doi: 10.1016/S0022-4359(97)90015-4.

Haigh, M. and M.A. Shapiro (2012), 'Carbon reporting: does it matter?', *Accounting, Auditing and Accountability Journal*, **25** (1), 105–125. doi: 10.1108/09513571211191761.

Hayes, T. and R. Mattimoe (2004), 'To tape or not to tape: reflections on methods of data collection', in Christopher Humphrey and Bill Lee (eds), *The Real Life Guide to Accounting Research: A Behind-the-scenes View of Using Qualitative Research Methods*, (1st ed.), Amsterdam, London, Boston: Elsevier, pp.359–372.

Hertz, R. (1997), *Reflexivity and Voice*, Thousand Oaks, CA: Sage.

Holstein, J.A. and J.F. Gubrium (2001), 'From individual interview to interview society', in James A. Holstein and Jaber F. Gubrium (1st ed.), *Handbook of Interview Research: Context and Method*, Thousand Oaks, Calif: Sage Publications, pp.3–32.

Holstein, J.A. and J.F. Gubrium (2003), 'Active interviewing', in James A. Holstein and Jaber F. Gubrium (1st ed.), *Postmodern Interviewing*, Thousand Oaks, Calif; London: Sage Publications, pp.66–81.
Holtzclaw, E.V. (2012), *Laddering: Unlocking the Potential of Consumer Behavior*, Hoboken, New Jersey: John Wiley and Sons.
Islam, M.A. and C. Deegan (2008), 'Motivations for an organisation within a developing country to report social responsibility information: evidence from Bangladesh', *Accounting, Auditing and Accountability Journal*, **21** (6), 850–874. doi: 10.1108/09513570810893272.
Jayasinghe, K. and D. Wickramsinghe (2011), 'Power over empowerment: encountering development accounting in a Sri Lankan fishing village', *Critical Perspectives on Accounting*, **22** (4), 396–414. doi: 10.1016/j.cpa.2010.12.008.
Johnson, J.M. (2001), 'In-depth interviewing', in James A. Holstein and Jaber F. Gubrium (1st ed.), *Handbook of Interview Research: Context and Method*, Thousand Oaks, Calif: Sage Publications, pp.103–119.
Keats, Daphne (2000), *Interviewing: A Practical Guide for Students and Professionals*, Sydney: UNSW Press.
Kvale, Steinar (2007), *Doing Interviews*, Thousand Oaks, Calif: Sage Publications.
Maccoby, E.E. and N. Maccoby (1954), 'The interview: a tool of social science', *Handbook of Social Psychology*, **1**, 449–487.
Mann, C. and F. Stewart (2003), 'Internet interviewing', in James A. Holstein and Jaber F. Gubrium (1st ed.), *Postmodern Interviewing*, Thousand Oaks, Calif; London: Sage Publications, pp.81–106.
Marshall, Catherine and Gretchen B. Rossman (2006), *Designing Qualitative Research*, California: Sage.
Mathews, M.R. (1997), 'Twenty-five years of social and environmental accounting research: is there a silver jubilee to celebrate?', *Accounting, Auditing and Accountability Journal*, **10** (4), 481–531.
Miles, Matthew B. and Michel A. Huberman (1994), *Qualitative Data Analysis: An Expanded Sourcebook*, (2nd ed.), Thousand Oaks: Sage.
Mir, M.Z. and A.S. Rahaman (2011), 'In pursuit of environmental excellence', *Accounting, Auditing and Accountability Journal*, **24** (7), 848–878. doi: 10.1108/09513571111161620.
Mitchell, M., A. Curtis and P. Davidson (2012), 'Can triple bottom line reporting become a cycle for "double loop" learning and radical change?', *Accounting, Auditing and Accountability Journal*, **25** (6), 1048–1068. doi: 10.1108/09513571211250242.
Momin, M.A. (2013), 'Social and environmental NGOs' perceptions of corporate social disclosures: the case of Bangladesh', *Accounting Forum*, **37** (2), 150–161.
Owen, D. (2008), 'Chronicles of wasted time?: a personal reflection on the current state of, and future prospects for, social and environmental accounting research', *Accounting, Auditing and Accountability Journal*, **21** (2), 240–267. doi: 10.1108/09513570810854428.
Parker, L.D. (2011), 'Twenty-one years of social and environmental accountability research: a coming of age', *Accounting Forum*, **35** (1), 1–10. doi: 10.1016/j.accfor.2010.11.001.
Passetti, E., L. Cinquini, A. Marelli and A. Tenucci (2014), 'Sustainability accounting in action: lights and shadows in the Italian context', *The British Accounting Review*, **46** (3), 295–308.
Platt, J. (2001), 'The history of the interview', in James A. Holstein and Jaber F. Gubrium (1st ed.), *Handbook of Interview Research: Context and Method*, Thousand Oaks, Calif: Sage Publications, pp.33–54.
Ranamagar, N., E. Barone and J.F. Solomona (2013), 'A Habermasian model of stakeholder (non)engagement and corporate (ir)responsibility reporting', *Accounting Forum*, **37** (3), 163–181.
Reynolds, T.J. and J. Gutman (1988), 'Laddering theory, method, analysis, and interpretation', *Journal of Advertising Research*, **28** (1), 11–34.
Rubin, Herbert J. and Irene Rubin (2005), *Qualitative Interviewing: The Art of Hearing Data*, Thousand Oaks, Calif: Sage Publications.
Saravanamuthu, K. and C. Lehman (2013), 'Enhancing stakeholder interaction through environmental risk accounts', *Critical Perspectives on Accounting*, **24** (6), 410–437. doi: 10.1016/j.cpa.2013.02.002.
Sargiacomo, M., L. Ianni and J. Everett (2014), 'Accounting for suffering: calculative practices in the field of disaster relief', *Critical Perspectives on Accounting*, **25** (7), 652–669.
Scheurich, J.J. (1995), 'A postmodernist critique of research interviewing', *International Journal of Qualitative Studies in Education*, **8** (3), 239–252.
Silverman, David (2001), *Interpreting Qualitative Data: Methods for Analysing Talk, Text and Interaction*, London: SAGE.
Solomon, J.F., A. Solomon, N.L. Joseph and S.D. Norton (2013), 'Impression management, myth creation and fabrication in private social and environmental reporting: insights from Erving Goffman', *Accounting, Organizations and Society*, **38** (3) 195–213.
Spence, L.J. and L. Rinaldi (2014), 'Governmentality in accounting and accountability: a case study of embedding sustainability in a supply chain', *Accounting, Organizations and Society*, **39** (6), 433–452.
Taylor, D., M. Tharapos and S. Sidaway (2014), 'Downward accountability for a natural disaster recovery effort: evidence and issues from Australia's Black Saturday', *Critical Perspectives on Accounting*, **25** (7), 633–651.
Van Maanen, John (1995), *Representation in Ethnography*, Thousand Oaks: Sage Publications.

Walker, Robert (1985), *Applied Qualitative Research*, New York: Gower Pub Co.
Warren, C.A.B. (2001), 'Qualitative interviewing', in James A. Holstein and Jaber F. Gubrium (1st ed.), *Handbook of Interview Research: Context and Method*, Thousand Oaks, Calif: Sage Publications, pp.83–101.
Yang, H.H., R. Craig and A. Farley (2014), 'A review of Chinese and English language studies on corporate environmental reporting in China', *Critical Perspectives on Accounting*, **28**, 30–48 doi: 10.1016/j.cpa.2014.10.001.

17. Participant observation as the data collection tool and its usage in the CSR researches
Ilke Oruc

INTRODUCTION

This chapter will focus on the participant observation method as one of the data collection tools for corporate social responsibility (CSR) research and it will present information oriented towards how we can use especially the participant observation method in our research. Indeed, as many qualitative researchers highlight, the observation is one of the activities that we experience mostly in our life; but, we do not think too much about this in a systematic way or what inferences we make as a result of these observations. When we approach the issue in methodological terms, the observation is a tool that can provide us with important data resources within the method that we chose based on the research problem. The participant observation method that we mostly emphasize constitutes one of the fundamental parts of ethnographic research, which Linne Marie Lauesen in Chapter 15, 'Ethnographic research methods in CSR research: building theory out of people's everyday life with materials, objects, practices, and symbolic constructions', this volume, has mentioned. Even though the usages of the method related to CSR have been explained in detail in Chapter 15, it is vital to make explanations regarding the concepts of ethnography and organizational ethnography in terms of providing the integrity of the issues here.

If we want to talk about participant observation methods, firstly, we should address ethnography (see Chapter 15) that is effectively used in this method and also the concept of field research, which the basic of this research methodology rests on. Of course, this method has a historical background, and the methodology has changed and developed with time. But instruction about this part here would obviously extend the study and delay the important discussion in this chapter. Therefore, regarding historical background, consult Chapter 15.

Ethnography means *writing about people* (ethos: people, race or cultural group, and graphia: writing, presentation) (Neuman 2003). It is defined as a method with a comprehensive discovery and definition of the culture of a particular group or people (Johnson and Christensen 2004; Payne and Payne 2004), and in particular it requires a systemic approach (Brewer 2000, p. 6). This method has been used by Malinovski, and he wanted to understand the world of indigenous people with references to their relationships with life. These studies have provided a basis for the generalizations regarding human behavior and social life by broadening our knowledge about the distribution of variety and diversity of human lives across the world (Yıldırım and Şimşek 2005, pp.70; Kottak 2008). Ethnography, as a method, is field-based, personal, multi-factored, longitudinal, inductive, dialogue-based and holistic (Angrosino 2007).

The purpose of ethnography is to understand and interpret groups' and society's culture and its elements based on their descriptions of their members and society with perspective both from within (emic) and from the outside (etic) point (Angrosino 2007). Ethnography is a good method for people to understand *why they are doing what they are doing* through participant observation, interpretation and writing of a culture, which constitute ethnographic work in different ways. Ethnographic perspective is obtained by the researcher in the area, where an event, or events, from everyday life occurs, and the natural flow of data that he or she will use is typically assembled by recording. After this process has been conducted and recorded alongside the collection of other data, it will all together generate a narrative regarding the field formed into a whole (Machin 2002, p. 3).

There are lots of studies conducted on organizational ethnography in the literature. These studies are aimed at revealing the realities involving the culture of working life by combining organizational field observations of routines and other events in many areas (Smith 2007). The researchers studying organizations soon realized the importance of studying daily routines in the organizations, since most researchers ignored such routines by assuming that they are insignificant or already established (Schwartzman 1993). Ethnographers concluded that employees finished their tasks in a different way than dictated by the administrators, and that they did not deliberately share some information with the administrators and engineers, and thus slowed down or blocked the production process, and finally that they played games and collaborated with their co-workers to finish the job (Smith 2007).

Van Maanen (1979), in a study on organizational ethnography, suggests that ethnography can be a useful method in generating theories based on realities in organizations. He also emphasizes that ethnographers believe in the effectiveness of participating in the organization field directly (*through participant observation, that is*). In organizational studies, the patterns of interest are typically the various forms in which people manage to do things together in observable and repeated ways. As mentioned earlier, ethnographic studies aim at defining these communities in detail by using certain advantages such as face-to-face communication, direct participation in some group activities, document analysis, informants who provide more valuable information than questionnaires, and observations. Van Maanen, in his study, rated the data based on representation and process in his organizational ethnography. According to this classification, theories and experimentalism were in the first category. At the experimental level, he suggests that it is necessary to examine the behaviors as well as the descriptions made by the members through observations. The second level includes attitudes, and they are the concepts used by the researcher in order to explain the patterns of the data obtained in the first level. Van Maanen calls this *the representation of representation*.

In short, workplace ethnographers, like other ethnographers, create research questions that we are generally familiar with. They make permanent and original contributions to social sciences by analysing the dynamic nature of workplaces; by identifying the routine in the complexity as well as the complexity in the routines; and by studying power and inequality. This point of view takes the following issues into consideration: organization, responsibilities, duration of work, relationships; and things that often do not come forward with other working methods (Smith 2007). The importance of these issues is thus crucial (Schwartzman 1993).

Conducting a study based on qualitative study principles requires detailed planning and acting accordingly. The use of ethnography in a study on organizations is often performed as a part of a grounded theoretical framework, a sound research design, data collection tools, effective analysis methods and validity-reliability calculations. Research design starts with the determination of the research question and related questions hereto, and then follows a cyclical process. There are various data collection methods that might be applied in an ethnographic study to be carried out on organizations such as field notes, reflective journals, informal interviews and participant observation. Among those, participant observation is one of the most important data collection methods. Researchers choose among these options depending on their research design. Although it is believed that providing detailed information about these tools will be useful to guide researchers, who are planning to apply quantitative research methods, it will increase the length of this chapter considerably. Organizational ethnography might provide valuable information not only for the place of CSR in working life, but also for many other themes. Therefore, researchers should benefit from the advantages of ethnography when approaching organizations – not only sociologically, but also in terms of capturing the dynamics of organizations as well.

Generally, we observe that in CSR research, the studies are typically based on the reports of the organizations: information that they share with their stakeholders, and the scales developed for the measurement of this information in the quantitative terms have been publicized (Barkay 2012). For CSR, only the studies integrating the daily procedure of organizations with the values they have more than the written sentences formed in corporate reports etc., are needed, and especially, it is required to determine how the understandings that can integrate these differences in a multi-cultural organizational field are operationalized. In the organizations, the real CSR research process includes the extremely complex processes, which cannot be fully documented by using only the quantitative research methods. For discovering a real organization, it is important to pay attention to the real experiences in its daily life (Lauring and Thomsen 2009). CSR is considered as the *all over the place and nowhere at the same time* field. Making a field survey in the CSR field means that we observe the connections and issues between the fields jointly formed (Garsten 2010). There will be many data collection techniques that we consider preferable in terms of our research, or that we want to use during the ethnographical field study based on any problems related to the CSR issues that we determine essential. With these techniques, the participant observation method, which is considered as almost equaling ethnography, will form our fundamental discussion point for this chapter. I will make inferences to the issue of how we can also use the participant observation method from my own gender based ethnographical field research, which has been conducted in an organization for my Ph.D. thesis on CSR. For this reason, I think that giving details about the issue of participant observation primarily will be meaningful.

PARTICIPANT OBSERVATION

One of the best ways of understanding a certain behavior is to experience and hear it directly (Karasar 1991). Through this, the most original data can be reached with the different appearances of the examined issue from the inside and outside (Altunisik et al. 2004). *Naturalness* is making an observation in the natural order of the subject (for example, the house where s/he works, the place where s/he works or public space etc.) (Kalof et al. 2008, pp.114–118), as a definition; it is the act of noticing a phenomenon by making records generally with the tools at hand for scientific purposes (Angrosino 2007, pp.53). Humans are mostly not aware of their behaviors, and for this reason, the observation ensures that we establish a connection with the things that the humans say and what they perceive. In the field of sociology, participant observation is the method of examining the interactions of the individuals with each other including the cultural rituals and events forming the extremely complicated relations network, which is called 'daily life' as a part of the community they live in. By directly participating in the daily activities, the researcher becomes part of that reality (DeWalt and DeWalt 2001). Participant observation (or the ethnographic field study) is considered the basis of cultural anthropology, and it requires the presence of a field researcher, who is close to the humans and who can record the observations and information that s/he has made regarding their lives (Bernard 1994).

Participant observation is a data collection tool, which is structured on the basis of a relatively long duration for constituting the research, and reports upon the experience, social life and social processes in a field. It not only includes the embedding of the researcher into the field taking place in the social world and providing the reaching into this field, but it is also defined as the production of the written explanations and definitions giving the versions of the world of the others (Emerson et al. 1995, p.353). In this observation method, the researcher gets support from various recording and data collection methods for the recording of the observations to the field notes (DeWalt and DeWalt 2001).

The participant observation starts with an open approach to a special place, culture or group. Then the researcher defines a certain place (location) for his/her observations. But, sometimes, it can be difficult to reach the determined places. Especially, in cases of extraordinary studies or in studies, in which the participants are unwilling to participate, this problem appears. In this situation, it is required to make interviews with the *gatekeepers* who can then provide the entrance to the research field. A researcher should decide how s/he will participate in a group or a team, and s/he should take a role, by which s/he will not take any risks within the group activities. The active participation in the field is called *being local*. The researcher also should take a more objective role; that is, s/he will not be active in the group in all terms and in which s/he can establish communication based on a certain distance with the group members. The way this role can be obtained by the researcher and the person, who makes it possible for the researcher to enter to the field, can also affect this decision (Kalof et al. 2008, pp.114–118).

How the observation research will be conducted is discussed by many ethnographers, and it is classified in different ways. Some researchers assert that there are two fundamental ways of the observation research: participant observation and direct observation. With participant observation, the researcher embeds him/herself into the research field and meets with the persons that s/he observes and becomes active (or participant) in the field. In direct observation, the researcher follows the humans, but s/he is not a participant. A direct participant is obliged to consider the effect of his/her existence in his/her observations (even probably being too little) and to know that s/he should not disturb the other people. Making video recordings behind a mirror by the researcher is an example of this. The usage of the visual and audio recording tools in such ways, however, can affect the human behaviors negatively. Especially in these methods, care should be taken to act ethically. The best example of this in terms of the organization is Hawthorne's research (see e.g., Corner and Hawthorn 1980). In some situations, it can be required for the researcher to be a participant rather than a direct observer (Kalof et al. 2008, pp.114–118). The most appropriate definition oriented for the classification of participant observation has been made by Raymond Gold (1958, cited by deMarrais and Lapan 2004). He defines the role of the researcher in participant observation in four different ways:

- complete participant
- the participant as observer
- the observer as participant
- complete observer.

Gold does not consider the participant observation a research method, but a strategy, which is a data collection tool in the field. To obtain the data collection, the researcher is thus required to harmonize his/her roles. The researcher can also apply the other data collection techniques to the community under research (such as questionnaire, archive records, interview), but even though s/he uses these other tools, s/he is required to be careful and attentive while observing the humans and the events around them (Angrosino 2007).

The study starts with the researcher trying to get used to being in the entered field. After the field is entered, the researcher will adapt to the environment and enter the networks of the relations in the field, and after that select the ways and the tools that will effectively record the data required. The insiders of the field can provide extremely rich information for the research, and this forms a basis for the researcher to form a report and to establish trust based relations with the group members. Often, one or a few persons are effective respondents in such research settings. They are often called the *key informants* (Kalof et al. 2008, pp.114–118). The most important question for the ethnography is whether a few respondents are sufficient enough for providing information regarding a culture, or if several are required. It depends basically on two things; selecting the persons who provide the best information, and asking them questions regarding the things that they know. In participant observation, the researcher should ensure that the people accept him/her. The participant observer does not have the purpose of controlling all elements of the research. S/he conveys the information, which is required in the research design, without intervening and in a way in which it happens in its natural environment. Some steps should be taken for ensuring orderliness in the participant observation and establishing the sensitivity of the definition of the study (Angrosino 2007):

1. The first step is the process of selecting the location. The field can be selected because the researcher can get answers to his/her research problem or it can be considered adequate for providing these answers.
2. The second step is to gain the rights to enter the community. Some communities are open for outsiders, and others are not open. If the researcher goes to a place, which may be difficult to be accepted in, additional preparations should be made. So-called *gatekeepers* (i.e. important persons that may provide the needed entrance to the field) may provide both formal and informal convergence. For this reason, it is required to gain their approval and support.
3. Once having gained access to the site, the individual researcher may begin observing immediately. Those working with teams may, however, need to take some time

for training, just to make sure everyone is doing his/her assigned task in the proper manner. If one is working in a situation requiring the assistance of translators or others who live in the community, it may be necessary to spend some initial time orienting them to the goals and operations of the research project. It may also be necessary to take some time to become accustomed to the site. The more exotic the locale, the more likely will it be that the researcher suffers from culture shock – a sense of being overwhelmed by the new and unfamiliar. But even when working close to home in reasonably familiar surroundings, the focus on observation that the researcher employs may result in a phase of 'shock' just because s/he is interacting with that setting in the role of researcher in ways quite different from those that characterized earlier encounters.

4. Another step is when the researcher finds it necessary to take notes probably regarding everything s/he finds during the observation. Recording of the notes by the researcher is an important requirement, but this does not have a generally accepted format. Some researchers prefer tools such as lists, networks, tables, and others prefer free format expressions. Some prefer software programs, and others prefer handwritten notes, index cards and other tools. Their crucial point is that the method chosen should be beneficial for collecting information, repetitions and analyses, which suits the researcher best. In the case of group projects, it can be necessary to have certain standards for collecting information.
5. Another step is to see the patterns in the field regarding the questions that will occur when the research advances; in the following stages of the research and in the additional observations or in the observations in the other meanings of the research.
6. The observation continues till it reaches the theoretical saturation. When the data repetitions get frequent, the field is to be left.

Even though it is classified in different ways, the field research fundamentally gets its shape according to the above-mentioned issues. Differing from these stages is up to the researcher and his/her argumentation of methodology. Focusing on a problem in the culture in which the researcher lives decreases the possibility of getting a cultural shock in the field of study. For this reason, it is difficult to assert that all the above-mentioned stages must be followed.

How much time should be spent in the field? In anthropological studies, the duration can go up to one year. But, this duration changes according to the repetition situation of the data gathering for answering the research question (Emerson et al. 1995). The skills that the participant observer is required to possess are learning another language, using the body language correctly, forming the tools oriented for the recording of the data or keeping the data in memory, theory development, developing the writing ability, embedding in the field and objectivity (Emerson et al. 1995; Angrosino 2007).

Participant observation provides some advantages for research. Firstly, it increases the quality of the data provided during the field study. Secondly, as many data collection tools can be used, it increases the quality of the analysis and interpretation of these data. The participant observation, for this reason, is both a data collection technique and an analytic tool. Thirdly, it provides the appearing of new research problems and approaching the issue from different angles (DeWalt and DeWalt 2001).

Like other research methods, this method also has limitations. Participant observation and being based in the field context takes more time than other data collection techniques. The observation processes change depending on the research, and it is uncertain as to whether the data repetition takes several weeks or even years. The records of the observer are extremely sensitive and it should also be considered in his/her comments that the different researchers can see different things. In field research, participation of the researcher in the activities creates ethical concerns, and it is required that the processes, in which the researcher can affect the investigated, should be approached with care and sensitivity.

Participant Observation in CSR Research

After giving that much explanatory information regarding participant observation, we can consider why we can use it in CSR research. Generally what we try to internalize above is that the ethnography provides a research method paying attention to the culture in which it exists. The organizations take place in the system as a part of the community in which we live. As of the 1980s, understanding the culture has become an important element in the organization studies (Patton 2002). The findings obtained from these studies have ensured the formation of the new understandings in the management approaches. After these researches, the studies examining the organizational culture have accelerated. Understanding the organizational culture as a reflection of a culture in which researchers exist requires both *etic* (*internal*) and *emic* (*external*) points of view. Because we cannot separate the culture of an organization from the macro-communal structure in which it exists, it is required that the ethnographical studies provide a perspective from the inside as well as from the outside, which should be generalized in the efforts of understanding it. When we approach issues of CSR, we can say that the CSR activities of the organizations are affected from whether they are multi-national companies (MNC), domestic, large or small sized. It is known that elements such as the education, culture, and social structure in the community in which they live also affect this structure of the organizations. Especially recently, where the enterprise scandals affected the stakeholders' trust negatively regarding working efficiency and enterprise profit, it appears clear why the enterprises are required to act much more sensitively with CSR issues. Generally, the way MNC and large sized enterprises care about CSR issues regarding stakeholders can give big advantages to the organizations in the long run, and it will ensure that the positive image in the eyes of the stakeholders will increase.

What is required to be asked now is how the organizations internalize the philosophy of CSR and how they put this into implementation and whether there is a difference between the mentioned outcomes and the real outcomes. Most times, from studies of what enterprises have realized regarding CSR, we can observe the implementations within and outside of the organization on the basis of the culture of the enterprise. In research settings based on ethnography and participant observation, we can find the opportunities to observe the ethical and CSR implementations within the businesses whether these are reflected outside or not.

Today, when websites with CSR issues are evaluated in sustainability studies seen from a communal perspective, they generally focus on issues which are considered deficient in the community, which are not cared for, or which are considered as important (Marrewijk 2003, pp.96–97; Ozturk 2003, pp.101). When we approach these issues from a stakeholder approach, it is seen that the things realized are extremely important, and it is observed that the CSR activities in companies oriented towards stakeholders remain in their communal focus in the revealing of them or the sharing of what they have accomplished. For this reason, ethnographical field survey also pays attention to the culture within the setting, the integrity and philosophy of the companies' CSR activities, and in researchers observing how it is situated in the organization. The participant observation method taking place within this setting can present important findings to the researcher and the ones who are interested in the issue.

The participant observation thought gets its shape after the selection of the ethnographical research method, and it is necessary to form the drafts oriented for how it will be realized. For this, primarily, it is required of the researcher instead to observe the environment closely. The explanations regarding the data collection methods that we can utilize while making participant observations are available below. But as highlighted before, the researcher can use many tools together and s/he can also use the data collection tools differently from the ways explained. Personally, I have used informal interviews, field notes and reflective diaries that provided me to make written participant observations. I used that together with participant observation in my ethnographical field research. It has been effective and useful for me, and for this reason, I want to present in the next section how we can make the informational interviews supporting my observations.

Informal Interviews

Making informal interviews is a way of interviewing, which is not structured like an open-ended interview (Patton 2002). In informal interviews, we talk with the informants of the study by using questions (Jorgensen 1989), and we get answers from the informants in a daily conversational way regarding the issues, we are interested in (Denzin 1989; McNamara 2009, p.183). Naturally, it is accomplished face-to-face and through the establishment of a relation as natural as possible (Brewer 2000). We can learn about the expressions in the field via the informal interview (Hammersley and Atkinson 1995).

That the interview is informal does not mean that the interview will not have a focus. The general intention behind the usage of the concept and the accomplishment of this interview form will give a certain idea to the researcher making the interview. The purpose of interviewing, then, is to allow us to enter into the other person's perspective. An evaluator can enhance the use of qualitative data by generating relevant and high-quality findings (Patton 2002). Therefore, the interview content (data) will change depending on the interviewer, interview time and other conditions. Even though the informal interviews are considered a technique, which is easily implemented, because it is based on the individual skills and the power of interpreting the cultural phenomena of the researcher, indeed it is not as easy as it seems to be (Fetterman 1997). It is clear that this interview type requires increased interviewer ability. The interviewer can feel the need for sustaining and controlling the situation. Also, due to the reciprocal interaction, it requires gaining the trust of the other party (the informants) and the development of good relations with him/her. Many situational coincidences happen in the daily life within a field. For this reason, it is required to think creatively depending on the situations of the research, and to design how one as researcher will obtain data (Brewer 2000). When the informal interview is implemented in a good way, it will provide the correct information about the lives and opinions of the humans in the field setting. Thus the researcher needs to collect and analyse data by creating the most natural situation and conditions as possible (Fetterman 1997). The researcher makes unstructured interviews with open-ended questions, and utilizes the issues appearing in the research field generated by his/her participation. The interview ways are determined by the researcher, and s/he aims to find answers regarding the problem of the research (O'Reilly 2005).

The most important data resources in the field are found when the researcher completes participant observation and is situated in the field setting with a certain identity and role given by those working in the field. In that respect, the informal interviews, which s/he has included within the process, are of vital importance to the research. The interview situation including the personal interactions between the researcher and the participants is realized as the conversations in the appropriate environment within the field takes place. We can use this as an approach to the research problem regarding CSR issues. For example, when we want to evaluate the responsibilities of the organization towards its workers, we can direct questions to the workers as a participant observer for them to define the behaviors of the organization towards them. For this to be effective, it will be beneficial for us as researchers to be a participant observer at the worker level and to 'work' there ourselves. If we are being perceived as part of the managerial level as a researcher sent by the management, we can encounter difficulties in the conveyance of information or data to us by the workers. For this reason, we should consider the importance of choosing the field that we will enter carefully and according to the specific CSR problem that we want to investigate. With the participant observation study, the field notes and keeping a reflective diary, we can convey the realities of the field that we have observed in an effective way. For this reason, these tools will be given detailed concerns in the next section.

How Can the Data in the Participant Observation be Made Written?

The first tool that can be used for recording the participant observation data and making them written is the field notes. These notes provide us with our observations and concerns in the field and provide more insight to the simultaneous writing of the events, experiences and the interactions going on in the field (Emerson et al. 1995, p.353). It is necessary to record the data obtained from the field for it not to be lost; to be remembered and to be analysed. For this reason, the researcher records his/her observations and his/her own feelings in the field study by keeping the field notes and diaries. This stage is important in terms of systematizing the execution of the study and to protect the data without them getting lost (Atkinson 1992, pp.17; Emerson et al. 1995, pp.8–10). The expressions obtained from the field, the events and the results based on these events are reflected through the ethnographer's gaze. This also causes the structuring of the events and situations in different ways by the different researchers (Emerson et al. 1995).

The observation method is widely based on the research notes and the interview transcripts. Keeping the field notes is one of the most fundamental tasks of the observer and it includes the definition of and reflection upon the observed matters. The observer should record everything that is necessary to be noted. The field notes that an observer keeps should give the details that will provide the basis for analysing the context of the issue, its framework and data (Patton 2002). The fundamental attribution of the field notes should generally be descriptive. The fundamental information such as the physical attributions of the place where the observation has been made and the personal characteristics of the observed persons (communal statuses, cultural identities, education levels, physical characteristics, etc.) should be written and dated. Firstly, the field notes require the recording with the words that will recall direct citation of what the informants say and what s/he says means for the cultural context via the formal interview or observation. Secondly, the field notes should include the importance of his/her own feelings, his/her reactions to the events encountered, his/her thoughts in personal terms, and the things that s/he has observed for the research. It should convey all feelings of the researcher about the events in the field with their intensity and naturalness. As a result, in qualitative research, the informant's own experiences of the observer also constitute a part of the data (Emerson et al. 1995; Patton 2002).

The other method that we can use for recording the data that we have obtained with participant observation is the reflecting diaries. A reflecting diary is characterized as an unstructured form of personal reflective writing. The building blocks of the reflecting implementation are the accumulation of the expressions of the thoughts and discoveries, and it is the reflecting and critical drawing up of the personal opinions under the experience and understandings such as by making a kind of reflective map. The writing form can be experienced such as by dialogues, metaphor expressions, visualization, and making a story of it (Bolton 2001).

After explaining all of these, I want to mention how I have made use of these kinds of tools. Firstly, I kept the field notes of the recording of the events, which I had been experiencing in the field and which I had been observing, which were extremely important. You should determine by yourself what the field notes can tell you about the events and the things encountered there as a researcher. I also chose to use memorizing words of this issue and record the sentences that I have considered as important. I realized that this was not possible in the working environments within the field. For this reason, I preferred to do this in the appropriate fields for myself at the breaks. Keeping the field notes in a regular way has provided me with important advantages in terms of recording the data in an orderly way. Then, by transferring all data that I have conveyed into field notes and to the reflecting diary every night regularly, I had ensured the recording of the data freshly, without being forgotten, and completely. This was one of the ways that I have selected for making all of my field data written. Also, this was important in terms of determining as to whether the data within the field has been repeated or not, and determining at what time I could leave the field. Besides, there has been descriptive information oriented for the informants and tools that I have used to support my data obtained in the unstructured interview with a human resources manager. In my reflecting diary, I have used three empty columns for making the data, events and coding. At the same time, I wrote descriptions of the relations of the individuals within the organizations and for determining the places where the events have happened I drew the dining hall and factory plan of the organization. As a result of all of these methodological data collection methods explained above, there will be texts composed of hundreds of pages at your hands available as research. If you use especially the interview method, their transcription will also take much of your time, and these texts will also be included in the data that you have obtained. Which result will we then reach? This means that we will pass on to another stage in

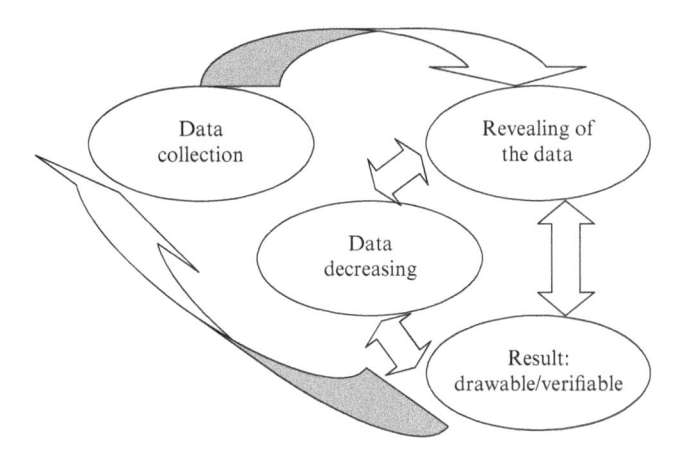

Figure 17.1   Components of the data analysis: interactive model

which we are required to advance carefully and in an attentive manner while making qualitative research.

Analysis of the Data

In qualitative research, the data analysis is conducted on the basis of a certain process and is cyclical. There is no single formula that can be used in the analysis chapter (Angrosino 2007), but it includes certain processes as we see in Figure 17.1.

In the data analysis process, firstly, the important thing is the management of the data in a robust way; in other words, it is the organizing of the data regularly and clearly (Angrosino 2007, p.70). In the data recording, the researcher can use a computer program that will assist analysis of the qualitative data and s/he can also use methods such as index cards and apply audio recordings into a computer analysing programme.

Another important step in the data analysis is the reviewing of the readings. The reviewing of the notes before the formal analysis is an important requirement. While collecting data, we can see the issues, which are overlooked or which are not considered as important as we refresh our memories. At the same time, we can query our pre- and post-study perceptions (Angrosino 2007, p.70). During the research, the obtaining of the data correctly and ensuring its validity and reliability is extremely important. For this reason, the studies oriented for providing the validity and reliability of the research in both qualitative and quantitative research constitute an important part of the research.

The individual reference environment of the researcher is extremely vital in terms of the quality of the research executed as being based on ethnography. Ethnographical field research is generally conducted by the participant observer balancing the objective data collection with the subjective points of views regarding the results as a kind of motion related to the things that the humans give meaning in their lives (Machin 2002; Angrosino 2007). At the same time, it requires the effective usage of the individual abilities of the researcher. For example, making observations, keeping the data in mind and recording them correctly, and writing ability are a part of these elements (Emerson et al. 1995;

Alvesson 1998; Angrosino 2007). While making research, whether the researcher has the required equipment for realizing the research conducted, appears to us as another element that affects the validity and reliability of the research. The researcher who wants to convey research based on qualitative inquiry in a valid and secure way is required to have knowledge of various qualitative research issues. This accumulation expressing the individual's reference framework can present an account regarding the validity and reliability of the researcher as being based on his/her undergraduate or master's education, the qualitative research courses and seminars that s/he has participated in, and the studies that s/he has conducted.

Situations such as the qualitative inquiry, the variety of the philosophical and theoretical harmony, and their intersection with the designed research objective require the provision of the quality and reliability of the research. The quality and credibility of the study can be examined in three groups. However, this is generally related to the inquiry; the philosophical beliefs of the evaluators regarding the paradigm based preferences such as the attentive techniques and methods regarding its validity, reliability and robustness for collecting and analysing the qualitative data; reliability, ability and perceived reliability of a qualitative researcher and subjectivity versus objectivity, approach towards honesty, and the paradigm based preferences such as the prediction against the generalization, which causes the evaluation of the validity and reliability of the research in the different dimensions. Also, this approach considers some general approaches and opinions of the data quality and reliability in the qualitative analysis. These special philosophical supports provide a general point of view to the specific paradigms and special aims for the qualitative inquiry and will include the additional or representative criteria for providing and querying the validity, reliability and credibility (Patton 2002).

Running the analysis of the data through again and again will increase the validity and reliability. In the selection of the data, the researcher tries over and over again and changes the validity indicators of the study before completion. The studies for the re-evaluation of the data present the information that will increase their values (Baker 1997). The validity is a key opinion, which is discussed in terms of the legality of qualitative research for a long time. If a qualitative research does not produce valid results, it does not meet the politics, programs or expectations of the academic community. There are three validity forms discussed in the qualitative research (Johnson 1997):

1. The descriptive validity means the correctness of the explanations made as reports by the qualitative researcher.
2. The interpretive validity is obtained with the reporting of and giving meaning to the point of view of the participants to the issue, his/her opinions, intention and degree of his/her experience by the researcher.
3. The theoretical validity is obtained with the theoretical explanations developed from the research study, which is harmonized with the data or with a degree of a theory. By this way, the creditability and justifiability are provided.

These forms of validity are available in qualitative research and, at the same time, they are discussed in the internal and external reality of the qualitative researcher. There are thus many strategies for discussing the validity of the qualitative research.

It is advisable to consult at least two other field experts other than the researcher in order to determine the validity and reliability of the data. This is expressed as part of the validity/reliability and is helpful in trying to determine whether the data recorded according to the subjective criteria is analysed correctly via the experts participating from the outside. With at least three field experts, it helps to form robustness in the correctness of the codes, giving correct meaning to the data and correct evaluation of the findings. The coding is depending on the problem of the research, and as a result of this, the themes and sub-themes that will give meaning to the research findings are determined. In my research, all written texts have been themed via the repetitive readings according to their line numbers and determined codes. For the validity and reliability of the research, the themes have also been asserted by an experienced expert other than me as researcher, and the separation points have compared. To which sub-themes the determined themes will be placed has been decided, and their provisions in the field study have been mentioned according to the line numbers and respondent or whether they are within the events or not and have been tried to be given.

Even though there are many different evaluations oriented towards the determination of the validity and reliability of the research, I have in my research considered that the formula of Miles and Huberman (1994) was the best. This formula has revealed which opinion differences I have had with the other field experts concerning the reliability of my research, and whether my research results are sufficient or not. This formula is Reliability = Consensus/Total consensus + Dissensus. The impetus of these kinds of results shows that you can provide reliability among the coders in an ethnographic research project.

The ethics and the politics of ethnography are not clearly separable. Questions about the right way to treat each other as human beings, within a research relationship, are not wholly distinct from questions about the values which should prevail in a society, and the responsibility of social scientists to make, or refrain from, judgements about these. For ethnographers, ethical issues are also inextricably related to views about the ontological and epistemological foundations of their work. Our assumptions about the nature of reality, the possible knowledge of that reality, the status of truth claims and so on, all have significant implications for our judgements about the ethnographer's responsibilities. The lack of consensus about methodology, which marks contemporary debates in and about ethnography, is reflected in discussions about its ethics. For this reason, the researcher should avoid damaging the participants; s/he should show respect to the values and beliefs of the participants; s/he should take justice as the basis by looking equally and behaving equally to the humans (Murphy and Dingwall 2007, pp.339–351). Primarily, remember not to mention the name of the field where the research is conducted; keep the names of the participants taking place in the research anonymous and instead use codenames (informant A; informant B, etc.), and get the required permissions for the publishing of the research and reporting the data you have obtained without diverging from the reality in which they are required. Other than this, many discussions can be made regarding ethical terms, but the important thing is that the researcher forms the research design in a robust way; that s/he has sufficient knowledge of the methodology, and that s/he effectively uses the data collection tools that s/he has selected and s/he can integrate his/her coding with his/her problems and s/he can realize these in an ethical framework.

The qualitative research process that we have tried to set out above has the multiple components forming the cyclical process as of the moment at which it starts. Other than the need of a strong research design that we have determined as depending on the research problem and our sub-problems, a feedback process is required continuously during the research. After the research objective and problem that we have determined regarding issues of CSR, the research methodology, sample group, data collection tools, data analysis, and providing of the validity and reliability of the research, we reach a result based on the findings. If we form our research design strongly, then it is possible for us to make inference with the correct steps without being obliged to continuously change the things we have determined in this design. The effective revealing and evaluation of the findings as a result of all of these are important in terms of making the qualitative research meaningful for the readers.

RESULT

This chapter has explored participant observation as a method to be used in field research for ethnographic studies of CSR. Indeed, the chapter has a structure integrated with the chapter of Linne Marie Lauesen. Lauesen's Chapter 15 has formed an important example of the implementation in the issue of CSR, and for this chapter, giving details regarding how we can use participant observation as a data collection tool, which I have used in my ethnographic study conducted from different angles, has been requested. Generally, it is considered that the book, which provides qualitative as well as quantitative research accounts for CSR studies, is to give readers an important starting point to research requests to various approaches to the issue seen from the different perspectives.

The most important point that we are required to highlight here is that we do not make generalizations about the fact that we can reveal all realities and operations in the field in which we have chosen to make the participant observation. For this reason, it is important for us to mention the limitations of our research in a clear way. The points that we have mentioned above can help us in the points we have discussed while we set off in our research, and it will also provide us with skills to develop our knowledge regarding qualitative research, to see many methodological frameworks and to use the tools effectively. Even though the study that we have realized expresses only the area in which we exist, it will ensure attention is payed to many elements which are not observed in the quantitative research. Also, the requirement that the ethical elements of our research should be dealt with carefully requires the researcher also to consider Chapter 4 on research ethics by David Crowther.

REFERENCES

Altunisik Remzi, Recai Coskun, Serkan Bayraktaroglu and Engin Yildirim (2004), *Sosyal bilimlerde arastirma yontemleri*, Adapazari: Sakarya Kitabevi, 3. Baski.

Alvesson, M. (1998), 'Gender relations and identity at work: a case study of masculinities and femininities in advertising agency', *Human Relations*, **51** (8), 969–1005.

Angrosino, Michael (2007), *Doing Ethnographic and Observational Research*, London: Sage Publications.

Atkinson, Paul (1992), *Understanding Ethnographic Texts. Qualitative Research Methods*, vol. 25, London: Sage Publications.

Baker, G. (1997), 'Membership categorisation and interview accounts', in David Silverman (ed.), *Qualitative Research: Theory, Method and Practice*, London: Sage Pub., pp. 162–176.

Barkay, T. (2012), 'Employee volunteering: soul, body and CSR', *Social Responsibility Journal*, **31** (1), 25–38.

Bernard, H. Russel (1994), *Research Methods in Anthropology Qualitative and Quantitative Approaches*, London: Sage Publications, 2nd ed.
Bolton, Gillie (2001), *Reflective Practice: Writing and Professional Development*, London: Paul Chapman.
Brewer, John D. (2000), *Ethnography*, NY: Open University Press.
Corner, J. and J. Hawthorn (eds) (1980), *Communication Studies: An introductory Reader*, London: Edward Arnold Publishers Ltd.
deMarrais, Kathleen and Stephen D. Lapan (eds) (2004), *Foundations of Research: Method of Inquiry in Education and the Social Sciences*, Mahwah, NJ: Lawrence Erlbaum Associates.
Denzin, Norman K. (1989), *Interpretive Biography*, Qualitative Research Methods Series 17, A Sage University Press, Newbury Park, CA: Sage Pub., Inc.
DeWalt, Kathleen M. and Billie R. DeWalt (2001), *Participant Observation: A Guide for Fieldworkers*, Lanham, MD: Altamira Press.
Emerson, Robert M., Rachel I. Fretz and Linda L. Shaw (1995), *Writing Ethnographic Fieldnotes*, USA: University of Chicago Press.
Fetterman, David M. (1997), *Ethnography: Step by Step*, London: Sage Publications, Inc., 2nd ed.
Garsten, C. (2010), 'Ethnography at the interface: corporate social responsibility as a anthropological field of enquiry', in Marit Melhuus, Jon P. Mitchell and Helena Wulff (eds), *Ethnographic Practice in the Present*, Oxford, UK: Berghahn Books, pp.56–68.
Gold, R. (1958), 'Roles in sociological field observation', *Social Forces*, 36, 217–213.
Hammersley, Martyn and Paul Atkinson (1995), *Ethnography: Principles in Practice*, 2nd ed., London: Routledge.
Johnson, B.R. (1997), 'Examining the validity structure of qualitative research', *Education*, **118** (3), 282–292.
Johnson, Burke and Larry Christensen (2004), *Educational Research: Quantitative, Qualitative and Mixed Approaches*, USA: Pearson Education Inc., 2nd ed.
Jorgensen, Danny L. (1989), *Participant Observation: A Methodology for Human Studies*, Applied Research Method Series vol.15, Newbury Park, CA: Sage Publications.
Kalof, Linda, Amy Dan and Thomas Dietz (2008), *Essentials of Social Research*, NY: Open University Press.
Karasar, Niyazi (1991), *Bilimsel arastirmalar yontemi: kavramlar, ilkeler, teknikler*, Ankara: Sanem Yayıncılık, 4. bs.
Kottak, Conrad Phillip (2008), *Antropoloji: insan cesitliligine bir bakıs*, (Çev. S. Altunek vd.), Ankara: Utopya Yayınları.
Lauring, J. and C. Thomsen (2009), 'Ideals and practices in CSR identity making: the case of equal opportunities', *Employee Relations*, **31** (1), 25–38.
Machin, D. (2002), *Ethnographic Research for Media Studies*, Great Britain: Arnold Publisher.
Marrewijk, M.V. (2003), 'Concepts and definitions of CSR and corporate sustainability: between agency and communion', *Journal of Business Ethics*, **44**, 95–105.
McNamara, C. (2009), 'General guidelines for conducting interviews', accessed at http://managementhelp.org/evaluation/interview.htm.
Miles, M.B. and A.M. Huberman (1994), *Qualitative Data Analysis: An Expanded Sourcebook*, CA: Sage Publications, 2nd ed.
Murphy, E. and R. Dingwall (2007), 'The ethics of ethnography', in Paul Atkinson, Sara Delamont, Amanda Coffey, John Lofland and Lyn Lofland (eds), *Handbook of Ethnography*, London: Sage Publications.
Neuman, W.L. (2003), *Social Research Methods: Qualitative and Qualitative Approaches*, USA: Pearson Education, Inc.
O'Reilly, K. (2005), *Ethnographic Methods*, NY: Routledge.
Ozturk, M. (2003), *Fonksiyonlar acisindan isletme yonetimi*, Papatya Yayincilik, Istanbul.
Patton, M.Q. (2002), *Qualitative Research and Evaluation Methods*, Thousand Oaks, CA: Sage Publications, 3rd ed.
Payne, G. and J. Payne (2004), *Key Concepts in Social Research*, London: SAGE Publications.
Schwartzman, H.B. (1993), *Ethnography in Organizations*, Qualitative Research Methods Series 27, A Sage University Paper, USA: Sage Publications.
Smith, V. (2007), 'Ethnographies of work and work of ethnographers', in Paul Atkinson, Sara Delamont, Amanda Coffey, John Lofland and Lyn Lofland (eds), *Handbook of Ethnography*, London: Sage Publications, pp.220–233.
Van Maanen, J. (1979), 'The fact of fiction in organizational ethnography', *Administrative Science Quarterly*, **24**, 539–550.
Yıldırım, A. and H. Şimşek (2005), *Sosyal bilimlerde nitel araştırma yöntemleri*, Ankara: Seçkin, 5. Bs.

18. Application of correspondence analysis to determinants of human resources disclosure
Esther Ortiz and José G. Clavel

INTRODUCTION

Today global capital markets require international consensus about disclosure requirements and other barriers to globalization. Business reporting has improved over the years and we are witnessing a wide range of disclosures of non-financial information. Research methods used in corporate social responsibility (CSR) are conditioned by the characteristics of this information. The information included in disclosure must be codified in order to analyse it. The principal studies have used content analysis in an effort to establish a relationship between non-financial disclosure and a wide range of factors, including industry, country, and listing. Social disclosure needs a specific methodology because it studies qualitative data, which limits the methods available. Instead of trying to use a regression to analyse the relationship between disclosure (obtained from the content analysis) and the other selected variables, we use 'correspondence analysis' (CA). CA is often referred to as the analogue of principal component analysis for categorical data. It is a method for studying a set of qualitative measurements whose primary goal is to transform a contingency table of frequencies into a graphical display, so facilitating the interpretation of the information.

Many steps have been taken to harmonize financial information. For example, the US Securities and Exchange Commission (US-SEC) no longer requires foreign companies to translate their annual reports to US Generally Accepted Accounting Principles (US-GAAP). Before 2007, foreign listers were required to fill in Form 20-F, the annual report required by the US-SEC, in which they had to translate at least the fundamental variables (net income and equity) from local Generally Accepted Accounting Principles (GAAP) to US-GAAP. In 1999 the US-SEC changed its requirements specifically regarding human resources, thus improving non-financial disclosure. So, the information provided today by foreign companies listed on the New York Stock Exchange (NYSE) means we can draw on two kinds of reports: Annual Report and 20-F. The items about employees included in Form 20-F are compulsory. There are other items published, either in Form 20-F or in the Annual Report, that are expected to be voluntarily reported. This allows us not only to take into account different independent variables which could show a relationship with human resources disclosure, but also to obtain an additional variable – the report in which companies disclose information about employees – which is synonymous with whether the information issued is compulsory or voluntary.

The remainder of this chapter is organized into four main sections. The first describes the background of primary interest to the study and summarizes relevant research results. The second, the methods section, presents and discusses the disclosure items, the hypotheses, and the research procedures and design. The results of the study are reported in the third section, and the final section contains a discussion of these results and some concluding remarks.

BACKGROUND

Companies that make voluntary disclosures choose to differentiate themselves by increasing the amount of business information they provide. Effective voluntary disclosures can provide more transparency and understanding about the company to investors and creditors. Thus, voluntary disclosure is understood as disclosures primarily outside the financial statements that are not explicitly required by GAAP.

Companies in the world have enlarged their annual reports to include a section on social issues. Companies use these sections to highlight their achievements in reducing pollution, protecting the environment, or addressing employees' welfare. In corporate social disclosure (CSD) the two most important areas are employees/human resources and environment. The main previous studies have used content analysis to measure the extent of CSD (for more on content analysis, see Neuendorf (2002)). Our analysis focuses on four dimensions: theme (environment and human resources, among others), evidence (monetary, non-monetary, declarative, and none), amount (page measurement), and location in the report (chairman review, separate sections, other sections, and separate booklet). Giegler and Klein (1994) state that correspondence analysis (CA) complies with all the necessary requirements to analyse disclosure through content analysis and includes additional information about the kind of disclosure. The main source to examine is the annual report, as in Singh and Ahuja (1983), Andrew et al. (1989), Lynn (1992), Gray et al. (1995a, 1995b), Kreuze et al. (1996), and Nafez and Naser (2000). Zeghal and Ahmed (1990) argue that using only the annual report as a basis to evaluate CSD is misleading. They use other sources like brochures and advertisements of the six largest banks and the nine largest petroleum companies in Canada. The studies examine the extent of CSD practices in specific markets: Singh and Ahuja (1983) present a sample with annual reports of Indian public industry companies; Teoh and Thong (1984) study CSD practices in Malaysia; Andrew et al. (1989) investigate CSD in a sample of Malaysian and Singapore companies; Zeghal and Ahmed (1990) carry out a content analysis of CSD of the six largest banks and the nine largest petroleum companies in Canada; Lynn (1992) examines CSD practices in Hong Kong; and Nafez and Naser (2000) companies listed on the Amman Financial Market. These are national data, but other studies use an international sample, as in Gray et al. (1995a, 1995b).

As we do in this chapter, other authors use the publicly available information on company websites issued by listed companies to study non-financial disclosure (Bonsón and Escobar 2002, Aranguren and Ochoa 2008, Briano and Rodríguez 2012). Firms' disclosure strategies are influenced by a wide range of factors (industry, country, date, level of detail, among others) and are also determined by other variables of influence (company size, shareholders' concentration, gearing, listing status, industry type, performance, raising of financing, or audit firm size). The link between disclosure and these variables may be left to intuition, but many studies try to establish an empirical relationship between them. Two different effects have been identified in the literature: size effect and exchange effect (Atiase 1987). Many authors believe that size is an important variable in explaining disclosure (Firth 1979, Chow and Wong-Boren 1987, Cowen et al. 1987, Cooke 1991, Malone et al. 1993, Hossain et al. 1994, Wallace et al. 1994). Agency theory shows that the company has to satisfy the needs of creditors and investors and so may provide more detail in its disclosure in order to avoid informative asymmetries (Jensen and Meckling 1976). Ali and Hwang (2000) establish relations between country-specific factors and value relevance. It is supposed that big firms generate greater interest. To satisfy this increasing interest a better level of disclosure is also supposed (McKinnon and Dalimunthe 1993). Firms entering international capital markets are large sized. These companies will want to at least match their competitors in terms of disclosure in order to enhance the success of their capital raising efforts. This will lead to 'follow the leader' practice (Gray et al. 1995, p. 45). As for political costs: bigger companies will be viewed as being of public interest, which will make them disclose more than smaller firms (Giner 1995). Operating in some industries requires even more disclosure, because the activities are of keen current interest, such as environmentally unfriendly activities, high risk new technology industries, and so on (Rajgopal 1999, Street and Bryant 2000). In terms of listing status, the a priori hypothesis suggests that those listed companies disclose more information because of the extra disclosures contained in the listing requirements; those companies which are multi-listed will disclose more information than those listed on only one exchange; and those which have foreign investors (which list on a foreign stock exchange) will have to satisfy their informative needs with more disclosure. Cooke (1989) shows that there is a significant association between the extent of disclosure and listing status between three categories of companies: unlisted, listed only on the Stockholm Stock Exchange, and multiple listed. Depoers (2000) proves the null hypothesis for the relationship between size and foreign activity and disclosure in the financial statements of French listed companies. Street and Bryant's (2000) findings are consistent with prior research pointing to a significant association between listing status and overall level of disclosure.

Choi (1973) (examining firm's published annual reports) concludes that 'at least the firms examined here significantly improve their financial disclosure on entry into the European capital market' (p. 170). Meek and Gray (1989) investigate the extent to which the disclosure requirements of the London Stock Exchange relating to company annual reports are complied with or exceeded by Continental European companies (Swedish, Dutch, German, and French companies) listed on their own exchanges. Gray and Roberts (1989) highlight the power of market pressures to enhance the voluntary disclosure of the British multinational companies, despite the costs of disclosure. Johnson and Khurana (1994) report that internationally listed companies disclose more voluntary information because capital markets value it positively. Although the markets are interconnected, at the same time, persistent national characteristics are evident. Consistent patterns of behaviour may be observed within each country. These patterns are shown not only in the disclosure of financial information, but also in a wide range of voluntary disclosures, which in some cases are substantial (Meek and Gray 1989).

DESIGN AND METHODOLOGY

Regardless of whether the information revealed had been obtained from Annual Reports or Form 20-F, the first condition for inclusion in the sample was to be listed on the NYSE (Form 20-F was the required annual report for foreign listed companies by US-SEC). We have chosen NYSE listed companies from three different European countries: Spain, United Kingdom, and Germany. When making the choice we tried to get a representation of the most different accounting systems in Europe: United Kingdom as an example of an Anglo-Saxon accounting system in Europe, while Germany and Spain represent a Continental accounting system.

The second step was to select the companies. The choice of Spanish and German companies was not difficult: there were only seven Spanish and eight German companies listed on the NYSE at 19 September 1998, which allows us to include the whole population in the sample. For the British companies, the selection was limited by matching one British firm to a Spanish and a German listed company.

Each company was contacted through its website and a copy of its Annual Reports and Forms 20-F for 1998 and 1999 were requested. The size of the companies guaranteed the existence of a website, from which it was possible to get the available released information. If anything else was necessary, we used the investors' relations link.

To sum up, 84 Annual Reports and Forms 20-F have been examined, 42 for each year. In our sample there are 21 firms: seven of each nationality.

Information about the audit company was obtained from the audit report included in financial statements (which can be found in both: Form 20-F or Annual Report). All the companies are audited by one of the big-five. The NYSE website offers the possibility of identifying the industry of the listed companies. We have reduced the 4-digit Standard Industrial Classification (SIC) Code to its correspondence division. Five divisions are represented in the sample, although in Division I (Services) only one company is included so we decided not to consider that division. The measurement criterion to classify companies by size was the total assets in 1998. US dollars are used to homogenize total assets reported in the balance sheet, using the exchange rates at the end of the tax year 1998. We have two size groups: companies whose assets are above the average and those whose assets are below. The last variable is the listing status. The stock exchanges on which sample companies list have been found in the old Form 20-F, Item 5: Nature of the Trading Market. The association has been made in another two groups: companies listed only on NYSE and Domestic Stock Exchanges and companies listed on more stock exchanges than NYSE and Domestic ones.

A scoring sheet was developed to capture disclosure practices and the extent of reporting in Forms 20-F and Annual Reports. The items of information on human resources are classified in two groups (Table 18.1):

- Group I: Disclosure required by the SEC in Form 20-F. In 1999 the SEC approved a new regulation on human resources disclosure, included in 20-F. Before this rule, which we refer to as 'old format', there was only the requirement to disclose Item 1. According to new Form 20-F, Item 6 should include different kinds of information about employees.
- Group II: Disclosure that might be expected to be voluntarily reported in both

Table 18.1 Categories in the scoring sheet

I. Required disclosure in Form 20-F	Old Form 20-F (Item 1)	Changes in number of employees in the various departments such as research and development, production, sales, or administration. A description of any material country risks which are unlikely to be known or anticipated by investors and could materially affect the registrant's operations
	New Form 20-F (Item 6)	Either a) number of employees at the end of the period or b) average for the period for each of the past three financial years c) If possible, breakdown of persons employed by main category of activity d) If possible, breakdown of persons employed by geographic location e) Any significant change in the number of employees f) Information regarding the relationship between management and labour unions g) If the company employs a significant number of temporary employees, number of temporary employees on average during the most recent financial year
II. Voluntary disclosure	A. Remuneration	A1: Pensions A2: Stock options A3: Incentives A4: Other non-monetary remunerations
	B. Training	B1: Relationships with universities B2: Specific courses B3: Promotions
	C. Employment conditions	C1: Flexible work schedule C2: Facilities, such as nursery gardens among others C3: Employment quality

documents (20-F and Annual Report). This group's information has been reclassified in the following sub-categories: A: Remuneration, B: Training, and C: Employment conditions.

The categories to score the information about employees, voluntarily reported, were obtained a priori from an in-depth analysis of the disclosure in Annual Reports and 20-Fs. This perception is supported by other relevant studies. Lev (2000) proposed a path information structure for human resources, in which the inputs would be: compensations (such as stock options), employee training (both on and off the job), and perks (such as healthcare or gyms). Wyatt (2000) did a survey in Europe and then in the USA in order to establish relationships between the effectiveness of a company's human capital management and shareholder value creation, after controlling for variables such as industry and country.

All the information obtained could be summarized in different contingency tables,

Application of correspondence analysis 313

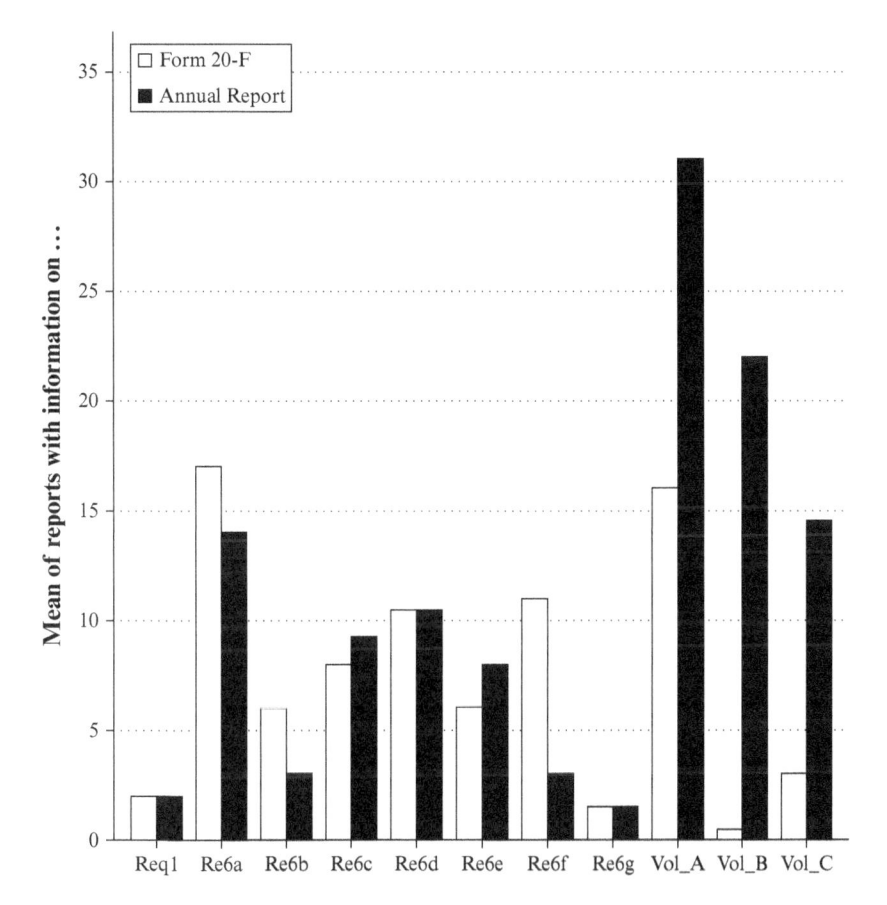

Note: (*) Req1: item 1 in old Form 20-F; Re6a to Re6g: different required disclosure in Form 20-F; Vol_A, Vol_B and Vol_C: other kinds of disclosure.

Figure 18.1 Number of reports with information about different issues. Means by type of report*

according to the sum criteria we choose. For example, if we aggregate depending on the type of report, the 21 (companies) x 11 (items) Total Table becomes a 2 x 11 contingency table that can easily be represented as it is shown in Figure 18.1.

The traditional content analysis just counts the data and looks for an explanation of the findings. For example, according to the results shown in Figure 18.1, there are more than 15 companies' reports in which information about the (a) 20-F item: 'number of employees at the end of the period' have been disclosed, but only 14 Annual Reports contain this information.

The problem with this approach is that we are looking just in one dimension: the type of report. Remember that information issued in these reports may depend on other features such as country, size, industry, and so on. That is why we propose to use another method, the analysis of correspondence, a methodological approach that has been used many times in other different fields.

Correspondence analysis (Greenacre 1984) is an exploratory method whose primary goal is to transform a table of numerical information into a graphical display, facilitating the interpretation of this information. Correspondence analysis (CA in advance) is often referred to as the analogue of principal component analysis for categorical data. But, whereas in principal component analysis, total variance is decomposed along principal axes, in CA total variation in the data is measured by the usual chi-squared statistic for row-column independence and it is the chi-squared which is decomposed along the principal axes.

The distances between the elements of the contingency table CA analyses is known as the chi-squared distance because of its analogy with the chi-squared concept of calculating squared differences between proportions relative to their expected values. In fact, this test is usually done. It is clear that the observed frequencies are always different from the expected frequencies. The question statisticians ask is whether these differences are large enough to reject the hypothesis that the rows are homogeneous, in other words whether the discrepancies between observed and expected frequencies are so large that it is unlikely that they could have arisen by chance alone. The sum of the differences for all the pairs is called the chi-squared test, where the hypothesis is that of no difference or homogeneity assumption.

To do this, there are a number of ways to compute the solution to CA: using the singular value decomposition (Eckart and Young 1936), or by an algorithm known as reciprocal averaging. The results are similar. We used the R package ca, (Nenadic and Greenacre 2007) to obtain the simple CA of the data. We are looking for a subspace of lower dimensionality, preferably not more than two or three dimensions, which lies close to all the profile points. This is why we only include in the figures of the CA results the first three dimensions of the space: the first three axes, called $k = 1$ in the titles of all the figures: the first dimension or axis; $k = 2$, the second dimension or axis; and $k = 3$, which would be the third dimension or axis. Once the subspace is determined, we project the profiles onto such a subspace and look at the profiles' projected positions as an approximation of their true higher-dimensional position. The output presents the coordinates of the profile points in that new subspace. The accuracy of display, the precision of the solution, is measured by the percentage of inertia represented in the subspace.

We are looking for a subspace of lower dimensionality, preferably not more than two or three dimensions, which lies close to all the profile points. So that we can project the profiles onto such a subspace and look at the profiles' projected positions in this subspace as an approximation to their true higher-dimensional position. The result presents the coordinates of the profile points on that new subspace and other statistics to facilitate the reading of the result.

The amount of information included in the initial contingency table is measured with the inertia. The inertia of a table is the weighted average of the squared chi-squared distances between the column profiles and the average profile, and it is the classical chi-squared statistic divided by the total of the table. We are on a maximization problem where the more inertia our final solution maintains, the better it is. The result provided also the precision of the solution, measured by the percentage of the initial inertia represented in the subspace. The component of inertia along a principal axis, called principal inertia, is the inertia of the row points (or columns points) projected onto the axis. Thus, each row (or column) makes a contribution to a principal inertia that could be expressed in relative amounts.

Besides the coordinates on the solution, the output gives us other information so useful to interpret like these maps related with the different contribution of the profile points to the principal inertia. The first possibility is to express each contribution to the k-th axis relative to the corresponding principal inertia. These results, labelled CTR, allow us to diagnose which points have played a major role in determining the orientation of the principal axis. The second one is to express each contribution to the k-th axis according to the corresponding point's inertia. On doing that we could diagnose the position of each point and whether a point is well represented in the map, in which case the point is interpreted with confidence, or poorly represented, and in which case its position is interpreted with caution. This concept is labelled as COR and they are squared cosines or squared correlations and facilitate the interpretation of each profile position.

RESULTS

The independence chi-squared test included as part of the CA allows us to test the following hypotheses:

- There is no significant difference within countries in disclosure about employees.
- There is no significant difference in disclosure about employees between various industry groupings.
- The level of disclosure about employees does not depend on the size of the companies.
- The level of disclosure about employees does not depend on the listing status of the companies.
- The level of disclosure about employees does not depend on the audit firm of the companies.
- There is no significant difference between SEC disclosure requirements included in Form 20-F (item about employees) and voluntary disclosure about human resources in the domestic Annual Reports of the companies listed on the NYSE.

Once the null hypothesis of independence is rejected, CA provides a full analysis of the relationships between the elements and interesting conclusions. We now present the main results obtained in each of the categories.

Global Analysis

The score given when a company discloses some category of information is 1, while non-disclosure is valued with a 0. This is because we count with different kinds of information: quantitative and qualitative, and compulsory and voluntarily disclosed. What we want is to use another methodology without introducing subjective valuation of this information and, therefore, any bias.

After a first analysis of the disclosure, we find that only 2 per cent of the total disclosure includes information required in the old Form 20-F, while the content of disclosure

Table 18.2 Countries' row contributions

Row	(*)	QLT MAS INR	k = 1 COR CTR	k = 2 COR CTR	k = 3 COR CTR
1	1	1000 62 113	642 659 151	−235 88 56	−290 135 114
2	2	1000 72 97	198 84 17	−394 332 182	223 107 78
3	3	1000 89 64	−389 603 79	−193 149 54	−10 0 0
4	4	1000 89 83	−477 702 119	29 3 1	−155 74 46
5	5	1000 84 127	571 622 161	396 300 215	−10 0
6	6	1000 86 123	560 635 160	354 253 176	53 6 5
7	7	1000 134 70	−378 785 113	87 41 17	−134 98 52
8	8	1000 146 79	−328 573 92	148 117 52	−111 66 39
9	9	1000 58 57	406 480 56	−357 370 120	−70 146
10	10	1000 53 79	353 240 39	−362 252 113	−181 63 38
11	11	1000 62 46	−127 64 6	79 25 6	442 770 265
12	12	1000 65 63	−141 59 8	−74 16 6	502 750 355

Notes: (*) 1: Spain 20-F 98; 2: Spain 20-F 99; 3: Spain Annual Report 98; 4: Spain Annual Report 99; 5: Germany 20-F 98; 6: Germany 20-F 99; 7: Germany Annual Report 98; 8: Germany Annual Report 99; 9: UK 20-F 98; 10: UK 20-F 99; 11: UK Annual Report 98; 12: UK Annual Report 99.

is mainly that which is required in the new one (55 per cent). Voluntary disclosure represents 42 per cent of the total disclosure, and within it, there is first information about remuneration (22 per cent), then information about training (11 per cent), and finally, information about employee conditions (9 per cent). Disclosure mainly required in Form 20-F is included in this form and voluntary disclosure is included in the Annual Report.

Differences by Countries

At first we hypothesize that there is no significant difference in disclosure about employees between various country groups, that is, between Spanish, German, and British companies. This is rejected at a 5 per cent level of significance[1] (chi-square statistic = 144.66, d.f. = 110). From dimension 1 (dimensions are always represented in figures as k, and are ranked according to importance) (Tables 18.2 and 18.3 include the information about row and column contributions in k = 1), we obtain a clear classification between disclosure in 20-F and Annual Report (Table 18.2, dimension 1 for 20-F is positive and for Annual Report it is negative) (Table 18.3, dimension 1 for required disclosure is positive and for voluntarily reported disclosure is negative).

After applying CA to classify disclosure between countries, we apply CA separately to the three different countries represented in the sample. The previous hypothesis that there is independence between disclosure and other variables in the cases of Spain and Germany can be rejected at a 5 per cent level of significance. For Spanish disclosure it is clear that dimension 1 (Table 18.4, k = 1) distinguishes disclosure in 20-F and Annual Report (disclosure in 20-F has positive coordinates, while Annual Report shows negative coordinates). The same can be done regarding the third dimension of the map about year of disclosure. There is a clear difference between disclosure in 1998 and 1999 (Table 18.4,

Table 18.3   Countries' column contributions

J	(*)	QLT MAS INR	k = 1 COR CTR	k = 2 COR CTR	k = 3 COR CTR
1	of	1000 14 66	266 456	1002 633 236	−195 24 12
2	a	1000 153 61	303 666 83	−103 78 27	−137 136 63
3	b	1000 48 121	348 138 34	−825 777 533	−194 43 39
4	c	1000 86 28	130 150 9	116 118 19	−223 436 93
5	d	1000 101 22	146 284 13	87 102 13	−13 2 0
6	e	1000 79 23	16 3 0	105 109 14	−223 494 86
7	f	1000 74 195	851 794 317	262 75 83	197 43 63
8	g	1000 10 50	132 10 1	272 41 12	−498 136 52
9	A	1000 235 94	−184 243 47	−104 77 41	239 411 293
10	B	1000 108 251	−843 880 451	8 18 12	−214 57 108
11	C	1000 91 88	−270 218 39	82 20 10	310 288 191

Notes: (*) of: required in old Form 20-F 'changes in number of employees in the various departments such as research and development, production, sales or administration. A description of any material country risks which are unlikely to be known or anticipated by investors and could materially affect the registrant's operations'; a: required in 20-F after changes 'either number of employees at the end of period'; b: required in 20-F after changes 'or average for the period for each of the past three financial years'; c: required in 20-F after changes 'if possible, breakdown of persons employed by main category of activity'; d: required in 20-F after changes 'if possible, breakdown of persons employed by geographic location'; e: required in 20-F after changes 'any significant change in the number of employees'; f: required in 20-F after changes 'information regarding the relationship between management and labour unions'; g: required in 20-F after changes 'if the company employs a significant number of temporary employees, number of temporary employees on average during the most recent financial year'; A: voluntary disclosure about 'remuneration'; B: voluntary disclosure about 'training'; C: voluntary disclosure about 'employment conditions'.

Table 18.4   Spain's row contributions

Row	(*)	QLT MAS INR	k = 1 COR CTR	k = 2 COR CTR	k = 3 COR CTR
1	f8	1000 200 382	669 746 421	−390 254 379	2 0 0
2	f9	1000 231 266	389 419 165	459 581 604	−9 0 1
3	A8	1000 285 168	−381 784 195	−3 9 85	196 208 515
4	A9	1000 285 184	−404 804 219	−59 17 12	−190 178 484

Notes: (*) f8: 20-F 98; f9: 20-F 99; A8: Annual Report 98; A9: Annual Report 99.

k = 3). The classification of German disclosure is the same: the first dimension establishes similarities and differences between disclosure in different reports (20-F or Annual Report) (Table 18.5, k = 1) and the second dimension between years of disclosure (Table 18.5, k = 2).

Table 18.5 Germany's row contributions

Row	(*)	QLT MAS INR	k = 1 COR CTR	k = 2 COR CTR	k = 3 COR CTR
1	f8	1000 186 331	625 912 327	−194 88 472	−181 14
2	f9	1000 191 302	585 899 295	195 100 490	241 24
3	A8	1000 298 193	−385 947 199	−337 22	8 546 481
4	A9	1000 324 175	−350 944 179	275 16	−81 51 481

Notes: (*) f8: 20-F 98; f9: 20-F 99; A8: Annual Report 98; A9: Annual Report 99.

Table 18.6 Industry row contributions

Row	(*)	QLT MAS INR	k = 1 COR CTR	k = 2 COR CTR	k = 3 COR CTR
1	f1	1000 54 169	656 569 133	375 185 207	−428 242 532
2	f2	1000 59 97	102 264	555 775 496	273 188 237
3	f3	1000 88 118	−522 845 137	202 126 98	18 12
4	f4	1000 86 137	−591 905 171	−400	−28 24
5	g1	1000 147 177	514 907 222	−132 60 70	−16 12
6	g2	1000 149 176	498 876 212	−83 24 28	151 80 184
7	g3	1000 196 54	−233 811 61	−758 430	−61 56 40
8	g4	1000 222 72	−220 619 61	−107 146 69	−200

Notes: (*) f1: Financial companies 20-F 98; f2: Financial companies 20-F 99; f3: Financial companies Annual Report 98; f4: Financial companies Annual Report 99; g1: Non-financial companies 20-F 98; g2: Non-financial companies 20-F 99; g3: Non-financial companies Annual Report 98; g4: Non-financial companies Annual Report 99.

Differences by Industry

Regarding our second hypothesis about independence between disclosure and industry, we have made two different industry groups: companies with SIC Code within Division H (finance, insurance, and real estate). There is no independence between disclosure of financial and non-financial companies because null hypothesis is rejected. As expected, the second dimension distinguishes disclosure between both industry groups (Table 18.6, k = 2) with the sole exception of the 1999 Annual Report, in which there is no difference between industry groups, but which is not statistically significant (the second dimension of row 4 is negative but its correlation and contribution has no value). The first dimension again classifies between the kinds of reports (20-F vs Annual Reports) (Table 18.6, k = 1).

Differences by Size

The third hypothesis is about the independence between company size and disclosure. It can be rejected and, as always, the first dimension highlights the distinction between categories of information disclosed in Form 20-F and in Annual Reports (Table 18.7,

Table 18.7 Size row contributions

Row	(*)	QLT MAS INR	k = 1 COR CTR	k = 2 COR CTR	k = 3 COR CTR
1	b1	1000 82 165	597 787 168	−68 10 16	−269 160 322
2	b2	1000 87 79	178 153 16	−268 350 259	316 487 471
3	b3	1000 124 131	−426 766 130	−200 168 206	−75 23 37
4	b4	1000 126 136	−469 912 161	−40 7 9	−112 52 87
5	s1	1000 117 177	544 870 200	183 98 163	62 11 24
6	s2	1000 119 174	553 935 211	−82 20 33	−41 5 11
7	s3	1000 169 87	−269 626 71	196 331 269	24 5 5
8	s4	1000 176 50	−207 664 43	80 98 46	67 70 43

Notes: (*) b1: Companies with total assets over the average 20-F 98; b2: Companies with total assets over the average 20-F 99; b3: Companies with total assets over the average Annual Report 98; b4: Companies with total assets over the average Annual Report 99; s1: Companies with total assets below the average 20-F 98; s2: Companies with total assets below the average 20-F 99; s3: Companies with total assets below the average Annual Report 98; s4: Companies with total assets below the average Annual Report 99.

signs of the coordinates in k = 1, positive sign only for Form 20-F and negative sign only for Annual Reports). Size effect is found in the second dimension, so there are also differences in disclosure depending on the size of the company (Table 18.7, k = 2 is negative for rows 1, 2, 3, 4, which represent disclosure of companies with total assets over the average, and k = 2 is positive for rows 5, 7, 8, which represent disclosure of companies with total assets below the average. The only exception (row 6) is 1999 Form 20-F of not so big companies).

Differences by Listing Status

Previously we made the hypothesis of independence between listing status and disclosure about employees. This hypothesis can be rejected as there is a relationship between listing status of a company and its way of disclosing human resources. No news in the first dimension. It highlights the differences in disclosure between kind of reports (20-F and Annual Report) (Table 18.8, k = 1) and the most important informative items are the same: relationship between management and labour unions in 20-F and training in Annual Report (Table 18.9, k = 1). It is the third dimension that highlights differences in disclosure about human resources between companies that list only on NYSE and their Domestic Stock Exchange or those that list on more Stock Exchanges than these two as a minimum (Table 18.8, k = 3), but it contains only 7.06 per cent of the total inertia while the effect of kind of report contains 74.5 per cent. The only exception is disclosure in 1999 Form 20-F of companies that only list on NYSE and Domestic Exchanges, where there are no differences in disclosure between listing status.

Differences by Audit Company

The hypothesis of independence between audit company and disclosure about human resources cannot be rejected at a 5 per cent level of significance (chi-square

320 Handbook of research methods in corporate social responsibility

Table 18.8 Listing status row contributions

Row	(*)	QLT MAS INR	k = 1 COR CTR	k = 2 COR CTR	k = 3 COR CTR
1	M1	1000 133 208	568 930 259	90 23 40	384 11
2	M2	1000 141 143	314 435 84	−348 533 623	58 15 28
3	M3	1000 204 143	−368 867 166	18 23	1158 4 159
4	M4	1000 197 142	−384 915 175	77 36 42	70 1
5	S1	1000 66 121	548 732 119	92 21 20	−297 215 341
6	S2	1000 66 145	587 700 136	295 177 209	183 68 130
7	S3	1000 89 53	−265 528 38	56 24 10	−227 387 271
8	S4	1000 105 45	−192 390 23	−117 145 53	−98 101 60

Notes: (*) M1: Companies that list on more stock exchanges than NYSE and Domestic Stock Exchanges 20-F 98; M2: Companies that list on more stock exchanges than NYSE and Domestic Stock Exchanges 20-F 99; M3: Companies that list on more stock exchanges than NYSE and Domestic Stock Exchanges Annual Report 98; M4: Companies that list on more stock exchanges than NYSE and Domestic Stock Exchanges 20-F 99; S1: Companies that only list on NYSE and Domestic Stock Exchange 20-F 98; S2: Companies that only list on NYSE and Domestic Stock Exchange 20-F 99; S3: Companies that only list on NYSE and Domestic Stock Exchange Annual Report 98; S4: Companies that only list on NYSE and Domestic Stock Exchange Annual Report 99.

Table 18.9 Listing status column contributions

Row	(*)	QLT MAS INR	k=1 COR CTR	k=2 COR CTR	k=3 COR CTR
1	of	1000 14 23	215 124 4	15 10	388 406 125
2	a	1000 155 79	310 843 90	128 143 92	−22 44
3	b	1000 47 79	454 551 58	−151 61 39	355 336 348
4	c	1000 84 26	169 415 15	−28 11 2	−89 114 39
5	d	1000 103 19	124 380 10	−41 42 6	9 2 1
6	e	1000 77 22	69 74 2	53 45 8	−208 678 198
7	f	1000 73 219	797 947 278	109 18 32	−82 10 29
8	g	1000 9 44	247 58 3	726 504 181	659 416 240
9	A	1000 230 92	−179 358 44	−234 613 459	15 3 3
10	B	1000 115 336	−780 934 421	200 61 168	31 1 6
11	C	1000 94 61	−366 917 76	59 24 12	−34 8 7

Notes: (*) of: required in old form 20-F 'changes in number of employees in the various departments such as research and development, production, sales or administration. A description of any material country risks which are unlikely to be known or anticipated by investors and could materially affect the registrant's operations'; a: required in 20-F after changes 'either number of employees at the end of period'; b: required in 20-F after changes 'or average for the period for each of the past three financial years'; c: required in 20-F after changes 'if possible, breakdown of persons employed by main category of activity'; d: required in 20-F after changes 'if possible, breakdown of persons employed by geographic location'; e: required in 20-F after changes 'any significant change in the number of employees'; f: required in 20-F after changes 'information regarding the relationship between management and labor unions'; g: required in 20-F after changes 'if the company employs a significant number of temporary employees, number of temporary employees on an average during the most recent financial year'; A: voluntary disclosure about 'remuneration'; B: voluntary disclosure about 'training'; C: voluntary disclosure about 'employment conditions'.

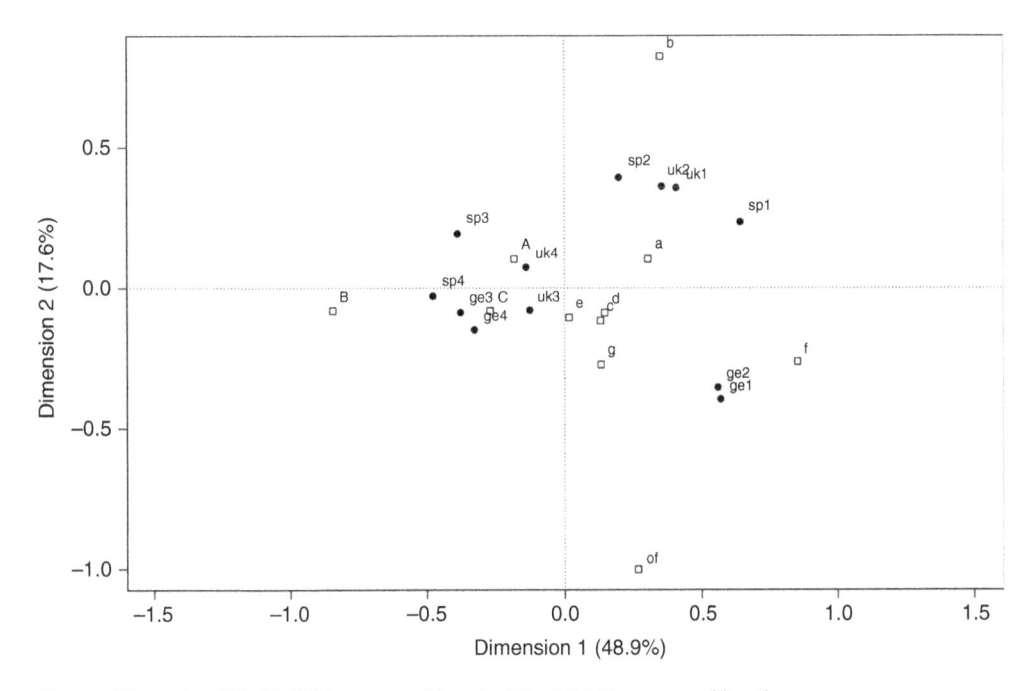

Notes: Dimension (Dim)1 48.94 per cent of inertia; Dim 2 17.63 per cent of inertia.
(*) sp1: Spain 20-F 98; sp2: Spain 20-F 99; sp3: Spain Annual Report 98; sp4: Spain Annual Report 99; ge1: Germany 20-F 98; ge2: Germany 20-F 99; ge3: Germany Annual Report 98; ge4: Germany Annual Report 99; uk1: UK 20-F 98; uk2: UK 20-F 99; uk3: UK Annual Report 98; uk4: UK Annual Report 99.

Figure 18.2 Country informative items (*)

statistic = 96.49, d.f. = 90). All the audit companies in our sample are one of the big-five, so we cannot distinguish between the big-five and non-big-five in order to find informative differences.

Differences Between Form 20-F: Old and New and Annual Reports

Bearing in mind any of the chosen variables, it can be seen that one axis always groups the disclosure items required in 20-F (it does not matter if it is the old or new one) and the voluntary items, as we have previously supposed. Hence, our last hypothesis may be rejected. In spite of the other different variables, the first dimension always highlighted differences in disclosure depending on the kind of report, whether 20-F or Annual Report.

Although in Figures 18.2, 18.3, 18.4, 18.5, and 18.6 the sample has been classified according to each of the chosen factors (country, industry, size, listing status, and audit company), if we look at them, the informative categories required by the SEC (of, a, b, c, d, e, f, g) are always located on the same side together with information disclosed in 20-F. In contrast, the other informative categories voluntarily disclosed (A, B, C) are only included in Annual Reports, because they are located together on the other side of the axis with the same sign in their coordinates.

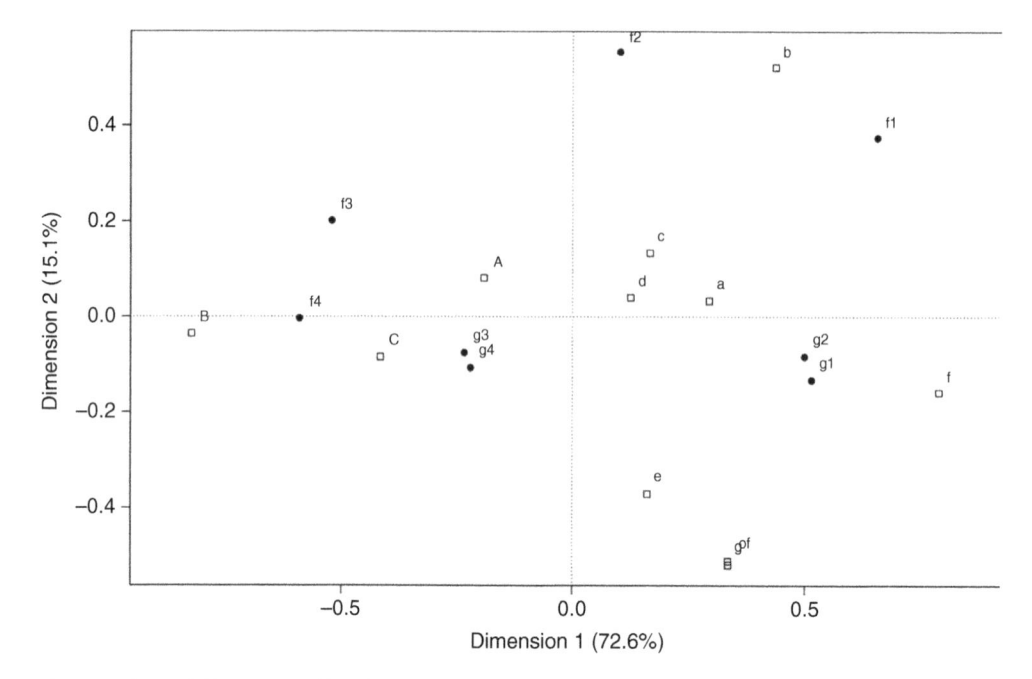

Notes: Dim 1 72.59 per cent of inertia; Dim 2 15.11 per cent of inertia.
(*) f1: Financial companies 20-F 98; f2: Financial companies 20-F 99; f3: Financial companies Annual Report 98; f4: Financial companies Annual Report 99; g1: Non-financial companies 20-F 98; g2: Non-financial companies 20-F 99; g3: Non-financial companies Annual Report 98; g4: Non-financial companies Annual Report 99.

Figure 18.3   Industry informative items (*)

Limitations of the Research

Some caution must be applied when analysing the results of the research. The primary limitation of this study comes from the sample: in the Spanish and German sample there can be no bias in the choice of the companies given the short list of candidates, but the British firms were chosen and there may be some kind of bias derived from the selection. The research may also be biased because of the few countries involved; it would have been desirable to expand the sample to more European countries. A second limitation is that we have categorized the types of voluntary disclosure, and the results depend on this classification, contained in the scoring sheet, which depends on the researcher who has categorized the informative items. We have chosen the most appropriate and objective methodology, bearing in mind that it is difficult to analyse qualitative information.

Figure 18.4 Size informative items (*)

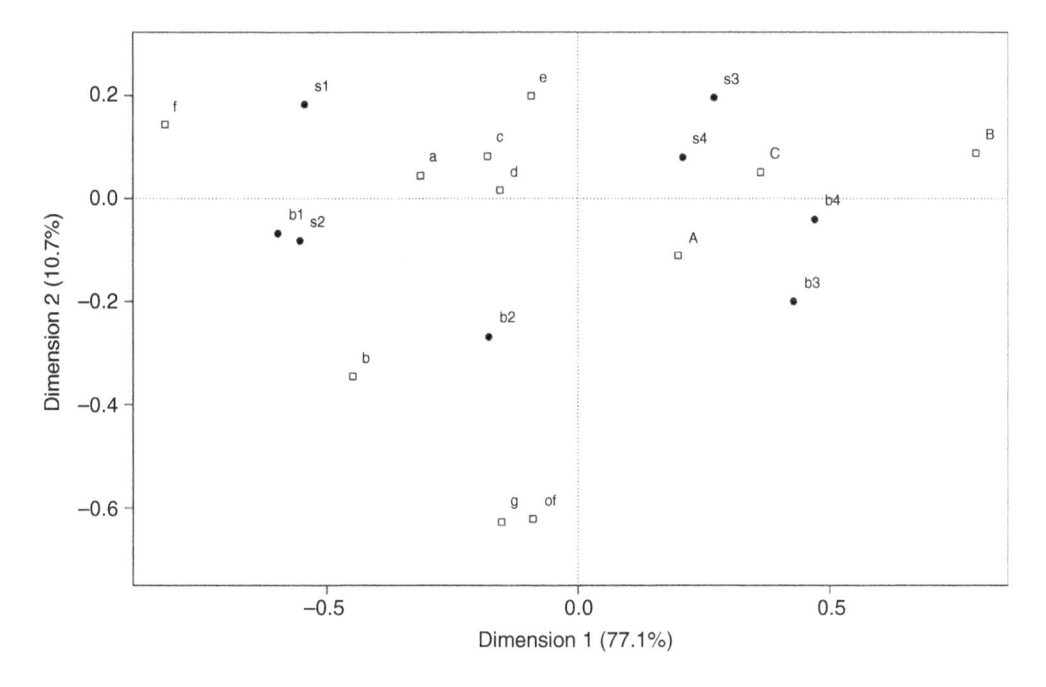

Notes: Dim 1 77.13 per cent of inertia; Dim 2 10.72 per cent of inertia.
(*) b1: Companies with total assets over the average 20-F 98; b2: Companies with total assets over the average 20-F 99; b3: Companies with total assets over the average Annual Report 98; b4: Companies with total assets over the average Annual Report 99; s1: Companies with total assets below the average 20-F 98; s2: Companies with total assets below the average 20-F 99; s3: Companies with total assets below the average Annual Report 98; s4: Companies with total assets below the average Annual Report 99.

CONCLUDING DISCUSSION

Subject to limitations that may be due to sample sizes, selection criteria, and assumptions underlying the methodology, the results presented suggest:

1. Consistent with prior intuitive expectations, the information required by Form 20-F is essentially different from information disclosed in domestic Annual Reports.
2. Factors like country, industry, size, or listing status shape the characteristics of disclosure. No relationship has been found between auditing company and disclosure, because all the auditing companies were one of the big-five.
3. There are different trends in disclosure about employees in financial and non-financial companies. The results may be indicating that in the last Annual Report examined (1999), the differences between financial and non-financial companies are narrowing.
4. This is in disclosures contained in Form 20-F, where the differences between companies whose assets are over and below the average are narrow. There are similarities in the way financial and big companies and non-financial and not so big companies

Figure 18.5 Listing status informative items (*)

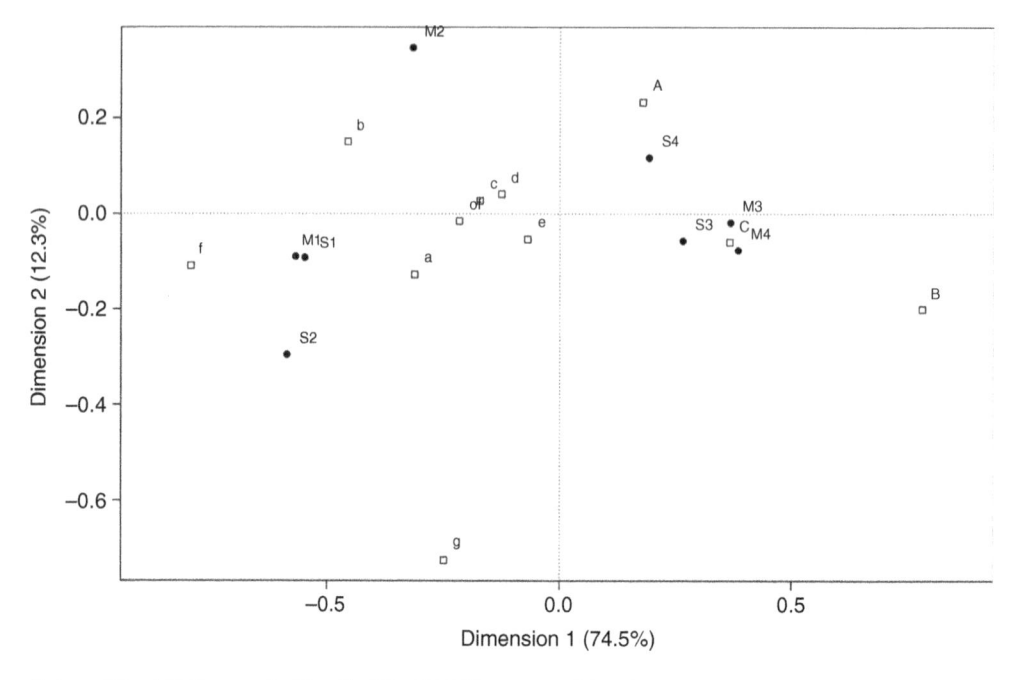

Notes: Dim 1 74.5 per cent of inertia; Dim 2 12.27 per cent of inertia.
(*) M1: Companies that list on more stock exchanges than NYSE and Domestic Stock Exchanges 20-F 98; M2: Companies that list on more stock exchanges than NYSE and Domestic Stock Exchanges 20-F 99; M3: Companies that list on more stock exchanges than NYSE and Domestic Stock Exchanges Annual Report 98; M4: Companies that list on more stock exchanges than NYSE and Domestic Stock Exchanges 20-F 99; S1: Companies that only list on NYSE and Domestic Stock Exchange 20-F 98; S2: Companies that only list on NYSE and Domestic Stock Exchange 20-F 99; S3: Companies that only list on NYSE and Domestic Stock Exchange Annual Report 98; S4: Companies that only list on NYSE and Domestic Stock Exchange Annual Report 99.

disclose. This may be due to a possible bias in the sample as financial companies are bigger than non-financial ones.

5. Listing status also generates differences in disclosure about human resources. It is logical that companies with multiple listing present a wider range of diversity in their Form 20-F.

To summarize, although the distances in disclosure about employees are smaller, there are many variables which continue to affect it and create diversity. In recent years, there have been efforts by different organizations to homogenize the disclosure of non-financial information, with attempts to cope with all these specific features and to add this information to the financial information in order to help get a better informed decision-taking process. The use of other statistical tools than the traditional ones, such as CA, might contribute to the race to make all company disclosure around the world comparable.

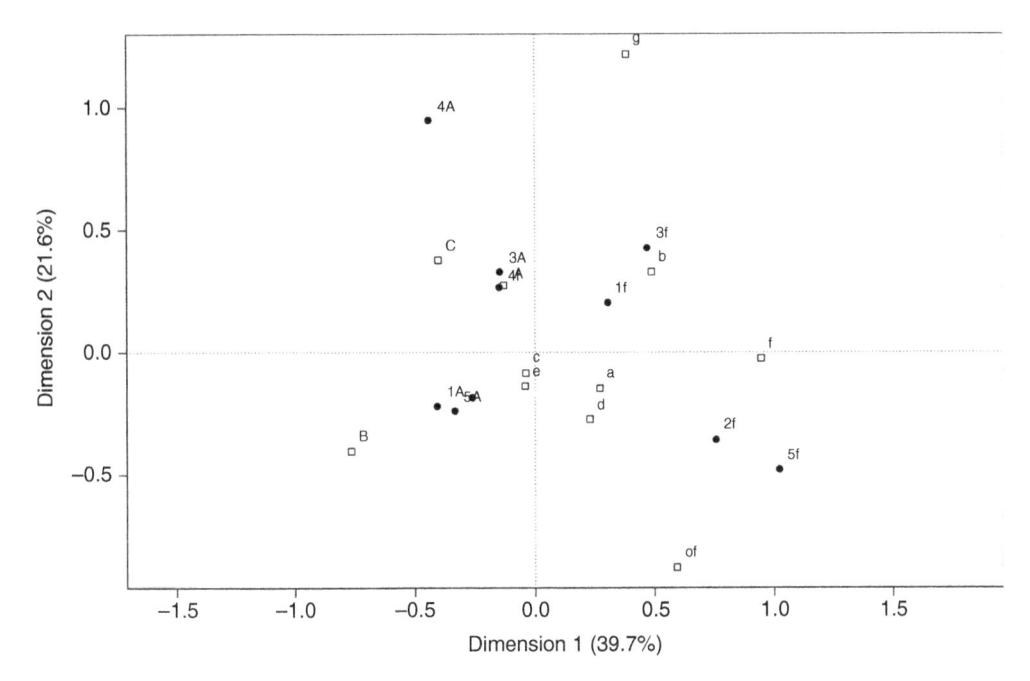

Notes: Dim 1 39.75 per cent of inertia; Dim 2 21.56 per cent of inertia.
(*) 1f: Arthur Andersen 20-F 99; 1A: Arthur Andersen Annual Report 99; 2f: KPMG 20-F 99; 2A: KPMG Annual Report 99; 3f: Coopers and Lybrand 20-F 99; 3A: Coopers and Lybrand Annual Report 99; 4f: Price Waterhouse 20-F 99; 4A: Price Waterhouse Annual Report 99; 5f: Ernst and Young 20-F 99; 5A: Ernst and Young Annual Report 99.

Figure 18.6 Audit company informative items (*)

NOTE

1. We will take a 5 per cent level of significance for all our research hypotheses.

REFERENCES

Ali, A. and L.S. Hwang (2000), 'Country-specific factors related to financial reporting and the value relevance of accounting data', *Journal of Accounting Research*, **38** (1), 1–21.
Andrew, B.H., F.A. Gul, J.E. Guthrie and H.Y. Teoh (1989), 'A note on corporate social disclosure practices in developing countries: the case of Malaysia and Singapore', *British Accounting Review*, **21** (4), 371–376.
Aranguren Gómez, N. and E. Ochoa Laburu (2008), 'Divulgación de información sobre empleados y medio ambiente en España y Alemania: Una nota de investigación', *Revista de Contabilidad*, **11** (2), 123–142.
Atiase, R.K. (1987), 'Market implications of predisclosure information: size and exchange effects', *Journal of Accounting Research*, **25** (1), 168–176.
Bonsón, E. and T. Escobar (2002), 'A survey on voluntary disclosure on the internet: empirical evidence from 300 European Union companies', *The International Journal of Digital Accounting Research*, **2** (1), 27–51.
Briano Turrent, G.C. and L. Rodríguez Ariza (2012), 'Corporate information transparency on the Internet by listed companies in Spain (IBEX 35) and Mexico (IPYC)', *The International Journal of Digital Accounting Research*, **12**, 1–37.

Choi, F.D.S. (1973), 'Financial disclosure and entry to the European capital market', *Journal of Accounting Research*, **11** (2), 159–175.
Chow, C.W. and A. Wong-Boren (1987), 'Voluntary financial disclosure by Mexican corporations', *The Accounting Review*, **LXII** (3), 533–541.
Cooke, T.E. (1989), 'Voluntary corporate disclosure by Swedish companies', *Journal of International Financial Management and Accounting*, **1** (2), 171–195.
Cooke, T.E. (1991), 'An assessment of voluntary disclosure in the annual reports of Japanese corporations', *International Journal of Accounting*, **26** (3), 174–189.
Cowen, S., L. Ferreri and L. Parker (1987), 'The impact of corporate characteristics on social responsibility disclosure: a typology and frequency based analysis', *Accounting, Organisations and Society*, **12** (2), 111–122.
Depoers, F. (2000), 'A cost-benefit study of voluntary disclosure: some empirical evidence from French listed companies', *European Accounting Review*, **9** (2), 245–263.
Eckart, C. and G. Young (1936), 'The approximation of one matrix by another of lower rank', *Psychometrika*, **1** (3), 211–218.
Firth, M. (1979), 'The impact of size, stock market listing and auditors on volume disclosure incorporate annual reports', *Accounting and Business Research*, **autumn**, 273–280.
Giegler, H. and H. Klein (1994), 'Correspondence analysis of textual data from personal advertisements', in Michael Greenacre and Jörg Blasius (eds), *Correspondence Analysis in the Social Sciences*, London: Academic Press.
Giner, Begoña (1995), *La divulgación de información financiera: una investigación empírica*, Instituto de Contabilidad y Auditoría de Cuentas, Madrid.
Gray, R., R. Kouhy and S. Lavers (1995a), 'Corporate social and environmental reporting: a review of the literature and longitudinal study of UK disclosure', *Accounting Auditing and Accountability Journal*, **8** (2), 47–77.
Gray, R., R. Kouhy and S. Lavers (1995b), 'Methodological themes: construction research database of social and environmental reporting by UK companies', *Accounting Auditing and Accountability Journal*, **8** (2), 78–101.
Gray, S.J. and C.B. Roberts (1989), 'Voluntary information disclosures and the British multinationals: corporate perceptions of costs and benefits', in Anthony G. Hopwood (ed.), *International Pressures for Accounting Change*, Hertfordshire: Prentice Hall, pp. 116–140.
Gray, S.J., G.K. Meek and C.B. Roberts (1995), 'International capital market pressures and voluntary annual report disclosures by U.S. and U.K. multinationals', *Journal of International Financial Management and Accounting*, **6** (1), 43–68.
Greenacre, Michael (1984), *Theory and Applications of Correspondence Analysis*, Academic Press: London.
Hossain, M., L.M. Tan and M. Adams (1994), 'Voluntary disclosure in emerging capital market: some empirical evidence from companies listed on the Kuala Lumpur Stock Exchange', *International Journal of Accounting*, **29** (4), 334–351.
Jensen, M. and W.H. Meckling (1976), 'The theory of firm: managerial behavior, agency costs and ownership structure', *Journal of Financial Economics*, **3** (4), 305–360.
Johnson, V.E. and I. Khurana (1994), 'Voluntary disclosures and the SEC: Rule 144A private debt placements', *The International Journal of Accounting*, **29** (2), 136–145.
Kreuze, J.G., G.E. Newell and S.J. Newell (1996), 'Environmental disclosures: what companies are reporting', *Management Accounting*, **78** (1), 37–46.
Lev, B. (2000), 'New accounting for the new economy', available at http://www.stern.nyu.edu/alt126blev (accessed 12 December 2013).
Lynn, M. (1992), 'A note on corporate social disclosure in Hong Kong', *British Accounting Review*, **2** (2), 105–110.
Malone, D., C. Fries and T. Jones (1993), 'An empirical investigation of the extent of corporate financial disclosure in the oil and gas industry', *Journal of Accounting, Auditing and Finance*, **8** (3), 249–273.
McKinnon, J.L. and L. Dalimunthe (1993), 'Voluntary disclosure of segment information by Australian diversified companies', *Accounting and Finance*, **33** (1), 33–50.
Meek, G.K. and S.J. Gray (1989), 'Globalization of stock markets and foreign listings requirements: voluntary disclosures by Continental European companies listed on the London Stock Exchange', *Journal of International Business Studies*, **20** (2), 315–336.
Nafez, A.B. and K. Naser (2000), 'Empirical evidence on corporate social disclosure (CSD) practices in Jordan', *International Journal of Commerce and Management*, **10** (3) (4), 18–34.
Nenadic, O. and M. Greenacre (2007), 'Correspondence analysis in R, with two- and three-dimensional graphics: the ca package', *Journal of Statistical Software*, **20** (3), 1–13.
Neuendorf, Kimberly (2002), *The Content Analysis Guidebook*, California, Thousand Oaks: Sage Publications.
Rajgopal, S. (1999), 'Early evidence on the informativeness of the SEC's market risk disclosures: the case of commodity price risk exposure of oil and gas producers', *The Accounting Review*, **74** (3), 251–280.
Singh, D.R. and J.M. Ahuja (1983), 'Corporate social reporting in India', *International Journal of Accounting Education and Research*, **18** (2), 151–169.

Street, D.L. and S.M. Bryant (2000), 'Disclosure level and compliance with IASs: a comparison of companies with and without U.S. listings and filings', *The International Journal of Accounting*, **35** (3), 305–329.

Teoh, H.Y. and G. Thong (1984), 'Another look at corporate social responsibility and reporting: an empirical study in a developing country', *Accounting Organizations and Society*, **9** (2), 189–206.

Wallace, R.S.O., D. Naser and A. Mora (1994), 'The relationship between the comprehensiveness of corporate annual reports and firm characteristics in Spain', *Accounting and Business Research*, **25** (97), 41–53.

Wyatt, W. (2000), 'The Human Capital Index: European Survey Report 2000', available at http://www.watsonwyatt.com (accessed 12 November 2013).

Zeghal, D. and S.A. Ahmed (1990), 'Comparison of social responsibility information disclosure media used by Canadian firms', *Accounting Auditing and Accountability Journal*, **3** (1), 38–53.

19. The application of survey methodology in CSR research
Christopher Boachie

INTRODUCTION

A survey in Corporate Social Responsibility (CSR) usually begins with the need for information where no data or insufficient data exist. Sometimes this need arises from within the statistical agency itself, and sometimes it results from a request from an external client, which could be another government agency or department, or a private organization. Typically, the researcher or CSR organization or the client wishes to study the characteristics of a population, build a database for analytical purposes or test a hypothesis. A survey can consist of several interconnected steps, which include defining the objectives, selecting a survey frame, determining the sample design, designing the questionnaire, collecting and processing the data, analysing and disseminating the data and documenting the survey.

Many CSR research methods are descriptive; that is, they set out to describe and to interpret what it is. Descriptive research, according to Best, is concerned with conditions or relationships that exist; practices that prevail; beliefs, points of views, or attitudes that are held; processes that are going on; effects that are being felt; or trends that are developing (Best 1970). At times, descriptive research is concerned with how 'what is' or 'what exists' is related to some preceding event that has influenced or affected a present condition or event (Best 1970). Such studies look at individuals, groups, institutions, methods and materials in order to describe, compare, contrast, classify, analyse and interpret the entities and the events that constitute their various fields of inquiry.

Typically, surveys gather data at a particular point in time with the intention of describing the nature of existing conditions, or identifying standards against which existing conditions can be compared, or determining the relationships that exist between specific events. Thus, surveys may vary in their levels of complexity from those that provide simple frequency counts to those that present relational analysis. The purpose of this chapter is to provide details on the application of survey in CSR research. This chapter should be read in conjunction with the chapters on sampling, questionnaires, interviews and data analysis techniques.

Many researchers reading this book will probably be studying for higher degrees within a fixed and maybe short time frame, which may render longitudinal study out of the question for them. Nevertheless, longitudinal study is an important type of research. More likely, researchers for higher degrees will find cross-sectional survey research appropriate, and it is widely used in higher degree research. This chapter defines the subject. It also discusses typical research objectives that may be accomplished with surveys and various advantages of the survey method. It explains survey and data-gathering techniques, ethical issues and the main potential errors that researchers must be careful to avoid. Finally, it presents the current applications of survey techniques in CSR research.

DEFINITION OF SURVEY RESEARCH

There are several ways of conducting research and collecting information, but one way that makes it really easy is by doing a survey. Survey research is one of the most important areas of measurement in applied social research. The broad area of survey research encompasses any measurement procedures that involve asking questions of respondents. A survey is defined as a brief interview or discussion with individuals about a specific topic (Dillman 2007). The term survey is unfortunately a little vague, so we need to define it better. It is often used to mean a collection of information. Surveys are commonly used in psychology and CSR research to collect self-report data from study participants. It may either focus on factual information about individuals, or aim to collect the opinions of the survey takers.

It can be administered in a couple of different ways. In one method known as a structured interview, the researcher asks each participant the questions. In the other method known as a questionnaire, the participant fills out the survey on his or her own.

Surveys can be 'exploratory', in which no assumptions or models are postulated, and in which relationships and patterns are explored (e.g. through correlation, regression, stepwise regression and factor analysis). They can also be 'confirmatory', in which a model, causal relationship or hypothesis is tested. It can be descriptive or analytic (e.g. to examine relationships). Descriptive surveys simply describe data on variables of interest, while analytic surveys operate with hypothesized predictor or explanatory variables that are tested for their influence on dependent variables. For example, if a researcher wants to develop a framework for identifying the CSR practices of companies operating in Africa or develop an index for measuring the CSR performance of companies in Africa, he or she may use descriptive survey. On the other hand, if one wants to investigate the relationship between CSR and Corporate Financial Performance (CFP) in companies or impact of CSR on CFP, he or she may use analytic surveys.

Most surveys will combine nominal data on participants' backgrounds and relevant personal details with other scales. Thus, they are useful for gathering factual information, data on attitudes and preferences, beliefs and predictions, behaviour and experiences – both past and present (Weisberg et al. 1996). The attractions of a survey lie in its appeal to generalizability or universality within given parameters, its ability to make statements which are supported by large data-banks and its ability to establish the degree of confidence which can be placed in a set of findings.

Surveys typically, though by no means exclusively, rely on large-scale data, for example, from questionnaires, test scores, attendance rates, results of public examinations, and so on, all of which enable comparisons to be made over time or between groups. This is not to say that surveys cannot be undertaken on a small-scale basis, as indeed they can; rather it is to say that the generalizability of such small-scale data will be slight. In surveys the researcher is usually very clearly an outsider, indeed questions of reliability must attach themselves to researchers conducting survey research on their own subjects, such as participants in a course that they have been running (e.g. Bimrose and Bayne 1995, Morrison 1997). Further, it is critical that attention is paid to rigorous sampling, otherwise the basis of the survey's applicability to wider contexts is seriously undermined. Non-probability samples tend to be avoided in surveys if generalizability is sought; probability sampling will tend to lead to generalizability of the data collected.

TYPES OF SURVEYS

Before initiating survey research, the investigator must determine the format that is most appropriate for the proposed investigation. Surveys are classified according to their focus and scope (census and sample surveys) or according to the time frame for data collection (longitudinal and cross-sectional surveys). Becoming familiar with the options enables the researcher to select the method that will provide the most useful data.

Surveys Classified According to Focus and Scope

A survey that covers the entire population of interest is referred to as a 'census', an example of which is the national census, undertaken by the governments. In research, however, 'population' does not refer to all the people of a country. The term population is used to refer to the entire group of individuals to whom the findings of a study apply. The researcher defines the specific population of interest. It is often difficult or even impossible for researchers to study very large populations. Hence, they select a smaller portion, a sample, of the population for study. A survey that studies only a portion of the population is known as a sample survey.

Surveys may be confined to simple tabulations of tangibles, such as the proportion of banks that spent at least $100,000 on CSR activities in a year (Werner 2011). The most challenging type of survey is one that seeks to measure intangibles, such as attitudes, opinions, values, or other psychological and sociological constructs. In such a study, one must bring to bear not only the skills involved in proper sampling but also the skills involved in identifying or constructing appropriate measures and employing the scores on these measures to make meaningful statements about the constructs involved. If one classifies surveys on the basis of their scope (census versus sample) and their focus (tangibles versus intangibles), four categories emerge: (1) a census of tangibles, (2) a census of intangibles, (3) a sample survey of tangibles, and (4) a sample survey of intangibles (Ary et al. 2009). Each type has its own contributions to make and its own inherent problems.

A Census of Tangibles

When you seek information about a small population, such as a single village, and when the variables involved are concrete, there is little challenge in finding the required answers. If a member of parliament (MP) wants to know how many desks are in the school, how many children ride the school bus, or how many teachers have master's degrees, a simple count will provide the information. Because the study covers the entire population, the MP can have all the confidence characteristic of perfect induction. Well-defined and unambiguous variables are being measured, and as long as the enumeration is accurate and honest, the MP can say, without much fear of contradiction, 'On the first of September there were 200 children's desks in our school' or 'Sixty-five percent of the present faculty has master's degrees.' The strength of a census of this type lies in its irrefutability. Its weakness lies in its confinement to a single limited population at a single point in time. The information provided by such a census may be of immediate importance to a limited group, but typically such surveys add little to the general body of knowledge in education (Ary et al. 2009).

A Census of Intangibles

Suppose the MP now seeks information about pupil achievement or aspirations, teacher morale, or parents' attitudes toward school. The task will be more difficult because this census deals with constructs that are not directly observable but must be inferred from indirect measures. Test scores and responses to questionnaires serve to approximate constructs such as knowledge and attitudes (Dillman 2007). An opinion inventory designed to measure student, teacher and parent attitudes and opinions about schools can be published annually. Administering the inventory to all the students, teachers, or parents in the school system would represent a census of intangibles.

The value of a census of intangibles is largely a question of the extent to which the instruments used actually measure the constructs of interest. Reasonably good instruments are available for measuring opinions and achievement in a variety of CSR research. Many other variables remain very difficult to measure.

Because researchers lack instruments that can meaningfully measure the constructs involved, many important questions may not be answered. Such variables as the success of CSR activities, managers' motivation, psychological adjustment, and leadership have been difficult to define and measure operationally.

A Sample Survey of Tangibles

When researchers seek information about large groups, the expense involved in carrying out a census is often prohibitive. Therefore, researchers use sampling techniques and use the information they collect from the sample to make inferences about the population as a whole. When sampling is done well, the inferences made concerning the population can be quite reliable. An example is seeking the opinions of senior managers on how much they spend on CSR in all listed pharmaceutical companies of a nation.

A Sample Survey of Intangibles

The public opinion polls are examples of studies measuring intangible constructs. Opinion is not directly observable but must be inferred from responses made by the subjects to questionnaires or interviews. Opinion polling began in the 1930s and has grown tremendously (Ary et al. 2009). Respondents are asked to rate companies according to their perception on CSR activities within a region, state or nation. Where respondents have been willing to reveal their preferences freely before elections, for instance, pollsters have been quite accurate in inferring public opinion from which they have predicted subsequent election results. These polls have provided excellent examples of the usefulness of sample statistics in estimating population parameters.

However, if people who support one candidate are reluctant to reveal their preference, whereas people who support the other candidate feel free to say so, considerable error is introduced into the results of the poll. For example, people are more willing to say they will vote against an incumbent than for him or her. Respondents are also reluctant to reveal a choice that may appear to be based on self-interest, prejudice, or lack of knowledge about the issues. How someone is going to vote is an intangible, but what is marked on a ballot is tangible. The television network news services have done very well in predicting how regions and states will vote when only a few precincts have reported because they can use tangible measures of a sample (i.e., how some ballots have been marked) to predict the vote of a population. Therefore, the risks are only those involved in estimating population parameters from sample statistics. However, pollsters who estimate how a population 'will' vote on the basis of how people 'say' they will vote have the additional handicap of measuring what is intangible at the time the measurements are made. Surveys of intangibles are limited by the fact that the data researchers collect are only indirectly measuring the variables they are concerned about. The seriousness of this limitation depends on how well the observations measure the intangible variable.

The same survey may study tangibles and intangibles at the same time. The survey on equality of CSR activities of companies asked the respondents to answer questionnaires and administered achievement tests in order to make inferences about social class, ability and achievement, as well as the relationship of these variables to each other and to tangible variables in the study.

Surveys Classified According to the Time Dimension

Surveys are also classified according to the time of data collection: longitudinal surveys, which study changes across time, and cross-sectional surveys, which focus on a single point in time (Ary et al. 2009).

Longitudinal Surveys

Longitudinal surveys gather information at different points in time in order to study the changes over extended periods of time. Three different designs are used in longitudinal survey research: panel studies, trend studies and cohort research.

Panel studies
In a panel study, the same subjects are surveyed several times over an extended period of time. For example, a researcher studying the amount of money spent on CSR activities over a ten-year period would select a sample of 100 profitable companies and administer a measure of the amount spent on CSR. This same group would be followed through successive amounts spent each year to assess how the amount spent each year develops over time. Researchers have studied how age affects IQ (intelligence quotient) by measuring the same individuals as adolescents and when they were college-aged, middle-aged and older. Because the same subjects are studied over time, researchers can see the changes in the individuals' behaviour and investigate the reasons for the changes. An example of a panel study is Simionescu and Gherghina's (2014) study of CSR and corporate performance: empirical evidence from a panel of the Bucharest Stock Exchange listed companies.

Trend studies
A trend study differs from a panel study in that different individuals randomly drawn from the same general population are surveyed at intervals over a period of time. For example, researchers who have studied national trends in CSR achievement sample about 80 percent of companies at various intervals and measure their CSR performance. Although the same individuals are not tested each time, if the samples from the population of com-

panies are selected randomly, the results each time can be considered representative of firm population from which the sample companies were drawn. Results from year to year are compared to determine if any trends are evident.

Another example of a trend study is the survey on CSR reporting conducted by both KPMG and PwC to provide a useful reflection of the current state of CSR reporting for other audiences who take an interest in the subject. KPMG looks at the 100 largest companies by revenue in 41 countries to explore how many companies are producing CSR reports and other issues, such as the drivers for reporting, sector variances, and the use of standards and assurance for CSR reports. Results indicate that CSR reporting is now undeniably a mainstream business practice worldwide, undertaken by almost three quarters (71 percent) of the 4,100 companies surveyed in 2013. This global CSR reporting rate is an increase of 7 percentage points since 2011 when less than two thirds (64 percent) of the companies surveyed issued CSR reports (KPMG 2013). Among the world's largest 250 companies, the CSR reporting rate is more or less stable at 93 percent (KPMG 2013).

Cohort studies
In a cohort study, a specific population is followed over a length of time with different random samples studied at various points. Whereas trend studies sample a general population that changes in membership over time, a cohort study samples a specific population whose members do not change over the duration of the survey. Typically, a cohort group has age in common. For example, the mining sector might follow the managers in charge of CSR in 2013 over time and ask them questions about contribution to the health sector, education, environment and donation to the disabled, and so on. From a list of all such managers, a random sample is drawn at different points in time, and data are collected from that sample. Thus, the population remains the same during the study, but the individuals surveyed are different each time.

Cross-Sectional Surveys

Cross-sectional surveys study a cross section or sample of a population at a single point in time with the intention of getting fair representation of the population. In a longitudinal study of CSR development, for example, a researcher would compare a measure of CSR activities in 2014 with one in 2015. A cross-sectional study would compare the amount spent on environmental cleanliness in different mine sites in 2015. The cross-sectional survey is the method of choice if you want to gather the data at one point in time.

Longitudinal surveys are more time-consuming and expensive to conduct because the researcher must keep up with the subjects and maintain their cooperation over a long period of time. Cross-sectional surveys, in contrast, do not require years to complete. Hence, they are less expensive. A major disadvantage of the cross-sectional method is that chance differences between samples may seriously bias the results. You may by chance draw a sample of first mine sites which are more mature than average and a sample of last mine sites which are less mature than average, with the result that the difference between the groups appears much smaller than it really is. However, researchers can usually obtain larger samples for cross-sectional studies than for longitudinal studies, and the larger samples mitigate the problem of chance differences.

SURVEY TECHNIQUE

The survey permits you to gather information from a large sample of people relatively quickly and inexpensively. Conducting a good survey, however, is not as easy as it might initially appear. It requires careful planning, implementation and analysis if it is to yield reliable and valid information.

Six Basic Steps Involved in Survey Research

Planning
Survey research begins with a question that the researcher believes can be answered most appropriately by means of the survey method. For example, 'How do investors feel about CSR activities in their company?' and 'What is the extent of CSR activities among listed companies in Ghana?' are questions that a survey could answer. The research question in survey research typically concerns the beliefs, preferences, attitudes or other self-reported behaviours of the people (respondents) in the study. A literature review reveals what other researchers have learned about the question.

Defining the population
One of the first important steps is to define the population under study. To whom will you distribute the survey? The population may be quite large, or it may be rather limited. For instance, the population might be all listed manufacturing companies in England or all banks in India. Or you might further restrict the population to 'all foreign banks in Indiana'. Defining the population is essential for identifying the appropriate subjects to select and for knowing to whom the results can be generalized.

Once the population has been defined, the researcher must obtain or construct a complete list of all individuals in the population. This list, called the sampling frame, can be very difficult and time-consuming to construct if such a list is not already available.

Sampling
Because researchers generally cannot survey an entire population, they select a 'sample' from that population. It is very important to select a sample that will provide results similar to those that would have been obtained if the entire population had been surveyed. In other words, the sample must be representative of the population. The extent to which this happens depends on the way subjects are selected. The sampling procedure that is most likely to yield a representative sample is some form of probability sampling. Probability sampling permits you to estimate how far sample results are likely to deviate from the population values.

Constructing the instrument
A major task in survey research is constructing the instrument that will be used to gather the data from the sample. The two basic types of data-gathering instruments are interviews and questionnaires.

Conducting the survey
Once the data-gathering instrument is prepared, it must be field tested to determine if it will provide the desired data. Also included in this step are training the users of the instrument, interviewing subjects or distributing questionnaires to them, and verifying the accuracy of the data gathered.

Processing the data
The last step includes coding the data, statistical analysis, interpreting the results and reporting the findings. Many considerations are involved in implementing the foregoing steps. The balance of this chapter discusses these considerations in detail.

DATA-GATHERING TECHNIQUES

There are two basic data-gathering techniques in survey research: interviews and questionnaires. Interviews involve some form of direct contact between the people in the sample group and the interviewer (the researcher or someone trained by the researcher), who presents the questions to each person in the sample group and records their responses. When a questionnaire is used, the questions are sent to all the members of the sample group, who record and return their responses to the questions.

Personal Interviews

In a personal interview, the interviewer reads the questions to the respondent in a face-to-face setting and records the answers. One of the most important aspects of the interview is its flexibility. The interviewer has the opportunity to observe the subject and the total situation in which he or she is responding. Questions can be repeated or their meanings explained in case they are not understood by the respondents. The interviewer can also press for additional information when a response seems incomplete or not entirely relevant. A greater response rate is another obvious advantage of the personal interview. The term response rate refers to the proportion of the selected sample that agrees to be interviewed or returns a completed questionnaire. With interviews, response rates are very high – perhaps 90 percent or better. Personal contact increases the likelihood that the individual will participate and will provide the desired information. With mailed questionnaires, the personal contact is missing, and people are more likely to refuse to cooperate. This results in many 'no-returns' (people who do not complete and return the questionnaire). The low response rate typical for a mailed questionnaire (less than 30 percent is common) not only reduces the sample size but also may bias the results (Fowler 2002). However, an interviewer can get an answer to all or most of the questions. Missing data represent a serious problem for the mailed questionnaire. Another advantage is the control that the interviewer has over the order with which questions are considered. In some cases, it is very important that respondents not know the nature of later questions because their responses to these questions may influence earlier responses. This problem is eliminated in an interview, in which the subject does not know what questions are coming up and cannot go back and change answers previously given. For individuals who cannot read and understand a written questionnaire, interviews provide the only possible information-gathering technique.

The main disadvantage of the personal interview is that it is more expensive than other survey methods. The selection and training of the interviewers, their salary and their travel to the interview site make this procedure costly. It takes a great deal of time to contact potential respondents, set up appointments and actually conduct the interview. Another disadvantage is the possibility of interviewer bias, which occurs when the interviewer's own feelings and attitudes or the interviewer's gender, race, age and other characteristics influence the way questions are asked or interpreted. As a general rule, interviewers of the same ethnic/racial group get the most accurate answers to race-related questions (Ary et al. 2009). On other issues, however, two studies found that blacks reported income from welfare and voting more accurately to white interviewers than to black interviewers (Fowler 2002). The gender of the interviewer may be a factor in surveys of opinions on abortion and gender equality issues. Women talking to women interviewers may express different opinions than they would if the interviewer were male. Researchers should consider the interaction between the subject matter of a survey and the demographic characteristics of the interviewers and respondents. If race, ethnicity or some other characteristic is very relevant to the answers to be given, then the researcher should consider controlling the relationship of interviewer and respondent characteristics.

Another problem is social desirability bias, in which respondents want to please the interviewer by giving socially acceptable responses that they would not necessarily give on an anonymous questionnaire. They may say what they think the interviewer wants to hear. For example, in preference polls in elections involving minority candidates, the proportion of respondents who said they would vote for the minority candidates was often higher than the proportion of votes these candidates actually received in the election. To account for this error, researchers speculate that white voters may have feared they would appear racist if they admitted to interviewers that they preferred a white candidate. Without realizing it, the interviewer also may verbally or nonverbally encourage or reward 'correct' responses that fit his or her expectations (Ary et al. 2009).

Focus Groups

A specific category of interviews is the focus group. Several subjects are interviewed at the same time. An advantage of a focus group is that participants respond not only to the researcher but also to other participants and their responses. The interaction between participants usually reveals more about the subjects' point of view than would be the case with a researcher-dominated interview. The focus group's interaction enables the researcher to see how subjects incorporate the viewpoints of the others in structuring their own understandings (Robson 1993). This method can provide the researcher with insight into how disagreements are or are not resolved (Fowler 2002). Sometimes the researcher can report a final consensus. Focus groups are often used in qualitative research. The researcher invites people who are interested in the same general topic to assemble to discuss it. They are assured that they will be free to express themselves in their own words and to respond not only to the researcher but also to other participants and their responses. In quantitative research, it is very difficult and often very expensive to assemble individuals who will gather in the same place at the same time to respond to the quantitative researchers' predetermined questions. Among those willing to bear the expense of assembling people to focus on a predetermined topic are manufacturers of consumer products who want to learn what product characteristics lead to high sales. Also, politicians often use focus groups to determine what stances might help get them elected or re-elected to public office. Researchers can also engage the focus group living closer to a mine site about their perception on CSR activities of the mine.

Telephone Interviews

The telephone interview is popular, and studies show that it compares quite favourably with face-to-face interviewing. In fact, the past 50 years have seen a gradual replacement of face-to-face interviewing with telephone interviewing as the dominant mode of survey data collection in the United States (Holbrook et al. 2003). Its major advantages are lower cost and faster completion, with relatively high response rates. The average response rate may reach 80 percent or higher (Neuman and Kreuger 2003). Telephone interviews can be conducted over a relatively short time span with people scattered over a large geographic area. For example, national polling organizations often use the telephone to obtain nationwide opinions among voters near election time. Large-scale surveys in major cities often use the telephone instead of sending interviewers into unsafe areas (DeVaus 2002). The phone permits the survey to reach people who would not open their doors to an interviewer but who might be willing to talk on the telephone. Another advantage is that respondents have a greater feeling of anonymity – and hence there may be less interviewer bias and less social desirability bias than with personal interviews.

The main disadvantage of the telephone interview is that there is less opportunity for establishing rapport with the respondent than in a face-to-face situation. It takes a great deal of skill to carry out a telephone interview so that valid results are obtained. The interviewer often finds it difficult to overcome the suspicions of the surprised respondents. It is recommended that you identify yourself right away and explain why you are doing a survey and are not asking for money (Ary et al. 2009). An advance letter that informs the potential respondents of the approaching call is sometimes used to deal with this problem, but the letter can induce another problem: the recipient has time to think about responses or to prepare a refusal to participate when the call comes. Another limitation of telephone interviews is that complex questions are sometimes difficult for respondents to follow. If they misunderstand the questions, the interviewer may not know. It is best that interview questions be short with a limited number of options. The phenomenon of multitasking may affect the quality of telephone interviews. Without the interviewer's knowing, the respondent may be watching television, stirring soup, or writing checks while answering the survey questions (Ary et al. 2009). Telephone interviews can be very time-consuming. If the sample is very large, a researcher will need a number of people to help with the interviews. Telephone interviews must be relatively brief.

Another disadvantage is that households without telephones, those with unlisted numbers and those with cell phones only are automatically excluded from the survey, which may bias results. Almost all homes in the developed countries have telephones, so this is not the problem it was years ago. In the developing countries, however, this is a major limitation. Neuman and Kreuger (2003) state that approximately 95 percent of the population can be reached by telephone. A technique known as 'random-digit dialling' solves the problem of unlisted numbers (although it does not reach households without a telephone). In random-digit dialling, a computer randomly generates a list of telephone numbers based on all possible numbers thought to be in use in an area (Ary et al. 2009). Because of the random determination, this technique ensures that every household with a telephone service has an equal chance of being included in the sample. Random-digit dialling has greatly improved the sampling in telephone surveys. See Fowler (2002) for a thorough discussion of random-digit dialling. Other limitations of telephone surveys arise from new technology that may make it increasingly difficult to reach potential respondents by phone. Services such as caller identification, phone number blocking and similar procedures enable residential phone customers to have much greater control over incoming calls. People may simply ignore calls from the unfamiliar number of the surveyor and telephone response rates may continue to drop.

Computer-Assisted Telephone Interviewing (CATI)

Computer and telecommunications technology has been applied to telephone surveys. Wearing earphones, the interviewer sits at a computer while it randomly selects a telephone number (through random-digit dialling or from a database) and dials (Smith et al. 2002). When the respondent answers, the interviewer reads the first question that appears on the computer screen and types the answer directly into the computer. The computer program displays the next screen containing the next question, and so on through the entire survey. Using CATI saves a great deal of time. The surveyor can fill in forms on a computer screen or type answers to open-ended questions very quickly. The major advantage is that CATI software immediately formats responses into a data file as they are keyed in, which saves the researcher time usually spent in coding and manually transferring responses from paper into the computer for analysis.

Conducting the Interview

Whether the interview is conducted in person or by telephone, the interviewer's main job is to ask the questions in such a way as to obtain valid responses and to record the responses accurately and completely. The initial task for the interviewer is to create an atmosphere that will put the respondent at ease. After introducing yourself in a friendly way, briefly state the purpose of the interview but avoid giving too much information about the study, which could bias the respondent (Zikmund et al. 2010).

It is well to begin the interview with fairly simple, non-threatening questions. The interviewer also has the responsibility of keeping the respondent's attention focused on the task and for keeping the interview moving along smoothly. This can best be done if you are thoroughly familiar with the questions and their sequence so that you can ask the questions in a conversational tone and without constantly pausing to find what question is coming next. Of course, you must refrain from expressing approval, surprise, or shock at any of the respondent's answers. Interviews can be more or less structured.

In a less structured interview, the same questions are asked of all respondents, but the interview is more conversational and the interviewer has more freedom to arrange the order of the questions or to rephrase the questions. If comparable data are to be obtained, however, the interviewer must standardize the procedure by using a structured interview schedule. A structured interview schedule contains specific questions in a fixed order, to be asked of all respondents, along with transition phrases and probes (questions used to clarify a response or that push a little further into a topic). For example, if the respondent starts to hedge, digress or give irrelevant responses, or if he or she has obviously misinterpreted the question, then the interviewer may use a fixed probe such as: 'Explain your answer a little further' or 'Can you tell me a little more about that?'

Another important technique besides the probe is the pause. A good interviewer needs skill in listening and is quiet at times until the respondent answers. In less structured interviews, any marked deviations from the protocol should be documented so that the information can be taken into account when analysing the interviewee's response. In using probes, take care not to suggest or give hints about possible responses. It takes less training time to teach interviewers to administer a structured interview than it does an unstructured one because everything they need to say or do is contained in the interview schedule. For this reason, the structured interview is the most widely used format for large studies with numerous interviewers.

Training the Interviewer

It is essential that potential interviewers receive training before being sent out to conduct interviews. Quality of interviewers is probably one of the least appreciated aspects of survey research. 'Interviewers have a great deal of potential for influencing the quality of the data they collect' (Fowler 2002, p.117). According to Fowler (2002) there are certain aspects of interviews that need to be standardized and, therefore, they should always be included in interviewer training:

1. Procedures for contacting respondents and introducing the study;
2. Instructions on asking questions so that interviewers ask all questions in a consistent and standardized way;
3. Procedures for probing inadequate answers in a nondirective way;
4. Procedures for recording answers to open-ended and closed-ended questions; and
5. Rules for handling the interpersonal aspects of the interview in a non biasing way.

To be able to answer respondents' questions, interviewers should also know the purpose of the project, the sponsorship, the sampling approach used and the steps that will be taken with respect to confidentiality. Interviewer trainees should be provided with written manuals on interviewing procedures. They should observe interviews being conducted by trained individuals and should be supervised in conducting practice interviews. In the practice interviews, the interviewees should be individuals drawn from the same population that will be used in the research project.

Mailed Questionnaires

The direct one-on-one contact with subjects in a personal interview is time-consuming and expensive. Often, much of the same information can be obtained by means of a questionnaire mailed to each individual in the sample, with a request that he or she complete and return it by a given date. Because the questionnaire is mailed, it is possible to include a larger number of subjects as well as subjects in more diverse locations than is practical with the interview. A mailed questionnaire has the advantage of guaranteeing confidentiality or anonymity, thus perhaps eliciting more truthful responses than would be obtained with a personal interview (Dillman 2007). In an interview, subjects may be reluctant to express unpopular or politically incorrect points of view or to give information they think might be used against them at a later time. The mailed questionnaire also eliminates the problem of interviewer bias.

A disadvantage of the mailed questionnaire is the possibility of respondents misinterpreting the questions. It is extremely difficult to formulate a series of questions whose meanings are crystal clear to every reader. The investigator may know exactly what is meant by a question, but because of poor wording or different meanings of terms, the respondent makes a significantly different interpretation. Furthermore, large segments of the population may not be able to read or may read only in another language and may not be able to respond to a mailed questionnaire. Only people with considerable education may be able to complete a very complex questionnaire. Another important limitation of mailed questionnaires is the low return rate. It is easy for the individual who receives a questionnaire to lay it aside and simply forget to complete and return it. A low response rate limits the generalizability of the results of a questionnaire study. It cannot be assumed that non-response is randomly distributed throughout a group. Studies have shown that there are usually systematic differences in the characteristics of respondents and non-respondents to questionnaire studies (Ary et al. 2009). Response rate is often higher among the more intelligent, better educated, more conscientious and those more interested or generally more favourable to the issue involved in the questionnaires. The goal in a questionnaire study is 100 percent returns, although a more reasonable expectation may be 40 to 75 percent returns. A number of factors have been found to influence the rate of returns for a mailed questionnaire, including (1) length of the questionnaire, (2) cover letter, (3) sponsorship of the questionnaire, (4) attractiveness of the questionnaire, (5) ease of completing it and mailing it back, (6) interest aroused by the content, (7) use of a monetary incentive, and (8) follow-up procedures used. We discuss these factors in more detail later.

Electronic Mail Surveys

As computers have become common, researchers have used electronic mail to deliver questionnaires. Dillman (2000) found that e-mail surveys have the advantage of prompter returns, lower item non-response and more complete answers to open-ended questions. Electronic mail surveys can be completed at a pace the respondents choose, and they cannot be mislaid like a mail survey.

The main disadvantage is that they are appropriate only when the researcher has e-mail addresses for all members of a finite population, such as all elementary teachers in a given school district or all members of a local union or fraternal lodge. Research shows that some of the factors found to be important for regular mail surveys are also important for e-mail surveys (Punch 2003). For example, people who received a prior e-mail notification about the survey were more likely to respond; also, surveys addressed individually to a person (rather than being part of a mailing list) had higher response rates.

Internet Surveys

The Internet has become a popular methodology for survey research. The questionnaire is placed on a website constructed by the investigator. Respondents are able to answer the questions and submit the questionnaire online. 'Web-based surveys' have a number of advantages. They have the potential of reaching large populations and permit the collection of larger amounts of data than would be possible with traditional survey methods (Smyth et al. 2006). They can be conducted quickly and easily and are less expensive than mailed surveys. The cost advantage increases as the size of the sample increases. Dillman (2000) states, 'Once the electronic data collection has been developed, the cost of surveying each additional person is much less, compared with both telephone interview and postal procedures. In some instances, these technologies may result in decisions to survey entire populations rather than only a sample' (p. 353).

Another important benefit is in the processing of survey data. Web-based surveys can significantly reduce the amount of time and effort and the costs associated with getting the data into a system for analysis. Furthermore, because they are available 24 hours a day, respondents can reply when and where they choose. The major limitation of Internet surveys is that samples are restricted to those with access to the technology and who choose to respond (Selm and Jankowski 2006). Samples are dominated by relatively affluent, well-educated, urban, white-collar, technically sophisticated young males (Flatley 2001). The large number of potential responses in a web survey does not overcome the problem of sampling error due to lack of representativeness. One needs to be sure the survey is reaching the desired respondents. There is somewhat conflicting evidence about response rates in web-based surveys. The consensus, however, is that response rates for web surveys are lower than rates obtained by other methods (Dillman 2007).

A meta-analysis of 68 web surveys found a mean response rate of 39.6 percent (Cook et al. 2000). Dillman and Bowker (2001) compared response rates to a questionnaire administered by telephone, mail or Internet. The response rate for the Internet was 50 percent compared with 80 percent for telephone and mail surveys. To generate enthusiasm and maximize response, one should send an introductory letter separate from the instrument that explains what the survey is about, that requests their cooperation, and that provides an incentive for completing the survey. The problem, however, is that the introductory letter is usually sent by e-mail and may be deleted before it is ever read by the potential respondent. Because of the relative anonymity provided by the Internet, it is more difficult to determine if respondents are who they say they are. It would also be possible for people to use different identities and respond more than once to a survey. The disadvantage is that the response rate appears to be low, but actually one cannot calculate the response in the usual way. The reader is referred to DeVaus (2002), who discusses a variety of applications for web-based surveys, as well as tips on designing the questionnaire.

Directly Administered Questionnaires

A directly administered questionnaire is given to a group of people assembled at a certain place for a specific purpose. Examples include surveying the new employees attending orientation at the company's training site. Surveys at universities are often administered in classrooms or in residence halls. The main advantage of directly administering questionnaires is the high response rate, which typically is close to 100 percent (Rosenberg et al. 2005). Other advantages are the low cost and the fact that the researcher is present to provide assistance or answer questions. The disadvantage is that the researcher is usually restricted in terms of where and when the questionnaire can be administered. Also, when a population is limited, the results of the survey will be equally limited in terms of generalizability. As we have seen, researchers have a choice among several data-collection methods for survey research. They choose the one best suited for their particular study. However, a multimode approach in which researchers use combinations of these methods in the same study is quite common. In fact, Fowler (2002) states that mixing modes is one of the best ways to minimize survey non-response, because it enables researchers to reach people who are inaccessible via a single mode.

SURVEY ERROR

The accuracy of a survey estimate refers to the closeness of the estimate to the true population value. Where there is a discrepancy between the value of the survey estimate and true population value, the difference between the two is referred to as the error of the survey estimate. The total error of the survey estimate results from the two types of error mentioned below:

- Sampling error, which arises when only a part of the population is used to represent the whole population; and
- Non-sampling error, which can occur at any stage of a sample survey and can also occur with censuses. Sampling error can be measured mathematically whereas measuring non-sampling error can be difficult.

In survey sampling, total survey error includes sampling variability, interviewer effects, frame errors, response bias and non-response bias. Total survey error is the difference between a population parameter (such as the mean, total or proportion) and the estimate of that parameter based on the sample survey or census. It has two components: sampling error and non-sampling error. Sampling error results from the variability inherent in using a randomly selected fraction of the population for estimation. Non-sampling error is the sum of all other errors, including errors in frame construction, sample selection, data collection, data processing and estimation methods. The survey literature decomposes non-sampling errors into five general sources or types: specification error, frame error, non-response error, measurement error, and processing error (Zikmund et al. 2010).

Most surveys try to portray a representative cross-section of a particular target population. Even with a technically proper random probability sample, however, statistical errors will occur because of chance variation in the elements selected for the sample. These statistical problems are unavoidable without very large samples (at least >400) (Ary et al. 2009). However, the extent of random sampling error can be estimated.

Systematic Error

The other major source of survey error, systematic error, results from some imperfect aspect of the research design or from a mistake in the execution of the research. Because systematic errors include all sources of error other than those introduced by the random sampling procedure, these errors or biases are also called non-sampling errors. A sample bias exists when the results of a sample show a persistent tendency to deviate in one direction from the true value of the population parameter. The many sources of error that in some way systematically influence answers can be divided into two general categories: respondent error and administrative error.

Respondent Error

Surveys ask respondents for answers. If people cooperate and give truthful answers, a survey will likely accomplish its goal. If these conditions are not met, non-response error or response bias, the two major categories of respondent error, may cause sample bias.

Non-Response Error

Few surveys have 100 percent response rates. In fact, surveys with relatively low response rates may still accurately reflect the population of interest. However, a researcher who obtains a one percent response to a five-page e-mail questionnaire concerning various CSR perceptions of a company may face a serious problem. To use the results, the researcher must believe that the investor, who responded to the questionnaire, is representative of all investors, including those who did not respond. The statistical differences between a survey that includes only those who responded, and a survey that also includes those who failed to respond, are referred to as non-response error. This problem is especially acute in mail and Internet surveys, but non-response also threatens telephone and face-to-face interviews.

ETHICAL ISSUES IN SURVEY RESEARCH

Survey research designs usually pose fewer ethical dilemmas than do experimental or field research designs (Bailey 1994). Potential respondents to a survey can easily decline to participate, and a cover letter or introductory statement that identifies the sponsors of, and motivations for, the survey gives them the information required to make this decision. Little is concealed from the respondents, and the methods of data collection are quite obvious. Only in group-administered survey designs might the respondents (such as students or employees) be, in effect, a captive audience, and so these designs require special attention to ensure that participation is truly voluntary. Those who do not wish to participate may be told they can just hand in a blank form.

Confidentiality is most often the primary focus of ethical concern in survey research (Cooper and Schindler 2001). Many surveys include some essential questions that might prove damaging to the subjects if their answers were disclosed. When a survey of employees asks: 'Do you think the senior management, especially your manager, is doing a good job?' or when student course evaluations ask: 'On a scale of 1 to 5, how fair would you say the professor is?' respondents may well hesitate; if the manager or professor saw the results, employees or students could be hurt.

To prevent any disclosure of such information, it is critical to preserve subject confidentiality. Only research personnel should have access to information that could be used to link respondents to their responses, and even that access should be limited to what is necessary for specific research purposes. Only numbers should be used to identify respondents on their questionnaires, and the researcher should keep the names that correspond to these numbers in a safe, private location, unavailable to staff and others who might otherwise come across them. Follow-up mailings or contact attempts that require linking the ID numbers with names and addresses should be carried out by the researcher or trustworthy assistants under close supervision. If an electronic survey is used, encryption technology should be used to make information provided over the Internet secure from unauthorized people. Usually confidentiality can be protected readily; the key is to be aware of the issue.

Few surveys can provide true anonymity, where no identifying information is ever recorded to link respondents with their responses. The main problem with anonymous surveys is that they preclude follow-up attempts to encourage participation by initial non-respondents, and they prevent panel designs, which measure change through repeated surveys of the same individuals (Dillman and Christian 2005). In-person surveys rarely can be anonymous because an interviewer must, in almost all cases, know the name and address of the interviewee. However, phone surveys that are meant only to sample opinion at one point in time, as in political polls, can safely be completely anonymous. When no future follow-up is desired, group-administered surveys also can be anonymous. To provide anonymity in a mail survey, the researcher should omit identifying codes from the questionnaire but could include a self-addressed, stamped postcard so the respondent can notify the researcher that the questionnaire has been returned without creating any linkage to the questionnaire itself (Mangione 1995, p. 69).

RECENT APPLICATIONS OF SURVEY TECHNIQUES IN CSR RESEARCH

CSR and other business researchers across all industries conduct surveys to uncover answers to specific, important questions. These questions are varied, cover a diverse range of topics, and can be asked in multiple formats. There are four main reasons to why CSR researchers conduct surveys:

1. To uncover answers;
2. To evoke discussion;
3. To base decisions on objective information; and
4. To compare results.

CSR activities include multiple stakeholders. In order to gather information from these stakeholders a survey needs to be conducted. Some of the recent works on the application of survey methodology are discussed below.

A unique study has been undertaken to examine the diffusion of environmental management initiatives in business and the motives and pressures reported by senior executives to adopt these practices in one industry. Babiak and Trendafilova (2011) framed these sustainable practices under the umbrella of CSR and examined the causal drivers of environmental behaviour. This study used a mixed-methods approach and included a survey and 17 in-depth interviews with a professional sports team and league executives. Results revealed both strategic and legitimacy motives to adopt environmental management practices.

The application of the survey method to CSR can be further highlighted by the study of Majid et al. (2013) where they explored the relationship between CSR and corporate reputation in the cement industry in Pakistan. The researchers approximated CSR to corporate reputation. The survey method was used to gather information through questionnaires. In this research, four dimensions of CSR were studied: environment oriented responsibilities, customer oriented responsibilities, community oriented responsibilities, and legal responsibilities. The collected data were analysed with the help of inferential statistics. Results indicated a strong relationship between CSR and corporate reputation in the cement industry of Pakistan.

Further, Crifo and Forget (2015) analysed the economics of CSR behaviours, namely the voluntary integration of environmental, social and governance factors in firms' strategy. They reviewed theoretical and empirical literature and provided a unified framework of the forces driving CSR, relying on three categories of market imperfections: the existence of externalities and public good; consumer heterogeneity; and imperfect contracts. The impacts of CSR on corporate performance and society were also surveyed. Understanding the economics of CSR is core to take a step out of the long lasting debate of whether engaging in CSR generates profits for corporations and to provide research paths to follow in order to understand how firms can succeed on both financial and social levels. They conclude that all countries should undertake to monitor and assess their own environment and integrate social, economic and environmental information to inform decision-making processes.

Quoting a research study undertaken by Lima Crisóstomo et al. (2011) that CSR is value destroying in Brazil, since a significant negative correlation exists between CSR and firm value. The paper examined the relationship between CSR and firm performance, taking into account firm value and financial accounting performance, in an emerging market – Brazil. Content analysis was conducted to extract data from two different sources, one relative to CSR data and another that provided financial data. CSR indexes and financial performance measures were calculated to allow the estimation of regression analysis conducted to examine the relationship between CSR and performance.

Aras et al. (2010) investigated the relationship between CSR and firm financial performance. The authors investigated the Istanbul Stock Exchange (ISE) 100 index companies and their social responsibility policy and financial indicators. The relationship between CSR and financial performance is empirically examined between 2005 and 2007 with different approaches and measurement methods. A survey method was used to estimate CSR from the listed companies of Istanbul. The authors show that some causality is related to lagging between periods for financial performance and CSR. Based upon previous empirical studies, this study conducts the analysis based on the assumption that there may be a relationship between firm size, profitability, risk level and CSR.

An empirical study by Chen and Wang (2011) pointed out that companies which undertake CSR activities respond quickly to the various stakeholders needs. The paper used data collected from 2007 to 2008 from Chinese firms to explore the relationship between CSR and corporate financial performance (CFP) empirically. Data for this study were obtained from self-designed questionnaires of CSR. After numerous steps of initial design, repeated modification, pilot survey, and so on, the authors began to implement the formal survey in March 2009. The core issue was the data concerning CSR and financial performance during 2007 and 2008. Respondents were senior executives from Guangdong enterprises of China. They adopted on-scene fill in and on-scene recycling to finish the survey. It took more than two months to accomplish the whole survey process. Results indicated that there exists a significant and reciprocal relationship between homophonous CSR and CFP in Chinese enterprises.

Bocquet et al. (2013) explored the relationship between CSR and innovation from a firm strategic perspective. Matching community innovation survey data with specific data collected about the CSR behaviour of Luxembourg firms, the authors identified two types of firms (strategic versus responsive) that differ in the intensity of their CSR adoption. A bivariate probit model, estimated to explain the different types of technological innovations (product and/or process), shows that firms with strategic CSR profiles are more likely to innovate in both products and processes. In contrast, adopting responsive CSR practices significantly alters firms' innovation, such that CSR may create barriers to innovation.

Another sector specific study in the sphere of CSR is undertaken by Ofori et al. (2014) for the banking sector. The authors examined the impact of CSR on financial performance using empirical evidence from the Ghanaian banking sector. The sample frame for the study was all banks licensed by the Bank of Ghana to operate commercial banking services in the country. The data-collection technique employed was the questionnaire survey method. In collecting information on the independent variable CSR, the primary data source employed was a questionnaire consisting of closed-ended questions. Research questions were designed as concisely as possible in order to obtain maximum information on management views and motives for CSR practices. The items in the questionnaire were thus used to measure their views on CSR practices, as well as their motivation for CSR practices. Questions covering views influencing the practice of CSR sought to understand the views behind this practice. The rest of the questions sought to examine the banks' motivation for practising CSR. For these questions on banks' views on CSR and their motivation for CSR activities, the authors adopted a 5-point Likert scale. The scale ranged from '1 = strongly agree' to '5 = strongly disagree'. The respondents were thus asked to indicate the extent to which they agreed with statements on the two main issues. The findings revealed that banks in Ghana view CSR practices to be a strategic tool; banks are motivated to practise CSR by legitimate reasons as much as they are motivated by profitability and sustainability reasons.

CONCLUSION

Survey researchers have long been aware that collecting data by asking questions is an exercise that may yield many surprises. Since the 1980s, psychologists and survey methodologists have made considerable progress in understanding the cognitive and communicative processes underlying question answering, rendering some of these surprises less surprising than they have been in the past. Yet, this does not imply that we can always predict how a given question would behave when colleagues and students ask for advice. In many cases, the given question is too mushy an operationalization of theoretical variables to allow for predictions (although we typically feel we know what would happen if the question were tinkered with, in one way or another, to bring it in line with theoretical models). Nevertheless, the accumulating insights (reviewed in Sudman et al. 1996, Tourangeau et al. 2000) alert us to likely problems and help us in identifying questions and question sequences that need systematic experimental testing before they are employed in a large-scale study.

There are a lot of ways to conduct research and collect information, but one way that makes it really easy is by doing a survey. Survey research is one of the most important areas of measurement in applied social research. This chapter presents different types of survey methods such as postal, interview, telephone and web-based surveys. A major difficulty in survey research is securing a sufficiently high response rate to give credibility and reliability to the data. The accuracy of a survey estimate refers to the closeness of the estimate to the true population value. Survey research designs usually pose fewer ethical dilemmas than do experimental or field research designs. Potential respondents to a survey can easily decline to participate, and a cover letter or introductory statement that identifies the sponsors of, and motivations for, the survey gives them the information required to make this decision. Little is concealed from the respondents, and the methods of data collection are quite obvious.

REFERENCES

Aras, G., A. Aybars and O. Kutlu (2010), 'Managing corporate performance', *International Journal of Productivity and Performance Management*, **59** (3), 229–254.
Ary, Donald, Lucy Cheser and Asghar Razavien (2009), *Introduction to Research in Education*, Belmont, CA, USA: Cengage Learning.
Babiak, K. and S.Trendafilova (2011), 'CSR and environmental responsibility: motives and pressures to adopt green management practices', *Corporate Social Responsibility and Environmental Management*, **18** (1), 11–24.
Bailey, Kenneth D. (1994), *Methods of Social Research*, 4th ed., New York, NY, USA: The Free Press.
Best, John W. (1970), *Research in Education*, 2nd ed., Englewood Cliffs, NJ, USA: Prentice Hall.
Bimrose, J. and R. Bayne (1995), 'A multicultural framework in counsellor training: a preliminary evaluation', *British Journal of Guidance and Counselling*, **23** (2), 259–265.
Bocquet, R., C. Le Bas, C. Mothe and N. Poussing (2013), 'Are firms with different CSR profiles equally innovative? Empirical analysis with survey data', *European Management Journal*, **31** (6), 642–654.
Chen, H. and X. Wang (2011), 'Corporate social responsibility and corporate financial performance in China: an empirical research from Chinese firms', *Corporate Governance: The International Journal of Business in Society*, **11** (4), 361–370.
Cook, C., F. Heath and R. Thompson (2000), 'A meta-analysis of response rates in web or Internet based surveys', *Educational and Psychological Measurement*, **60** (6), 821–836.
Cooper, Donald C. and Pamela. S. Schindler (2001), *Business Research Methods*, 7th ed., New York, NY, USA: McGraw-Hill.
Crifo, P. and V.D. Forget (2015), 'The economics of corporate social responsibility: a firm-level perspective survey', *Journal of Economic Surveys*, **29** (1), 112–130.
DeVaus, David A. (2002), *Conducting Surveys Using the Internet*, Thousand Oaks, CA, USA: Sage.
Dillman, Don A. (2000), *Mail and Internet Surveys: The Tailored Design Method*, 2nd ed., New York, NY, USA: John Wiley and Sons.
Dillman, Don A. (2007), *Mail and Internet Surveys: The Tailored Design Method*, 2nd ed., Hoboken, NJ, USA: John Wiley and Sons.

Dillman, D.A. and D.K. Bowker (2001), 'The web questionnaire challenge to survey methodologists', in Ulf-Dietrich Reips and Michael Bosnjak (eds), *Dimensions of Internet Science*, Lengerich, Germany: Pabst Science, pp.53–71.

Dillman, D. A. and L.M. Christian (2005), 'Survey mode as a source of instability in responses across surveys', *Field Methods,* **17** (1), 30–52.

Dillman, D.A., J.D. Smyth, L.M. Christian and M.J. Stern (2003), 'Multiple answer questions in self-administered surveys: the use of check-all-that apply and forced-choice question formats', paper presented at the American Statistical Association, San Francisco, CA. August 14.

Flatley, J. (2001), 'The Internet as a mode of data collection in government social surveys: issues and investigation', paper presented at the International Conference on Survey Research Methods, Latimer, UK, May 11–12.

Fowler, Floyed J. (2002), *Survey Research Methods*, 3rd ed., Thousand Oaks, CA, USA: Sage.

Holbrook, A., M. Green and J. Krosnick (2003), 'Telephone versus face-to-face interviewing of national probability samples with long questionnaires', *Public Opinion Quarterly*, **67** (1), 79–125.

KPMG (2013), 'Survey of corporate responsibility reporting', accessed 5 April 2014 at www.kpmg.com/sustainability.

Lima Crisóstomo, V., F. de Souza Freire and F. Cortes de Vasconcellos (2011), 'Corporate social responsibility, firm value and financial performance in Brazil', *Social Responsibility Journal*, **7** (2), 295–309.

Majid, A., M. Yasir and M. Arshad (2013), 'Corporate social responsibility and corporate reputation: a case of cement industry in Pakistan', *Interdisciplinary Journal of Contemporary Research in Business*, **5** (1), 843–857.

Mangione, Thomas W. (1995), *Mail Surveys: Improving the Quality*, Thousand Oaks, CA, USA: Sage.

Morrison, G.L. (1997), 'TRNSYS extensions (TRNAUS)', Report STEL/1 1997, School of Mechanical and Manufacturing Engineering, University of New South Wales, Sydney, Australia.

Neuman, Lawrence W. and Larry W. Kreuger (2003), *Social Work Research Methods: Qualitative and Quantitative Approaches,* Boston, MA, USA: Allyn and Bacon.

Ofori, D.F., R.B. Nyuur and M.D. S-Darko (2014), 'Corporate social responsibility and financial performance: fact or fiction? A look at Ghanaian banks', *Acta Commercii*, **14** (1), 1–11.

Punch, Keith (2003), *Survey Research: The Basics,* London, UK, Thousand Oaks, New Delhi, India: Sage.

Robson, Colin (1993), *Real World Research: A Resource for Social Scientists and Practitioner–Researchers*, Oxford, UK: Blackwell Publishers.

Rosenberg, S.L., D.J. Heck and E.R. Banilower (2005), 'Does teacher content preparation moderate the impacts of professional development? A longitudinal analysis of LSC teacher questionnaire data', accessed 24 February 2015 at http://www.horizon-research.com/pdmathsci/htdocs/reports/Rosenberg_heck_banilower_2005.pdf.

Selm, V. and N.W. Jankowski (2006), 'Conducting online surveys', *Quality and Quantity,* **40** (3), 435–456.

Simionescu, L.N. and S.C. Gherghina (2014), 'Corporate social responsibility and corporate performance: empirical evidence from a panel of the Bucharest Stock Exchange listed companies', *Management & Marketing*, **9** (4), 439–458.

Smith, Sean P., Eric R. Banilower, Kelly C. McMahon and Iris R. Weiss (2002), *The National Survey of Science and Mathematics Education: Trends from 1977 to 2000*, Chapel Hill, NC, USA: Horizon Research.

Smyth, J.D., D.A. Dillman, L.M. Christian and M.J. Stern (2006), 'Comparing check-all and forced-choice question formats in web surveys', *Public Opinion Quarterly*, **70** (1), 66–77.

Sudman, Seymour, Norman M. Bradburn and Norbert Schwarz (1996), *Thinking about the Answers: The Application of Cognitive Processes to Survey Methodology,* San Francisco, CA, USA: Jossey-Boss.

Tourangeau, Roger, Lance J. Rips and Kenneth Rasinski (2000), *The Psychology of Survey Response*, Cambridge, England: Cambridge University Press.

Weisberg, Michael K., Martin Prinz, Robert N. Clayton, Toshiko K. Mayeda, Mayeda M. Grady, Ian Franchi, Colin T. Pillinger and Gregory W. Kallemeyn (1996), 'The K (Kakangari) chondrite grouplet', *Geochimica et cosmochimica acta*, **60** (21), 4253–4263.

Werner, C.A. (2011), *The Older Population: 2010*, US Department of Commerce, Economics and Statistics Administration, US Census Bureau.

Zikmund, William G., Barry J. Babin, Jon C. Carr and Mitch Griffin (2010), *Business Research Methods*, 8th ed., Mason, OH, USA: South-Western Cengage Learning.

20. Content analysis method: a proposed scoring for quantitative and qualitative disclosures[1]
Juniati Gunawan and Kumalawati Abadi

INTRODUCTION

Corporate Social Responsibility (CSR) has become an important aspect of businesses wishing to remain relevant in today's global environment. In Indonesia, CSR activities are not mandatory for all companies doing business in the country; however, for certain companies such as those in the mining sector that exploit natural resources, CSR has become compulsory in accordance with the Indonesian Government Regulation No. 47/2012. In fact, regardless of the presence or absence of regulations, CSR becomes very important when a company is aware and is committed to maintaining its survival, both from the economic or social and environmental aspects.

Companies in Indonesia should not only think of corporate responsibilities as mere economic performances offered to its shareholders in terms of profit and share price, or as legal responsibilities to the government of having to pay taxes or as compliance with 'environmental impact assessment' requirements. It is more than that. If companies wish to be acknowledged and accepted, they should also pay attention to their social responsibilities.

Responsibility to the environment can be realized by reporting the company's activities through a sustainability report. A sustainability report contains information on CSR activities in the social, economic and environmental fields. It also maintains the company's commitment to sustainability and minimization of risks. This report is important for stakeholders in order to obtain an overview of the company's CSR activities, as well as its strategies in maintaining sustainability, both internally and externally.

The Sustainability Reporting Guidelines (SRG) issued by the Global Reporting Initiative (GRI) is used widely as a guide in preparing sustainability reports. In addition, GRI is used to assess sustainability activities through the reports. GRI has explained the details of the indicators related to the disclosures of sustainability reports from the aspects of good corporate governance, economics, social and environment.

In assessing the performance in regard to sustainability through sustainability reports, the content analysis (CA) method has been widely used with a number for scoring. This method can be regarded as the only method of transferring qualitative information into quantitative information in order to be further examined.

Krippendorff (2004, p. 18) explains the meaning of CA: 'Content analysis is a research technique for making replicable and valid inferences from texts (or other meaningful matter) to the contexts of their use.' The weakness of the CA method is the level of subjectivity when applying scores (Gunawan, Djajadikerta and Smith, 2009; Smith, Yahya and Amiruddin, 2007). The scoring process is undertaken through the use of a guideline interpretation. The interpretation is very important when conducting analysis in measuring disclosures. Thus, subjectivity in interpreting the guideline and disclosed information in the reports accrued when the level of understanding of the scorers are different or when the guideline for awarding scores is not clear.

Subjectivity can be minimized by a particular process. In previous studies, Perry and Bodkin (2000) describe how subjectivity can be minimized and how to perform an analysis of information in the form of a narrative. Similarly, Gunawan, Djajadikerta and Smith (2009) illustrate quite clearly that subjectivity can be minimized by making a clear guideline and applying more than one scorer during awarding scores.

Based on the importance of CA, this study proposes a guideline to conduct the score application process for more than two coders. In addition, the scoring method has also been improved from prior studies to be more applicable to measure the quality of information in reports. After developing a proposed guideline and scoring method, further examination has been conducted using this new guideline by analysing sustainability reports from mining industries. Hence, it is expected that this study will provide insights to conduct better CA process by applying more than one coder, particularly in awarding detailed scores to measure the quality of report disclosures, both quantitative and qualitative.

THEORETICAL REVIEW

Corporate Social Responsibility (CSR)

Although becoming a global issue, there is so far no one single definition of CSR that is accepted globally. Etymologically, CSR can be defined as the responsibility of the company or corporation.

CSR activities cannot be separated from the corporation, community and environment. In relation with it, CSR activities should be handled accountably as they affect people, community and environment (Lawrence, Weber and Post, 2005). A corporation's contribution to the environment through its business brings a very positive impact on its survival. Kotler and Lee (2005) state that CSR is a commitment to improve community well-being through discretionary business practices and contributions of corporate resources. Responding to a variety of definitions of CSR, the World Business Council for Sustainable Development (WBCSD) has been constantly updating the definition of CSR from year to year.

The WBCSD's definition of CSR:

> Corporate Social Responsibility is the continuing commitment by business to contribute to economic development while improving the quality of life of the workforce and their families as well as of the community and society at large. (WBCSD, 2002, p. 3)

In Indonesia, CSR practices are voluntary, although there are many regulations which relate to the key aspects of CSR. The understanding of CSR in Indonesia is much more in external activities rather than internal. Thus, CSR practices in Indonesia are still tailored to the circumstances of each company, based on its types and needs. CSR has many aspects and requires a significant amount of knowledge to understand well. Openness to continue to improve CSR activities is expected to be one of a company's business strategies that can be evaluated on an ongoing basis, particularly through reports.

CSR and Reporting

Forms of CSR embodied in some company activities should be disclosed in a public report so that the company's stakeholders can understand the benefits from the company implementing these activities. In Indonesia, there is a wide range of form of reports describing different companies' CSR activities, for example: social reports, environmental reports, corporate social and environmental reports, and annual reports.

Pruzan (2001) provides a very useful description of 'social report' stating its basic characteristics. According to Pruzan (2001), a social report measures how well an organization inform the existing values, which are created together with stakeholders. A social report also provides an extensive overview of an organization's relationship with its stakeholders and, thus, will create the opportunity for it to thrive and survive in the long term.

The continued development of social reports, environmental reports or similar reports, initiates the Global Reporting Initiative (GRI) to provide a guideline to make sustainability reporting a tool that can be used to communicate between the company and its stakeholders.

Very few companies understand how the presentation of the sustainability report works. Thus, the report can often be understood only by a certain group of people. The importance of knowing the stakeholders who will read a certain sustainability report is essential to help companies understand and realize the importance of continual improvement progress.

With proper understanding of the importance of continual improvement progress, a company will then be more careful in presenting the information in its sustainability report. The choice of words, tones, narratives, analyses and quantitative data that will be included in sustainability reports must describe the actual condition of the company, so that the company's goal to communicate CSR activities and its commitment to sustainability can be achieved.

Sustainability Report

The GRI (2006) defines a sustainability report as a practice measurement, disclosure and accountability to the organization's internal and external stakeholders for organizational performance towards the goal of sustainable development. A sustainability report is a report that is used to describe the implications of economic, environmental and social activities, complemented by strategies to minimize corporate risks and maximize the whole aspects of sustainability.

A sustainability report should also provide a balanced and fair description of the organization's performance, including both its positive and negative impacts. A sustainability report is intended to meet the information needed by stakeholders. Items that are outlined in the sustainability report are not only a history or list of past performances of a business unit, but they are also of the current state and the business's commitment in the future. Commitment in the future can be taken from the minutes of the meetings or the company's strategy.

All-important CSR activities that have been undertaken by the company should be disclosed in the sustainability report, as well as when the activity has to end. Challenges or barriers faced by the company that result in suspended CSR programmes should also be disclosed in the report along with their impact on sustainability. Furthermore, the company is expected to inform about its commitment in ensuring sustainability that includes economic, social and environment in the sustainability report.

Content Analysis

Content analysis is a method of codifying the text (content) of a manuscript into several categories according to the specified criteria. Krippendorff explains the definition of CA as the research techniques used to make valid inferences from the text to the context of its use. According to Krippendorff (2004, p. 18), 'content analysis is a research technique for making replicable and valid inferences from texts (or other meaningful matter) to the contexts of their use'. Krippendorff also explains that the research using CA should be allowed to be re-researched on the same phenomenon by different researchers.

According to Holsti (1969), there are three objectives of CA, namely: (a) to describe the characteristics of the communication, (b) to make the conclusion of the causes of communication and (c) to make the conclusion of the impact of communication (cited in Krippendorff, 2004). CA is useful to understand the symbolic messages in the form of documents, writing, dance, song, literature, articles, and so on, including unstructured data, as well as to compare the contents of more than two books on the same topic but by different authors at the same time. Furthermore, Krippendorff (2004) describes some of the many advantages of applying CA, which include:

1. It is a method that is not contaminated by the procedure of data.
2. Its use of unstructured data.
3. It is sensitive to context.
4. It can be used to process symbolic forms. Symbolic phenomena in their native context can be understood. In this way, researchers cannot ignore the context of time, place and circumstances of events. Thus analytical construction or experiences of context can be developed to make inferences of the study.
5. It can be applied to numerous data.

However, all research methods have limitations in addition to having definite advantages. Limitations of the CA method have been noted by all studies, in terms of having subjectivity in understanding the measurement guideline and the meaning of information they read. Consequently, it is possible that the CA process conducted by two different researchers can result in different conclusions for the same case study.

Zuchdi (1993) describes the limitations of the CA method, which are:

1. The process is time-consuming and costly.
2. The analysed material is sometimes very weak and not representative enough to produce valid findings.
3. The results depend largely on the nature of the research question, but a question may involve the use of the unit analysis of a theme. Sometimes it is very difficult to identify themes. In addition, good research questions may require various disciplines to answer and also require a relatively long time and serious work. Thus, it is quite hard to obtain a good question that is in accordance with the purpose of the research.

Table 20.1 Sample of companies

No.	Name of Company
1	PT. Adaro Indonesia
2	PT. Aneka Tambang, Tbk
3	PT. Petrosea, Tbk
4	PT. Timah (Persero), Tbk
5	PT. Kaltim Prima Coal
6	PT. International Nickel Indonesia, Tbk

Source: Indonesia Sustainability Reporting Award Event (2012).

RESEARCH METHODS

This study is considered as an exploratory qualitative research which aims to develop a more detailed guide to implement the CA process, especially in awarding scores. To examine the created guide, sustainability reports are used as samples.

Sample

Six sustainability reports (Table 20.1) were examined using the new proposed guideline. These reports were obtained from the company websites of all the Indonesian mining companies that participated in the Indonesia Sustainability Reporting Award (ISRA), including listed and non-listed companies. Mining companies are the major type of industry which publish sustainability reports.

Scoring Analysis Method

Sustainability reports were measured using the sustainability report guideline from GRI, version 3, which includes economic, environmental and social aspects. The scoring measurement was taken from Raar (2002). Raar developed a measurement of quantities using numbers (scores) 1–5, while the quality measurement using numbers (scores) 1–7, is described in Table 20.2.

In Raar (2002), the measurement of score, both quantitative and qualitative, needs to be improved by providing more clear explanation. The quantitative scores 3, 4 and 5 provide ambiguous interpretation if the report has a picture, graph or table, then 'half page' will not properly represent the awarded score number 3, 4 or 5. On the other hand, the qualitative scores 1, 2 and 6 do not explain the description of narrative information. This causes difficulties in putting scores when narrative information is always disclosed in the sustainability report. Through the process of awarding a score based on Table 20.2, this study finds some important improvements to provide better and clearer explanations. This scoring is very essential since there is no comprehensive scoring method available, while scoring is one of the most important tools for conducting CA.

Based on the above reasons, Table 20.2 is improved into Table 20.3 accordingly to provide a more comprehensive and clear explanation in the scoring process. In the

Table 20.2 Quantity and quality scoring index

Quantitative	Qualitative
1 = sentence	1 = monetary
2 = paragraph	2 = non-monetary
3 = half page of A4	3 = qualitative only
4 = one page of A4	4 = qualitative and monetary
5 = more than one page of A4	5 = qualitative and non-monetary
	6 = monetary and non-monetary
	7 = qualitative, monetary and non-monetary

Source: Raar (2002).

Table 20.3 Proposed quantitative and qualitative scoring index

Quantitative	Qualitative
0 = no information is disclosed in accordance with the indicators	
1 = sentence	1 = only qualitative
2 = paragraph	2 = qualitative and monetary
3 = 2–3 paragraphs	3 = qualitative and non-monetary
4 = 4–5 paragraphs	4 = qualitative and diagram (table/chart)
5 = > 5 paragraphs	5 = qualitative, monetary and non-monetary
	6 = qualitative, monetary and diagram (table/chart)
	7 = qualitative, non-monetary and diagram (table/chart)
	8 = qualitative, monetary, non-monetary and diagram (table/chart)

Source: Raar (2002) with improvements and amendments.

quantitative scores 3, 4 and 5, the description of 'page' has been improved by directly providing the number of paragraphs. In the qualitative scoring, all information has been added into more comprehensive description and results in 8 scores, instead of 7 as a maximum score.

The explanation for each scoring index in Table 20.3 is as follows:

Quantitative measurement

1. A score of 0 is given if the information in the report is not disclosed in accordance with the indicator measurement; in this case, the GRI items.
2. A score of 1 is given if the disclosure contains at least one word and as much as one sentence. A diagram (figure, table or chart) reveals one word, it is considered a sentence.
3. A score of 2 is given if the disclosure contains at least two sentences; considered as one paragraph.
4. A score of 3 is given if the disclosure contains two to three paragraphs.

5. A score of 4 is given if the disclosure contains four to five paragraphs.
6. A score of 5 is given if the disclosure contains more than five paragraphs.

Qualitative measurement

1. A score of 1 is given if the disclosure only reveals a description or narrative.
2. A score of 2 is given if the disclosure reveals a description and also informs the nominal value of a particular currency.
3. A score of 3 is given if the disclosure reveals a description and informs the size of particular units, such as weight, volume, size and percentage.
4. A score of 4 is given if the disclosure reveals a description and presents a picture, graph, chart or table.
5. A score of 5 is given if the disclosure reveals a description, mentions the nominal value of a particular currency, and also includes other units than currency.
6. A score of 6 is given if the disclosure reveals a description, mentions the nominal value of a particular currency, and presents either a picture, graph, chart or table.
7. A score of 7 is given if the information reveals a description, mentions the size of a particular unit except the currency (such as weight, volume, size, percentage) and presents either a picture, graph, chart or table.
8. A score of 8 is given if the information reveals a description, mentions the nominal value of a particular currency, informs the size of a unit apart from currency, as well as presents either a picture, graph, chart or table.

Content Analysis Process Development

The method of CA used in this study is applied by assigning two different coders to reduce subjectivity (Gunawan, Djajadikerta and Smith, 2009; Krippendorff, 2004). The coders use the proposed scoring index developed in this study (Table 20.3). The purpose of this evaluation is to provide evidence that assigning more than one coder will result in a better score in measuring reports. The most important process in assigning more than one coder is providing a clear guideline for each coder to minimize different interpretations.

A coder's role is to analyse the information disclosed in the report and provide professional assessment in determining the score in accordance with the guidelines used. The importance of the CA process greatly affects the results of any study that applies this method. Therefore, each stage of the process's application is crucial. The process of determining the coder, either coder 1 or 2, is selected by explaining the purpose and objective of conducting a CA method. The coder should have an adequate understanding of the information context described in the guideline and all possible information disclosed in the report. Competencies of coders determine the quality of scores awarded, and this is related to the quality of the result.

The guidelines that govern the implementation of the procedure set out to obtain a total score in a reliable and systematic manner that is capable of describing the quantity and quality of disclosed information. Similarly, scores were expected to be more similar given the instructions reference standards used; in this case, it is the standard SRG issued by the GRI. The process of developing guidelines is conducted by discussing with the two coders on building a consensus to be consistent in applying scores through the process of CA

(Gunawan, Djajadikerta and Smith, 2009). The discussion includes a general explanation on the method of CA, which guidelines to be applied in scoring are used, and information that is interpreted. In summary, there are three stages in the process of CA. They are the creation of general guidelines, the scoring process and the evaluation process.

Phase 1: general guideline
Each coder is required to understand and be thorough in following every step in the established guidelines. Each coder must be independent, especially when finding difficulties and ambiguities in understanding the guidelines that have been set.

As a general guideline, it must be understood by both coders. Each coder should read the company's sustainability report to understand the type of information disclosed in the report. This first stage is an exploration for each coder; they should be able to express their opinions on whether or not they quite understand and are interested to proceed to the next stage.

Phase 2: guideline for scoring
The guideline for awarding scores emphasizes the aspects that are considered important to organize a systematic CA procedure, which provides insight and clarity (Krippendorff, 2004). The scores were determined according to the applied guideline.

In relation to the purpose of this study, the scoring process can be illustrated in Figure 20.1. Explanation of Figure 20.1:

1. Read the text in the 2009 sustainability reports of the six mining companies selected for this study.
2. Understand all 79 performance indicators of the GRI sustainability reporting guideline.
   (i) Analyse whether there is information disclosed in the sustainability report that is in accordance with GRI performance indicators.
3. Ignore all the irrelevant information and provide a score of 0 (zero) if the disclosed information is not relevant to the GRI performance indicators.
   (i) Award scores (in accordance with the determined quantitative and qualitative scoring) when there is disclosed information that is relevant to the GRI performance indicators.
   (ii) Sum the scores to describe the level of disclosures in a sustainability report. The higher the score, the more it illustrates the company's sustainability report and provides more comprehensive information in accordance with the GRI performance indicators.

The scoring process for quantitative and qualitative disclosures is described as follows.

Quantitative disclosures: There are five levels in awarding scores for quantitative disclosures used in this study based on how much information is disclosed in the sustainability report. The scores are explained in Table 20.3. The maximum total score that can be achieved for total quantity is 395. This total number is obtained by multiplying the maximum score (5) for any information disclosed with the total of 79 indicators.

Qualitative disclosures: Awarding scores for qualitative disclosures is undertaken after completing the quantitative scoring process. If the score for the quantitative disclosure

Content analysis: scoring for quantitative and qualitative disclosures 357

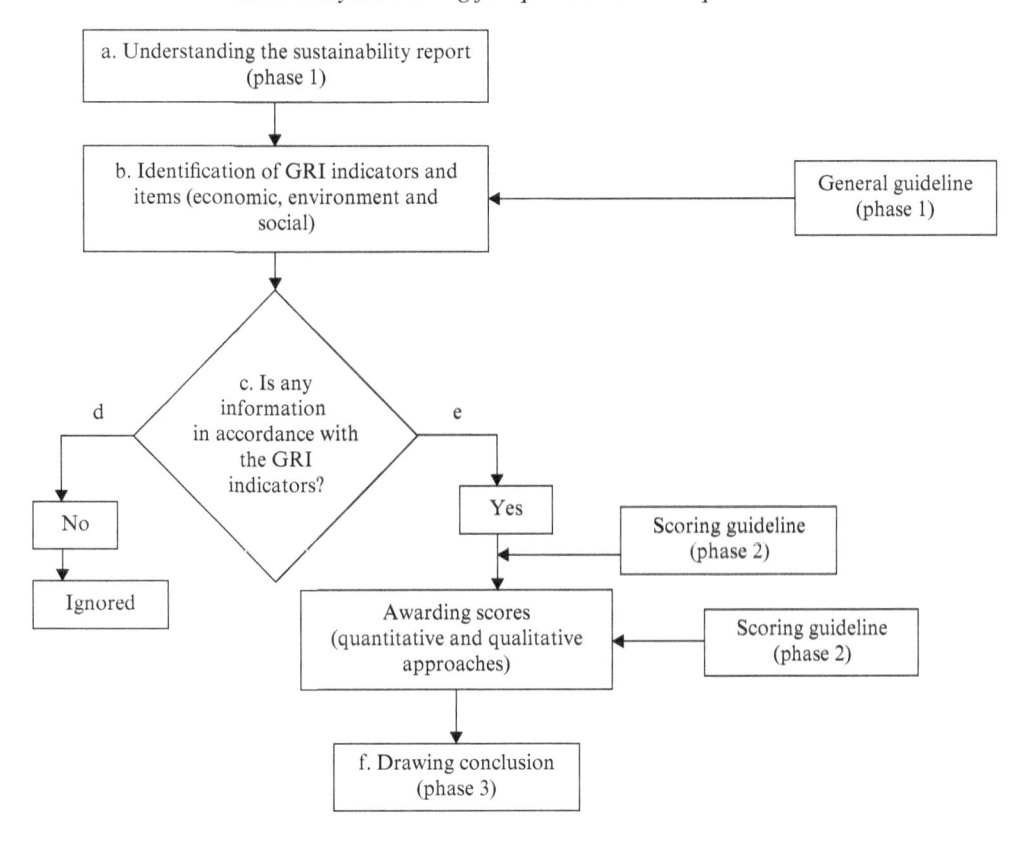

```
┌─────────────────────────────┐
│ a. Understanding the        │
│ sustainability report       │
│ (phase 1)                   │
└─────────────────────────────┘
              │
              ▼
┌─────────────────────────────┐         ┌─────────────────────┐
│ b. Identification of GRI    │◄────────│ General guideline   │
│ indicators and items        │         │ (phase 1)           │
│ (economic, environment and  │         └─────────────────────┘
│ social)                     │
└─────────────────────────────┘
              │
              ▼
         ◇ c. Is any
    d  information  e
       in accordance with
       the GRI
       indicators?
       
       │ Yes
       ▼
┌─────────────────────┐                  ┌─────────────────────┐
│ No                  │                  │ Scoring guideline   │
└─────────────────────┘                  │ (phase 2)           │
       │                                 └─────────────────────┘
       ▼
┌─────────────────────┐    ┌─────────────────────────────┐    ┌─────────────────────┐
│ Ignored             │    │ Awarding scores             │◄───│ Scoring guideline   │
└─────────────────────┘    │ (quantitative and qualitative│    │ (phase 2)           │
                           │ approaches)                  │   └─────────────────────┘
                           └─────────────────────────────┘
                                         │
                                         ▼
                           ┌─────────────────────────┐
                           │ f. Drawing conclusion   │
                           │ (phase 3)               │
                           └─────────────────────────┘
```

Source: Adapted from Gunawan, Djajadikerta and Smith (2009) with improvements.

Figure 20.1   Scoring process

is 0 (zero), then it is not necessary to put any score for qualitative because it means there is no information relevant to the guidelines. The scores are explained in Table 20.3. The maximum total score that can be achieved is 632. This score is obtained by multiplying the maximum score, which is 8 for any information disclosed with the total of 79 indicators.

During the scoring process, if identical information is spread over several pages of the report, the scores should be awarded to the most numbers of (quantitative) and the most comprehensive (qualitative) piece of information. This provision is based on the premise that equal information which is presented repeatedly is considered as waste information. Repetitive information can even be confusing, so the report may not be interesting to read. The information disclosed in the report should be solid, clear, transparent, concise and easily understood.

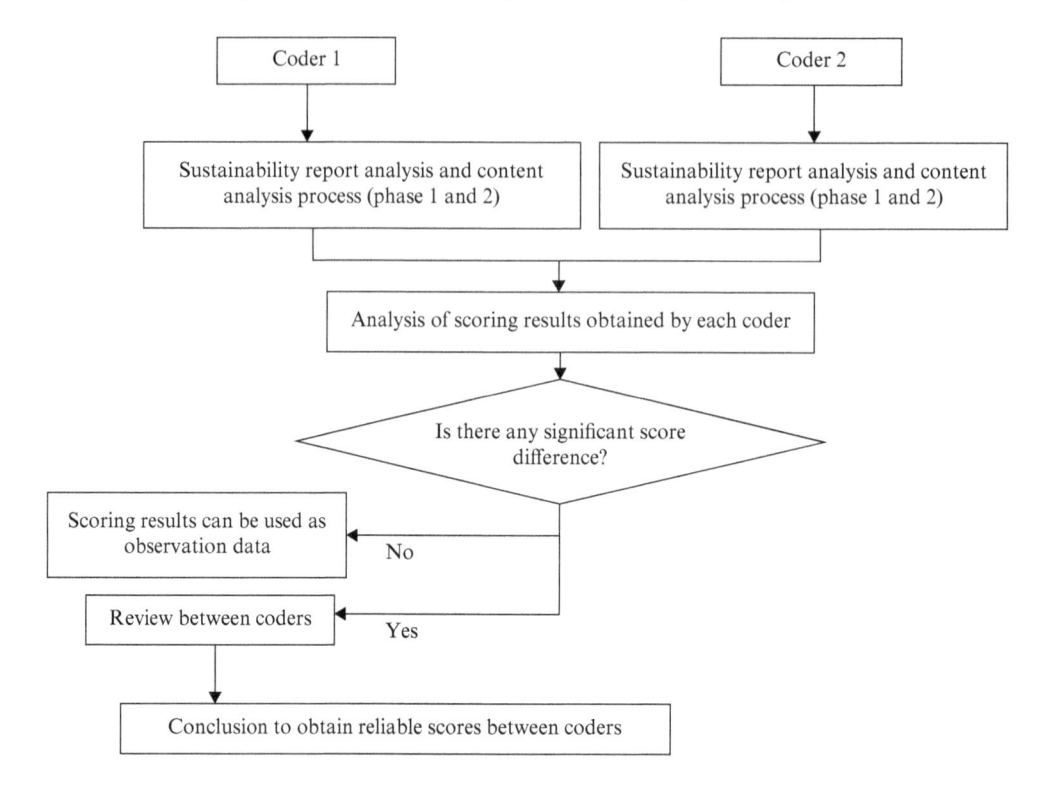

358 *Handbook of research methods in corporate social responsibility*

```
                    ┌─────────┐                              ┌─────────┐
                    │ Coder 1 │                              │ Coder 2 │
                    └────┬────┘                              └────┬────┘
                         ▼                                        ▼
          ┌──────────────────────────────┐        ┌──────────────────────────────┐
          │ Sustainability report        │        │ Sustainability report        │
          │ analysis and content         │        │ analysis and content         │
          │ analysis process             │        │ analysis process             │
          │ (phase 1 and 2)              │        │ (phase 1 and 2)              │
          └──────────────┬───────────────┘        └──────────────┬───────────────┘
                         └───────────────┬──────────────────────┘
                                         ▼
                  ┌──────────────────────────────────────────┐
                  │ Analysis of scoring results obtained     │
                  │ by each coder                            │
                  └────────────────────┬─────────────────────┘
                                       ▼
                              ╱ Is there any ╲
                             ╱ significant    ╲
                            ╱ score            ╲
                             ╲ difference?    ╱
                              ╲              ╱
   ┌────────────────────────┐     │     │
   │ Scoring results can be │◄────┘ No  │ Yes
   │ used as observation    │           ▼
   │ data                   │    ┌─────────────────────┐
   └────────────────────────┘    │ Review between      │
                                 │ coders              │
                                 └──────────┬──────────┘
                                            ▼
                  ┌──────────────────────────────────────────┐
                  │ Conclusion to obtain reliable scores     │
                  │ between coders                           │
                  └──────────────────────────────────────────┘
```

Source: Adapted from Gunawan, Djajadikerta and Smith (2009) with improvements.

Figure 20.2 Total scores evaluation process

Phase 3: evaluating total scores
To complete the process of CA, it is necessary to evaluate the total score that is described in Figure 20.2.

SUPPORT RESULTS AND DISCUSSIONS

After conducting the CA with the procedure developed in this study, six sustainability reports were evaluated to examine whether the guideline can be well implemented. Two coders were assigned to conduct CA with the new proposed guideline. Two coders had been selected through over five discussions and evaluations following the general guideline. After the coders agreed to assist the study, the scoring process began independently.

The scoring process was performed in the span of three weeks. This time was used to provide scores starting from each coder, followed by discussions and re-evaluation of the reports to reduce subjectivity. Each coder awarded scores in sustainability reporting information from the sample selected, with reference to the GRI guideline. Then, the results of the total scores from the two coders were compared. According to the results,

Table 20.4 Quantitative disclosures for economic aspect by coder 1 and 2

Indicator	Item Description	Score CODER 1	Score CODER 2
EC1	Economic value retained and distributed	14.00	11.00
EC2	Financial implication due to climate change	3.00	6.00
EC3	Benefits plan obligations	10.00	5.00
EC4	Financial assistance from government	4.00	4.00
EC5	Minimum wages	10.00	9.00
EC6	Local suppliers	10.00	11.00
EC7	Local employees	13.00	15.00
EC8	Infrastructure investments	14.00	13.00
EC9	Indirect economic impact	14.00	16.00

Source: Data process.

Table 20.5 Qualitative disclosures for economic aspect by coder 1 and 2

Indicator	Item Description	Score CODER 1	Score CODER 2
EC1	Economic value retained and distributed	42.00	40.00
EC2	Financial implication due to climate change	2.00	7.00
EC3	Benefits plan obligations	9.00	6.00
EC4	Financial assistance from government	3.00	3.00
EC5	Minimum wages	22.00	19.00
EC6	Local suppliers	20.00	17.00
EC7	Local employees	22.00	29.00
EC8	Infrastructure investments	13.00	19.00
EC9	Indirect economic impact	26.00	20.00

Source: Data process.

the total scores obtained by the two coders did not have significant differences; the scores should not differ by more than 10 per cent (as professional judgement). This result may indicate that the guideline applied in this study proves to be quite reliable as proven by the two independent coders.

The results of quantitative and qualitative measurement of the disclosed information in sustainability reports using GRI indicators from each coder are presented as follows.

Economic Aspect

The results of total scores from the information disclosed for economic aspects are presented in Tables 20.4 and 20.5 based on item indicators from the GRI guideline.

Environmental Aspect

The results of total scores from the disclosed information for environmental aspects are presented in Tables 20.6 and 20.7 based on aspect indicators from the GRI guideline.

Table 20.6 Quantitative disclosures for environmental aspect by coder 1 and 2

Indicator	Aspect Description	Score CODER 1	Score CODER 2
EN1–EN2	Material	15.00	17.00
EN3–EN7	Energy	47.00	53.00
EN8–EN10	Water	26.00	30.00
EN11–EN15	Biodiversity	42.00	52.00
EN16–EN25	Emission, effluent and waste	90.00	91.00
EN26–EN27	Product and service	16.00	20.00
EN28	Compliance	6.00	7.00
EN29	Transport	12.00	14.00
EN30	Overall	10.00	11.00

Source: Data process.

Table 20.7 Qualitative disclosures for environmental aspect by coder 1 and 2

Indicator	Aspect Description	Score CODER 1	Score CODER 2
EN1–EN2	Material	46.00	51.00
EN3–EN7	Energy	88.00	90.00
EN8–EN10	Water	61.00	62.00
EN11–EN15	Biodiversity	70.00	82.00
EN16–EN25	Emission, effluent and waste	142.00	158.00
EN26–EN27	Product and service	15.00	23.00
EN28	Compliance	3.00	4.00
EN29	Transport	11.00	9.00
EN30	Overall	32.00	32.00

Source: Data process.

Social Aspect

The results of total scores from the disclosed information for social aspects are presented in Tables 20.8 and 20.9 based on aspect indicators from the GRI guideline.

Having completed the CA conducted by two coders, the result shows that economic performances obtain the highest scores, both for quantitative and qualitative approaches, compared to other aspects, which are environment and social (Table 20.10). This result may suggest that economic performance is still a priority for the Indonesian mining companies. These companies could think that economic information is needed more by stakeholders, therefore they disclose it greatly in their sustainability reports.

CONCLUSION

Studies using CA have limitations in terms of subjectivity and scoring numbers. The prior studies often simply apply dichotomous scores of 1 and 0 for disclosed and non-disclosed

Table 20.8 Quantitative disclosures for social aspect by coder 1 and 2

Indicator	Aspect Description	Score CODER 1	Score CODER 2
LA1–LA10	Employment	114.00	112.00
LA11–LA14	Training and education	48.00	41.00
HR1–HR9	Human rights	65.00	70.00
SO1–SO8	Society	61.00	58.00
PR1–PR9	Product responsibility	63.00	63.00

Source: Data process.

Table 20.9 Qualitative disclosures for social aspect by coder 1 and 2

Indicator	Aspect Description	Score CODER 1	Score CODER 2
LA1–LA10	Employment	175.00	159.00
LA11–LA14	Training and education	66.00	64.00
HR1–HR9	Human rights	45.00	50.00
SO1–SO8	Society	59.00	50.00
PR1–PR9	Product responsibility	51.00	56.00

Source: Data process.

Table 20.10 Quantitative and qualitative total average of disclosure level

Performance Indicator	Quantitative Disclosure Score	Qualitative Disclosure Score
Economic	10.11	17.78
Social	9.33	16.32
Environment	8.69	9.69

Source: Data process.

information. This scoring method is not enough to provide comprehensive analysis when CA is performed. Therefore, it is important to develop a clear guideline and scoring method as a platform to conduct CA, especially to measure the quality of reports. This study develops a more comprehensive step-by-step guideline when performing CA by more than one coder, as well as providing more comprehensive scoring numbers and descriptions to award a score.

In awarding quantitative scores, more description has been developed from previous study (Table 20.2). Rather than only describing 'half' or 'full' page, the number of paragraphs has been stated. In awarding qualitative scores, prior study (Table 20.2) scores 1, 2 and 6 cannot be applied as there is no 'narrative' description. After conducting a comprehensive scoring process, more description is added by 'narrative' explanation, so the scores 1, 2 and 6 can be applied. Further, a score of 8 is also added to provide a chance for the coder when there is qualitative, monetary, non-monetary information and diagram (table/chart) disclosed in the report (see Table 20.3).

This study, then, develops a more structured guideline to conduct a step-by-step CA process when more than one coder is assigned. Using the new proposed scoring numbers and the guideline steps, a process of CA was performed that was more comprehensive, clear and adequate to measure the report disclosure quality. This process provides evidence that subjectivity can be minimized through the clear, detailed and structured guideline. Commitment and communication between two coders is indispensable to reduce subjectivity. This is shown by the total scores produced by the different coders, but resulted in insignificant score differences. In sum, this study has proposed an update on CA guidelines, in terms of scoring and procedures, which was developed from previous studies.

Other additional findings show that 'economic' performance is still considered more important for Indonesian mining companies. They disclosed much of this economic information in their sustainability reports. In contrast, environmental disclosures were minimal compared to social performance information. This result may inform that economic performance is still considered the most important performance that the companies should achieve, while social and environmental performance may follow after the economic condition is stable.

LIMITATION AND FURTHER STUDY

This study aims to develop a new and clear guideline to conduct CA by proposing more comprehensive scoring numbers and methods, rather than only a dichotomous method. By applying different numerals, it is expected that a CA method can be undertaken more precisely. However, the subjectivity in awarding scores cannot be totally removed but rather minimized.

Since this is a preliminary study with limited number of samples, there is a need for further studies to apply this guideline in conducting CA, especially for measuring sustainability reports. The description of the procedure and number scoring guideline can be the most important contribution of this study, and yet, more exploration and evidence are required. Different types of industries and more samples should be used to apply this guideline and scoring method.

NOTE

1. This chapter was presented at the *International Conference on Governance*, organized by Trisakti University, Jakarta, 13–14 February 2014.

REFERENCES

GRI (2006), *Sustainability Reporting Guideline*, Amsterdam: Global Reporting Initiative.
Gunawan, J., H. Djajadikerta and M. Smith (2009), 'The examination of corporate social disclosure by Indonesian listed companies', *Asia Pacific Centre for Environmental Accountability Journal*, **15** (1), 13–34.
Holsti, O. R. (1969), 'Content analysis for the social sciences and humanities', Reading, MA: Addison-Wesley.
Indonesia Sustainability Reporting Award (2012), http://www.ncsr-id.org/2012/12/26/8th-sustainability-reporting-awards-2012/ (accessed on 10 January 2013).

Kotler, Philip and Nancy Lee (2005), *Corporate Social Responsibility: Doing the Most Good for Your Company and Your Cause*, New Jersey: John Wiley & Sons.

Krippendorff, K. (2004), *Content Analysis: An Introduction to Its Methodology*, 2nd edn., CA: Sage Publication, Inc.

Lawrence, Anna T., James Weber and James E. Post (2005), *Business and Society: Stakeholder Relations, Ethics and Public Policy*, McGraw-Hill College.

Perry, Monica and Charles Bodkin (2000), 'Content analysis of 100 company web sites', *Corporate Communications: An International Journal*, **5** (2), 87–97.

Pruzan, P. (2001), 'Corporate reputation: image and identity', *Corporate Reputation Review*, **4** (1), 50–64.

Raar, J. (2002), 'Environmental initiatives: towards triple-bottom line reporting', *Corporate Communications: An International Journal*, **7** (3), 169–183.

Smith, M., K. Yahya and A.M. Amiruddin (2007), 'Environmental disclosure and performance reporting in Malaysia', *Asian Review of Accounting*, **15** (2), 185–199.

WBCSD (2002), http://www.wbcsd.org/work-program/business-role/previous-work/corporate-social-responsibility.aspx (accessed on 20 December 2012).

Zuchdi, D. (1993), 'Panduan Penelitian Analisis Konten', Yogyakarta: Lembaga Penelitian IKIP Yogyakarta.

21. Focus groups in social accounting as a stakeholder engagement tool
Sara Moggi

INTRODUCTION

The focus group is a qualitative method that involves interviews and communication among participants. Like other qualitative methods, focus groups aim to collect empirical data by questioning people, by entering their context, and by observing the world through their eyes. In this technique, researchers look for data from the interaction among the subjects involved in the meeting, not just the responses and reactions that they might obtain from an individual interviewee. According to Morgan (1988, p. 25), 'focus groups are useful when it comes to investigating *what* participants think, but they excel at uncovering *why* participants think as they do'. Similarly, Kitzinger (1995, p. 1) stated that 'the method is particularly useful for exploring people's knowledge and experiences and can be used to examine not only what people think but how they think and why they think that way'. From focus groups emerge opinions, motivations, and feelings regarding the issues discussed and the related social processes and norms of the context of analysis. Researchers must consider both single points of view and common views, as well as the network between them. Kitzinger (1995, p. 2) thought focus groups reveal different typologies of communication commonly used by people every day, such as 'jokes, anecdotes, teasing, and arguing', especially if the subjects involved know each other.

Focus groups are often incorrectly considered synonymous with group interviews. A specific historical reminder may serve to clarify the origin and nature of this method. The former of the focus group technique is considered to be Robert King Merton. In 1941, Paul Felix Lazarsfeld called Merton at the Office of Radio Research to observe the evaluation of a recorded audio program by a selected group of people. Each participant had to press a red button when something heard aroused a negative feeling and to press a green button for a positive response. At the end of the first evaluation, a researcher asked the participants about the motivations for their choices. Merton, as a silent observer, explained to Lazarsfeld how his assistant's conduct of the interviews had influenced the replies of the participants.

During World War II, Merton was called on to interview groups of soldiers about their responses to specific training films, called 'morale films'. From this research, the concept of the 'focused interview' with individuals as well as groups was born (Merton and Kendall 1946), with which the term 'focused' referred to interviews that concentrated on a specific topic of discussion and analysis. As indicated by Merton (1987, p. 555), '*groups* in the sociological sense are people having a common identity or continuing unity, shared norms, and goals'. He noted that, at first, the focused interview of groups sought to obtain the single opinions of the subjects at the meeting and to observe how the group influenced their single opinions. It was the study proposed by Morgan and Spanish in 1984 in which the term 'focus group' was first used in its present sense. Morgan and Spanish (1984, p. 253) defined focus group sessions as 'tape-recorded group discussions among four to ten participants who share their thoughts and experiences on a set of topics selected by the researcher'. They underlined the importance of this method, both as a new tool to collect data from subjects with mutual interests and as an important opportunity to encourage triangulation in data collection. Despite the potential and efficacy of this method in social studies, several authors (Kitzinger 1994, Merton 1987, Morgan and Spanish 1984) stated that the technique was at first largely confined to market research, such as customer satisfaction and advertising evaluation.

From market research, Calder (1977) identified three different kinds of focus groups that can also be applied in other social sciences:

1. an 'exploratory' focus group that aims to generate hypotheses;
2. a 'clinical' focus group that provides the unconscious motivations of participants; and
3. a 'phenomenological' focus group, in which researchers can identify the common ideas of participants related to their everyday point of view.

The last typology is the closest to the common use of focus groups as increasingly used in several fields.

Since the 1980s, the technique has also been applied in medical research and, in particular, to the evaluation of educational aspects of medicine. Barbour (2005) stated how focus groups were initially applied as an exploratory phase of surveys in this field and have gradually acquired relevance as independent methods of research.

Despite the wide use of focus groups in social sciences, little is known regarding the employment of this technique in social accounting studies (Agyemang et al. 2009). Ball et al. (2012) cited just a few studies on engagement research from a methodological point of view, and Gray (2002) called for further studies regarding stakeholder engagement. In light of this research gap, this chapter aims to provide a guide for researchers in social accounting who may be considering this method for data collection. In analysing the main features of the technique, the present study provides examples derived from the social accounting process implemented in Sirio, an international nonprofit organization (NPO) based in northern Italy, with more than 2,000 members and 50 branches. Then, the main aspects of organizing, managing, and analysing focus groups have been described. Specifically, it summarizes several studies and describes the most important issues to consider in defining a focus group, the research approach, and coding of the data collected. The following section explains the focus group method as part of engagement research and its specific employment in social accounting studies, giving several examples from Sirio. In addition, the strengths and weaknesses of the method in this field have been identified. The chapter concludes with a discussion of some of the lessons learned from the case study and offers suggestions on further application of this method, both in academic research and in accounting practices.

FOCUS GROUP ORGANIZATION

Several authors have identified the main features and organization of effective focus groups (Barbour 2005, Fern 2001, Kitzinger 1995). There may be no single framework that is the best; hence, the aim of this section is to outline a range of options for building and managing a focus group, the steps that should be followed in this process, and the behavior that researchers must exhibit before and during group meetings.

Composition

First, the best composition of a focus group depends on the aim of the study. The composition of the group is not a scientifically derived sample, but a balanced group of subjects. The heterogeneity of participants should be ensured to guarantee a stimulating discussion and comparison between data collected from different groups (Barbour 2005).

The choice of participants must consider the social and demographic characteristics of each. Following the framework proposed by Fern (2001), the researcher selects participants taking into account the following: social status, age, ethnic/racial differences in cultural value orientation, gender, personality, and the interaction among these aspects. Fern (2001, p. 23) also noted that 'group composition is usually considered in terms of how individual member characteristics will affect group cohesion or compatibility and subsequently how the group interacts'. Consequently, the recruitment of individuals for the group sessions must be done with care. As indicated by Agyemang et al. (2009), in a rural context or in undeveloped countries, it is difficult to identify the best participants in a focus group because of the lack of a formal database that permits a balanced choice.

In market research studies, a group of people who do not know one another is preferred, whereas in social sciences, the preference is for people who know one another or are part of the same context. Social background plays an important role in the choice of participants. Depending on the aim of the study, the researcher can insert people from different or similar social environments. If the aim is to understand issues in a complex context, the group can be composed of strangers who will provide different points of view on the same phenomenon, whereas a group of acquaintances may provide a common opinion, with rarely conflicting views (Kitzinger 1994). In all these cases, the composition of the group is defined in order to create interaction and follow the discussion through both verbal and nonverbal messages.

Size, Duration, and Location

There is no best size in terms of the number of participants in a focus group. Several authors believe that it is usually better for a group to consist of four to eight people (Fern 2001), whereas the number of total focus group meetings depends on the saturation level that could be reached for different quantities of the data collected (Morgan and Spanish 1984); this cannot be defined in advance (Krueger and Casey 2000).

According to Kitzinger (1994), the duration of a focus group meeting should not exceed two hours, which usually corresponds to the natural length of the discussion. Morgan and Spanish (1984) also suggested a short break in the middle of the meeting. In addition, to better understand the timing and duration of each question to be discussed, it is recommended to test the list of questions with a pilot focus group, usually in a well-known context.

Location plays an important part in a good focus group's organization. A comfortable place for the participants supports an open approach and helps to develop confidence in answering questions. For example, it should be a place that is easy to locate and well-lit, with comfortable seating and a round table where people can converse face-to-face. To obtain a useful recording of the discussion, it is important to choose a room with as little external noise interference as possible and to request participants to switch off their mobile phones.

Follow-Up

The first interaction with participants is the follow-up. The best way to meet the chosen subjects is to call them and inform them about their involvement into the focus group, avoiding the use of technical terms. Once the ice has been broken, the researchers usually send an email explaining the aim of the research, the organization of the meeting, the location, and the duration, stressing that it is important for the subject to be present, not delegating a substitute.

Depending on the approach decided by the researcher, the questions that will be posed for discussion during the focus group can be given in advance to the subjects. Usually, to ensure spontaneous behavior, it is sufficient to be clear in defining the study's aims (Barbour 2005). If participants know the precise detail of the questions, the researcher must consider this issue when analysing the data, as it can influence the participants' responses.

The framework for the questions is typically the same as for interviews. The questions can be standardized to enable comparison of the results from the different groups or they may be tailored differently according to the people in the group. In the first case, the aim is to arrive at an in-depth analysis of a particular context. In the second case, the focus is to collect a common opinion on a particular issue. Typically, the researcher has a list of the questions to be presented, not necessarily in the order written, referring to the main topics and subtopics that will be discussed. The researcher should make himself or herself familiar with the questions before the meeting to avoid having to check them during the discussion.

In social studies that employ qualitative methods in data collection, a framework of structured or semi-structured questions can be used. Semi-structured group interviews are preferred for maintaining the core of a question's vagueness. As suggested by Bohnsack (2004), this vagueness can be useful, giving participants more freedom to answer questions and express their opinions; by contrast, the researcher can lead more precisely defined questions in a particular direction.

The researcher who manages the focus group, described by Barbour (2005) as the gatekeeper, takes the role of moderator or facilitator of the discussion, depending on the attitudes shown by participants during the meeting. The researcher's approach is also defined by the aim of the study. This person can be passive or take an active role in the discussion. As a moderator, the researcher tries to curtail lengthy or irrelevant debates that can hinder the regular flow of the discussion, which becomes crucial if there is a strong discussion leader who prevails over others (Morgan 1988). In the role of moderator, the gatekeeper must take care that his or her moderation does not control the direction of the discussion. As a facilitator, the gatekeeper also tries to involve individuals who are reticent about voicing their opinion, which increases the disclosure level of the conversation.

At the beginning of the session, the gatekeeper explains the rules to follow during the meeting, specifying whether the discussion will be recorded and the aim of the process (sharing and analysing the data with other researchers). When the subjects involved are strangers, it is suggested that participants and the researcher all introduce themselves. Focus groups can employ stimulus materials, such as newspapers, pictures, and advertisements, in order to provoke a reaction and stimulate conversation on a related topic.

One problem identified in focus groups in Italy is that participants are commonly late arriving for the meeting, however clearly the starting time has been specified. For this reason, the first quarter of an hour is typically dedicated to informal chats as a warm-up, while waiting for all participants to be present.

During the meeting, the researcher asks questions and manages the flow of the discourse in case participants stray from the topic. Interventions are only necessary when there is a diversion or dispute that the group cannot manage on its own. Despite Morgan and Spanish's (1984, p. 267) notion that focus groups 'can be conducted by assistants who possess only minimal expertise', my opinion corresponds with Kitzinger's studies (1994, 1995), which emphasized the importance of experience in conducting focus groups. Accordingly, she suggested a period of training as an observer in order to learn the rules and tricks of the method.

At the end of the focus group, the gatekeeper thanks the participants and asks if there are any questions. During this debriefing, participants tend to be more relaxed, forgetting the presence of a recorder and speaking more openly about the issues raised.

After the Meeting

When the meeting ends, the researcher writes notes about the general flow of the discussion, the roles taken by participants and the location, timings, and first impressions of the interactions between the subjects. As in other qualitative methods, the hermeneutic unit includes recorded and transcribed conversations, a taken for granted list, and the researcher's notes, which should include records of the participants' social demographic characteristics, behavior, and attitudes. These notes, together with the taken for granted list and transcriptions of the discussion, are an important resource for the researcher to develop a view of the flow of the discussion and the attitudes of the participants.

This qualitative method, though flexible, originally did not attract researchers (Morgan and Spanish 1984) because the results were perceived to lack reliability. In the last ten years, the rigor of focus groups applied in social sciences has made progress thanks to the validation of results that have to come from the people interviewed (Barbour 2001). Depending on the subjects involved, the sharing of results follows distinct procedures, such as a complete validation of the recorded and transcribed conversation or through feedback on their preliminary opinions. In negative or positive returns, the notes provided by participants are included in the hermeneutic unit.

In the analysis of the data collected, the researcher considers the results in terms of two different types of behavior (Bohnsack 2004): interaction among participants and interactions in the social context. This may mean analysing the results at two different times, using different lenses and consequently different coding. To avoid overlapping these two different evaluations, the researcher should carry out the coding at two separate times. In order to increase understanding of the data collected, Vicsek (2007) suggests the analysis of situational factors, such as interaction among participants, environment, time, content, personal characteristics of the participants, and features of the moderator.

ENGAGING THE STAKEHOLDER IN THE SOCIAL ACCOUNTING PROCESS

In the last ten years, with the aim of building a bridge between academic studies and the real world, the field of applied studies in social accounting has seen the increasing application of 'engagement research', defined by Ball et al. (2012, p. 191) as 'research aiming to speak directly and persuasively to audiences outside academic life on issues which academics identify as pressing and substantive'. This approach permits the application of several methodologies (Correa and Larrinaga 2015), such as participant observation (Dey 2007) or action research (Adams and McNicholas 2007). In such research, stakeholders can be engaged in several modes, including identifying issues that should be disclosed in social reports, how to communicate organizational performance (Thomson and Bebbington 2005), and website interaction on social, environmental, economic, and ethical responsibilities (Unerman and Bennett 2004).

According to Ball et al. (2012, p. 206), 'the cloth of engagement research must be cut according to the needs of each project' and there is no agreement on what type of engagement enhances accounting change. Bebbington et al. (2007) stressed that there is a lack of literature in regard to the potential of engagement and related processes in social and environmental accounting. Engagement is considered a tool for organizational change. Consequently, managing this process correctly has become crucial for organizations, both in governance and accounting issues (Owen et al. 2001). From a two-way dialogue, parties involved in stakeholder engagement learn from each other and increase their awareness of the reporting process and of the social and environmental impact of the organization (Bebbington et al. 2007).

As emphasized by Gray et al. (1997), stakeholder engagement is based on a stakeholder dialogue in which each group has a voice. Accordingly, focus groups seek to hear the voice of the stakeholder on reporting issues. In social sciences, focus groups are generally considered a good opportunity to involve actors such as local community or organization members who are usually excluded from local projects in which they can express their critical opinions (Reed et al. 2006). The social reporting process occurs in several phases, which may include stakeholder engagement practices (Moggi et al. 2015). When an organization decides to follow this path, the inclusion of the subjects in the definition of the stakeholder map and the aims and contents of the social report is an important element to consider (Schiller et al. 2013). According to Adams and McNicholas (2007), the process of social and environmental reporting and the sharing of the related results increase awareness of sustainability principles. Furthermore, as emphasized by Bebbington et al. (2007, p. 372), 'A focus on stakeholders and their participation in organizational processes may also reflect a more dialogic framing of accountability'.

The process involves subjects employed in different organizational functions, who may be internal or external stakeholders. By providing different perspectives, stakeholder engagement increases the value of the reporting; conversely, it is a challenge for the organization that decides to apply the technique. As suggested by Thomson and Bebbington (2005), this activity is better carried out by external experts, because managing the engagement in its several forms and analysing the data collected are highly time-consuming. In this case, academics can be helpful supporters; the partnership develops studies in the field by direct contact with the real world.

As Gray (2002, p. 693) has pointed out, little has appeared in the literature on social accounting in regard to stakeholder engagement in practice, although it is considered 'one of the principal characteristics of social accounting'. In light of the efficacy that focus groups can have in obtaining and sharing opinions and experiences, this method is frequently used in stakeholder engagement. In accordance with the accounting framework, 'the stakeholders are those with rights to the account and it is for them the account is prepared' (Gray et al. 1997, p. 330); and the accountability perspective depends primarily on the definition of the stakeholder map of the accountable organization.

SIRIO'S SOCIAL ACCOUNTING PROCESS AND STAKEHOLDER ENGAGEMENT

In order to examine how stakeholders can be involved at the start of the social accounting process, this study presents the case of Sirio, an international NPO with more than 2,000 members and funds of more than 400,000 euros collected yearly. Sirio, under the supervision of a five-person research group at the University of Verona (Italy), started the social reporting process using focus groups as a tool for stakeholder engagement for the purpose of defining the stakeholders map and social report features.

Sirio has a complex hierarchical structure, with 50 branches in northern Italy. It operates in response to the needs of local and international communities, helping people in states of disease or poverty caused by natural disasters and deprivation and disadvantage. The geographical spread of its work, the large number of its members, and the numerous activities it carries out in international and local communities underline the need for a high level of accountability to a large number of stakeholders. The board of Sirio therefore asked the team of researchers from the University of Verona to carry out the social report process.

From the beginning, the willingness to engage a large number of organizational members to attain a strong awareness of the social reporting process and commitment to their activities was clear (Adams and McNicholas 2007). A staff of four junior researchers and one expert was involved from the early stages of the process and throughout the methodology of the action research, which permitted a better understanding of all phases of the difficult path ahead (Dey 2000, Dey et al. 1995). As Adams and McNicholas (2007) observed, action research 'allows the researchers to remain focused on the problem and allows the organization to take immediate remedial action'.

Because no social accounting system or any form of consolidated financial statement was available for this NPO, the first step was to consider what data to collect and how to collect it in order to build the social account, in view of the various activities undertaken by each branch. The second step was dedicated to mapping stakeholders, identifying the main features of the relationships between these subjects and Sirio. The expert researcher, together with the 'social report staff', attended a number of meetings to draft the process and choose the people who were to be involved, identifying focus groups as the best method to engage stakeholders. The key stakeholders considered for participation were members of the 50 branches, members of the similar NPO composed of young people (Sirio JR), and some beneficiary organizations of their activities in the local community.

As identified by O'Dwyer (2005), the main resistance to stakeholder engagement participation was shown by internal stakeholders, who, in this case, were members of Sirio. The researchers overcame this resistance by carefully explaining the aim of the engagement and stressing the importance of their pivotal role in the reporting process.

In nine meetings, there were three to six participants in each focus group, making a total of 37 people involved. The choice of these subjects was undertaken with care. Sirio is formally divided into eight geographical areas, and the governance of the organization changes completely every year. For these reasons, a focus group was organized for each area, involving those who had had a position of responsibility in each of the branches during the previous year. This was a successful strategy, because problems related to hierarchy were eliminated by including people with similar responsibilities, levels of education, mixed gender, and shared values, covering Sirio's entire territorial area of action. Thanks to their past duties, these people had a broad grasp and understanding of the activities carried out in the accounting period.

Under the supervision of the expert researcher, each junior researcher was responsible for organizing and managing two focus groups. The small number of meetings to manage gave them the opportunity to carefully consider each aspect of the method. During the process, the supervisor was updated constantly on progress in reporting by both the other researchers and the 'social reporting staff'. The five researchers were able to organize their own focus groups independently and with some flexibility as to dates of the meetings. Given that a number of meetings were organized for each branch and area, a technique referred to as piggy-backing by Krueger and Casey (2000) was applied in a few cases, which permits the occasional area meeting at which focus groups can take place before or after the meeting.

The dimension chosen for each focus group enhanced good conversations, which were also easy to follow in the typing phase and in the data analysis. In fact, as underlined by Agyemang et al. (2009), when meetings are overpopulated, it is a challenge for the researcher to follow the flow of the discourse, to manage the meeting, and to transcribe the dialogue. Therefore, the number of participants was limited to fewer than seven, which made it easier for the researcher to mediate in the case of controversial issues and created a good environment that enhanced a high level of interaction between the subjects.

An unexpected effect of selecting participants by geographical area was that they spoke a common dialect. This helped to create a more comfortable and relaxed atmosphere in which to present their opinions informally and share their experiences. No problems were found in regard to gender, age, or the fact that they were strangers.

In addition to the eight focus groups with organization members, the researchers organized a focus group with members of the Sirio JR and three interviews were conducted with selected beneficiaries of Sirio's activities in the territory. These permitted the evaluation of relationships between stakeholders and Sirio from a more detached point of view.

The researcher attended the focus groups with a list of semi-structured questions to guide the conversation. The main topics discussed during the meeting were the definition of the stakeholders linked to the organization (stakeholder mapping) and the features expected of their first social report. One of the first difficulties encountered was misunderstanding of the term 'stakeholder', for which the Italian language does not have an equivalent word and which can be translated as 'bearer of interests'. Researchers overcame this concern with examples provided by the participants and by avoiding correction of the 'wrong answers'.

This engagement in social accounting helped the researchers to shape social report characteristics, depending on the context and expectations of members and external stakeholders. At the same time, it partially increased the awareness of the subjects involved in the process of reporting and allowed the stakeholders map to be created. This method also helped to reduce members' mistrust of researchers and others outside Sirio. The data analysis showed that, in the majority of cases, focus groups shared experiences, knowledge, values, and common problems and as a result became a veritable example of group identity. The Sirio case study has provided an example of engagement in the social reporting process, suggesting actions and behaviors that could be carefully adapted to a different context.

STRENGTHS AND WEAKNESSES OF THE FOCUS GROUP TECHNIQUE

Focus groups are suitable for various study objectives, but all methods for data collection have their strengths and weaknesses. Two problems are encountered in regard to the engagement studies. The first problem is how to become aware of possible engagement activity; the second concerns the possibility to publish the results of the research (Bebbington et al. 2007). Regarding the first issue, in most cases, the opportunity to apply the focus group method is linked with providing a consultancy to an organization that, for example, wants to draw up a social accounting system or to start the process of social reporting. This method provides researchers with the opportunity to enter into the organization and directly collect original data, taking care not to influence the context studied. Concerning the second issue, rigor and reliability in the data collection and analysis may help in attaining the objective of publishing the results.

One of the most important and powerful features of focus groups is the interaction between participants, which increases understanding of the phenomena studied, thanks to the group's dynamism (Lewin 1947). The participants tend to integrate one another into the group and offer a wide range of answers to the questions posed by the researcher. From this holistic point of view, the researcher should consider the influence of the social context on participants' answers.

A group discussion can cause different reactions in people. Shy subjects can be pushed to engage in the conversation because they are part of a group (the 'safety in numbers' factor); on the other hand, some people may feel dominated by the leader's behavior and remain silent. The researcher cannot know the behavior of focus group members in advance, and it is essential to modulate his or her mediating role, for example encouraging more reticent participants to get involved. It is the researcher's responsibility to read the data carefully, as this method usually yields a unique voice on a particular topic, as well as criticisms (Watts and Ebbutt 1987). If the aim of the study is to obtain the opinion of a single subject, the individual focused interview would probably be more suitable than the focus group method.

Using focus groups, the researcher can perceive social, cultural, and behavioral differences that can be only partially studied using other qualitative methods. For Morgan and Spanish (1984, p. 259), this method 'also showed us what happened when people took differing individual experiences and attempted to make collective sense of them'. Additionally, this method facilitates discussion of taboo topics that are usually difficult to discuss in face-to-face conversation. In fact, during a focus group, a participant often helps the shyer subjects by attempting to start a conversation (Kitzinger 1995). The downside of this feature is that each group has norms that can silence the opinion of an individual (Kitzinger 1995).

According to Barbour (2005), one of the most common myths regarding focus groups is that they produce outcomes more quickly and cheaply than other research methods. According to Kitzinger and Barbour (1999), costs in terms of time (e.g., transcription) and resources (e.g., room lease) may be considerable in this research method. Even with the expertise of the moderator, conversations during a focus group are difficult to transcribe and, for every one and a half hours of conversation, eight hours are typically needed for transcription.

Considering the artificial environment in which discussion takes place, focus groups are by definition an unnatural method of data collection. The artificial construction of the group should, if possible, be ignored by participants during the discussion, as it is difficult for the researcher to discern the difference between the real opinions of the subjects and responses that may be a consequence of the setting.

It is often claimed that the focus group method lacks reliability. Lunt and Livingstone (1996, p. 92) stated that 'focus groups are unreliable because different conversations would occur if groups were repeated' and one can also obtain different results from the same group posing the same questions at different times. This weakness could be overcome through rigor in data collection, which helps the replicability of the method (Bohnsack 2004).

As already mentioned, stakeholder engagement using focus groups can attain a high level of involvement for these subjects in tailoring social reports. However, even though this method is not easy to implement and despite the experience of the facilitator, the results are never as expected. One of the things often neglected in the process of stakeholder engagement is the choice of the right stakeholders to be involved in the right phase of the reporting process (Moggi et al. 2015). For example, in Sirio, members were carefully selected and were involved in the former phase of social accounting. However, the same subjects were not considered in the final phase of the diffusion of the social report. In what Adams and McNicholas (2007, p. 386) defined as 'a lack of communication between individuals', the result was an incomplete sharing of the results of their activities and an inability to use the report as a fundraising tool. According to these authors, researchers recognized the limited experience of Sirio's members involved in the social reporting process as one of the key barriers. This issue has hindered their awareness of both the social reporting process and Sirio's activities.

CONCLUSIONS

Although the main features of this technique and its application in social science have been much reported in the literature, very few studies have been published in social accounting, and those that do exist usually focus on the principle of engagement research, rather than on how to carry out the method in practice. The interaction provided by focus groups, considering the external (and internal) institutional pressures to increase the level of accountability to stakeholders, has recently interested researchers and practitioners. The method provides insights to researchers into the real world; at the same time, it enlarges the organization's awareness of stakeholder claims that can influence its strategies. Consequently, the involvement of these subjects in the organization through stakeholder engagement practices, such as in the social reporting process, is positively viewed. In light of the lack of studies on how stakeholders are involved into the process, it has become important to understand the bond between organizations and these subjects and how to improve the dialogue between them (Agyemang et al. 2009). Researchers are the formers of learning, and by attending stakeholder engagement occasions, they benefit from the reciprocity of the process.

It is clear from this analysis that the organization and management of focus groups are difficult, requiring researchers with appropriate experience. However, the flexibility of this tool and its correct management yields results from interaction among participants. By contrast, inexperienced moderators increase the risk of inadequate disclosure and determine a low reliability level of results. It is essential for researchers to define specific rules that must be followed in the definition of a group, in its management, and in their posture. On the other hand, they must realize that an overly rigid framework can reduce the effectiveness of the method (Kitzinger and Barbour 1999). Among the varieties of qualitative research techniques, focus groups can be usefully conducted as exploratory research, before interviewing and after participant observation (Morgan and Spanish 1984) or as part of triangulation with other qualitative methods, thereby increasing reliability.

As shown by the Sirio case study, the existing aspirations of stakeholder groups, such as local communities, must be considered at the starting point of social reporting (Thomson and Bebbington 2005). The main purpose of stakeholder engagement is to create a dialogue between the organization and stakeholders, share experiences, open a channel of discussion, and increase reciprocal awareness. The focus group method is a sharing process that can help the subjects to explain their opinions in a way that is not possible in a one-on-one interview. In this sense, social reporting should represent a form of stakeholder accountability that, responding to stakeholders' claims, enhances the accountability change (Gray et al. 1997).

In the light of the sharing of common values, the focus groups organized in Sirio were also considered as an identity tool. The meetings highlighted the importance of each subject as a member of a social group and the presence of norms that regulated the way they thought, acted, and related to others, which also consequently influenced Sirio's social reporting.

This chapter has explained the features and organization of focus groups, using the case of Sirio's contribution to studies in the field, thereby helping to fill a gap in the literature on methods that can be successfully applied to social accounting. According to Morgan and Spanish (1984, p. 268), '[t]here is really only one test for such methodological merit: does the technique provide new or improved means of asking and answering sociological questions?'

The challenge for future methodological studies in social accounting will be to identify the best methods of increasing comprehension of the dynamics between stakeholders and organizations. Stakeholder engagement as a potential means of dialogue can strengthen the bridge between these subjects, as well as between academic studies and practices in corporate, nonprofit, and the public sector.

REFERENCES

Adams, C.A. and P. McNicholas (2007), 'Making a difference: sustainability reporting, accountability and organisational change', *Accounting, Auditing and Accountability Journal*, **20** (3), 382–402. doi: 10.1108/095 13570710748553.

Agyemang, G., M. Awumbila and B. O'Dwyer (2009), 'A critical reflection on the use of focus groups as a research method: lessons from trying to hear the voices of NGO beneficiaries in Ghana', *Social and Environmental Accountability Journal*, **29** (1), 4–16. doi: 10.1080/0969160x.2009.9651804.

Ball, A., V. Soare and J. Brewis (2012), 'Engagement research in public sector accounting', *Financial Accountability and Management*, **28** (2), 189–214. doi: 10.1111/j.1468-0408.2012.00542.x.

Barbour, R.S. (2001), 'Checklists for improving rigour in qualitative research: a case of the tail wagging the dog?', *BMJ: British Medical Journal*, **322** (7294), 1115–1117. doi: http://dx.doi.org/10.1136/bmj.322.7294.1115.

Barbour, R.S. (2005), 'Making sense of focus groups', *Medical Education*, **39** (7), 742–750. doi: 10.1111/j.1365-2929.2005.02200.x.

Bebbington, J., J. Brown, B. Frame and I. Thomson (2007), 'Theorizing engagement: the potential of a critical dialogic approach', *Accounting, Auditing and Accountability Journal*, **20** (3), 356–381. doi: 10.1108/09513570710748544.

Bohnsack, R. (2004), 'Group discussion and focus groups', in Uwe Flick, Ernst von Kardoff and Ines Steinke (eds), *A Companion to Qualitative Research*, London: Sage, pp. 210–221.

Calder, B.J. (1977), 'Focus groups and the nature of qualitative marketing research', *Journal of Marketing Research*, **14** (3), 353–364.

Correa, C. and C. Larrinaga (2015), 'Engagement research in social and environmental accounting: sustainability accounting', *Management and Policy Journal*, **6** (1), 5–28.

Dey, C. (2000), 'Bookkeeping and ethnography at Traidcraft plc: a review of an experiment in social accounting', *Social and Environmental Accountability Journal*, **20** (2), 16–18. doi: 10.1080/0969160x.2000.9651638.

Dey, C. (2007), 'Social accounting at Traidcraft plc: a struggle for the meaning of fair trade', *Accounting, Auditing and Accountability Journal*, **20** (3), 423–445. doi: 10.1108/09513570710748571.

Dey, C., R. Evans and R. Gray (1995), 'Towards social information systems and bookkeeping: a note on developing mechanisms for social accounting and audit', *Journal of Applied Accounting Research*, **2** (3), 36–69.

Fern, Edward. F. (2001), *Advanced Focus Group Research*, London: Sage Publications.

Gray, R. (2002), 'The social accounting project and accounting organizations and society: privileging engagement, imaginings, new accountings and pragmatism over critique?', *Accounting, Organizations and Society*, **27** (7), 687–708. doi: 10.1016/S0361-3682(00)00003-9.

Gray, R., C. Dey, D. Owen, R. Evans and S. Zadek (1997), 'Struggling with the praxis of social accounting: stakeholders, accountability, audits and procedures', *Accounting, Auditing and Accountability Journal*, **10** (3), 325–364. doi: 10.1108/09513579710178106.

Kitzinger, J. (1994), 'The methodology of focus groups: the importance of interaction between research participants', *Sociology of Health and Illness*, **16** (1), 103–121. doi: 10.1111/1467-9566.ep11347023.

Kitzinger, J. (1995), 'Qualitative research: introducing focus groups', *BMJ: British Medical Journal*, **311** (7000), 299–302. doi: http://dx.doi.org/10.1136/bmj.311.7000.299.

Kitzinger, J. and R. Barbour (1999), 'Introduction: the challenge and promise of focus groups', in Rosaline S. Barbour and Jenny Kitzinger (eds), *Developing Focus Group Research: Politics, Theory and Practice*, Thousand Oaks, CA: Sage, pp. 1–20.

Krueger, R.A. and M. Casey (2000), *Focus Groups: A Practical Guide for Applied Research*, Thousand Oaks, CA: Sage.

Lewin, K. (1947), 'Frontiers in group dynamics: channels of group life, social planning and action research', *Human Relations*, **1** (2), 143–153.

Lunt, P. and S. Livingstone (1996), 'Rethinking the focus group in media and communications research', *Journal of Communication*, **46** (2), 79–98.
Merton, R.K. (1987), 'The focussed interview and focus group: continuities and discontinuities', *Public Opinion Quarterly*, **6** (4), 7–13.
Merton, R.K. and P.L. Kendall (1946), 'The focused interview', *American Journal of Sociology*, 541–557.
Moggi, S., C. Leardini and B. Campedelli (2015), 'Social and environmental reporting in the Italian higher education system: evidence from two best practices', in Walter Leal Filho, Luciana Brandli, Olga Kuznetsova and Armida M. Finisterra do Paço (eds), *Integrative Approaches to Sustainable Development at University Level*, Berlin: Springer, pp. 81–96.
Morgan, David L. (1988), *Focus Groups as Qualitative Research*, Newbury Park, CA: Sage.
Morgan, D.L. and M.T. Spanish (1984), 'Focus groups: a new tool for qualitative research', *Qualitative Sociology*, **7** (3), 253–270.
O'Dwyer, B. (2005), 'The construction of a social account: a case study in an overseas aid agency', *Accounting, Organizations and Society*, **30** (3), 279–296. doi: 10.1016/j.aos.2004.01.001.
Owen, D.L., T. Swift and K. Hunt (2001), 'Questioning the role of stakeholder engagement in social and ethical accounting, auditing and reporting', *Accounting Forum*, **25** (3), 264–282. doi: 10.1111/1467-6303.00066.
Reed, M.S., E.D. Fraser and A.J. Dougill (2006), 'An adaptive learning process for developing and applying sustainability indicators with local communities', *Ecological Economics*, **59** (4), 406–418. doi: 10.1016/j.ecolecon.2005.11.008.
Schiller, C., M. Winters, H.M. Hanson and M.C. Ashe (2013), 'A framework for stakeholder identification in concept mapping and health research: a novel process and its application to older adult mobility and the built environment', *BMC Public Health*, **13** (428), 1–9. doi: 10.1186/1471-2458-13-428.
Thomson, I. and J. Bebbington (2005), 'Social and environmental reporting in the UK: a pedagogic evaluation', *Critical Perspectives on Accounting*, **16** (5), 507–533. doi: 10.1016/j.cpa.2003.06.003.
Unerman, J. and M. Bennett (2004), 'Increased stakeholder dialogue and the internet: towards greater corporate accountability or reinforcing capitalist hegemony?', *Accounting, Organizations and Society*, **29** (7), 685–707. doi: 10.1016/j.aos.2003.10.009.
Vicsek, L. (2007), 'A scheme for analyzing the results of focus groups', *International Journal of Qualitative Methods*, **6** (4), 20–34.
Watts, M. and D. Ebbutt (1987), 'More than the sum of the parts: research methods in group interviewing', *British Educational Research Journal*, **13** (1), 25–34.

22. A phenomenological study of moral discourse, social justice and CSR
Julia J.A. Shaw

INTRODUCTION

The corporate social responsibility (CSR) research field is characterized by a range of methodologies and this chapter will explore the application of a broadly qualitative approach. Phenomenological inquiry constitutes a naturalistic method that aims to understand and clarify phenomena in context-specific settings. Not based on any particular conceptual framework or series of techniques, it is creatively informed by a broad range of liberal and humanistic disciplines such as philosophy, anthropology, sociology, politics, socio-legal theory, psychology and history. Defined as 'any kind of research that produces findings not arrived at by means of statistical procedures or other means of quantification', qualitative researchers engage in the intellectual pursuit of enlightenment and insight rather than causal determination and assured predictable outcomes (Strauss and Corbin 1990, p.17). Arising from a post-positivist repudiation of a single or objective truth, focus is placed on the social meaning and experiences of individuals, communities and sub-cultures, and the significance of words and texts. In order to explore the concept of moral duty and CSR this chapter adopts a phenomenological mode of inquiry, which is useful for reimagining over-familiar problems and, importantly, provides a contextual and flexible interdisciplinary framework within which to investigate diverse perspectives and practices for generating knowledge.

The Enlightenment project of achieving universal human freedom from natural necessity (the struggle for material substance) and freedom from social necessity (against the oppression of human by human) has failed. The modern business environment is characterized by rapacious multinational corporations, whose activities are coordinated to a large extent by government policies that seem principally targeted towards maintaining a secure business environment for investments at all costs. Enron, the epitome of an unethical business, put a human face to the suffering of people whose retirement plans were ruined by the deceptive actions of the company.

The intrinsic violence of neo-corporate regulation and configuration of current economic power relations militates against Karl Marx's utopian vision of each person 'moving around himself as his own true sun' and Immanuel Kant's humanism; specifically, Kant's idea that all individuals comprise a 'kingdom of ends' because of their intrinsic value or inner worth and dignity (Shaw 2015, p.99). The corporatist mindset has created a performance culture whereby a person is valued on the basis of what they earn. At the same time, the labour of the worker comprises a sacrifice of their life and vitality, a form of self-abasement, as the 'production of the object [is] as loss of the object to an alien power, an *alien* person . . . who is *alien* to labour and the worker' (Marx 1978, p.31).

Whilst both enslavement and empowerment are built into the logic of narratives of economic progress, for Emmanuel Levinas the corporate culture's focus on the performance principle is exploitative and constitutes metaphorical economic enslavement (1969, pp. 197–199). Levinas's metaphor applies not only to the poorest of the world, millions of whom are trafficked into slavery and a life of extreme hardship and drudgery, but also the typical middle-class consumer who shuffles along the workhouse treadmill, living in order to work and working in order to consume (Wolcher 2013, p. xvi). Contrast the treatment of the richly remunerated, largely unregulated global financial sector and tacit acceptance of its extreme ethical laxity, against the creeping surveillance of ordinary citizens in the wake of rapidly expanding regulatory state powers which threaten basic human rights. The consequent reimagining and recalibration of the fundamental concepts of democracy, freedom, fairness and justice have exacerbated the imbalance of power, fostered feelings of alienation and resulted in the destabilization of society.

According to situationists like Guy DeBord, this diminution of human existence was produced by the regime of representation in the 'society of the spectacle' which transformed 'being' into 'having' and further commodified 'having' into 'appearance' (Shaw 2017, p. 97). Capitalism was viewed as having turned all relationships into the merely transactional; society had been divided into actors and spectators, producers and consumers, operating under a hierarchical system of masters and slaves. Qualitative researchers may turn to the imaginative arts such as poetry and literature to channel the creativity of individuals who have become disheartened by the stifling regimes of power and narratives of dominance imposed by corporate and state actors.

This chapter engages the philosophy of Immanuel Kant and other neo-Kantians in explicating the landscape of corporate social responsibility in an age of disenchantment. Immanuel Kant is commonly associated with moral imperatives and just organizations, and it is intended to examine the work of key modern neo-Kantians in terms of their relevance to social responsibility and ethical organizations. The critique will begin by exploring aspects of John Rawls's *A Theory of Justice*, in which his formulation of 'reflective equilibrium', the 'original position' and 'veil of ignorance' advances a complex and important set of ethical principles with which to found and organize all aspects of social life. His efforts comprise the establishment of a regulative conception of ethics, for the promotion of just social organizations, which is alleged to be able to provide a unanimous and 'common point of view from which all claims [relating to just conduct] may be adjudicated' (Rawls 1971, p. 5).

Many corporations have a reductive view of CSR, maintaining a narrow conception which operates only at the level of management values, methods, regulations and practices; after all, Milton Friedman famously advised that the social responsibility of a company is to increase its profits (1970, pp. 32–33, 122–124). Nevertheless, there are some good examples of companies assuming a moral obligation such as US firm TOMS Shoes, which donates one pair of shoes to a child in need for every pair a customer purchases. US ice cream producer Ben & Jerry's is another such example, in the development of a dairy farm sustainability programme in its home state of Vermont, and in its commitment to use only fair trade ingredients.

Since companies have a different idea of what constitutes CSR, Rawls's conception of the role of public consensus in forming standards relating to moral and conscionable behaviour and morality may be useful in managing disparate moralities and blending these into a unified whole. He deals with this question in *A Theory of Justice* in an attempt to elaborate how a just society can stabilize itself and promulgate fair regulations and transparent processes taking into consideration the de facto pluralism of worldviews. To this end, he begins by asking what is necessary to achieve a consensus on identifying what are fair, right and just actions in a globalized, diverse and homogenous modern environment. This is especially useful, given differing constitutional frameworks and secular versus religious business environments which allow for a variety of corporate regulatory standards, often producing divergent views on what constitutes 'good' CSR practice. Rawls resolves many of these seemingly incompatible and irreconcilable perspectives by appealing, like his predecessor Kant, to the faculty of human reason; to be applied to an expanded view of the role of corporations in constructing ethical institutions. Other theorists within this tradition are explored in terms of how it is possible to identify and prioritize key values, in determining a minimum standard of fair and just practice extending to all stakeholders as a benchmark or even prerequisite for good CSR practice.

THE DUTY OF RESPECT FOR EVERY INDIVIDUAL AS A BINDING MORAL OBLIGATION ON ALL SOCIAL ACTORS

The language of ethical dues and rights has a long pedigree. Influential Enlightenment figure, Immanuel Kant, famously attempted to release metaphysics from its mystical, and therefore pre-reflective and antithetical, standing; towards rendering it potentially accessible to and utilizable by all other disciplines. Since qualitative research is not subject to the same rigorous tests for validity as quantitative research, it is necessary in most instances to fix the parameters carefully as to what can and cannot be the proper object of evaluation. In this case, it is important to first distinguish this particular version of neo-Kantianism from that of his avowed successor, Hans Kelsen (Shaw 2014, p. 195). Kant's project was one of synergy, not of separation, and thus it is argued that to equate Kant with Kelsen is to condemn Kant's moral philosophical works to a narrow, arbitrary and positivistic interpretation.

This comparison would allegedly negate the moral and ethical core fundamental to Kant's entire philosophical oeuvre; as set out in his second critique in the form of the 'categorical moral imperative'. In keeping his theory of law 'pure', Kelsen denied the conceptually necessary connection between law and morality. Alternatively, John Rawls and Jürgen Habermas are also credited with being influenced by Kant's moral philosophy, and irrespective of the extent to which they can be described as neo-Kantians, it is impossible to develop a serious account of applied moral philosophy without at least considering their contribution to the debate:

> Rawls' and Habermas' moral visions are recognisably attenuated, pared-down, cleverly diminished versions of the great Kantian doctrine that must be counted among the few that truly dominate the moral imagination of the West. They are pared-down so far that Kant's transcendental excesses never quite afford a reasonable target; and they are so robust in the Kantian spirit that they never quite seem vulnerable in the way of ideology. (Margolis 1996, p. 11)

This section will examine some key elements of John Rawls's theory of justice and right, taken from his 1971 *A Theory of Justice*, in which he advances a complex and important set of ethical principles from which to found and organize social and political life. His endeavours comprise the establishment of a regulative conception of justice and fairness, which can serve unanimously as 'a common point of view from which all claims may be adjudicated' (1971, p. 5). For Rawls, the modern social and political order is characterized by a range of disparate moralities and is commonly split into a range of incompatible and irreconcilable religious, philosophical and moral dogmas. From a seemingly impossible position of irreconcilable divisions, his work explores the possibility of public consensus and universality. To this end, he begins by inquiring as to what is social unity, and whether a just and stable society is a credible aim in our diverse and homogenous modern environment; moving on to uncovering the conditions under which social unity may be realizable. Whilst still upholding the idea of autonomous self-regulation by means of the implementation of self-regulatory norms and standards, this Kantian perspective has much to offer CSR scholarship and practice.

It is suggested that a Kantian architectonic affords the best possibility of fostering a genuine commitment to corporate social responsibility and accountability, because of its ability to prescribe a set of ethical duties which are to be extended towards all stakeholders in any multi-stakeholder model of corporate governance, as a moral imperative. The most incisive and compelling of Kant's moral principles is the second formulation of his categorical moral imperative, 'Act in such a way that you treat humanity, whether in your own person or in the person of any other, always at the same time as an end and never merely as a means to an end' (2002, pp. 229–230). To treat someone as 'a means' describes self-interested behaviour which is concerned more about achieving a particular goal than the welfare of the person used to reach that objective. A person is merely instrumental in this case, whereas treating someone as 'an end' entails acknowledging their right to be considered as an equal human with their own interests and character that ought not to be disregarded. Rawls is equally concerned with questions concerning the appropriateness, fairness and legitimacy of rules and regulatory processes – without being overly concerned with form or procedure, such as the institutional dimension of a hard law backed by sanctions. He refers to neither institutionalized decision-making processes nor to social and political developments. Rather, towards realizing the possibility of a rational justification of universal liberal rights, Rawls prioritizes the moral imperatives of right, and justice itself becomes a conception of right. The priority of justice and right over all other values derives from the concept of freedom, as a prerequisite of every human end.

In the Kantian tradition, Rawls concerns himself with the notion of 'natural duties of justice' which we 'have' and 'obligations' which we 'take on' (1971, pp. 114, 334). Moral obligations, like Kant's juridical obligations, 'arise as a result of our voluntary acts . . . however the content of obligations is always defined by an institution or practice, the rules of which specify what it is that one is required to do'; alternatively natural duties, which are ethical in nature, 'hold between persons irrespective of their institutional relationships; they obtain between all as equal moral persons' (Rawls 1971, pp. 113, 115). In each case, autonomous rational members of a society are obliged to treat each other with respect in order to affirm one's own value as a moral person (Rawls 1971, pp. 337–339). In recognition of this principle, a CSR policy which is heavily informed by ethical rights will highlight the general rights and moral dignity of all actors likely to be impacted by the behaviour of the business. Respect for all affected actors, as proper rights-bearers, is therefore the core concern here; and of particular relevance to multinational corporations in a global context where there is a multiplicity of beliefs, traditions and cultures. Although there are many different forms of respect, the question a company might ask of its model of corporate governance is 'how do we respect the rights of actors who are directly affected by our activities?' In conjunction with the assumption of responsibility for respecting the rights of every affected individual, is the principle of accountability, which involves the scrutiny of all significant actions and inactions and a commitment to ensuring that leading members of an organization are held to account for their choices.

A KANTIAN FORMULATION OF CSR AS 'AN END' AND NEVER SOLELY AS A 'MEANS' TO AN END

Although the concept of CSR is largely unsettled and subject to much disagreement as to the proper nature of business-society relationships, most companies accept its importance in any corporate portfolio of activities. Even so, a utilitarian attitude prevails; for example, many stakeholder theories hold that businesses have no or minimal social or moral duties beyond compliance with legislation and seek to abstract moral considerations from business relationships. Yet, since a company is an agglomeration of people it is appropriate to hold those individuals, whose actions directly impinge on the well-being of others, morally accountable. The deployment of CSR policies is, however, too often instrumental and, to use Kantian terminology, CSR is not treated as 'an end' in itself. That is not to say CSR ought to be mandatory; the moral philosophy of Kant and the neo-Kantians is based on the promotion of free choice, in which case moral right-holders are both entitled to be allowed to do something or permitted to have something done for them. Through rational deliberation and respect for the dignity of all individuals, it is hoped that moral human agents (as CEOs, managers, shareholders and employees) will freely choose to act in the interests of others, in sympathetic recognition of their equal membership of the 'kingdom of ends'.

John Rawls's theory of justice and fairness has its basis in morality, and Kant's conception of right provides the intellectual foundation for Rawls's first principle of justice, which provides, 'the most extensive basic liberty compatible with a similar liberty for others' universally and for everyone. Whilst he insists on adherence to the moral requirement to obey the law, such obedience is deserved on the basis of political institutions which operate according to the 'principle of fairness'. The principle of fairness is based upon the generation of moral requirements from the sacrifices of others which is viewed as necessary for the mutual production of benefits (Klosko 1994, p. 253). Rawls defines obligations as moral requirements incurred through voluntary actions (1971, p. 113). These hold both individually and collectively so that duties are owed by all individuals to all individuals, regardless of contingent differences, for example, race, class, sex, religion, ability. Rawls considers these factors to be irrelevant. Such arbitrary distinguishing characteristics have no place in constructing a definition of moral personhood and are placed behind a 'veil of ignorance' (1971, pp. 136–142) in order to uphold the 'original position' (1971, pp. 17–22) in which the essence of society is one of total equality, impartiality and sameness:

> The principles of justice for the basic structure of society are . . . [those] principles that free and *rational* persons concerned to further their own interests would accept in an initial position of equality as defining the fundamental terms of their association. (1971, p. 11)

By constructing the original position, which serves as a heuristic device for attenuating the principles of justice, Rawls has taken the Kantian moral concept of a person as autonomous, free and equal. The original position formulation seeks to identify principles of practical rationality in order to make these norms of 'moral reasonableness' universally available and applicable in order to enable people to act autonomously. Also emulating Kant in his critical theory of justice, society is stripped to its moral core; removing all of its contingencies, complications and potential for conflict in order to facilitate the ideal of a fair system of cooperation. All choices must be considered behind a veil of ignorance, obliterating from view any factors which may cause an individual to prosper or suffer under one principle or another. Decisions are made by 'idealised beings' abstracted from their contingent concrete circumstances which would otherwise allow the use of systems of rules and procedures as a tool of oppression. Status, natural assets, religious beliefs, general predisposition and proclivities, for example, are veiled so that persons are able to live in a well-ordered society founded on unanimous consensus as to the principles of justice. In their rationality and essential freedom, moral agents are indistinguishable from one another and have the capacity and duty to determine 'how they are to regulate their claims against one another and what is to be the foundation charter of their society' (1971, p. 11).

Rawls's original position has dramatized the procedural conditions of moral discourse and assumes that, if these conditions are satisfied and certain rules of rationality are adhered to, moral discourse then results in his two principles of justice. The first principle, the 'liberty principle', holds that each person is to have an equal right to the most extensive system of basic liberties that is compatible with a similar system for everyone else. The second principle imposes a moral obligation. Referred to as the 'difference principle' (or sometimes the priority rule), it holds that social and economic inequalities are only fair so far as they work to the advantage of the least advantaged people in society (1971, p. 250). The first principle expresses a belief in the just foundations of society. It also bears a close similarity to Kant's definition of right, in that each person should be able to enjoy maximum freedom so that 'the choice of one can be united with the choice of another in accordance with a universal law of freedom' (1991, p. 56). In this case, no person would have a self-interested reason to choose any principle but maximum liberty for all; and it is this principle that rational individuals – with an equal vote – would choose behind a veil of ignorance. The concept of a law, for Rawls, makes explicit the idea of equal treatment which is already embodied within the concept of right. For example:

> Behind the veil of ignorance, in considering possible restrictions on freedom, one adopts the perspective of the one who would be most disadvantaged by the restrictions, in this case the perspective of the alien who wants to immigrate. In the original position, then, one would insist that the right to migrate be included in the system of basic liberties for the same reasons that one would insist that the right to religious freedom be included: it might prove essential to one's life plan. (Carens 1997, p. 258)

A Rawlsian account of corporate governance would not confer a position of privilege and dominance on shareholders vis-à-vis other actors who also share an interest in an organization's activities; rather the company's existence would be dependent on serving the interests of multiple stakeholders. In the form of universal and abstract laws, hard and soft regulation, all subjects would be entitled to the same level of consideration and be capable of receiving the same rights. For Rawls, a just society can be stabilized under a set of laws constructed upon liberal ideas of justice, for example, the priority of equal opportunity and freedom over utilitarian claims of the general good. To facilitate this aim, Rawls adopts Kant's concept of the 'autonomy of morals' in so far as moral discourse needs the free universal acceptance of general principles to inform and guide individual conduct and attitudes towards the actions of others. The capacity for autonomous action and the ability to formulate and pursue a rational life plan defines the moral personality. For Rawls, a person is responsible for choosing the principles of justice which govern his actions and is morally obligated to give effect to these; 'by acting from these principles persons are acting autonomously: they are acting from principles that they would acknowledge under conditions that best express their nature as free and equal rational beings' (1971, p. 515).

Rawls's *A Theory of Justice* concurs with Kant's identification of the fundamental formal features which a moral judgement must exhibit in order to be valid, namely, autonomy, universality and an unconditional nature. It is this unconditionality which enables self-legislation; in turn the subject as self-legislator guarantees the legitimacy of Rawls's conception of justice. The author and recipient of lawful actions are interchangeable; each has the capacity for universal rational choice, and a consensus as to the definition of justice can be established because of this equality. A rational agent is, therefore, required to choose ends in abstraction from his own personal desires or inclinations as a subject prior to, and independent of, his objects. This independence allows and enables such an agent to be free and autonomous. Rawls takes on board this Kantian doctrine, but replaces the idealist metaphysics of Kant's noumenal subject by a subject placed in a situation of choice which is characterized by empirical circumstances, for example, the circumstances in which justice arises or those which invoke the self-interested motivation of an agent.

A RAWLSIAN REIMAGINATION OF THE CORPORATION AS AN AGENT OF SOCIAL TRANSFORMATION

A company has legal personality and is sanctioned by law to perform actions that impinge on others. As a legal 'person' (and just as an individual has particular obligations in relation to their stakeholder groups of family, friends and significant others), it is a reasonable expectation that a business may assume a greater share of social responsibilities that reach beyond its immediate family of shareholders. Through the activities of its owners, managers and employees, the corporate citizen enters into relationships with individuals and groups, and these relationships carry a range of responsibilities. The concept of self-legislation, for Rawls, implies the exercise of moral autonomy as a property of the individual will. A Kantian definition of the term 'moral autonomy' relates to the capacity to impose the objective moral law on oneself and is hypothesized as a necessary organizing principle for all morality. Used in many different ways and applied to a variety of philosophical and practical contexts, moral autonomy is translated into political autonomy at the level of collective will-formation and vice versa. Even though the 'moral will' is assimilated into practical reason, the rationally grounded 'political will' retains a contingent aspect in that it is founded on context-dependent reasons. The Rawlsian approach parallels Kant's formulation, however, it substitutes a disembodied transcendental self for an ordinary rational subject. In Habermasian terms, referred to later in the chapter, this explains why the common ground of shared beliefs, achieved discursively in different political arenas, also generates what he refers to as 'communicative power'.

The original position embodies in its definition a set of conditions, for example, an absence of knowledge about the kind of subject one is, along with a necessary ignorance of an individual's identity and of their particular personal circumstances. This is a form of bracketing-out, phenomenological reduction or epoch; commonly referred to as 'bracketing'. It is a method used by qualitative researchers which relates to the gathering, inclusion and exclusion of particular constructions, preconceptions and assumptions. For Edmund Husserl, this method enables a 'return to philosophical questioning [and provides] a way to see the world anew' as it is in reality or 'lived experience' (1931). Excluding classifying characteristics, via a process of bracketing-out, sets the limits for what actions can be chosen, both rationally and a priori by requiring respect for the interests of all parties; it also justifies Rawls's requirement for a minimum set of conditions to be applicable to all reasonable societies. Even in his later transitional work, Rawls continues to reveal his Kantian roots, stating that the procedures according to which first principles are chosen 'must be founded on practical reason' (1971, p. 560). This is because morality is an aspect of practical reason and the search for moral principles consists in reasoning practically, not in seeking out independent moral facts. So then, a valid decision is right or wrong according to the nature of one's practical reason; referred to by Rawls as the 'rational' and the 'reasonable'.

Rawls also favours, what he refers to as, 'Kantian constructivism' in its holding that moral objectivity is to be understood in terms of a suitably constructed social point of view that all can accept. Constructivism is much like Kantian rationalism in that it claims objectivity for morality and, at the same time, holds that this objectivity is radically different from the objectivity of empirical judgements. It also looks to the nature of practical choice as a basis for moral judgement by joining:

> The content of justice with a certain conception of the person; and this conception regards persons as both free and equal, as capable of acting both reasonably and rationally, and therefore as capable of taking part in social cooperation among persons so conceived. In addressing the public culture of a democratic society, Kantian constructivism hopes to invoke a conception of the person implicitly affirmed in that culture, or else one that would prove acceptable to citizens once it was properly presented and explained. (Rawls 1980, p. 569)

In addition, the selective application of a set of refined emotions, and resistance of any contrary inclinations, is essential for stimulating ethical behaviour which is consistent with moral ends.

The principles of justice and fairness are, for Rawls, determined from the vantage point of an original position, behind a veil of ignorance with the emphasis placed on the value of equality – the striving to overcome the tension between individuality and the universal notion of equality – which leads Rawls to search for the common root of all humanity in rational action. To this end, he formulates a particular hypothetical model with which to justify the claim that the principles or maxims for ethical action that parties would choose, under similar circumstances, are valid principles of justice. His constructivism can be interpreted as a particular view of what would constitute this justification, in that rational self-interested actors would most certainly surrender their short-term benefits for long-term security. In his article 'Justice as fairness', Rawls commends Kantian constructivism in its employment of a 'method of avoidance' in order to overcome the problem of 'truth' in moral philosophy and the controversy between realism and subjectivism:

> The hope is that, by this method of avoidance, as we might call it, existing differences between contending political views can at least be moderated, even if not entirely removed, so that social cooperation on the basis of mutual respect can be maintained. Or if this is expecting too much, this method may enable us to conceive how, given a desire for free and uncoerced agreement, a public understanding could arise consistent with the historical conditions and constraints of our social world. (Rawls 1985, p. 231)

The validity of qualitative research rests on the integrity of the researcher to present research findings that allow for critical reflection. With this in mind, it is important to highlight some of the limitations of a Rawlsian perspective. Onora O'Neill criticizes Rawls for drawing a somewhat negative picture, accusing him of inter alia doing little more than 'abstracting from', rather than adding helpful evaluative information in relation to, agents in the original position; and that the veil of ignorance merely obscures and limits claims about agents in that they simply 'know less'. In addition, she claims that the way in which he does this is governed by a 'certain ideal, a certain theory' which may unwittingly result in the 'privileging [of] certain sorts of human agent and life by presenting their specific characteristics as universal ideals' (O'Neill 1989, pp. 209–212). She further suggests Rawls omits in both *A Theory of Justice* and *Political Liberalism* any discussion of those theories that concern the confirmation or legitimation of the supposed neutrality, universality and objectivity of the principles of rational justice he promotes. He is also alleged to have explicitly rejected 'idealised accounts of agents, their rationality and their mutual independence' and having failed to appeal, however obliquely, to 'transcendent moral claims' (O'Neill 1989, p. 218). Margolis accuses Rawls of arbitrariness in his moral constructivism, specifically in 'the complete absence of any effort on Rawls's part to explain exactly why we should suppose practical reason to be invariantly ordered' and claims that, unlike Rawls, 'Kant is never arbitrary' (1996, p. 35). It has also been suggested that Rawls's Kantianism does little more than give 'a rubber stamp of approval to conventional morality' (Morton 1996, pp. 311–312). Rorty has even challenged Rawls's Kantian credentials; asserting that his approach to political theory in *A Theory of Justice* is less Kantian than he would have us believe and that, rather, his arguments appeal to 'a conception of Deweyan pragmatism' as opposed to Kant's universal practical rationality (2004, p. 197).

To include such criticisms is part of the evaluative process and emphasizes the point that moral philosophy comprises a speculative approach and provides merely a starting point for comparing diverse theories, before it is possible to even consider attempting a reasoned summary or judgement. The philosophical methodology does not even claim to provide definitive answers to particular problems. What can be stated with precision, however, is the increasing significance of organizations, and specifically companies, to social improvement and societal welfare (Shaw 2014, p. 158). The transformative interplay of a range of state, public and private actors along with the global corporation, for example, has led to the growing use of political theories and moral philosophy in helping to determine their ethical obligations and refine corporate social responsibilities in tackling global political and environmental challenges.

CSR AS A MORAL DISCOURSE (CMR): A HABERMASIAN MODEL

For Jürgen Habermas, social transformation is best achieved through 'communicative action' because of its preoccupation with the avoidance of distortion and manipulation, towards achieving mutual understanding and agreement through the use of language. The aspiration to attain consensus by means of an 'ideal speech situation' first requires others to be treated as meaningful subjects rather than mere objects. Habermas's critical social theory of communicative action is based on the ontological and linguistic notions of discourse theory. In common with Rawls, Habermas has also been labelled 'neo-Kantian', even accused of being a pragmatist who is unable to escape the shadow of 'the Kantian grid' (Rorty 1985, p. xx). Not all of his scholarship has paid homage to Kant, as his earlier work was oriented towards supporting Hegelian-Marxist social theory, however, his later writing bears strong Kantian overtones. In presenting what is essentially a transcendental argument for moral principles in his communicative ethical theory he has, like Kant, 'gone further and claimed that engagement in practical discourse per se presupposes a commitment to specific substantive moral principles' (Brownsword and Beyleveld 1994, p. 126). Whereas Kant's theory of justice focuses on the principle of reason and the legitimation of all general 'norms' at the universal level, Habermas shifts the focus of the 'critique of reason' from forms of transcendental consciousness to forms of interpersonal communication as a subtle reformulation of Kant's original thesis. The social world, as the totality of legitimately ordered interpersonal relations, is accessible only from the perspective of the participant; it is inextricably interwoven with the intentions and beliefs, the practices and languages of its members (Habermas 1999, p. 38).

Organizations, both public and private, exert a powerful influence over the lives of those on the inside and outside. In the case of corporations, their attitudes and activities are frequently isolated from the alternative contexts (social, political, philosophical and aesthetic) in which they exist; rather assuming a purity and inviolability which puts them beyond the reach of any challengers (Shaw and Shaw 2014, p. 45). Habermas argues that such a predisposition would fail to provide the necessary conditions, assumed by both speaker and listener, which allow natural speakers the ability to communicate rationally. These conditions, 'universal pragmatics' or validity claims underpin all ordinary speech and, in constructing the framework for human understanding, are essential for social progress. The validity claims comprise truth, sincerity, understandability and appropriateness. For Habermas, rational discourse is possible because of this shared sphere of communication from within which the public practice of argumentation enables valid principles relating to conscionable behaviour to be established freely and intersubjectively. These principles are the result of reasoned argument in pursuit of intersubjective recognition for claims of a persuasive 'better' argument, leading to the development of a discourse theory which privileges truth and justice. The next developmental stage is the establishment of institutions and practices which are capable of giving effect to socially appropriate forms of theoretical and practical discourse. As 'ideal' presuppositions of rational practices these would be effective in redefining, for example, the proper function of the company in its social situation; in this way ideas of reason would form part of social reality.

Like Rawls, Habermas situates the abstract principle of equality as the fundamental discourse principle which underpins his theory of justice and, similarly, he replaces the Kantian transcendental self with the empirical (Habermas 1996, p. 138). The accompanying necessary conditions of universality and impartiality reveal an underlying moral principle not unlike Kant's imperative to treat people as ends in themselves. The norm of equal respect for autonomous rational agents is, according to Habermas, the moral principle which gives expression to an individual right – one which is more fundamental than a political right as the familiar object of explicit constitutional guarantees. Habermas asserts that individual rights make possible democratic self-rule and, importantly, they give a concrete expression to the most basic individual right namely that of equal respect, which in itself underpins our political self-understanding. Therefore, discourse is not central to our moral and political self-understanding; rather it is the moral principle of respect for persons. Equal respect, then, makes democratic self-rule the proper form of political association and citizens can understand themselves as the source of law, as a result of accepting this principle and judging the validity of their collective decisions from this basis. Habermas connects the legitimacy of legal norms to what everyone might agree to in public discussions, taking into account the interests of all equally; in doing so he places Kant's 'united will of a people' as a core ideal within his discourse theory.

Individual passions, wants and inclinations of affected communities are to be included and have a place in the content of, or 'belong to', practical discourse because, according to Habermas:

> While the degree of solidarity and the growth of [general] welfare are indicators of the quality of communal life, they are not the only ones. Just as important is that equal consideration be given to the interests of every individual in defining the general interest. Going beyond Kant, discourse ethics extends the deontological concept of justice by including in it those structural aspects of the good life that can be distinguished from the concrete totality of specific forms of life. (1990, p. 203)

Habermas's modified version of Kantianism reconstructs the universalized moral point of view; only his discourse ethics determines 'what is moral' or right by means of an intersubjectivist frame of reference. This universal and intersubjective context relies on the normative presuppositions of communicative interaction which are alleged to be capable of providing the conditions for the ideal speech situation. In relation to company reporting, the application of such frameworks that approximate the ethical principles of communicative action admit the examination not only of reported results, but also reveal the processes involved in achieving such outcomes. Such a development would make stakeholders a central component of the discourse rather than marginal to the process. They would become participants in a discourse that is transparent, fair and egalitarian which would be a significant step for social progress, towards a moral corporate discourse.

Habermas follows in the Kantian tradition by postulating the moral principle of equal respect for the rational autonomous agent as a property of the innermost part of our moral consciousness. It forms the historically situated point of departure for our moral reflection, and the framework within which it is possible to conceive of moral argument (Mendelson 1996, p. 303). The problem of justice and equal treatment, however, is not a problem of communities or history, rather for Habermas it is necessarily one of justification – to be explicated according to the logic of public argumentation. In his *Theory of Communicative Action*, Habermas is making a universalistic claim in proposing these general linguistic social constructs. His idea of a 'discourse ethics' can be interpreted as an attempt to reconstruct Kant's categorical imperative in introducing this principle of universalism, particularly in its aim to achieve a rational consensus in the context of a possible plethora of conflicting opinions so that a norm is right when it is able to correspond with a universal interest. It is only valid when, in the context of practical discourse, it is determined by rational consensus (Habermas 1979, p. 3). Empathy in coming to a reasoned agreement is necessary in what is a very public process and, unlike Rawls's Kantian constructivism, Habermas's representation of practical discourse does not involve the monological process of individuals cautiously contracting behind a veil of ignorance; rather, moral agents must proactively attempt to put themselves in another's shoes.

The focus shifts from what can be willed without contradiction as a general rule or maxim for action, to what everyone can agree upon as a general social norm. Within this construct, the idea of the autonomous individual is intersubjective; individuals must participate in the practice of mutual recognition of 'exposedness and vulnerability' in order to 'reciprocally stabilise their fragile identities' (Habermas 1990, p. 207). Communication processes shape rational will-formation, and for Habermas:

> Argumentation insures that all concerned in principle take part, freely and equally, in a cooperative search for truth, where nothing coerces anyone except the force of better argument . . . it is a public affair, practised intersubjectively by all involved [encouraging] the simultaneous growth of the autonomous individual subject and his dependence on interpersonal relations and social ties. (1990, pp. 198, 199)

This idea has profound implications for the evolution of CSR towards engaging the wider social environment in business decision-making, as part of an on-going discourse between the corporation and its stakeholders (Shaw and Shaw 2015, p. 246). Such an initiative would entail looking beyond the usual gestures of corporate philanthropy, community initiatives and political lobbying towards achieving fully integrated external engagement; perhaps even inviting community consultation on aspects of product design, recruitment policy and project implementation.

CONCLUSION

Considering the broad configuration of the global capitalist system, corporate social responsibility is too often a perfunctory gesture, providing yet another reason for business as usual; justifying the deeper extension of market forces into an already imploding social body. A phenomenological investigation of the possible conditions for the necessary evolution of CSR arises, therefore, within the context of accusations that it is failing to deliver, in the case of both companies and society. Reports of unfair or discriminatory business behaviour and a growing number of social and environmental scandals, particularly those relating to the financial sector, have proliferated. This self-interested behaviour was neatly encapsulated as 'the corporation has evolved to serve the interests of whoever controls it, at the expense of whoever does not' (Dugger 1989, p. 36). Yet the globalized world collapses traditional distinctions concerning the division of labour between the political and economic contexts and arguably necessitates a new perspective on the role of the corporation in society. This wider assumption of responsibility must arguably go further than the traditional economic nature and operational concerns of a company; even beyond a stakeholder perspective which relates to an identifiable cohort of those most affected by its activities. After all, a genuine interest in CSR would imply a concomitant concern for society, which is comprised of all people who inhabit the world and their natural habitat; and this conception would, ideally, be the starting point for an integrated business and community engagement strategy.

Many stakeholder perspectives are concerned with the moral responsibility of companies in relation to creating social benefits for wider society, and this chapter contrasts the procedural ethical stance of Rawls and Habermas who were similarly influenced by Kant's metaphysics of morals and theory of justice. Using different frames of reference they articulate a modern morality of intersubjective principles of right and fairness which, although implicit, are not actualized in social practice. Consequently, both attempt to lay the groundwork for a morally just and fair society in which each individual ought to be in a position to manage their own affairs as well as being able to conceive and pursue outcomes acceptable to all parties affected by them in an environment of mutual respect under appropriately equal conditions. For the corporation, this moral aim would necessitate full disclosure of their objectives, interests and attitudes in the spirit of transparency and accountability.

All corporate actors who engage in moral discourse would, importantly, attempt to understand and respect the opinions of other participants; being cognizant of their unequal power relationships and specific vulnerabilities. Common CSR activities such as formulating corporate codes of conduct might be undertaken in collaboration with critical third parties such as non-governmental organizations, academics and activist groups. Such groups of external stakeholders as informed participants would be invited to ask questions, debate areas of concern and their responses may even influence company policymaking and future development. As well as seeking to forge strong alliances with community actors, corporate decision-making may be purposefully linked to public discourses relating to wider societal and environmental concerns and challenges. Accordingly, the adoption of a more widely conceived corporate moral discourse may even lead to significant social transformation. This form of exploratory, speculative or hypothetical research benefits from a broadly qualitative approach, not least of all because it is less bounded (in respect of, for example, practical evidence and validation demands) and is, therefore, better able to freely engage with an eclectic assortment of interdisciplinary perspectives and methodologies.

REFERENCES

Brownsword, Roger and Deryck Beyleveld (1994), *Law as a Moral Judgment*, Sheffield: Sheffield Academic Press.
Carens, Joseph H. (1997), 'Aliens and citizens: the case for open borders', *Review of Politics*, **49** (2), 251–273.
Dugger, William M. (1989), *Corporate Hegemony*, New York: Greenwood Press.
Friedman, M. (1970), 'The social responsibility of business is to increase its profits', *New York Times Magazine*, September 13: 32–33, 122–124.
Habermas, Jürgen (1979), 'What is universal pragmatics?', *Communication and the Evolution of Society*, Thomas McCarthy (trans.), Boston: Beacon Press.
Habermas, Jürgen (1990), 'Discourse ethics: notes on a program of philosophical justification', in Christian Lenhardt and Shierry W. Nicholsen (trans.), *Moral Consciousness and Communicative Action* Cambridge: Polity Press, pp. 43–116.

Habermas, Jürgen (1996), *Between Facts and Norms*, Cambridge, Massachusetts: MIT Press.
Habermas, Jürgen (1999), *The Inclusion of the Other: Studies in Political Theory*, Cambridge, Massachusetts: MIT Press.
Husserl, Edmund (1931), *Ideas: General Introduction to Pure Phenomenology*, W.R. Boyce Gibson (trans.), London: George Allen and Unwin.
Kant, Immanuel (1991), *Metaphysics of Morals*, Mary J. Gregor (trans.), Cambridge: Cambridge University Press.
Kant, Immanuel (2002), *Groundwork for the Metaphysics of Morals Kant*, Arnulf Zweig (trans.), Oxford: Oxford University Press.
Klosko, G. (1994), 'Political obligation and the natural duties of justice', *Philosophy and Public Affairs*, **23** (3), 251–270.
Levinas, Emmanuel (1969), *Totality and Infinity*, The Hague: Martinus Nijhoff.
Margolis, Joseph (1996), *Life Without Principles*, Oxford: Blackwell.
Marx, Karl (1978), 'Economic and philosophic manuscripts of 1844', in Robert C. Tucker (ed.), *The Marx–Engels Reader*, New York: W.W. Norton, pp. 67–125.
Mendelson, Jack (1996), 'The Habermas-Gadamer debate', in Seyla Benhabib (ed.), *Critique, Norm and Utopia*, New York: Columbia University Press, pp. 102–146.
Morton, Adam (1996), *Philosophy in Practice*, Oxford: Blackwell.
O'Neill, Onora (1989), *Constructions of Reason: Explorations of Kant's Practical Philosophy*, Cambridge: Cambridge University Press.
Rawls, John (1971), *A Theory of Justice*, Cambridge, Massachusetts, USA: Harvard University Press.
Rawls, John (1980), 'Kantian constructivism in moral theory', *Journal of Philosophy*, **77** (9), 515–572.
Rawls, John (1985), 'Justice as fairness: political not metaphysical', *Philosophy and Public Affairs*, **14** (3), 223–251.
Rorty, Richard (1985), 'Habermas and Lyotard on postmodernism', in Richard J. Bernstein (ed.), *Habermas and Modernity*, Cambridge: Polity Press, pp. 161–176.
Rorty, Richard (2004), 'Trapped between Kant and Dewey: the current situation of moral philosophy', in Natalie Brender and Larry Krasnoff (eds), *New Essays on the History of Autonomy*, Cambridge: Cambridge University Press, pp. 195–214.
Shaw, Hillary J. (2014), *The Consuming Geographies of Food: Diet, Food Deserts and Obesity*, London: Routledge.
Shaw, Julia J.A. (2015), 'Compassion and the criminal justice system: stumbling along towards a jurisprudence of love and forgiveness', *International Journal of Law in Context*, **11** (1), 92–107.
Shaw, Julia J.A. (2017), 'Aesthetics of Law and Literary License: an anatomy of the legal imagination', *Liverpool Law Review: a Journal of Contemporary Legal and Social Policy Issues*, **38**(2): 83–105.
Shaw, J.J.A. and H.J. Shaw (2014), 'A Philosophical Foundation for Corporate Social Responsibility', in D. Crowther, R. Said and A. Amran (eds), *Ethics, Governance and Corporate Crime: Challenges and Consequences*, Bingley, UK: Emerald Publishing Limited.
Shaw, J.J.A. and H.J. Shaw (2015), 'The politics and poetics of spaces and places: mapping the multiple geographies of identity in a cultural posthuman era', *Journal of Organisational Transformation & Social Change*, **12** (2), 234–256.
Strauss, Anselm and Juliet Corbin (1990), *Basics of Qualitative Research: Grounded Theory Procedures and Techniques*, Newbury Park, CA, USA: Sage Publications, Inc.
Wolcher, Louis E. (2013), *Law's Task: The Tragic Circle of Law, Justice and Human Suffering*, Aldershot, UK: Ashgate Publishing.

23. Social network analysis in CSR research
Duygu Türker

INTRODUCTION

As a viable multidisciplinary method, social network analysis (SNA) has been frequently used to reveal the nature and structure of relationships among different actors in a network or to analyse the network itself for a long time. This network perspective together with considering the relational aspects of phenomena can be particularly useful to conceptualize and analyse the social, economic, or political structures of social units. Therefore, this social network perspective can also be used in the analysis of the relational context of social responsibility and ethical issues. The purpose of the current study is to provide a viable understanding of the application of SNA for corporate social responsibility (CSR) literature. In doing so, this study first provides a conceptual framework of SNA and then briefly discusses its paradigmatic stance and methodological approach based on the relevant literature. In the second section, it is analysed whether and how SNA can address our CSR related research problems over three selected research mainstreams: stakeholder management, collaborative social responsibility projects, and ethical conduct among employees.

SOCIAL NETWORK ANALYSIS

Conceptual Framework

The notion of social network provides a useful paradigm for the various disciplines of social sciences including sociology, anthropology, business, or economics, and so on. Wasserman and Faust (1994, p. 3) state that most researchers adopt a network perspective since it allows 'new leverage for answering standard social and behavioral science research questions by giving precise formal definition to aspects of the political, economic, or social structural environment'. From this perspective, a social phenomenon cannot be isolated from its relations within the social context. Taking the actors or links within a network, or the network itself, as the unit of analysis utterly changes how researchers perceive social phenomena and gets them much closer to explore the mystery of complex social problems around us.

SNA has evolved by the contributions of scholars who attempt to explain diverse social phenomena over the last century (Borgatti et al. 2009). During this time period, it has derived some of its basic notions from the theoretical perspectives of sociometry, anthropology, and structural sociology, which emphasize the role of structural constraints over human behaviors (Mizruchi 1994). Tracing back to the studies of early sociologists such as Durkheim, Marx, and Simmel, structural sociologists assume that social structures, constraints, and opportunities have a more explicit impact over human actions than subjective states (Mizruchi 1994). Therefore, studying social structures 'shifts attention away from seeing the world as composed of egalitarian, voluntarily chosen, two-person ties and concentrated instead on seeing it as composed of asymmetric ties bound up in hierarchical structures' (Wellman 1983, p. 157). Although this deterministic perspective of structural sociology leaves little room for individual choice (Casciaro et al. 2014), most structural sociologists accept that objective factors can be more significant to explain human behaviors (Mizruchi 1994). Therefore, from a sociological point of view, a social network refers to 'a specific set of linkages among a defined set of persons, with the additional property that the characteristics of these linkages as a whole may be used to interpret the social behavior of the persons involved' (Mitchell 1969, p. 2) and SNA can be defined as 'a type of structural sociology based on an explicit notion of the effects of social relations on individual and group behavior' (Mizruchi 1994, p. 330).

In addition to its use in sociology, network perspective has been adopted by other disciplines through the increasing need for 'more relational, contextual and systemic understandings' rather than 'individualist, essentialist and atomistic explanations' (Borgatti and Foster 2003). According to Galaskiewicz and Wasserman (1993), network analysis contributes particularly to the fields of political sociology, interorganizational relations, social support, social influence, and epidemiology. However, its use in these diverse fields of social sciences requires revisiting the definition of concept to encompass all relations among different entities. For instance, Laumann et al. (1978, p. 458) define social network as 'a set of nodes (e.g., persons, organizations) linked by a set of social relationships (e.g., friendship, transfer of funds, overlapping membership) of a specified type'. Obviously, the adoption of concept by other disciplines widens its use and enhances the knowledge generated through SNA.

Although SNA appeared in the mid-1930s as a distinct research method, it has captured a growing interest since only the 1990s (Wasserman et al. 2005). Its use particularly in organization studies can vary from micro to macro issues including the categories of social capital, embeddedness, network organizations, board interlocks, joint ventures/inter-firm alliances, knowledge management, social cognition, and group processes (Borgatti and Foster 2003). Briefly, SNA has been used to reveal the nature and structure of interpersonal, intergroup, and interorganizational relations in the organizational field. For example, at the interorganizational level, the scholars use a social network perspective to analyse supply chain networks (Borgatti and Li 2009, Galaskiewicz 2011, Giannakis 2012, Kim et al. 2011), interlocking directorates (Everard and Henry 2002, Galaskiewicz and Wasserman 1989), or multinational organizations due to their geographically dispersed structure (Ghoshal and Bartlett 1990), and so on.

Despite this increasing interest, SNA is not fully explored by the scholars from the organizational field. However, it has significant potential to shed new light on our current understanding of the diverse topic of organizational studies. The current study is focusing specifically on how SNA can be conceptualized and used in the corporate social responsibility (CSR) literature. As a concept, which requires a close collaboration between the organization and its stakeholders to integrate social, environmental, ethical, human rights, and consumer concerns into action (CEC 2011), CSR can also be analysed from this relational perspective at the actor, dyadic, triadic, subset, and network levels.

Characteristics of Network Analysis

Paradigmatic stance

The paradigmatic stance of network research is still under debate. For some authors, searching a single paradigm for network research might restrict its theoretical potential (Parkhe et al. 2006) due to the mutually exclusive nature of these meta-theories (Burrell and Morgan 1979). Depending on the dominance of the structuralist sociologists, network research mainly focuses on the consequences of networks, which determine the actors' context with providing opportunities or constraining their behaviors (Borgatti and Foster 2003). Therefore, these actors, as the interdependent units of a social, economic, or political structure, transfer some resources through their linkages into other actors within a network and, so, the network research helps us to conceptualize these structures and their deterministic nature over the behaviors of actors (Galaskiewicz and Wasserman 1994). Based on this stance, Wellman (2002, p. 82) states that the theory of structural or network analysis has five paradigmatic characteristics:

- Behavior is interpreted in terms of structural constraints on activity rather than in terms of inner forces within units (e.g., 'socialization to norms') that impel behavior in a voluntaristic, sometimes teleological push towards a desired goal.
- Analyses focus on the relations between units, instead of trying to sort units into categories defined by the inner attributes (or essences) of these units.
- A central consideration is how the patterned relationships among multiple (actors) alter jointly affect network members' behavior.
- Structure is treated as a network of networks that may or may not be partitioned into discrete groups.
- Analytic methods deal directly with the patterned, relational nature of social structure in order to supplement – and sometimes supplant – mainstream statistical methods that demand independent units of analysis.

This paradigmatic approach towards network research is, however, found insufficient by some scholars; for instance, the actors and their personalities can be considered as an essential dimension of a network (Mehra et al. 2001). Following a Lakatosian philosophy of science (Lakatos 1970), Kilduff et al. (2006, p. 1033) provide a new approach to the construction of the protective belt for SNA by emphasizing 'the recursive complexity and distinctiveness of both actors and networks and the ongoing mutual constitution of perceived and actual structures'. According to the authors, the four main principles of social network research are 'the primacy of relations between organizational actors, the ubiquity of actors' embeddedness in social fields, the social utility of network connections, and the structural patterning of social life' and these principles nurture two sets of protective belt theories as 'the structural configuration of the network system itself' and 'the centrality of individual actors' within the system (Kilduff et al. 2006, p. 1033). This multi-lensed perspective of SNA can contribute to increase our understanding in diverse levels of analysis.

Methodological approach

Although SNA is sometimes criticized as being 'merely descriptive' or 'just methodology' (Borgatti et al. 2009), the strength of network analysis lies in 'its integrated application of theoretical concepts, ways of collecting and analyzing data, and a growing, cumulating body of substantive findings' (Wellman 2002). Therefore, the adoption of a network perspective to address a given research problem in social sciences is the first step and must be followed by a grounded methodological approach. Integrating Wellman's (2002) paradigmatic characteristics with Galaskiewicz and Wasserman's (1994) assumptions, Rowley (1997) provides the following methodological issues in SNA:

- What are the boundaries of the network under study?
- What type(s) of relations will be measured? Do the relations measured represent the range of relevant components of the construct?
- Will binary or value data be collected? Does the operationalization of the relationship construct(s) require assessing the strength of the ties?
- Are the ties directional or non-directional? Are the exchange ties between network partners reciprocal?

In order to understand these points, some key concepts and major methodological tenets of SNA are briefly introduced in this section. The researcher must determine the set of actors who belong to this network based on the reasonable limits, such as the membership in this network or the relative frequency of interaction, and so on, to specify the boundary of a network (Wasserman and Faust 1994, p. 31). Deriving its mathematical roots from graph theory (Gross and Yellen 2006), SNA provides an analysis approach for all levels including the actor in complete or ego networks, dyad and triad levels, subgroups, and network (Prell 2012). Therefore, depending on the unit of analysis in the research question, the actors (or nodes) can be real people as well as teams or organizations. A tie between each of these actors can be classified in terms of different criteria; it can be either directed or undirected and dichotomous or valued (Borgatti and Foster 2003). Depending on its context in social sciences, these ties in a network can represent similarities (location, membership, attribute), social relations (kinship, friendship, affective or cognitive attitudes), interactions (e.g., talked with, advice to), and flows (e.g., information, beliefs, personnel, resources) (Borgatti et al. 2009). Despite all these ties seeming to be empirically the same, their attributed meanings in a given network can significantly change their functioning and so the interpretation; 'for example, centrality in the "who has conflicts with whom" network has different implications for the actor than centrality in the "who trusts whom" network' (Borgatti and Foster 2003, p. 992).

Although SNA is usually thought of as a tool for visualization, it goes beyond with providing critical knowledge on the nature and structure of relationships. For instance, it is stated above that centrality is one of the most widely used tools at the node-level analysis. Searching the antecedents and consequences of an actor's centrality in a network might have some important implications for the research question. Wasserman and Faust (1994) identify and elaborately explain the four major groups of SNA: structural and locational properties, roles and positions, dyadic and triadic methods, and statistical dyadic interaction models. All these analysis methods provide a precious evaluation for the various research questions.

Since SNA is interested in the relations among actors, its data collection method is somewhat different than other methods in social sciences. Usually, the data are collected by observing, interviewing, or questioning actors on their links with other actors in a network and then modeled at the levels of actor, dyad, triad, subgroup, or whole network. Based on the research objective, one may use either questionnaires, interviews, observations, archival records, experiments, or other techniques during the data collection process (Wasserman and Faust 1994). Many commercial and free software packages are available for the analysis of the collected data. In their study, Huisman and van Duijn (2005) make an overall comparison among 27 packages in terms of their objective, data format (type, input format, missing values), functionality (visualization techniques, analysis methods), and support. Due to their generalizability, the authors analyse the features of six packages (UCINET, Pajek, NetMiner II, STRUCTURE, MultiNet, and StOCNET) in more detail and score them objectively. According to the authors, since each package has some pros and cons, the researchers should choose the best analysis tool depending on the objective of their study (Huisman and van Duijn 2005).

SOCIAL NETWORK ANALYSIS IN CSR RESEARCH

It is clear that the aforementioned theoretical and methodological approach of SNA can be very useful to address many research problems within CSR literature. However, SNA is rarely used by the scholars due to the dominant methodological assumptions in this field of social sciences. The current approach usually narrows down the methodological scope of CSR literature and most scholars have either limited knowledge of the existence of other methods or lack of experience of their applicability into this field of study. Since using a network metaphor can enhance our way of understanding, in this section it is tried to figure out how SNA can be applied to the specific research problems within CSR literature. In doing so, three important CSR research mainstreams were chosen and their relational aspects were configured from the SNA perspective.

Stakeholder Relations

In the literature, CSR is usually taken as a framework between a business and its stakeholders; the analysis of various CSR definitions points out that the stakeholder dimension is an integral part of CSR conceptualization (Dahlsrud 2008) and most scholars and practitioners think that balancing the diverse interests of a business's stakeholders is an essential part of CSR. However, in real life, the nature or structure of stakeholder management can be problematic for any firm that engages in CSR. Considering the limits of a firm, the first and foremost problem might appear in identifying the priority of stakeholders and managing their diverse needs in a balanced manner. At the theoretical level, while Mitchell et al. (1997, p. 854) suggest that the power of the stakeholder over the firm, the legitimacy of its relation with the firm, and the urgency of its claim on the firm are together sufficient to assess the stakeholder salience, Driscoll and Starik (2004) add a new dimension of 'proximity'. Although many studies follow these frameworks (e.g., Elias et al. 2002, Harvey and Schaefer 2001, Friedman and Mason 2004, Ryan and Schneider 2003), a network perspective is rarely adopted by the scholars. However, as Reed et al. (2009, p. 1937) state, SNA can be 'used to identify the network of stakeholders and measuring relational ties between stakeholders through use of structured interview/ questionnaire'. For instance, the study of Türker (2014) analyses the nature of power inequalities among stakeholders to achieve finely balanced decisions in stakeholder management. The study focuses on the relational sources of power and analyses the relative power of each stakeholder in a given set with identifying the centrality measures based on the frequency of interaction and trust.

Since the relationship among diverse stakeholders constitutes a structure, another line of inquiry in stakeholder management is about this structure and its impact over the firm's responses. Following a SNA perspective, Rowley (1997, p. 888) argues that the area of research through 'the density of the stakeholder network surrounding an organization' and 'the organization's centrality in the network influence its degree of resistance to stakeholder demands'. According to Rowley (1997), an organization is embedded into a network of stakeholders and each of these stakeholders has their own stakeholder network and so on. Therefore, the position of the organization in this network within networks can be viewed as a significant factor that shapes the firm's behavior. From the lenses of network perspective, the author proposes that the network density positively affects 'the ability of focal organization's stakeholders to constrain the organization's actions' and the centrality of focal organization positively affects 'its ability to resist stakeholder pressures'. Therefore, depending on the level of network density and its centrality within that network, an organization either becomes a compromiser (both high), commander (low density – high centrality), subordinate (high density – low centrality), or solitarian (both low). SNA can provide both the conceptualization and methodological toolkit for the solutions of such questions at the empirical level.

Collaborative Social Responsibility Projects

A company has several alternative governance mechanisms to execute its social responsibility activities; it may either '(1) outsource CSR through corporate charitable contributions, (2) internalize CSR through in-house projects, or (3) use a collaborative model' (Husted 2003, p. 483). It is clear that each of these governance modes have some strengths or weaknesses. However, considering the complexity of today's environmental, economic, and social problems, building cooperation among organizations that have complementary skills and expertise might increase the effectiveness of CSR and contribute to the creation of social capital in the long run. The literature clearly suggests that following this type of governance model can create joint value, help to exchange core competencies, and contribute to the social transformation (Austin 2000, Berger et al. 1999, Sakarya et al. 2012). However, since this type of governance model includes diverse organizations from public, for-profit, and non-profit organizations (NGOs), or the organization from different industries, some problems might appear during the formulation, implementation, or evaluation stages of this longstanding collaboration process. For instance, the study of Jamali and Keshishian (2009) on the relations between businesses and NGOs at five CSR partnerships in Lebanon demonstrates that such partnerships can be problematic in terms of systematic involvement/preparation in the first stage, negotiations, persuasion, expectations/motivations, and so on; therefore, the authors point out that 'the partnerships crafted were mostly symbolic and instrumental rather than substantive and integrative' (Jamali and Keshishian 2009, p. 289).

Due to the involvement of various organizations in such models, we need to address how the nature and structure of these models affect the obtained results. Network perspective can be particularly useful to advance our understanding of these models. For instance, one might scrutinize the link between the effectiveness/efficiencies of a CSR project and the network structure, type, or density, and so on. On the other hand, considering the diverse occupational areas, goals, expectations, or cultures of organizations in a CSR network, the relational aspects such as power or trust can be analysed by SNA. Moreover, the role and effect of individual actors over the network can be determined through the centrality analysis.

Ethical Conduct among Employees

Based on the famous model of Carroll (1979, 1991), the ethical dimension is one of the major elements of social responsibility conception; a business organization should be ethical in its every conduct and operation. However, the increasing number of unethical problems in the corporate world during the last decades shows that most businesses are far away from developing their own ethical stances. There are many reasons underpinning the spread of unethical conduct among or within the organizations. For some, it is partly explained by focusing on the relational context of the unethical conduct in organizations. The social relations can affect the unethical behaviors as an 'organizational/contextual' factor (Trevino et al. 2006) and the counterproductive work behaviors (CWB) as a group-level factor (O'Boyle et al. 2011). In their study, Brass et al. (1998) examine how the type (in terms of strength, status, multiplexity, and asymmetry) and the structure of relations (such as density, cliques, structural holes, and centrality) can add constraints over the unethical conduct (Brass et al. 1998). For instance, based on the review of literature and logical inferences from the social network perspective, Brass et al. (1998, p. 18) propose that 'strong relationships foster empathy and psychological proximity, and they decrease the likelihood of unethical behavior' or the multiplexity of a relationship can increase the costs of breaking the relationship, such as 'acting unethically toward a business partner may also result in a lost friendship when the relationship is multiplex'.

Although Brass et al. (1998) build a strong theoretical foundation on using SNA for ethical behaviors in organizations, few scholars empirically take an SNA perspective in the analysis of the ethical behaviors in organizations. For instance, the study of Türker and Altuntas (2014) attempts to articulate how unethical behaviors spread among the key actors of a given network. The authors conducted a study of the Turkish medical sector as one of the highly performance-oriented sectors in Turkey and found that the unethical behavior tends to spread from the focal dyad between physicians and sales representatives through the other actors in the same network and the cliques among these key actors, which can manifest itself in terms of frequency of interaction, information sharing, or level of trust, and so on, and might result in initiation or maintenance of the secret unethical behaviors among the members.

CONCLUSION AND FUTURE IMPLICATIONS

Since SNA can enable us to better understand the behavior of actors within a relational context (Granovetter 1985), today, an increasing number of scholars from various disciplines adopt this perspective into their own research areas. As this study tries to configure that SNA can be very useful to analyse the key questions in CSR literature by taking their relational context into account. It is clear that most scholars conceptualize CSR as a relationship between a business and its stakeholders. Therefore, SNA can provide invaluable knowledge about the stakeholder management in terms of diverse relational aspects among members including their needs, expectations, or the level of trust, conflict, or power, and so on. Moreover, it can provide a useful tool to evaluate the relational base of CSR projects, which fall into Husted's (2003) collaborative models; SNA can increase our knowledge for explaining how these collaborations can be formed among various public, private, or NGOs and, more importantly, how the quality and quantity of such collaboration can increase. Even the nature and trends in CSR literature can be identified through the SNA perspective (Ma 2009).

However, like all other methods, SNA has both some pros and cons. According to Reed et al. (2009), while SNA helps to 'gain insight into the boundary of stakeholder network/ the structure of the network and identifies influential stakeholders and peripheral stakeholders', the data collection process can be time-consuming for both researchers and respondents, and the analysis of collected data requires the involvement of specialists in this method. For instance, in the use of questionnaires, since the respondents must fill a matrix on their evaluation of relations with other actors in terms of frequency of interaction, trust, or power, it can take a much longer time than usual questionnaire forms. Therefore, the process of data collection can be very problematic for the researchers. However, in line with the trend towards becoming a citizen of the global network during the last decades, the people or organizations are getting more and more interconnected through diverse communication technologies in the future. In such a socially networked world, we cannot analyse our critical research questions on CSR without considering its social and relational context anymore. Therefore, it is believed that SNA can be more widely used among CSR researchers in the future.

REFERENCES

Austin, J.E. (2000), 'Strategic collaboration between nonprofits and business', *Nonprofit and Voluntary Sector Quarterly*, **29** (1), 69–97.
Berger, I.E., P.H. Cunningham and M.E. Drumwright (1999), 'Social alliances: company/ nonprofit collaboration', *Social Marketing Quarterly*, **5** (3), 48–53.
Borgatti, S.P. and P.C. Foster (2003), 'The network paradigm in organizational research: a review and typology', *Journal of Management*, **29** (6), 991–1013.
Borgatti, S.P. and X. Li (2009), 'On social network analysis in a supply chain context', *Journal of Supply Chain Management*, **45** (2), 5–22.
Borgatti, S.P., A. Mehra, D.J. Brass and G. Labianca (2009), 'Network analysis in the social sciences', *Science*, **323 (April)**, 892–895.
Brass, D., K. Butterfield and B. Skaggs (1998), 'Relationships and unethical behavior: a social network perspective', *Academy of Management Review*, **23 (1)**, 14–31.
Burrell, Gibson and Gareth Morgan (1979), *Sociological Paradigms and Organizational Analysis*, London: Heinemann.
Carroll, A.B. (1979), 'A three dimensional conceptual model of corporate social performance', *Academy of Management Review*, **4** (4), 497–505.
Carroll, A.B. (1991), 'The pyramid of corporate social responsibility: toward the moral management of organizational stakeholders', *Business Horizons*, **34** (4), 39–48.
Casciaro, T., F. Gino and M. Kouchaki (2014), 'The contaminating effects of building instrumental ties: how networking can make us feel dirty', *Administrative Science Quarterly*, DOI: 10.1177/0001839214554990.
Commission of the European Communities (CEC) (2011), 'Communication from the Commission to the

European Parliament, the Council, the European Economic and Social Committee and the Committee of the Regions – A renewed EU strategy 2011–14 for Corporate Social Responsibility', available at http://ec.europa.eu/enterprise/policies/ sustainable-business/files/csr/new-csr/act_en.pdf (accessed 7 October 2014).

Dahlsrud, A. (2008), 'How corporate social responsibility is defined: an analysis of 37 definitions', *Corporate Social Responsibility and Environmental Management*, **15** (1), 1–13.

Driscoll, C. and M. Starik (2004), 'The primordial stakeholder: advancing the conceptual consideration of stakeholder status for the natural environment', *Journal of Business Ethics*, **49** (1), 55–73.

Elias, A.A., R.Y. Cavana and L.S. Jackson (2002), 'Stakeholder analysis for R&D project management', *R&D Management*, **32 (4)**, 301–310.

Everard, A. and R. Henry (2002), 'A social network analysis of interlocked directorates in electronic commerce firms', *Electronic Commerce Research and Applications*, **1** (2), 225–234.

Friedman, M.T. and D.S. Mason (2004), 'A stakeholder approach to understanding economic development decision making: public subsidies for professional sport facilities', *Economic Development Quarterly*, **18 (3)**, 236–254.

Galaskiewicz, J. (2011), 'Studying supply chains from a social network perspective', *Journal of Supply Chain Management*, **47** (1), 4–8.

Galaskiewicz, J. and S. Wasserman (1989), 'Mimetic processes within an interorganizational field: an empirical test', *Administrative Science Quarterly*, **34** (3), 454–479.

Galaskiewicz, J. and S. Wasserman (1993), 'Social network analysis concepts, methodology, and directions for the 1990s', *Sociological Methods & Research*, **22** (1), 3–22.

Galaskiewicz, J. and S. Wasserman (1994), 'Introduction', in Stanley Wasserman and Joseph Galaskiewicz (eds), *Advances in Social Network Analysis: Research in the Social and Behavioral Sciences*, Thousand Oaks, CA: Sage, pp. xi–xvii.

Ghoshal, S. and C.A. Bartlett (1990), 'The multinational corporation as an interorganizational network', *The Academy of Management Review*, **15** (4), 603–625.

Giannakis, M. (2012), 'The intellectual structure of the supply chain management discipline: a citation and social network analysis', *Journal of Enterprise Information Management*, **25** (2), 136–169.

Granovetter, M. (1985), 'Economic action and social structure: the problem of embeddedness', *American Journal of Sociology*, **91 (3)**, 481–510.

Gross, Jonathan L. and Jay Yellen (2006), *Graph Theory and Its Applications*, USA: Taylor & Francis Group.

Harvey, B. and A. Schaefer (2001), 'Managing relationships with environmental stakeholders: a study of U.K. water and electricity utilities', *Journal of Business Ethics*, **30** (3), 243–260.

Huisman, M. and M.A.J. van Duijn (2005), 'Software for social network analysis', in Peter J. Carrington, John Scott and Stanley Wasserman (eds), *Models and Methods in Social Network Analysis*, UK: Cambridge University Press, pp. 270–316.

Husted, B.W. (2003), 'Governance choices for corporate social responsibility: to contribute, collaborate or internalize?', *Long Range Planning*, **36 (5)**, 481–498.

Jamali, D. and T. Keshishian (2009), 'Uneasy alliances: lessons learned from partnerships between businesses and NGOs in the context of CSR', *Journal of Business Ethics*, **84 (2)**, 277–295.

Kilduff, M., W. Tsai and R. Hanke (2006), 'A paradigm too far? A dynamic stability reconsideration of the social network research program', *Academy of Management Review*, **31** (4), 1031–1048.

Kim, Y., T.Y. Choi, T. Yan and K. Dooley (2011), 'Structural investigation of supply networks: a social network analysis approach', *Journal of Operations Management*, **29** (3), 194–211.

Lakatos, I. (1970), 'Falsification and the methodology of scientific research programs', in Imre Lakatos and Alan Musgrave (eds), *Criticism and the Growth of Knowledge*, New York: Cambridge University Press, pp. 91–132 (cited in Kilduff et al. (2006)).

Laumann, E.O., J. Galaskiewicz and P.V. Marsden (1978), 'Community structure as interorganizational linkages', *Annual Review of Sociology*, **4 (1)**, 455–484.

Ma, Z. (2009), 'The status of contemporary business ethics research: present and future', *Journal of Business Ethics*, **90** (3), 255–265.

Mehra, A., M. Kilduff and D.J. Brass (2001), 'The social networks of high and low self-monitors: implications for workplace performance', *Administrative Science Quarterly*, **46 (1)**, 121–146.

Mitchell, J.C. (1969), 'The concept and use of social networks', in J. Clyde Mitchell (ed.), *Social Networks in Urban Situations: Analysis of Personal Relationships in Central African Towns*, Manchester: Manchester Univ. Press. (cited in Laumann et al. (1978)), pp. 1–50.

Mitchell, R.K., B.R. Agle and D.J. Wood (1997), 'Toward a theory of stakeholder identification and salience: defining the principle of who and what really counts', *The Academy of Management Review*, **22** (4), 853–886.

Mizruchi, M.S. (1994), 'Social network analysis: recent achievements and current controversies', *Acta Sociologica*, **37 (4)**, 329–343.

O'Boyle, E.H., D.R. Forsyth and A.S. O'Boyle (2011), 'Bad apples or bad barrels: an examination of group- and organizational-level effects in the study of counterproductive work behavior', *Group & Organization Management*, **36** (1), 39–69.

Parkhe, A., S. Wasserman and D. Ralston (2006), 'New frontiers in network theory development', *Academy of Management Review*, **31 (3)**, 560–568.

Prell, Christina (2012), *Social Network Analysis: History, Theory and Methodology*, London: Sage Publications Ltd.

Reed, M.S., A. Graves, N. Dandy, H. Posthumus, K. Hubacek, J. Morris, C. Prell, C.H. Quinn and L.C. Stringer (2009), 'Who's in and why? A typology of stakeholder analysis methods for natural resource management', *Journal of Environmental Management*, **90 (5)**, 1933–1949.

Rowley, T.J. (1997), 'Moving beyond dyadic ties: a network theory of stakeholder influences', *The Academy of Management Review*, **22** (4), 887–910.

Ryan, L.V. and M. Schneider (2003), 'Institutional investor power and heterogeneity: implications for agency and stakeholder theories', *Business & Society*, **42 (4)**, 398–429.

Sakarya, S., M. Bodur, O. Yildirim-Oktem and N. Selekler-Goksen (2012), 'Social alliances: business and social enterprise collaboration for social transformation', *Journal of Business Research*, **65** (12), 1710–1720.

Trevino, L.K., G.R. Weaver and S.J. Reynolds (2006), 'Behavioral ethics in organizations: a review', *Journal of Management*, **32** (6), 951–990.

Türker, D. (2014), 'Analyzing relational sources of power at the interorganizational communication system', *European Management Journal*, **32** (3), 509–517.

Türker, D. and C. Altuntas (2014), 'Analysis of unethical behaviors in social networks: an application in the medical sector', *Procedia: Social and Behavioral Sciences*, **150**, 1177–1186. [10th International Strategic Management Conference, Rome/Italy (19–21 June 2014).]

Wasserman, Stanley and Katherine Faust (1994), *Social Network Analysis: Methods and Applications*, Cambridge: Cambridge University Press.

Wasserman, S., J. Scott and P.J. Carrington (2005), 'Introduction', in Peter J. Carrington, John Scott and Stanley Wasserman (eds), *Models and Methods in Social Network Analysis*, UK: Cambridge University Press, pp. 1–7.

Wellman, B. (1983), 'Network analysis: some basic principles', *Sociological Theory*, **1**, 155–200.

Wellman, B. (2002), 'Structural analysis: from method and metaphor to theory and substance', in John Scott (ed.), *Social Networks: Critical Concepts in Sociology*, London: Routledge, pp. 81–122.

24. Theoretical storytelling as a meta-frame for all research methods in corporate social responsibility
Linne Marie Lauesen

INTRODUCTION

As co-editor of this and other book volumes, as author of books and papers in various academic journals, and especially as a reviewer for journals publishing corporate social responsibility papers, I often wonder why some authors have the finest data material, the best intentions for weaving it together, and a solid research method filled with rigour and trustworthiness in all facets, but still manage to write a poor overall story that makes a good, but boring contribution that I do not remember and especially do not cite afterwards in my own works? And why a paper filled with statistics about a certain medical problem, which I really should not care about, stays in my mind for years waiting for the right moment for me to cite it if ever appropriate? The answer to these questions is very simple: the first was poorly written and the latter great in terms of providing a splendid overall (theoretical) story.

It is not as if some authors are born good writers and others not. Writing skills are not genetically inherited although one tends to think so, when glancing over how little emphasis universities – and especially some departments – put on teaching students how to write well. It is rarely a part of the curriculum, and often such courses are placed as voluntary summer courses for those who want to write better assignments. Writing is a technique for writing good academic papers, but it needs theoretical and practical rehearsal over and over again. Just like learning to play the piano, it is not something that we just 'can'. But we can learn it.

So what does it take to write a good overall theoretical story? It is not as hard as it seems, because unlike what one might think, there is a method behind this too. We just need to consult another field in order to rehearse such techniques, which are rarely displayed in academic research besides in editorials of journals with editors that are well educated in qualitative methodology. What puzzles me is that it is not required for scholars, to be a qualitative researcher, to learn how to write a good (theoretical) story. But of course, storytelling is most often seen in qualitative work. However, great work of quantitative accounts is not just based on authors with talented writing skills. If they are, the writer surely has a good gut feeling about what constitutes a good story, and that is not bad either. However, it might not be that all are so skilfully equipped, so for all of the rest of us, I will provide an account of theoretical storytelling theory as a meta-frame for all research methods in corporate social responsibility.

The rest of this chapter is structured as follows. In the next section, I will justify my request for better writing styles by referring to editors and good academic writers in order to underpin my claim that all research can be improved by exercising good storytelling. Next, I will present some theoretical and practical ideas of how to write a good story. It does not matter whether it is a fictional story or a scientific/academic story – the tricks are the same. It is all based on the author having good data – either in terms of measures, good or enough respondents, interviews, observations, archival texts for the academic scholar, and similarly: a good plot for the fiction writer. It is hard not to find one or more good stories within a good set of data acquired by sound research methodologies as those presented earlier in this volume. The main activity for creating such a story – fiction or 'real' – is to use the so-called 'Narrative Arc'. I present this model and use it for further analysis of two exemplars of writings for you to see that they have actually – consciously or unconsciously – been used in these accounts.

The first story, I will show you, is a short fiction story written by my own son, who had 'storytelling' as a subject in eighth grade in our local public school. It is amazing how knowing just a little of these writing techniques can produce a good story out of a small idea (a plot) he initially had as a 15-year-old. I did only help him a little: the ending was disappointing. During the entire story he had built up a story about a boy as a hero and potential rescuer (a story character), and in the end an adult came and took all the credit for solving the problem. That could have been the real ending of a documentary story, but then the rest of the story was wrongly composed. If the point of the story was that adults always come to rescue troubled children, then the story should be told in another way. But it was not what he wanted: it was to sustain the heroism of the boy solving the problem, and not the story of the coincidental adult just coming by. When telling him this theoretical flaw, he ended up changing the end of the story, so that the reader could get his or her expectations relieved. The story was rewarded with an A in class. This story – albeit fictional – serves to illustrate how storytelling is built around the Narrative Arc template, which works for both fiction and scientific stories because its format is compelling: it talks to our heart and our minds.

To illustrate how this is done in academic writing using the same template, I will show you an editorial of David Crowther's from 2015 on publishing CSR papers in the *Social Responsibility Journal* that uses the exact same mechanism as the short story in order to make them effectual and memorable.[1]

A REQUEST FOR BETTER STORIES IN ACADEMIA

In sociology, business management, and organization studies, as well as many other science fields, we find more and more accounts of storytelling. It surrounds instances and contexts, in which humans participate, because people tend to create interesting interactions with one another and the things they care about.[2] Lately, we also find editors especially asking for and providing good accounts of how to write papers for their journals with the aim of creating a good story as a meta-frame for presenting one's research findings regardless of research methodology.

What place do stories have in an evidence-based world, the psychiatrist Glenn A. Roberts asked in the traditional quantitatively based medical journal, *Advances in Psychiatric Treatment* (2000). He suggests that '[n]arrative- and evidence-based approaches may initially appear to be in tension, even competition. The view advanced here is that they are necessary and complementary companions' (Roberts 2000, p. 432). Stories are the means for research with their generality reaching individuals through their particularity (Brody

1987; cited from the above), because '[e]ach has the potential to leaven, challenge, sharpen and enrich the other; each highlights the other's blind spots – both are needed' (ibid.). In our own world of business management and organization studies, Pratt (2009, p. 856) likewise resonates that 'it is possible to analyse qualitative data quantitatively, just as we analyse quantitative data qualitatively when constructing stories around the numbers, we present'.

However, we need to strengthen our skills on how to write things up in an interesting way, and thus the need for clear accounts of theoretical storytelling is much required as a meta-frame for any kind of research methodology. Showing tables and templates does not provide it in itself – it is the text surrounding it, explaining it, showing what it was, that made the researcher do his or her research initially, how it all ended (the results), and how it adds to our knowledge, that triggers our curiosity for reading and publishing their material. As Dyer and Wilkins (1991, p. 617) argue, 'stories are often more persuasive and memorable than statistical demonstrations of ideas and claims'.

The above should not be taken as a critique of quantitative methods, but merely pointing to the need for all kinds of studies to contain some kind of storytelling surrounding the data we present – qualitative or quantitative. In Dyer and Wilkins's critique of Eisenhardt's then relatively novel approach to post-positivistic case study methodology, they add the importance of storytelling:

> we hope that many scholars will continue to tell good stories that have theoretical import. If researchers apply the paradigm of hypothesis testing to case study work without the goal of telling good stories, they are likely to miss both the calibre and the quantity of theory we have seen result from classic storytelling through case studies in the past. (Ibid., p. 618)

'All research is interpretive!' is the headline of Evert Gummesson's 2003 paper in the *Journal of Business & Industrial Marketing* arguing that 'interpretation exists in all types of scientific studies, be they quantitative or qualitative', which makes strong emphasis of researchers framing their findings in telling a good and trustworthy story out of their data in order to persuade the readers and reviewers. Few editors, however, have taken the steps of offering guidelines for researchers of how to frame such stories and assist them in where to put these stories in journals besides the aforementioned and Trish Reay.

Trish Reay, an editor of the *Family Business Review*, gives us a rich account of how she considers a good paper[3] for this journal (Reay 2014). Despite aiming at the audience for this particular journal, we can learn a lot for our own field of CSR by listening to her requests. Reay shows us seven steps of how to compose a good paper (pp. 95–102):

1. Ensuring you have sufficient high quality data
2. Setting up an appropriate research question to guide your article
3. Grounding one's study in the relevant literature
4. Explaining one's methods and showing one's work
5. Telling an intriguing empirical story
6. Telling a convincing theoretical story
7. Showing a clear contribution to the . . . literature.

These seven points are thoroughly investigated in her editorial, and if we surpass the first four points, because these are dealt with in other chapters throughout this volume, and the last one, which is fairly obvious, we see that storytelling – whether empirical and/or theoretical – is crucial for making your paper work for the audience (and especially us reviewers and editors). Reay highlights the dangers of turning one's 'inherently interesting story into something dull and dreary' (2014, p. 99) because the scholar has learned that the first four and the seventh points are the most important. One of the tricks to stay tuned into on the potential story of your data is to 'keep focus on what you (and others) have found surprising about your findings' (p. 100). Where do we do that in academic journals, we wonder? Reay suggests that we do it in two steps: (1) in the Introduction[4] in order to hook our readers, and (2) in the Findings section, where you are allowed to tell a longer, detailed empirical story.

Next, Reay points to a crucial point in storytelling, which we will come to in the next section, but in further details than she presents it: 'showing' versus 'telling'. She emphasizes the 'telling' over the 'showing', which is the opposite in fiction writing, where the importance lies on 'showing' and not 'telling'. I will come back to this difference, but highlight what Reay means. In good academic writing, it is important to 'tell the frame of the story (including your interpretations)' (p. 100), and in addition you must show your data and explain how they support your story.

Regarding establishing a convincing theoretical story, Reay (2014, p. 100) directs us to the Discussion section of our paper.

> It is here that you compare and contrast your empirical findings with the established literature. This means that you explain how your findings are similar or different from the literature that you reviewed in the literature review section.

Now, we must remember that the editorials are limited accounts of writing, and Trish Reay was framing seven types of things necessary in order to compose a good overall paper, so we do not get much more out of it without consulting some fuller accounts of good scholarly writing techniques. If we want to dig more into what really constitutes good writing despite the advice we get from editorials such as the above, we must go from 'where' to put our story in a scholarly paper into 'what' to put in the story.

STORYTELLING TECHNIQUES: THEORY AND PRACTICE

It is crucial to know not only about writing techniques that create a good story, but also to know the differences in such techniques, which strongly depends upon the genre (and thus paradigm) one writes within. With genre we not only distinguish between fiction and science; we also distinguish between different genres within each of these two meta-genres. As Van Maanen said about writing good ethnography:

> Literary standards are different [than scientific], but they are not shabby and second-rate. When taken seriously they may require even more from an ethnographer than those formulated by the profession. Fidelity, coherence, generosity, wisdom, imagination, honesty, respect, and verisimilitude are standards of a high order. (Van Maanen 2011, p. 33)

Narrative Voice

Notice the voice I use when writing this chapter. This is one of many conscious choices an author should make when addressing his or her audience. I mainly use 'direct voicing':

first person (myself) addressing the reader (second person: you) as if I was a teacher in a writing class.[5] But I mix it with 'indirect voicing': non-personal voice, because the audience of this volume comes from different paradigms, and I want to address all. See the examples from the Introduction below:

- Direct voice: first person (author) addressing second person (reader): the use of 'I', 'you', 'we', and 'they':
  - 'I will show you an editorial of David Crowther's from 2015 . . . that uses the exact same mechanism as the short story in order to make them effectual and memorable.'
  - 'Now, we must remember that the editorials are limited accounts of writing, and Trish Reay was framing seven types of things necessary in order to compose a good overall paper.'
- Indirect voice: invisible, authoritative person (author) addressing an invisible audience (reader) framing everything in the third person or non-person: the use of the imperative form (authority) and 'he'/'she' or surnames only:
  - 'Writing is a technique for writing good academic papers, but it needs theoretical and practical rehearsal over and over again.'
  - 'The rest of this chapter is structured as follows.'

None of these narrative voices are better than the other: it is the effect of persuasion of the reader that differs and addresses different audiences' expectations. Direct voices are often used in qualitative writing styles, and indirect voices in quantitative, which is perfectly in tune with their respective paradigms and their journals' unspoken writing requirements for publishing their papers. The author using the direct voice aims to persuade the reader about his or her point by explaining and interpreting it using this voice, because all interpretive paradigms rest on subjective opinions that need qualification and persuasion. The direct, subjective voice speaks directly to its audience, and the argument this voice delivers is the subjectively interpreted 'evidence' in this respect. The author using the indirect voice asserts the idea that writing within paradigms that consider them being objective, is supported by objective, non-personal, assumable non-interpretive styles.[6] Again, the narrative voice supports the paradigmatic typology of 'evidence': objective evidence, objective voice. If you have read the former chapters in this volume, you would probably have detected this difference already.

Showing versus Telling

Often, in fiction writing, the 'first law' – if we can call it that – is: show, don't tell! (Wells 1999, Goodall 2000, Warren 2011). Bud Goodall, a famous academic writer, said:

> *Show, don't tell*: Don't lecture the reader. Develop scenes, describe details, give voice to characters and let actions speak instead of making arguments about it.
> *Describe before you evaluate or analyse*, otherwise known as 'show me the data'. Readers like to reach their own conclusions rather than have the meaning summed for them. Rich descriptions of scenes, details about characters and events – all of these are data in a story. (Goodall 2012, p. 30)

Van Maanen illustrates the point in his ethnographic writing:

> To say 'the police sometimes kill people for mistaken reasons' is, flatly, not a story. To say 'Officer Allen shot Officer Roberts while both men were on a drug stakeout' is a story. (Van Maanen 2011, p. 105)

Van Maanen's point is that the first sentence is 'telling', whereas the second sentence is 'showing'. If we meet the first sentence in an academic paper as a reviewer, we would think (or ought to think): where is the evidence for this claim? The second sentence provides exactly this evidence, because it is presented and synthesized into the story.

As presented earlier, Trish Reay argued otherwise, emphasizing telling over showing, however, my point is that balancing the telling part (your interpretation) and the showing part (the evidence) is crucial in academic storytelling. If you continue telling how everything is going to be understood throughout a paper, we miss the evidence and you lack trustworthiness of your claims. So mix the telling and the showing in your writing style. A good trick is:

1. Show first (the evidence)
2. Then tell (your interpretation).

Characters

A vivid writing composition technique that has come forward during the last decade especially in organization studies, and strictly borrowed from fiction writing, is the use of storytelling characters in academic disciplines of analysing and writing. I would like to draw your attention to three especially outstanding scholars in this field, whose works stand out immensely in terms of guiding other scholars in that particular direction. Since the volume of their authorships is too much to account for in detail in this chapter, I suggest you read *Narratology* by Mieke Bal (2009), *Narrating the Organisation* by Barbara Czarniawska (1997), and *Storytelling Organizations* by David M. Boje (2008).

The essence of how to use characters in storytelling – whether it concerns organizational stories or writing academic papers – is using the unspoken fictional characters directly in your telling and writing. Most stories comprise at least one 'hero' and one 'villain' – technically referred to as the 'protagonist' versus the 'antagonist'. Besides these, we often find the characters of the 'helper' – both of the hero and villain – and the 'victim(s)', just to mention the most important characters to enact a story. Basically, a good story can be summarized into a villain conducting a sort of crime involving one or several victims, which is solved by the hero assisted by his or her helpers to eliminate the villain. It may sound primitive, but if you analyse most good writing – even scientific writing – you will find such elements in it despite there being no such direct characters in terms of human beings directly in the paper (Bal 2009, Czarniawska 1997, Boje 2008). Let me show you an example of a summary of a paper that most business management scholars are familiar with: the Michael E. Porter and Mark R. Kramer famous 2006 *Harvard Business Review* paper, 'Strategy and society: the link between competitive advantage and corporate social responsibility', in which the authors present their idea of Shared Value for the first time:

Governments, activists, and the media have become adept at holding companies to account for the social consequences of their actions. In response, corporate social responsibility has emerged as an inescapable priority for business leaders in every country. Frequently, though, CSR efforts are counterproductive, for two reasons. First, they pit business against society, when in reality the two are interdependent. Second, they pressure companies to think of corporate social responsibility in generic ways instead of in the way most appropriate to their individual strategies. The fact is, the prevailing approaches to CSR are so disconnected from strategy as to obscure many great opportunities for companies to benefit society. What a terrible waste. If corporations were to analyze their opportunities for social responsibility using the same frameworks that guide their core business choices, they would discover, as Whole Foods Market, Toyota, and Volvo have done, that CSR can be much more than a cost, a constraint, or a charitable deed—it can be a potent source of innovation and competitive advantage. In this article, Michael Porter and Mark Kramer propose a fundamentally new way to look at the relationship between business and society that does not treat corporate growth and social welfare as a zero-sum game. They introduce a framework that individual companies can use to identify the social consequences of their actions; to discover opportunities to benefit society and themselves by strengthening the competitive context in which they operate; to determine which CSR initiatives they should address; and to find the most effective ways of doing so. Perceiving social responsibility as an opportunity rather than as damage control or a PR campaign requires dramatically different thinking—a mind-set, the authors warn, that will become increasingly important to competitive success. (Porter and Kramer 2006[7])

The 'hero' in this summary is the authors presenting a solution to the problem, as they see it: corporations do not exercise social responsibility, because the (then) CSR concepts, templates, ideas within it, and their effects do not match the core activities of business making. The solution is to get companies to enact shared value in terms of synthesizing optimization of their competitive advantage by finding business opportunities that benefit society. The 'villain' is the CSR literature until then, which the authors think has failed as a means for solving societal problems (society is presented as the 'victim' here), and the 'helper' is the solution of the new concept of Shared Value.

The references that it has achieved so far[8] alone prove the effect and powerfulness it has had on the entire scholarly community of CSR.

Plot-Making Using the Narrative Arc

A 'plot' is defined in the *Merriam-Webster Dictionary* as 'a series of events that form the story in a novel, movie, etc'.[9] From this definition we see that nothing prevents theoretical or academic story-writing from using a technique mostly referred to as being applied in fiction writing.

However, to assist writers creating a plot I would like to present the story-framing template – the Narrative Arc[10] – normally used for analysing stories in literature studies, but is especially used as a means for constructing stories in fields such as journalism – as a means for creating good academic stories as well.[11]

Many literary writers have written about the Narrative Arc as an analytical template, however, I will direct your attention to one of these to assist you in getting on with exploring this template further.

First of all, the Narrative Arc is a template aiming at understanding how a story plot is developed over time (see Figure 24.1). On the X-axis, we see the time line understood as how you develop your story during the length of your paper. The time thus comprises

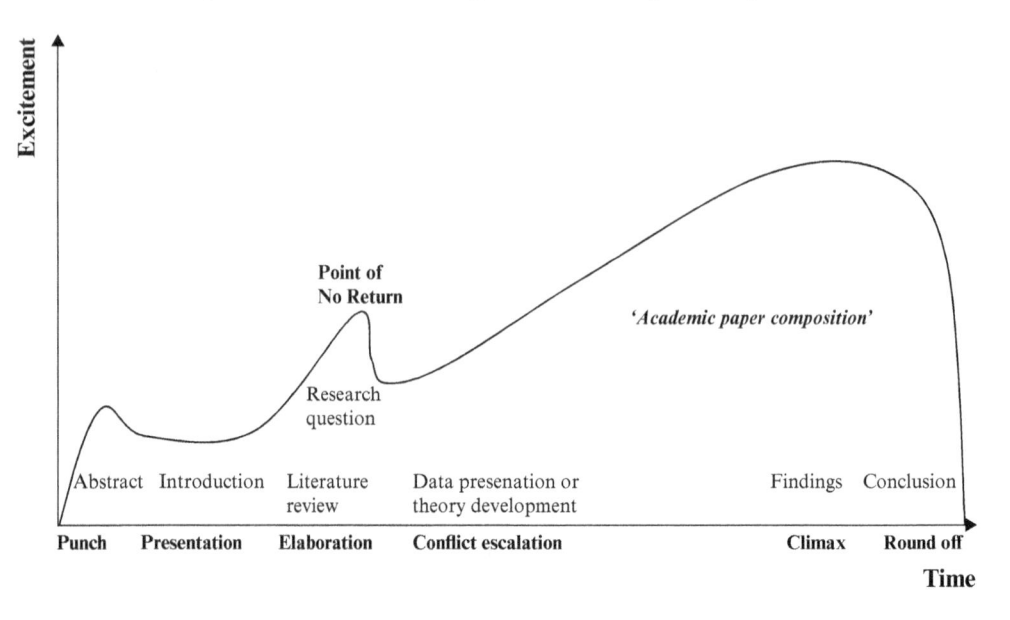

408 *Handbook of research methods in corporate social responsibility*

Figure 24.1 The Narrative Arc illustrated by the author and framing academic paper composition within it

each step during your story. The Y-axis represents the altitude of excitement while you present your story.

Jim Bizzochi (2007) used the following explanations for the phases (on the X-axis) within the Narrative Arc:

> Each stage has a distinct function, and the authors of the work agonize over the order, timing, and exact details of each step:
>
> - the setup introduces the characters and the storyworld they inhabit
> - the complication introduces a challenge to be overcome
> - the development is the long phase that dominates the bulk of the storytelling, as the protagonist works towards her goal
> - the resolution or climax is the culmination of the struggles of the development phase, often resulting in some form of victory or defeat
> - the denouement or falling action ties up the story's loose ends, and allows the narrative experience to gracefully end. (Bizzochi 2007, no page number).

In Bizzochi's interpretation, it is clear that he talks about how to write a fiction story. If we want to utilize these steps as a means for composing our academic theoretical story, we must interpret these steps into our own types of genre. This is what I have illustrated above the X-axis, which I explain below:

1. Punch

The first thing readers of academic papers and books (fiction as well as non-fiction) look at is your headline, and if it is convincing enough, then they will read your abstract (or the first page of your novel). Here, you must show all your best achievements for drawing the reader in. It is your punch of the story. Many scholars begin glancing over a range of abstracts before they decide what to read. You must in a very limited space show the reason for your inquiry, what you did to collect the best data to investigate it, and which results you had, and why they are so compelling not only to you, but to the entire community of readers that you address.

2. Presentation

If the readers have decided that your paper or book is worth reading, you must then continue holding them on to it, which is the next step you will achieve in your introduction. As a scholar, you can now elaborate more on why you were attached to the problem you saw, and here you must exercise the right balance of telling and showing, because telling alone does not guarantee your readers will stay hooked. The best thing is to advance the showing part (crucial in fiction writing) by referring to who else has supported you, saying that the problem you have is worth investigating. You must still convince your readers that you picked up an interesting study and how you now plan to invite the reader to follow you all the way through.

3. Elaboration

Now, if readers have not left you by this point, you are as a scholar now on the way of grounding your study in the literature of relevance. Keep in mind the need to continue having your readers' attention not by what I call 'name-dropping' – that is, saying this researcher said this, another said that – but by creating a storyline of its own even here. There are lots of books on how to make a good literature review, so consult them. The point is: the way you compose your literature review must equal a storyline as well, as fiction writers by now must have established the reader's interest in the plot. There must be a natural development, so that the last review you do in this section naturally leads up to the next, and most essential for scholars: the gap you want to fill in the literature.

4. The 'point of no return'

You have now reached the highest point in excitement for a short moment, whether you are a fiction or non-fiction writer. The scholar must have pointed out at least through the literature review showing how he or she wants to fill a gap in the literature, which is the 'point of no return'. You cannot disappoint your reader now. You must present a compelling research question, which the rest of your paper is concerned about answering. Comparing this point with fiction literature, it is here the hero faces the ultimate challenge: to fight the villain. He must take up the challenge, or the entire story is a waste. Cowardice is never rewarded.

5. Conflict escalation

The excitement curve drops a little, which indicates that you are now allowed a little background support for holding your story together. Soon, however, you must take up the lead you have initiated and even in your methodology or theory development sections continue to escalate the excitement leading up to the climax of your story: the findings for the scholar; the final combat for the fiction writer.

6. Climax

As a scholarly writer, your results are the uttermost exiting things you need to present here in the Findings part of your paper. It does not get much more thrilling. You must really do a good job balancing your showing with your telling. See before about first showing, then telling your interpretation of your data analysis. This is where you answer your research question. See that it is properly done, and if not, change your research question for this paper to fit your findings. Compared to fiction writing, this is the scene that settles everything. The hero must win. Unless you write a tragedy like Shakespeare's (1603) *The Tragedy of Hamlet, Prince of Denmark*, where Prince Hamlet dies together with Laertes in the last scene after their crucial and deadly fencing duel.

7. Round off

All good stories must end, and your discussion and conclusion serves to round off your story. It is celebration time (in fiction: the hero out-conquered the villain) and you want to show how your findings have led the academic world to a more knowledgeable place (in fiction: the hero restored the peace and is now collecting the reward), and what you see as future perspectives, your findings will give as reward to the academic audience. Here you can really tell. This is your moment to dictate. You have proven your skills as a researcher, and you are allowed to impose your visions on how you see the future of this particular research field.

Next, I will use these seven points as an analytical framework to illustrate how they work both in fiction and non-fiction academic writing. Due to the limitations of this chapter, I cannot re-publish an entire academic paper, so I will use a short story of fiction[12] and an editorial within CSR research as examples.[13] In square brackets you will find numbers referring to the points in the Narrative Arc similar to the seven points listed above. The numbers indicate when each of the steps have been finished.

STORIES

The Bicycle Cellar

By Sophus Bech Lauesen

> The baseball bat swung through the air. It hit the bikes with a bang, and the children froze.
> It resounded in the dark bicycle storage, and the children began slowly to move away from them.
> –Alright, then. Now we're in charge down here! We don't want anyone come running and disturb us – so from now on, you only come and get your damn bikes at four o'clock! Is that clear?! And not a word to the teachers – otherwise: we'll show you! [1]
> Jasper and Benny had conquered the bicycle cellar since Spring, and Jonas clearly remembered them from the incident happening.
> They were both kicked out of school in the eighth grade, and because they did not have anything to do with themselves, they chose to take control of the bike cellar and make it their hang-out. Ever since, there had been a rotten atmosphere down there, and even ninth grade did not dare to say or do anything about it. [2]
> It was half past twelve, and Jonas sat motionless at his seat in the classroom waiting for the bell to ring for the next break. There weren't many in class today. The right side was almost empty, and

the rest looked as stoned as he. Mr. Thompson was almost about to fall off of his soft armchair, and he would have done if it weren't for the shrilling bell that suddenly gave life back to people again. It was lunch time, and Jonas knew just where he could find Tim.
He went up on to the first floor, and indeed Tim sat in the corner waiting for him.
–What the hell took you so long?
–It's my damn bag! It is so packed that I can only go half pace with it on.
–Well, all right then . . . Come and sit here. Then I'll tell you where I was yesterday.
Tim smiled a little when he said it. He always had something to tell. Jonas struggled over to the corner and took a place.
–Now listen: I was down in the bike cellar yesterday, and of course the two morons were waiting for me. I ran to my bike as fast as I could, but I can still see them running after me, and I cry unto them: What the hell you doing man? It's over four! – But they didn't listen, so I just sat up and raced away.
–They're fucking insane.
Jonas handed down for his lunch packet while Tim told more, but to his agony, it wasn't there.
–Oh fuck, damn! I completely forgot that there wasn't room for my lunch in the bag . . .
–Where the hell have you left it then?
–Hmm, I think I–
He hesitated. [3]
–. . . I forgot the damn thing down on my bike! What a bugger I am!
–To hell, Jonas – what are you going to do?
–I should probably just wait until after school to pick up the . . .
–No way! Hurry, though, just go there and take it – they will probably not notice it.
Jonas didn't know what to do, but went down the stairs anyway . . . [4]
The door that read 'Bicycle storage' was slightly worn. No one approached this part of the building during school hours, for who knew what or who were waiting at the entrance?
When people came in the morning, they came early. Put their bikes and hurried up before Jasper and Benny woke up. It was bigtime chaotic.
The door creaked when Jonas stepped into the dark room. Only little daylight crept through some small windows that Jasper had smashed with his baseball bat long time ago. However, one could clearly see where their hang-out was: in one of the corners. Overturned bicycles, blankets and empty chips bags were laying all over the place. And right there in the middle the two sat deeply engrossed in doing something on a laptop. Jonas saw his chance to run over to his bike, but he reached only ten meters before he heard Benny's voice:
–Hey Japps – see the fat idiot who thinks he can reach his bike!
–Ha – he thinks, he is something, huh?
Steps approached rapidly, and Jonas could suddenly feel a hot breeze coming from Benny's mouth. He tried to step aside, but stumbled, fell, and was now on all fours. When he looked up, he saw the two big boys jumping about in front of him.
–That's a shame, huh?
–Did you really think you could run away, you somnolent scam?
Jonas' confidence had plummeted within seconds, and it made things far worse.
–I-I would really like to have my food . . . It is on my bike . . .
–Well, now would you really? Don't you know that it is forbidden for you to come down here during school hours?
Jonas didn't listen. He didn't even look up. He had seen the thing he tripped over. It was not a stone, tile or some of the usual stuff from the cellar. It was something made out of wood and had a slightly strange cylinder form . . . Damn, it was Jasper's baseball bat! What the hell did it do here? Perhaps he had thrown it after someone or something – he always did.
–Look at us when we talk to you, kiddo! Stand up like a man, so we can see what you are made of!
Jonas quickly pushed the bat onto his left hand, and rose gently, while he hid the bat behind his back.
–Japps – show the kid how we deal with someone like him?
. . . Jasper hesitated, but then tried to give a sign to Benny, who just stood and smiled contentedly. [5]

–I don't have my fucking bat, Benny. Where did you put it?!
–I surely haven't taken your bat, Japps! Damn, I never dream of taking that!
There came the chance. Jonas took the bat back and swung dangerously with it above his head. Jasper and Benny took a hasty step back, and appeared suddenly much less powerful. They stepped further back, and Jonas saw for the first time the fear in their eyes.
–Help!, it came from both of them.
–Hell, then help us, God dammit! He has a baseball bat!
The door opened at the other end, and the caretaker came for the first time in a long time into the bicycle cellar.
–What the hell is that noise?! Couldn't you be quiet, for God's sake?!
It wasn't long before he saw them. But instead of coming to their aid, he stared directly at Jasper and Benny. He captured his gaze as he slowly trudged over to them.
–Help us, please! He stands there and threatens us with a baseball bat!, it came from them interchangeably, but the caretaker was indifferent. He stood between them and took them both in their earlobes.
–I've been looking for you two since I don't know for how long. Now it's bloody end to you making trouble! And what the hell is this shit you've made back there in the corner? Go and clean this up!
–But, but, but–
–No 'but's! I put a guard on here in the bicycle cellar, and if you ever approach this school again, I'll personally take care of you! [6]
Jonas was relieved and just threw the bat in the trash pile. He walked over to his bike, took his lunch bag and went smoothly up the stairs again. Tim sat gazing into the air when Jonas came back.
–What the hell – did you really survive these two?
–You know what Tim? They weren't that damn dangerous after all. [7]

Editorial

By David Crowther

This Editorial was originally published in the *Social Responsibility Journal*, Vol. 11 Iss: 3.

Readers of the paper will notice that this volume seems much bigger than usual, while online readers will notice that there seem to be more papers included. This is, in fact, true as this issue contains 15 papers; this demonstrates the continuing growth and popularity of the Journal. [1] At the beginning of this year – after ten successful years of growth and development – we increased the size of each issue from 10 papers to 11 papers. But even that is not sufficient to publish all the high-quality papers which we accept for publication and so for this issue and the next, we have increased the size to include 15 papers. [2]

This means that this year – 2015 – we will publish 52 papers in the Journal, making it one of the largest academic journals. This reflects the continuing increase in popularity of the Journal to such an extent that we are unable to publish all the good-quality papers which are received. So over time, we have become more discriminating and only accept the very best papers. [3]

The nature of the papers we accept and publish reflects the diverse nature of the topic of social responsibility as we are interested in all aspects of this very important subject. Our readers and writers are similarly interested in the breadth of the subject. And it is a subject of global importance so we receive contributions from every part of the world, making it a very diverse and international Journal. Moreover, we reflect this in our Editorial Advisory Board membership, as we believe that a topic of global importance should be treated globally by international experts. We also believe that the quality of the Journal and its contributions has increased during the decade of its existence and that improvement should be continuous. So if you have any suggestions, then please contact me to discuss. And if you are interested in serving on the Editorial Advisory Board, then please contact me to express your interest and outline how you believe you can contribute to the continuing improvement of the Journal. [4]

Please note, however, that *Social Responsibility Journal* is the official journal of the Social Responsibility Research Network and you should ideally already be a member of the network and familiar with its aims and objectives. If you do not know about the Network, then have a look at our Web site – http://www.socialresponsibility.biz which can also be accessed from the Journal Web site. [5]

The Network also has a book series – *Developments in Corporate Governance and Responsibility* and this also is published by Emerald. You can find full details from the Web site also. Volume 7 – *Corporate Social Responsibility in the Digital Age* has just been published and Volume 8 is currently in press. Call for papers for future books have also been issued so if you are interested in contributing to these, then also please check the details and contact me. This is also the same if you are interested in editing a volume yourself. This is quite a lot of information which I have provided – hopefully much for you to think about and I look forward to hearing from you at some point in the future. In the meantime, here is an extra-large number of papers about some interesting topic. [6]

So I will finish at this point and leave you to read the papers and then join in the discourse. [7]

CONCLUSION

Hopefully, the two examples above illustrate well how the Narrative Arc can be used both as an analytical template as well as assisting scholars in composing their journal papers or book chapters. It should not be understood as if every good writing needs to have clearly defined characters such as heroes, villains, victims, and helpers or being able to be analysed as clearly in terms of applying the Narrative Arc as suggested above. Neither should the many references I have drawn upon mainly for qualitative writers be understood as if good writing styles only apply to scholars of qualitative inquiries. My claim is that all scholarly writers can benefit from learning some basic storytelling writing techniques, which should not be restricted for qualitative writers alone. Many good quantitative papers and book chapters, as you will find in this volume, are excellently written. This chapter is meant as inspiration for all kinds of scholars to consider while writing for publication, because if these elements can be detected analytically after reading your paper through, it – in my opinion – may enhance its impact on the reviewers and readers and success rate for publication.

NOTES

1. The best, of course, would have been for me to present a full academic paper and analyse it to strengthen my point, but the limitations of this chapter do not allow me to present such lengthy exemplars. However, try to do the same analysis of one of your favourite papers written by yourself or others and see if this does comprise the elements of the Narrative Arc or not. I would not be surprised if it did in one way or another.
2. Of course we also find good stories in the natural and technical sciences, but here we concentrate on the sciences involving human interaction.
3. In this instance, Reay refers primarily to qualitative papers – but it could as easily be said for quantitative papers, for these often need just as thorough an overhaul as qualitative papers do.
4. Notice how I presented a small bit of the story I am going to tell you in the next section already in the Introduction to this chapter. Are you not interested in knowing how a 15-year-old can use an established technique on a good plot and write an A-grade story that probably will amaze you too? Well, you will have to wait a little (oh, what a teaser).
5. I consider writing as a qualitative art usable for both qualitative *and* quantitative writing styles.
6. Despite that we already know that no (or at least few) academic fields (besides mathematics) can be said to be free of interpretation.

7. Summary achieved from https://hbr.org/2006/12/strategy-and-society-the-link-between-competitive-advantage-and-corporate-social-responsibility, accessed 12 May 2016.
8. As of Google Scholar, accessed 11 May 2016, it has received 6,404 citations: https://www.google.dk/#q=How+many+has+cited+%22the+link+between+competitive+advantage+and+corporate+social+responsibility.
9. http://www.merriam-webster.com/dictionary/plot.
10. It is unclear who invented or coined the term and idea within the Narrative Arc, but do not credit me for inventing it. Its origin can be traced all the way back to Aristotle's (ca. 335 BC) *Poetics*, where he talks about the Greek Tragedy and its composition. I present it here inspired by recent developments others have made of it, but I have added my own drawing, and I will interpret academic paper-writing into it. Some will say that this figure may happen multiple times during a long play or a novel, but my point is that a good story contains this development at least once.
11. I first presented this model as an academic writing tool at the 5th Organizational Governance Conference and 14th International Conference on Social Responsibility in Tekirdag, Turkey, 9–12 September 2015.
12. Disclaimer: Be aware that the tone of the fiction story is that of teenagers – it may sound 'blasphemous' to some readers, but it is not intended or meant by the author to offend nor provoke any reader: rather, it is meant to show how a certain Western teenage culture actually speaks to one another – like an American 'gang' subculture. Even in Danish public school yards.
13. All permissions for (re-)publication have been given by the respective authors and editors of the written exemplars.

REFERENCES

Bal, Mieke (2009), *Narratology: Introduction to the Theory of Narrative*, Toronto: University of Toronto Press.
Bizzochi, J. (2007), 'Games and narrative: an analytical framework', *Loading...*, **1** (1), no page number, accessed 12 May 2016 at http://journals.sfu.ca/loading/index.php/loading/article/view/1/1.
Boje, David M. (2008), *Storytelling Organizations*, London: Sage.
Brody, H. (1987), *Stories of Sickness*, Newhaven, CT: Yale University Press.
Crowther, D. (2015), 'Editorial', *Social Responsibility Journal*, **11** (3), accessed 12 May 2016 at http://www.emeraldinsight.com/doi/full/10.1108/SRJ-06-2015-0077.
Czarniawska, Barbara (1997), *Narrating the Organization: Dramas of Institutional Identity*, Chicago: University of Chicago Press.
Dyer, W.G. and A.L. Wilkins (1991), 'Better stories, not better constructs, to generate better theory: a rejoinder to Eisenhardt', *Academy of Management Review*, **16** (3), 613–619.
Goodall, Jr., H. Lloyd (2000), *Writing the New Ethnography*, Walnut Creek, CA: AltaMira Press.
Goodall, Jr., H. Lloyd (2012), *Writing Qualitative Inquiry: Self, Stories, and Academic life*, vol. 6, California: Left Coast Press.
Gummesson, E. (2003), 'All research is interpretive!', *Journal of Business & Industrial Marketing*, **18** (6–7), 482–492.
Porter, M.E., and M.R. Kramer (2006), 'Strategy and society: the link between competitive advantage and corporate social responsibility', *Harvard Business Review*, **Dec.**, 78–92. Summary referred to accessed 12 May 2016 at https://hbr.org/2006/12/strategy-and-society-the-link-between-competitive-advantage-and-corporate-social-responsibility.
Pratt, M.G. (2009), 'From the editors: for the lack of a boilerplate: tips on writing up (and reviewing) qualitative research', *Academy of Management Journal*, **52** (5), 856–862.
Reay, T. (2014), 'Publishing qualitative research', *Family Business Review*, **27** (2), 95–102, first published on 2 April 2014.
Roberts, G.A. (2000), 'Narrative and severe mental illness: what place do stories have in an evidence-based world?', *Advances in Psychiatric Treatment*, **6** (6), 432–441.
Shakespeare, William (1603), *The Tragedy of Hamlet, Prince of Denmark*, play accessed 12 May 2016 at http://www.william-shakespeare.info/shakespeare-play-hamlet.htm.
Van Maanen, John (2011), *Tales of the Field: On Writing Ethnography*, 2nd ed., Kindle version, Chicago: University of Chicago Press.
Warren, Jerianne (2011), *Show Don't Tell: A Guide to Purpose Driven Speech*, US: Jerianne Warren.
Wells, Gordon (1999), *How To Write Non-fiction Books*, Woodston, Peterborough: Writers' Bookshop.

PART IV

FUTURE RESEARCH AGENDA

David Crowther and Linne Marie Lauesen

We have covered a lot of ground in this book and we have explored a wide variety of methodologies for research into the area of CSR. All of these methods have been used by some in this field, and have certainly been used by the authors of the respective chapters. As we have stated some have been little used whereas others are commonly used; we make no claims concerning the validity of any of these methods. All are equally useful in undertaking research in this field and choice must be dependent upon the context and circumstances of any research project coupled with the preferences of the researcher. We hope that the wide range of methods discussed will increase the repertoire of researchers and hopefully lead to some interesting research.

But it is not sufficient to consider how research can be conducted: it is also necessary to consider what can – or should – be considered as suitable for research in this field. In his classic book about the philosophy of science Paul Feyerabend (1975) argued against scientific method and epistemological conformity in claiming that science is an anarchic enterprise. In other words he claimed that progress came from stepping outside the established tradition. This was echoed by Derrida (1978) who claimed that critique came from within and led outside. This is a step forward in the developing of theory from the seminal works of Kuhn (1962) and Popper (1959) who were concerned with explaining paradigm shifts.

With the development of CSR as a discipline in the late 1990s and early 2000s academics turned their attention to both defining what was meant by CSR and how it might differ from corporate responsibility, environmental concern, corporate governance and latterly sustainability. Although there is an undoubted panoptical element (Bentham 1789) to the need for academics to publish and mark their territory, we argue that academics are in serious danger of marginalising themselves through their desire to legitimate their knowledge through the development of theory integral to each particular discipline and thereby limiting both what is researched and how it is researched. Whatever terms are adopted it is clear that CSR continues to be prominent in corporate activity and continues to evolve (Seifi and Crowther 2011). We want to argue in this book that theorising must also evolve to keep up with practice. In other words we consider that theorising is not simply about monitoring what has happened with reference to the past. It is more about developing predictive ability for the future.

With this in mind we have completed this book with a short section which we hope will be thought provoking. In this section we have invited experienced and well-respected international academics to make contributions. In doing so we gave them an open brief to write what they considered to be important for the future of CSR research.

This section therefore begins with Nicholas Capaldi's 'Philosophical prolegomena to all future research in CSR', where he defines CSR and shows the present chaotic and conflicting analyses provided by rival theorists. What we seek is a clear definition unencumbered by private agendas, he asserts. In order to accomplish this we need to: (1) have an understanding of 'social' institutions, (2) a definition of a corporation as a 'social' entity, specifically as a 'commercial' entity, (3) an account of how corporations relate to other social institutions (including political and legal ones), (4) some understanding of what it means to evaluate the performance of social institutions in general and commercial ones in particular, and (5) the disambiguation of legal responsibility from 'social' responsibility. To come to terms with this, Capaldi presents 15 research implications for researchers to consider in the field of CSR from disregarding the possibility to know any objective and universal truth about corporations to considering contemporary norms, environmental impact, globalisation, inequality, greed, legal policies, ownership and investment, political state, competition, metrics of measurements, and company cultures and sub-cultures.

Jacob Dahl Rendtorff continues the invited chapters by taking us beyond strategic CSR and exploring the concept of responsibility as the foundation of ethics: political, technological and economic responsibility for the future of humanity. Jacob argues in his chapter that the future research agenda in CSR will move beyond strategic responsibility and become a major ethical concern at all levels of society. His chapter demonstrates the importance of the concept of responsibility as the foundation of ethics, in particular in the fields of politics and economics in modern civilisation marked by globalisation and technological progress. He considers that the concept of responsibility in the future will be the key notion in order to understand the ethical duty in a modern technological civilisation. We can indeed observe a moralisation of the concept of responsibility going beyond a strict legal definition in terms of imputability. Moreover, this implies that corporate responsibility cannot solely be defined strategically in terms of profits or shared values. The chapter begins by discussing the humanistic foundations of such a concept of responsibility. It looks at the historical origins of responsibility and it relates this concept to the concept of accountability. On the basis of this historical determination of the concept, Jacob presents the definition of the concept of responsibility as a fundamental ethical principle that has increasing importance as the foundation of the principles of governance in modern welfare states. In this context his chapter discusses the extension of the concept of responsibility towards institutional or corporate ethical responsibility where responsibility does not only concern the responsibility of individuals but also deals with the responsibility of institutional collectivities.

As the last invited chapter, Martin Samy and Fiona Robertson explore the emerging trends in CSR from positivism to social constructivism in Chapter 27. In this chapter, the authors chart the history of CSR activities over the decades, review methods undertaken by researchers and discuss the direction for future research methods. The theme of this chapter is to develop an argument shifting from positivism to social constructivism in CSR research. In this journey the research design is arguably biased towards a phenomenological approach that encompasses abductive paradigms. The authors take a case study design as findings are considered situational and contemporary and would build a stronger argument for mimetic actions among corporations in our society. When undertaking a case study, it is vital to adopt a systematic approach incorporating reliability and validity of data collection and analysis. The authors anticipate that future research in CSR would arguably have an impact on society if researchers undertake in-depth analysis by adopting a critical realism design to document, investigate and highlight contributions made by individual corporations. Reporting the CSR practices of multinationals through this case study design and process would reveal the best practices that could be modelled for other organisations. It would also highlight deficiencies and recommend changes.

REFERENCES

Bentham, Jeremy (1789), *An Introduction to the Principles of Moral and Legislation*, London: Clarendon Press.
Derrida, Jacques (1978), *Writing and Difference*, trans. Alan Bass, London: Routledge & Kegan Paul.
Feyerabend, Paul (1975), *Against Method*, London: New Left Books.
Kuhn, Thomas S. (1962), *The Structure of Scientific Revolution*, Chicago: University of Chicago Press.
Popper, Karl R. (1959), *The Logic of Scientific Discovery*, London: Routledge.
Seifi, S. and D. Crowther (2011), 'The future of corporate social responsibility', in Maria A. Costa, Maria J. Santos, Fernando M. Seabra and Fatima Jorge (eds), *Responsabilidade Social: Uma Visão Ibero-Americana*, Lisbon: Almedina, pp. 749–772.

25. Philosophical prolegomena to all future research in CSR
Nicholas Capaldi

INTRODUCTION

In order to conduct research on corporate social responsibility (CSR) one must first define CSR. At present there are admittedly chaotic and conflicting analyses provided by rival theorists. What we seek is a clear definition unencumbered by private agendas. In order to accomplish this, we need the following:

1. an understanding of 'social' institutions;
2. a definition of a corporation as a 'social' entity, specifically as a 'commercial' entity;
3. an account of how corporations relate to other social institutions (including political and legal ones);
4. some understanding of what it means to evaluate the performance of social institutions in general and commercial ones, in particular the disambiguation of legal responsibility from 'social' responsibility.

BRIEF HISTORY

The US origin of CSR can be traced back to the University of California-Berkeley in the 1960s, where several of the early leaders of the nascent 'business and society' field worked or were trained (Epstein 1999). Their research on CSR was designed to bring about reforms in perceived inequalities thought to be inherent in capitalism (Jones 1980). Scholars in business schools' Management departments established the broader 'social issues in management' field that later spawned the more specialized area of business ethics.

There are both pro-market and anti-market approaches in the field (Capaldi 2013). The most influential criticism of pro-market thinking is known as 'stakeholder theory'. It maintains that the corporate executive's job is to balance the needs and desires of various corporate constituencies (Donaldson and Preston 1995). This so-called theory has its roots in the classic Berle and Means (1932[1991]) argument that, with the separation of ownership and control, managers were no longer beholden to 'owner' control. This led to the question to whom firms were ultimately responsible.

SOCIAL INSTITUTIONS

Let us begin by denying that 'social' institutions reflect a supernatural order (otherwise they would require theological analysis), and by denying that they reflect an objective natural order (as understood by classical and medieval thinkers who subscribed to a teleological understanding of the universe). Social institutions are an example of 'spontaneous' order as articulated by Hayek (1945) (i.e. unplanned origin, historically evolving, without a telos, and incapable of being modelled either mechanically or organically). As such, social institutions cannot be studied scientifically in the sense that they do not have structures that can be understood independently of the meaning that participants give to them (Dilthey (2010), see discussion of *Geisteswissenschaften*; Weber (1904[1949]), see *Verstehen*). The notion of planning a 'social' institution is illusory. Any imposed plan (and any law) will have unintended and sometimes unpredictable consequences.

In what follows, research implications are designated by 'R' followed by a number.

R_1 It is not possible to research universal timeless truths about corporations. Research must focus on context and settle at best for highly qualified generalizations. How then are we to judge or evaluate the performance of a social institution and how are we thereby to make sense of the notion of 'improving' performance? We do so through explication. 'Explication' is the clarification of what is routinely taken for granted, namely our ordinary understanding of our practices, in the hope of extracting from our previous practice a set of norms that can be used reflectively to guide future practice (Wittgenstein (1969), Ryle (1949), see distinction between 'knowing how' and 'knowing that'; Oakeshott (1991), see essay on 'Rationalism in politics'). Explication is a way of arriving at a kind of practical knowledge that takes human agency as primary. It seeks to mediate practice from within practice itself. Explication is a form of practical knowledge and presupposes that practical knowledge is more fundamental than theoretical knowledge. Explication presupposes that efficient practice precedes the theory of it. All reflection is ultimately reflection on primordial practices that existed prior to our reflecting on them.

R_2 Research on CSR can only explicate the current norms in a specific context. Taking 'social' in the broadest possible way, norms can be understood as either legal or non-legal (ethical).

R_3 'Advocacy' of what those norms should be in evolving and novel contexts is not a form of research (i.e., not descriptive) but a normative activity. There is nothing inherently illegitimate about advocacy or normative activity. But it is intellectually dishonest to present this as 'research'. To what extent do activist organizations (e.g., Greenpeace, etc.) misrepresent the facts and to what extent is advocacy a mask for a private political agenda? The same questions can be asked of organizations that critique activist organizations.

Any present norm can be challenged but only by reference to another previously agreed-upon norm. Unfortunately, we live in an irredeemably morally pluralistic world. This is not only true of different cultures but within cultures themselves. Research can reveal or uncover what norms are held and by whom but not what the norms should be.

It is widely recognized that there are significant substantive ethical disagreements. These disagreements are not resolvable through sound rational argument. Many of these disagreements depend upon different fundamental metaphysical commitments. Even when there is agreement on metaphysical foundations, there are disagreements on different rankings of the good. Even here, however, resolution of these disagreements is not possible without begging the question, arguing in a circle, or engaging in infinite regress. We cannot appeal to consequences without knowing how to rank the impact of different approaches with regard to different ethical interests (liberty, equality, prosperity, security, etc.). Nor can we appeal to preference satisfaction unless one already grants how one will correct preferences, compare rational versus impassioned preferences, and calculate the discount rate for preferences over time. Appealing to disinterested observers, hypothetical choosers, or hypothetical contractors will not help because if such decision makers are truly disinterested, they will choose nothing. In order to choose, one must already have a particular moral sense or thin theory of the good. Intuitions will always be met with contrary intuitions. Any balancing of claims can be countered with a different approach to achieving a balance.

R_4 To the extent that we engage in normative activity we must show the extent to which any suggested future permutation is consistent and coherent with past practice. Past practice (R_1) does not entail future practice. The past practice may reflect not only the norms of previous corporate practice but the norms of more encompassing social practices if there are any. Random analogies to other social practices are misguided unless the advocate can persuade us that the other practice(s) are not random but part of a larger social narrative. Identifying a practice and a larger social context is, intellectually speaking, a philosophical activity and not the result of empirical research.

THE CORPORATION

The following philosophical account is a reflection on Anglo-American business practice of the last two centuries. How this relates to other cultural contexts will be addressed below.

Understood legally, a 'corporation' is a discrete entity established either by legislation or through legal registration. Corporations have rights and responsibilities distinct from those of their members. Corporations can engage in activities as enumerated in their charter either as profit-seeking businesses or as not-for-profit entities. As profit-seeking commercial enterprises, corporations ('company' in British Commonwealth Countries) have investors ('shareholders' are one example of investors) whose liability is limited to their investment. Investors typically elect or appoint a board of directors to control the corporation in a fiduciary capacity. Limited liability is not unique to corporations but can be found in other legal entities such as limited partnerships. In addition to providing economies of scale, corporations function to bring together entrepreneurs (who lack capital) with investors (not able/willing to be entrepreneurs themselves).

CORPORATIONS IN THE LARGER SOCIAL CONTEXT

How are we to understand contemporary business enterprises and their relationship to other social institutions?

Typically, researchers view CSR either as a form of value creation (sustainable business model), risk-management, or philanthropy. While all of these perspectives are useful, we maintain that these perspectives merely focus on the fact that corporations do in fact impact other social institutions. Might corporations have a positive obligation to transform other social institutions?

> Rather than assume that corporations only have an obligation to conform to the present structure and meaning of social institutions might they be obliged to ask if those institutions as presently constituted are fit participants in a global economy?

What follows is a larger thesis about the role of firms in a market economy in the world in which we live (Shamir 2011; Capaldi 2004, 2013).

$$TP \to ME \to LG \to RL \to PA$$

Since the Renaissance, the Western world has adopted the technological project. The 'technological project' (TP) is the program articulated by Descartes in the *Discourse on Method* (2004 [1637]), namely that what we seek is to make ourselves the 'masters and possessors of nature'. Instead of the classical view that nature is an organic process to which we must conform, Descartes proclaimed the modern vision of controlling nature for human benefit.

The TP has had four important consequences: first, remarkable technological advantages (military and commercial) have been achieved; second, those advantages have enabled initial subscribers to the project (Western Europe and American) to dominate the entire globe. Subsequently, the rest of the world has largely come to embrace the project. This is the origin of globalization. It is 'the' fact with which all theorists must come to terms. Third, we have largely progressed from seeing the economy as zero-sum to viewing it in terms of growth (IMF, WTO, World Bank, free trade agreements, etc.). Finally, we have seen a growing emphasis on innovation.

R_5 The implicit norms of the TP are that human beings strive to live longer, healthier, more prosperous lives and with greater personal freedom, to all of which there are no, as yet, apparent theoretical limits. With regard to this set of interlocking norms, I maintain the following:

1. My account is a philosophical explication. I do not claim that everyone does or would accept this explication, but then they are required to provide a rival explication.
2. There may be rival explications, as opposed to carping complaints, but my explication is compatible with people choosing to live side by side and pursuing rival lives precisely because my set of norms provides for limited government with the rule of law in a culture that respects personal autonomy.
3. I further claim that the consequences of the TP (longevity, health, prosperity, and individual freedom) are irresistible and over time will become the dominant norms for the foreseeable future (empirical claim/prediction). If there are other and non-economic values how do they relate to the aforementioned economic goods (longevity, individual freedom, etc.)? Can one prioritize these values or are they precisely the ones that reflect individual choices? In the evaluation of any present or suggested future policy on the part of corporations, one must show three things:

a. Does the policy work to achieve one or more of the agreed-upon goals or norms?
b. Is this the only way to achieve the norm?
c. Does the policy conflict with other norms?

The TP has created three distinct sets of problems each of which is subject to research:

1. R_6 Environmental impact (sustainability): How effective are the laws on environmental impact? As in the case of all laws, are any of them counter-productive? (Sunstein 1997). To what extent, if any, does the TP do irreversible (that is, cannot be overcome by present and future developments of the TP) damage to the planet Earth? What is meant by 'damage'? To what extent is the environment of humanity limited to the planet Earth? (Simon 1996). The TP has created products of extraordinary complexity and potentially dangerous consequences if misused. To what extent are these problems best handled by demanding more of the producer and to what extent do we need an additional focus on 'consumer responsibility'?
2. R_7 Globalization: To what extent and why is it (a) rejected/resisted; (b) resented; and (c) the basis of national reform?
3. 'Inequality'[1]: The TP has transcended if not dramatically altered the socio-economic picture of the pre-industrial world and exclusively resource-based economies. It has led to dramatic improvements in longevity, quality of life, and prosperity, but this improvement has been more rapid for some than for others. For subscribers to globalization and TP, and on the assumption that growth is not zero-sum, the questions are:

    R_8 Is 'inequality' per se objectionable? To whom? Why? How does this relate to R_7 (a) and (b)? Is it the case that present 'more-haves' have permanently prevented or are actively discouraging present 'less-haves' from improving, catching up, or exceeding the achievements of the 'more-haves'?

    R_9 What legal policies and social practices increase or decrease the rate of improvement or opportunities for improvement? Such studies would have to be national, regional, or cultural specific.

The 'market economy' (no central allocation of resources): since 1989, the implosion of the Soviet Union and the end of the Cold War, it is now asserted almost everywhere that a market economy is the most efficient method for engaging in the TP.

The ME within the TP as Schumpeter rightly observed is a form of creative destruction. Everything changes: new personae (leader, entrepreneur, manager, director, marketer, accountant, financier, investor, employee, union, in-house counsel, etc.), new forms of property (e.g., intellectual property), new forms of corporate governance (bureaucracy, contract, collective bargaining vs right to work, etc.), and new forms of social relationship (families where more than one person works full-time). It is this more than anything else that has raised the question of corporate social responsibility.

R_{10} Are we researching the right questions?[2] What conceptual changes are required in light of creative destruction? Does it any longer make sense to talk about owners as opposed to investors? In light of the foregoing, does it any longer make sense to conceptualize issues in terms of a debate between shareholders and stakeholders as opposed to a director-centric model of the corporation? What board composition improves productivity? Do corporations have constituencies or a set of overlapping contractual arrangements? Given mergers, acquisitions, and start-ups, what is the shelf life of a corporation? Are unions and collective bargaining giving way to mobile contract oriented personnel? What personnel problems are created by multi-national corporations?

Given the TP and its accompanying requirement of constant innovation, are not corporations constrained to prioritize the production of profitable products or services (much clearer than simply talking about 'profit')? Given the potential for infinite growth, are we not forced to conceptualize issues about resource allocation in terms of cost-benefit analysis? (Porter and Kramer 2006). What effect has benchmarking had? Does benchmarking remove competitive advantage?

What is the most effective way within a company to address social issues (e.g., ethics officer, ethics-training, public relations, risk-management)? To what extent is CSR a collective action problem that requires co-ordination within an industry, particularly local (e.g., chamber of commerce), or among businesses? (Olson 1965; Maitland 1985). Is CSR a one-way transfer of corporate resources to non-profits or should corporate leaders be encouraged to suggest/implement the reorganization of other institutions including universities? Should universities be reorganized as businesses? Do so-called non-profits have special or unique social obligations?

Given the enormous impact on all other social institutions (e.g., family, education, etc.) what changes in resource allocation are required in marketing, recruitment, and retention of employees? In a global economy, what community (local, national, international) are we talking about and what does 'community' now mean? Is it right for citizens in country X to encourage citizens of country Y to invest in country X as opposed to investing nationally in country Y? Does the previous question make sense in a global market economy? Does it make sense to put the emphasis on what companies 'owe' to the community when different communities, including nation-states, vie with each other to give special economic incentives in order to convince companies to relocate to their geographical locale?

A market economy flourishes best under 'limited government', that is, legitimated by election, restricted to security, and enhancing a market economy through a legal system that enforces contracts and resolves disputes. The most important limitation on government is the 'rule of law', here understood generically as procedural restraints on all government officials and actions. We believe that it is important to recognize the distinction (Oakeshott 1975) between states that are enterprise associations (have a collective goal) and states that are civil associations (no collective goal and the state provides the context for individuals to pursue their private goals).

R_{11} What is the right size of the political state in a global economy? We have seen the evolving nature of the political state in light of the TP and the ME (e.g., dissolution of old states, creation of new states, and new associations of states, e.g., the EU). To what extent would redrawing state boundaries increase economic productivity and/

or decrease ethnic tension (e.g., should Catalonia be allowed independence or secession)? Do states in the modern global economy have to have contiguous boundaries? Is there a one-size-fits-all model or are there independent variables? To what extent are some states client states of other states? Which political model enhances economic growth – the civil association or the enterprise association? Should corporations consider themselves solely and ultimately responsible to national governments or is their responsibility to a larger conception of community an overriding one?

How are we to conceptualize the 'social' role of nation-states? Should corporations evaluate themselves in a mercantilist fashion or in global terms? Is it possible to identify a collective common good for all mankind (global telos) in terms of which we can measure the contribution of specific social entities including corporations? Hayek's (1945) critique of equilibrium and social justice as well as Schumpeter's (1943) conception of creative destruction would seem to point otherwise. Until someone clearly identifies the whole of which corporations are a part it is not clear what is being measured.

What are the effects on emigration and immigration? How effective are economic aid or loans when given from one state or national entity to another? (Easterly 2006). How effective are the WTO, IMG, World Bank, and so on at promoting economic growth? Which form of aid has been more effective: state to state or wholly private? Do former colonial powers owe reparations to former colonies? Should former colonies be asked to reimburse their former colonial rulers for the R&D costs of all the medical and technological advances the latter have created and exported? That is, to what extent were former colonies 'exploited' or net 'beneficiaries' of colonialism? Is it better for former colonial powers to engage in paternalism (e.g., World Bank, etc.) or embrace a 'sink or swim' attitude? Should we create and examine the category of 'national global responsibility' for countries that fail to repay loans, manipulate their currencies, borrow more than they can possibly repay?

To what extent is the Continental EU less/more productive because it still retains the vestiges of an enterprise association in the form of a corporatism of the state, business, and labour? (Mazzucato 2013). How well do states that are civil associations handle social issues as opposed to enterprise associations? What are the effects of international trade agreements? How effective have non-governmental organizations been in addressing economic and social issues? Which legal tradition is more commerce friendly, the Anglo-American case law tradition or the more widespread Continental model with its emphasis on law as legislation? How does this impact civil and criminal law? Is there convergence?

Within each state we may want to research the role, nature, extent, and effectiveness of 'regulatory' agencies (Armstrong and Green 2013). What is the nature, cause, and consequences of corruption? We acknowledge that there is individual corruption and government corruption, but is there such a thing as a 'corrupt culture'? How important is respect for intellectual property? Should industrial espionage and cyber-theft be criminalized?

The final piece of the narrative is the rise of 'individual or personal autonomy'. Economically, this is seen in the growing importance of the entrepreneur. Politically and legally it is seen in the increasing importance attributed to individual rights. Socially this is seen in the emancipation of women. Increasingly, it is taken for granted that individuals choose their profession, their place of habitation, and their spouse. This is part of what Schumpeter meant by 'Creative Destruction'.

Up until now we have largely relied on the Anglo-American framework in our discussion.

R_{12} Are there alternative frameworks (e.g., so-called Rhine model or the East-Asian model)? (Williams and Aguilera 2008). Is there growing convergence or a healthy/unhealthy competition? How might the role of the corporations be viewed differently in different frameworks? Will dominance reflect success with the TP? Is competition more consistent with TP?

R_{13} What are the metrics for making comparisons?

R_{14} To what extent does past and present research reflect political agendas or unacknowledged parochial perspectives?

R_{15} Which cultures, subcultures, and so on are better adapted for TP, ME, LG, RL, PA? Which cultures are more effective: those that promote private philanthropy social entrepreneurship as opposed to those which promote mandatory action on the part of businesses per se?

NOTES

1. 'Inequality' is not understood here as the opposite of 'equality'. The onus is on advocates of 'equality' to explain what kind of equality they are advocating, why, and what kind of research agenda if any could support their advocacy.
2. This could be researched in part by a poll (of academics? corporate executives? etc.) and by a literature review.

REFERENCES

Armstrong, J. and K. Green (2013), 'Effects of corporate social responsibility and irresponsibility policies', *Journal of Business Research*, **66** (10), 1922–1927.
Berle, Adolf Augustus and Gardiner Coit Means (1932[1991]), *The Modern Corporation and Private Property*, revised ed., New Brunswick: Transaction Publishers.
Capaldi, N. (2004), 'The ethical foundations of free market societies', *The Journal of Private Enterprise*, **XX** (1), 30–54.
Capaldi, N. (2013), 'Pro-market vs. anti-market approaches to business ethics', in Christoph Luetge (ed.) *Handbook of the Philosophical Foundations of Business Ethics*, The Netherlands: Springer, pp. 1223–1238.
Descartes, R. (2004) [1637], *A Discourse on Method: Meditations and Principles*. Translated by Veitch, John. London: Orion Publishing Group.
Dilthey, William (2010), *Understanding the Human World: Selected Works of Wilhelm Dilthey*, ed. Rudolf A. Makkreel and Frithjof Rodi, vol. II, NJ: Princeton University Press.
Donaldson, T. and L.E. Preston (1995), 'The stakeholder theory of the corporation: concepts, evidence, implications', *Academy of Management Review*, **20**, 65–91.
Easterly, William R. (2006), *The White Man's Burden*, London: Penguin.
Epstein, E.M. (1999), 'The continuing quest for accountable, ethical, and humane corporate capitalism', *Business & Society*, **38**, 253–267.
Hayek, F.A. (1945), 'The use of knowledge in society', *The American Economic Review*, **35** (4), 519–530.
Jones, T.M. (1980), 'Corporate social responsibility revisited, redefined', *California Management Review*, **22** (3), 59–67.
Maitland, I. (1985), 'The limits of business self-regulation', *California Management Review*, **27** (3), 132–147.

Mazzucato, Mariana (2013), *The Entrepreneurial State: Debunking the Public vs. Private Myth in Risk and Innovation*, London: Anthem.
Oakeshott, Michael (1975), 'The vocabulary of a modern European state', *Political Studies*, **23** (2–3), 319–341.
Oakeshott, Michael (1991), *Rationalism in Politics and Other Essays*, Indianapolis: Liberty Fund.
Olson, Mancur (1965), *The Logic of Collective Action: Public Goods and the Theory of Collective Action*, Cambridge, MA: Harvard.
Porter, M. and M. Kramer (2006), 'Strategy and society: the link between competitive advantage and corporate social responsibility', *Harvard Business Review*, **84** (12), 78–92.
Ryle, Gilbert (1949), *Concept of Mind*, London: Hutchinson.
Schumpeter, J. (1943), *Capitalism, Socialism and Democracy*, London: Allen and Unwin, Chapter 7.
Shamir, R. (2011), 'Socially responsible private regulation: world-culture or world-capitalism?', *Law & Society Review*, **45** (2), 313–336.
Simon, J. (1996), 'Can the supply of natural resources be infinite?', in Julian L. Simon (ed.) *Ultimate Resource 2*, Princeton: Princeton University Press, pp. 54–69.
Sunstein, C.R. (1997), 'Paradoxes of the regulatory state', in Cass R. Sunstein (ed.) *Free Markets and Social Justice*, Oxford: Oxford University Press, pp. 271–289.
Weber, Max (1904[1949]), 'Objectivity in social science and social policy', in E.A. Shils and H.A. Finch (eds) *The Methodology of the Social Sciences*, New York: Free Press, pp. 50–112.
Williams, C.A. and R.V. Aguilera (2008), 'Corporate social responsibility in a comparative perspective', in Andrew Crane, Abagail McWilliams, Dirk Matten, Jeremy Moon and Donald S. Siegel (eds) *The Oxford Handbook of Corporate Social Responsibility*, Oxford: Oxford University Press, pp. 452–472.
Wittgenstein, Ludwig (1969), *On Certainty*, Oxford: Blackwell.

26. Beyond strategic CSR: the concept of responsibility as the foundation of ethics – political, technological and economic responsibility for the future of humanity
Jacob Dahl Rendtorff

INTRODUCTION

In this chapter, I would like to argue that the future research agenda in corporate social responsibility (CSR) will move beyond strategic responsibility and become a major ethical concern at all levels of society. The chapter will demonstrate the importance of the concept of responsibility as the foundation of ethics in particular in the fields of politics and economics in the modern civilization marked by globalization and technological progress. I consider that the concept of responsibility in the future will be the key notion in order to understand the ethical duty in a modern technological civilization. We can indeed observe a moralization of the concept of responsibility going beyond a strict legal definition in terms of imputability. Moreover, this implies that corporate responsibility cannot solely be defined strategically in terms of profits or shared values. In my work on corporate social responsibility and business ethics, I have tried to demonstrate this point at several occasions in books (Rendtorff 2007; Rendtorff 2009) and presentations, working papers and articles that contain previous developments of my ideas for this chapter (Rendtorff 2016).

The chapter begins by discussing the humanistic foundations of such a concept of responsibility. It looks at the historical origins of responsibility and it relates this concept to the concept of accountability. On the basis of this historical determination of the concept I would like to present the definition of the concept of responsibility as a fundamental ethical principle that has increasing importance as the foundation of the principles of governance in modern welfare states. In this context the chapter discusses the extension of the concept of responsibility towards institutional or corporate ethical responsibility where responsibility does not only concern the responsibility of individuals but also deals with the responsibility of institutional collectivities. In this way the chapter is based on the following structure: (1) the ethical foundation of the concept of responsibility, (2) towards global ethics: Technological, political and economic responsibility and (3) conclusion and discussion.

ETHICAL FOUNDATION OF THE CONCEPT OF RESPONSIBILITY

In his important book, *Betrachtungen über das Eine*, the well-known Japanese philosopher Tomonobo Imamichi discusses the origins of the concept of responsibility in order to lay the foundations of a modern humanism (Imamichi 1968). He presents the problem of responsibility as a central problem for ethics. In Western thought there was not really a discussion of the concept of responsibility before modernity. Imamichi makes research into the close relation between person and responsibility. He argues that historically there was not really a close relation between the two concepts. Even though the thought of Socrates and Seneca did contain the fact of its implication there was not really a clear notion defining responsibility in the classical world (Imamichi 1968, p. 31). The adjective 'responsible' can only be found in the 13th century in French and in the 14th century in English. The concept of responsibility is only found in French in 1787 and later in English. In German we can only find '*Verantwortlichkeit*' at the end of the 19th century. In the work of John Stuart Mill, responsibility means 'Accountability'. In the 19th century, the concept is closely linked with the social contract. Accordingly, Professor Imamichi concludes that in the Western world we can find a reflection about the human person, but we cannot say that there was profound philosophical reflection on the concept of responsibility.

On the contrary, in the oriental and Eastern thought there was not really a reflection about the concept of the person, but the concept of responsibility is central to the philosophy of Confucius (Imamichi 1968, p. 32). In his philosophy, responsibility manifests itself as a fundamental virtue. Responsibility is a part of inter-individuality ('*l'inter-individualität*'). The five virtues in Confucius's philosophy are 'love, responsibility, ethical habit, intelligence and devotion'. Not to act with responsibility implies the loss of human dignity and man is acting like an animal. With this we can nearly say that the concept of responsibility becomes the most important concept in human dignity and in the respect for the human person in the humanistic philosophy.

In fact, a philosopher, who was very close to this position, was Pico della Mirandola, who also treated the problem of the risk of losing human dignity. In the philosophy of Pico, the most important aspect of human existence is human freedom (Pico 1955, p. 4). According to him, freedom signifies that Man can raise himself to the divine and that he can lose his dignity so he reaches the level of the animals. Accordingly, we can say that the attribution of moral subjectivity is linked to freedom. Later, in the philosophy of Kant, we find a similar analysis of the relation between freedom, imputability (*imputatio moralis*) and human dignity that is the foundation of the Kantian morality (Kant 1979, p. 61). According to Kant, the degrees of responsibility depend on the level of human freedom. However, following Imamichi, we can argue that Kant has very well developed a notion of the human person that is based on rather a legal notion of responsibility as a position of attribution of action without having a focus on the moral dimension of this concept.

In his semantic analysis of the concept of responsibility, Paul Ricœur gives us the foundations for understanding this juridical limitation of the concept in classical civil law. The concept refers to the obligation to repair damage because one has made a fault (Ricœur 1995, p. 41). In penal law the concept refers to the obligation to accept punishment. Ricœur reminds us that 'impute' signifies the attribution to someone of the blame for an action and the attribution to them of the corresponding punishment. In this classical juridical sense responsibility signifies retribution and attribution of an action to a person (Ricœur 1995, p. 44). Imputation means that ignorance does not excuse and that the person can be seen as the agent of an action. Accordingly, in this sense responsibility means '*zurechnen*' and 'Accountability'. Ricœur emphasizes that the legal sense of 'imputation' goes back to the Kantian concept of freedom without causality in the sense that it is the free action of the agent that is at the origin of the attribution of imputation to a specific agent. In this sense it is possible to have a pure legal conception of responsibility that can be distinguished from a moral conception of responsibility. This is, for example, the case with legal positivism in the thought of Hans Kelsen, who only accepts the legal concept based on objective imputation as acceptable (Ricœur 1995, p. 51).

In fact, we can say that it is only with phenomenological philosophy that the concern for responsibility is fundamentally developed in modern Western thought. In modern phenomenology, responsibility is the very significance of freedom. Therefore, it is possible to demonstrate the development of an ethical notion of responsibility that is very far from the legal concept of responsibility. In this phenomenological approach to responsibility, we can observe a reintroduction of the theme of 'inter-individuality' proposed by Professor Imamichi in his analysis of the Confucianist virtues.

In the phenomenology of responsibility in the thought of Sartre and Levinas, we find the project of being engaged in world and the concern for the other as fundamental concepts of responsibility. The two phenomenological philosophers can help us in understanding the space and the frame for the ethical reflection concerning responsibility. The concept of responsibility is for both of the philosophers situated at the fundamental level of phenomenological ontology.

In *L'Etre et le Néant*, Sartre defines humanity or human reality as freedom: '*L'homme ne saurait tantôt libre et tantôt esclave. Il est tout entier et toujours libre ou il n'est pas*' (Sartre 1943, p. 463). In this way, Sartre indicates that there is a fundamental relation between freedom as liberty and negation and responsibility. Even though he uses the common sense of responsibility (as to be contentious, to be the non-contestable author of an event or an object) (Sartre 1943, p. 639), Sartre emphasizes that the original choice of human beings as project implies an absolute responsibility. In *L'Etre et le Néant*, Sartre puts emphasis on this ontological responsibility and he emphasizes that the self chooses freely and authentically the project in relation to the project of existence. When I chose myself, I chose the world as such and I chose myself as responsible for the world as I have chosen it.

Sartre continues with a moralization of the ontological concept of responsibility in *L'Existentialisme est un humanisme*. He says that the engagement of freedom cannot be limited to subjective interiority, but that the freedom of being responsible for the way it has chosen to make explicit the sense of the world is also responsible for the other and in this way for the whole of humanity. Sartre says with his strong formulations about responsibility: '*Elle engage l'humanité entière*' (Sartre 1946, p. 26). '*Ainsi je suis responsable pour moi-même et pour tous, et je crée une certaine image de l'homme que je choisis; en me choisissant, je choisi l'homme*' (Sartre 1946, p. 27). Accordingly, for Sartre the responsibility becomes total responsibility: '*Cela signifie ceci: l'homme qui s'engage et qui se rend compte qu'il est non seulement celui qu'il choisit d'être mais encore un législateur choisissant en même temps que soi l'humanité entière, ne saurait échapper au sentiment de sa totale et profonde responsabilité*' (Sartre 1946, p. 27).

Accordingly, for Sartre, the existential choice implies an absolute responsibility, a freedom that one sets the values and the norm of good and evil oneself. To choose is to affirm the value that one has chosen. This is why we can never chose evil as such. According to this interpretation the authentic choice implies the choice of the freedom of the other. In the authentic choice I assume my responsibility for the freedom of the other. I cannot choose to dominate the other, but I have to choose to respect his or her liberty.

According to Levinas in *Totalité et infini: Essai sur l'extériorité*, the fundamental responsibility for the other manifests itself in the break with the metaphysics of identity (Levinas 1961). Levinas moves from ontology towards ethics that he considers as primordial philosophy. In this primary philosophy absolute responsibility for the other human being becomes a fundamental fact of life. Levinas considers traditional metaphysics as a movement from being as essence and massivity towards the other that is expressed in the indefinite conception of the infinite in the face of the other. According to Levinas, responsibility is something that imposes itself on the self with the view of the face of the other. Levinas says that one is *'ligoté'*, *'otage d'autrui'* – slave of the other – when one has been confronted with the infiniteness of the demand of the other in the face of the other. With the phenomenology of the face, Levinas shows us how the ethical demand is concretely manifested in human life (Levinas 1961).

This constitutes the foundation of the conception of Levinas of ethics as primary philosophy, which emphasizes the infinite responsibility for the other as fundamental for the realization of the self in the relation with the other and with the world. The desire for the infinite of the self cannot be satisfied if it becomes a possibility for the other that helps to break with the immanence of the self.

I can only become myself in the meeting of the other who limits my activities. As a consequence, the realization of the ethical demand is a presupposition for becoming oneself. The exteriority of the other in relation to the self is a condition for the possibility of the self to become oneself as an ethical being (Levinas 1961, 1991, p. 28). It is the other that I meet as a limit and an opening in relation to the infinite that is the foundation of the universal ethical responsibility of human beings.

Apart from the differences of ontologies, Levinas and Sartre share an absolute conception of responsibility as important for human dignity in inter-individuality. But the foundation of this conception is very different in the thought of the two philosophers. For Sartre, the ability of the freedom of the individual for choosing life and existence is central for the ethical concern for the other, while for Levinas it is the existence of the other as such that gives us the foundation of the absolute responsibility of human beings.

With this foundation of ethical responsibility, we see that research in CSR in the future must move beyond pure legal or strategic concepts of responsibility in order to take its point of departure in this fundamental ethical significance of responsibility where responsibility expresses an existential relation of human beings to the world. In order to be important research and practice on CSR must have this ethical significance of the infinite character of responsibility in mind as the foundation of responsibility in private and public organizations.

TOWARDS GLOBAL ETHICS: TECHNOLOGICAL, POLITICAL AND ECONOMIC RESPONSIBILITY

However, even though Sartre and Levinas are aware of the infinite character of the concept of responsibility they do not really develop this concept to give it a significance that can be a basis for technological ethics. It is only with the German philosopher Hans Jonas that we can reach such a conception of responsibility. In his book *Prinzip Verantwortung. Versuch einer Ethik der technischen Zivilisation* (1979), Jonas has defended a global and metaphysical conception of responsibility. He proposes the argument that the technological and scientific development implies a need for increased responsibility for humanity that is much greater than at other times in the history of humanity (Jonas 1979, p. 15). Because the technological and scientific civilization has so much power to destroy the globe, the responsibility of humanity has become even more great (Jonas 1979, p. 31). This dimension of responsibility is essential for understanding the future of CSR research. We must focus on the importance of responsibility for the future of humanity. There is a close connection between social responsibility and environmental responsibility for future sustainability of the Earth.

Technological Responsibility and Sustainable Development

Accordingly, Hans Jonas proposes an important foundation of bioethics and ethics of science in relation to technological civilization with his new formulation of the categorical imperative as an imperative to ensure existence of human beings forever on Earth: 'Act in this way that there will always be authentic human life on earth' (Jonas 1979, p. 36). This implies an extenuation of the concept of responsibility that concerns not only the present in time and space but also in particular in relation to the future including future human beings as well as animals and the integrity of nature and the biosphere in its totality. Instead of the dominant technological optimism, Jonas proposes a heuristics of fear in relation to the technological and scientific progress (Jonas 1979, p. 392). One can say that Jonas makes an integration of the concern for the weak and fragile important in order to develop a foundation of responsible human action in relation to the future. Indeed, in times of climate change, global poverty and concern for the future of humanity this becomes an important dimension of responsibility.

The work on the concept of sustainable development in international politics can be considered in this perspective (Elkington 1997). Here, responsibility for the future of humanity becomes an essential element of social and political action. This dimension of responsibility will be important in the future since CSR and social responsibility is not only focused on individuals but indeed on the future of human existence on the planet.

In international politics, the work on sustainable development can be considered in this perspective. The world commission on the environment, the 1987 Brundtland Commission, defined the concept of sustainable development as the fundamental aim of the international community (World Commission 1987). Sustainable development is defined as the respectful use of natural resources with the aim of respecting the good life conditions for future generations on Earth. We will have to ensure that future human beings can have the same or better life conditions than present generations. In this sense, sustainable development has since 1987 been a very important concept for the international community.

We can in particular mention the close link between economic, social and environmental development that is expressed in the idea of 'the triple bottom-line'. According to which a corporation or an organization does not only search to deal with its profits and economic gains, but also to include its influence on the environment and its social relations with the employees, with the local community and with the government in the evaluation of its economic success and of the general economic wealth of the organization (Elkington 1999). In this context, it is the general intention of the concept of sustainable development to integrate the social, economic and environmental concerns in a general policy of responsibility for sustainable development in the world.

Political Responsibility in the Welfare State

With the thought of Hans Jonas following the phenomenological concept of responsibility by Sartre and by Levinas and with its application to the concept of sustainable development in international politics we face a change and a radicalization of the reach of the concept of responsibility. We can say that we are not only responsible in the strict legal sense of attribution and imputation of an action. Responsibility is not only based on the fault or on an action that is not justifiable and punishment is not sufficient as retribution. Our responsibility is much more heavy. We are responsible for the survival of humanity in all our actions (Ricœur 1994, Ricœur 1990, p. 270). This development of the concept of responsibility can also be shown in the context of the modern welfare state.

On the basis of this change Ricœur has emphasized that we should rethink the semantic and juridical content of the concept of responsibility (Ricœur 1994). Even though the strict legal significance still exists, Ricœur makes the point that the meaning of responsibility has changed a lot with the thought of Levinas and Jonas where we move beyond the strict obligation of being submitted to punishment. It is time to propose a new conceptualization of the concept of responsibility within the politics of the welfare state. Ricœur reminds us that the project of philosophical and legal positivism was to demoralize the attribution of responsibility to the individual. However, with the ethical notions of responsibility this project was destroyed and we are facing a new moralization of the concept of responsibility. Today we can talk of the emergence of a responsibility without fault (Ricœur 1995, p. 45).

The strict legal responsibility opens for a much larger social responsibility. This is important for the future of research in CSR. The conceptions of vulnerable human beings of Levinas and of the fragile and suffering agent by Ricœur can help us to understand the anthropological foundations of this concept of responsibility. It is the responsibility for the other human being and for the future generations that we find again in law. This change is also present in the legal development of the notion of the protection of the human person not only in penal law but also in health law. François Ewald shows in his book *Histoire de l'Etat Providence. Les origines de la solidarité* how the emergent welfare society compensates risks of labour accidents, disease and health risk and social problems by developing strong systems of insurance of work and health insurance based on collective systems of treatment and responsibility that oblige corporations and society to offer compensation for the poor and vulnerable (Ewald 1986).

We can say that we face a concept of law that goes beyond the contract of the individual liberal responsibility that is based on principles of community and solidarity (Delmas-Marty 1995). This state responsibility implies an interpretation of sustainable development and of the heuristics of fear where the respect for autonomy, dignity, integrity and vulnerability in the framework of responsibility is determined as the framework of the scientific and technological development of a society of protection of future generations (Rendtorff and Kemp 2000). In this way, we can observe a collective responsibility that goes beyond the singular responsibility of individuals and we face a development of this responsibility beyond the nation state towards common responsibility in the international sphere of cosmopolitan community (Rendtorff 2009).

Accordingly, future research in CSR must include not only individual engagement in universal responsibility and future-directed focus on sustainability and sustainable develoopment, but it also moves beyond focus on private corporations to include states and public organizations, institutions and administrations. Social responsibility is not only limited to the private sector but it also includes the public sector and different organizations and institutions in the public sector. Ethical responsibility should be central to public management and governance.

Corporate Social Responsibility as Institutional Accountability

The debate about the social responsibility of the corporation as based on ethical responsibility for the future of humanity also manifests an indication of a change of the concept of responsibility going beyond a strict legal definition in terms of attribution of action to the individual. Here we face an institutional attribution of responsibility to a corporation (Rendtorff 2007, 2009). In addition, this responsibility is proposed as a voluntary and moral responsibility that goes beyond the positive responsibility by law. A responsible action is in this sense a free and voluntary act. In the future this idea of voluntary responsibility will be more important in the sense that ethical responsibility, based on values and personal consciousness, is much stronger as a binding responsibility. This is the case of the politics of the European Union and in the principles of the Global Compact of the United Nations where voluntary subscription to binding policies of CSR has been very strong. In this sense the social responsibility of the corporation includes the respect for sustainable development, nature and future generations in the sense that Paul Ricœur calls the 'good life with and for the other in just institutions' as a vision of the judgement and 'phronesis' of practical reason (Ricœur 1990, p. 202). So the institutionalization of ethical responsibility moves corporations and organizations well beyond the strategic ideas of CSR. Social responsibility is based on voluntary commitment to the ethical responsibility for the future of humanity.

The concept of CSR goes beyond the juridical concept of imputation and adds that the corporation is a political and moral actor that has to respond to its duty to live as a good citizen with respect for its collective duties. Lynn Sharp Paine from Harvard makes in the book *Value Shift: Why Companies Must Merge Social and Financial Imperative to Achieve Superior Performance* (2002) the argument that there is a change of values in the modern capitalist economy where we no longer consider the corporation as an instrument for profit maximization or as a fictive legal person, but as a responsible moral actor with its values and ethical principles (Paine 2002).

According to a famous article by Archie B. Carroll, who is a pioneer of the ethics and responsibility of the corporation, we would have to distinguish between (1) economic responsibility, (2) legal responsibility, (3) ethical responsibility, and (4) philanthropic responsibility (Carroll 1979; Capron and Quairel-Lanoizeelée 2004, p. 105; Crane and Matten 2004, p. 44).

This is the basis for what one according to the classical tradition of political philosophy can call the republican conception of the corporation as a good corporate citizen, which is not only concerned with economic profits but also takes an ethical position in relation to the political, social and ecological problems of its surroundings (Zadek 2006). This concept of CSR implies that the corporation does not only have to obey the law, but engage in a constructive manner for the social perfection of society.

In this moral sense, the concept of responsibility is linked to the power and capacity of the corporation to be imputable and take over its own action. The argument for taking into consideration the responsibility of the corporation is based on the realization of the enormous capacity and power of a large modern enterprise in a global context. In this context it is possible to distinguish between the institutional responsibility of the corporation, the responsibility of the directors and managers of the corporation and finally the responsibility of the employees of the corporation. The concept of the moral responsibility of the corporation goes further than a specific legal responsibility and includes a large number of responsibilities that are ethically defined in relation to the stakeholders of the corporation.

CONCLUSION AND DISCUSSION

The conclusion is that we can say that the virtue of responsibility has been liberated from its legal closure and that it has become important as the foundation of the discussion of the intersubjective relation, sustainable development, responsibility of science and technology and in relation to the politics of responsibility of the state in the economic life as an institutional responsibility for the common good in society. The future of CSR is demonstrated by the fact that the concept moves from strategic responsibility to ethical responsibility for the future of humanity. In this sense, CSR is not only something that happens in particular firms, but it moves beyond the economy towards the social and political dimensions of society.

It is the significance of the virtue of responsibility by Confucius that is important (Imamichi 1968, p. 32). With the virtues we go beyond a strict separation of morals and the system of actions. We can say that politics and economics have been dominated by a conception of governance as founded on technological rationality. Responsibility was not a governance virtue as such but rather a concept of professional responsibility and of vocation in the Weberian sense of responsibility of politics where responsibility was defined as objective neutrality. Moreover, responsibility is not defined in the sense of Milton Friedman and Michael Porter with his idea of shared value as a fidelity to the professional principles of the officers of the corporation. We can no longer restrict social responsibility to creating shared value where the social responsibility of the manager is to ensure profits for shareholders as well as it being the task of the union leader to fight for the interests of the members of the union.

Today and in the future, responsibility has moved beyond this selective and restrictive concept of responsibility, which is limited to the strategic dimension of responsibility. CSR is more than strategic thinking. It has become ethical responsibility for the good life in organizations.

An important aspect of the change of the meaning of the concept of responsibility is the emergence of the collective and institutional responsibility (Rendtorff 2007, 2009). Even if we are not dogmatic collectivists we can admit that responsibility without fault goes beyond the individuals and can be attributed to the public or private organizations or institutions without having a reference to a precise individual culpability. Ethical responsibility is a collective responsibility for the future of humanity that can be promoted by groups of individuals in common. With this collective dimension, we have found the link between the individual and institutional responsibility with regard to the assurance of the progress of humanity towards the common good of present and future generations.

Thus, we can document strong changes of the concept of responsibility with implications for future CSR research in the 21st century. CSR research does not have to justify itself on the basis of corporate strategic thinking since the agenda of CSR has moved to the forefront of ethical discussions of the future of humanity. CSR is not only about corporate action, but it is also about social responsibility in the whole of society by all the different institutions and organizations in society. CSR is not only a duty of law or a strategic concern, but it is a fundamental dimension of human ethical action for the future of sustainability on the planet.

REFERENCES

Capron, Michael and Françoise Quairel-Lanoizeelée (2004), *Mythes et réalités de l'entreprise responsable. Acteurs, Enjeux, Stratégies*, Paris: La Decouverte.
Carroll, Archie B. (1979), 'A three-dimensional conceptual model of corporate performance', *Academy of Management Review*, 4 (4), 497–505.
Crane, Andrew and Dirk Matten (2004), *Business Ethics*, Oxford, UK: Oxford University Press.
Delmas-Marty, Mireille (1995), *Pour un droit commun*, Paris: Editions du Seuil.
Elkington, John (1997, 1999), *Cannibals with Forks: The Triple Bottom Line of 21st Century Business*, Oxford: Capstone.
Ewald, François (1986), *Histoire de L'Etat Providence. Les origines de la solidarité*, Paris:Le Seuil.
Imamichi, Tomonobu A. (1968), *Betrachtungen über das Eine*, Tokio Universität, Japan: Institut der Ästhetik, Philosophische Fakultät.
Jonas, Hans (1979), *Das Prinzip Verantwortung: Versuch einer Ethik für die technologische Zivilisation*, Frankfurt/M.: Insel Verlag. Neuauflage als Suhrkamp Taschenbuch.
Kant, Immanuel (1979), *Lectures on Ethics*, trans. L. Infeld, London: Methuen.
Levinas, Emmanuel (1961, 1991), *Totalité et infini, Essai sur l'extériorité*, Den Haag : Martinus Nijhoff, 2nd Edition : 1991 : Paris: Le Livre de Poche.
Paine, Lynn Sharp (2002), *Value Shift: Why Companies Must Merge Social and Financial Imperative to Achieve Superior Performance*, New York, NY: McGraw-Hill.
Pico della Mirandola, G. (1955), 'Oration on the dignity of Man', in G.J. Miller and D. Carmichael (eds) *On the Dignity of Man, On Being and the One, Heptaplus*, trans. C.G. Wallis, P. W. Miller and D. Carmichael, Indiana: Hackett Publishing.
Rendtorff, Jacob Dahl (2007), *Virksomhedsetik. En grundbog i organisation og ansvar*, København: Samfundslitteratur.
Rendtorff, Jacob Dahl (2009), *Responsibility, Ethics and Legitimacy of Corporations*, Copenhagen: Copenhagen Business School Press.
Rendtorff, Jacob Dahl (2016), 'Responsibility as the Foundation of Ethics: Political, Technological and Economic Responsibility'. Revista do Programa de Pós-Graduação em Direito da Universidade Federal da Bahia, 26 (28), 23–38.
Rendtorff, Jacob Dahl and Peter Kemp (2000), *Basic Ethical Principles in European Bioethics and Biolaw*, Vols I–II, Copenhagen and Barcelona: Center for Ethics and Law.
Ricœur, Paul (1990), *Soi-même comme un Autre*, Paris: Le seuil.
Ricœur, Paul (1994), 'Le concept de responsabilité', in *Esprit*, Novembre 1994 / Les équivoques de la responsabilité *Esprit*.
Ricœur, Paul (1995), *Le Juste*, Paris: Editions Esprit.
Sartre, Jean-Paul (1943), *L'Etre et le Néant*, Paris: Gallimard.
Sartre, Jean-Paul (1946), *L'Existentialisme est un humanisme*, Paris: Nagel.
The World Commission on the Environment (1987), *Our Common Future*, New York: Oxford University Press.
Zadek, Simon (2006), *The Civil Corporation*, London: Earthscan.

27. From positivism to social constructivism: an emerging trend for CSR researchers
Martin Samy and Fiona Robertson

INTRODUCTION

In this chapter, the authors chart the history of corporate social responsibility (CSR) activities over the decades, review methods undertaken by researchers and discuss the direction for future research methods. The theme of this chapter is to develop an argument shifting from positivism to social constructivism in CSR research. In this journey the research design is arguably biased towards a phenomenological approach that encompasses abductive paradigms. We take a case study design as findings are considered situational and contemporary and would build a stronger argument for mimetic actions among corporations in our society.

Early research in CSR adopted the philosophical paradigms of positivism as a logical derivative to measuring the success of Social Responsibility activities. However, in the last decade, a new paradigm for CSR has emerged; a social constructivism approach advocates that corporations construct the extent of what is CSR; why they undertake CSR activities and how they should report. It is now recognized that CSR research cannot rely on positivist mainstream quantitative techniques which are too shallow to address its complexity, as they can rely on: too few variables; do not put studied phenomena in their proper context and natural setting; and ignore the human aspects, individual personalities, collective consciousness and roles that govern CSR practices. Particularly, Weick (2007, p. 14) correctly asserts, 'richness has power but we are not powerless to evoke it'.

Several academics argue that CSR theories have been developed without engaging with organizations that implement it, despite recognizing that the attitudes of participants and corporate culture are important to determining the extent of accountability discharged through CSR practices (Varenova et al. 2013, Adams and Larrinaga-González 2007). They therefore call for engagement research conducted inside organizations focusing on the micro/internal processes.

In all levels of academic research, it is essential to consider the different research philosophies or paradigms, in particular the parameters of ontology and epistemology, as they are essential in understanding the area of the research problem (Easterby-Smith et al. 2012, Flowers 2009). The philosophical position of an individual should be the guiding force in developing the methodology that suits the research problem. That guiding force is inherent in the mindset of the researcher and it is based on values and beliefs and most of the time is enveloped by their experiences and exposure to the real world. As Weick (1995) stated, as individuals we view the world through talk, discourse and conversation. The problem a researcher would have is when one fails to appreciate their own thinking of the problem and relies on the views of other writers without the element of critical thinking.

As shown in Figure 27.1, the researcher's thoughts are made up of values and beliefs

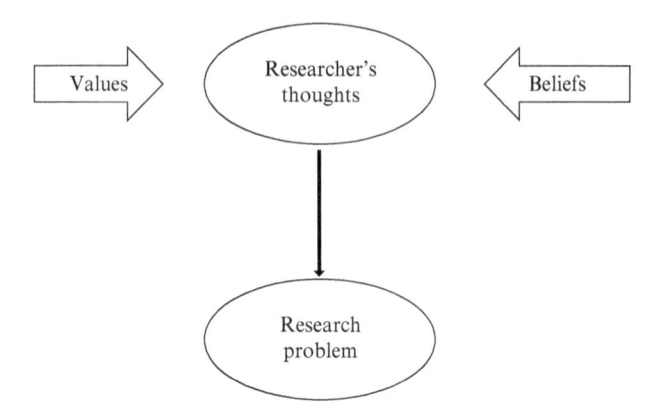

Figure 27.1   Mindset of the researcher

that construct the mindset of an individual who then formulates the problem(s) to be investigated. This development of the mind is essential to motivate and focus the researcher to undertake an independent research to uncover the truth.

DEVELOPMENTS OF CSR

The concept of CSR was first defined in 1953 by Howard Bowen. According to Lee (2008) the concept of CSR has gone through several stages of development: social responsibilities of businessmen in the 1950s–1960s; enlightened self-interest in the 1970s; corporate social performance model in the 1980s and strategic management in the 1990s. Carroll (1999) defines stages differently:

> [T]he modern era of social responsibility begins: the 1950s; CSR literature expands: the 1960s; definitions of CSR proliferate: the 1970s; the 1980s: fewer definitions, more research, and alternative themes; the 1990s: CSR further yields to alternative themes. (Carroll 1999, pp. 269, 270, 273, 284, 288)

The rationale for looking at the history of the development of the CSR concept is that of understanding the developmental changes in conceptualization of CSR as a practice. The theoretical developments over the decades have given the impetus for academics to fervently explore the nature of CSR in a much more practical stance. The development of the CSR concept can be presented schematically in Table 27.1.

PARADIGMS

A novice researcher who starts the process of thinking about the research problem would ultimately develop a view of the expectations of society according to his own beliefs and values. This critical thinking process is extremely vital in appreciating the published research and forming the questions and/or hypothesis.

Table 27.1 Historical developments of CSR

		CSR DEVELOPMENT		
1950–1970	1970–1980	1980–1990	1990–2000	2000–2011
Identifying what CSR means and how important it is for business and society	Rationale for being socially responsible and first CSR frameworks	Expansion of CSR research and development of alternative themes	Further development of alternative themes	New research
Abrams (1951): business to take into account interests of various groups	Wallich and McGowan (1970): develop enlightened self-interest model	Jones (1980): CSR is a process, not an outcome	Carroll (1991): introduces the pyramid of corporate social responsibility	Schwartz and Carroll (2003): introduce the intersecting circles model of CSR
Bowen (1953): defines social responsibilities of businessmen	CED (1971): business to serve the needs of society as the latter consents to business operating. Concentric circles model of CSR	Tuzzolino and Armandi (1981): framework to assess corporate social performance, based on Maslow's hierarchy of human needs	Wood (1991): criticizes CSP models by Carroll (1979) and by Wartick and Cochran (1985) and produces her model of CSP	Margolis and Walsh (2003), Hahn et al. (2010): suggest a trade-off between CSP and CFP. Samy et al. (2010): identifies a causal link between CSP and CFP.
Frederick (1960): identifies 5 conditions for business to satisfy to be socially responsible	Davies (1973): business to be socially responsible for its long-term interest	Strand (1983): model relating CSR and corporate environment	Clarkson (1995): applies stakeholder theory to evaluate CSP	Cacioppe et al. (2008), Hine and Preuss (2009): explore perceptions on CSR
Davies (1960): defines CSR	Sethi (1975): CSR framework to classify corporate behaviour. Introduces the term 'corporate social performance'	Freeman (1984); Freeman and Reed (1983): develops stakeholder theory, defining narrow and wide view of stakeholders	Berman et al. (1999): suggest strategic and intrinsic stakeholder management models	

Table 27.1 (continued)

		CSR DEVELOPMENT		
1950–1970 →	1970–1980 →	1980–1990 →	1990–2000 →	2000–2011
Identifying what CSR means and how important it is for business and society	Rationale for being socially responsible and first CSR frameworks	Expansion of CSR research and development of alternative themes	Further development of alternative themes	New research
	Carroll (1979): three-dimensional model of corporate social performance	Drucker (1984): introduces 'doing well by doing good'		
	Attempts are made to find the relationship between CSR and CFP	Research into relationship between CSR and CFP expands	Research into relationship between CSR and CFP becomes the main theme	Research into relationship between CSR and CFP is still popular

Source: Varenova et al. (2013).

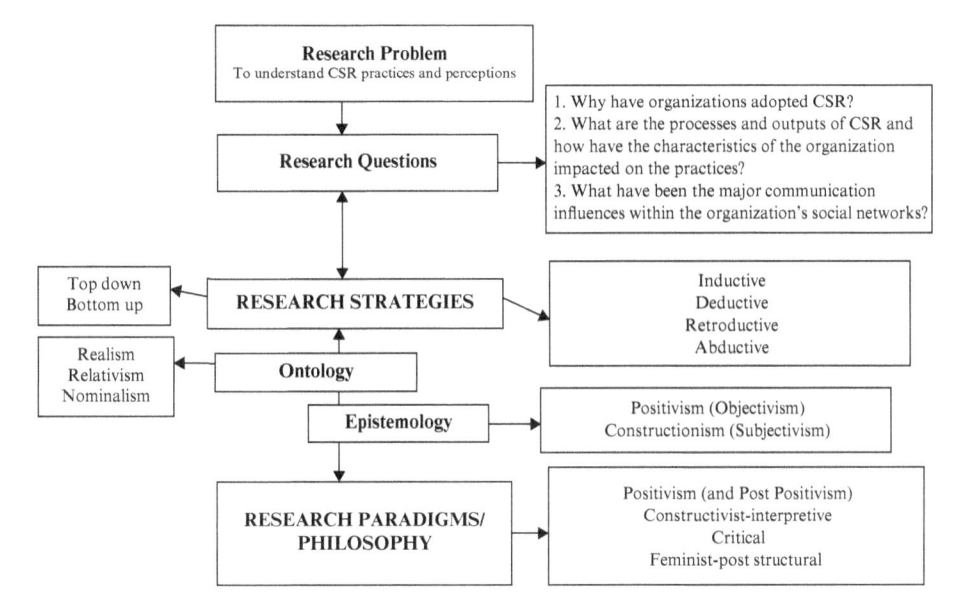

From positivism to social constructivism: an emerging trend 441

```
                    ┌─────────────────────────┐
                    │    Research Problem     │
                    │ To understand CSR       │
                    │ practices and perceptions│
                    └───────────┬─────────────┘
                                │
                                ▼
                    ┌─────────────────────┐    1. Why have organizations adopted CSR?
                    │ Research Questions  │───▶ 2. What are the processes and outputs of CSR and
                    └─────────────────────┘       how have the characteristics of the organization
                                ▲                 impacted on the practices?
                                │              3. What have been the major communication
                                │                 influences within the organization's social networks?
                                │
 ┌──────────┐                   ▼                       ┌──────────────┐
 │ Top down │◀──┐  ┌─────────────────────┐              │  Inductive   │
 │ Bottom up│   └──│ RESEARCH STRATEGIES │─────────────▶│  Deductive   │
 └──────────┘      └─────────────────────┘              │ Retroductive │
 ┌──────────┐                   ▲                       │  Abductive   │
 │ Realism  │◀──┐               │                       └──────────────┘
 │Relativism│   └──│  Ontology  │
 │Nominalism│      └────────────┘
 └──────────┘              ▲
                           │                       ┌───────────────────────────┐
                    ┌──────────────┐               │ Positivism (Objectivism)  │
                    │ Epistemology │──────────────▶│Constructionism (Subjectivism)│
                    └──────┬───────┘               └───────────────────────────┘
                           │
                           ▼                       ┌───────────────────────────┐
                ┌─────────────────────┐            │Positivism (and Post Positivism)│
                │ RESEARCH PARADIGMS/ │───────────▶│ Constructivist-interpretive│
                │    PHILOSOPHY       │            │          Critical         │
                └─────────────────────┘            │ Feminist-post structural  │
                                                   └───────────────────────────┘
```

Source: Adapted from Blaikie (2007, p. 27), Easterby-Smith et al. (2012), Crotty (1998), Denzin and Lincoln (1998).

Figure 27.2 Research choices

A paradigm covers three elements: epistemology, ontology, and methodology (Denzin and Lincoln 1998). Guba and Lincoln (1998, p. 195) consider the research method to be secondary to questions of paradigm which they define as 'the basic belief system or worldview that guides the investigator, not only in choices of methods but in ontologically and epistemologically fundamental ways'. As these parameters describe perceptions, beliefs, assumptions and the nature of reality and truth, it is therefore important to understand and discuss these aspects to ensure research approaches adopted are congruent with the nature and aims of the research objectives, and that researcher biases are understood, highlighted and reduced (Flowers 2009). Particularly, James and Vinnicombe (2002) warn that researchers all have inherent biases that may influence research design. Figure 27.2 highlights the choices that social researchers must consider for a research project.

RESEARCH STRATEGY

Research strategies provide a starting point for answering the research questions, which Blaikie (2007) categorizes into four approaches as highlighted in Table 27.2.

The abductive approach incorporates what inductive and deductive strategies ignore, being the meanings and interpretations that social actors ascribe to their motives and actions. Blaikie (2007) labels this a 'bottom up' approach, which involves deriving concepts and theories from the situation, as opposed to a 'top down' approach, where the researcher's ideas, concepts or mechanisms are tested to establish whether they represent reality. This research strategy can be used to answer both 'what' and 'why' questions which

Table 27.2   Logics of the four research strategies

	Inductive	Deductive	Retroductive	Abductive
Aim	To establish universal generalizations to be used as patterns of explanation	To test theories, to eliminate false ones and corroborate the survivor	To discover underlying mechanisms to explain observed regularities	To describe and understand social life in terms of social actors' motives and understanding
Start	Accumulate observations or data	Identify a regularity to be explained	Document and model a regularity	Discover everyday lay concepts, meanings and motives
	Produce generalizations	Construct a theory and deduce hypotheses	Construct a hypothetical model of a mechanism	Produce a technical account from lay accounts
Finish	Use these 'laws' as patterns to explain further observations	Test the hypotheses by matching them with data	Find the real mechanism by observation and/or experiment	Develop a theory and test it iteratively

Source: Blaikie (2007, p. 8).

are contained in a phenomenological research. It is advocated by a number of prominent social scientists including Weber (1964), Schutz (1963) and Winch (1958). Further, the relationship between theory and research differs in an abductive research strategy, compared to the other three strategies. Particularly, Blaikie (2010, p. 156) asserts that 'the two are intimately entwined; data and theoretical ideas are played off against each other in a developmental and creative process. Research becomes a dialogue between data and theory mediated by the researcher'. Underlying research strategy are ontological and epistemological assumptions which, for an abductive approach, are based on a relativist ontology and a constructionism epistemology (Blaikie 2007). The researcher's philosophical stance will inform the methodology and provides context for the research approach (Crotty 1998). There is an inter-dependency between both ontology and epistemology, as each informs and depends on the other and social researchers draw on different ontological and epistemological assumptions when developing their research methodologies (Easterby-Smith et al. 2012, Hatch and Cunliffe 2006).

ONTOLOGY

Debates of philosophical standpoints regarding social reality usually commence with ontology (Easterby-Smith et al. 2012) and each research paradigm holds a view of the world that is underpinned by ontological assumptions. Ontology, in relation to social sciences, is about the nature of reality and existence and involves assertions about what exists, what it looks like, how it is made up and how the different elements interact with each other (Blaikie 2007, Easterby-Smith et al. 2012). According to Blaikie (2007, p. 13), ontologies answer the question: 'What is the nature of social reality?' Ontological assumptions therefore make claims regarding the types of social phenomenon that do or can exist, the conditions of their existence and their inter-relationships. Therefore, social researchers must consider whether the reality being investigated is objective and factual in nature and external to the individual or whether the reality is subjective in nature and a product of the individual mind (Burrell and Morgan 1987). Philosophical debates among social scientists are often reduced to two opposed and mutually exclusive positions, realism and relativism, and are concerned with different positions regarding truth and facts (Blaikie 2007, Easterby-Smith et al. 2012).

From a realist perspective, both natural and social phenomena are assumed to exist independently from the activities of the human observer (Blaikie 2007). This perspective therefore asserts that realities exist outside the mind (Crotty 1998). There are several categories of realism which start with a traditional position that takes a worldview as being concrete and external where science can only progress through observations that have a direct relationship to the phenomena being investigated (Easterby-Smith et al. 2012). This position has been modified in recent decades to encompass different perspectives and Blaikie (2007) highlights that categories of realism are not universal in the literature and indeed contain alternative categories with different definitions. This is evidenced by Guba and Lincoln (1998) who classify realism perspectives into three categories as naïve, critical and historical realism while Blaikie (2007) considers five categories being shallow, conceptual, cautious, depth and subtle realism. Easterby-Smith et al. (2012) simplifies these categories into two perspectives along the continuum being the traditional perspective which assumes a single truth where facts exist and can be revealed, and an internal realism perspective that assumes a single reality where it is not possible to access that reality directly, and thus gathering of indirect evidence is necessary. Relativism goes further along the continuum to assert that there are fundamental differences between natural and social phenomena and that humans, unlike nature, have cultural influences and live in a world of their shared interpretations (Blaikie 2007). Therefore, this perspective asserts that realities take the form of multiple social constructions that are local and specific in nature (although elements can be shared among individuals and across cultures) and are dependent on the form and content of the individual and groups holding the constructions (Guba and Lincoln 1998). Social action involves a process of meaning-giving and it is the creation and maintenance of those meanings and their interpretations that give rise to the reality of social actors (Blaikie 2010). Therefore, different observers may hold different perspectives and therefore truth and experiences can vary (Easterby-Smith et al. 2012). Therefore, Crotty (1998, p. 64) asserts that we should accept social constructionism as relativist as 'the way things is really just the sense we make of them' and historically and cross-culturally there are 'very divergent interpretations of the same phenomena'.

While relativism assumes that there are many truths and the facts depend upon the viewpoint of the observer, a more extreme position, termed nominalism, proposes that there are no truths and facts are all human creations (Easterby-Smith et al. 2012). Therefore, the nominalist position asserts that the individual understanding of the external world consists of nothing more than names, concepts and labels that are used to construct reality through language and discourse (Burrell and Morgan 1987, Easterby-Smith et al. 2012).

While ontology considers the differing perspectives on what constitutes reality, it is also important to consider what constitutes knowledge of that reality and how it is measured, which involves considerations of epistemology.

EPISTEMOLOGY

Epistemology is concerned with the optimal ways of enquiring into the nature of the world and considers knowledge in terms of how (sources of knowledge) and what it is possible to know (limits of knowledge) and requires consideration of ways that reliable and verifiable knowledge is produced (Chai 2002, Easterby-Smith et al. 2012, Eriksson and Kovalainen 2008). Epistemological assumptions are therefore concerned about how this knowledge can be obtained and provide criteria for how knowledge can be judged to be both adequate and legitimate (Crotty 1998, Blaikie 2007). Therefore, researchers need to identify, explain and justify the epistemological stance they have adopted (Crotty 1998). In that respect, social researchers must consider whether it is possible to identify and communicate the nature of knowledge as being 'hard, real and capable of being transmitted in tangible form, or whether knowledge is of a softer, more subjective, spiritual or even transcendental kind, based on experience and insight of a unique and essentially personal nature' (Burrell and Morgan 1987, p. 2–3). There are two contrasting views among researchers regarding how social science should be conducted, which are positivism (or objectivism) and constructionism (Easterby-Smith et al. 2012, Crotty 1998). Positivism assumes that the social world is external and that its properties should be measured objectively based on observed facts (Easterby-Smith et al. 2012). Conversely, constructionism proposes that there is no meaning without a mind and therefore meaning is not discovered but constructed. Therefore, constructionism proposes that understanding can only be derived by considering the frame of reference of social actors and therefore understanding comes from the inside rather than externally (Burrell and Morgan 1987). Therefore, this world view is not conceived of as a fixed constitution of objects, but rather as 'an emergent social process – as an extension of human consciousness and subjective experience' (Burrell and Morgan 1987, p. 253). In this respect, different people may construct meanings in different ways, even in relation to the same phenomena (Crotty 1998). Therefore, the mindset of different individuals would construct the society that we want to have and live in varying ways. Large corporations, especially the multinationals, are able to influence the fabric of a society through their products and services. Arguably the cultural practices of a large organization can be transferred to the society's acceptance into norms because individuals make up that society. An interesting example is India's recent amendments on child labour laws to allow children as young as 14 years old to work in family enterprises. Easterby-Smith et al. (2012) highlight a trend from positivism to constructionism among social researchers and indeed many prominent authors have argued that research in the pursuit of improved environmental, social and economic performance requires closer engagement with actual practice (Adams and Larrinaga-González 2007, Gray 2002).

The links between ontology and epistemology assumptions are referred to as research philosophies (Saunders et al. 2007) or research paradigms (Blaikie 2007), and are located within the broader framework of theoretical and philosophical perspectives that consider different methods of making connections between ideas, social experience and social reality (Blaikie 2007, Guba 1990).

RESEARCH PARADIGMS

Research paradigms are described by Denzin and Lincoln (2003), as an interpretative framework derived from a basic set of beliefs that guide action. Interpretive studies reject the possibility of an 'objective' account of events and situations, seeking instead a relativistic, albeit shared, understanding of phenomena (Orlikowski and Baroudi 1991). Denzin and Lincoln (1998) highlight four major interpretive paradigms in qualitative research being positive and post positivist; constructivist-interpretive; critical; and feminist-post structural.

Current researchers such as Robertson and Samy (2015) advocate a constructionism paradigm, which is an interpretive method, described as anti-positivist, as it respects the differences between people and the objects of natural science (Hatch and Cunliffe 2006). Social constructivism has its roots in the work of Max Scheler and Karl Mannheim and was subsequently developed by prominent works from Berger and Luckmann (1967) and Lincoln and Guba (1985). Constructivists consider how people create meaningful ways of understanding themselves and the world, which they in turn use to navigate everyday life (Raskir and Bridges 2004). However, debates exist as to whether constructions primarily originate from individuals or the social context. While constructivism has a focus on the internal, cognitive processes of individuals, social constructionism considers the collective generation of meanings that transpire between the dynamic interplay of culture, language and ongoing relationships (Crotty 1998, Raskir and Bridges 2004). The two approaches can be viewed as similar due to their focus on sense-making (McNamee 2004) and confusion and inconsistency in terminology appears to exist in the literature, where in many cases both terms are viewed as one and the same (Crotty 1998).

For example, Creswell (2009, p. 8) states that social constructivists consider subjective meanings that are not simply imprinted on the individual but are formed through interaction with others. Particularly, Fish (1990) highlights that all objects are made, not found, and the means by which they are made are social and conventional. Crotty (1998, p. 52) therefore emphasizes that these means 'are institutions which precede us and which are already embedded and that it is by inhabiting them or being inhabited by them, that we have access to the public and conventional senses they make'. Particularly, Greenwood (1994, p. 85) states that with regards to social constructionism 'social realities, therefore, are constructed and sustained by all social interactions involved ... Social reality is, therefore, a function of shared meanings: it is constructed, sustained and reproduced through social life.' Therefore, the 'social' element in social constructionism concerns the mode of meaning generation and not the type of object that has meaning (Crotty 1998). A social constructionism position assumes that many different realities exist and therefore the researcher aims to increase the general understanding of the situation by gathering the views and experiences of diverse individuals in a small number of case studies chosen for specific reasons to assess the complexity of 'whole situations' (Easterby-Smith et al. 2012). Therefore, the aim is to understand how members of a social group, through their participation in social processes, enact their particular realities and assign them with meaning, and to show how these meanings, beliefs and intentions of the members help to explain their social action (Orlikowski and Baroudi 1991). The interpretive perspective of this research therefore attempts to understand 'the intersubjective meanings embedded in social life ... [and thus] to explain why people act the way they do' (Gibbons 1987, p. 3).

Table 27.3 Contrasting implications of positivism and social constructionism

Factor	Positivism	Social constructionism approach
The observer	must be independent	is part of what is being observed
Human interests	should be irrelevant	are the main driver of the science
Explanations	must demonstrate causality	aim to increase general understanding of the situation
Research progresses through	hypotheses and deductions	gathering rich data from which ideas are induced
Concepts	need to be defined so that they can be measured	should incorporate stakeholder perspectives
Units of analysis	should be reduced to the simplest terms	must include complexity of 'whole' situations
Generalization through	statistical probability	theoretical abstraction
Sampling requires	large numbers randomly selected	small number of cases chosen for specific reasons

Source: Easterby-Smith et al. (2012, p. 24).

The implications of this approach, as contrasted with a positivism approach are demonstrated in Table 27.3.

This philosophy implies that social phenomena are constantly revised, and their meanings are continually influenced by social interaction (Bryman and Bell 2011). It therefore attempts to understand the subjective meaning of social action and is referred to by Habermas (1970) as an interpretive method. An interpretative approach will be adopted which 'looks for culturally derived and historically situated interpretations of the social life-worlds' (Crotty 1998, p. 67). Interpretivism, based on the work of Max Weber (1864–1920), attempts to interpret social action to arrive at a casual explanation of its course and effects (Weber 1968, p. 3). In particular, Weber was primarily interested in the motivational understanding on rational action. For example, statistical data produced by qualitative data, such as Frias-Aceituno et al. (2013), who found that company size had a positive impact on potential Integrated Reporting (IR) adoption and additionally found that size and diversity of the board was an important indicator of IR adoption, are not understandable on their own. Therefore, Weber (1964) specified that there must be a relevant action (e.g. decision to adopt or not) and a meaning attached to that action (e.g. reputational) that must be identified to link a relationship like IR adoption to company size and board size and diversity. Weber (1964, p. 98) defined a motive as 'a complex of subjective meaning which seems to the actor himself or to the observer as adequate grounds for the conduct in question'.

Building on the work of Weber, Schutz sought to consider how it was possible to form objective concepts and theories from subjective meanings (Schutz 1963). Schutz argued that Weber failed to differentiate between 'the meaning a social actor *works with* when action is taking place, the meaning that a social actor *attributes* to completed act or some future act, and the meaning that a sociologist *attributes* to the action' (Blaikie 2007, p. 128, italics in original). Schutz (1963) considered that social researchers must interpret the world of social actors by systematic scrutiny rather than by living experience and that the subjective meanings can be experienced only on their typicality from where social theories can be constructed. Therefore, interpretivists propose that social regularities can be understood by constructing models of 'typical meanings used by typical social actors engaged in typical courses of actions in typical situations' (Blaikie 2007, p. 131). The viewpoint of weak constructionism asserts that interpretive research can complement positivist research, by generating hypotheses and theories for further investigation, and by filling in the knowledge gaps that positivist research cannot reveal, such as the contextual exigencies, the meaning systems, and the interaction of various components of a system (Orlikowski and Baroudi 1991). In this respect, Astley (1985, p. 498) asserts, 'we can perceive nothing except through the knowledge structure in which perception is embedded'. Weak constructionism is similar to Longino's (2002) idea of what constitutes scientific knowledge where she bridges the dichotomy between rational and social epistemologies of knowledge and advocates a middle ground approach that recognizes both the rational and social aspects of knowledge. This differs from a strong constructionism position that assumes there is no pre-existing reality, and the research aim is therefore to investigate how social actors invent structures to make sense of their world through attention to language and conversations (Easterby-Smith et al. 2012). In this respect, the role of interpretive research is to replace, rather than complement, positivist investigations (Orlikowski and Baroudi 1991). This philosophical position recognizes the subjectivity in the relativism of the environment and takes into consideration the cultural perspectives of individual, organization and society.

Between the poles of positivism and social constructivism is arguably critical realism which undermines one's view to not be scientifically objective on one spectrum to an idealist position on the other. Bhaskar and others promoted the idea of dialectic realism as a way forward for social sciences research (Bhaskar 1998). Based on the extension of critical realism, the dialectical approach takes a deeper meaning to social constructs in order to understand the human interactions and conflicts of both the positive and negative and perceptions of individuals and the society that accepts it as a norm. Therefore, adopting a dialectic design would allow the researcher to investigate the nature of the reasoning for the phenomena through the quest of what is the truth and the ethical expectations of individuals in a society. Bhaskar (1998) argues that the concept of 'personalism' in dialectical realism brings about the responsibility of an individual's actions on the society and the resultant punishment imposed which clearly ties in with the legitimacy framework or the social licensee to operate for organizations in our society. These axiological issues of morality and ethics which are one's values are embedded in the society and therefore understanding them through thematic, discourse analysis, narrative and ethnographical means is vital.

The links between ontology, epistemology, research paradigm and methodology for this study are highlighted in Table 27.4.

RESEARCH METHODOLOGY

One of the common methods adopted in the ontological and epistemological positions of relativism is complemented by the situational context of the research and hence the adoption of a case study approach.

Table 27.4 Link between ontology, epistemology and methodology

Ontologies	Realism	Internal realism	Relativism	Nominalism
Epistemology	Strong positivism	Positivism	Constructionism	Strong constructionism
Research paradigm			Social constructionism-interpretivism	
Methodology:				
Aims	Discovery	Exposure	Convergence	Invention
Starting points	Hypotheses	Propositions	Questions	Critique
Designs	Experiment	Large surveys; multi-cases	Cases and surveys	Engagement and reflexivity
Data types	Numbers and facts	Numbers and words	Words and numbers	Discourse and experiences
Analysis/ interpretation	Verification/ falsification	Correlation and regression	Triangulation and comparison	Sense-making and understanding
Outcomes	Confirmation of theories	Theory testing and generation	Theory generation based on the environment	New insights and actions

Source: Adapted from Easterby-Smith et al. (2012, p. 25).

Merriam (1998) highlights that 'there is little consensus on what constitutes a case study or how this type of research is done' (p. 26). According to Hammersley et al. (2000), its meaning has overlapped significantly with ethnography; participant observation; fieldwork; qualitative research; and life history.

While Stake (2005) views case study research as a choice of what is to be studied, the case itself, other case research authors consider it as a strategy of inquiry, a methodology, or a comprehensive research strategy (Denzin and Lincoln 2003, Merriam 1998, Yin 2003). Yin (2003, p. 13) defines a case study as an empirical inquiry that investigates a contemporary phenomenon (the case) within its real-life context, especially when the boundaries between phenomenon and context are not clearly evident. In addition, Goode and Hatt (1952) highlighted that the case study is a method of organizing data that preserves the unitary character of the social object being studied. They identified that a case study involves the notion of a social unit and the manner in which it is studied, with a social unit being defined as an individual, social event or group of people; and that the individual, group or event should be treated as a whole. Therefore the focus of a case study may be a single individual or a set of actors engaged in a sequence of activities over time which allows researchers to retain the holistic and meaningful characteristics of real-life events – such as individual life cycles, organizational and managerial processes, neighbourhood change, international relations and the maturation of industries (Yin 2003).

This view is consistent with Creswell (2009, p. 13) who defines a case study as 'a strategy of inquiry in which the researcher explores in depth a program, event, activity, process or one or more individuals'. Therefore, case study research seeks to obtain a holistic view of a specific phenomenon or series of events (Gummesson 2000). As Valdelin (1974, p. 47) states:

> detailed observations entailed in the case study method enable us to study many different aspects, examine them in relation to each other, view the process within its total environment and also utilise the researchers capacity for 'verstehen'. Consequently, case study research provides us with a greater opportunity than other available methods to obtain a holistic view of a specific research project.

Verstehen relates to empathy, being understanding the meaning of actions and interactions from the members' own points of view (Eckstein 2000).

Lincoln and Guba (1985) highlight that qualitative research is based on the view that social phenomena, human problems and the nature of cases are situational, therefore choosing a case will invariably involve studying its situation. Thus, qualitative understanding of cases requires experiencing the activities of the case as they occur in its context and particular situation which is expected to shape the activities, as well as the experiencing and the interpretation of the activity (Stake 2006). Therefore, case study research involves the study of a real situation (Ritchie and Lewis 2006), with the behaviour of social actors viewed in the context of all the interactions going on around them in their natural setting (the organization) rather than in isolation (Rowley 2002, Cassell and Symon 2004).

Yin (2003) distinguishes between three types of case studies: exploratory, descriptive and explanatory research. Since a number of organizational issues are related to the intersection of human agents and organizational structures, the distinctive need for case studies arises out of the desire to understand complex social phenomena by capturing the holistic and meaningful characteristics of real-life events in greater detail, with its unique strength being the ability to analyse a variety of evidence and variables compared to other approaches (Yin 2003, Sjoberg et al. 1991, Galliers 1992).

Yin (2003, pp. 13–14) therefore contends that case study is a comprehensive research strategy that:

- copes with the technically distinctive situations in which there will be many more variables of interest than data points;
- relies on multiple sources of evidence, with data needing to converge in a triangulating fashion; and
- benefits from the prior development of theoretical propositions to guide data collection and analysis.

In line with Creswell (2009), Yin defines case study research as a strategy rather than techniques of data collection and analysis, which Blaikie (2010) highlights as a major deficiency of the early discussions of case studies. In particular, Stake (2006) places emphasis on a case study being defined as an interest in individual cases, rather than on the techniques of inquiry.

CASE STUDY STRATEGY

By defining the case study as a research strategy, Yin (2003) has been able to argue that it is a comprehensive method that encompasses not just data collection techniques, but also design logic and specific approaches to data analysis. Therefore, the connection between the elements in the research design is facilitated by the research strategy (Maxwell 2005), which becomes 'a way of linking ideas and evidence to produce a representation of some aspect of social life' (Ragin 1994, p. 48). In particular, Yin argues that case study strategy should not be confused with qualitative research, and that research evidence 'can include, and even be limited to quantitative evidence' (Yin 2003, p. 14). Therefore, a broad spectrum of research methods are applied in case studies (Teddlie and Tashakkori 2012, Woodside 2010) which reflects the huge variety of research problems and phenomena (Dubois and Gadde 2014). Case study evidence may be quantitative, qualitative or a mix of both, and may be drawn from ethnographic, field research, unstructured interviews, observation, archival searches or highly structured surveys, with all techniques of evidence gathering being interpretive (Eisenhardt 1989, Gerring 2007). The in-depth focus on the case(s), as well as the desire to cover a broader range of contextual and other complex conditions, produce a wide range of topics to be covered by any given case study which extends beyond the study of isolated variables. Therefore, the relevant case study data are likely to come from multiple and not singular sources of evidence from one or a few cases (Yin 2003, Hammersley et al. 2000). Connolly (1998, p. 124) views quantitative and qualitative approaches as complementary, and claims that quantitative work 'aims to produce generalizations but can tell us little about causal relations, while qualitative work can help to identify relations of causality, but it is unable to generalize from these' and that causal relations can be found by direct study of particular cases – and, in particular, of the interpretations, intentions and motives of social actors.

The use of mixed or multiple methods in case study research usually contributes to increasing accuracy and complexity/coverage in a study more so than generality, and a mixed-method approach is likely to provide confirmation and disconfirmation of some beliefs and feelings of participants collected during interviews by examining data collected using alternative methods within the same context (Woodside 2010). This method contrasts with the social survey where a relatively small amount of data is gathered from a large number of cases (usually individual respondents) (Hammersley et el. 2000). A further contrast can be seen between case studies and experimental research, where the latter also usually involves the investigation of a small number of cases but is distinguished from case study by its direct control of variables compared to case study where researchers construct cases out of naturally occurring social situations (Hammersley and Gomm 2000). Therefore, while experimental research isolates the phenomena from their context, case studies highlight the rich, real-world context in which the phenomena occur (Eisenhardt and Graebner 2007). A comparison of case studies with experimental and survey approaches is detailed in Table 27.5.

Case study, as a strategy of inquiry, has a long history and has been used in many fields including social anthropology, political science, sociology, education and organizational management and strategy (Blaikie 2010, Gummesson 2000, Yin 2003, Merriam 1998). Gerring (2007) argues that in the social sciences field, there is a shift from a variable-centred approach to causality towards a case-based approach. Case studies are used to

Table 27.5 *A schematic comparison of case study with experimental and survey approaches*

Experiment	Case study	Survey
Investigation of a relatively small number of cases	Investigation of a relatively small number of cases (sometimes just one)	Investigation of a relatively large number of cases
Information gathered and analysed about a small number of features of each case	Information gathered and analysed about a large number of features of each case	Information gathered and analysed about a small number of features of each case
Study of cases created in such a way as to control the important variables	Study of naturally occurring cases or in 'action research' form, study of cases created by the actions of the researcher but where the primary concern is not controlling variables to measure their effect	Study of a sample of naturally occurring cases selected in such a way as to maximize the sample's representativeness in relation to some larger population
Quantification of data is a priority	Quantification of data is not a priority. Indeed qualitative data may be treated as superior	Quantification of data is a priority
The aim is either theoretical inference – the development and testing of theory – or the practical evaluation of an intervention	The main concern may be with understanding the case studied in itself, but with no interest in theoretical inference or empirical generalization. However, there may also be attempts at one or both of these. Alternatively, the wider relevance of the findings may be conceptualized in terms of provision of vicarious experience as a basis for 'naturalistic generalization' or 'transferability'	The aim is empirical generalization from a sample to a finite population. Though this is sometimes seen as a platform for theoretical inference

Source: Hammersley et al. (2000, p. x).

study complex social phenomena (Yin 2003, Gummesson 2007) and are especially useful for studying behaviour in organizations and new or emerging behaviour (Wagner et al. 2011), particularly in new situations where only little is known about the phenomenon and in situations where current theories seem inadequate (Easton 1995, Eisenhardt 1989, Yin 2003). Gummesson (2000) advocates case study research as a useful strategy for studying organizational processes and also for explanatory purposes as it allows the study of contextual factors and process elements in the same real-life situation (Halinen and Törnroos 2005).

It is important that case researchers apply methodological rigour and provide an account of methodology used to allow readers to evaluate the research adequately (Dubois and Gadde 2014, Eisenhardt 1989). Beverland and Lindgreen (2010, p. 61), in their longitudinal study of case research published in *Industrial Marketing Management*, concluded that 'there were many cases that provided relatively little detail by which readers could make informed judgments'. While Piekkari et al. (2010), in a review of use of the case study approach in 145 case studies in key industrial marketing journals over a 10-year period (1997–2006), concluded that 80 of these papers did not explain their methods for data analysis and 39 papers included no methodological references at all. As a research strategy, Yin advocates key guidelines, which have been further developed by Halinen and Törnroos (2005) to consider areas of best practice in the case study process when looking at business networks. Piekkari et al. (2010) consider not only best practice, but also innovative practice in their review of use of the case study approach.

These phases of the case study methodology and recommendations for both best and innovative practice are shown in Table 27.6.

SINGLE AND MULTIPLE CASES

Eckstein (1975) distinguishes case studies from comparative research on the basis of whether one or a number of cases are used. Yin (2003) regards single case studies as being of five types: critical, extreme, typical, longitudinal and revelatory. Therefore, single cases selected are either unusually revelatory, extreme exemplars, or opportunities for unusual research access (Yin 2003). Eisenhardt (1989, p. 542) considers that 'each case is analogous to an experiment, and multiple cases are analogous to multiple experiments'. Stake (2005) identifies case studies as intrinsic, instrumental or collective. Intrinsic case studies are used where the case itself is of primary, not secondary, interest, and where we wish to learn about the case itself rather than by studying to learn about other cases or about a general issue (Stake 2005). Instrumental case studies aim to provide insight into an issue or to seek a greater understanding of something else, perhaps to support a developing generalization or theory, whereas collective case studies are also instrumental but involve joint study of a number of cases that represent some phenomenon, population or general condition where the aim is likely to be theory generation, which may apply to an even wider collection of such cases (Blaikie 2010). Therefore, attempts to categorize case studies would specify that their use ranges from descriptive, which usually involves single cases, to explanatory, which normally requires multiple cases. The explanatory nature of multiples cases can be used to explain the phenomena and the complexity of organizational culture and practices. The authors assert that '[m]ultiple cases are generally regarded as more rigorous than single case studies, in that comparisons across cases allow for a greater robustness in the development of insights and a consideration of their context dependency' (O'Connor and Rice 2001, Yin 2003). However, multiple case studies can also be time-consuming and more complex and expensive to conduct. Multiple case study research is particularly appropriate when there is the need to explore new topics and issues. Similarly, Eisenhardt (1989, p. 545) advocates multiple case design, suggesting that 'a number between 4 and 10 cases usually works well', without further justification. She argues that the multiple case designs draw together several patterns where 'the researcher can draw a more complete theoretical picture' (Eisenhardt 1989, p. 620). They enable comparisons that clarify whether an emergent finding is simply unique to a single case or consistently replicated by several cases and enable broader exploration of research questions and theoretical elaboration. Therefore, multiple cases are selected for theoretical reasons such as replication, extension of theory,

Table 27.6 A model of case study research

Phases of case study process	Key decisions	Best practice recommendations	Innovative practice approaches
Relating theory to empirical data	Research purpose	Clarity of research purpose: exploratory, explanatory, descriptive. Theory development prior to data collection.	Abductive and theory-testing case studies.
Choosing and justifying empirical cases	Number of case studies	Decision on use of single or multiple cases prior to data collection. Choice of single vs. multiple case design driven by research purpose.	The selection of case studies is based on empirical research (e.g. survey, interviews or focus groups) that the authors undertake with the purpose of selecting information rich case studies.
	Sampling strategy	Purposeful sampling. Use of literal or theoretical replication.	Population studies, i.e. the researcher investigates the whole population relevant to the study.
Establishing case boundaries	Defining the case (unit/s of analysis, temporal scope)	Specification of unit of analysis: holistic or embedded. Longitudinal or cross-sectional designs.	
Selecting appropriate data sources	Multiple sources of evidence	Use of multiple data sources to ensure triangulation and convergence on a single explanation. The selection of interview respondents ensures that data is collected from actors with different perspectives with respect to investigated phenomena (e.g. employees, management, internal and external actors of a firm, etc.).	Case study research combines qualitative and quantitative data: interviews, questionnaire survey, observation and archival records. Qualitative pre-studies, including pilot focus groups, are used to identify key issues for investigation through case study research and complement case study data sources.
Analysing findings and data reduction	Method/process of data analysis	Application of analytic techniques, e.g. pattern matching to ensure systematic approach. Use of initial theoretical propositions to steer appropriate analytical strategy.	The authors employ critical event analysis, processual or historical analysis.

Table 27.6 (continued)

Phases of case study process	Key decisions	Best practice recommendations	Innovative practice approaches
Ensuring quality of data	Method of verification	The authors explain the process of data analysis; more sophisticated methods to data analysis are employed: pattern matching and constant comparison of findings with theory. The coding process is often conducted using specialized software such as Nudist, NVivo or Decision Support Analysis software. Construct validity, external validity, internal validity, reliability.	Follow-up interviews conducted to validate case study findings and case study report.
Writing up and presenting case data	Presentation and discussion of findings	Choice of report structure should be aligned to research purpose and case audience. Case report may not need to include rich narrative. Findings are presented using: within and/or cross-case study analysis, case history analysis, thematic analysis, comparison between theory and data.	

Sources: Halinen and Törnroos (2005), Yin (2003), Piekkari et al. (2010).

contrary replication, and elimination of alternative explanations as researchers argue that the number of cases selected will depend on the complexity of the phenomenon and the conditions in which it occurs; the greater the complexity, the greater the number of cases that will be necessary to achieve confidence in the testing of the theory. Therefore, cases must be carefully selected to either predict similar results (a literal replication) or predict contrasting results but for predictable reasons (a theoretical replication). Schofield (2000) argues that choosing sites on the basis of their fit with a typical situation is far preferable to choosing on the basis of convenience, which is a common practice among novice or emerging researchers. However, Kennedy (1979) considers that findings emerging from the study of several very heterogeneous sites would be more robust and more likely to be useful in understanding various other sites than one emerging from the study of several very similar sites (Kennedy 1979). Gomm et al. (2000) argue that it is possible for case study researchers to improve the quality of their empirical generalizations and provide evidence in support of them by attempting to account for probable relevant heterogeneity within their target population in at least two complementary ways being:

1. By using theoretical ideas and information about the case and the population in their analyses; and
2. By selecting cases for study on the basis of such ideas and information.

They suggest that where information about the larger population is available it should be used and, if it is not available, then the potential risk involved in generalization still needs to be highlighted, preferably via specification of likely types of heterogeneity that could render the findings unrepresentative (Gomm et al. 2000). Another strategy, they suggest, is to study a small sample of cases that have been selected to cover the extremes of the expected relevant heterogeneity within the population and that cases do not all have to be studied in the same depth; one or two may be investigated in detail, with others investigated specifically to check the likely generalizability of findings from the main case study (Gomm et al. 2000). Schofield (2000) also highlights that the target population may be an actually existing population of cases or it could be a population that seems likely to or might exist in the future which will clearly have implications for the cases that should be selected for study. For studying what may or could be, cases which represent the leading edge of change could be selected on the basis that they represent a good generalization to a future population (Schofield 2000).

By comparing cases, researchers can establish the range of generality of a finding or explanation and, at the same time, pin down the conditions under which that finding will occur (Miles and Huberman 1994, p. 172), allowing potential for both greater explanatory power and greater generalizability than a single case study can deliver. However, while the use of a number of cases may strengthen the research undertaken, and make the findings more convincing, their use is only appropriate when replication, rather than sampling logic, is used (Blaikie 2010).

The aim of case study research is to understand the deeper structure of a phenomenon to inform other settings, rather than generalization from the setting (usually only one or a few cases) to a population (Orlikowski and Baroudi 1991). Therefore, instead of statistical representativeness, case studies offer depth and comprehensiveness for understanding the specific phenomenon (Easton 1995, p. 475). Indeed, Gummesson (2007, p. 230) states 'it is correct, as is often pointed out, that one or a few cases cannot answer the questions of how often, how much, and how many. But is it not better to understand a phenomenon in depth than to know how often the not understood phenomenon occurs?'

Therefore, the focus is on analytical (the findings specific to the research context) rather than statistical generalizations (Gerring 2007). Such analytical generalization is based on either corroborating, modifying, rejecting or otherwise advancing theoretical concepts referenced in designing the case study or new concepts that arose upon the completion of the case study (Yin 2003 p. 40).

STEPS IN ANALYSIS

When undertaking a case study approach, the researchers should adopt a methodological and systematic process to ensure the focus is clear and the objectives are achievable within a time frame. The following is a guide to follow in most types of case studies:

1. Identify the research questions.
    a. In this step, a limited number of practical and achievable questions needs to be identified. The project needs to be planned according to reasonable time allocated for data collection and analysis.
2. Identify the data to be collected for the research questions.
    a. It is vital to understand the data to be collected, the process and feasibility which is to ensure accessibility to such data. This can be documents, interviews of selected respondents, observation of meetings, and so on.
    b. At this point, themes and sub themes from prior literature (if applicable) should be identified and clearly denoted to the data collection process. It should be individually broken down to the data and analysis process that is linked to the appropriate research question.
3. Consider the analysis to be undertaken according to the data to be collected for the individual research questions.
    a. During this process, the issues of reliability and validity considerations of where the data is collected, who collects it, how and who will analyse the data are important planning stages.
    b. Analysis by a methodological process such as content analysis or thematic analysis as recommended by Braun and Clarke (2006) or software such as NVivo should be identified.
4. Finally report the findings according to the research questions and discuss with an existing literature review.

VALIDITY AND RELIABILITY

Yin (2003) asserts that the development of case study design needs to maximize four conditions related to research quality:

1. Construct validity;
2. Internal validity (for explanatory or causal case study only);

3. External validity; and
4. Reliability.

These conditions are highlighted in Table 27.7 and will be applied as appropriate in the research design process of this study.

Table 27.7 Quality criteria for case research

Design test	Theoretical explanation of the concept	Case study tactic	Phase of research when tactic occurs
Construct validity	To secure that correct operational measures have been established for the concepts that are being studied	1. Triangulation through multiple sources of data or interviews.	Data collection
		2. Providing readers with a chain of evidence using cross-case tables or quotes from informants.	Data collection
		3. Allowing interviewees to review the draft case and give feedback.	Composition
Internal validity	To make sure that a causal relationship – certain conditions lead to other conditions – has been established. Internal validity is a concern of explanatory or causal case studies but not for exploratory or descriptive cases that do not attempt to make causal statements	1. Pattern matching through cross-case analysis.	Data analysis
		2. Searching for negative cases, ruling out or accounting for alternative explanations.	Data analysis
		3. Explanation building.	Data analysis
		4. Use logic models.	Data analysis
External validity	To prove that the domain to which a case study's findings belong can be generalized	1. Specification of the population of interest.	Research design
		2. Replication logic in multiple case studies.	Research design
Reliability	Demonstrating that the findings from a case study can be replicated if the case study procedures are followed	1. A standardized interview protocol.	Data collection
		2. Constructs well defined and grounded in extant literature.	Data collection
		3. Providing an audit trail by providing access to data within a database.	Data collection

Sources: Beverland and Lindgreen (2010, p. 57), Yin (2003).

Beverland and Lindgreen (2010) believe that addressing research quality is important for several reasons:

- leads to better practices in the field;
- results in richer insights and therefore better theory;
- active debate over research quality is a sign of a healthy research community, and thus will improve the status of the method; and
- having explicit standards of quality will improve the legitimacy of case research.

CONCLUSION

The objective of this chapter was to develop an understanding of undertaking research adopting a social constructivism paradigm. In this process the authors introduce the hallmarks of research design based on the premises of a case study. When undertaking a case study, it is vital to adopt a systematic approach incorporating reliability and validity of data collection and analysis. We anticipate that future research in CSR would arguably have an impact on society if researchers undertake in-depth analysis by adopting a critical realism design to document, investigate and highlight contributions made by individual corporations. Reporting the CSR practices of multinationals through this case study design and process would reveal the best practices that could be modelled for other organizations. It would also highlight deficiencies and recommend changes.

REFERENCES

Abrams, F.W. (1951), 'Management's responsibilities in a complex world', *Harvard Business Review*, **29** (3), 29–34.
Adams, C. and C. Larrinaga-González (2007), 'Engaging with organisations in pursuit of improved sustainability accounting and performance', *Accounting, Auditing & Accountability Journal*, **20** (3), 333–355.
Astley, W.G. (1985), 'Administrative science as socially constructed truth', *Administrative Science Quarterly*, **30**, 497–513.
Berger, Peter L. and Thomas Luckmann (1967), *The Social Construction of Reality: A Treatise in the Sociology of Knowledge*, Garden City, N.J: Anchor.
Berman, S.L., A.C. Wicks, S. Kotha and T.M. Jones (1999), 'Does stakeholder orientation matter? The relationship between stakeholder management models and firm financial performance', *Academy of Management Journal*, **42**, 488–506.
Beverland, M. and A. Lindgreen (2010), 'What makes a good case study? A positivist review of qualitative case research published in Industrial Marketing Management, 1971–2006', *Industrial Marketing Management*, **39**, 56–63.
Bhaskar, R. (1998), 'International association of critical realism', available at https://criticalrealism.wikispaces.com/Roy++Bhaskar. Accessed on 15th May 2017.
Blaikie, Norman (2007), *Approaches to Social Enquiry*, 2nd ed., Cambridge: Polity Press.
Blaikie, Norman (2010), *Designing Social Research*, 2nd ed., Cambridge: Polity Press.
Bowen, H.R. (1953), *Social Responsibilities of the Business Man*, New York: Harper and Row.
Braun, V. and V. Clarke (2006), 'Using thematic analysis in psychology', *Qualitative Research in Psychology*, **3** (2), 77–101.
Bryman, Alan and Emma Bell (2011), *Business Research Methods*, 3rd ed., Oxford: Oxford University Press.
Burrell, Gibson and Gareth Morgan (1987), *Sociological Paradigms and Organizational Analysis*, Aldershot: Gower Publishing Company Ltd.
Cacioppe, R., N. Forster and M. Fox (2008), 'A survey of managers' perceptions of corporate ethics and social responsibility and actions that may affect companies' success', *Journal of Business Ethics*, **82**, 681–700.

Carroll, A.B. (1979), 'A three-dimensional conceptual model of corporate performance', *Academy of Management Review*, **4** (4), 497–505.
Carroll, A.B. (1991), 'The pyramid of corporate social responsibility: toward the moral management of organisational stakeholders', *Business Horizons*, **34** (July–August), 39–48.
Carroll, A.B. (1999), 'Corporate social responsibility: evolution of a definitional construct', *Business and Society*, **38** (3), 268–295.
Cassell, Catherine and Gillian Symon (2004), *Essential Guide to Qualitative Methods in Organizational Research*, London: Sage Publications.
Chai, R. (2002), 'The production of management knowledge: philosophical underpinnings of research design', in David Partington (ed), *Essential Skills for Management Research*, 1st ed., London: SAGE Publications Ltd, pp. 1–19.
Clarkson, M.B.E. (1995), 'A stakeholder framework for analyzing and evaluating corporate social performance', *Academy of Management Review*, **20**, 92–117.
Committee for Economic Development (CED) (1971), *Social Responsibilities of Business Corporations*, New York: Charles Allen & Co Inc. Accessed on 15th May 2017 at https://www.ced.org/reports/single/social-responsibilities-of-business-corporations.
Connolly, P. (1998), '"Dancing to the wrong tune": ethnography, generalization and research on racism in schools', in Paul Connolly and Barry Troya (eds), *Researching Racism in Education*, Buckingham: Open University Press, pp. 255–264.
Creswell, John W. (2009), *Research Design*, 3rd ed., London: Sage.
Crotty, Michael (1998), *The Foundations of Social Research*, London: Sage Publications Ltd.
Davies, K. (1960), 'Can business afford to ignore social responsibilities?', *California Management Review*, **2**, 70–76.
Davies, K. (1973), 'The case for and against business assumption of social responsibilities', *Academy of Management Journal*, **16**, 312–322.
Denzin, N.K. And Y.S. Lincoln (1998), *Strategies of Qualitative Research*, Thousand Oaks, CA: Sage Publications.
Denzin, Norman K. and Yvonne Lincoln (2003), *Collecting and Interpreting Qualitative Materials*, 2nd ed., California: SAGE Publications, Inc., pp. 1–45.
Drucker, P.F. (1984), 'The new meaning of corporate social responsibility', *California Management Review*, **26**, 53–63.
Dubois, A. and L. Gadde (2014), '"Systematic combining": a decade later', *Journal of Business Research*, **67**, 1277–1284.
Easterby-Smith, Mark, Richard Thorpe and Paul R. Jackson (2012), *Management Research*, 4th ed., London: SAGE Publications Ltd.
Easton, G. (1995), 'Methodology and industrial networks', in Kristian K. Möller and David T. Wilson (eds), *Business Marketing: An Interaction and Network Perspective*, Norwell (MA): Kluwer Academic Publishing, pp. 411–491.
Eckstein, H. (1975), 'Case study and theory in political science', in Fred I. Greenstein and Nelson W. Polsby (eds), *Handbook of Political Science, vol. 7, Strategies of Inquiry*, Reading, MA: Addison-Wesle, pp. 79–137.
Eckstein, H. (2000), 'Case study and theory in political science', in Roger Gomm, Martyn Hammersley and Peter Foster (eds), *Case Study Method*, London: Sage, pp. 119–164.
Eisenhardt, K.M. (1989), 'Building theories from case study research', *The Academy of Management Review*, **14** (4), 532–550.
Eisenhardt, K.M. and M.E. Graebner (2007), 'Theory building from cases: opportunities and challenges', *Academy of Management Journal*, **50** (1), 25–32.
Eriksson, Päivi and Anne Kovalainen (2008), *Qualitative Methods in Business Research*, 1st ed., Oxford: SAGE Publications Ltd.
Fish, S. (1990), 'How to recognise a poem when you see one', in David Bartholomae and Anthony Petrosky (eds), *Ways of Reading: An Anthology for Writers*, Boston: Bedford Books of St Martin's Press, pp. 178–191.
Flowers, Paul (2009), 'Research philosophies: importance and relevance', accessed 8 May 2015 at http://www.networkedcranfield.com/cell/Assigment%20Submissions/research%20philosophy%20-%20issue%201%20-%20final.pdf.
Frederick, W.C. (1960), 'The growing concern over business responsibility', *California Management Review*, **2**, 54–61.
Freeman, R. Edward (1984), *Strategic Management: A Stakeholder Approach*, Boston: Pitman.
Freeman, R.E. and D.L. Reed (1983), 'Stockholders and stakeholders: a new perspective on corporate governance', *California Management Review*, **25** (3), 88–106.
Frias-Aceituno, J., L. Rodriguez-Ariza and I. Garcia-Sanchez (2013), 'The role of the board in the dissemination of integrated corporate social reporting', *Corporate Social Responsibility and Environmental Management*, **20** (4), 219–233.

Galliers, Robert D. (1992), *Information Systems Research: Issues, Methods and Practical Guidelines*, Oxford, UK: Blackwell Scientific.
Gerring, John (2007), *Case Study Research: Principles and Practice*, New York: Cambridge University Press.
Gibbons, M.T. (1987), 'Introduction: the politics of interpretation', in M.T. Gibbons (ed.), *Interpreting Politics*, New York: New York University Press, pp. 1–31.
Gomm, R., M. Hammersley and P. Foster (2000), 'Case study and generalization', in Roger Gomm, Michael Hammersley and Paul Foster (eds), *Case Study Method*, London: Sage, pp. 98–116.
Goode, William J. and Paul K. Hatt (1952), *Methods in Social Research*, New York: McGraw Hill.
Gray, R. (2002), 'The social accounting project and accounting organizations and society: privileging engagement, imaginings, new accountings and pragmatism over critique?', *Accounting, Organizations and Society*, **27** (7), 687–708.
Greenwood, J. (1994), 'Action research and action researchers: some introductory considerations', *Contemporary Nurse*, **3** (2), 84–92.
Guba, E. (1990), 'The alternative paradigm dialogue', in Egon Guba (ed.), *The Paradigm Dialogue*, Newbury Park, C.A.: Sage, pp. 17–30.
Guba, E. and Y. Lincoln (1998), 'Competing paradigms in qualitative research', in Norman K. Denzin and Yvonne S. Lincoln (eds), *Handbook of Qualitative Research*, Thousand Oaks, CA: Sage, pp. 195–220.
Gummesson, Evert (2000), *Qualitative Methods in Management Research*, Thousand Oaks, CA: Sage.
Gummesson, E. (2007), 'Case study research and network theory: birds of a feather – qualitative research', *Organization and Management: An International Journal*, **2** (3), 226–248.
Habermas, J. (1970), 'Knowledge and interest', in D. Emmett and A. MacIntyre (eds), *Sociological Theory and Philosophical Analysis*, London: MacMillan, pp. 36–54.
Hahn, T., F. Figge, J. Pinkse and L. Preuss (2010), 'Editorial. Trade-offs in corporate sustainability: you can't have your cake and eat it', *Business Strategy and the Environment*, **19**, 217–29.
Halinen, A. and J.A. Törnroos (2005), 'Using case methods in the study of contemporary business networks', *Journal of Business Research*, **58**, 1285–1297.
Hammersley, M., R. Gomm and P. Foster (2000), 'Case study and theory', in Roger Gomm, Michael Hammersley and Paul Foster (eds), *Case Study Method*, London: Sage, pp. 234–258.
Hatch, Mary Jo and Ann L. Cunliffe (2006), *Organizational Theory*, 2nd ed., Oxford: Oxford University Press.
Hine, J.A.H.S. and L. Preuss (2009), '"Society is out there, organisation is in here": on the perceptions of corporate social responsibility held by different managerial groups', *Journal of Business Ethics*, **88**, 381–393.
James, K. and S. Vinnicombe (2002), 'Acknowledging the individual in the researcher', in David Partington (ed.), *Essential Skills for Management Research*, 1st ed., London: SAGE Publications Ltd, pp. 84–98.
Jones, T.M. (1980), 'Corporate social responsibility revisited, redefined', *California Management Review*, 22 (3) Spring, 59–67.
Kennedy, M.M. (1979), 'Generalizing from single case studies', *Evaluation Quarterly*, **3** (4), 661–678.
Lee, M.P. (2008), 'A review of the theories of corporate social responsibility: its evolutionary path and the road ahead', *International Journal of Management Reviews*, **10** (1), 53–73.
Lincoln, Yvonne S. and Egon G. Guba (1985), *Naturalistic Inquiry*, Newbury Park, CA: Sage Publications.
Longino, Helen E. (2002), *The Fate of Knowledge*, Oxford: Princeton University Press.
McNamee, S. (2004), 'Relational bridges between constructionism and constructivism', in J. Raskir and S. Bridges (eds), *Bridging the Personal and Social in Constructivist Psychology*, New York: Pace University Press, pp. 37–50.
Margolis, J.D. and J.P. Walsh (2003), 'Misery loves companies: rethinking social initiatives by business', *Administrative Science Quarterly*, **48**, 268–305.
Maxwell, Joseph A. (2005), *Qualitative Research Design: An Interactive Approach*, Thousand Oaks, CA: Sage.
Merriam, Sharan B. (1998), *Qualitative Research and Case Study Applications in Education*, San Francisco: Jossey-Bass.
Miles, Matthew B. and Michael A. Huberman (1994), *Qualitative Data Analysis: An Expanded Source Book*, 2nd ed., Thousand Oaks, CA: Sage.
O'Connor, G.C. and M.P. Rice (2001), 'Opportunity recognition and breakthrough innovation in large established firms', *California Management Review*, **43** (2), 95–116.
Orlikowski, W. and J. Baroudi (1991), 'Studying information technology in organizations: research approaches and assumptions', *Information Systems Research*, **2** (1), 1–27.
Pedersen, E.R. (2010), 'Modelling CSR: how managers understand the responsibilities of business towards society', *Journal of Business Ethics*, **91**, 155–166.
Pedersen, E.R. (2011), 'All animals are equal, but . . .: management perceptions of stakeholder relationships and societal responsibilities in multinational corporations', *Business Ethics: A European Review*, **20** (2), 177–191.
Pedersen, E.R. and P. Neergaard (2009), 'What matters to managers? The whats, whys, and hows of corporate social responsibility in a multinational corporation', *Management Decision*, **57** (8), 1261–1280.

Piekkari, R., E. Plakoyiannaki and C. Welch (2010), 'Good case research in industrial marketing: insights from research practice', *Industrial Marketing Management*, **39**, Case Study Research in Industrial Marketing, pp. 109–117.
Ragin, Charles C. (1994), *Constructing Social Research*, Thousand Oaks, CA: Pine Forge Press.
Raskir, Jonathan D. and Sara K. Bridges (2004), *Studies in Meaning 2: Bridging the Personal and Social in Constructivist Psychology*, New York: Pace University Press.
Ritchie, Jane and Jane Lewis (2006), *Qualitative Research Practice*, London: Sage Publications.
Robertson, F. and M. Samy (2015), 'Factors affecting the diffusion of integrated reporting: a UK FTSE 100 perspective', *Sustainability Accounting, Management and Policy Journal*, **6** (2), 190–223.
Rowley, J. (2002), 'Using case studies in research', *Management Research News*, **25** (1), 16–27.
Samy, M., E.G. Odemilin and R. Bampton (2010), 'Corporate social responsibility: a strategy for sustainable business success: an analysis of 20 selected British companies', *International Journal of Business in Society*, **10** (2), 203–217.
Saunders, Mark, Philip Lewis and Adrian Thornhill (2007), *Research Methods for Business Students*, 4th ed., Harlow: Prentice Hall Financial Times.
Schofield, J. (2000), 'Increasing the generalizability of qualitative research', in Roger Gomm, Michael Hammersley and Paul Foster (eds), *Case Study Method*, London: Sage, pp. 69–97.
Schutz, A. (1963), 'Common sense and scientific interpretation of social action', in Maurice A. Natanson (ed.), *Philosophy of the Social Sciences*, New York: Random House, pp. 302–346.
Schwartz, M.S. and A.B. Carroll (2003), 'Corporate social responsibility: a three domain approach', *Business Ethics Quarterly*, **13** (4), 503–530.
Sethi, S.P. (1975), 'Dimensions of corporate social performance: an analytic framework', *California Management Review*, **17** (Spring), 58–64.
Sjoberg, G., N. Williams, T.R. Vaughan and A.F. Sjoberg (1991), 'The case study approach in social research', in Joe R. Feagin, Anthony M. Orum and Gideon Sjoberg (eds), *A Case for the Case Study*, Chapel Hill: UNC Press, pp. 27–79.
Stake, Robert E. (2005), *The Art of Case Study Research*, London: Sage.
Stake, Robert E. (2006), *Multiple Case Study Analysis*, New York: Guilford Press.
Strand, R. (1983), 'A systems paradigm of organizational adaptations to the social environment', *Academy of Management Review*, **8**, 90–96.
Teddlie, C. and A. Tashakkori (2012), 'Common "core" characteristics of mixed methods research: a review of critical issues and call for greater convergence', *The American Behavioral Scientist*, **56** (6), 774–788.
Tuzzolino, F. and B.R. Armandi (1981), 'A need-hierarchy framework for assessing corporate social responsibility', *Academy of Management Review*, **6**, 21–27.
Valdelin, Jan (1974), *Produktutveckling och marknadsföring*, Stockholm: EFI.
Varenova, D., M. Samy and A. Combs (2013), 'Corporate social responsibility and profitability: trade-off or synergy – perceptions of executives of FTSE All-Share companies', *Sustainability Accounting, Management and Policy Journal*, **4** (2), 190–215.
Wagner, H., S. Morton, A. Dainty and N. Burns (2011), 'Path dependent constraints on innovation programmes in production and operations management', *International Journal of Production Research*, **49** (11), 3069–3085.
Wallich, H.C. and J.J. McGowan (1970), 'Stockholder interest and the corporation's role in social policy', in William J. Baumol (ed.), *A New Rationale for Corporate Social Policy*, New York: Committee for Economic Development, pp. 39–60.
Wartick, S.L. and P.L. Cochran (1985), 'The evolution of the corporate social performance model', *Academy of Management Review*, **10** (4), 758–769.
Weber, Max (1964), *The Theory of Social and Economic Organization*, New York: Free Press.
Weber, Max (1968), *On Charisma and Institution Building: Selected Papers*, Chicago: University of Chicago Press.
Weick, K.E. (1995), 'South Canyon revisited: lessons from high reliability organizations', *Wildfire*, **4** (4), 54–68.
Weick, K.E. (2007), 'The generative properties of richness', *Academy of Management Journal*, **50** (1), 14–19.
Winch, Peter (1958), *The Idea of Social Science and its Relation to Philosophy*, London: Routledge and Kegan Paul.
Wood, D.J. (1991), 'Corporate social performance revisited', *Academy of Management Review*, **16** (4), 691–718.
Woodside, A. (2010), 'Bridging the chasm between survey and case study research: research methods for achieving generalization, accuracy and complexity', *Industrial Marketing Management*, **39**, 64–75.
Yin, Robert K. (2003), *Case Study Research: Design and methods*, 3rd edn, Thousand Oaks, CA: Sage.

Index

accountability 65, 369, 374, 380–381, 389, 429, 437
action research 7, 10, 286, 369, 370
Adams, C.A. 369–370, 373
Agadi, K. 227–228
agency theory 20, 310
Aguinis, H. 56
Agyemang, G. 366, 371
Ahmed, S.A. 309
Ahuja, J.M. 309
Aktouf, O. 98
Ali, A. 310
Allen, D.B. 222
Altunas, C. 397
Alvesson, M. 284
Amoako, G.K. 108–109
analysis of current research 21–22
Anderson, L. 231, 233, 238
Andrew, B.H. 309
anonymity 68, 131, 337, 340, 344
applied research 11
applied thematic analysis (ATA) *see* grounded theory (GT)
Aras, G. 197, 271–272, 345
archival records 136, 395
Astley, W.G. 447
autoethnography (self-reporting) 225, 231–239, 266, 270–271
   analytic autoethnography 225, 233–234, 238
   'back region' of performative space 236–237, 238
   Brazilian mining sector 225, 231, 234–238
   commitment to theoretical understandings 234, 238
   control of information 237
   critical thinking 225, 231–232, 238
   divergent perspectives 232
   'front region' of performative space 236–237
   impression management performances for 'researcher-as-audience' 234, 235–238
   meta-autoethnography 234, 238
   official accounts 232
   purposive sampling 234
   reflection 225, 231, 233–234, 238
   reflexivity 225, 231–232, 233–234, 238
   researcher's visibility 233
   subjective and confessional style 232
   textual visibility 238
   values and beliefs 231
autonomy 382, 383
Aybars, A. 197

Babiak, K. 345
Baker, C.R. 241, 243, 246
Bal, M. 406
Ball, A. 365, 369
Barbour, R.S. 365, 367, 373
Barnett, M.L. 223
Barthes, R. 247, 249, 252, 253
Baudrillard, J. 243
Beattie, V. 242
Bebbington, J. 243, 369–370
Bédard, R. 97
Behl, A. 109
Belkaoui, A. 246, 251
Ben & Jerry's 378
Berger, P.L. 445
Berle, A.A. 419
Best, J.W. 328
Beverland, M. 451–452, 458
Bhaskar, R. 2, 447
Bhattacharya, S. 107, 109
bias 149, 289, 322, 324, 441
   social desirability bias 336, 337
   survey research 333, 335, 336, 337, 340, 343
Billington, R. 250
Billo, E.R. 273–274
Bizzochi, J. 408
Blaikie, N. 441–443, 449
Boachie, C. 108–109, 227
Bochner, A.P. 265, 266
Bocquet, R. 346
Bodkin, C. 350
Bohnsack, R. 367
Boje, D.M. 406
Borel, E. 112
Botero, L.F. 103
Botosan, C.A. 242–243
Bourdieu, P. 76, 82, 83
Bowen, H. 272, 438
Brahe, T. 81
Brammer, S.J. 222
Brannan, M. 265
Brass, D. 397
Briggs, C. 52

Brignall, S. 89, 91
Brown, R. 89, 91
Brundtland Commission (1987) 432
Bryant, S.M. 310
Bryer, A.R. 286
Bryman, A. 193
Buckminster Fuller, R. 63
Buhmann, K. 276
Burns, R.B. 4, 7
Burns, T. 85–86
Burrell, G. 7
Butland, B. 173
Butler, D. 18
Buxton, D. 251

Cable, V. 50–51
Calder, B.J. 365
Capaldi, N. 416
carbon footprinting 13
carbon trading 117, 124
Carens, J.H. 382
Carroll, A.B. 39, 67, 272, 434, 438
case studies 272–276, 280, 285–286, 345–346, 450–456
 see also positivism and social constructivism
Casey, M. 371
Catlin, D.W. 133
Certified Emission Reductions (CERs) 117
Chandler, D. 251
Charmaz, K. 25, 29, 34–36, 38–40
Chen, H. 196–197, 346
Chenhall, R.H. 89–90
chi-square statistical test 188, 189–190, 215, 314–315
Chia, R. 88
Chicago School 269
Choi, F.D.S. 310
Chomsky, N. 251
Christiansen, L.H. 274–275
Chua, W.F. 86, 88–89
Clark, V.L.P. 59
Clavel, J.G. 227, 267
Claydon, J. 25–26
Clean Development Mechanism (CDM) 117
climate change see global warming, climate change and greenhouse gases
Clinton, B. 115
cluster analysis see statistical methods
coding 35, 36–38, 289, 305, 369
 see also grounded theory (GT)
Cohen, L. 182, 186
cohort studies 127, 133–135, 333
confidentiality 10, 46, 68, 71, 74, 131
 survey research 340, 343–344

Confucius 429, 435
Connolly, P. 450
consent 68–69, 74, 75, 155
constructivist approach 25, 231
 see also positivism and social constructivism
content analysis 99, 268, 280, 345
 correspondence analysis and human resources disclosure 308, 309, 313
 interview techniques 285, 287
 see also content analysis method for quantitative and qualitative disclosures
content analysis method for quantitative and qualitative disclosures 227–228, 349–362
 advantages 352
 coders 355, 356, 358–359, 360, 361–362
 CSR and reporting 350, 351
 economic aspect 353, 359, 362
 environmental aspect 353, 359, 360, 362
 evaluation process 356
 general guidelines 356
 Global Reporting Initiative (GRI) Sustainability Reporting Guidelines (SRG) 349, 351, 353, 354, 355, 356, 358, 359, 360
 Indonesia Sustainability Reporting Award (ISRA) 353
 Indonesian mining sector 227, 349, 350, 351
 limitations 352
 narrative 350
 objectives of content analysis 352
 process development 355–358
 qualitative disclosures 227, 228, 353–354, 355, 356–357, 359, 360, 361
 quantitative disclosures 351, 353–355, 356–357, 359, 360, 361
 research methods 353–358
 sample of Indonesian companies 353
 scoring guideline 227, 356
 scoring index 353–354, 355
 scoring method 350, 353–355, 361
 scoring numbers 227, 228, 360
 scoring process 356, 357, 358
 social aspect 351, 353, 360, 361, 362
 subjectivity 227, 228, 349–350, 352, 355, 360, 362
 support results 358–360
 sustainability reports 227, 228, 349, 351–352, 353, 358, 362
 theoretical review 350–353
 total scores evaluation 358
Cooke, T. 310
Cooper, C. 246
Corbin, J.M. 25, 29, 32, 34, 38–40
Cordy, T. 163
Coronado, G. 274

corporate financial performance (CFP) 56, 196–197, 222, 223
corporate governance (CG) 55–56, 60, 415
corporate reputation 222
corporate social disclosure (CSD) 309
corporate social performance (CSP) 56, 222
correspondence analysis 267
  see also correspondence analysis and human resources disclosure
correspondence analysis and human resources disclosure 227, 308–325
  amount (page measurement) 309
  analysis of correspondence 313–314
  annual reports 227, 308–313, 316, 318–319, 321–322, 323
  assets 323
  audit company 319, 321–322
  audit report 311, 321, 323, 325
  background 309–310
  bias 322, 324
  chi-squared test 314–315, 319
  company selection 311
  company size 311, 318–319
  compulsory disclosure 315
  content analysis 308, 309, 313
  contingency table 313–314
  corporate social disclosure (CSD) 309
  countries 310, 316–318, 321, 323
  design and methodology 311–315
  dimension or axis 314
  employees/human resources 309
  environment 309
  evidence 309
  exchange effect 310
  follow the leader practice 310
  Form 20-F 227, 308, 311–313, 315–319, 321–322, 323–324
  generally accepted accounting practice (GAAP) 227, 308, 309
  Germany 310, 311, 316, 317–318, 322
  global analysis 315–316
  industry 318, 321, 322, 323
  inertia 314
  international financial reporting standards (IFRS) 227
  limitations of research 322–323
  listing status 310, 311, 319, 320, 321, 323, 324
  location in report 309
  number of reports with information about different issues 313
  political costs 310
  principal component analysis 314
  principal inertia 314–315
  R package ca 314
  reciprocal averaging 314
  results 315–323
  scoring sheet categories 311–312, 322
  singular value decomposition 314
  size of company 309–310, 318–319, 321, 323
  social issues 309
  Spain 311, 316, 317, 322
  subspace 314
  theme 309
  total disclosure 315–316
  transparency 309
  United Kingdom 310, 311, 316, 322
  US Securities and Exchange Commission (US-SEC) 308, 311, 321
  value relevance 310
  voluntary disclosure 309, 315–316, 322
corruption 21
Cournot, A. 112
Courtés, J. 258
Cramer, D. 193
creative accounting 63
credibility 52, 304
Creswell, J.W. 59, 445, 448–449
Crifo, P. 345
Crisóstomo, L. 345
critical incident techniques 286, 288
critical theory 100, 101, 438
Cronbach, L.J. 193
cross-sectional design 129
Crotty, M. 443, 445
Crowther, D. 11, 26, 243, 271–272, 274, 306, 402, 412–413
CSR reports (CSRR) 226, 241–243, 244–246, 254
CSR-based management research process 9–20
  conducting research 11
  environmental issues 12–14
  governance problems 15–16
  human rights issues 14–15
  organisational and regional studies 16–18
  Social Responsibility Research Network perspectives 11–12
  stakeholder perspectives 18–20
Czarniawska, B. 234, 406

data-gathering techniques see survey research
Davison, J. 241, 246–247
De Bord, G. 378
De Neve, G. 274
deductive approach 3–5, 6
  application 4
  conducting research 11
  empirical observation – data collection 4–5
  falsification and discarding theory 5

nomothetic methods 7
positivism and social constructivism 442
theory/hypothesis formation 4
Deegan, C. 287
Delamont, S. 232
Deming, E. 141
Denzin, N.K. 445
Depoers, E. 310
Derrida, J. 415
Descartes, R. 422
descriptive statistics 178, 182–185, 196, 197, 203
descriptive studies 57, 205
DeVaus, D.A. 341
Dietz, T. 113, 117–118
Dillman, D.A. 340
direct observation 296
disclosure 21, 70–71
   see also content analysis method for quantitative and qualitative disclosures; correspondence analysis and human resources disclosure
Djajadikerta, H. 350
document analysis
   ethnographic research methods 267, 268, 272, 273
   interview techniques 283, 285, 286
Donaldson, L. 79
Donkin, A. 162, 165
Doucouliagos, H. 57
Driscoll, C. 295
Duarte, F. de P. 225, 266
Duijn, M.A.J. van 395
Duisit, L. 253
Dumay, J. 284
Dyer, W.G. 403

Easterby-Smith, M. 2, 443, 444
Eckstein, H. 452
Eco, U. 247, 251
ecological footprint 13
economic, social and environmental factors 104, 272, 432, 444
   content analysis (CA) method for quantitative and qualitative disclosures 353, 359, 362
   methodological and epistemological perspectives 94, 96, 98, 104
   see also social and environmental accounting
Eisenhardt, K.M. 403, 452
Ellis, C. 265, 266
empirical studies 4–5, 205
Enron 65, 67, 74–75, 377
environmental factors 12–14, 125, 206, 309, 415

content analysis method for quantitative and qualitative disclosures 353, 359, 360, 362
impact measurement 18
impact (sustainability) 423
performance 205
protection 16
reports 17
see also economic, social and environmental factors
epistemological approach 2, 11, 44, 46–47
   positivism and social constructivism 437, 441, 442, 444, 447–448
   see also methodological and epistemological perspectives and CSR in Colombia
errors
   non-sampling 283
   recall 132
   statistical methods 180, 190, 191
   survey research 331, 341, 342–343
   see also sampling and sampling procedures
ethics in research process 10, 25, 26, 63–75
   codes of conduct 67
   codes of ethics 72–74
   confidentiality 68, 71, 74
   consent 68–69, 74, 75
   corporate behaviour 67
   deontological ethics 65
   disclosure of findings 70–71
   ethical approval form 73–74
   ethical dilemmas 74
   ethical objectivism 65, 66–67
   ethical relativism 65, 66
   honesty, respect and confidence 64
   litigation 71–72
   loyalty 72
   managers and business ethics 63–64
   opportunities for further work 71–72
   participant observation methods and ethnography 305–306
   positivism and social constructivism 447
   replicability 69–70
   in research process, codes or values 10
   social network analysis (SNA) 397
   survey research 343–344
   teleological ethics 65
   transparency of purpose 69
   University Ethics Committee 73
   utilitarianism 65–66
   'what' and 'why' of ethics 64–65
ethnographic research methods 226, 265–277
   case studies 272–276
   content analysis 268
   correspondence analysis 267
   cultural artefacts 270

definition 265–266
digital ethnography 266, 270, 272–273, 274
facts 269
in-depth studies 276
interviewing 226, 267, 268–269, 273–275
laws 265
'meaning' 265, 269–270
organisational culture 270
participant observation 226, 267, 268–269, 273–275
review 268–271
review of used in CSR 271–276
surveys 269
textual or document analysis 267, 268, 272, 273
urban ethnography 269
visual ethnography 226, 267, 270
see also auto-ethnography (self-reporting)
ethnography 7, 10, 99, 448
interview techniques 283, 286
theoretical storytelling 404, 406
see also ethnographic research methods; participant observation methods and ethnography
EU CSR Alliance 276
Eugénio, T. 280, 285
Euske, K.J. 89–90
Ewald, F. 433
experimental research 186, 395, 450–451
extractive industries 13–14, 23

factor analysis 197, 199
Fallon, W. 274
falsification and discarding theory 5
Faust, K. 391, 394
Feld, L.P. 57
feminist-post-structuralism 445
Fern, E.F. 366
Feyerabend, P. 76, 81, 83, 88–89, 415
fiduciary duty 19
Field, A.P. 59
field notes 34, 300, 301–303, 448
Financial Accounting Standards Board (FASB) 242
financial performance 21–22, 58, 197, 205, 222, 223
Fiol, C.M. 243, 256
Fish, S. 445
Fisher, J. 95
Floch, J.-M. 256
focus groups 48–50, 286, 336–337
aims and strengths 49–50
control characteristics 49
definition and composition 48–49
full group 48

mini-group 48–49
mixed methods approach 44, 45–46, 48–50, 53
sampling, representativeness and validity 50
telephone group 48
see also focus groups in social accounting as stakeholder engagement tool
focus groups in social accounting as stakeholder engagement tool 228, 364–375
accountability 369, 374
clinical focus group 365
coding 369
composition 366
duration 366
exploratory focus group 365
facilitator 367–368
follow-up 367–368
gatekeeper 367–368
location 366
moderator 367–368
organisation of focus group 366–369
phenomenological focus group 365
post-meeting 368–369
reliability 373
replicability 373
semi-structured questionnaires 367, 371
Sirio (Italy) social accounting process and stakeholder engagement 228, 370–372
size 366
social background 366
social and environmental reporting 369
stakeholder engagement 365, 369–370
Sirio (Italy) 365
stakeholder map 369
strengths 372–373
structured questionnaires 367
sustainability principles 369
validation 368
weaknesses 372–373
Fontana, A. 284
food deserts in British cities 108, 159–175
community and government initiatives to improve food access 174–175
consequences 161
data narratives: diet and obesity 170–174
definition of food deserts 159–161
demographic and geographic characteristics 162–165, 166
diet 159, 161–162, 165, 166, 168, 169, 170–174, 175
diseases 161
ethnicity 159, 162, 163–165, 168, 169–170, 174

fast lane syndrome 173
FFV (fresh fruit and vegetables) 165, 167, 169, 170–171, 172–173, 174, 175
food cost and food knowledge 173
'food time' 173
green stores 160
health 159–160, 166
Low Income Diet and Nutrition Survey 161
Low Income Project Team (LIPT) 159
methodology 165–166
Middle Level Super Output Areas (MLSOAs) 163–166, 169
Modifiable Areal Unit Problem (MAUP) 166
Neighbourhood Statistics 159, 165
obesity 159, 161–162, 165–175
policy direction 175
poverty indicators 160, 162, 165, 168, 170, 172, 173
psychiatric problems 161
residents affects 160–161
results: correlations 166–174
  demography related 166
  geographical/access related 166
  health related 166
  partial correlations as social transects 169–170
  wealth related 167–169
retailers 160
shop-to-residence distance 165–166, 169, 170, 172, 173
SMEs 159
socio-demographic factors 169
socio-economic factors 159, 161–162, 165–166, 167
time and food effects 173–174, 175
Forget, V.D. 345
formal surveys 197
Fowler, F.J. 339, 342
Freedman, M. 242
Freeman, R.E. 272
Frey, J.H. 284
Frias-Aceituno, J. 446
Fricker, R.D. 153, 155
Friedman, M. 64, 378, 435
Frooman, J. 56
Frost, C. 18
funding of research 23
future research agenda 22–23, 415–458
  philosophical prolegomena 419–426
  positivism and social constructivism 437–458
  responsibility as foundation of ethics 428–436

Gackston, D. 197
Galaskiewicz, J. 392, 394
Gallagher, M. 162
game theory and sustainability 107, 111–124
  auctions 113
  Bayes theorem 111
  climate problem 116–117, 123–124
  collaboration 122–123
  competition 122
  complete information 115–116
  cooperative strategy 119
  decision theory 107, 112
  deductive logic 107, 112
  defect strategy 119
  discrete/continuous games 116
  dominance strategy 118–120
  extensive, normal, characteristic function 114
  history and impact of game theory 112–113
  importance of game theory 116–122
  inductive logic 107, 112
  infinitely long game 116
  intrasensitivity 124
  limitations 122
  linear compensation proposition (LinC) 118
  mathematical techniques 111
  mechanism design theory 113–114
  Nash equilibrium 118, 121–122
  non-cooperative game theory 112
  one-player/many-player games 116
  open game 122
  Pareto optimality 124
  partition function 114
  payoffs, staggered 119
  perfect/non-perfect game 115–116
  Prisoner's Dilemma 114, 115, 118–119, 120, 121
  quality choice 120–121
  risk analysis 111, 122
  risk factors 113–114
  simultaneous/sequential games 115
  strategic decision-making 122
  sustainability and sustainable development 123
  symmetric/asymmetric games 114, 120
  'winning the game' 112
  zero-sum/non-zero-sum games 115, 122
Garfinkel, H. 84
Geertz, C. 269–270
Generally Accepted Accounting Principles (GAAP) 227, 308, 309
Gerring, J. 450
Gherghina, S.C. 332
Giegler, H. 309
Gilbert, N. 2

Gill, J.L. 8–9, 177
Gillett, R. 59
Girard, R. 101
Glaser, B.G. 25, 29, 32, 36, 38–40, 41
Glass, G. 58
Glavas, A. 56
global financial crisis (2008) 15, 50, 67
global governance 15
Global Reporting Initiative (GRI) Sustainability Reporting Guidelines (SRG) 349, 351, 353, 354, 355, 356, 358, 359, 360
global warming, climate change and greenhouse gases 12–13, 23, 116–117, 123–124
Goffman, E. 235–237, 238
Gold, R. 297
Gomm, R. 455
Goodall, B. 405
Goodall Jr, H.L. 271
Goode, W.J. 448
governance 12, 15–16
  see also corporate governance (CG)
Gray, R. 242, 284–285, 309, 365, 369–370
Gray, S.J. 310
Green, M. 26
Greenbaum, T. 48
greenwashing 14
Greenwood, J. 445
Greimas, A.J. 245, 247, 252, 258
grounded theory (GT) 25, 29–41, 286
  applied thematic analysis (ATA) 29, 36–38
  axial coding 33, 35, 40
  classic grounded theory 29–32
  classic methodology 29
  code notes 34
  construction of 38–40
  constructivist grounded theory 35–36
  data interpretation (conceptualization) 40–41
  focused coding 35, 39
  Glaserian 36
  initial coding 35
  interpretive character 36
  open coding 33
  selective coding 34
  social constructivist methodology 29
  structured methodology 29
  structured (Straussian) grounded theory 32–34
group effect 49
group interviews 364
Guba, E.G. 441, 443, 445, 449
Gubrium, J. 288
Gummesson, E. 10, 403, 451, 455–456

Gumperz, J.J. 246
Gunawan, J. 227–228, 350
Guthrie, J. 242
Guy, C. 162

Habermas, J. 379, 386, 389, 446
Hackston, D. 242, 243
Halinen, A. 452
Hamlett, J. 173, 174
Hammersley, M. 448
Hanson, N.R. 81, 83
Harsanyi, J. 113
Hasseldine, J. 243
Hatch, M.J. 78
Hatt, P.K. 448
Hawthorne Experiments at General Electric Company (USA) 8
Hayek, F.A. 420, 425
Hayes, T. 289
Hébert, L. 255, 261
Heckemeyer, J.H. 57
Hegel, G.W.F. 101
Ho, S.S.M. 243
Höllerer, M. 273
Holman-Jones, S. 233
Holstein, J.A. 288
Holsti, O.R. 352
Holt, N.L. 233
Hooks, J. 243
Howard, K. 9
Hubbert, M.K. 23
Hubbert's Peak 14, 23
Huberman, M.A. 289, 305
Hughes, B. 115
Huisman, M. 395
human rights issues 14–15, 16
Husserl, E. 384
Husted, B.W. 222, 398
Hwang, L.S. 310
Hyunwoo, L. 162

ideographic research 7, 11
Imamichi, T. 428–429, 430
in-depth interviews 44–45, 50–53, 101, 276, 345
  aims and strengths 52
  definition and composition 50–51
  sampling, representativeness and validity 52–53
inductive approach 6, 7, 11, 442
Inglis, V. 173
Inoue, Y. 223
internal organisation culture 10
International Accounting Standards Board (IASB) 242

470 *Handbook of research methods in corporate social responsibility*

International Emission Trading (IET) 117
interpretive interactionism 288
interpretivism 44, 46–47, 445, 446–447, 448
interview techniques 285, 364
   computer-assisted telephone interviewing (CATI) 338
   conducting 338–339
   duration 51
   ethnographic research methods 226, 267, 268–269, 273–275
   in-depth *see* in-depth interviews
   informal 300–301
   logistical considerations 51
   mixed methods approach 45–46
   personal 335–336
   social network analysis (SNA) 394–395
   structured interviewing 51, 282–283, 284, 329, 338–339
   survey research 334
   telephone 337–338
   unstructured interviewing 51, 282–284, 286, 301–302
   see also interview techniques and management motivation for corporate social and environmental reporting
interview techniques and management motivation for corporate social and environmental reporting 226, 280–289
   active interviewing 288
   bias 289
   convergent interviews 286, 288
   creative interviewing 288
   critical incident techniques 286, 288
   cultural interviews 284
   definition of interview as research method 281–282
   document analysis 283
   emotional cost 284
   empathetic approach 283, 284
   ethnographic studies 283
   focus group interviews 286
   global context 287–288
   'how' of interviews 288
   in-depth interviews 280, 286–287, 288
   internet interviews 288
   interpretation issues 289
   interpretive interactionism 288
   interviewer effect 283
   laddering technique 288
   limitations 288–289
   neopositivist approach 284
   open-ended design 284
   polyphonic interview 288
   rapport 283
   reconceptualizing interview 284
   reflexivity 281, 284, 288, 289
   reliability 288–289
   romanticist approach 284
   semi-structured interview *see* semi-structured interview
   social and environmental accounting (SEA) research 284–287
   structured interview 282–283, 284
   topical interviews 284
   translating and transcribing interview data 289
   unstructured interview 282–283, 284, 286
Islam, M.A. 226, 267, 287

Jain, T.N. 246, 261
Jamali, D. 396
James, K. 441
Jayasinghe, K. 286
Johnson, J.M. 284
Johnson, P. 8–9
Johnson, V.E. 310
Joiner, T.A. 134
Joint Implementation (JI) 117
Jonas, H. 431–432, 433
Jones, R.E. 244–245, 257, 260

Kalinauskaitė, R. 107–108
Kant, I. 377–379, 380, 381–389, 429
Kapelus, P. 237
Kelsen, H. 379, 430
Kennedy, M.M. 455
Kennett-Hensel, P. 136
Keshishian, T. 396
Khan, H.Z. 108
Khan, Md. R. 108
Khurana, I. 310
Kilduff, M. 393
Kincaid, H. 77
Kitzinger, J. 364, 366, 368, 373
Klein, H. 309
Kotler, P. 350
Kramer, M.R. 406–407
Kreuger, L.W. 337
Krippendorff, K. 197, 349, 352
Krueger, R.A. 371
Kuder, G.F. 192
Kuhn, T.S. 76, 80–81, 83, 415
Kutlu, O. 197
Kvale, S. 284
Kyoto Protocol 13, 117, 123

Lacey, R. 136
Lather, P. 78, 84
Lauesen, L.M. 226, 229, 293, 306
Lauesen, S.B. 410–412

Laumann, E.O. 392
Lay, K. 74–75
Lazarsfeld, P.F. 125–126, 364
Lee, G. 162
Lee, M.P. 438
Lee, N. 350
Lee, S. 223
legal rules 67
Lehman, C. 286
Lehman, G. 243
Lev, B. 312
Lévi-Strauss, C. 251, 252
Levinas, E. 378, 430–431, 433
Levine, D.K. 113–114
Levinson, S.C. 246
Likert scale 86, 88, 90, 181, 193, 197, 346
Lincoln, Y.S. 441, 443, 445, 449
Lindgreen, A. 451–452, 458
Livingstone, S. 373
longitudinal study design 107–108, 125–136
  age effects 134
  application of in CSR 135–136
  archival method 136
  case studies 451
  cause-and-effect relationships 127, 129–130
  change 128–129
  cohorts 127, 133–135
  concept and definition 125–126
  cross-sectional design 129
  disadvantages 130–133
    anonymity 131
    attrition and missing data 130–131
    cost 131
    panel conditioning 132–133
    retrospective study, weaknesses of 131–132
  generations 133–135
  gross change 128–129
  intervals: length and periodicity 126–127
  net change 128
  'on' and 'in' organisations 129–130
  panel 126, 131, 132
    attrition 136
    designs 128
    members 126
    study 127, 134
    survey 126
    technique 126
  period effects 126–127, 134
  prospective studies 125, 132, 136
  purpose and advantages in organisations 127–130
  recall error 132
  repeated measures 126
  retrospective 136
  short- and long-term effects 127
  social change 134
  subjective measures 132
  time series 126, 128
  trend studies 126
  waves 127, 128, 130–131, 132, 133
Lovelock, J. 13
Lozano, E. 99
Luckmann, T. 445
Lucy, J.A. 246
Lukman, R. 26
Lunt, P. 373
Lynn, M. 309
Lynne, L. 134

Maccoby, E.E. 281
Macintosh, N.B. 241, 243, 246
Macve, R. 18
Majid, A. 345
Malinowski, B. 268, 293
management research, types of 7–9
Manion, L. 182, 186
Mannheim, K. 445
Marens, R. 19–20
Margolis, J. 56, 379, 385
Marshall, C. 289
Marx, K. 377
Masten, D.L. 270
mathematical techniques 111
  see also statistical techniques
Mattimoe, R. 289
Maupin, J.R. 133
Mazutis, D.D. 135
McCoy, C.S. 63
McGlone, T. 134
McGoun, E.G. 246
McNamee, S. 447
McNicholas, P. 369–370, 373
Means, G.C. 419
Medina, L.C. 102–103
Meek, G.K. 310
Mejia, C. 100
memos 34, 35–36
Merriam, S.B. 448
Merton, R.K. 364
meta-study 25, 26, 55–60
  academic research 57–59
  corporate financial performance (CFP) 56
  corporate governance (CG) 55–56, 60
  corporate social performance (CSP) 56
  data extraction 55
  implications 60
  materials and method 60

meta-analytical approach 56
meta-communicative events 53
meta-data analysis 55, 57, 58–59, 60
meta-method 55, 57, 58, 60
meta-synthesis 55, 57, 59, 60
meta-theory 55, 57, 58, 60
mixed methods approach 57, 58, 60
step-by-step approach 57, 59
methodological and epistemological perspectives and CSR in Colombia 26–27, 94–105
  assumptions and nature of realities of CSR 95–99
  'Care for Your Health SAS' 102
  case studies 99
  classic methodology 29
  conceptualization of social responsibility 101
  content analysis 99
  critical theory 100, 101
  deductive analytics 100
  empirical study 101
  epistemological approach 103
  ethnography 99
  financial capitalism and globalization 102–103
  government and general interest groups 97
  in-depth interviews 101
  Inclusive Business 100
  ISO 26000 102
  legitimacy/illegitimacy 94, 98, 104
  methodological approaches 94, 99–103
  non-participatory observation 100, 101
  objectivity 104
  paternal responsibility 101–102
  proactive point of view 97
  production and creation 97
  productive scenario 98
  protection and security 97
  reactive point of view 97
  secondary data 99
  semi-structured interviews 99–100, 103
  social justice 94, 98, 104
  Social Policy 100
  Socially Responsible Management 102
  socio-environmental and economic problems 94, 96, 98, 104
  source data 99
  structural tensions 103
  subjectivity 99, 104
  telecommunications sector 101–102
  triangulation 101
methodological pluralism 8–9
methodology planning 10, 22, 25–105
  ethics in research process 63–75

grounded theory (GT) 29–41
meta-study 55–60
methodological and epistemological perspectives and CSR in Colombia 94–105
mixed methods approach 44–54
quantitative and qualitative approaches in management accounting 76–91
Michell, L. 45, 46
Miles, M.B. 289, 305
Milgram, S. 69, 70
Mill, J.S. 429
Miller, G. 84
Milne, M.J. 197, 242, 243
Mitchell, R.K. 395
mixed methods approach 25–26, 44–54, 57–58, 60, 285, 345, 450
  aims 53
  debtors and debt collectors 44
  epistemological considerations: interpretivism 46–47
  focus groups 44, 45–46, 48–50, 53
  in-depth interviews 50–53
  National Debtline 47–48
  online surveys 47–48
  strengths 53
Modell, S. 89
Moggi, S. 228
moral discourse see phenomenological study of moral discourse and social justice
Morgan, D.L. 45, 49–50, 364–365, 366, 368, 373, 374–375
Morgan, G. 7
Morgenstern, O. 112
Morrison, K. 182, 186
Muñoz, A. 101
Murthy, D. 270, 274

Nafez, A.B. 309
Nagel, E. 65
Naser, K. 309
Nash, J. 112–113, 123
neopositivist approach 284
Neufeld, M.A. 58
Neuman, L.W. 337
Neumann, J. von 111, 112, 123
nominalism 443, 448
nomothetic research 7, 11
non-governmental organisations (NGOs) 396, 398
non-participatory observation 100, 101
non-response 149, 150, 155

objectivist approach 104, 303–304, 405, 444, 446

O'Dwyer, B. 371
Ofori, D.E. 346
Ohlsson, C. 132
Oikonomou, I. 135
O'Neill, O. 385
online surveys 44, 45, 47–48, 53
ontological orientation 2–3
  positivism and social constructivism 437, 441, 442–444, 447–448
  semiotics 256, 257, 258–260
organisational culture 270, 299
organisational model 85
organisational structure 21
organisational studies 16–18
Orlitzky, M. 56
Ortiz, E. 227, 267
Oruc, I. 226–227, 267
Ospina, D. 26–27
Ospina, J. 26–27

Paine, L.S. 434
Paldam, M. 57
panel *see* longitudinal study design
Panozzo, F. 86
Parker, L.D. 242, 280, 285
participant observation 369, 448
  see also participant observation methods and ethnography
participant observation methods and ethnography 226, 267, 268–269, 273–275, 281, 293–306
  ability of researcher 304
  advantages 298
  being local 296
  credibility 304
  CSR research 299–300
  culture shock 298
  data analysis 303–306
  data recording 303
  direct observation 296
  duration in field 298
  ethics 305–306
  ethnographers 296
  ethnography 293–295, 297, 299–300, 303, 305–306
  etic (internal) and emic (external) points of view 299
  evaluator 300
  field notes 300, 301–303
  field research 293
  gatekeepers 296, 297
  informal interviews 300–301
  key informants 297
  limitations 298–299
  location 296, 297

naturalness 295–296
objectivity 303–304
open approach 296
orderliness 297
organisational culture 299
organisational ethnography 293–295
politics 305
quality of research 204
reference environment 303
reflective diaries 300, 301, 302
reliability 303–305
representation of representation 294
review of readings 303
rights to enter community 297
robustness 304–305
sensitivity 297
stakeholder approach 299–300
sub themes 305
subjectivity 303–304
themes 305
unstructured interviews 301–302
validity 303–305
visual and audio recording tools 296
Pavelin, S. 222
Pearson, K. 178
peer feedback 46
Peirce, C.S. 248–249, 251, 252, 261
performance evaluation 19
Perry, M. 350
personalism 447
Pfeiffer, T. 118
phenomenological approach 437
  see also phenomenological study of moral discourse and social justice
phenomenological study of moral discourse and social justice 228, 377–389
  accountability 380–381, 389
  autonomy 382, 383
  bracketing 384
  categorical moral imperative 379–380, 388
  communicative power 384, 386
  cooperation 382
  critical theory of justice (Kant) 382
  CSR as moral discourse (CMR): Habermasian model 386–388
  Deweyan pragmatism 385
  difference principle 382
  discourse ethics 386, 387–388
  equality 382, 383, 384, 386–387
  ethical principles 379
  fairness 379–380, 381, 389
  freedom 380, 381, 382, 383, 384
  Hegelian-Marxist social theory 386
  impartiality 381, 387
  just organisations 378

justice 379–380, 381, 387
  Kantian constructivism 384–385
  Kantian formulation of CSR as 'an end' and not a 'means' to an end 381–383
  Kantian perspective 380, 387
  legitimacy 383, 387
  liberty principle 382
  minimum set of conditions 384
  moral accountability 381
  moral autonomy 383
  moral constructivism 385
  moral discourse 382–383
  moral duty 377
  moral imperatives 378
  moral obligation 382
  moral philosophy 379
  naturalistic method 377
  neo-Kantians 378–379, 381, 386
  original position 378, 381–382
  practical reason – rational and the reasonable 384
  priority rule 382
  public consensus 378, 380
  rationality 382
  Rawlsian reimagination of corporation as agent of social transformation 383–385
  reflective equilibrium 378
  respect 379–381, 387, 389
  right, conception and definition of 379, 380, 381, 382, 389
  sameness 381
  self-legislation 383, 387
  shared beliefs 384
  transparency 389
  unconditionality 383
  universality 380, 386, 387
  validity 385, 386
  veil of ignorance 378, 381–382, 384–385, 388
philosophical prolegomena 416, 419–426
  advocacy 420
  commercial entity, corporation as 419
  conceptual changes 424
  corporate governance, new forms of 423
  corporations 421–426
  creative destruction 423–424, 425
  environmental impact (sustainability) 423
  explication 420, 421, 422
  globalization 423
  historical background 419
  inequality 423, 426
  legal responsibility and social responsibility 419
  limited government 424, 426
  market economy 423, 424, 426
  norms 420, 422–423
  past practice 421
  personae, new 423
  political state, size of 424–425
  property, new forms of 423
  rule of law 424, 426
  social institutions 419–421
  social relationship, new forms of 423
  stakeholder theory 419
  technological project (TP) 422–424, 426
Pico della Mirandola, G. 429
Piekkari, R. 452
Platt, J. 281
Plowman, T.M. 270
Popper, K.R. 5, 415
Porter, M.E. 406–407, 435
positivism and social constructivism 282–283, 416–417, 437–458
  abductive approach 437, 441–442
  accountability 437
  anti-positivism 445
  bias 441
  bottom up approach 441
  case study
    approach 447–449
    descriptive 449
    exploratory 449
    research model 453–454
    strategy 450–452
  constructionism/constructivism 442, 444, 445, 447, 448
    see also social constructionism/constructivism
  contrasting implications 446
  critical paradigm 445
  critical thinking 438
  CSR development 438, 439–440
  deductive strategy 442
  environmental, social and economic performance 444
  epistemology 437, 441, 442, 444, 447–448
  ethnography 448
  experimental research 450–451
  explanatory research 449
  feminist-post-structuralism 445
  field work 448
  inductive strategy 442
  interpretivism 445, 446–447, 448
  knowledge 444, 447
  life history 448
  logical positivism 77
  methodological and systematic process 441, 456
  mindset of researcher 44, 438
  morality and ethics 447

nominalism 443, 448
objectivist approach 444, 446
ontology 437, 441, 442–444, 447–448
paradigms 438, 441, 444–447
participant observation 448
personalism 447
phenomenological approach 437
positivism 444, 445–446, 447, 448
post-positivism 445
quality criteria for case research 457
relativism 442, 443, 447, 448
reliability 417, 457, 458
replication 455
research choices 441
research methodology 447–449
research paradigms 444, 445–447
research philosophies 444
research strategy 441–442
retroductive strategy 442
single and multiple cases 452, 455–456
social action 443, 446
social constructionism/constructivism 443, 445–446, 447, 448, 458
subjectivity 446–447
survey 451
top down approach 441–442
traditional perspective 443
truth and fact 443
validity 417, 456–458
values and beliefs 437–438
'what' and 'why' questions 441
Post, J.E. 244–245, 257, 260
post-positivism 445
pragmatism 25, 269
Pratt, M.G. 403
Preston, A. 88
Preston, L.E. 244–245, 257, 260
Price, R. 245, 246
principal component analysis 314
Prisoner's Dilemma 114, 115, 118–119, 120, 121
privatisation 21
problem centred/practical research 8–9
Propp, V.I. 252, 253
Pruzan, P. 351
Pugh, D. 77
Puxty, A. 246

Qu, S.Q. 284
qualitative approach 6, 7, 22, 25, 204, 225–414
   analytic autoethnography 231–239
   autoethnography 239
   content analysis method 349–362
   correspondence analysis 308–325
   ethnography 265–277

focus groups 336, 364–375
grounded theory (GT) 29, 33, 40
interview techniques 280, 281, 282, 283, 285, 286
interviews and management motivation 280–289
longitudinal study design 108, 125, 128, 136
meta-study 57, 58, 59, 60
methodological and epistemological perspectives 99–100, 102, 104
mixed methods approach 45, 50, 51, 52
moral discourse and social justice: phenomenological study 377–389
participant observation methods and ethnography 293–306
phenomenological study 228, 377, 378, 379, 384, 385, 389
positivism and social constructivism 448–449, 450
sampling and sampling procedures 157
semiotics 241–261
social network analysis (SNA) 391–398
statistical methods 180, 182–183
survey methodology 328–347
theoretical storytelling 229, 401–414
see also quantitative and qualitative approaches
quantitative approach 6, 7, 10, 22, 25, 107–223
   correspondence analysis 315
   ethnography 276
   focus groups 336
   food deserts in British cities 159–175
   game theory and sustainability 111–124
   longitudinal study design 125–136
   meta-study 57, 58, 59, 60
   mixed methods approach 45
   participant observation methods and ethnography 303, 306
   positivism and social constructivism 450
   regression techniques 205–223
   sampling and sampling procedures 139–158
   statistical methods 177–203
   theoretical storytelling 229, 402–403, 405, 413
   see also quantitative and qualitative approaches
quantitative and qualitative approaches 26, 76–91
   action research 91
   analytic methods 79
   closed questions 88, 89, 91
   commensurability 76, 91
   epistemological approach 85, 91
   ethnography 91
   interpretivist approach 78

legitimacy 76
management and management accounting 83, 84–85
    broader research 89–91
    objectivist research 76, 79–80, 85–89
    qualitative research methods, limitations of 90–91
    subjective aspects 87–88
mathematical techniques 89
neo-positivist approach 77
objectivist approach 76, 77, 79–80, 84–89, 90, 91
    challenges to 83
ontological approach 85, 91
open questions 91
organisation 76
paradigm 89, 91
positivist approach 77, 79, 88–89
qualitative methods 76, 77, 81, 83, 84–85, 86, 89, 91
qualitative ontologies, epistemologies and methodologies 78
quantitative methods 77, 79, 81, 82, 83, 85, 86, 89, 91
quantitative ontologies, epistemologies and methodologies 76–78
questionnaires 77, 79, 86
reflective practice 84
reflexivity 84, 91
scientific knowledge 80–82
scientific methodology 79, 83
statistical and mathematical techniques 79, 80, 81, 83, 86, 90
subjectivist approach 78, 79–80, 86, 90–91
    problems with 83–85
surveys 77, 79
triangulation 89, 91
questionnaires 186, 280, 282, 285, 398
    directly administered 341–342
    mailed 339–340
    semi-structured 367, 371
    structured 367

Raar, J. 353
random-digit dialling 154, 337–338
rapport 283, 337
Rathje, Professor 173
Rawls, J. 65, 378–386, 389
realism 443, 448
    critical 2, 443, 447, 458
reasons for research 1
Reay, T. 403–404, 406, 413
Reed, M.S. 395, 398
reflective diaries 300, 301, 302
reflectivity 47, 225, 231, 233–234, 238

reflexivity
    autoethnography 225, 231–232, 233–234, 238
    interview techniques 281, 284, 288, 289
    mixed methods approach 47, 53
regional studies 16–18
regression techniques 109, 205–223
    ability to predict 206
    AMOS software 221
    analysis of variance (ANOVA) 208
    basic regression concept in social sciences 206
    binary logistic regression: logit and probit models 212–216, 223
        estimated coefficients, estimation of 215–216
        likelihood ratio test 216
    chi-square 215
    coefficients of correlation 207
    correlation and prediction 207–208
    descriptive studies 205
    Developmental Well-being Index 207–208
    domestic violence in India based on National family health survey 212–214
    empirical studies 205
    error in estimation 209
    factor analysis 219
    fixed effects 217
    Freedom House Rule of Law 210–211
    goodness-of-fit 216, 218, 219
    hierarchical regression 222
    'how' question 206
    instrumental studies 205
    likelihood ratio (LR) 212, 215
    McFadden's-R^2 statistic 215, 216
    maximum likelihood estimation 212
    measurement error 220
    multiple regression 209–211
    non-linear regression model 216–217
    odds ratio 212
    ordinary least squares (OLS) regression 209–211, 212, 216, 222
        pooled 217, 222
    panel data regression (pooled data, micro panel data, longitudinal data, event history analysis or cohort analysis) 217–218
    path coefficient 220
    path dependence 223
    path diagrams 220
    Pearson's product moment correlation (Pearson's r) 207
    percent correct predictions statistic 215
    pseudo-R^2 statistic 215
    random effects 217–218

recall ability 211
recent applications in CSR research 221–223
regression coefficient 209–210, 212
regression intercept 209
regression weight 209
residual 209, 220
residual error 220
sample mean 207
scatter plot 207–208
simple linear regression equation 208–209
Spiritual Well-being Index 207
SPSS output 207, 210–212, 215
standard deviations 207
statistical methods 178, 184, 185
structural (simultaneous) equation models (SEM) 218–221
subjective well-being 210–211
t-test 208, 216
un-standardized coefficients 210
variables 205
  continuous predictor 215
  dichotomous 207, 211, 212
  dummy predictor 215
  input (independent, predictor, or explanatory) 205, 208–210, 212, 215, 221
  k predictor 210
  latent 218–219
  observed 219–220
  output (dependent, criterion or outcome) 205, 208, 209–210, 221–222
  quantitative 207
  unobserved 219–220
Wald statistic for β coefficient 212
'when' question 206
z-value 216
relativism 442, 443, 447, 448
reliability
  disclosure 243
  focus groups 373
  inter-rater 194
  interview techniques 288–289
  participant observation methods and ethnography 303–305
  positivism and social constructivism 417, 457, 458
  split-half 192, 193
  statistical methods 191, 193, 197
  survey research 329
Rendtorff, J.D. 416
replication 69–70, 373, 452, 455
representativeness 48, 50, 52–53
research planning 25
response effect 283

response rates 335, 340, 341, 342, 347
responsibility as foundation of ethics 416, 428–436
  absolute responsibility 430–431
  accountability 429
  civil law 429
  collective responsibility 433, 435
  common responsibility 433
  Confucianist virtues 430
  CSR as institutional accountability 434–435
  directorial and managerial responsibility 435
  economic responsibility 434
  economic, social and environmental development 432
  employee responsibility 435
  ethical foundation of concept of responsibility 428–431
  ethical responsibility 434, 435
  freedom 429–431
  fundamental responsibility 431
  global ethic 431–435
  globalization 428
  human dignity 429, 431
  imputation 429–430
  individual responsibility 436
  infinite responsibility 431
  institutional responsibility 435–436
  inter-individuality 430–431
  legal responsibility 430, 434, 435
  moral responsibility 430, 434, 435
  moral subjectivity 429
  ontological responsibility 430
  penal law 429
  philanthropic responsibility 434
  political (state) responsibility in the Welfare State 433–434
  professional responsibility 435
  respect 429
  social responsibility 434, 435, 436
  strategic responsibility 435
  sustainability and sustainable development 432–434, 435
  technological progress 428
  technological responsibility 432–433
  total responsibility 430
  universal responsibility 434
  virtue of responsibility 435
  voluntary responsibility 434
reward schemes 20
Rhoades, D.L. 56
Richardson, M.W. 192
Ricœur, P. 429, 433, 434
Rinaldi, L. 286
Rincón, L.D.C. 102

Ringov, D. 222
Roberts, C.B. 310
Roberts, G.A. 402
Robertson, F. 416–417, 445
Robson, C. 4
Robson, F. 163
robustness 304–305
Rorty, R. 385
Rossman, G.B. 289
Roulston, K. 52
Rowe, M. 265
Rowley, T.J. 394, 396
Rubin, H.J. 281, 284
Rubin, I. 281, 284

St. Pierre, E.A. 78, 84
Sairally, B.S. 188
sampling and sampling procedures 108, 139–158
　advantages 141
　bias 149
　census 140
　cluster sampling 145–146, 154
　consent 155
　convenience sampling 142, 147, 155, 156
　entertainment polls 155
　errors 148–151, 153
　　biased error 149
　　non-sampling errors 148, 150–151
　　random sampling error 148
　　reduction of 149–150
　　sources of 149
　　unbiased error 149
　faulty formulation 149
　focus groups 50
　in-depth interviews 52–53
　judgement (purposive or expert choice) sampling 50, 142, 147, 234
　knowledge networks 155
　mixed (hybrid) sampling 148
　multi-stage sampling 146–147, 154
　Neyman sampling 145
　non-probability sampling 142, 147–148, 153, 155, 156, 329
　　convenience (opportunity, accidental or haphazard) sampling 142, 147, 155, 156
　　judgement (purposive or expert choice) sampling 142, 147
　　quota sampling 142, 147–148
　　snowball sampling 142, 148
　non-response 149, 150, 155
　online surveys 48
　parameter 140
　periodicity 143
　pilot survey 141
　population or target population 139, 156–157
　probability sampling 141–147, 148, 153, 155, 156
　　cluster sampling 145–146, 154
　　equal allocation 144–145
　　multi-stage sampling 146–147
　　Neyman allocation 145
　　optimum allocation 145
　　proportional allocation 145
　　sample size allocation in different strata 144–145
　　simple random sampling (SRS) 142
　　stratified sampling 143–144, 145, 146
　　systematic sampling 142–143
　　two-stratum population 144
　probability survey research 329
　quota sampling 142, 147–148
　random digit dialling (RDD) 154
　random sampling 141, 148
　rejection of certain items 149
　sampling 139–140
　sampling frame (working population) 140, 156–157
　sampling techniques 156–157
　sampling units 140, 157–158
　selective factor, presence of 149
　simple random sampling 142
　size of sample 139, 149–150, 151–152, 153, 156–157, 158
　snowball sampling 142, 148
　statistic 140
　statistical methods 177
　stratified sampling 143–144, 145, 146, 154
　substitution 149
　surveys 141
　　census (complete enumeration) 140
　　harvested e-mail list 155–156
　　intercept 155
　　internet-based 153–154
　　list-based sampling frame 153–154
　　non-list-based random sampling 154
　　pre-recruited panel 155
　　unrestricted self-selected 156
　systematic sampling 142–143, 148, 155
　theoretical sampling 40
　volunteer (opt-in) panels 156
Samy, M. 416–417, 445
Sapir, E. 261
Saravanamuthu, K. 286
Sartre, J.-P. 430–431, 433
Saunders, M. 3
Saussure, F. de 247, 249, 250, 251, 252, 261
Sayer, A. 2

Schaltegger, S. 17
Schein, E.H. 270
Scheler, M. 445
Schelling, T. 119
Schofield, J. 455
Schumpeter, J. 423, 425
Schutz, A. 446–447
Schwartz, B.N. 242
Seale, C. 84
segment marketing 198
Seifi, S. 107
Selten, R. 113
Semeen, H. 226, 267
semi-structured interviews 282–283, 284, 286–287, 288
  methodological and epistemological perspectives 99–100, 103
  mixed methods approach 45, 51
  survey research 338–339
semiotics 225–226, 241–261, 272
  action/idea 254
  actual world 255–256
  analyst ratings 241–242
  Barthesian semiotics 252–253, 260
  being 258–261
  characteristics 258
  competence 254–255, 257, 258
  computer-assisted methodology 242
  connotation 249
  corporate reporting as language of business 246–247
  corporation/stakeholder model 245
  counterfactual world 255–256
  criticisms 250–251
  CSR reports (CSRR) 226, 241–243, 244–246, 254
  cultural meaning 250
  denotation 249
  dialectics 255
  dialogics 255
  disclosure 244, 246
    quality 241–243
    quantity 242
    reliability 243
  evaluative stage 245
  expectation gap 244–245
  firm/society relationship 244–245
  folktales/stories 253–254, 260
  forward-looking information 256–257
  framework 245
  functional fixation 261
  further developments 249–250
  Greimas semiotics 247, 252–260
    canonical narrative schema 245, 254–255, 256, 260
  CSRR-quality semiotic framework 253–254, 256, 259
    framework 255–260
    narrative semiotic method 253–254, 257
  iconic elements 248
  illusory status 258–259, 260, 261
  indexical elements 248
  interpretant 248–249
  Linguistic Relativity hypothesis 261
  linguistic sign 247–248
  linguistic turn 241, 246
  manipulation 254–255, 257, 258
  meta-terms 258, 260–261
  modality 255, 258
  morphological perspective 255
  myth 249
  narrative 253–255
  not-being 258–261
  not-seeming 258–261
  object 248–249, 254, 258
  ontological status 256, 257, 258–260
  orders-of-simulacra theory 243
  paradigmatic values 250, 252–253, 260
  Peirce semiotics 248–249
  performance 254–255, 257, 258
  possible world 255–256
  quality of framework 242, 261
  radical semiotics 243
  real status 260
  reciprocal presupposition 255
  referent 249
  relational values – syntagmatic and paradigmatic 250, 252–253
  representamen 248–249
  reward 254–255, 258
  sanction phase 254–255, 258
  Sapir-Whorf hypothesis 246
  Saussure semiology 247–248
  secret status 258–259, 261
  seeming 258–261
  semantic perspective 255
  semantic unit 256
  semiosis 248
  semiotic square of veridiction (Veridictory Square) 258–260
  signification 249, 250, 252–253, 256, 257, 259, 260
  signified 247–249, 251
  signifier 247–249, 251
  spatial structure of narrative 255
  structuralism 261
  subject 254, 258
  symbolic elements 248
  syntagmatic approach 250, 252–253, 255, 260

temporal structure of narrative 255
textual analysis 243, 250
triadic model of the sign 248–249
truth/falseness 253, 255, 258–259, 261
values 250, 261
veridictory status 255–256, 258–260, 261
Seneca 429
Sethi, M. 109
Shachar, M. 59
Shanks, G. 245, 246
Sharp, J.A. 9
Shaw, H. 108
Shaw, J. 228
Siegel, D.S. 222
Silverman, D. 46, 51, 53, 84
Simionescu, L.N. 332
Simons, D.J. 69
Simons, R. 79, 85–86, 87, 88, 89, 90, 91
Singh, D.R. 309
Smith, K. 174
Smith, M. 350
Smith, T. 63
social accounting *see* focus groups in social accounting as stakeholder engagement tool
social constructivism *see* positivism and social constructivism
social desirability bias 336, 337
social and environmental accounting 17–18, 284–287
social and environmental reporting 365, 369
social factors 309, 353, 360, 361, 362
  see also economic, social and environmental factors
social justice *see* phenomenological study of moral discourse and social justice
social network analysis (SNA) 228–229, 391–398
  actor 395
  advantages 398
  archival records 395
  centrality 394, 396
  characteristics 393–395
  collaborative social responsibility projects 396–397, 398
  conceptual framework 391–392
  CSR research 395–397
  data collection method 394–395, 398
  disadvantages 398
  dyadic method 394, 395
  ethical conduct among employees 397
  experiments 395
  flows 394
  future implications 397–398
  interactions 394

internalizing CSR 396
interviewing 394–395
methodological approach 393–395
network density 396
observing 394–395
outsourcing CSR 396
paradigmatic characteristics 393, 394
principles 393
protective belt theories 393
questioning 394–395
roles and positions 394
similarities 394
social relations 394
software packages 395
stakeholder relations 395–396
structural and locational properties 394
subgroup 395
ties – directed, undirected, dichotomous or valued 394
triadic method 394, 395
social responsibility principles 16, 67
Social Responsibility Research Network perspectives 11–12
Socrates 429
Solarte, R.M.R. 101
Spanish, M.T. 364–365, 366, 368, 373, 374–375
Sparkes, A.C. 233
Sparks, A. 162
Spence, L.J. 286
Staden, C.J. van 243
Stagliano, A.J. 242
Stake, R.E. 448, 449, 452
Stakeholder Influence Capacity (SIC) construct 223
stakeholder perspectives 10–11, 17–20, 299–300
  see also focus groups in social accounting as stakeholder engagement tool
Stalker, G.M. 85–86
Stanford Prison experiment 69, 75
Stanwick, P.A. 205
Stanwick, S.D. 205
Starik, M. 295
statistical methods 10, 108–109, 177–203
  accuracy 197
  alpha coefficient 193
  analysis of time series 179
  analysis of variance (ANOVA) 201, 202
  arithmetic average or mean, median and mode 178
  bar charts 187
  Bartlett Test of Sphericity 197
  behavioural observation 194
  bivariate normal distribution 196

box plots 187
chi-square statistical test 188, 189–190
classification 198
cluster analysis 197–203
　algorithms 201
　dissimilar clusters 201
　distance measures 200
　extension chapters on advanced techniques 198–199
　hierarchical cluster analysis 199–200, 201
　K-means clustering 201–202, 203
　membership variable 202
　non-hierarchical clustering methods 203
　SPSS activity 202
　squared Euclidean distance 201
　Ward's method 201
coefficient of contingency 179
coefficient of correlation 178
coefficient of standard deviation 178
coefficient of variation 178
Cohen's Kappa 194
common factors 196
contingency table 189
continuous data 183
Cronbach's Alpha 193
Cronbach's values 197
cross-tabulations 187, 188–189
　in CSR 177–178
　data 196–197
dendogram 199–200, 201–202
dependent variables 184–185
descriptive statistics 178, 182–185, 196, 197, 203
discovery phase 177
discrete data 183
discriminant analysis 198
dissimilarity (distances) 199
distribution free test 186
Euclidean distance 199, 200, 201
expected frequencies 189
F values 202
factor analysis 197, 199
false negative errors 190
false positive errors 190
fitness for audience 187
frequencies/frequency tables 183, 187
fusion process 200, 201
geometric mean and harmonic mean 178
graphs 187
histograms 183, 187
hypothesis testing 184
independent observation 196
independent variables 184–185
index numbers 179

inferential statistics (sampling statistics) 178, 184–185, 203
inter-rater reliability 194
inter-relationships 198
internal consistency or reliability 193, 197
interval scales 180, 181, 186, 196
interview techniques 283
Islamic finance 188
KMO (Kaiser–Meyer–Olkin) test 197
Kuder–Richardson Formula 20 (K–R 20) 192–193
kurtosis 178, 184, 185
Likert scale 181, 193, 197
line graphs 187
linkage points 199–200
mean 178, 183
mean deviation 178
measurement error 180, 191
measures of central tendency 178
median 178, 183
metric 181
minimum and maximum 183
mode 178, 183
multi-regression 197
multiple correlation coefficient 178
nominal variables 180, 186, 190
observed frequencies 189
ordinal variables 180–181, 186
parametric and non-parametric data 185–188
　exploratory data analysis: frequencies, percentages and cross-tabulations 186–188
partial correlation coefficient 178
Pearson correlation coefficients 196
percentages 187
pie charts 187
power calculations 190–191
probability 189, 194
Pythagoras' theorem 201
range 178
rating scales 180–181
ratio variables 181–182, 186, 196
regression analysis 178, 184, 185
relative analysis 197
reliability 191, 197
reproducibility 197
　in research 178–179
sample size 190–191
sampling and sampling procedures 156
scales of data 180–182
scatterplots with regression lines 187
significance level 190
similarity (distances) 200
skewness 178, 184, 185

Spearman–Brown formula 192
split-half reliability 192, 193
squared Euclidean distance 199, 200–201
stability 197
standard deviation 178, 183
standard error of the mean 184
statistical data 179
statistical inference 109, 177
Statistical Package for Social Sciences
    (SPSS) 188, 190, 199–200, 201
statistical significance 189, 190–191
statistics of attributes 178
statistics of variables 178
survey instrument or indicator validity
    195
triangulation 195
unique factors 196
validity 191, 195–196, 197
    constructing validity 197
    content validity 195, 197
    criterion validity 195
    factor analysis 196
variables 180, 196, 198
variance 178, 183, 193
Yule's coefficient of association 178
statistical relationships 280, 285
Stengel, B. von 115
Strauss, A.L. 25, 29, 32, 34, 38–40, 41
Street, D.L. 310
structuralism 261
subjectivist approach
    content analysis method 227, 228, 349–350,
        352, 355, 360, 362
    critical subjectivity 231
    ethical relativism 66
    interview techniques 289
    longitudinal study 132
    methodological and epistemological
        perspectives 99, 104
    participant observation methods and
        ethnography 303–304
    positivism and social constructivism
        446–447
    theoretical storytelling 405
Sulkunen, P. 256
Sullivan, P. 266
Sun, L. 185
survey research 227, 280, 328–347
    analytic survey 329
    anonymity 337, 340, 344
    bias 333, 335, 337
        interviewer 336, 340
        response 343
        sample 343
        social desirability 336, 337

case studies 345–346
census 330–331
cohort studies 333
conducting the survey 335, 338–339
confidentiality 340, 343–344
confirmatory survey 329
constructing the instrument 334
cross-sectional survey 227, 328, 332, 333
data-gathering techniques 335–342
    computer-assisted telephone interviewing
        (CATI) 338
    conducting the interview 338–339
    directly administered questionnaires
        341–342
    electronic mail surveys 340
    focus groups 336–337
    internet (web-based) surveys 341
    mailed questionnaires 339–340
    personal interviews 335–336
    telephone interviews 337–338
    training the interviewer 339
definition 329
descriptive survey 328, 329
disadvantages 336
errors 331, 341, 342–343
ethical issues 343–344
ethnicity/racial issues 336
ethnographic research methods 269
exploratory survey 329
focus classification 330
gender issues 336
group-administered surveys 344
in-depth interviews 345
in-person surveys 344
interview techniques 282, 285, 334
large-scale data 329
longitudinal surveys 227, 328, 332–333
mail surveys 344
mailed questionnaires 335
mixed method approach 345
no-returns 335
non-probability sampling 329
online see online surveys
opinion polling 331
panel studies 332
phone surveys 344
pilot 197
planning 334
population of interest 330, 334
positivism and social constructivism 451
probability sampling 329
probes and pauses 339
questionnaire surveys 329, 334, 345, 346
random-digit dialling 337–338
rapport 337

recent applications in CSR research 344–346
reliability 329
response rates 335, 340, 341, 342, 347
sample survey 330–332
sampling 329, 334
scope classification 330
semi-structured interviews 338–339
social 450
statistical methods 186
structured interviews 329, 338–339
survey technique 334–335
time dimension surveys 332
trend studies 332–333
see also sampling and sampling procedures
sustainability reports 227, 228, 349, 351–352, 353, 358, 362
sustainability and sustainable development 12, 14, 21–22, 369, 415, 432–434, 435
see also game theory and sustainability

Tang, Z. 135
Tauginienė, L. 25
Tengblad, S. 132
Teoh, H.Y. 309
textual analysis 267, 268, 272, 273
theoretical research 11, 34
theoretical storytelling 229, 401–414
   characters 406–407
   climax 408, 410
   Conclusion 408
   conflict escalation 408, 409
   direct voicing 404–405
   Discussion section 404
   elaboration 408, 409
   ethnography 404, 406
   evidence-based approach 402, 406
   Findings section 404, 408
   helpers 406–407, 413
   heroes 406–407, 413
   indirect voicing 405
   interpretation 406
   Introduction 404, 408
   narrative approach 229, 402
   Narrative Arc 229, 402, 407–410, 413, 414
   narrative voice 404–405
   plot-making 407–410
   'point of no return' 408, 409
   points for composing a good paper 403–404
   presentation 408, 409
   punch (headline) 408–409
   rounding off 408, 410
   'showing' versus 'telling' 404, 405–406
   stories 410–413
   techniques: theory and practice 404–410
   victim(s) 406–407, 413
   villains 406–407, 413
theory building research 8
theory testing research 8
theory/hypothesis formation 4
Thomson, I. 370
Thong, G. 309
TOMS Shoes 378
Törnroos, J.A. 452
Törrönen, J. 256
transparency 21, 69, 309, 389
Trendafilova, S. 345
Türker, D. 228–229, 395–396, 397
Turocy, T.L. 115
Tylor, Sir E.B. 268

United Nations definition of CSR 271–272
United Nations Framework Convention on Climate Change (UNFCCC) 123–124
United Nations Global Compact 15–16, 276, 434

Valdelin, J. 449
validity
   construct validity 197, 456–457
   content validity 195, 197
   criterion validity 195
   descriptive validity 304
   external validity 457
   focus groups 50
   in-depth interviews 52–53
   internal validity 456–457
   interpretive validity 304
   mixed methods approach 53
   online surveys 48
   participant observation methods and ethnography 303–305
   phenomenological study of moral discourse and social justice 385, 386
   positivism and social constructivism 417, 456–458
   statistical methods 186, 191, 195–196, 197
   theoretical validity 304
values and beliefs 231, 250, 261, 437–438
Van der Stede, W.A. 88
Van Maanen, J. 265, 268, 269, 294, 404, 406
Vansina, J. 87
Vargas, L.M.S. 102–103
variables 180, 196, 198
   confounding 166
   dependent 109, 184–185
   independent 109, 184–185

nominal 180, 186, 190
ordinal 180–181, 186
ratio 181–182, 186, 196
see also regression techniques
Velthuis, L. 118
Venkatesh, V.G. 109
Vicsek, L. 369
Vienna Circle 77, 80
Vinnicombe, S. 441
Vitaliano, D.F. 222
Volkswagen 14
voluntarism 222

Walden, W.D. 242
Wall, S. 233
Wang, X. 196–197, 346
Ward Jr, J.H. 199
Warren, C.A.B. 284
Wasserman, S. 391, 392, 394
Watson, T.J. 266
Weber, M. 446
Weick, K.E. 437
Wellman, B. 393, 394
Wells, P.E. 10
Whetten, D.A. 67
White, M. 165
Whorf, B.L. 261

Wickramsinghe, D. 286
Wicks, A. 19–20
Wilkins, A.L. 403
Wong, K.S. 243
Wood, D.J. 244–245, 257, 260
World Business Council for Sustainable development (WBCSD) CSR definition 350
Worthington, F. 265
Wright, R. 115
Wrigley, N. 162
Wyatt, W. 312

Yanow, D. 78, 266
Yekini, K.C. 225–226
Yin, R.K. 448, 449, 450, 452, 456
Yusoff, H. 243

Zaheer, S. 126
Zehal, D. 309
Zenk, S. 162
Zhao, J. 113, 117–118
Zikmund, W. 143
Zimbardo, P. 69, 70, 75
Zollo, M. 222
Zuchdi, D. 352
Žydžiūnaitė, V. 25